iOS 8 by Tutorials

By the raywenderlich.com Tutorial Team

Soheil Azarpour, Ricardo Rendon Cepeda, Tammy Coron, Sam Davies, Jake Gundersen, Mike Katz, Chris Lowe, Vincent Ngo, Ryan Nystrom, Cesare Rocchi, Audrey Tam, Chris Wagner, Nicholas Waynik, & Jack Wu

iOS 8 by Tutorials

Soheil Azarpour, Ricardo Rendon Cepeda, Tammy Coron, Sam Davies, Jake Gundersen, Mike Katz, Chris Lowe, Vincent Ngo, Ryan Nystrom, Cesare Rocchi, Audrey Tam, Chris Wagner, Nicholas Waynik, & Jack Wu

Notice of Rights

Notice of Liability

Trademarks

ISBN: 978-0-9896751-7-8

Table of Contents:

Dedications

"To my lovely, always supportive wife Elnaz, and our son Kian."

– Soheil M. Azarpour

"To my ninja kittah, Dexter, who sat upon my hat
and worked out all the math."

– Tammy Coron

"To Scarlett, my wonderful and supportive wife."

– Jack Wu

"To my dearly departed dog, Kiwi. You inspired my first app and
I loved our time spent together."

– Ricardo Rendon Cepeda

"To my loving wife Stacy and daughter Sophie."

– Mike Katz

"To my parents. Thank you for all of the support you have
given me throughout the years."

– Chris Wagner

"To my beloved parents Victor & Iris, sister Brittany, and anyone
who has encouraged and supported me over the years."

– Vincent Ngo

"To my wonderful wife Allison and son Preston.
Thank you for always being supportive in everything I do."

– Nicholas Waynik

"To Pui."

– Sam Davies

"To my parents, who taught me how to be a parent."

– Cesare Rocchi

"To my magnificent wife, Laura, and spunky daughter, Hailey."

– Chris Lowe

"To the buddies, John and Eli, for making life so much fun."

– Jake Gundersen

"To my amazing wife and family who encourage me to never stop."

– Ryan Nystrom

"To my parents and teachers, who set me on the path that
led me to the here and now."

– Audrey Tam

Introduction

This year at WWDC, Tim Cook declared iOS 8 the most significant change for developers since the introduction of the original iPhone OS SDK. Not only does iOS 8 introduce an entirely new programming language—Swift—but it also introduces a wide range of new technologies and APIs that allow entirely new classes of apps to be developed.

For example, App Extensions allow you to share your app's functionality with other apps – for example customers could use your custom photo editor within Apple's stock Photo app. Customers will be searching for apps that contain useful and interesting extensions, and Apple will certainly promote extensions that do the best job at showcasing this new technology. An opportunity like this doesn't come around very often, so be prepared to grab it by the horns and hang on for the ride!

In addition, the iPhone portfolio has grown once again to include new devices with larger screens, and customers will expect your apps to work seamlessly across all of their devices and screen sizes. Don't panic – Apple's got your back with Adaptive Layout technologies. New changes to Interface Builder and UIKit mean your apps can take full advantage of these new screens by intelligently adapting themselves to various screen sizes and resolutions - with far less effort than you'd expect.

iOS 8 also introduces a ton of other new APIs and frameworks which makes the learning curve of this release appear steep. That's why the Tutorial Team has been hard at work researching all of the new APIs since the day they were announced at WWDC. We've condensed all of that information into a format that can bring you up to speed quickly and easily so you can focus on what you do best – developing high quality apps!

Get ready for your own private tour through the amazing new features of iOS 8. By the time you're done, your iOS knowledge will be completely up-to-date and you'll be able to benefit from the amazing new opportunities in iOS 8.

Sit back, relax and prepare for some high quality tutorials!

What you need

To follow along with the tutorials in this book, you'll need the following:

- **A Mac running OS X Mavericks or later.** You'll need this to be able to install the latest version of Xcode.
- **Xcode 6.1 or later.** Xcode is the main development tool for iOS. You'll need Xcode 6.1 or later for all tasks in this book as Xcode 6 is the first version of Xcode to supports iOS 8. You can download the latest version of Xcode for free on the Mac app store here: https://itunes.apple.com/app/xcode/id497799835?mt=12
- **One or more devices (iPhone, iPad, or iPod Touch) running iOS 8 or later, and a paid membership to the iOS development program [optional].** Most of the chapters in the book let you run your code on the iOS 8 Simulator that comes with Xcode. However, a few chapters later in the book require one or more physical iOS devices for testing.

Once you have these items in place, you'll be able to follow along with every chapter in this book.

Who this book is for

This book is for intermediate or advanced iOS developers who already know the basics of iOS and Swift development but want to upgrade their iOS 8 skills.

- **If you are a complete beginner to iOS development,** we recommend you read through *The iOS Apprentice, 3rd Edition* first. Otherwise this book may be a bit too advanced for you.
- **If you are a beginner to Swift,** we recommend you read through either *The iOS Apprentice, 3rd Edition* (if you are a complete beginner to programming), or *Swift by Tutorials* (if you already have some programming experience) first.

If you need one of these prerequisite books, you can find them on our store here:

http://www.raywenderlich.com/store

The tutorials in this book are in Swift. We realize that some of you might not be quite ready to move to Swift, so we have provided Objective-C versions of the sample projects as well. This way, you can read the chapters but follow along with the Objective-C versions of the sample projects if you would like.

How to use this book

This book can be read from cover to cover, but we don't recommend using it this way unless you have a lot of time and are the type of person who just "needs to know everything". (It's okay; a lot of our tutorial team is like that, too!)

Instead, we suggest a pragmatic approach – pick and choose the chapters that interest you the most, or the chapters you need immediately for your current projects. Most chapters are self-contained, so you can go through the book in a non-sequential order.

Looking for some recommendations of important chapters to start with? Here's our suggested Core Reading List:

- Chapter 2, "Beginning Adaptive Layout"
- Chapter 3, "Intermediate Adaptive Layout"
- Chapter 8, "Introducing Extensions"
- Chapter 9, "Today Extensions"
- Chapter 15, "Beginning CloudKit"
- Chapter 17, "Beginning Scene Kit"
- Chapter 19, "Beginning Photos"

That covers the "Big 7" topics of iOS 8; from there you can dig into other topics of particular interest to you.

Book overview

iOS 8 has a host of killer new APIs and techniques you'll want to start using right away. Here's what you'll be learning about in this book:

Section I: Adaptive Layout

In this section, you'll learn a completely new approach to building user interfaces for iOS 8; ones that are completely independent of device, screen size, resolution or device orientation. You'll be introduced to trait collections, size classes and universal storyboards, each of which will not only help you build the best interfaces for the current crop of iOS devices, but for future ones as well.

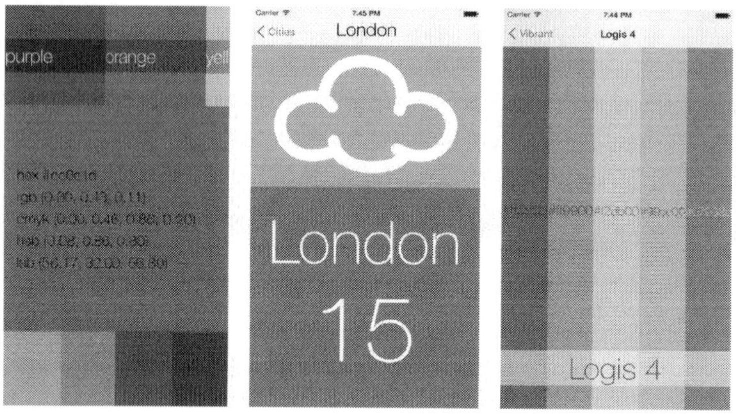

Here's a quick overview of the chapters in this section:

1. **Chapter 1, Introducing Adaptive Layout**: Before you dive into any code, you'll be given an overview of what Adaptive Layout is and the reasons why you should give serious consideration to this new design paradigm.
2. **Chapter 2, Beginning Adaptive Layout**: You'll learn how to use Interface Builder to create user interfaces that seamlessly adapt to different devices, resolutions and orientations.
3. **Chapter 3, Intermediate Adaptive Layout:** You'll take Adaptive Layout to the next level and learn about self-sizing table view cells, installable views, trait collections, and size-class dependent assets.
4. **Chapter 4, Adaptive View Controller Hierarchies**: Adaptive Layout affects not only your views, but view controllers as well. In this chapter you'll learn about

UISplitViewController, which is now available on iPhone, and how to upgrade a legacy application to take advantage of it.

5. **Chapter 5, Transition Coordinators**: You'll learn about the significant upgrades to transition coordinators, which were first introduced in iOS 7 and how to implement the new layout transitions as well.
6. **Chapter 6, Introducing Presentation Controllers**: You'll dig into iOS 8 approach of presenting view controllers and how the new APIs natively support adaptive layouts.
7. **Chapter 7, Custom Presentations:** Building on Chapter 6, this chapter shows you how to add polish to your apps with custom presentations.

Section II: App Extensions

App Extensions are one of the most anticipated features of iOS 8; they let you extend your app's content and functionality throughout the rest of the OS. Such extensions allow you to present custom functionality in other apps and gives users the power of your applications when and where they need it most. Once you've completed the following seven chapters you'll no doubt wonder how you ever survived without App Extensions – both as a developer *and* as a user.

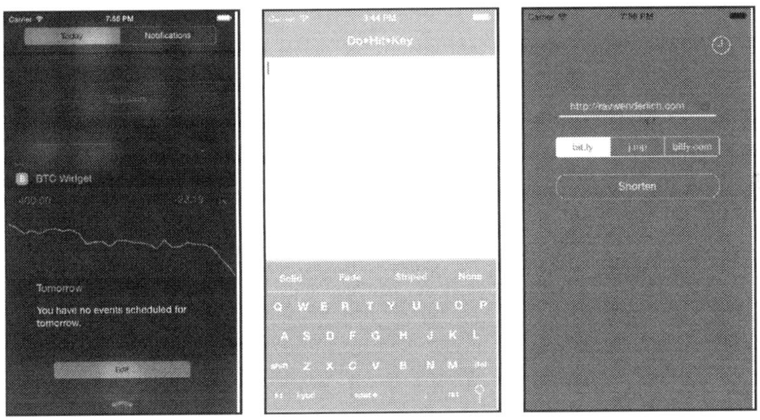

Here's a quick overview of the chapters in this section:

8. **Chapter 8, Introducing Extensions**: Get a quick overview of what App Extensions are, their API, some of the limitations imposed by Apple, and an overview of how to add one to an existing app.

9. **Chapter 9, Today Extensions**: You'll learn how to create Today Extensions, the iOS equivalent of desktop widgets. They're a great way to provide immediate and up-to-date information to your users.
10. **Chapter 10, Share Extensions**: You'll see how to craft extensions that let users share content directly to your web service from within whichever app they're using at the time.
11. **Chapter 11, Action Extensions**: Build exciting extensions that let users view, transform, or manipulate content within the context of the host app. Think Google Translate, but in real-time, in-place, without ever leaving the web page.
12. **Chapter 12, Photo Editing Extensions:** Does your app offer photo filters, or some other kind of photo manipulation functionality? Ever wish you could provide that same functionality to other third-party apps, or even Apple's stock apps? Well now you can! You'll learn how to create extensions to do exactly this.
13. **Chapter 13, Document Provider Extensions**: Learn how to build extensions that allow users to send and receive files between apps. You'll also learn how to present cloud storage services as if they were the local file system. Document Providers allow iOS apps to share, edit, and update each other's files.
14. **Chapter 14, Keyboard Extensions**: You'll replace the system keyboard with one of your own; iOS is now open to the world of intelligent swipe, Emoji, and animated GIF keyboards.

Section III: Major New Features

In this section, you'll learn about the biggest and most important new features and frameworks in iOS 8 not already covered in this book. You'll cover Apple's entry into the BaaS (Backend as a Service) sector, a new and highly performant way to render 3D content in your app, a much improved way to access and manipulate users' photos, how to render your custom views and controls in Interface Builder and much, *much* more.

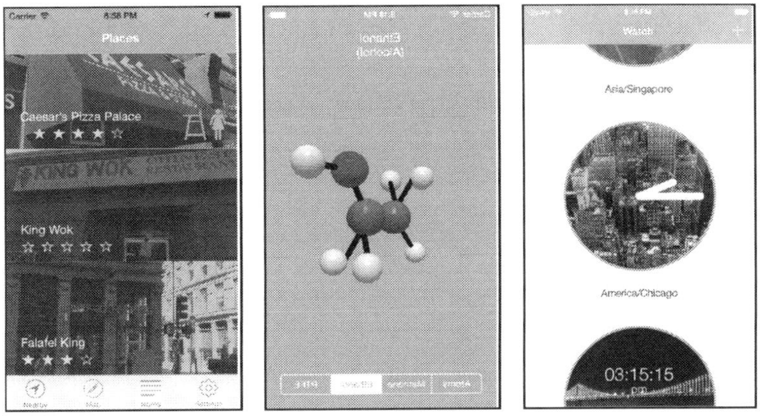

Here's a quick overview of the chapters in this section:

15. **Chapter 15, Beginning CloudKit**: You'll learn what CloudKit is, why you should use it and gain a solid overview of the CloudKit convenience APIs.
16. **Chapter 16, Intermediate CloudKit**: You'll take a deeper dive into CloudKit, learn about the lower-level APIs that allow fine-grained control of your data as well as some of the limitations of the API and how best to work around them.
17. **Chapter 17, Beginning Scene Kit**: Scene Kit has been available on OS X since 2012, but it's now debuted in iOS 8 as well. Take advantage of this battle-tested framework to add 3D visualizations to your UIKit based apps.
18. **Chapter 18, Intermediate Scene Kit**: You'll learn how to introduce physics to your 3D visualizations, how to import 3D models and take advantage of the amazing Scene Kit support in Xcode 6.
19. **Chapter 19, Beginning Photos**: The Assets framework has often been the Achilles' heel of developers when working with photos on iOS. Apple has changed all of this by introducing a brand spanking new and modern framework, which aims to remove *all* the pain points of working with Assets. You'll learn the basics of it in this chapter.
20. **Chapter 20, Intermediate Photos**: Here you'll take a closer look the new Photos framework, explore all four corners of the API, and learn about such things as asset caching and change requests.
21. **Chapter 21, Beginning Live Rendering:** Interface Builder now renders custom views and controls just as if they were Apple's own – *finally!* You'll learn how

to set up Live Rendering, how to expose your custom controls' properties and then delve into creating custom controls using `CALayer`.

22. **Chapter 22, Intermediate Live Rendering:** You'll learn how to mix your custom views and controls with Apple's stock controls for the purposes of Live Rendering, and you'll see how Live Rendering can seriously speed up the development process.
23. **Chapter 23, Handoff:** You'll discover what Handoff is, see how it works, gain a solid overview of the API, and learn how to add this near-magical functionality to your iOS apps.
24. **Chapter 24, Beginning WebKit:** Apple has *finally* replaced `UIWebView`! You'll get to experience the long-awaited and modern WebKit as you create a bespoke web browser.
25. **Chapter 25, Intermediate WebKit:** The new WebKit framework is useful beyond simply loading up web pages. You'll learn how to hook into the page loading process to execute custom JavaScript, which allows you to bend any web page to your will.

Section IV: Bonus Chapters

And that's not all – on top of the above, we have some bonus chapters for you!

These bonus chapters come as an optional PDF download, which you can download for free here:

- http://www.raywenderlich.com/store/ios-8-by-tutorials/bonus-chapters

In these bonus chapters, you'll learn about further additions to your iOS developer tool belt. You'll implement some real-time blurring, take in-depth look at all things Xcode 6, before rounding out the section with an overview of the new and shiny bits Apple added to the testing framework introduced in iOS 7.

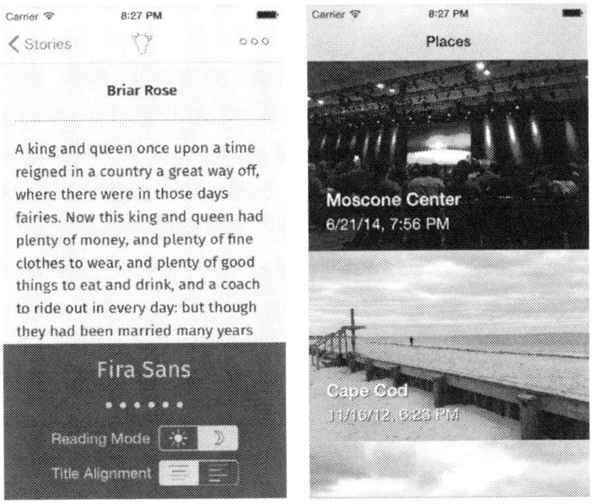

26. **Chapter 26, iOS 8 Visual Effects**: You'll learn how to efficiently add static blurs to your app, then take advantage of the brand new `UIVisualEffectView` to add real-time blurring and vibrancy to your app as well.

27. **Chapter 27, An In-depth Look at Xcode 6**: You'll get up-to-speed on the most important updates in the latest revision of Apple's development suite. There's an absolute ton of changes, including a whole new programming language!

28. **Chapter 28, Xcode 6 & Swift**: You'll discover how Swift integrates with Xcode, what Playgrounds are and how they should be used, and you'll be introduced to the Swift REPL, which among other things, lets you run Swift from the command line.

29. **Chapter 29, What's New with Testing**: You'll learn all about the updates to XCTest, Apple's testing framework, including asynchronous testing and performance testing.

30. **Chapter 30, What's New with iTunes Connect:** Learn about some exciting new features in iTunes Connect, such as adding videos to your App Store pages, TestFlight beta testing, and more.

Book source code and forums

As mentioned earlier, this book comes with Swift *and* Objective-C versions of the source code for each chapter. You can get the source code for the book here:

- http://www.raywenderlich.com/store/ios-8-by-tutorials/source-code

Some of the chapters have starter projects or other required resources, so you'll definitely want them close at hand as you go through the book.

We've also set up an official forum for the book at raywenderlich.com/forums. This is a great place to ask questions about the book, discuss making apps with iOS 8 in general, share challenge solutions, or to submit any errors you may find.

PDF Version

We also have a PDF version of this book available, which can be handy if you ever want to copy/paste code or search for a specific term through the book as you're developing.

And speaking of the PDF version, we have some good news!

Since you purchased the physical copy of this book, you are eligible to buy the PDF version at a significant discount if you would like (if you don't have it already). For more details, see this page:

- http://www.raywenderlich.com/store/ios-8-by-tutorials/upgrade

License

By purchasing *iOS 8 by Tutorials*, you have the following license:

- You are allowed to use and/or modify the source code in *iOS 8 by Tutorials* in as many apps as you want, with no attribution required.
- You are allowed to use and/or modify all art, images, or designs that are included in *iOS 8 by Tutorials* in as many apps as you want, but must include this attribution line somewhere inside your app: "Artwork/images/designs: from the iOS 8 by Tutorials book, available at http://www.raywenderlich.com".

Acknowledgements

We would like to thank many people for their assistance in making this possible:

- **Our families**: For bearing with us in this crazy time as we worked all hours of the night to get this book ready for publication!
- **Everyone at Apple**: For developing an amazing operating system and set of APIs, for constantly inspiring us to improve our apps and skills, and for making it possible for many developers to have their dream jobs!
- And most importantly, **the readers of raywenderlich.com — especially you!** Thank you so much for reading our site and purchasing this book. Your continued readership and support is what makes all of this possible!

About the authors

Tammy Coron is an artist, a writer, a musician, and a developer. Not too many people get an opportunity to do what they love. She considers herself to be one of the lucky ones! Check out her blog at http://www.justwritecode.net.

Soheil Azarpour is an independent iOS developer. He's worked on iOS applications for clients as well as his own personal apps. He enjoys making apps, hanging out with his family, and watching movies.

Christopher Lowe is a Social Media/Mobile Technical Lead at USAA, by day. By night, he's a UI and iOS consultant through his own company, Hashtag Studios. When not working, you can find Chris spending time with his wife, young daughter, and his two crazy dogs.

Jack Wu is the lead mobile developer at Extreme Innovations. He has built dozens of iOS apps and enjoys it very much. Outside of work, Jack enjoys coding on the beach, coding by the pool, and sometimes just having a quick code in the park.

Jake Gundersen is an independent iOS and OS X developer. He is the creator of Factor Samurai, a math game for classrooms and Co-Founder of Third Rail Games. He works on apps for DJs, educational games, and image processing applications. When not working on apps he spends time with his wife and twin boys.

Mike Katz envisions a world where mobile apps always work, respect users' privacy, and integrate well with their users' life. When not coding, he can be found with his family playing board games, brewing, gardening, and watching the Yankees. He has a B.S. and M.Eng in Electrical Engineering from Cornell University, and a M.S. in Neuroscience from Brandeis University.

Nicholas Waynik is an independent iOS developer, and has done everything from network administration to web development. He started writing iOS apps when the iPhone SDK was first released. Since then he has gone on to start his own business focusing on iOS development. He loves spending his free time with his wife Allison and son Preston, and sometimes playing golf.

Ricardo Rendon Cepeda is a Mobile Application Developer at Idean, an awesome UX/UI design studio in Palo Alto, CA. He specializes in iOS & OpenGL ES.

Ryan Nystrom is a Software Engineer at Facebook working on their iOS applications. He is a passionate open source contributor where he builds UI controls and frameworks for others to use and learn from. In his spare time he enjoys flying planes as a private pilot.

Sam Davies is a Technical Evangelist for ShinobiControls - purveyors of the finest UI controls for iOS and Android - including charts, grids and much more. By day you'll find him attending conferences, writing tutorials, meeting people and generally being a good guy. By night he's likely to be out entertaining people, armed with his trombone and killer dance moves.

Cesare Rocchi is a speaker, writer, UX designer and developer specializing in web and mobile applications. He began working on interactive applications while he was a researcher in the academia. He runs Studio Magnolia, an interactive studio that creates compelling web and mobile applications. He blogs at http://upbeat.it.

Vincent Ngo is a full time iOS software engineer at IBM. He graduated from Virginia Tech with a Computer Science degree. He has passion for developing, and learning about the iOS SDK. Outside of that, he likes playing video games, strumming his guitar, and chilling with friends.

Chris Wagner currently works as the lead iOS developer at Infusionsoft and started "programming" by playing with QBASIC and the Lego Mindstorms kit (thanks Dad). After graduating with a Computer Systems Engineering degree from ASU he worked as a Java web app developer before moving on to leading multiple iOS development teams.

Audrey Tam retired at the end of 2012 from a 25-year career as a computer science academic. Her teaching included Pascal, C/C++, Java, Java web services, web app development in PHP and MySQL, user interface design and evaluation, and iOS programming. Before moving to Australia, she worked on Fortran and PL/1 simulation software at IBM's development lab in Silicon Valley. Audrey now teaches short courses in iOS app development to non-programmers, and organizes venues for the Melbourne Cocoaheads' monthly meetings.

About the editors

Brian Moakley was a tech editor for this book. He is not only an iOS developer and fiction writer; he also holds the honor being Razeware's first fulltime employee. Brian joined Razeware with experience from companies such as ESPN's online fantasy team and Disney's Internet Group. When not writing or coding, Brian enjoys story driven first person shooters, reading some great books, and produces his own Minecraft Let's Play video series on YouTube.

Scott Atkinson was a tech editor for this book. He is a software developer in Alexandria, VA. In his day job, he is the iOS developer for Homesnap, a really great real estate discovery app. When he's not writing software, he spends time rowing on the Potomac river, exploring new restaurants, and cooking great food.

Chris Belanger was an editor for this book. He has been a coder for over a quarter century, which makes him feel kind of old. He's also a prolific writer, dabbles in electronic and organic music composition, and occasionally even manages to get real work done as a developer of real-time control systems.

Wendy Lincoln was an editor for this book. She is a full-time project manager by trade, and before that was a prolific, adept copywriter and editor. She has an unusual background that involves a cooking show, culinary school, a passion for writing and teaching, and thousands of miles walked as a political activist. When she's not glued to her computer working or editing brilliant developers' writing in her spare time, you'll find her working on her Date Night-themed cooking show.

Mic Pringle was a final pass editor for this book. He is a Yorkshire-born developer with a passion for aesthetics and the user experience. Currently working at The Infinite Kind, he's been handcrafting exquisite iOS apps since 2011. When not knee-deep in Objective-C, he enjoys spending time with his wife and daughter, as well as attending the odd football match.

Ray Wenderlich was a final pass editor for this book. He is an iPhone developer and gamer, and the founder of Razeware LLC. Ray is passionate about both making apps and teaching others the techniques to make them. He and the Tutorial Team have written a bunch of tutorials about iOS development available at http://www.raywenderlich.com.

About the artists

Ryan Holmes was the designer for this book. Beyond being a great designer, his adventures include starting a hackerspace in Tampa, Florida and more recently working on a cube satellite to let people play in outer space.

Vicki Wenderlich created many of the illustrations in this book. Vicki discovered a love of digital art several years ago, and has been making app art and digital illustrations ever since. She is passionate about helping people pursue their dreams, and makes free app art for developers available on her website, http://www.gameartguppy.com.

Section I: Adaptive Layout

In this section, you'll learn a completely new approach to building user interfaces for iOS 8; ones that are completely independent of device, screen size, resolution or device orientation. You'll be introduced to trait collections, size classes and universal storyboards, each of which will not only help you build the best interfaces for the current crop of iOS devices, but for future ones as well. Read on with an open mind, and prepare to be amazed.

Chapter 1: Introducing Adaptive Layout

By Sam Davies

Ah, the good old days of the iPhone; when there was only one device, with one screen size and one resolution. You could design your interfaces down to the very last pixel, with the guarantee that what you saw on your single test device would be the same thing that all your users around the world would see.

Designing apps was *so* simple back then, you could lay out your interface controls in code using just their frames, or you could use the Interface Builder and pack it all into a single NIB, relying on Springs and Struts to *do the right thing*. The most difficult thing you had to deal with was rotation, which usually meant you had two completely different designs.

Two different designs? I say, old chap!

But history shows the good times never last; Apple introduced the iPad. Building your layouts started to feel clumsy, at best. You had a choice: you could create two NIBs – one for the iPhone and one for the iPad:

Or you could continue to lay out your view in code using a liberal sprinkling of idiom checking, like so:

```
if (UI_USER_INTERFACE_IDIOM() == UIUserInterfaceIdiomPad) {
  ...
}
```

Just seeing that code sends shivers down my spine!

Neither of these solutions was particularly elegant, and it was often easier to create two entirely separate apps; one for the iPad and one for the iPhone.

Auto Layout soon followed, which let you define layouts in a more semantic way, detailing relationships between the size and position of UI elements, rather than specifying each control's size and position individually. However, Auto Layout is a rather complex beast with a steep learning curve; it struggled to gain the widespread adoption that Apple had hoped for.

And so here we are, the present day. Consider how you would adapt your existing apps to yet another new device, with yet another screen size. When you find yourself repeating the same design process a third time, adding a third storyboard or NIB and many more `switch` statements based on device idioms, you know something has gone terribly wrong.

Well, my developer friend, rejoice! iOS 8 introduces Adaptive Layout to address this very problem; that of design bloat. The underlying concept is simple – designing for individual form factors simply isn't scalable, so instead move towards a more abstract layout based on relationships between the various UI elements. The new universal storyboards and size-classes let you create a single layout, adaptable to *any* iOS device with *any* screen size or orientation – even future devices that haven't been *designed* yet.

This section of the book covers the following key components of Adaptive Layout in iOS 8:

- **Adaptive Layout:** Size classes, trait collections and universal storyboards let you design one layout that works on *every* iOS device. You'll see how to configure your layout in terms of abstract size classes so that it transfers seamlessly to both current and future iOS devices.
  You'll create an app that employs adaptive layout from scratch, including refreshing your knowledge of auto layout along the way.

  You'll then go on to build an app to get weather updates for more than just one city – leveling up your knowledge of adaptive enhancements to UIKit along the way.

- **Transition Coordinators**: The demise of orientation and rotation methods introduces a new paradigm to the concept of rotation. In an adaptive world, rotation is nothing more than a simple bounds change. You'll find out how this affects your apps along with some examples of how to create amazing custom rotation effects.

  To learn about transition coordinators, you'll take an existing color helper app, and add some polish via complex rotation animations.

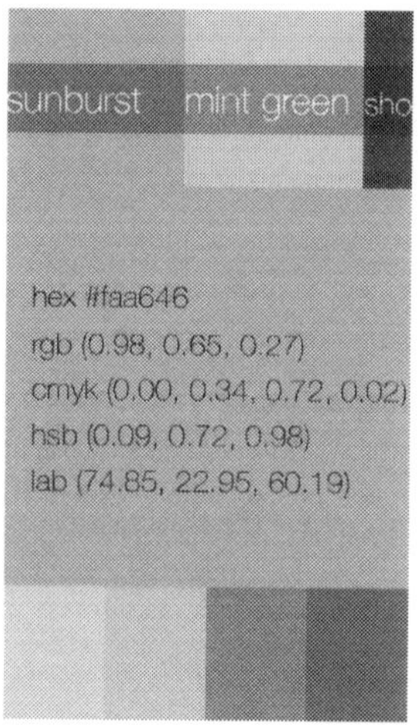

- **Adaptive View Controller Hierarchies**: The iPhone rolls out the red carpet for `UISplitViewController`. View controller hierarchies can adapt to their surroundings just as layouts do. You can now represent the same complex view controller with different hierarchies on different device configurations.

  Taking a step-up on the color picker app, in this chapter you'll be enhancing an existing color palette app, which you can use to assist in choosing entire sets of colors. The app is a master-detail app created from the template in Xcode 5, and you'll discover how to upgrade it to the adaptive world of iOS8, before fully customizing its functionality.

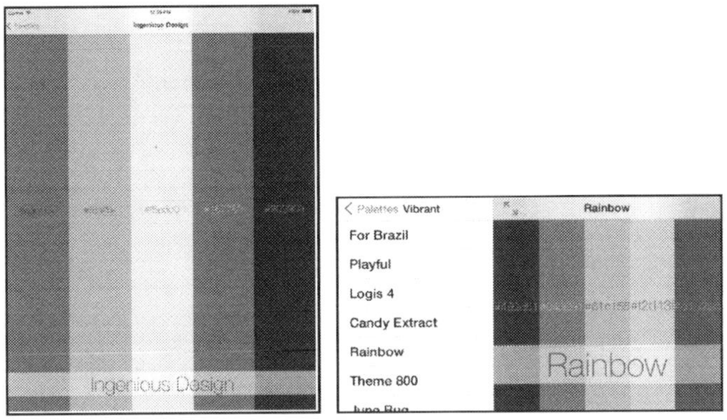

- **Presentation Controllers**. Popovers, alerts and search controllers are brought closer than ever before. When a new view controller appears on screen it's now said to be **presented**; you can use presentation controllers to completely customize this whole process.

  You'll start out by learning about updates to alerts, popovers and search controllers by building a quiz app to test your knowledge of the countries of the world.

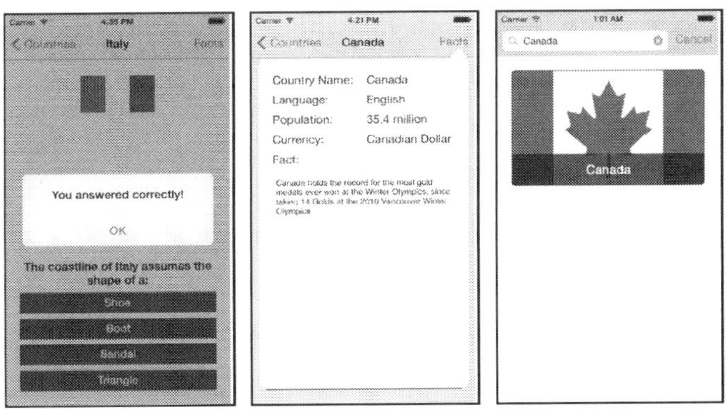

Once you have mastered this you'll move on to creating your own custom presentations, complete with cool bouncy animations.

It might seem like there's a lot to absorb here, but Adaptive Layout will be critical in the next generation of app design and development. Understanding and embracing these new technologies will let you build apps that work on any future devices released by Apple. As an added bonus, you'll find that Adaptive Layout has a positive impact on your development workflow.

You're embarking on an exciting new frontier of iOS app design; designing for iOS will never be the same again.

What are you waiting for? Westward ho, Adaptive Layout pioneers!

Chapter 2: Beginning Adaptive Layout

By Sam Davies

The introduction of Adaptive Layout in iOS 8 is a huge paradigm shift for iOS app designers. Apps now have the ability to adapt their layout to a particular device and device orientation. When designing your app, you can create a single layout, which works on all current iOS 8 devices.

This chapter serves as your introduction to Adaptive Layout. You'll learn about universal storyboards, size classes, layout and font customizations and the ultra-useful Preview Assistant Editor.

You'll create the user interface for a simple weather app in this chapter – and you'll build it completely from scratch. If you're not a fan of Auto Layout, don't worry; the first part of this chapter provides you with a gentle step-by-step approach to build an interface using Auto Layout. You'll be amazed at how much you can accomplish without writing a single line of code!

Universal storyboards

Universal storyboards are the first step on your journey towards Adaptive Layout. The same storyboard can now be used for both iPads and iPhones running iOS 8. There's no need to keep per-device storyboards in sync with each other – a monotonous process which can be fraught with error.

Open Xcode and select **Create a new Xcode project** like so:

Select **iOS\Application\Single View Application,** then click **Next:**

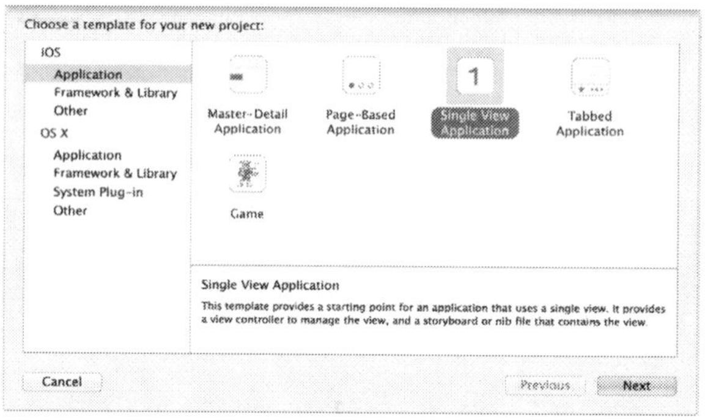

Set **Product Name** to **AdaptiveWeather, Language** to Swift and ensure that **Devices** is set to **Universal,** as shown below:

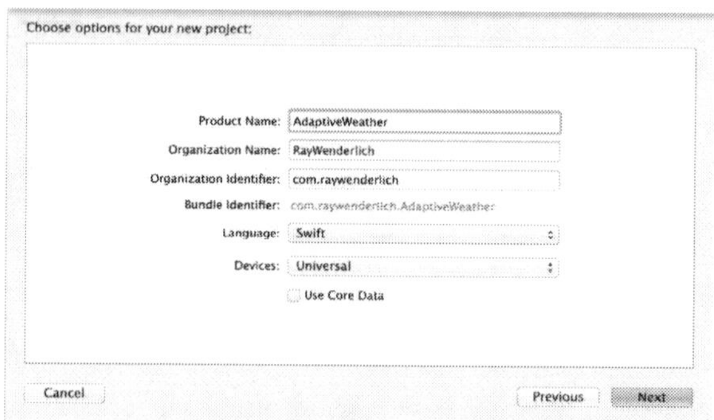

Once the project opens, take a look at the **Project Inspector** and you'll see just a single storyboard file.

Main.storyboard is the single storyboard for all devices, no matter their screen size. Open the storyboard and you'll see that it contains a single view controller, but of an unfamiliar size:

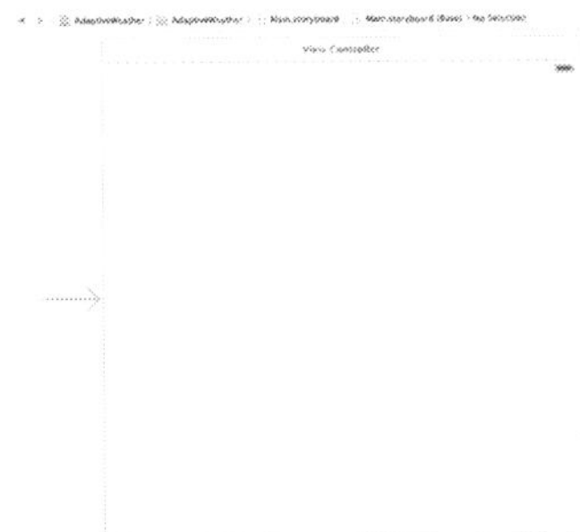

That's right – it's now a rough square! Storyboards in previous versions of Xcode had to match the screen size of the target device. This clearly isn't possible with the "*one storyboard to rule them all*" approach, so the storyboard is given an abstract size instead. The **Use Size Classes** option, found in the **File Inspector**, enables this new format for your project; select the storyboard, open the **File Inspector** and you'll see the checkbox option as shown below:

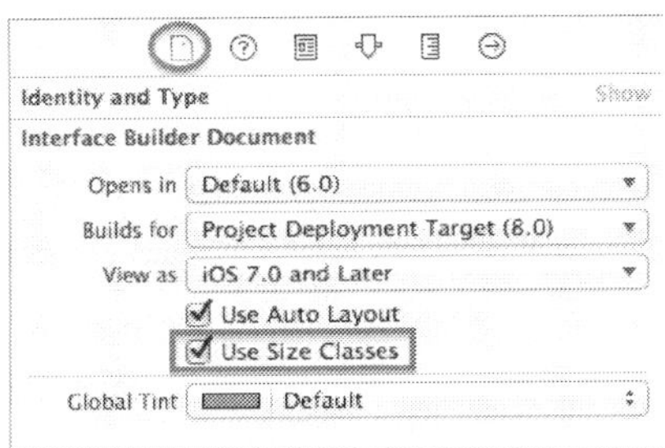

This option is enabled by default for all new iOS 8 projects. You can turn this option on yourself when upgrading your old projects to use the new storyboards. To learn how to update your old storyboards for iOS8, check out Chapter 4, "Adaptive View Controller Hierarchies" in this book.

To start, open **Main.storyboard** and drag an **Image View** from the **Object Library** onto the view controller canvas. In the **Size Inspector**, set the X position to **150** and the Y position to **20**. Set the **Width** to **300** and the **Height** to **265**.

Next, drag a **View** from the Object Library and place it below the image view. In the **Size Inspector**, set the X position to **150** and the Y position to **315**. Set the **Width** to **300** and the **Height** to **265**.

Select the view you just added, open the **Identity Inspector** and enter **TextContainer** in the **Label** field. Note that the **Document** pane might be collapsed – if so press the **Show** button to reveal it. This gives the view a name and makes it easier to see in the **Document Inspector**. This view will eventually hold the city and temperature labels of your app.

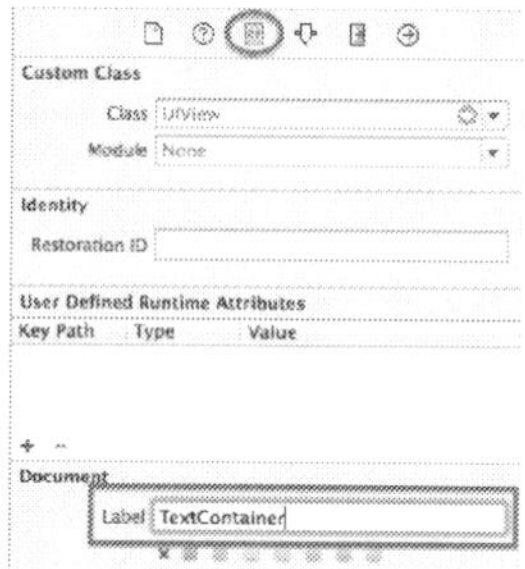

It's often hard to see views after dragging them in from the Object Library as their default background color is white, the same as the view controller's view. To fix this, select the view controller's view, open the **Attributes Inspector** and set its background color to **Red: 74, Green: 171, Blue: 247**.

Next, select the TextContainer view and set its background color to **Red: 55, Green: 128, Blue: 186**.

Your view controller should now look like the screenshot below:

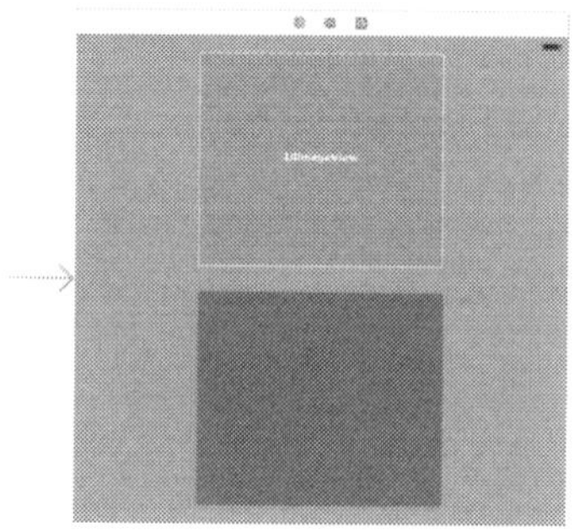

These two views are the only direct descendants of the view controller's view; your task now is to give them some layout constraints.

Adding layout constraints

Select the image view and press the **Align** button in the auto layout toolbar. **Check** the **Horizontal Center in Container**, ensuring the value is set to **0**. Then press the **Pin** button and add a top spacing to nearest neighbor constraint of 0, as so:

The constraints you added above ensure that the image view has a fixed size margin from the top and that it is centered left to right. Now you need to configure the space between the image view and the text container view. **Ctrl-drag** from the image view down to the container view, like so:

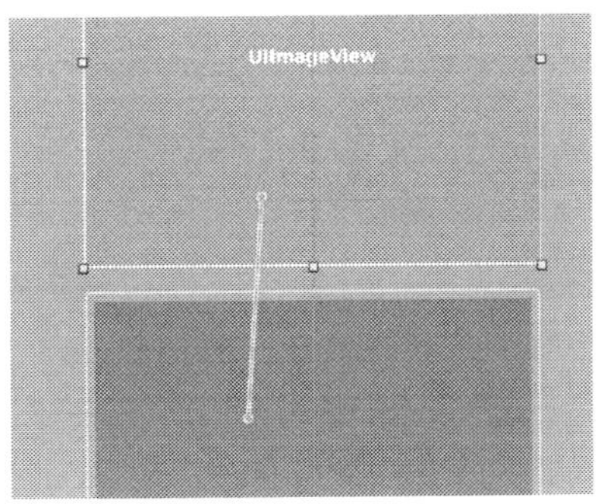

This displays the constraint context menu again. Select **Vertical Spacing** as shown below:

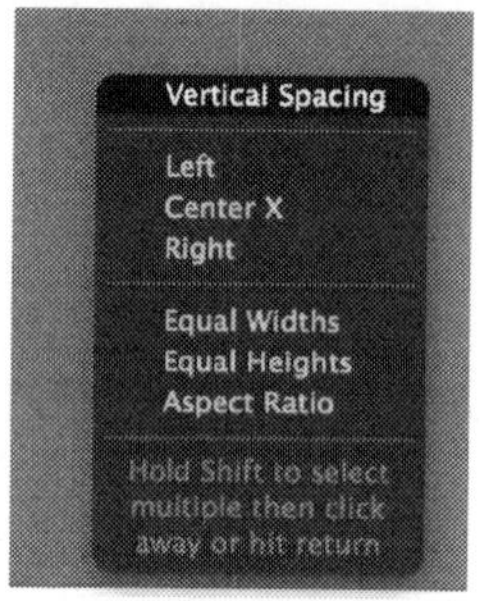

This constraint determines the amount of vertical space between the bottom of the image view and the top of the TextContainer view.

The Size Inspector looks a bit different in Xcode 6. Select your image view and open the **Size Inspector** to see how it looks now:

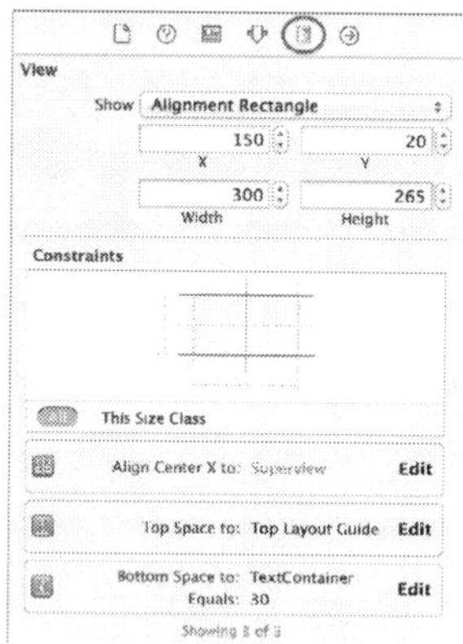

You'll see the three constraints you just added to your layout; you can easily configure each constraint from within the size inspector. Press the **Edit** button in the **Bottom Space To: TextContainer** constraint; you'll be presented with a dialog to configure the constraint properties. Set **Constant** equal to **20** as shown below:

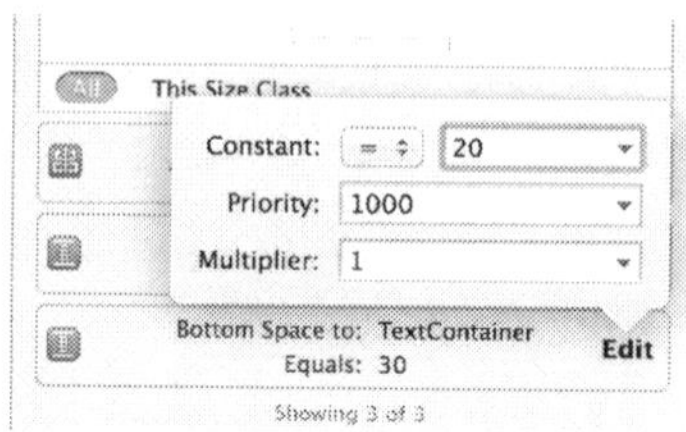

Click away from the dialog to close it.

You've already configured your TextContainer view to have a gap of 20 points away from the bottom edge of the image view, but you also need to add constraints to the other three sides of the view.

Select your TextContainer view then click the **Pin** icon in the bottom bar to show the **Add New Constraints** dialog. In the **Spacing to nearest neighbor** section, set the **left**, **right** and **bottom** spacing to **0**. Ensure that **Constrain to margins** is **unchecked**; this removes padding from around your view.

For reference, the dialog should now look like the following:

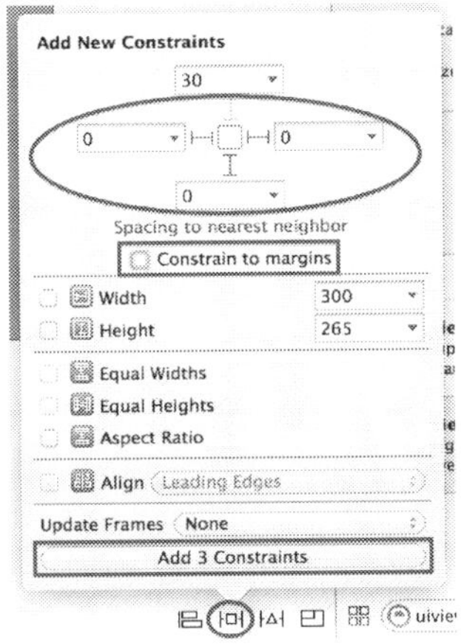

Click **Add 3 constraints** to add the new constraints to your view. This pins the text container view to the left, right and bottom edges of the view controller's view.

Your storyboard should now look like the screenshot below:

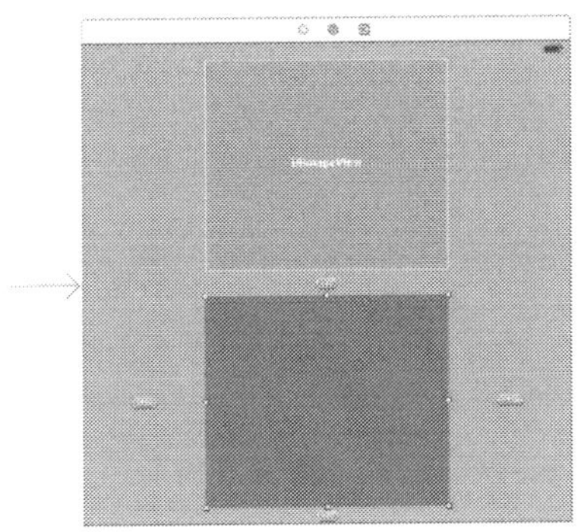

You'll notice a few orange constraints on your view; this indicates there are issues with these constraints that need your attention. It's possible to have the storyboard automatically update the frames of the contained views to satisfy these constraints, but if you do this right now your image view will shrink to zero size. That's because your image view doesn't yet have any content – which means it has an intrinsic height and width of zero. Auto Layout relies on a view's intrinsic size to determine its width and height if no physical width or height constraints are supplied.

In the **Project Navigator**, open **Images.xcassets**, then click on the **+** sign at the bottom of the left panel and select **New Image Set** from the popup menu:

Double-click the title **Image** in the top-left corner of the detail view and rename **Image** to **cloud**, as shown below:

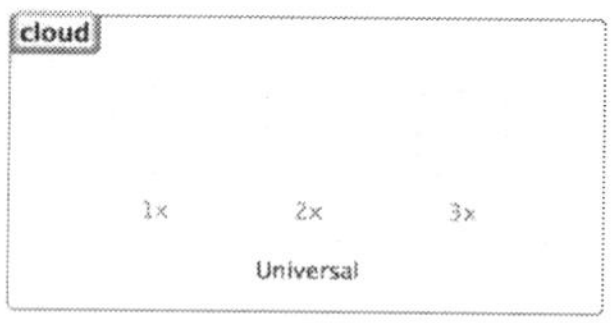

Your new image set is simply a collection of image files, where each file has a purpose for a particular scenario. For example, an image set may have non-Retina, Retina and Retina HD versions of the same image. Since asset libraries are well integrated with UIKit, you refer to the entire image set by name and let iOS choose the correct file at runtime.

> **Note:** If you've used an asset library in the past then you'll notice something strange here – what's this *3x* all about? This new display scale is known as Retina HD and is found on the iPhone 6 Plus. This means that in each direction, there are actually 3 pixels making up one point – i.e. there are 9 times more pixels in a *3x* image than a *1x* image!

Your cloud image set is currently empty. Locate **cloud_images.zip**, which accompanies this chapter, and unzip it. Inside you'll find five files. Drag **cloud_small.png** from the finder to the **1x** box in the **cloud** image set like so:

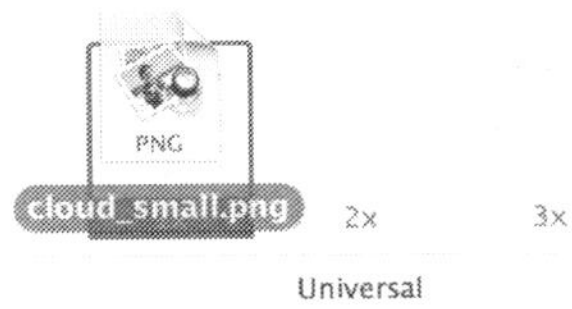

Since the cloud image is white with a transparent background, you won't be able to see it easily in the asset library. However, you can preview the image in QuickLook. Select the **1x** box and press **space**:

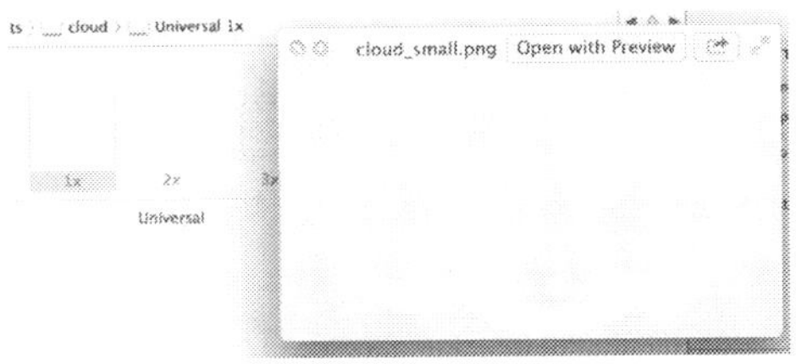

Now drag **cloud_small@2x.png** to the **2x** box, and **cloud_small@3x.png** to the **3x** box. Again, you won't be able to clearly see the images, but you can check using QuickLook.

You can now use your image set to populate your image view. Head back over to **Main.storyboard** and select your image view. Switch to the **Attributes Inspector**, type the name **cloud** into the **Image** field, and select **Aspect Fit** in the **View\Mode** drop down list, like so:

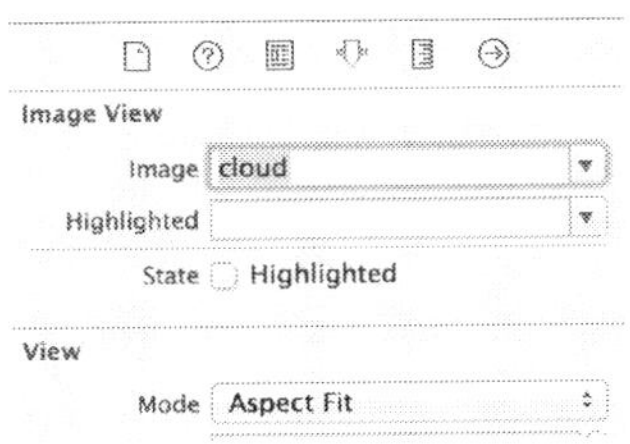

Your storyboard now should look like the following:

There's your image – but as you can tell from the orange constraints, you still have a bit of work to do. First select the view controller's view, then select the **Resolve Auto Layout Issues** icon in the bottom bar. Finally, select **All Views\Update Frames** from the dialog as shown:

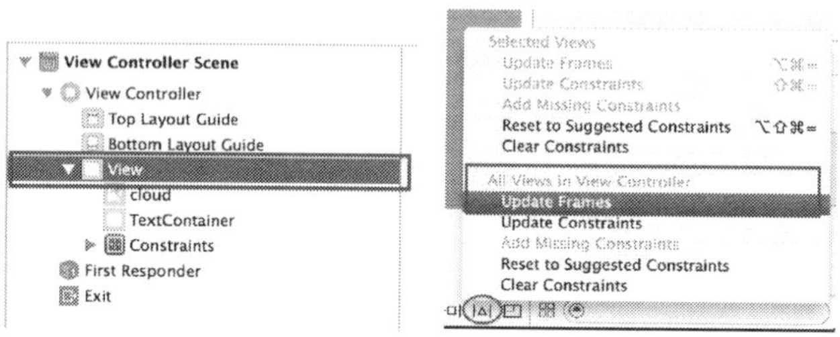

The view controller re-arranges the views to automatically resolve the unsatisfied constraints, which should leave your storyboard looking like this:

The Preview Assistant Editor

Normally you'd now build and run your project on the iPad, iPhone 4s, 5s, 6 and 6 Plus simulators – in both orientations – in order to test this new universal storyboard. This process is laborious at best, but Xcode 6 gives you a much better option with the new Preview Assistant Editor.

Open **Main.storyboard** then click the **Assistant Editor** icon in the menu bar:

This splits the screen into two panes. Click **Automatic** in the **Jump Bar** and choose **Preview** from the drop down menu. Finally select **Main.storyboard**, like so:

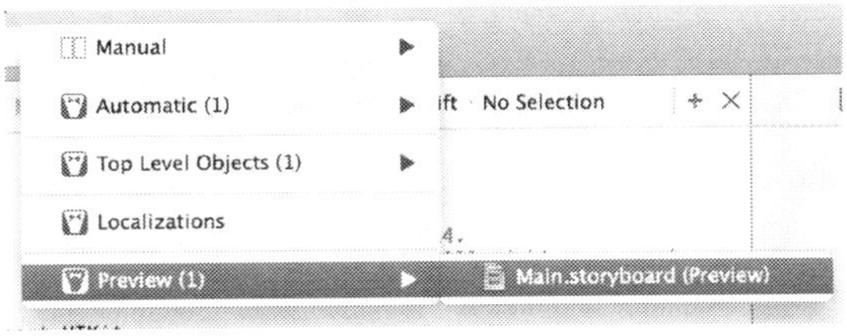

The assistant editor now displays a preview of the storyboard on the 4-inch iPhone screen, as shown below:

Rotate this preview by clicking on the **rotation icon** at the bottom of the preview panel alongside the preview name, in this case **iPhone 4-inch**. The preview will now display in the landscape orientation, like so:

This is a huge improvement over firing up multiple simulators – but wait! There's more! Click the + icon at the bottom left of the preview editor to reveal the list of available previews:

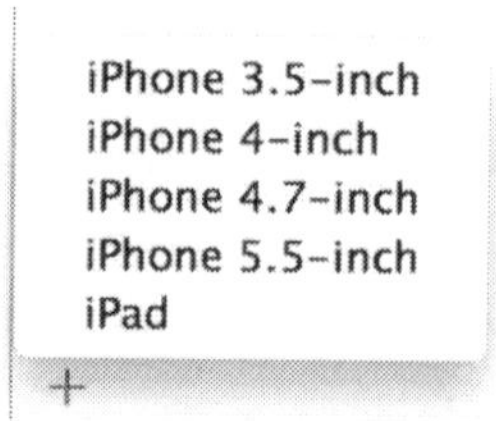

Select **iPhone 5.5-inch** and then **iPad** from this list to add their previews into the mix as shown below:

Notice anything odd about the landscape iPhone preview? That's right – the cloud image is far too big. To fix this you'll add a new constraint to the image view.

Head back to the storyboard. **Ctrl-drag** from the image view to the view controller's view to create a new constraint. From the context menu, select **Equal Heights** as shown below:

A number of constraints on the storyboard are now colored red. This is because the constraint you just added conflicts with the existing constraints, as it's not possible for the image view to have the same height as the view controller's view and maintain the vertical margins you created earlier.

Select the constraint you just added in the **Document Outline** and open the **Attributes Inspector**. If the **First Item** is not set to **cloud.Height** then select **Reverse First and Second Item** in the **First Item** dropdown as shown below:

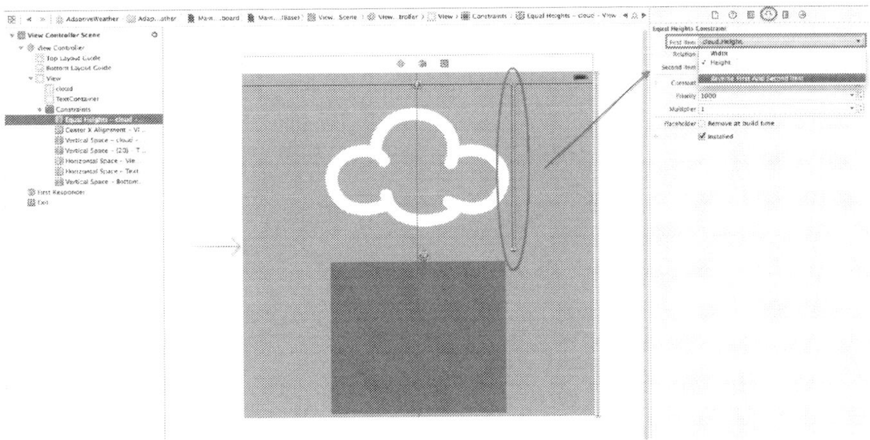

Next, select the **Relation** to be **Less Than or Equal** set **Multiplier** to **0.40** as shown below:

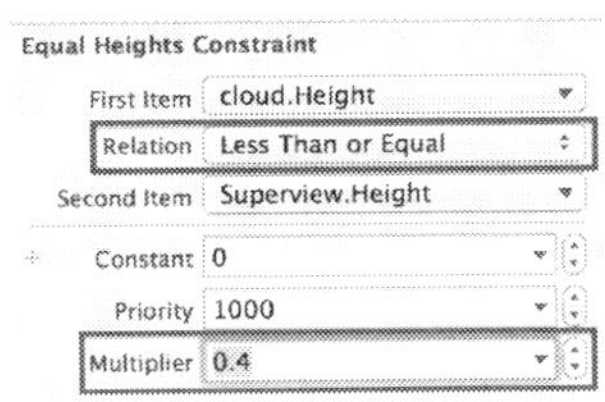

This means that the cloud image will either be the intrinsic size of the image, or be 40% of the height of the screen, whichever is smaller.

You'll notice that the preview pane automatically refreshes as soon as you update the constraint, as demonstrated below:

So you can get multiple device previews that also update automatically? Yep, the new Preview Assistant Editor is quite an improvement!

Since this is supposed to be a weather app, you should probably add some labels to show the city name and the current temperature.

Adding content to the TextContainer

In **Main.storyboard** drag two **Labels** from the **Object Library** onto the **TextContainer** view, and arrange them roughly as shown below:

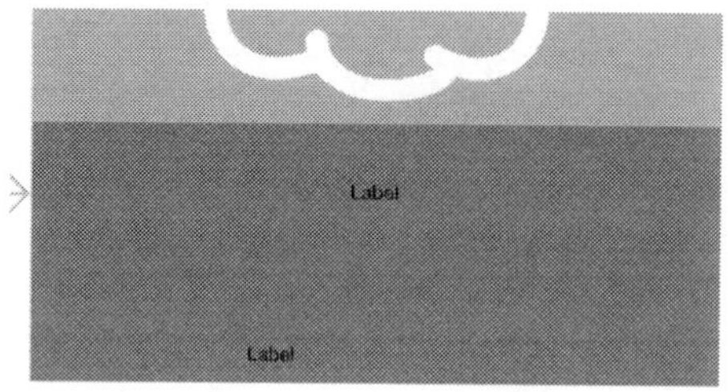

Select the topmost label and use the **Align** and **Pin** menus to **center** the label **horizontally** and add a **top spacing to nearest neighbor** of **10**, as shown below:

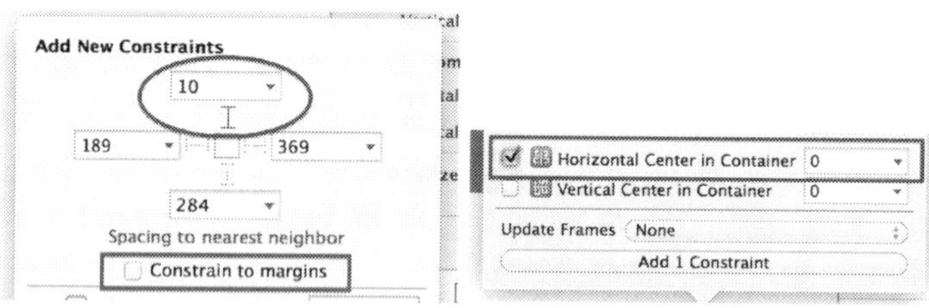

Next, select the **Attributes Inspector** and set **Text** to **Cupertino**, **Color** to **White**, and the font to **Helvetica Neue, Thin** with **Size** of **150.**

You've probably noticed the text is currently illegible, and this is due to the frame of the label. However, you'll resolve this shortly.

Now select the other label, and again use the Align and Pin menus to center it horizontally, and set a bottom space to nearest neighbor of 10. Check that the **Size Inspector** matches the following:

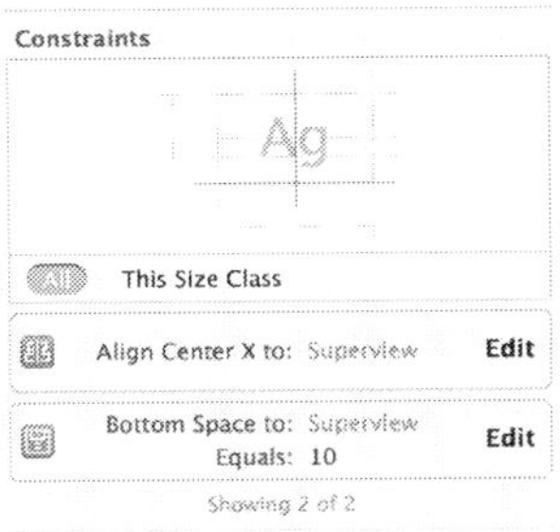

Use the **Attributes Inspector** to set the **Text** to **28C**, the color to **White**, and the font to **Helvetica Neue, Thin** with a size of **250**.

Now you need to resolve the label frame issues mentioned earlier. Select the view controller's view, click the **Resolve Auto Layout Issues** button at the bottom of the storyboard, and select **All Views\Update Frames.** You'll see the storyboard update as follows:

The labels overlap a little in the storyboard, which isn't the look you're going for. However, take a look at the preview in the assistant editor before you fix anything. The iPad version is looking pretty good:

Predictably, the font size is far too big for the iPhone:

You'll correct these sizing issues in the next section of this chapter.

Size classes

Universal storyboards are great – but you've already discovered that creating one single layout for all displays is a bit of a challenge. However, Adaptive Layout has a few more tools and tricks to solve these issues.

One of the core concepts behind adaptive layout is **size classes**. A size class is a property applied to any view or view controller that represents the amount of content that can be displayed in a given horizontal or vertical dimension. Xcode 6 provides two size classes: **Regular** and **Compact**. Although they are related to the *physical* dimensions of a view, they also represent the *semantic* size of the view.

The following table shows how the size classes apply to the different devices and orientations:

	Vertical Size Class	**Horizontal Size Class**
iPad Portrait	Regular	Regular
iPad Landscape	Regular	Regular
iPhone Portrait	Regular	Compact
iPhone Landscape	Compact	Compact
iPhone 6 Plus Landscape	Compact	Regular

These are the size classes that the device hands down to the app. However, you can override these size classes at any point in the view hierarchy. This can be useful when using a view controller in a container which is significantly smaller than the screen – you'll see an example of this in the Intermediate Adaptive Layout chapter.

What does that mean for you and the design of your app? Although your app is aware of size classes, the layout you've built is size class agnostic – that is, your layout remains the same for all size classes.

This is an important point when it comes to the design phase of your adaptive layout. You should build a base layout *first* and then customize each specific size class based on the individual needs of that size class. **Don't** treat each of the size classes as a completely separate design. Think of an adaptive layout as a hierarchy, in which you put all of the shared design into the parent and then make any necessary changes in the child size classes.

There's been almost no mention of configuring layouts for specific devices so far. This is because a core concept of adaptive layout is that size classes are abstracted away from device-specific characteristics. This means that a view that supports adaptive layout could be used in a full-screen view controller as well as in a contained view controller, albeit with different appearances.

This also benefits Apple, as there is room to expand the range and characteristics of their devices without forcing developers and designers to re-engineer their apps.

You'll use size classes to customize the landscape layout for iPhone since the current layout doesn't cope well when restricted vertically.

Working with class sizes

Click on **w Any h Any** in the bottom bar in the Interface Builder; you'll see the size class selector as shown below:

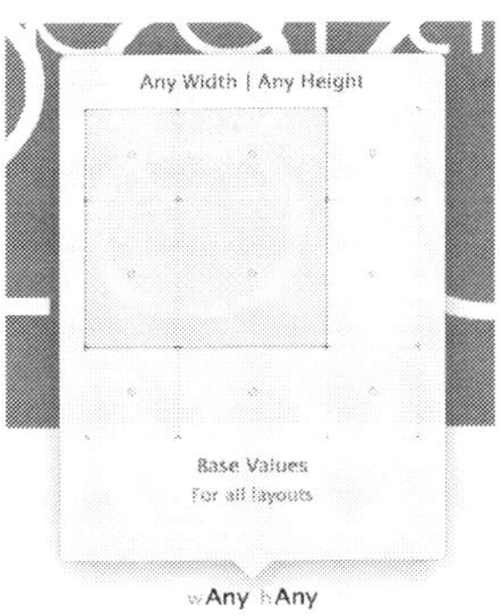

Here you can choose which size class to show in the storyboard by selecting cells within the grid. There are nine possible options: you have three choices for vertical (any, regular or compact) and three for horizontal, resulting in a total of 3x3 = 9 size class combinations.

> **Note:** There is a slight discrepancy in nomenclature at this point. Size classes are always referred to as *horizontal* and *vertical* - you'll learn about the underlying class, `UITraitCollection`, in the next chapter. However, IB uses the terms *width* and *height*. There's an obvious parallel (*width* = *horizontal*; *height* = *vertical*); just be aware that there are two terms for the same concept.

Your current layout doesn't work properly for compact heights. To fix this, choose the cells shown below to select the **Any Width | Compact Height** size class:

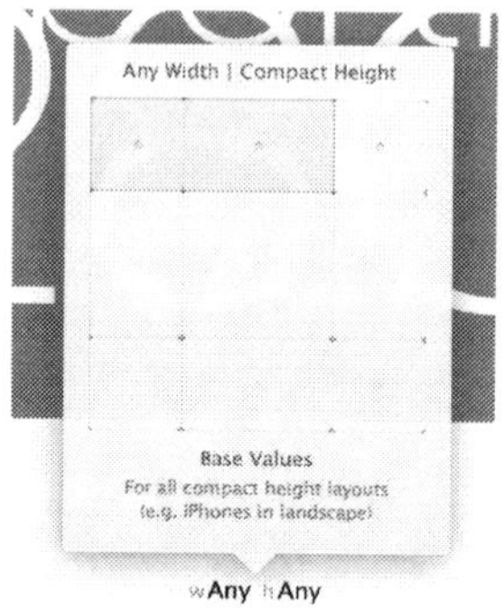

You'll immediately notice two changes in the editor:

1. The shape of the canvas changes to represent the new size class
2. The bottom bar turns a rather fetching shade of blue. This indicates that you're now working on a size-class specific layout.

In order to change the layout, you'll need to temporarily change a few constraints. In Auto Layout terminology this is known as **installing** and **uninstalling** constraints. A constraint is installed if it is currently active, whereas an **uninstalled** constraint is not currently active within the current size class.

Click on the image view to select it, and open the **Size Inspector**. You can see a summary of the constraints which affect this view:

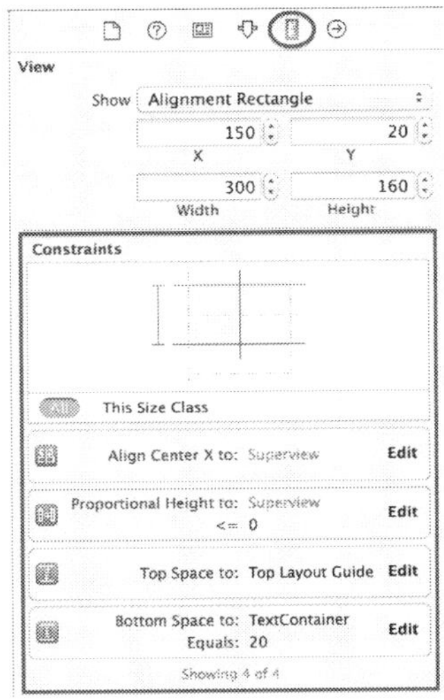

Select the **Align Center X to: Superview** constraint by single clicking it, and then press **Delete** to uninstall the constraint for the current size class. The constraint immediately disappears from the storyboard view and becomes grayed out in both the Document Outline and the view's Size Inspector:

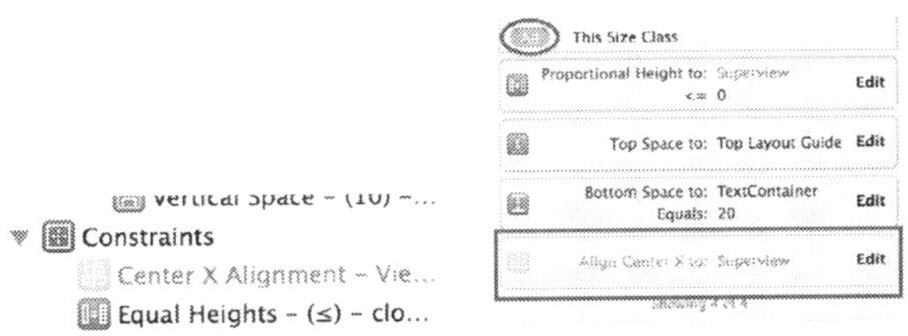

> **Note:** You might have to toggle from **This Size Class** to **All** in the Size Inspector to see the uninstalled constraint.

Double click on the uninstalled constraint in the Size Inspector to select the constraint. There's an additional line at the bottom as shown below:

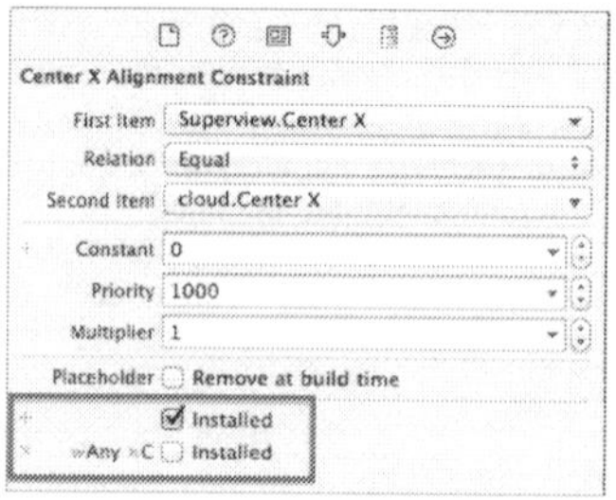

This indicates the constraint is installed for the base layout, but not for the **Any Width | Compact Height** layout – that is, the one you're currently editing.

Repeat the same procedure to uninstall the other three constraints associated with the image view. Your document outline and image view's Size Inspector should resemble the following images:

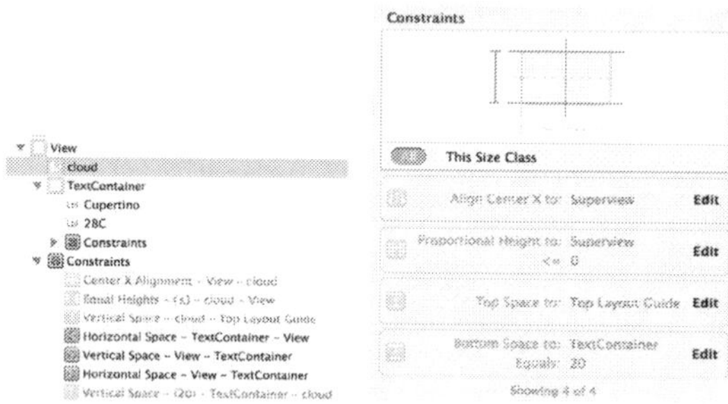

Now you can add the constraints required for this size class. Use the **Align** and **Pin** menus to **Vertically Center in the Container**, and to set a left spacing to nearest neighbor of 10:

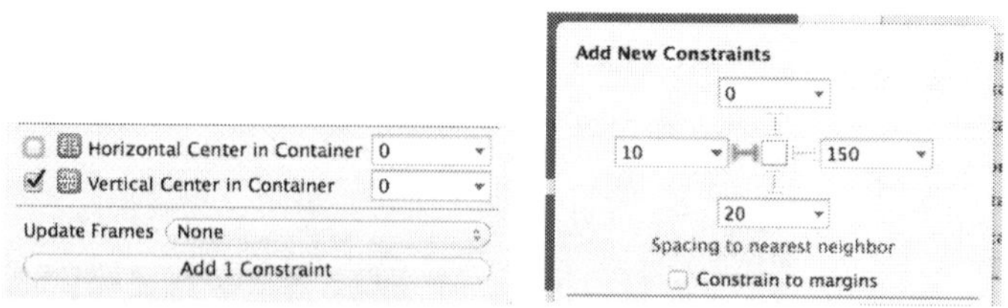

Ctrl-drag from the image view to the view controller's view and then select **Equal Widths** in the popup menu.

Open the **Size Inspector** for the image view and **double-click** the **Equal Width to: Superview** constraint to reveal its properties. If the **First Item** isn't **cloud.Width**, then use the drop down menu to **Reverse First and Second Item**. Then **update** the **Multiplier** to equal **0.45**.

The constraints for the image view are now setup correctly for all size classes, but the text container still needs a bit of attention. You'll need to alter the constraints for this size class to move the label to the right hand side.

The **TextContainer** view has internal constraints to position the labels, which work fine as-is. However, the three external constraints – pinning it to the left, right and bottom sides of the view – aren't quite working properly. To pin the view to the bottom right hand side of the parent view you'll need to uninstall the left-hand constraint.

Select the left-hand constraint, either from the document outline or on the storyboard, as shown below:

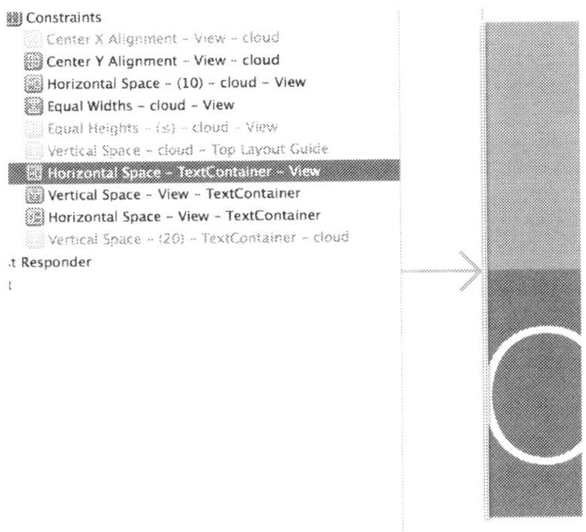

Then press **Cmd-Delete** to uninstall the constraint. As before, any uninstalled constraints appear grayed out in the Document Outline.

You now need to add two constraints to your TextContainer to position it correctly. The view should be half the width of its superview, the view controller's view, and pinned to the top. In theory, you could simply Ctrl-drag from the TextContainer view to the view controller's view as you've been doing all along. However, in practice it's often difficult to grab just the view when there's content in the way. It's much easier to use the document outline to do your dirty work.

Ctrl-drag from **TextContainer** in the document outline up to the view controller's view, as seen on the next page:

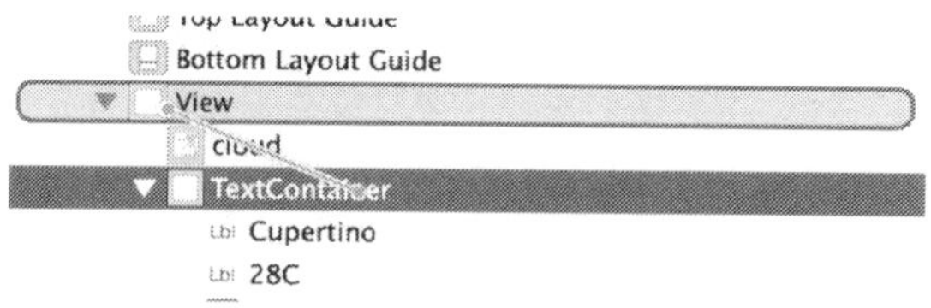

Shift-click on Top Space to Top Layout Guide and Equal Widths as shown below:

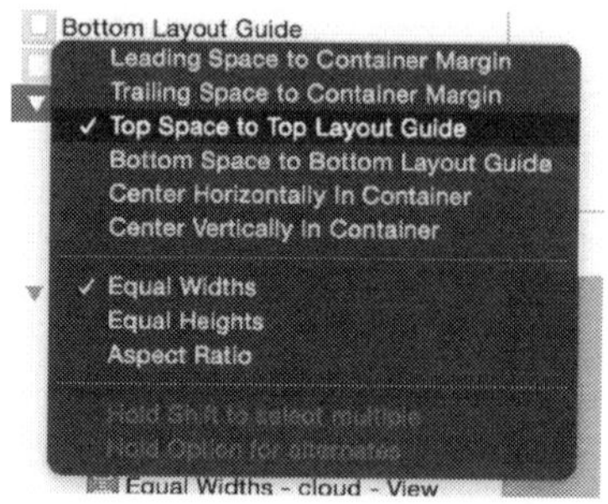

Open the **Size Inspector** for your **TextContainer** and update the two new constraints you've just created as follows:

- **Top Space to: Top Layout Guide** should have a **Constant** of **0**
- **Equal Width to: Superview** should have a **Multiplier** of **0.5**. Note that you might have to switch the first and second items in this constraint, as you have done before. Simply **double click** on the constraint and choose to **Reverse First and Second Item**.

Click the **Resolve Auto Layout Issues** icon in the bottom bar, and select **All Views\Update frames**. The storyboard updates and displays the new layout as shown below:

The layout has changed completely; you're closer to the finished product now. There are still a few issues to correct with the font sizes – you'll address these in the next section.

Adaptive fonts

The current font sizes in your TextContainer look pretty good in the iPad view using a container with regular size classes, but the font size is too large for compact size classes. Fear not – it's also possible to override font sizes within your size classes!

> **Note:** Unlike layout overrides, changing the font configuration will *always* affect the base layout. Changes to the font configuration don't respect the current size class overrides in interface builder. Instead, use the method prescribed below.

Click the size class button in the bottom tool bar and select the squares shown below to choose the base **Any Width | Any Height** size class. The bottom bar of your view turns gray to indicate that you're back to the base layout.

Select the Cupertino text label and open the **Attributes Inspector**. Click the small **+** to the left of the **Font** as shown below:

This reveals a menu for selecting the size class combination in which you'll override the font size. Navigate to **Compact Width > Any Height** like so:

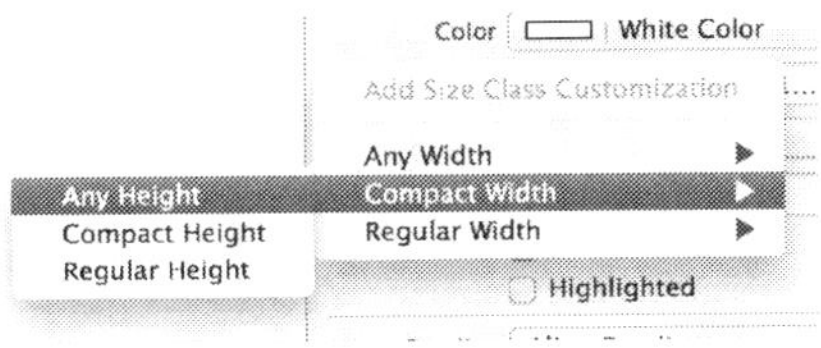

This creates a second font selector box that will apply to the specified size class combination. Update the font size in the new selector box to **90** as shown below:

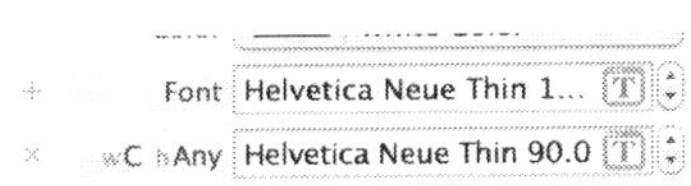

Now select the temperature text label and repeat the same process; this time, set a font size override of **150** for **Compact Width > Any Height**.

The preview updates automatically to show the effect of the changes you made:

Well, it's looking a *little* better, but the **Cupertino** label is clipped. Fiddling with the font sizes until it fits perfectly isn't a particularly scalable option. Cupertino is quite a long place name, but Washington, D.C. is longer – and Kleinfeltersville, PA is longer still! What's a designer to do?

Once again, Auto Layout comes to the rescue! You simply need to limit the width of the two text labels to match the width of the TextContainer. **Ctrl-drag** from the Cupertino label to the TextContainer, and select **Equal Widths**.

Repeat the process with the temperature label. The preview updates to show the effects of your changes as follows:

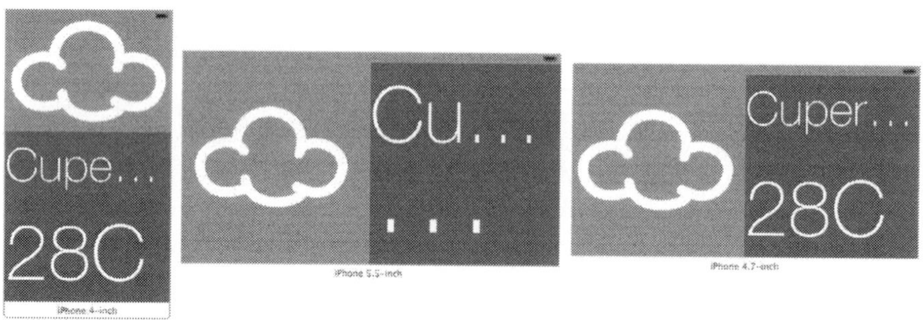

Hmm, having the text truncate is not exactly what you want. This is the default behavior for labels that contain more text than will fit in the available space. However, there is an option to automatically adjust the font size to fit the content.

Select the Cupertino label and open the **Attributes Inspector**. Change the **AutoShrink** drop down to **Minimum font scale** and ensure that it is set to **0.5**.

Also update the **Text Alignment** to **Centered.** Your Attributes Inspector should look as follows:

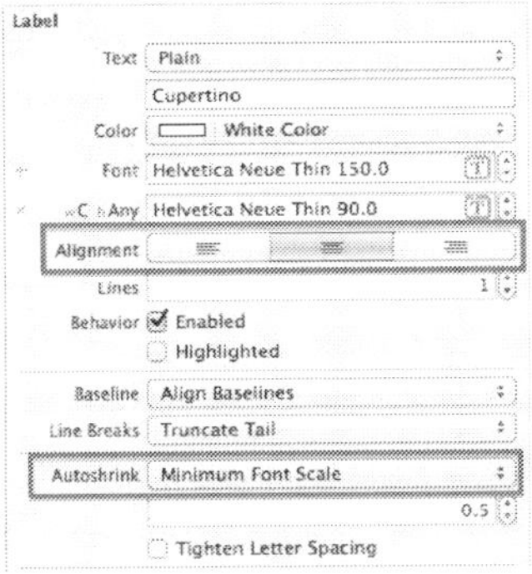

Repeat exactly the same procedure for the temperature label.

Take a look at the preview pane; the iPhone layouts look much better now:

Working with the preview editor is great, but this is probably a good time to build and run your project to see that everything is still working correctly. The iPhone screens look like everything is sizing correctly:

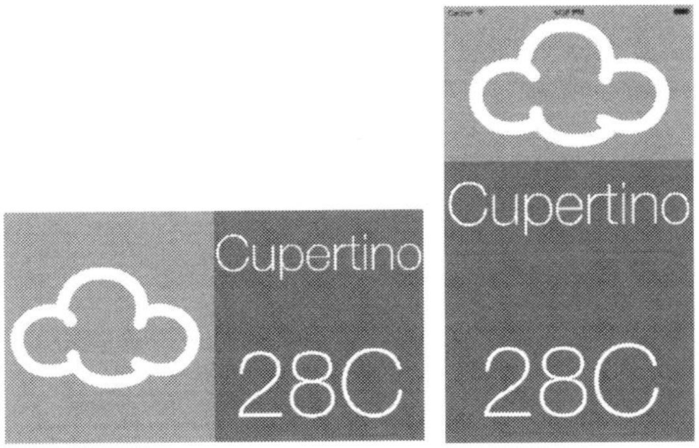

However, take a look at the iPad preview. The cloud image looks comically small, especially in portrait mode:

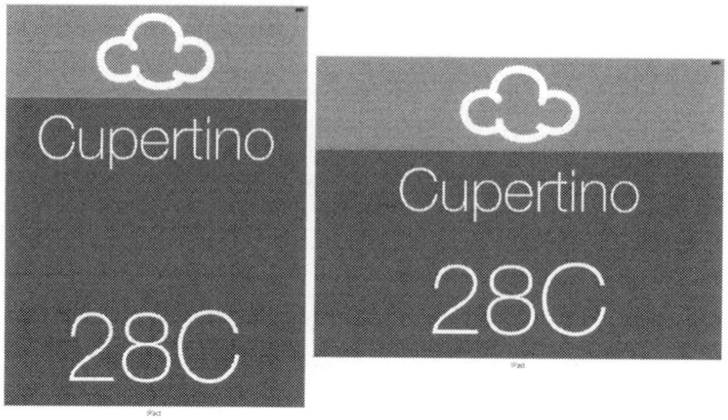

This is because you're using exactly the same image on the iPad as on the iPhone. In the next section you'll learn how you can change this to improve the image appearance on the iPad.

Device-dependent images

The fact that asset catalogs can provide different images for specific devices is not new to iOS8, but it's exactly the tool you need to solve this issue. With this feature you can refer to the same image name in your app and the asset library will *automagically* provide the appropriate image for the current device.

Open **Images.xcassets** and select the cloud image set on the left hand side. You'll see the three images you've already associated with this set – one standard density image, one Retina version as well as the new Retina HD version.

Select the cloud image set and open the **Attributes Inspector**. Change the **Devices** drop-down from **Universal** to **Device Specific**, and **check** the boxes next to **iPhone** and **iPad**:

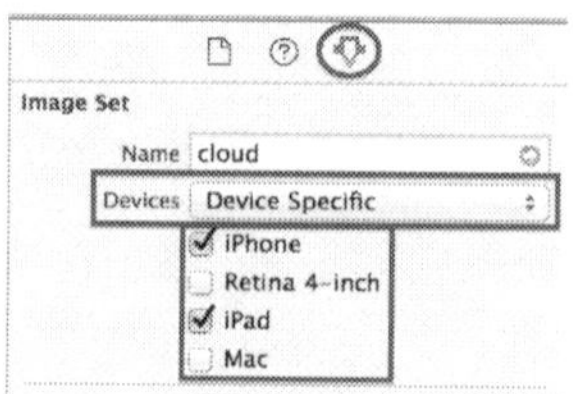

This adds groups for the device specific files, and moves the existing files to the iPhone section:

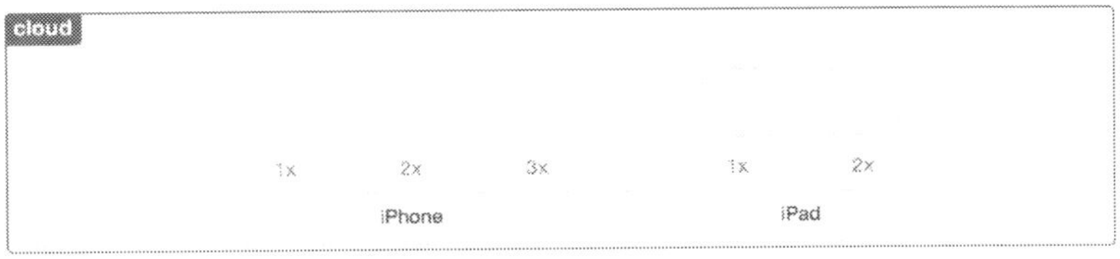

Head back to the files that you unzipped early and drag **cloud_big.png** from the finder to the **1x** box in the iPad section of the cloud image set like so:

Then drag **cloud_big@2x.png** to the **2x** box.

> **Note:** Apple is yet to release an iPad with a Retina HD screen, hence you only need two different images are required.

Build and run your app under the iPad simulator to ensure that the layout works as you expected:

The device-dependent approach seems to be a great solution to the problem presented in this tutorial. However, it *feels* a little wrong to have to specify different images for different devices. The main thrust of Adaptive Layout is to abstract the design of the app away from the display limitations of different devices and into the paradigm of size classes instead.

The next chapter deals with this paradigm shift and an alternative approach to this problem that follows the size class school of thought.

Conclusion

Take a moment to think about the app you've built. In particular, consider that it looks really good on *all* devices, in *both* orientations, using only *one* storyboard file! If nothing else convinces you that Adaptive Layout is the way of the future, consider the fact that this layout will also look good on future devices that *haven't even been released yet.*

The takeaway from this chapter is that, as a developer, you will need to change your approach to app design. Rather than working towards pixel-based layouts, you should be considering the relationship between the UI elements on the screen.

Does this sound a lot like Auto Layout? It should. If you've had a tough time with Auto Layout in the past, it's time to give Adaptive Layout a try in your apps. The trick is to take a moment and think about what you want your constraints to *do* instead of how you want the app to *look*. A little care and attention up-front can help your app avoid becoming an impenetrable forest of conflicting constraints.

This chapter has only scratched the surface of what you can achieve with Adaptive Layout in iOS 8. Chapter 3, "Intermediate Adaptive Layout" will introduce you to more advanced approaches to managing your app layouts – without resorting to pixel-pushing.

Chapter 3: Intermediate Adaptive Layout

By Sam Davies

The previous chapter gave you a brief introduction to Adaptive Layout, and the supporting functionality in Interface Builder.

This chapter introduces you to the more advanced concepts of Adaptive Layout, including the following:

- Auto-sizing table view cells
- Installable views
- Overriding trait collections for child view controllers
- Size-class specific images in asset catalogs
- Auto-hiding navigation bars
- Customizing the appearance of navigation bars using appearance proxies and trait collections

As usual, a starter project for this chapter is provided to get you up and running. **WorldWeather** is a basic master-detail app, which displays the weather for a collection of cities around the world. The data layer is already implemented, and the detail view controller looks very similar to the one in the previous chapter.

Self-sizing table view cells

Before iOS 7, you had to use either the `rowHeight` property on `UITableView`, or the `tableView(_:, heightForRowAtIndexPath:)` delegate method to specify the height of a table view cell; to make matters worse, you often needed complex calculations to determine the height of each cell at runtime.

iOS 7 introduced the concept of estimated row heights via the `estimatedRowHeight` property on `UITableView`, and the `tableView(_:, estimatedHeightForRowAtIndexPath:)` delegate method. This allowed for just-in-time row height delegate method calls just as the cell was about to come into view. Although this was a major improvement, it still placed the responsibility of calculating row height on the delegate instead of the cell. Since a cell is responsible for its own layout, surely it should also determine its own height?

And this is precisely what happens in iOS 8. By ensuring the Auto Layout constraints used in the cells layout properly determine the cells height, you can let UIKit handle the rest.

You'll use this technique to create a custom cell to represent each city in the master view controller.

Open the **WorldWeather** starter project in Xcode 6, and then open **Main.storyboard**. You'll see a familiar arrangement of view controllers that make up a master-detail project in iOS 8, along with two other view controllers, as shown below:

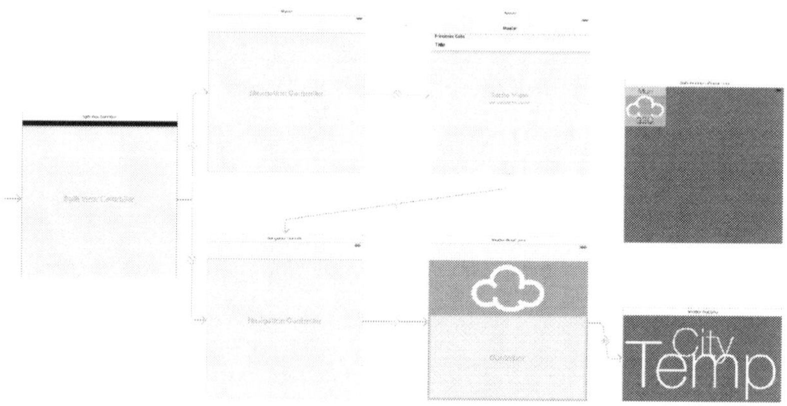

You'll get your hands dirty with the master table view controller.

Creating custom cells

You're going to create a custom cell containing the name of a city, and have an image of that city as the background.

In the storyboard, select the view controller called **Master** that contains a table view. Then, select the prototype cell in the table view and in the **Attributes Inspector** change the **Cell Style** to **Custom** and the **Cell Selection Style** to **None**, as shown below:

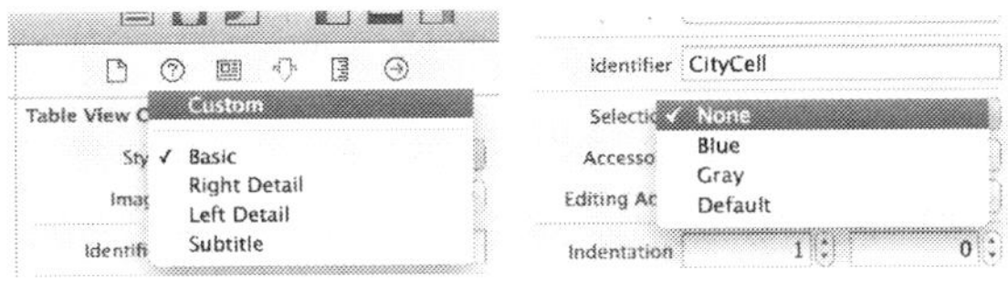

Drag an **Image View** from the **Object Library** onto the cell. With the image view selected, click the **Pin** button on the tool bar at the bottom of the storyboard canvas, and in the popup dialog choose constraints of **0** for **top**, **left**, **bottom** and **right**. Ensure that the **Constrain to margins box** is not checked, as shown below:

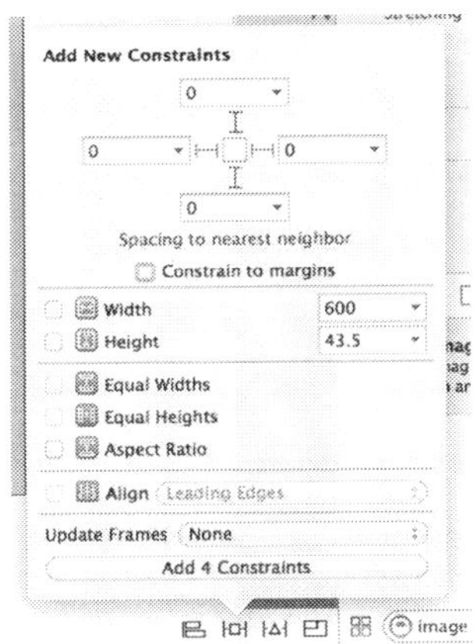

The constraints will appear orange in the storyboard because they're not currently satisfied; you'll fix that shortly. Go back to the **Object library**, and drag a **Label** onto the cell, like so:

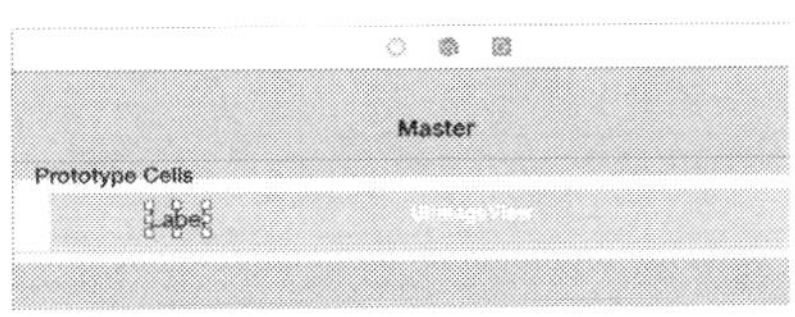

In the **Document Outline**, **ctrl+drag** from the **Label** to the **Content View**, as shown below:

When presented with the popup menu, hold down **shift** and click

- **Leading Space to Container Margin**
- **Trailing Space to Container Margin**
- **Top Space to Container Margin**
- **Bottom Space to Container Margin**

To select them, like so:

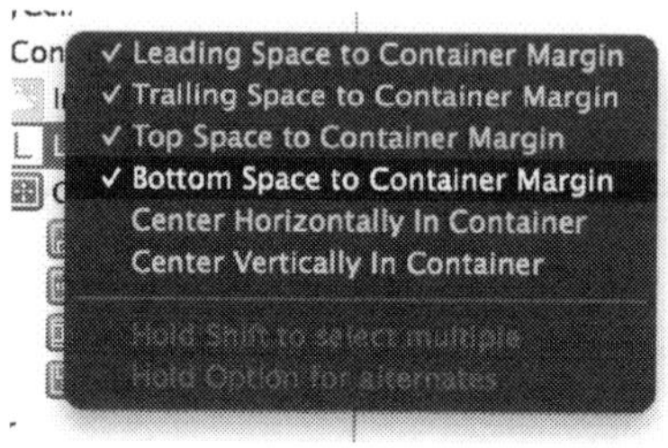

You've now created the constraints, but just like those before them, they won't yet have the correct settings, so don't panic if they turn orange.

Updating the constraints

Select the label in the cell and then open the **Size Inspector**. Use the **Edit** button on each constraint to update them to the following settings:

- **Trailing space to: Superview** -> a constant of **0**
- **Leading space to: Superview** -> a constant of **40**
- **Bottom space to: Superview** -> a constant of **40**
- **Top space to: Superview** -> constant of **40**

You'll notice that two of the constraints are now red, indicating a conflict. This is illustrated below:

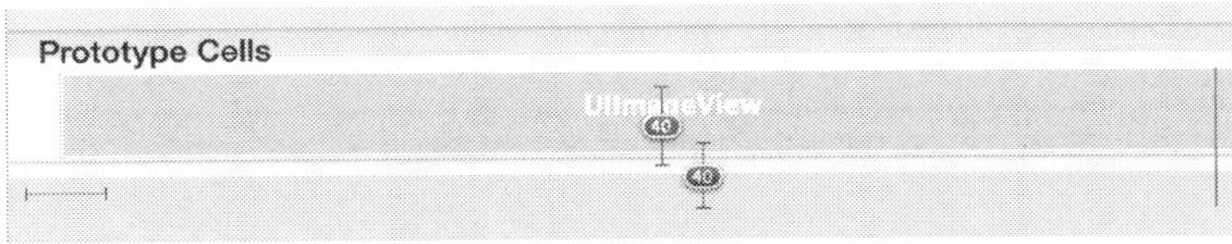

This is because the cell isn't tall enough to satisfy the constraints. Select the cell, and using the central grab handle, increase its height to **120**. This height is only a placeholder that's relevant in Interface Builder; Auto Layout will automatically calculate the actual cell height at runtime.

Now you can update the view to reflect the constraints. Click the **Resolve Auto Layout Issues** button in the bottom toolbar and choose **All Views in Master View Controller\Update Frames**, like so:

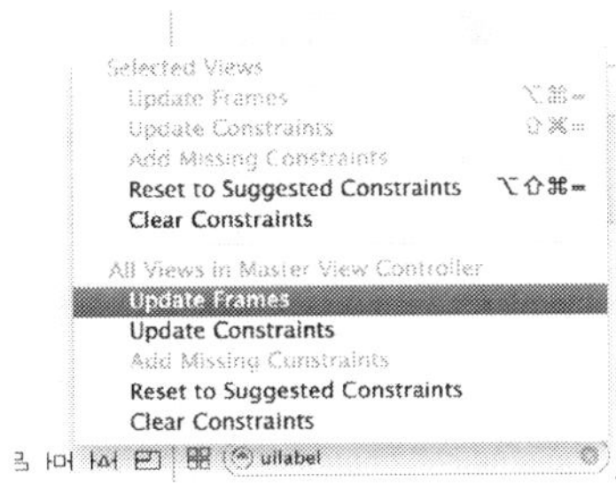

You'll now make a few changes to the appearance of the two new controls.

First select the label, open the **Attributes Inspector** and change **Text** to **City Name**. You'll set this to the actual city name in code later, but setting it here makes things a little easier to understand while designing your layout.

Then set **Font** to **Helvetica Neue Light** with a size of **30**, and set **Color** to **R:55, G:128, B:186**. Set **Background** to **R:255, G:255, B:255** with an opacity of **75%**.

Now select the image view and use the **Attributes Inspector** to set **Image** to **Bangkok** and **Mode** to **Aspect Fill**.

Your cell will now look like the following:

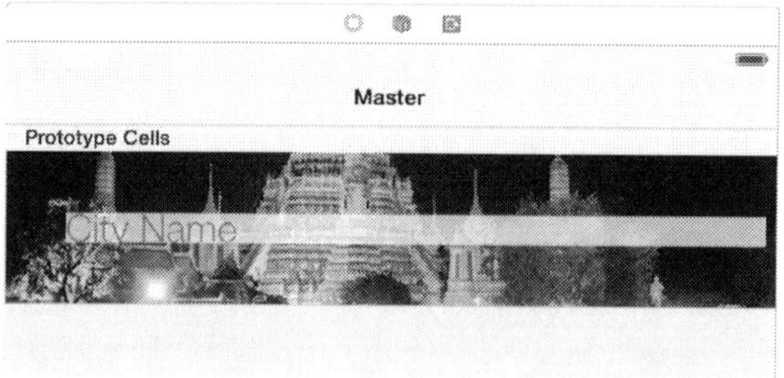

The final change is to remove the separator between the cells. Select the **Table View**, and then in the **Attributes Inspector** set **Separator** to **None**.

Now you need a custom class for this custom cell you've created.

Creating a custom class

In the **Project Navigator**, right click on the **Master View** group and select **New File...**. Choose **iOS\Source\Cocoa Touch Class** and name it **CityTableViewCell**. Also make it a subclass of `UITableViewCell`, like so:

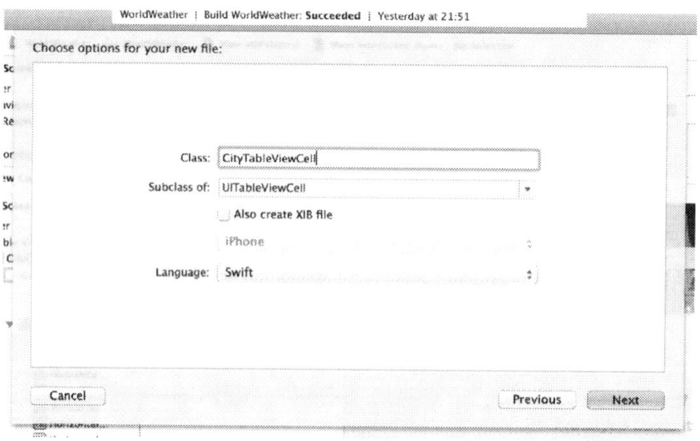

Make sure the **Language** is set to **Swift** and click **Next**, and then **Create**.

Open **CityTableViewCell.swift** and replace the contents with the following:

```
import UIKit
class CityTableViewCell: UITableViewCell {
  // MARK: - IBOutlets
```

```
  @IBOutlet weak var cityImageView: UIImageView!
  @IBOutlet weak var cityNameLabel: UILabel!

  // MARK: - Properties
  var cityWeather: CityWeather? {
    didSet {
      configureCell()
    }
  }

  // MARK: - Utility methods
  private func configureCell() {
    cityImageView.image = cityWeather?.cityImage
    cityNameLabel.text = cityWeather?.name
  }
}
```

The above class is relatively straightforward:

- `cityImageView` and `cityNameLabel` are `IBOutlets` which will be used to connect the controls in the custom cell you just created in Interface Builder to this class.
- `cityWeather` is a property of type `CityWeather`, a model class that's part of the data layer. It provides a city name and an image representing that city. You also provide a custom `didSet` method that calls `configureCell()`.
- `configureCell()` updates the image view and label with the properties of the `CityWeather` instance.

That's all the code you need in this custom class; all that's left is to wire it up in the storyboard.

Open **Main.storyboard** and once again find your custom cell. Open the **Identity Inspector** to set **Class** to `CityTableViewCell`.

Next open the **Connections Inspector** and find the two outlets you created in code. Drag from **cityNameLabel** to the **label** in the cell to make the connection, as shown below:

Now drag from **cityImageView** to the **image view** in the cell.

The **Connections Inspector** will now display the new connections, as shown here:

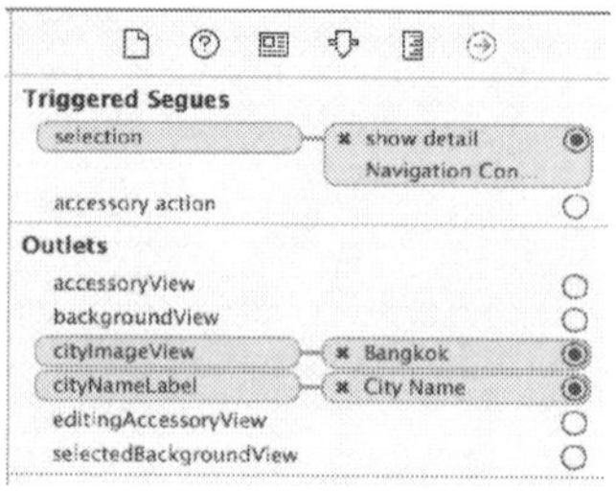

You now need to update the table view's data source to reflect the changes you've made to the cell.

From the **Project Navigator**, open **MasterView\MasterViewController.swift**, find `tableView(_:, cellForRowAtIndexPath:)`. First, replace this line:

```
let cell = tableView.dequeueReusableCellWithIdentifier(
"CityCell", forIndexPath: indexPath) as UITableViewCell
```

With this line:

```
let cell = tableView.dequeueReusableCellWithIdentifier(
"CityCell", forIndexPath: indexPath) as CityTableViewCell
```

And then this line:

```
cell.textLabel.text = city.name
```

With this line:

```
cell.cityWeather = city
```

The modifications to the code are:

- When you dequeue the cell you now cast it directly to an instance `CityTableViewCell`
- Instead of setting the text of the label directly, you're now setting the new `cityWeather` property and letting the cell update itself

Build and run. You'll see your new custom cells working perfectly:

Oh, wait just a minute! The cells didn't size themselves properly; the images are 200pts tall. *So what gives?*

It turns out there are two more changes you need to make in order to achieve self-sizing cells:

- The table views `rowHeight` property needs to be set to `UITableViewAutomaticDimension`
- The `estimatedCellHeight` needs to be set to a non-zero value

Add the following to the end of `viewDidLoad()` in `MasterViewController`:

```
tableView.rowHeight = UITableViewAutomaticDimension
tableView.estimatedRowHeight = 100
```

`estimatedRowHeight` doesn't have to be exact, just an approximation in-order for self-sizing to work. Setting the `rowHeight` to `UITableViewAutomaticDimension` simply provides a hint to the table view that the cells are self-sizing and should be treated as such.

Build and run. Hooray for self-sizing cells!

That looks much better. The cells match the height of the images and the labels have stretched accordingly.

Here's what you need to remember about self-sizing table view cells:

- The table view determines the width
- Your Auto Layout constraints **must** define the height, without any ambiguity
- The `rowHeight` property on the table view must be set to `UITableViewAutomaticDimension`
- `estimatedRowHeight` must be set to non-zero, but you should try and set this a close approximation, as too big a difference between the estimate and the actual will cause the table view to jump when scrolling. This value is used solely to calculate the length of the scroll bar in the tableview – a process that would otherwise require calculating the height of each cell individually.

Your master view controller is looking pretty good. In the next section you'll turn your attention to the detail view controller.

Conditionally installing views

In the Beginning Adaptive Layout chapter you learned how to customize your layouts using size classes and conditionally installed Auto Layout constraints.

However, when using a Universal storyboard (one that services both iPhone and iPad) there is a limit to what you can accomplish by rearranging the layout. Larger views simply require more content to look good.

Just as you can install and uninstall layout constraints, you can also install and uninstall *views*. This means you can have views that only appear for particular size classes.

In this section, you'll discover how to display a weather summary view, but only when the vertical size class is **Regular**.

The summary view is a just standard collection view provided by the starter project

Open **Main.storyboard** and locate the **Weather Text View**:

This view controller contains the city name and temperature labels. You're going to add a container view to it that will *contain* the collection view.

Drag a **Container View** from the **Object Library** onto this view and place it like so:

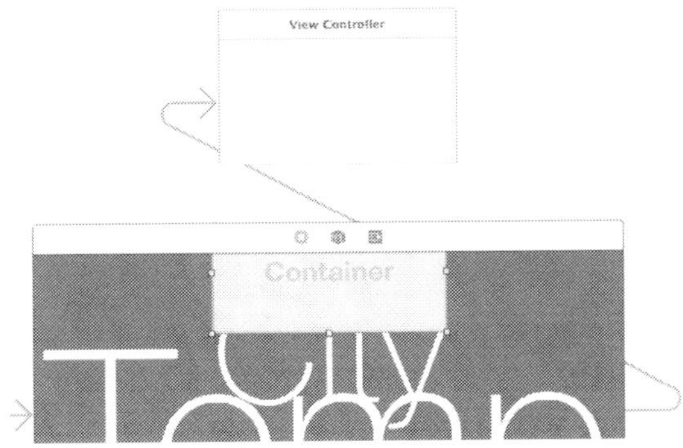

To properly position the container, click the **Pin** button in the bottom toolbar, and in the popup dialog to set the following constraints:

- Top distance to **0**
- Left distance to **0**
- Right distance to **0**
- **Height** to **150**

Additionally, make sure that **Constrain to margins** is unchecked, as seen on the next page:

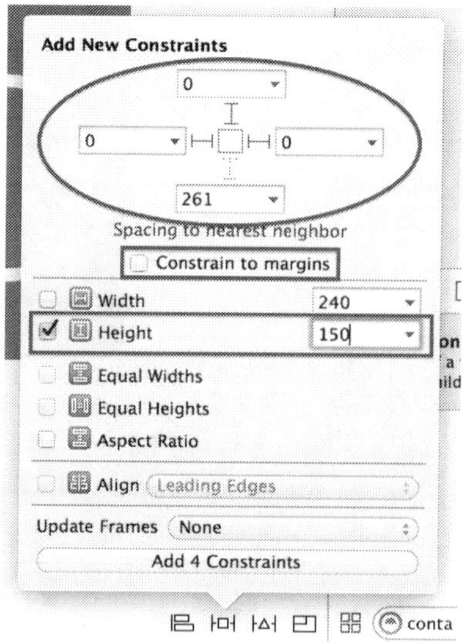

To update the frames, click the **Resolve Auto Layout Issues** button and select **All views\Weather Text View Controller\Update frames.**

Your view controller should look like this:

When you add a container view, Interface Builder automatically creates a blank view controller of the correct size and links it to the container view, as shown below:

In this instance you don't need this view controller, so select it and hit **delete** to remove it from the storyboard.

You can now embed the collection view controller in the container view. **Ctrl-drag** from the **Container** view to the **Daily Weather Collection View**, as shown below:

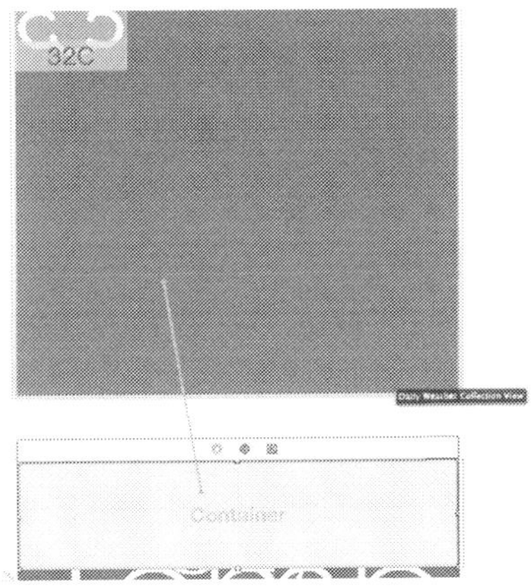

In the popup menu that's displayed, select **embed** to connect the two by creating an Embed segue. Notice how the collection view controller updates its size to match that of the container view, as shown here:

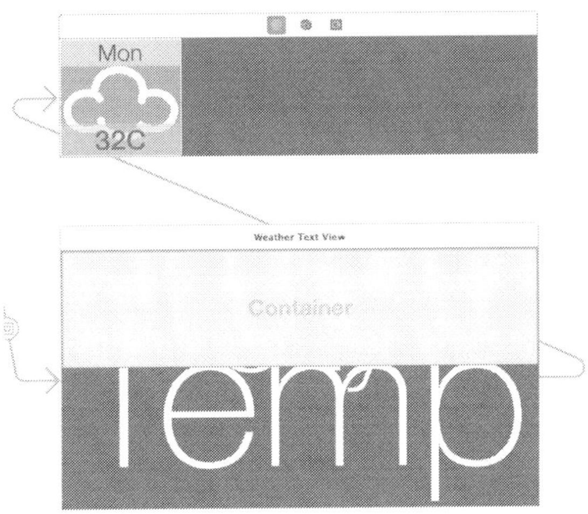

Correcting the alignment

You've likely noticed that the container view obstructs the existing labels. The top of the city name label should be aligned with the bottom of the container view instead of the top of the view controller.

It's a bit tricky to select the city label since it's behind the container view. Luckily, Interface Builder can help you out. **Ctrl+shift** click on the container view and a context menu pops up to let you select any elements underneath the mouse pointer, like so:

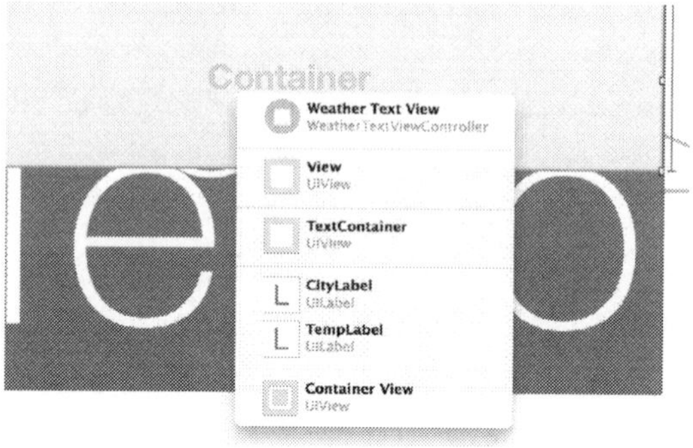

Select **CityLabel** from the menu. Open the **Size Inspector** to view the four constraints relating to this view:

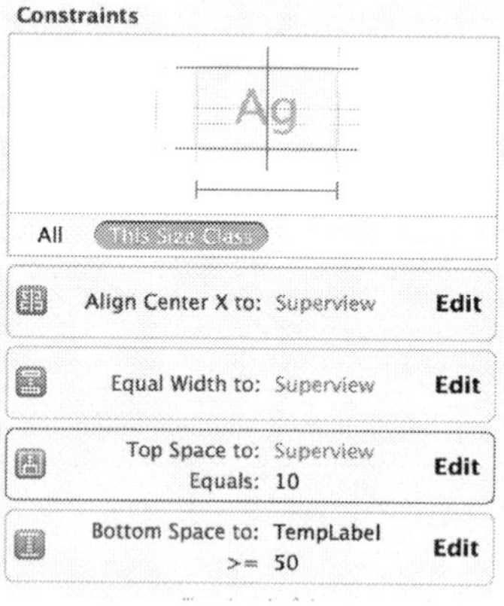

Select the **Top space to: Superview** constraint and hit **delete** to *uninstall* it. You'll see a cluster of orange lines on your storyboard as you've now created a fair bit of layout ambiguity. You'll fix this now.

> **Note:** Even though you used the delete key to remove the layout constraint, it hasn't been deleted. It's simply been uninstalled from the current size-class.

In the **Document Outline**, **ctrl-drag** from **CityLabel** to **Container View**, like so:

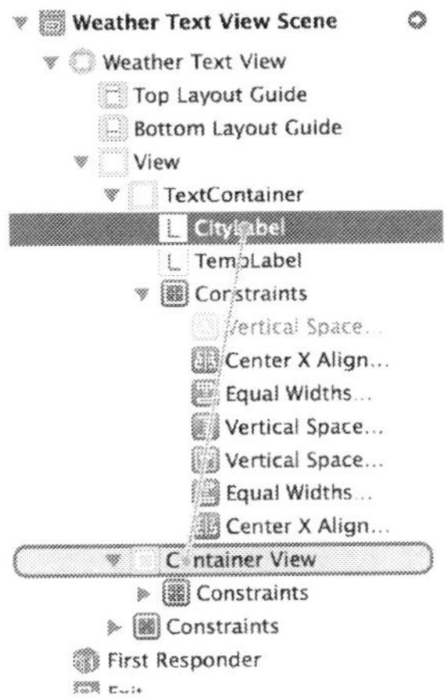

Select **Vertical Spacing** from the popup menu. Find this new constraint in the **Size Inspector** – it'll be called "Top Space to: Container View" – click **Edit** and set **Constant** to **0**:

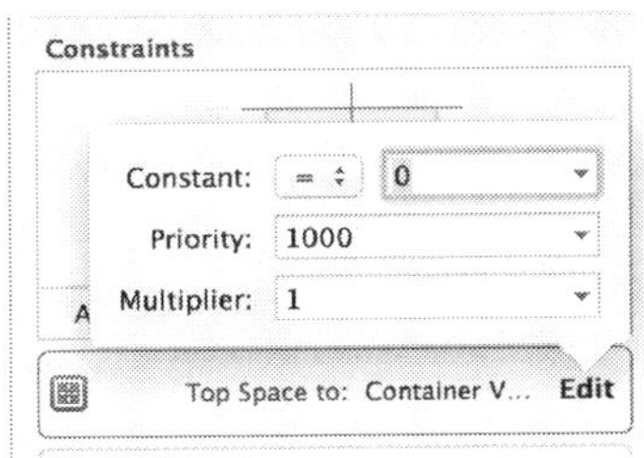

The layout is now complete; it should resemble the following:

At this point you're probably itching to add some data to your collection view.

The `DailyWeatherCollectionViewController` class exposes a `dailyWeather` property, which takes an array of `DailyWeather` objects. You need to pass this data from `WeatherTextViewController` to the collection view.

Open **DailyWeatherCollectionViewController.swift** and add the following protocol definition to the top, just below the `import` statements:

```
@objc protocol WeeklyWeatherContainer {
  var dailyWeather: [DailyWeather] { get set }
}
```

Using the above protocol you can check for conformance instead of relying on a specific class, resulting in looser coupling between classes. This protocol includes the `@objc` attribute as required for runtime conformance checking – i.e. checking that a particular object adopts a protocol at runtime, as opposed to compile time. You're going to use it here to discover which child view controllers require weather data, and then provide it to them. Using protocols leads to much looser coupling between classes – meaning that the parent view controller doesn't need to know the specifics of its children – just whether or not they require the weather data.

Update the declaration of `DailyWeatherCollectionViewController` so it conforms to this new protocol:

```
class DailyWeatherCollectionViewController:
UICollectionViewController, WeeklyWeatherContainer {
```

Next, you need to update the weather text view controller to provide all the necessary data.

Open **WeatherTextViewController.swift** and add the following method to the end of `WeatherTextViewController`:

```
private func provideDataToChildViewControllers() {
  for vc in childViewControllers {
    if let weeklyWeatherContainer = vc as?
WeeklyWeatherContainer {
      if let weeklyWeather = cityWeather?.weather {
        weeklyWeatherContainer.dailyWeather = weeklyWeather
      }
    }
  }
}
```

This method iterates over all of the view controllers' child view controllers attempting to cast each one as an instance of `WeeklyWeatherContainer`. If successful, it extracts the weather data from the `cityWeather` property, and sets it on the `weeklyWeatherContainer`.

Now you need to update the `cityWeather` property to call this method whenever it's set. Add the following line to the bottom of the `didSet` closure:

```
provideDataToChildViewControllers()
```

Build and run. The app is looking pretty sharp on an iPad, in portrait:

But if you re-run the app on the iPhone simulator, and rotate to landscape, you'll see there simply isn't room for the collection view when the vertical size-class is **Compact**:

You'll fix this by *uninstalling* the collection view for the **Compact** vertical size class.

Uninstalling views and constraints for size classes

Switch back to **Main.storyboard** and use the size class selector to choose **Any Width | Compact Height**:

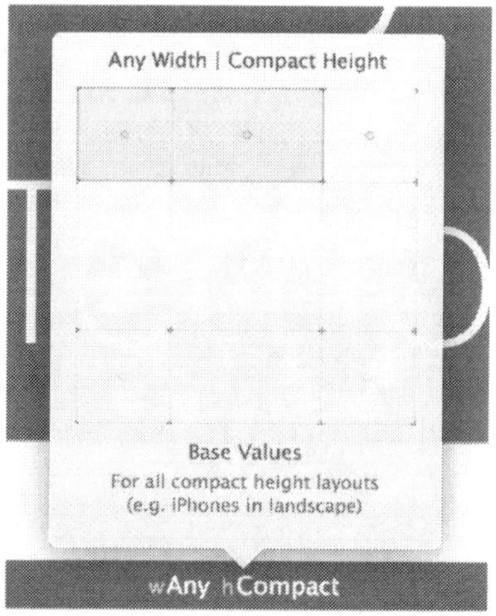

Select the container view in the **Weather Text View Scene** and hit **cmd+delete** to uninstall it.

> **Note:** You used **cmd+delete** to uninstall the view, rather than **delete** as previously. When you have selected an entity (be it a view or a constraint) in IB **cmd+delete** will uninstall it. However, the Size Inspector of a view allows you to "pseudo-select" a constraint by single clicking on it. At this point, **delete** will uninstall that constraint, whereas **cmd+delete** will attempt to delete the storyboard file. This seems confusing, but it's pretty easy to get used to.

You'll see it's no longer displayed in the view controller:

You'll also need to uninstall the constraints that relate to this container view, which makes sense since the view is no longer installed. Select **Container View** in the **Document Outline** as illustrated below:

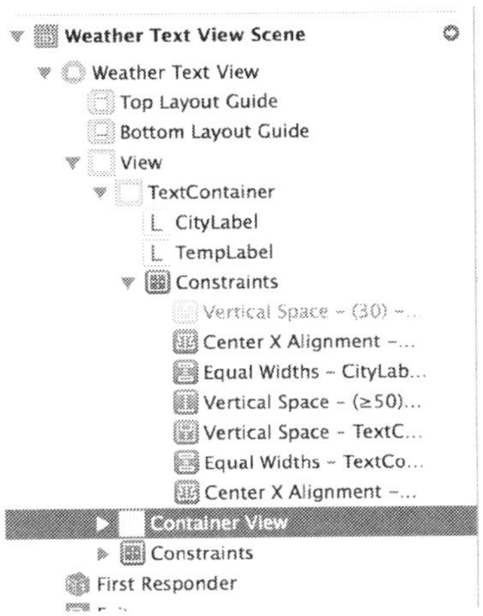

Open the **Size Inspector** to see the five constraints that relate to this view in the **Constraints** panel. Uninstall each one in turn; click the constraint to select it, and then press **delete** to uninstall it.

This leaves the city name label with an ambiguous layout. Recall that you uninstalled the top space constraint when you added the container view. Now's the time to reinstall it.

Select the **CityName** label and open the **Size Inspector**.

Click the **All** option in the scope bar to make sure uninstalled constraints are also displayed:

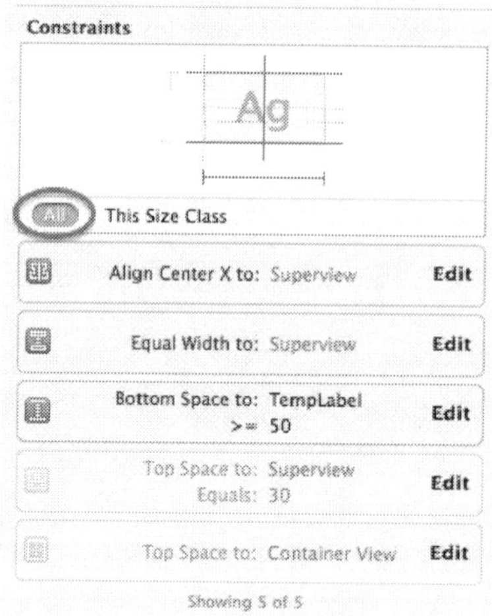

Double-click the **Top Space to: Superview** constraint to make the constraint the target of IB's Inspectors, and then click the **+** button to the left of the **Installed** check box:

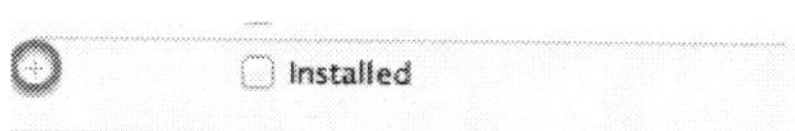

Select the **Any Width | Compact Height** size-class, which happens to be the current size class, from the popup menu, like so:

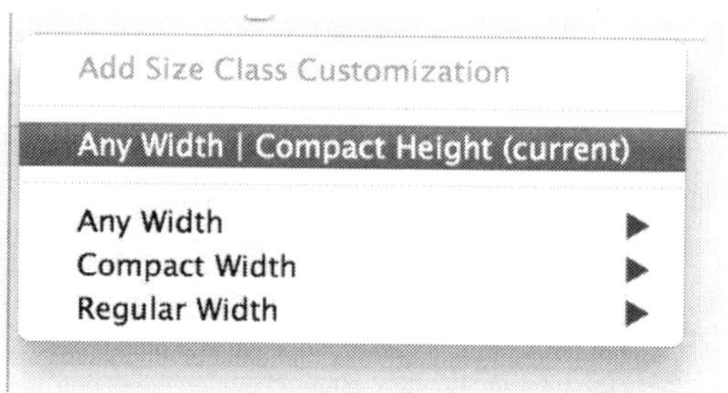

Ensure the **Installed checkbox** *is* checked in order to install the constraint in the corresponding size-class as shown:

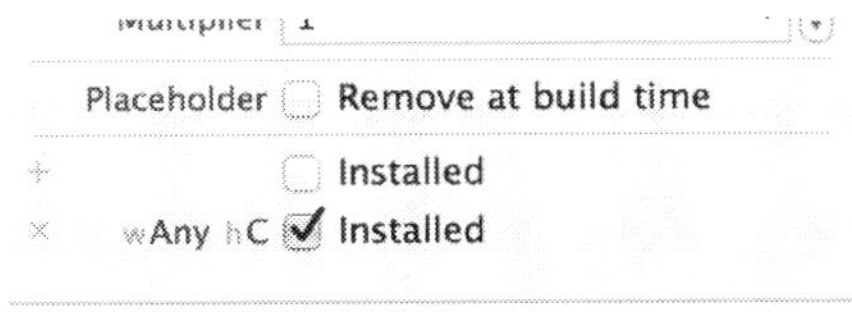

Build and run using the iPhone simulator. Rotate to landscape and note how the collection view has disappeared. *David Blaine, eat your heart out!*

However, if you rotate the simulator to portrait you'll see the collection view remains installed, and there isn't enough room for it:

This is because the iPhone has a vertical size-class of **Regular** when in portrait, matching the iPad. The weather text view is only about half the height of the entire screen, so it shouldn't necessarily share the same vertical size class.

In the following section you'll learn how to override the size-class of a child view controller, which as you'll see can be an incredibly useful tool in your Adaptive Layout tool belt.

Overriding size classes

Size-classes are part of a **trait collection**. A trait collection is a set of characteristics that describe the current environment. These include the horizontal and vertical size-classes, the screen scale, and the device idiom. The `UITraitCollection` class wraps these in a nice, convenient object.

Trait collections can be obtained from any object conforming to the `UITraitEnvironment` protocol. This includes `UIViewController` and `UIView`, which means you can get hold of the current trait environment at any time.

Devices have an intrinsic trait collection for a given orientation, and this is passed down through the view controller and view hierarchies. However, it is possible to override the trait collection of a child view controller using `setOverrideTraitCollection(_:, forChildViewController:)`. You'll use this to override the vertical size class.

To support Adaptive Layout, `UIViewController` - `viewWillTransitionToSize(_:,withTransitionCoordinator)` is called when the bounds of a view change during rotation. You can exploit this method, using it to hook in to the transition animation.

> **Note:** For a more in-depth look at transition coordinators, please check out Chapter 5, Transition Coordinators.

Open **DetailViewController.swift** and add the following method to the end of `DetailViewController`:

```
private func configureTraitOverrideForSize(size: CGSize) {
  var traitOverride: UITraitCollection?
  if size.height < 1000 {
    traitOverride = UITraitCollection(verticalSizeClass:
.Compact)
  }
  for vc in childViewControllers as [UIViewController] {
    setOverrideTraitCollection(traitOverride,
forChildViewController: vc)
  }
}
```

This is a utility method that takes a `CGSize` as an argument. If the height of this size is less than 1000 then it creates an instance of `UITraitCollection` with a **Compact** vertical size class.

> **Note:** The value of 1000 was chosen empirically using the resizable simulator – altering the height to discover the point at which the vertically regular layout no longer works. This makes the device and view controller hierarchy agnostic.

Next, it iterates over the view controller's child view controllers calling `setOverrideTraitCollection(_:, forChildViewController:)` on each one. Note that you don't have to provide a complete trait collection to this method; here you're simply providing a trait collection with only its vertical size-class set, so this is the only trait that'll be overridden.

Providing `nil` to the first parameter will reset any previous overrides and the trait collection will return to its default behavior, that is, deferring to the trait collection of the container's parent.

You'll need to call the method you just added from two places.

First, add the following to the very bottom of `viewDidLoad()`:

```
configureTraitOverrideForSize(view.bounds.size)
```

Then, add the following method to the `DetailViewController` class:

```
override func viewWillTransitionToSize(size: CGSize,
withTransitionCoordinator coordinator:
UIViewControllerTransitionCoordinator) {
  configureTraitOverrideForSize(size)
}
```

This simply makes sure the new method is call when a rotation takes place.

Build and run. Notice that on the iPhone simulator in portrait the view no longer includes the weather summary, since the view's height is less than 1000 (see image on next page):

Both orientations on iPad look different as well; but they still look great:

Take a closer look at the screenshot on the left; the large image representing the current weather is the same image used in the collection view cells.

In Beginning Adaptive Layout you learnt how to specify different images for different devices in an asset catalog. However, you can accomplish much the same thing using size-classes instead.

Size class dependent images

Asset catalogs in Xcode 6 now support size-class dependent images. You'll change the current device dependent image sets into size-class dependent image sets instead.

Open **Images.xcassets** and select the **sun** image set from the **weather images** group. Open the **Attributes Inspector** and change **Width** to **Any & Compact**, like so:

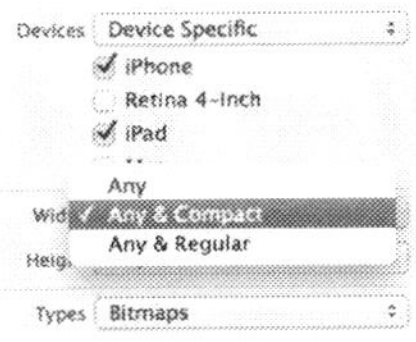

This states that the image set contains images for both **Any** and **Compact** horizontal size-classes. All iPhone orientations (except iPhone 6 Plus) use a horizontally compact size class.

Take a look at your image set; it now contains five new placeholders that represent the second size-class, as shown below:

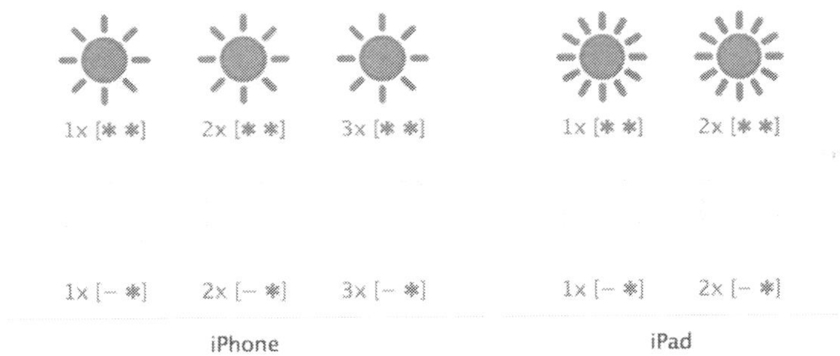

The notation is a bit strange: the two characters between the square braces represent the size-classes; the left character is the horizontal size-class, and the right character is the vertical size-class.

Each character can be one of the following:

- * Any
- – Compact
- + Regular

Judging by the notation, your image set supports the **Any** vertical size-class along with both the **Any** and **Compact** horizontal size-classes. Don't worry about there still being device-specific sections – you'll configure the iPhone section appropriately before making the asset universal later on.

When the size-class is **Compact**, you'll use the smaller, less complex images. They're not in the correct image slots, however. Drag each of the images in the [**] row in the iPhone section down into its respective placeholder in the [-*] row, and then drag the two iPad images to the recently vacated [**] row. When you're finished, your image set will look like this:

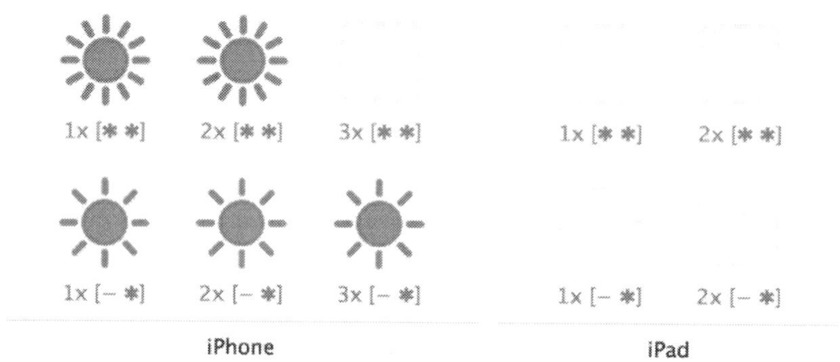

You'll notice that you're missing an image in the 3x [**] cell. You can find an image in the **additional_images.zip** file that accompanies this project. Unzip the file and drag **sun_big@3x.png** from the finder into the empty cell.

Back in the **Attributes Inspector**, change **Devices** from **Device Specific** to **Universal**, as shown below:

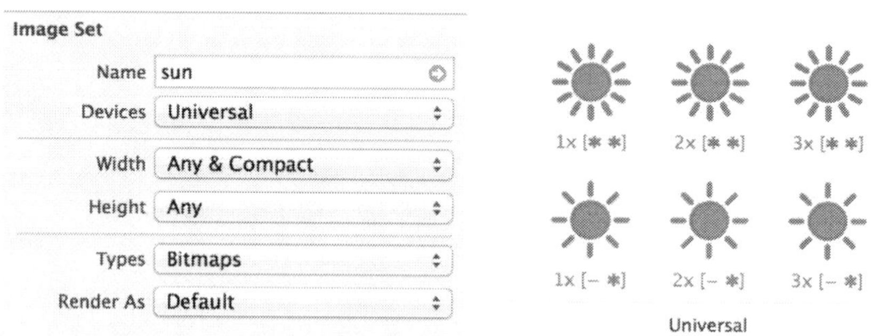

This updates the image set. Notice that the iPad and iPhone division has disappeared, and all the images have been successfully grouped into one Universal section.

Now repeat the above steps for both the **cloud** and **lightning** images sets.

Build and run. Make sure you try it on both the iPhone and iPad simulators. You'll see that nothing has changed yet. *What gives*?

To have the collection view use the appropriate images you'll have to override the trait collection to force the desired behavior. This time, you'll override the trait collection associated with the weather summary collection view so it always assumes a **Compact** horizontal size-class.

Open **WeatherTextViewController.swift** and add the following to the bottom of `viewDidLoad()`:

```
let traitOverride = UITraitCollection(horizontalSizeClass:
.Compact)
for vc in childViewControllers as [UIViewController] {
  setOverrideTraitCollection(traitOverride,
forChildViewController: vc)
}
```

This simply creates a trait collection with a **Compact** horizontal size-class, then iterates over the view controller's child view controllers and overrides the trait collection on each.

Build and run, this time using the iPad simulator. The summary collection view now uses the proper images:

Now run the app on the iPhone simulator and rotate to landscape. You'll see the navigation bar appears compressed, which increases the space available. In iOS 8 you can go one stage further and remove the navigation bar completely.

Showing or hiding the navigation bar

Open **Main.storyboard**, and from the **Document Outline**, expand **Navigation Controller Scene** and select **Navigation Controller**. You'll then see the navigation controller selected in the storyboard canvas:

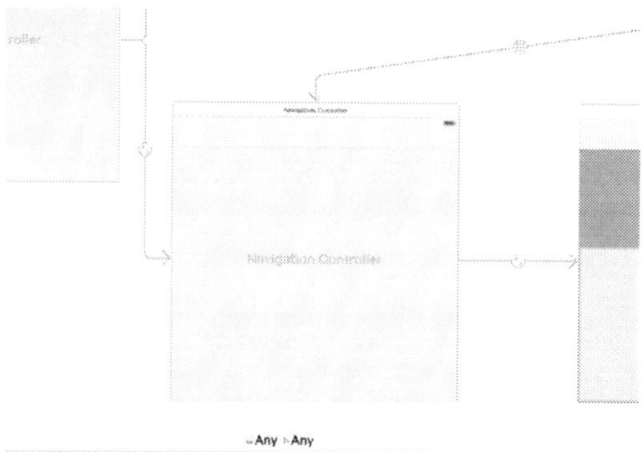

Open the **Attributes Inspector** and find the **Navigation Controller** section.

Check both the **Hide Bars\When Vertically Compact** and **Hide Bars\On Tap** checkboxes, as shown below:

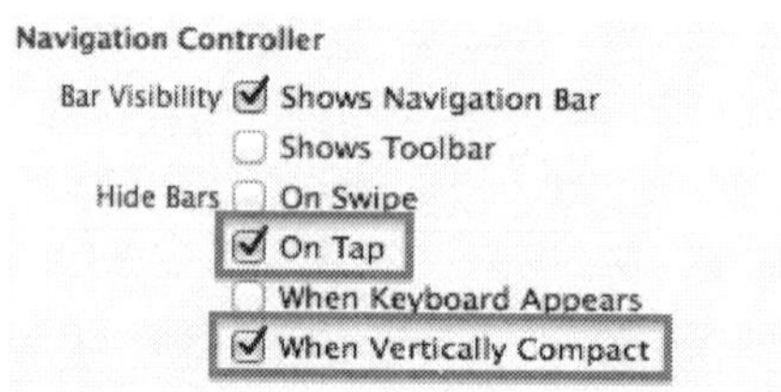

Build and run using the iPhone simulator. Rotate to landscape. Note how the navigation bar disappears entirely:

Tap anywhere to display the navigation bar. This tap-to-hide functionality works across all devices, and in both orientations.

> **Note:** It's also possible to use swipe gestures to show and hide the navigation bar; check out the `UINavigationController` API documentation on Apple's Developer Center for further details.

UIAppearance and size classes

iOS 8 updates the `UIAppearance` protocol to take full advantage of size-classes. For the unfamiliar, `UIAppearance` lets you apply styling details to an appearance proxy of an interface control such as `UIButton` or `UINavigationBar`; this style is then used by every instance of that control in your app.

> **Note:** You can learn about UI customization using appearance proxies in Adam Burkepile's excellent tutorial on raywenderlich.com at http://www.raywenderlich.com/21703/user-interface-customization-in-ios-6

Adding trait collection support lets you specify that certain styles are only applied in particular trait environments. This is invaluable for things like font size, which you'll definitely want to change in different size classes.

You're going to use the new functionality of `UIAppearance` to provide a custom font for your navigation bars. Since the bars change height depending on the vertical size-class, you'll provide a different font size for both **Compact** and **Regular** size classes.

Open **MasterViewController.swift** and add the following method to the `MasterViewController` class:

```
private func prepareNavigationBarAppearance() {
  let font = UIFont(name: "HelveticaNeue-Light", size: 30)!

  let regularVertical = UITraitCollection(verticalSizeClass:
.Regular)
  UINavigationBar.appearanceForTraitCollection(regularVertical).
titleTextAttributes = [NSFontAttributeName: font]

  let compactVertical = UITraitCollection(verticalSizeClass:
.Compact)
  UINavigationBar.appearanceForTraitCollection(compactVertical).
titleTextAttributes =
[NSFontAttributeName:font.fontWithSize(20)]
}
```

`appearanceForTraitCollection()` expects an instance of `UITraitCollection` and returns an appearance proxy – in this case, a proxy for `UINavigationBar` configured for the **Regular** vertical size-class – and sets `titleTextAttributes` to the specified font. You repeat this process for the **Compact** vertical size-class, only applying a smaller font size.

UI controls will only adopt appearance proxy settings when they are first rendered, so the proxy must be configured before the navigation bars are initially loaded.

Add the following statement to the bottom of `awakeFromNib()` in `MasterViewController`:

```
prepareNavigationBarAppearance()
```

This simply ensures the appearance proxies are configured before any navigation bars are instantiated and rendered.

Build and run, this time using the iPhone simulator. In portrait the vertical size-class is **Regular**, so the font is rendered using the larger size:

But in landscape the size-class is **Compact**, the font is rendered using the smaller size:

Note the larger font size will always be used on the iPad since it's vertically size-class is always **Regular**, regardless of orientation:

Where to go from here?

You covered a huge amount of material in this chapter by starting with more fundamental concepts of Adaptive Layout, and then exploring ways to use these concepts to great effect in your app. You've also gained more experience with Auto Layout, and hopefully some appreciation of its power.

Adaptive Layout is a fundamental part of iOS 8. As you progress through the rest of the Adaptive Layout chapters in this section, you'll soon realize that the future of app design *is* adaptive, and the historical way of building layouts will become increasingly untenable.

With the introduction of the iPhone 6 and iPhone 6 Plus, you now need to support a total of 10 screen sizes (4 iPhone, 1 iPad; each in both portrait and landscape). The size class architecture abstracts these away from device specifics and allows you to design for the future – safe in the knowledge that your designs will look great – no matter what Apple throws at you.

The first two chapters of this section on adaptive UI have concentrated on adaptive layout – i.e. updating the positions and sizes of the UI components. Adaptive UI doesn't stop there though – you might want to completely alter the view controller hierarchy based on the current size class. In the next chapter you'll learn how UIKit gives you the power to do just that with adaptive view controller hierarchies – paying particular attention to the split view controller.

Chapter 4: Adaptive View Controller Hierarchies

By Sam Davies

The preceding few chapters in the Adaptive Layout section of this book have shown you how the concepts apply to the **layout** of apps; however, that's not the only aspect of your interface that can benefit from this new UI design paradigm.

In this chapter you'll discover how to introduce Adaptive Layout into your view controller hierarchies; as the trait collections of your view controller's change, the view controllers that comprise the view can change as well.

The most common use of this technology is `UISplitViewController`, which is now supported on *all* devices – no longer is it exclusive to the iPad. In a Compact horizontal size class, the split view controller collapses to take on the form of a navigation controller, and expands back to its traditional two-view state when in a Regular horizontal size class.

In this chapter you'll learn how to do the following:

- Convert a legacy Master-Detail app to use the new universal split view controller in iOS 8
- Override trait collections to implement an expanded split view controller on an iPhone
- Create your own default detail view controller to be displayed when there's no content to display
- Deal with other interface controls when transitioning between the collapsed and expanded states of a split view controller
- Understand the behavior of the new `showViewController(_, sender:)` and `showDetailViewController(_, sender:)` methods

Adaptive view controller hierarchies are relatively complex to implement, so starting completely from scratch and covering everything in a single chapter would be a challenge. Therefore, you have a great little starter application from which to begin. **KhromaPal** provides a range of color palettes for a user to browse through; selecting a palette shows a large swatch of that palette along with its relevant color codes.

At this point you have a choice to make. The sample app comes in two forms: the first is a master-detail project from Xcode 5 that you'll first learn how to upgrade to use the new `UISplitViewController`. If you're not interested in learning about the upgrade process then you want to choose the second starter project, and skip to the second section *Expanding a split view on an iPhone.*

Upgrading a master-detail app to iOS 8

This section uses the starter project in the **Starter_From_Xcode5** directory. The app was built using the universal master-detail template in Xcode 5 and then converted to Swift. No iOS 8 features were implemented in this initial conversion, which means you can learn how to upgrade this existing master-detail app to iOS 8.

Launch Xcode 6 and open **KhromaPal.xcodeproj**. Since all devices can share a single storyboard in Xcode 6, delete **Main_iPhone.storyboard** by selecting it in the project navigator and pressing **delete**. Select **Move to Trash** in the dialog that appears:

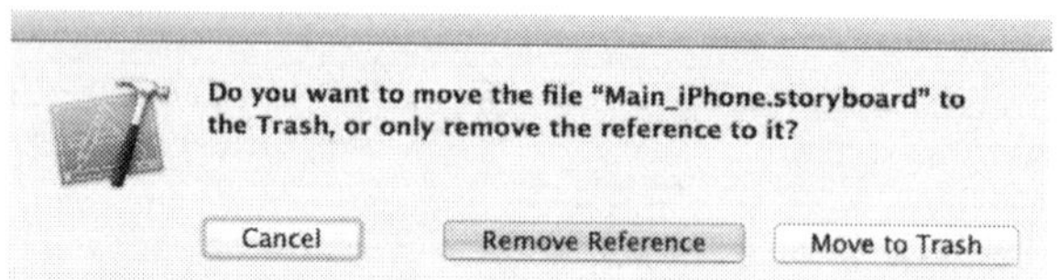

Then rename **Main_iPad.storyboard** to **Main.storyboard**, by selecting it in the project navigator and hitting **enter**.

You now need to update the project settings to use this new universal storyboard. Select your project in the **Project Navigator**, and then select the **KhromaPal** target. Open the **General** tab on the settings pane and in the **Deployment Info** section select the **iPhone** option in the scope bar. Change **Main Interface** to **Main.storyboard**:

Now select **iPad** in the scope bar and set **Main Interface** to **Main.storyboard** as well. Both targets now use the same storyboard.

Since the storyboard was designed for iOS 7 it doesn't yet understand the concept of size classes, which are required for using universal storyboards. To enable size classes, open the storyboard, and then open the **File Navigator**. In the **Interface Builder Document** section enable size classes by checking **Use Size Classes**, as shown below:

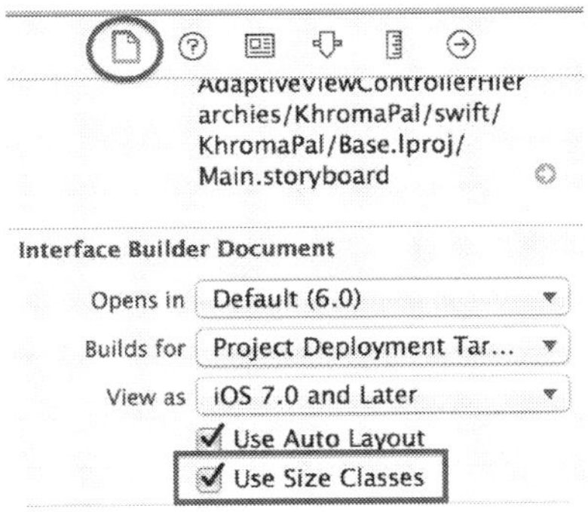

You'll be presented with the following confirmation dialog:

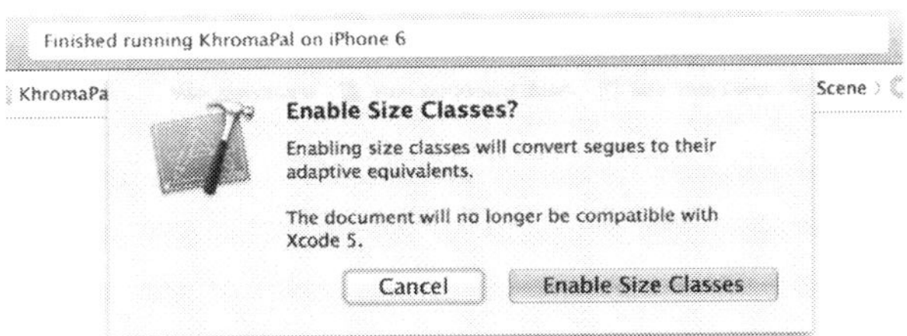

Click **Enable Size Classes**. There's no looking back now! :]

Note: As the confirmation kindly points out, once you enable size classes your storyboard will no longer be compatible with Xcode 5. If you work as part of a team, make sure *everyone* is using Xcode 6 before making this change.

You'll immediately notice that the view controllers inside the storyboard all change to the square abstract shape you've seen in previous chapters.

You might also notice there's no longer a segue between the table view that represents the master content and the navigation controller that contains the detail views. Prior to iOS 8, you would display the detail content by updating the detail view controller in the `tableView(tableView:, didSelectRowAtIndexPath:)` delegate method, like so:

```
override func tableView(tableView: UITableView!,
didDeselectRowAtIndexPath indexPath: NSIndexPath!) {
  if UIDevice.currentDevice().userInterfaceIdiom == .Pad {
    let palette = paletteCollection.children[indexPath.row] as
ColorPalette
    detailViewController!.colorPalette = palette
  }
}
```

iOS 8 now makes this step obsolete by providing `showViewController(_, sender:)` and `showDetailViewController(_, sender:)` on `UIViewController`. Calling `showDetailViewController(_, sender:)` on `UISplitViewController`, or a subclass of `UISplitViewController`, displays the passed view controller as the detail view controller.

There's also an accompanying segue which you'll use to link the table view to the detail navigation controller.

Open **Main.storyboard**. Find **Master Scene** in the **Document Outline** and select the **Master** view controller; this should bring it into view.

> **Note:** Enabling size classes has probably messed up the layout of view controllers in the storyboard. To make your life easier, rearrange them to match the following standard layout for master-detail projects:
>
> 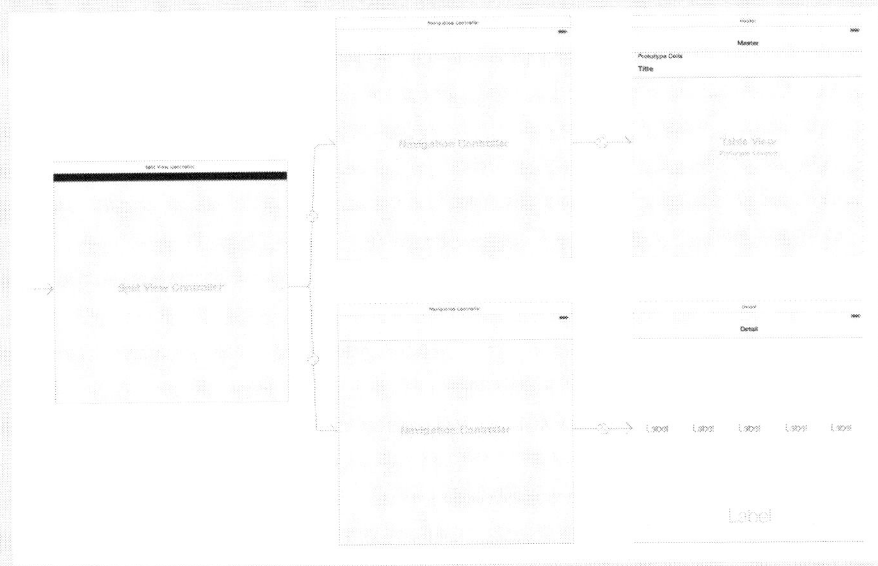

Ctrl+drag from the prototype table cell in the table view to the **Navigation Controller** containing the detail view controller, as shown below:

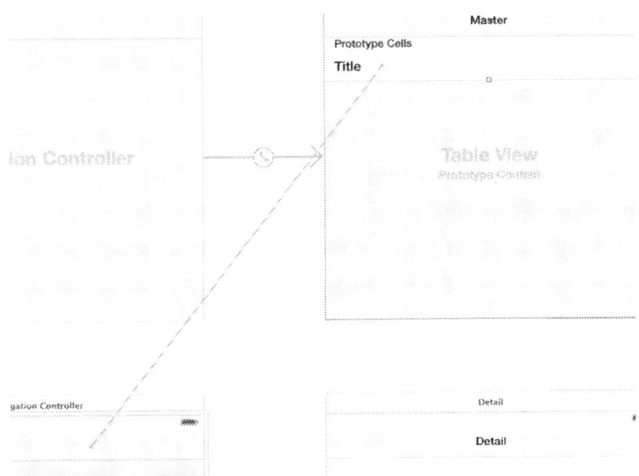

A menu that appears displays the options for the type of segue you're creating; many of which are new in iOS 8. Select **show detail** from the **Selection Segue** section:

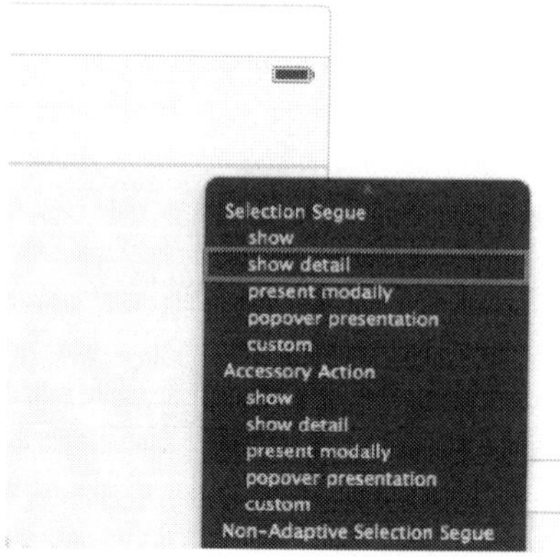

Once created, select the new segue in the storyboard, and then open the **Attributes Inspector**. Set **Identifier** to **showDetail**. Providing an identifier allows you to reference your segue in code.

You need to utilize this segue to pass the chosen color palette to the detail view controller. Open **MasterViewController.swift** and locate `prepareForSegue(segue:, sender:)`. Replace the existing implementation with the following:

```
override func prepareForSegue(segue: UIStoryboardSegue,
                              sender: AnyObject?) {
  if segue.identifier == "showDetail" {
    if let indexPath =
                  self.tableView.indexPathForSelectedRow() {
      let detailNav = segue.destinationViewController as
                      UINavigationController
      let detailVC  = detailNav.topViewController as
                      DetailViewController
      let palette   = paletteCollection.children[indexPath.row]
                      as ColorPalette
      detailVC.colorPalette = palette
    }
  }
}
```

The only difference between the two is that detail view controller is now contained within its own navigation controller, so you need to account for that.

Your project is now very close to being a universal app – in fact, you're ready to remove all the idiom checks.

Open **AppDelegate.swift** and update `application(application:, didFinishLaunchingWithOptions:)` and remove the `if` statement. Your implementation should now look like the following:

```
func application(application: UIApplication,
                 didFinishLaunchingWithOptions launchOptions:
NSDictionary?) -> Bool {
  let splitViewController = window!.rootViewController as
UISplitViewController
  let navigationController =
splitViewController.viewControllers.last as
UINavigationController
  let splitDelegate = navigationController.topViewController as
UISplitViewControllerDelegate
  splitViewController.delegate = splitDelegate
  return true
}
```

Open **MasterViewController.swift** and replace the implementation of `awakeFromNib()` with the following:

```
override func awakeFromNib() {
  super.awakeFromNib()
  title = "Palettes"
}
```

Next, find `tableView(tableView:, didSelectRowAtIndexPath:)` and remove the `else` branch of the `if` statement. The method should then match the following:

```
override func tableView(tableView: UITableView,
 didSelectRowAtIndexPath indexPath: NSIndexPath) {
  if rowHasChildrenAtIndex(indexPath) {
    let childCollection =
paletteCollection.children[indexPath.row]
                      as ColorPaletteCollection
    let newTable = storyboard
          .instantiateViewControllerWithIdentifier("MasterVC")
          as MasterViewController
    newTable.paletteCollection = childCollection
    newTable.title = childCollection.name
    navigationController.pushViewController(newTable, animated:
true)
  }
}
```

Build and run using the iPad simulator. Play around with it for a bit and you should see that nothing has changed:

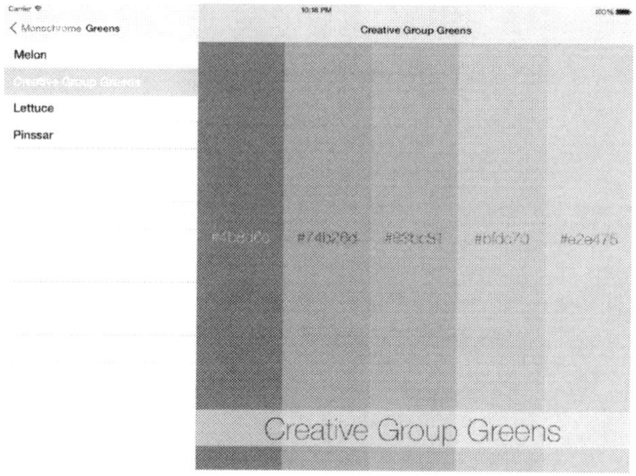

But that's exactly the result you wanted, wasn't it? You made some considerable modifications to the code and storyboard without affecting the app's functionality; *bravo!*

Expanding a split view on an iPhone

If you have skipped the previous section, and are starting out here, then you need to open the **KhromaPal** project inside the **Starter_From_Xcode6** directory. The remaining sections of this chapter will show you how to use `UISplitViewController` on iPhone.

How does a split view controller *know* that it should render as a navigation stack on an iPhone, but render as two separate view controllers on an iPad? The horizontal size class of the split view controller governs this:

- **Compact:** The split view controller assumes the appearance of a navigation controller. The detail view is pushed on to the navigation stack
- **Regular:** The split view controller appears as two separate view controllers, with a selection of display modes

The horizontal size class of all iPhones except the iPhone 6 Plus is always **Compact** regardless of its orientation; therefore the split view controller will always appear as a navigation controller. An iPhone 6 Plus has a Regular horizontal size class when in landscape; if you build and run the app on an iPhone 6 Plus in landscape, you'll see the expanded split view:

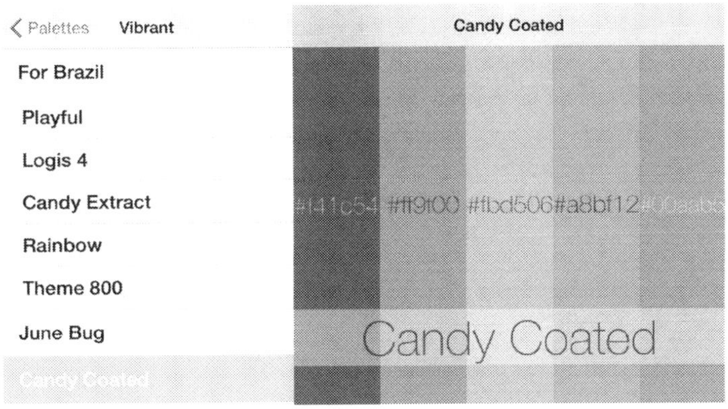

In order to display both the master *and* detail view controllers on *all* iPhone in landscape, you'll need to override the horizontal size class so that it matches that of the iPhone 6 Plus.

You cannot override the size classes of a view controller directly, but `UIViewController` provides `setOverrideTraitCollection(_, forChildViewController:)` to allow you to override trait collections for child view controllers; therefore you'll need a new view controller to host your existing split-view controller.

Open **Main.storyboard** and drag a **View Controller** from the **Object Library** onto the storyboard canvas. Open the **Attributes Inspector** and set **Title** to **Trait Override VC**. Also check **Is Initial View Controller**. Drag a **Container View** from the **Object Library** onto the view controller you just added, as shown below:

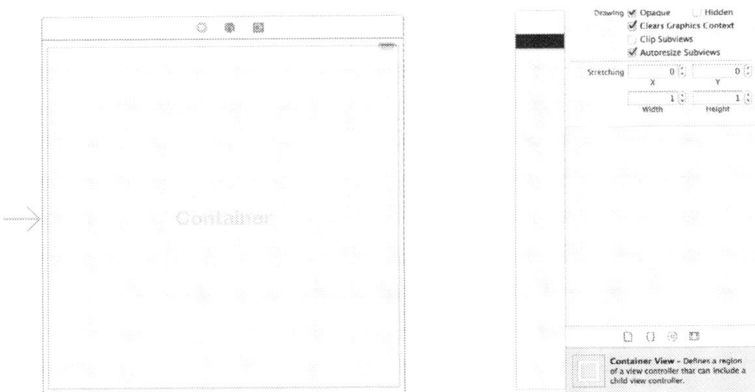

You don't need the view controller that belongs to the container. Select it and hit **delete** to remove it.

With the container view selected, click the **Pin** button in the bottom toolbar and set all the constraints' constants to **0**. Ensure **Constrain to margins** is not checked, and that **Update Frames** is set to **All Frames in Container** so the constraints are immediately applied to the storyboard:

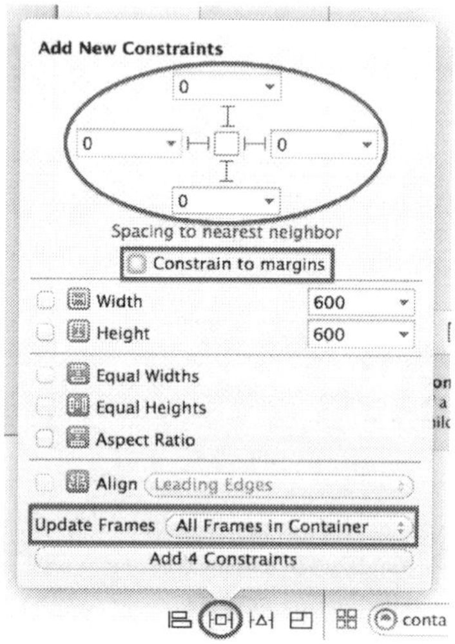

This will cause the container view to fill the available space.

Now you'll wire the split view controller into the view controller hierarchy as a child of the newly created trait override view controller. **Ctrl+drag** from the container view to the split view controller and select **embed** from the popup menu:

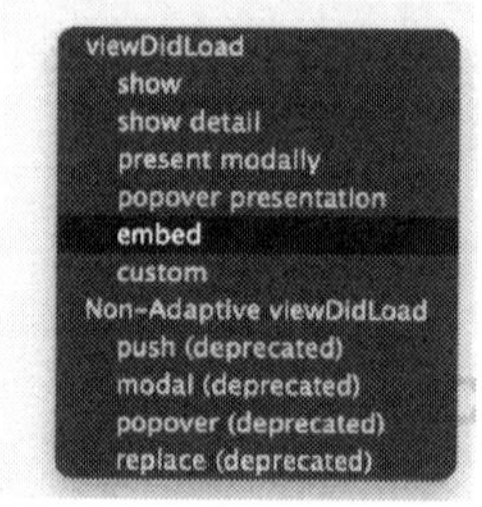

In order to override the trait collection, you need a custom class for the containing view controller. Select **File\New\File...** and then **iOS\Source\CocoaTouch**. Set **Class** to `TraitOverrideViewController` and **Subclass** to `UIViewController`. Make sure **Language** is set to **Swift** and then click **Next**, followed by **Create**.

Open **TraitOverrideViewController.swift** and replace the contents with the following:

```
class TraitOverrideViewController: UIViewController {
  override func viewWillTransitionToSize(size: CGSize,
        withTransitionCoordinator coordinator:
                  UIViewControllerTransitionCoordinator) {
    var traitOverride: UITraitCollection? = nil
    if size.width > 414 {
      traitOverride = UITraitCollection(horizontalSizeClass:
                                        .Regular)
    }
    setOverrideTraitCollection(traitOverride,
         forChildViewController: childViewControllers[0] as
                                 UIViewController)
    super.viewWillTransitionToSize(size,
                       withTransitionCoordinator: coordinator)
  }
}
```

In the code above you've implemented a single method – `viewWillTransitionToSize(_, withTransitionCoordinator:)` – which is new to iOS 8. This method is part of the `UIContentContainer` protocol, which is adopted by `UIViewController`. A content container (such as `UIViewController`) is responsible for managing the content for an area of the screen, and can therefore form a hierarchy. A parent container informs its children when the layout changes and they should resize using `viewWillTransitionToSize(_, withTransitionCoordinator:)`. The most common occurrence of this is rotation – where a bounds change in the window propagates down through the view controller hierarchy.

> **Note:** It is also possible to hook into this system yourself, but that is beyond the scope of this chapter. For more information, check out the API documentation for `UIContentContainer`.

Size classes are part of the `UITraitCollection` class; in the code above you've created a new trait collection with a Regular horizontal size class – provided the size the view controller is transitioning to is wide enough. You then call `setOverrideTraitCollection(_, forChildViewController:)` to enable the override. Since your view controller has just a single child view controller, you obtain it by grabbing the first object in the `childViewControllers` array.

Finally, you call `viewWillTransitionToSize(size:, withTransitionCoordinator:)` on the superclass to ensure the call propagates through the view controller hierarchy appropriately.

You now need to update your storyboard so it uses `TraitOverrideViewController`.

Open **Main.storyboard** and find **Trait Override VC** in the **Document Outline**. Use the **Identity Inspector** to set **Class** to `TraitOverrideViewController`.

Can you run up your app at this point? It *looks* like everything has been hooked up. No, but you're almost there – you have just a few more things to take care of.

When you create an app using the Master-Detail template, Xcode automatically sets the detail view controller as the delegate of the split view controller in the application delegate. By introducing the new trait override view controller as the initial view controller, this relationship is now broken. Therefore, you'll need to create a custom subclass of `UISplitViewController` and have it act as its own delegate.

Open **AppDelegate.swift** and delete everything in `application(application:, didFinishLaunchingWithOptions:)` apart from `return true`.

Select **File\New\File...** and then **iOS\Source\CocoaTouch**. Set **Class** to `SplitViewController`, **Subclass** to `UISplitViewController`, and **Language** to **Swift**. Finally click **Next**, followed by **Create**. Open **SplitViewController.Swift** and replace its contents with the following:

```
// 1
class SplitViewController: UISplitViewController,
                           UISplitViewControllerDelegate {

  override func viewDidLoad() {
    super.viewDidLoad()
    // 2
    delegate = self
  }
  // 3
  func splitViewController(splitController:
                                 UISplitViewController,
      collapseSecondaryViewController secondaryViewController:
                                 UIViewController,
      ontoPrimaryViewController primaryViewController:
                                 UIViewController) -> Bool {
    return true
  }
}
```

Taking each numbered comment in turn, you'll see that the code above does the following:

1. Declare the class adopts the `UISplitViewControllerDelegate` protocol
2. Set the `delegate` to `self`
3. Implement `splitViewController(collapseSecondaryViewController:, ontoPrimaryViewController:)` delegate method. This method is called when a split view controller is collapsing down into a navigation controller, and governs the behavior of the detail view controller. Returning `true` indicates that you have handled the collapse, whereas returning `false` enforces UIKit's default behavior, which is to push the detail view controller on top of the navigation stack. Here you're returning `true`, but not providing any other implementation. This means the detail view controller will be discarded on rotation of an iPhone from landscape to portrait.

Now you need to set the class of the split view controller in the storyboard to that of the class you just created above.

Open **Main.storyboard**. Find and select the split view controller in the **Document Outline**, open the **Identity Inspector**, and set **Class** to `SplitViewController`:

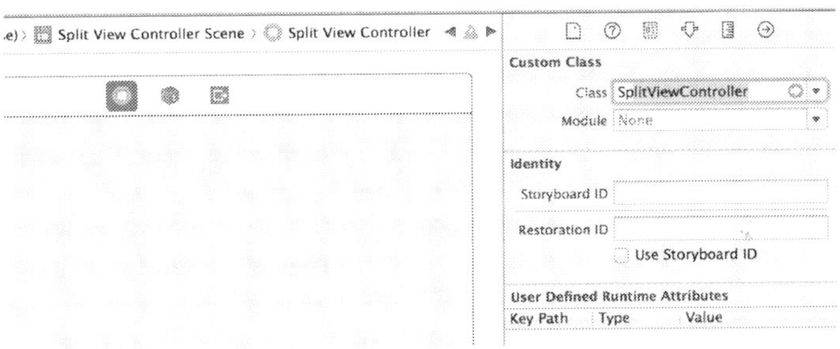

Finally, open **DetailViewController.swift** and remove `UISplitViewControllerDelegate` from the class declaration. It should now look like the following:

```
class DetailViewController: UIViewController {
```

Now delete the following two `UISplitViewControllerDelegate` methods:

- `splitViewController(splitViewController:, willHideViewController:, withBarButtonItem:, forPopoverController:)`
- `splitViewController(splitViewController:, willShowViewController:, invalidatingBarButtonItem:)`

Build and run, this time using the iPhone simulator. Rotate to landscape and check out your nifty split view controller:

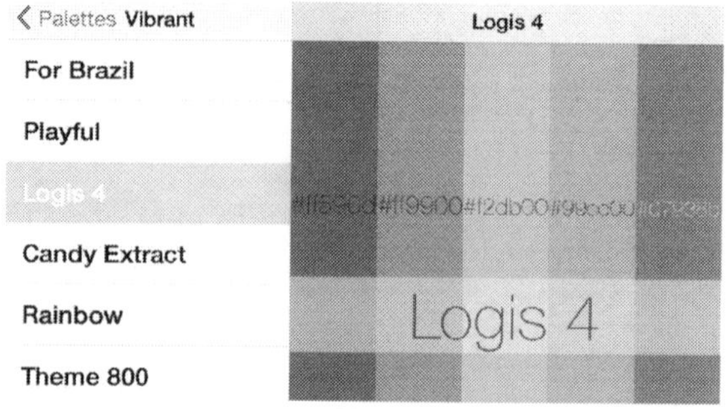

Providing a custom default view

You've likely noticed that in landscape on iPhone – and in both orientations on iPad – the detail view is simply blank before you select a palette. Your task in this section is to create a new view controller and use this as the default when nothing is selected.

Along the way, you'll learn how to deal with changes in device orientation, which modify the view controller hierarchy, starting with the portrait to landscape rotation on the iPhone. This rotation causes the split view to expand – that is to change from a navigation controller to the traditional split view controller – with both the primary and secondary controllers visible. This means you need to show additional content, but where should it come from?

- When the top view controller is a palette (i.e. a detail view controller) then it should move over to the secondary position on expansion.
- When the top view controller is a table view controller – that is, a level of the master view controller – then the secondary view controller should show a new *empty state* view controller on expansion.

To begin with, you'll create the *empty state* view controller. Open **Main.storyboard** and drag a **View Controller** from the **Object library** onto the storyboard canvas.

Although this view controller will reside in the storyboard, it won't be linked to any other scenes. Instead, you'll instantiate it in code. To this end, select the view controller use the **Identity Inspector** to set its **Storyboard ID** to **NoPaletteSelected**:

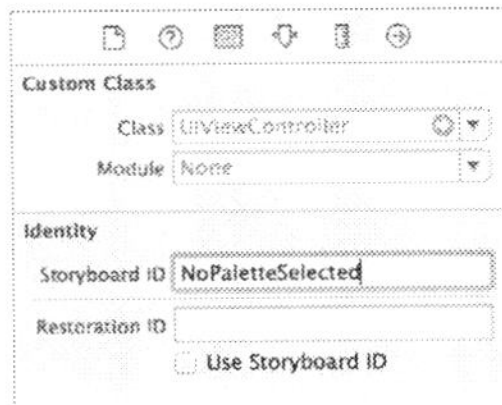

Next, drag a **Label** from the **Object Library** onto the view controller you just created. Double-click it and change the text to **No Palette Selected**.

With the label selected, open the **Attributes Inspector** and set **Font** to **Helvetica Neue Light**, with a size of **32**. Set **Alignment** to **Center**, and set **Color** to **Light Gray Color.** Change **Autoshrink** to **Minimum Font Scale**, with a value of **0.5**, as shown below:

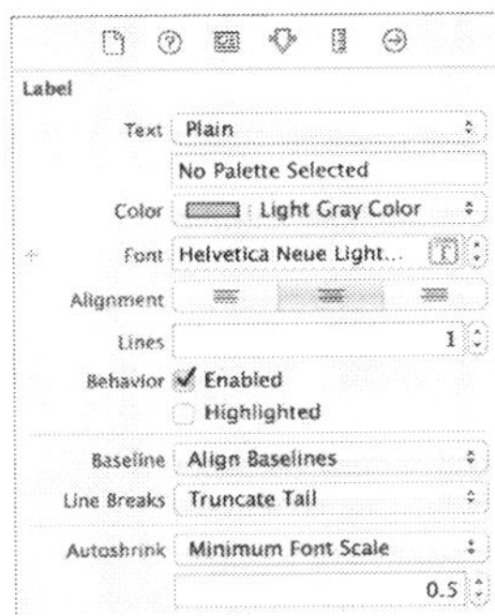

You need to provide layout constraints for the label; **select** the label and use the **Pin** menu to set **left** and **right** constraints to **0**, and ensure that **Constrain to margins** is **checked**:

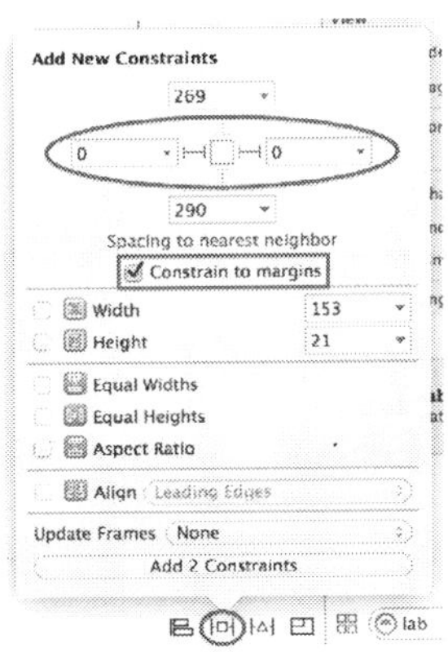

Then, use the **Align** menu to specify that the label should vertically centered; **check** the **Vertical Center in Container** box, checking that the associated value is **0**. Before adding the constraint, change the **Update Frames** menu to show **All Frames in Container** so that IB will re-layout the view controller:

This will leave you with a simple yet effective *No Palette Selected* view:

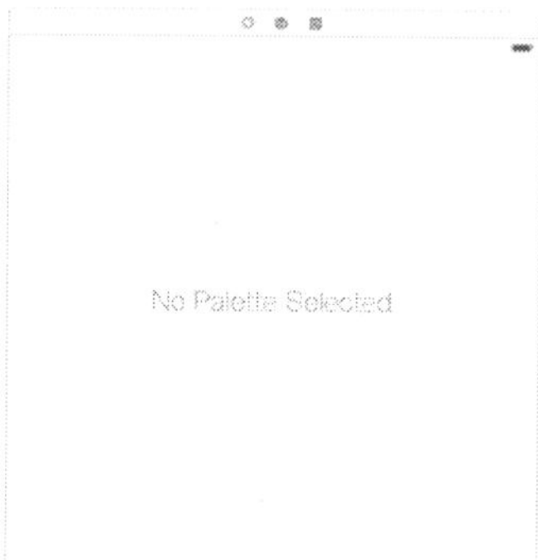

The first problem to solve is how to use this view controller in place of a seemingly empty view controller. Take a look at `configureView()` in **DetailViewController.swift**:

```
private func configureView() {
  if let palette = colorPalette {
    makeAllContentHidden(false)
    ...
  } else {
    makeAllContentHidden(true)
    ...
  }
}
```

`configureView()` uses a utility method to show or hide all sub-views of the detail view controller depending on whether or not it `colorPalette` is `nil`. Instead of hiding content, you'll display the new *No Palette Selected* view controller instead.

Replace the `else` branch of the `if` statement in `configureView()` with the following:

```
} else {
  if let empty = storyboard?
                    .instantiateViewControllerWithIdentifier(
                    "NoPaletteSelected") as? UIViewController {
    showViewController(empty, sender: self)
  }
  makeAllContentHidden(true)
}
```

Here, you use the storyboard identifier you specified earlier to create an instance of the new view controller. This approach lets you use a storyboard to lay out your views without needing to join the scenes together using segues. Finally, you use the new `showViewController(_:, sender:)` method to display the view controller.

> **Note:** The new `showViewController(_:, sender:)` and `showDetailViewController(_:, sender:)` methods of `UIViewController` can be used in place of methods such as `pushViewController(_:, animated)` on `UINavigationController`. These new methods are contextually aware, which means that they'll *do the right thing* no matter where you call them.

You can put this tactic to use immediately. Open **MasterViewController.swift** and replace the call to `pushNavigationController(_:, animated:)` with `showViewController(_:, sender:)` in `tableView(_:, didSelectRowAtIndexPath:)`.

So, find this line:

```
navigationController.pushViewController(newTable, animated:
true)
```

And replace it with this one:

```
showViewController(newTable, sender: self)
```

> **Note:** You'll notice that `showViewController(_, sender:)` doesn't have an `animated` argument, like `pushViewController(_, animated:)` does. This is because `showViewController(_, sender:)` is a semantic method for showing a view controller – the mechanics of the display are left to the view controller which is actually responsible for the presentation. You could configure the animation associated with a particular view controller by overriding `showViewController(_, sender:)`.

Rotate the iPhone simulator to landscape then build and run. Notice the *No Palette Selected* view now appears as expected:

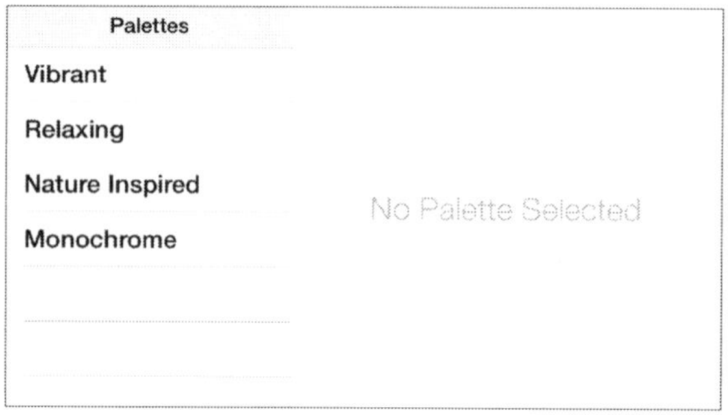

Kill the app. Rotate the simulator to portrait and re-run. Tap the **Nature Inspired** category to see the list of available palettes. Then rotate to landscape; you'd expect to see the same list of palettes in the master table with the *No Palette Selected* view in the detail view, *right?* But instead you see this:

That's not what you expected. Unfortunately, the default behavior of the transition between the collapsed and expanded states of the split view controller doesn't work for you in this case.

By default, a split view controller asks the primary view controller to provide the secondary view controller as it transitions from collapsed to expanded; a `UINavigationController` responds by popping the top view controller off its navigation stack. This works fine for most cases, *unless* you have a master navigation tree with a depth greater than one.

Why? In the simplest case, where the navigation stack depth is exactly one, if you can pop from the navigation stack, the returned object *must* be a detail view controller. This is because you cannot pop the final view controller off the navigation stack. This isn't the case for **KhromaPal**; instead, you'll need to override the default behavior.

There are two cases to handle when expanding from the collapsed state:

1. The top view controller is displaying a palette that you want popped so it becomes the secondary view controller.
2. The top view controller is navigating the tree of palettes and *not* displaying a palette; therefore the secondary view controller should be the *No Palette Selected* view controller.

To do this, you need a way to determine whether a given view controller is displaying a palette. You're going to create a protocol that determines whether an adopter is currently 'displaying' a palette, and have some of the view controller subclasses adopt it.

Select the **Protocols** group in the **Project Navigator**, then select **File\New\File...**, then **iOS\Source\Swift File**. Name the file **PaletteContainer.swift**, click **Create** and then open it in Xcode.

Add the following protocol definition to **PaletteContainer.swift**:

```
@objc protocol PaletteDisplayContainer {
  func rwt_currentlyDisplayedPalette() -> ColorPalette?
}
```

This is a simple protocol; it declares a single method that, when implemented, returns either the current palette, or `nil`. Note that this protocol is annotated with `@objc`, which is necessary to be able to check whether an object conforms to a protocol.

You'll need to update two view controllers so they adopt this protocol.

Open **DetailViewController.swift** and update the class declaration so it adopts the new protocol:

```
class DetailViewController: UIViewController,
                            PaletteDisplayContainer
```

And then add the required method:

```
func rwt_currentlyDisplayedPalette() -> ColorPalette? {
    return colorPalette
  }
}
```

Now you're going to make the navigation controller adopt this protocol, since both the primary and secondary view controllers in the split view controller are navigation controllers, but what does it mean for a navigation controller to be displaying a palette? A navigation controller is said to be displayed a palette if and only if its top view controller is, so this implementation will simply delegate to the top view controller in the navigation stack. At the moment, both split view child view controllers are using the base `UINavigationController` class. Your task is to create your own subclass of `UINavigationController` that adopts the `PaletteDisplayContainer` protocol.

Using the same process as before, create a new **Cocoa Touch** class, making sure it's a subclass of `UINavigationController`, and name it `NavigationController`. Open **NavigationController.swift** and replace its contents with the following code:

```
class NavigationController: UINavigationController,
                            PaletteDisplayContainer {
  func rwt_currentlyDisplayedPalette() -> ColorPalette? {
    if let tvc = topViewController as? PaletteDisplayContainer {
      return tvc.rwt_currentlyDisplayedPalette()
    }
    return nil
  }
}
```

The only method you need in your navigation controller subclass is the one declared in the `PaletteDisplayContainer` protocol. Here, the implementation attempts to cast the `topViewController` of the navigation controller to an object conforming to the `PaletteDisplayContainer` protocol, and if successful calls that view controllers implementation of the protocol method. Otherwise it returns `nil`.

In this way you can ask a navigation controller for the currently displayed palette, and it will return the palette displayed by the top view controller – which makes perfect sense when you think about it, since if any other view controller in the navigation stack displayed a palette then you wouldn't be able to see it!

Now you need to specify that the class of both navigation controllers in the storyboard is your new subclass. Open **Main.storyboard**, select each navigation controller in turn and use the **Identity Inspector** to set its **Class** to `NavigationController`.

You've now laid all the necessary groundwork to implement the custom behavior of your expanding split view controller. You'll control your split view controller using `UISplitViewControllerDelegate`, which you've already begun to implement in your custom `SplitViewController` class.

Open **SplitViewController.swift** and add the following delegate method to the `SplitViewController` class:

```
func splitViewController(splitViewController:
                              UISplitViewController,
separateSecondaryViewControllerFromPrimaryViewController
primaryViewController: UIViewController!) -> UIViewController? {
  if let paletteDisplayCont = primaryViewController as?
                              PaletteDisplayContainer {
   if paletteDisplayCont.rwt_currentlyDisplayedPalette() != nil{
      return nil
    }
  }
  let vc = storyboard?
    .instantiateViewControllerWithIdentifier(
      "NoPaletteSelected") as UIViewController
  return NavigationController(rootViewController: vc)
}
```

Expanding a collapsed split view controller calls this method to return the view controller to be used as the secondary view controller. The default behavior is to pop the top view controller from the primary navigation stack.

First you determine whether the primary view controller is displaying a palette. You do this by casting the primary view controller to a `PaletteDisplayContainer` then requesting the currently displayed palette.

If a palette is being displayed, you return `nil` to trigger the default behavior. If there's no palette being displayed, create an instance of the *No Palette Selected* view controller, pop it into an instance of `NavigationController`, and return that instead.

Build and run. Try both orientations, and navigate to various views. Rotating from portrait to landscape on iPhone now shows the appropriate secondary view controller in all circumstances:

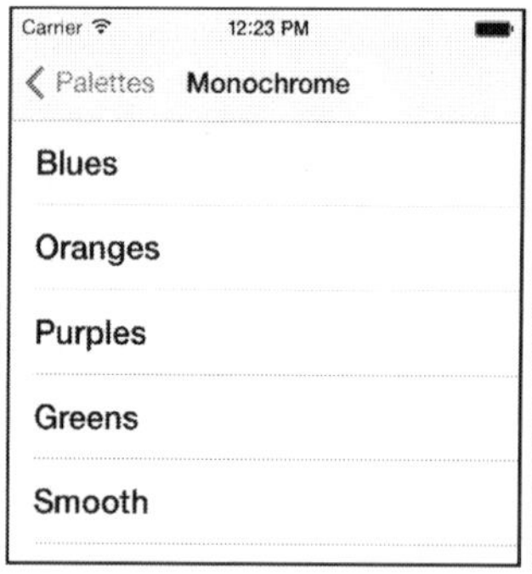

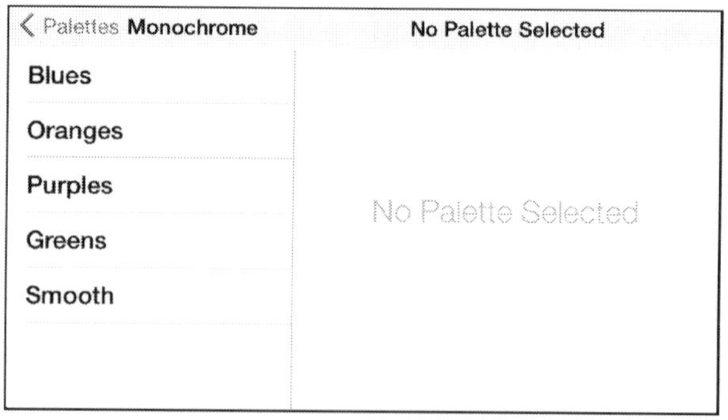

It's likely you've noticed that returning from landscape to portrait doesn't always behave as you might expect; you'll correct this in the next section.

Persisting selection on collapse

A split view controller is expanded in landscape on iPhone; in portrait, it's collapsed. The previous section customized the expansion process and ensured the relevant view controller was used as the secondary view controller. This section deals with the reverse process – how to specify which view controller should appear on the top of the navigation stack when the split view controller collapses.

As in the previous section, there is some background work to do before implementing the necessary `UISplitViewControllerDelegate` method. In the same way that you created a protocol to find which palette is currently displayed, you're going to create a protocol to find which palette is currently selected.

Open **PaletteContainer.swift** and add the following protocol definition:

```
@objc protocol PaletteSelectionContainer {
  func rwt_currentlySelectedPalette() -> ColorPalette?
}
```

This is much like the `PaletteDisplayContainer` protocol, only this time you want to determine whether or not a palette is selected.

Open **MasterViewController.swift**. Update the class declaration to declare it adopts the new protocol:

```
class MasterViewController: UITableViewController,
                            PaletteSelectionContainer {
```

And then add the required method to the class itself:

```
func rwt_currentlySelectedPalette() -> ColorPalette? {
  let selectedIndex = tableView.indexPathForSelectedRow()
  if let indexPath = selectedIndex {
    if !rowHasChildrenAtIndex(indexPath) {
      return paletteCollection.children[indexPath.row] as?
               ColorPalette
    }
  }
  return nil
}
```

This finds the index path of the selected row, if one exists. If the row has no children then you know the selection is a palette. If so, then you return the associated `ColorPalette` object from the `ColorPaletteCollection` belonging to the `MasterViewController`.

In the same way that your custom navigation controller, `NavigationController`, adopted `PaletteDisplayContainer`, you also need it to adopt `PaletteSelectionContainer`.

Open **NavigationController.swift**. First, modify the class declaration:

```
class NavigationController: UINavigationController,
                            PaletteDisplayContainer,
                            PaletteSelectionContainer {
```

And then add the required method :

```
func rwt_currentlySelectedPalette() -> ColorPalette? {
  if let tvc = topViewController as?
                 PaletteSelectionContainer {
    return tvc.rwt_currentlySelectedPalette()
  }
  return nil
}
```

The above implementation follows the same pattern as the display container. If the top view controller adopts the protocol then delegate the response to that controller; otherwise, return `nil`.

The existing implementation of the delegate method `splitViewController(_:, collapseSecondaryViewController:, ontoPrimaryViewController:)` still returns `true` in all cases. The return value of this method should only be `true` if you're handling the collapsing yourself; if you return `false` then it'll fall back into its default behavior. A return value of `true` means the framework will do nothing: the primary view controller will be left untouched and the secondary view controller will be discarded.

Open **SplitViewController.swift** and replace the existing implementation of `splitViewController(_:, collapseSecondaryViewController:, ontoPrimaryViewController:)` with the one shown below:

```
func splitViewController(splitController: UISplitViewController,
  collapseSecondaryViewController secondaryViewController:
    UIViewController!,
  ontoPrimaryViewController primaryViewController:
    UIViewController!) -> Bool {
  if let selectionCont = primaryViewController as?
                  PaletteSelectionContainer {
    if let displayCont = secondaryViewController as?
                  PaletteDisplayContainer {
      let selectedPalette =
                   selectionCont.rwt_currentlySelectedPalette()
      let displayedPalette =
                   displayCont.rwt_currentlyDisplayedPalette()
      if selectedPalette? != nil &&
          selectedPalette == displayedPalette {
          return false
      }
    }
  }
  // We don't want anything to happen. Say we've dealt with it
  return true
}
```

The above method determines whether the primary view controller has a selected palette and whether the secondary view controller is displaying that palette.

If the selected palette is the same as the palette being displayed, then you push the detail view on to the navigation stack. Since this is the default behavior of the framework, you return `false`.

Otherwise, discard the secondary view controller – it doesn't represent the currently selected palette so it shouldn't appear on the top of the collapsed split view. This is achieved by returning `true`.

Build and run on the iPhone. Play around with the app and notice the following rotation use cases now behave as expected:

1. Navigate to a palette in portrait and rotate to landscape – the palette will appear in the right hand side.

2. Select a palette in landscape and rotate to portrait. The palette will remain as the top of the navigation stack.

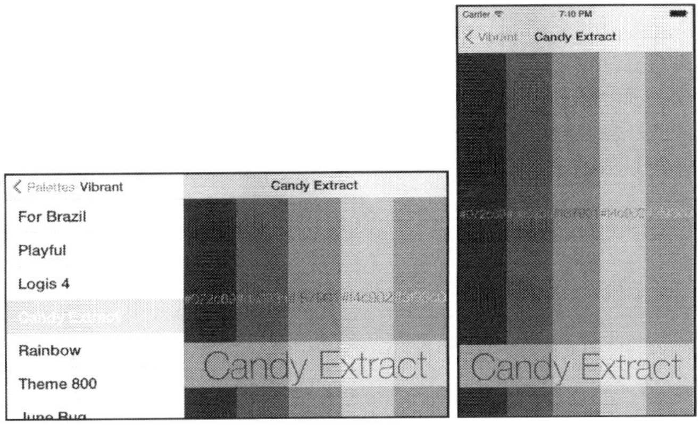

3. Navigate to the *Nature Inspired* palette collection in portrait and rotate to landscape. The secondary view controller will display "*No Palette Selected*".
4. In landscape, select a palette, and then navigate to a different palette collection. Rotate to portrait, and you'll see the current palette collection as the top view controller – not a palette.

Your user experience is really starting to come together, but there's still one issue you haven't addressed: disclosure indicators.

Adaptive disclosure indicators

Table views inside of navigation controllers are a widely-used paradigm on iOS. An important part of this paradigm is the **disclosure indicator**; the arrow that appears at the right side of a table view cell indicating there's more content available, as shown in the following screenshot:

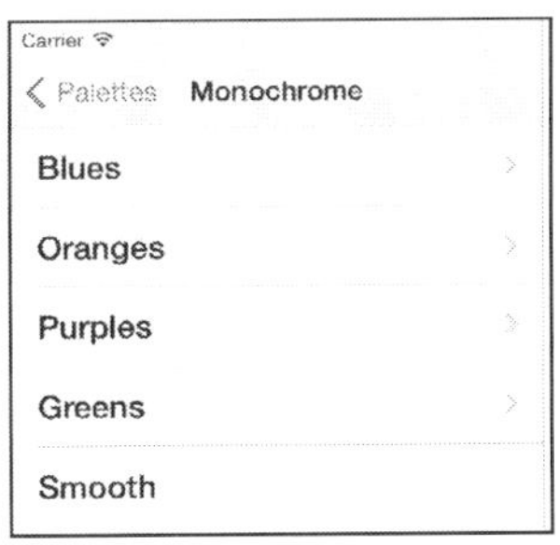

The disclosure indicators are controlled by the last piece of code containing idiom checks, found in **MasterViewController.swift**:

```
override func tableView(tableView: UITableView!,
  willDisplayCell cell: UITableViewCell!,
    forRowAtIndexPath indexPath: NSIndexPath!) {
  // Make sure that we see the disclosure indicators on iPad
  if(UIDevice.currentDevice().userInterfaceIdiom == .Pad) {
    if rowHasChildrenAtIndex(indexPath) {
      cell.accessoryType = .DisclosureIndicator
    } else {
      cell.accessoryType = .None
    }
  }
}
```

The above method belongs to the `UITableViewDelegate` protocol. It's considered your last chance to make any changes to a table view cell before it's displayed.

When the app runs on iPad, the disclosure indicators are shown only on cells that represent a collection, as opposed to those that represent a palette. This works because the split view controller is *always* expanded on iPad. This isn't true on iPhone; therefore you need to update the display logic.

Take a moment and think about what the disclosure indicator actually represents. In a completely generic sense it depends on whether or not selecting that cell will result in a push on the navigation controller stack. This rule holds true for split views in both collapsed and expanded states.

Therefore, determining whether or not a disclosure indicator should be shown is equivalent to determining whether a tap will result in a push.

Earlier in this chapter you were introduced to the new `showViewController(_:, sender:)` and `showDetailViewController(_:, sender:)` methods. These can be considered contextually aware, in that they behave differently depending on the environment from which they're called. A call to either of the methods will work its way up the view controller hierarchy to determine whether there is an ancestor that provides an implementation.

The following table shows which of the standard `UIViewController` subclasses in UIKit provide implementations for each of the methods:

	`ShowViewController(_, sender:)`	`showDetailViewController(_, sender:)`
`UINavigationController`	`pushViewController(_, animated:)`	-
Expanded `UISplitViewController`	-	redirect to `showViewController(_, sender:)` on secondary
Collapsed `UISplitViewController`	-	redirect to `showViewController(_, sender:)` on primary
Default `UIViewController`	`presentViewController(_, animated:, completion:)`	`presentViewController(_, animated:, completion:)`

Note that the default behavior for `UIViewController` will only occur if none of the view controllers in the view controller hierarchy provides their own implementation. This ensures that both `showViewController(_:, sender:)` and `showDetailViewController(_:, sender:)` will always result in the view controller appearing.

In order to work out where to send a particular call, you'll use the new `UIViewController` method `targetViewControllerForAction(_:, sender:)`. The default behavior of this method is to walk up the view controller hierarchy until it finds a view controller willing to respond to the given selector.

You'll use this functionality to determine whether calling `showDetailViewController(_:, sender:)` will result in a push or not. You'll implement this as an extension on `UIViewController`, which is the Swift equivalent of an Objective-C category; that is, a way to add new functionality to an existing class.

Using the all-too-familiar process, create a new Swift file in the **Extensions** group and name it **UIViewControllerShow.swift**. Open it, and add the following:

```
extension UIViewController {
  func rwt_showVCWillResultInPush(sender: AnyObject?) -> Bool {
    if let target =
```

```
    targetViewControllerForAction("rwt_showVCWillResultInPush:",
     sender: sender) {
      return target.rwt_showVCWillResultInPush(sender)
    } else {
      return false
    }
  }

  func rwt_showDetailVCWillResultInPush(sender: AnyObject?)
                                                   -> Bool {
    if let target =
targetViewControllerForAction("rwt_showDetailVCWillResultInPush:
"
  , sender: sender) {
      return target.rwt_showDetailVCWillResultInPush(sender)
    } else {
      return false
    }
  }
}
```

This defines two new methods on `UIViewController` - `rwt_showVCWillResultInPush(_)` and `rwt_showDetailVCWillResultInPush(_)`. These both follow the same pattern:

- Use `targetViewControllerForAction(_, sender:)` to walk the view controller hierarchy and try to find an ancestor which implements the method in question (either `rwt_showVCWillResultInPush(_)` or `rwt_showDetailVCWillResultInPush(_)`). If it does, then return the result of calling that method on the view controller discovered to implement it.
- Otherwise, return `false`. You can see from the previous table that neither `showViewController(_:, sender:)` nor `showDetailViewController(_:, sender:)` result in a push when it falls through to the default `UIViewController` implementation – instead, both methods get routed to `presentViewController(_, animated:, completion:)`.

With just this single extension, the result will always be `false`, since there are no view controllers in the hierarchy that would return anything other than `false`.

Add the following `UINavigationController` extension to **UIViewControllerShow.swift**:

```
extension UINavigationController {
  override func rwt_showVCWillResultInPush(sender: AnyObject?)
                                                   -> Bool {
```

```
    return true
  }
}
```

This extension overrides just one of the new methods you defined on `UIViewController`. Referring to the previous table again, you can see that a navigation controller does not implement `showDetailViewController(_:, sender:)`, therefore you don't have to override `rwt_showDetailVCWillResultInPush(_)`. It does, however, perform a push for a `showViewController(_:, sender:)` call; therefore you've overridden `rwt_showVCWillResultInPush(_)` to return `true`.

There are two rows of the table which describe behavior which you are yet to capture in your view controller extensions – and they relate to `showDetailViewController(_:, sender:)` on `UISplitViewController`. Therefore, you also need to extend the split view controller. Still working in **UIViewControllerShow.swift**, add the code shown below:

```
extension UISplitViewController {
  override func rwt_showDetailVCWillResultInPush(sender:
                                        AnyObject?) -> Bool {
    if collapsed  {
      if let primaryVC = viewControllers.last as?
                                   UIViewController {
        return primaryVC.rwt_showVCWillResultInPush(sender)
      }
      return false
    } else {
      return false
    }
  }
}
```

This single overridden function handles the following differences in logic between the expanded and collapsed states of a split view controller:

- **Collapsed:** The split view controller converts the `showDetailViewController(_:, sender:)` call into `showViewController(_:, sender:)` and redirects it to the primary view controller. This is the behavior you'll see on iPhone when in portrait: your app pushes the detail view on to the top of the navigation stack.
- **Expanded:** The split view controller displays the new view controller in the secondary view controller. Ergo no push.

This might seem like a lot of effort, but the real value is that you've abstracted all of the logic controlling the behavior out of your view controller. This means that these same view controller subclass extensions (i.e. the contents of **UIViewControllerShow.swift**) can be used not only across multiple split view controllers within your app, but even in different apps. These extension methods have no reliance on your data model, and in fact are intrinsically true within UIKit.

You're now ready to replace that final piece of idiom checking code. Open **MasterViewController.swift** and replace the existing `tableView(_:, willDisplayCell:, atIndexPath:)` implementation with the following one:

```
override func tableView(tableView: UITableView,
  willDisplayCell cell: UITableViewCell,
    forRowAtIndexPath indexPath: NSIndexPath) {
  var segueWillPush = false
  if rowHasChildrenAtIndex(indexPath) {
    segueWillPush = rwt_showVCWillResultInPush(self)
  } else {
    segueWillPush = rwt_showDetailVCWillResultInPush(self)
  }
  cell.accessoryType = segueWillPush ?
                            .DisclosureIndicator : .None
}
```

First, you define a variable to track whether tapping this cell will result in a push. If the selected row has children, the result of calling `showViewController(_:, sender:)` controls what happens with the push event. However, if the row doesn't have any children, then the result of calling `showDetailViewController(_:, sender:)` determines what happens with the push. Finally, if a tap results in a push you display a disclosure indicator.

Build and run using the iPhone simulator. You'll see that the app now behaves like you'd expect:

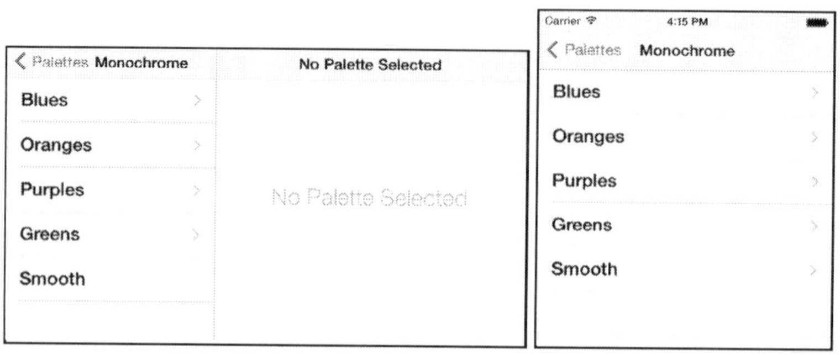

When the simulator is in landscape, you will see disclosure indicators next to rows that represent palette collections; color palettes themselves (i.e. rows which update the detail view controller, not the master view controller) don't have disclosure indicators. In portrait every row has a disclosure indicator – since tapping on a row always pushes a new view controller onto the navigation stack.

As you play with the app, you might find that you can get it to misbehave. When in landscape, navigate to **Monochrome,** then immediately rotate to portrait. Notice how the disclosure indicators aren't displaying correctly, as shown in the image below:

This is because rotating your device collapses the `UISplitViewController`, meaning you'll need to update the disclosure indicators.

It's okay though – this is easier to fix than you initially might think. `UIViewControllerShowDetailTargetDidChangeNotification` is a new notification fired when a `UISplitViewController` expands or collapses – i.e. the point at which the disclosure indicators need updating. Subscribing to this notification and updating the display of the disclosure indicators will fix the problem.

Add the following line to the end of `viewDidLoad()` in `MasterViewController`:

```
NSNotificationCenter.defaultCenter().addObserver(self,
    selector: "handleShowDetailVCTargetChanged:",
    name: UIViewControllerShowDetailTargetDidChangeNotification,
    object: nil)
```

Still within the same file, implement `deinit` as shown below:

```
deinit {
  NSNotificationCenter.defaultCenter().removeObserver(self,
    name: UIViewControllerShowDetailTargetDidChangeNotification,
    object: nil)
}
```

This ensures that the master view controller unsubscribes from the notification when it's disposed of.

Add the following to `MasterViewController`:

```
func handleShowDetailVCTargetChanged(sender: AnyObject?) {
  if let indexPaths = tableView.indexPathsForVisibleRows() {
    for indexPath in indexPaths as [NSIndexPath] {
      let cell = tableView.cellForRowAtIndexPath(indexPath)
      tableView(tableView, willDisplayCell: cell!,
                forRowAtIndexPath: indexPath)
    }
  }
}
```

The above method is quite simple; you loop through all visible cells and update their disclosure indicators by manually calling `tableView(tableView:, willDisplayCell:, forRowAtIndexPath:)`.

Build and run. You should now see that your previous disclosure indicator issue has been resolved:

That takes care of all of the iPhone-specific quirks. You now have a great-looking split view controller on the iPhone version of your app, and you cleaned up the resulting fallout.

It's not time to call it a day just yet. There are a few things you need to fix in the iPad version before you can ship it!

Correcting inconsistencies on the iPad

Build and run using the iPad simulator in portrait. You'll see the *No Palette Selected* view controller, as you'd expect. However, there is a rogue *back* button in the navigation bar, shown below, which takes you to an empty detail page:

This is because of the way you're adding the empty detail view controller. Take another look at `configureView()` in **DetailViewController.m**:

```
func configureView() {
```

```
  if let palette = colorPalette {
    ...
  } else {
    if let empty = storyboard
.instantiateViewControllerWithIdentifier("NoPaletteSelected")
                         as? UIViewController {
      showViewController(empty, sender: self)
    }
    makeAllContentHidden(true)
  }
}
```

When there is no palette to display, you create the *No Palette Selected* view controller and then pass it to `showViewController(_:, sender:)`. Since the navigation controller contains the detail view, this view controller ends up being pushed onto the navigation stack.

You *could* change this call to `showDetailViewController(_:, sender:)` instead; this would replace the navigation controller with the *No Palette Selected* view controller. However, this approach isn't ideal since you'd have an inconsistent user interface as the navigation bar would appear and disappear.

You could alternatively return a new navigation controller with the *No Palette Selected* view controller at its root, but the best approach is to update the *No Palette Selected* view controller to hide the back button.

Create a new **Cocoa Touch** class. Make sure it's a subclass of `UIViewController` and name it `NoPaletteSelectedViewController`. Open it and replace the contents of the file with the following:

```
class NoPaletteSelectedViewController: UIViewController {
  override func viewDidLoad() {
    super.viewDidLoad()
    navigationItem.hidesBackButton = true
  }
}
```

This is a very simple class; it simply ensures that the back button is hidden for the navigation item associated with this view controller.

You now need to associate this class with its storyboard representation.

Open **Main.storyboard**, select the **No Palette Selected** view controller and set the **Class** to `NoPaletteSelectedViewController` in the **Identity Inspector**.

Build and run using the iPad simulator. Notice that the *back* button has disappeared on the *No Palette Selected* view controller:

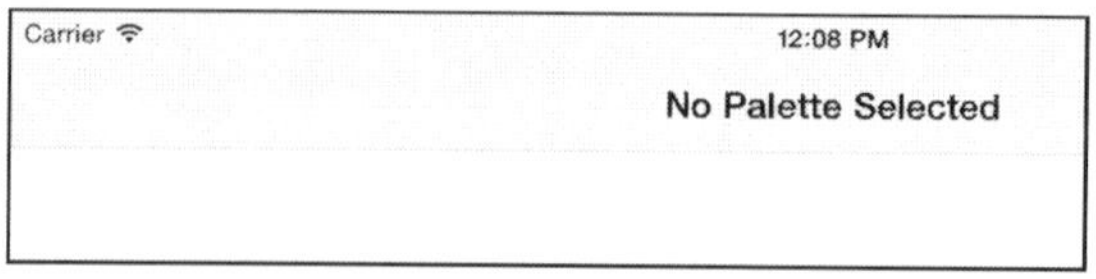

You also might have noticed that when in portrait on iPad, the only way to see the master palette list is to swipe right. This is okay, but it would be better to add a button in the navigation bar that performs the same action.

iOS 8 add `displayModeButtonItem()` to `UISplitViewController`; this provides you with an instance of `UIButtonItem` configured for the most appropriate action for an expanded split view controller. You'll use this method to populate the navigation bar associated with the detail view.

There are two different view controllers that can be associated with the detail view of the split view controller – `DetailViewController` and `NoPaletteSelectedViewController`, and they both need updating to display the split view controller's button item.

Open **NoPaletteSelectedViewController.swift** and add the following method to the class:

```
override func viewWillAppear(animated: Bool) {
  super.viewWillAppear(animated)
  if let svc = splitViewController {
    navigationItem.setLeftBarButtonItem(
                    svc.displayModeButtonItem(), animated: true)
  }
}
```

If this view controller exists within a split view controller, then it grabs the `UIBarButtonItem` returned by `displayModeButtonItem()` and sets it as the left bar button item on the navigation item.

`DetailViewController` is slightly more complicated; it's displayed in both expanded and collapsed states, whereas the *No Palette Selected* view controller is only displayed when the split view controller is expanded.

Add the following method to **DetailViewController.swift**:

```
override func viewWillAppear(animated: Bool) {
  super.viewWillAppear(animated)
```

```
    if let svc = splitViewController {
      if !svc.collapsed {
        navigationItem.setLeftBarButtonItem(
          svc.displayModeButtonItem(), animated: true)
        navigationItem.leftItemsSupplementBackButton = true
        navigationItem.hidesBackButton = false
      }
    }
  }
```

This code adds the display mode button item, sets the *back* button to visible, and that the left item you've added should appear *in addition* to the back button. By default, providing a left bar button item will replace the back button, but here you want both. The end result is that when the detail view is shown in a collapsed state on iPhone, the more familiar back button replaces the display mode button.

Build and run on the iPad simulator. You can see the new bar button when the iPad is in portrait, and the primary view controller is hidden. Tapping the button will slide the primary view controller in over the top of the secondary. When you rotate the iPad to landscape, the bar button disappears, because the split view controller is shown always-expanded – there is no need for the button.

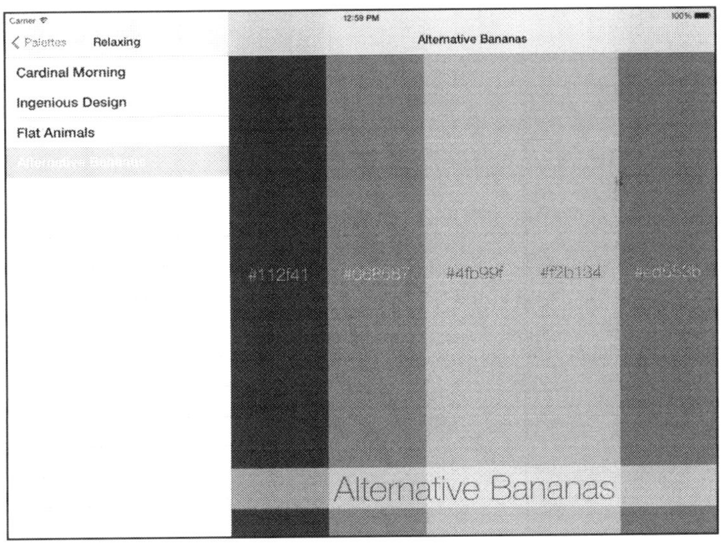

As an added bonus, you've gained some neat additional functionality on the iPhone version:

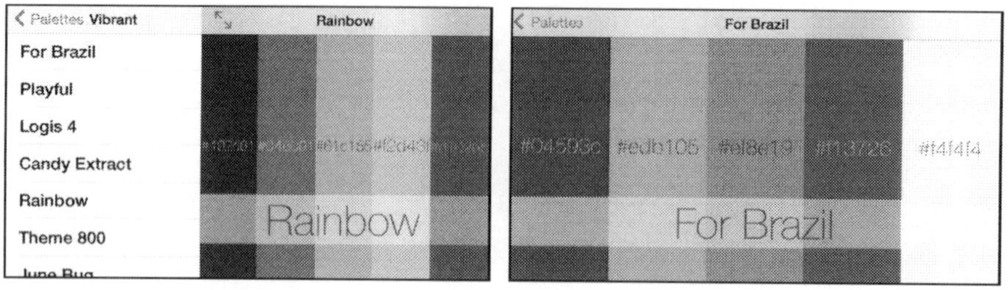

See the double-ended arrow that appears when the primary view controller is visible? Tapping this will expand the detail view controller to fill the entire screen, and then tapping the back arrow that appears will reveal the primary view controller.

Since the display mode bar button is now contextually aware, it changes its functionality as the state of the split view controller changes. The concept of display mode is only applicable when the split view is in an expanded state.

To summarize, the behavior of the different modes of the app is as follows:

- **All Visible:** Both the primary and secondary view controllers are visible. This is the default state for iPad when in landscape.
- **Primary Hidden:** Only the secondary view controller is visible.
- **Primary Overlay:** Both view controllers are visible, but the primary view controller is overlaid on the secondary.

When the iPad is in portrait, the default behavior toggles between primary hidden and overlay when the user swipes or taps the display mode button.

Where to go from here?

KhromaPal now has a really nice user interface that doesn't rely on idioms in order to behave differently the each device. You've learned a great deal in this chapter, including the following:

- How to upgrade an existing master-detail project to iOS8
- How to use the new universal features of `UISplitViewController`
- How to change the appearance of `UISplitViewController` by overriding trait collections
- How the new `showViewController(_:, sender:)` and `showDetailViewController(_:, sender:)` methods
- How to add a custom detail view when there's no active selection
- How to cope with transitions between different view controller hierarchies
- How to manage disclosure indicators in a contextually-appropriate fashion
- How to switch between the different display modes available in an expanded split view controller

The most significant part of this chapter is that `UISplitViewController` is now available on all devices – and is device agnostic. This is achieved via the new size class system, and the simplification of code that results is fantastic. No longer do you write two separate navigation routes in the same app – the same code will work seamlessly irrespective of device, both current and future.

This actually just scrapes the surface of adaptive view controller hierarchies; the new APIs in UIKit actually allow you to create your own, completely custom, adaptive view controller hierarchies. In many cases this won't be necessary, and you'll find the functionality you require within the new split view controller.

The next chapter moves away briefly away from the details of implementation for adaptive UI, and instead looks at one of the most powerful consequences – the deprecation of view controller rotation methods. This might sound concerning since you've almost certainly implemented custom rotation behavior in some of your existing apps – but fear not – the sample app is super cool and will really help you get to grips with the new technology.

Chapter 5: Transition Coordinators

By Sam Davies

Transition coordinators were introduced in iOS 7, made available via protocols such as `UIViewControllerTransitionCoordinator`. iOS 8 delivered Adaptive Layout, and with it a new use for transition coordinators in the form of layout transitions.

In addition to transitions between two controllers, iOS 8 now supports transitions that alter in the layout or size of a single view controller. This includes device rotation as well, since this is nothing but a change to the bounds of the view.

In this chapter you'll learn how to do the following things:

- Manage the new transition-based approach to device rotation.
- Leverage the power of the new transition coordinators to create some spectacular effects.
- Harness container size change notifications to implement rotation effects that are identical across both iPad and iPhone .
- Build views that adapt their padding, i.e. the space between the content of a view and the edge, according to their size class.

In this chapter you'll add all of the above functionality to a starter project named **KhromaLike**, which is an iOS 8 universal storyboard app. The app displays a selection of colored tiles; when a tile is selected the app displays details about that color along with a palette of complimentary colors. You can imagine that this app would be extremely handy for your next design project!

KhromaLike utilizes an adaptive layout; when the vertical size class is **Regular**, the collection view of colored tiles presents itself across the top of the view and scrolls horizontally like so:

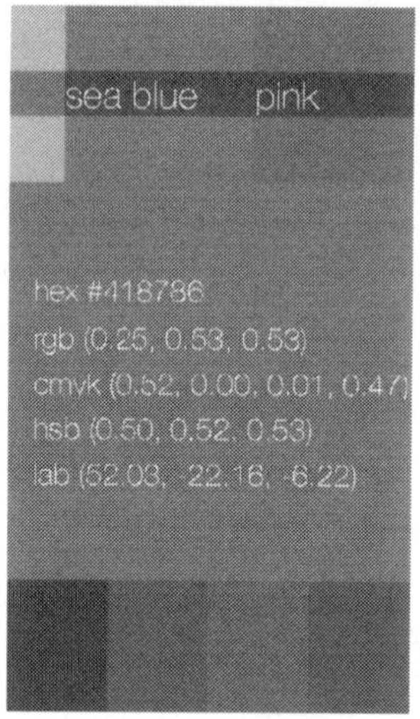

But when the vertical size class is **Compact**, the tiles appear down the left hand side, and scroll vertically, as shown below:

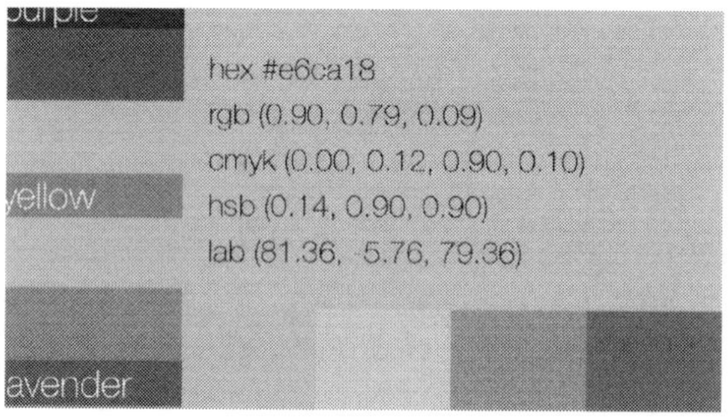

Find the KhromaLike starter project and open it in Xcode. The layout of the app was built completely within the storyboard using the techniques demonstrated in the previous Adaptive Layout chapters. Although the app is fully adaptive, at this time it still relies on legacy rotation methods.

Your first task is to update the app to use the new layout transitions instead.

Deprecated rotation methods

iOS 8 deprecates all the rotation methods of `UIViewController`. Yup – seriously. Take a look at **ColorSwatchCollectionViewController.swift**; you'll see that it implements `didRotateFromInterfaceOrientation()`. Since this method is now deprecated, you'll need to replace it. You'll focus on the iPhone elements for the first part of this tutorial, so use one of the iPhone simulators until you move on to the iPad coding.

iOS 8 didn't just deprecate the rotation methods – it deprecated the whole darn concept of *rotation* as well. In a fully adaptive interface, rotation loses all meaning; the physical *screen* must be rotated to ensure it is in the correct orientation, but the *content* itself only needs to be resized appropriately. Once you get your head wrapped around this, handling rotation in adaptive layouts becomes a lot easier. In fact, often you won't use anything other than the adaptive layout implementation you've already created in the storyboard.

iOS 8 adds the `UIContentContainer` protocol, and `UIViewController` adopts it. This protocol represents an object that can display content on the screen and is used as a mechanism to communicate changes that affect content, such as trait collection and size changes.

`willTransitionToTraitCollection(_, withTransitionCoordinator:)` is your go-to method for this; it's called when the trait collection of a content container belonging to the view controller hierarchy changes. Since the layout is adaptive to size classes, the layout change occurs when the trait collection changes.

From the **CollectionView** group, open **ColorSwatchCollectionViewController.swift** and delete `didRotateFromInterfaceOrientation()`. Replace it with the following:

```
override func willTransitionToTraitCollection(
                newCollection: UITraitCollection,
                withTransitionCoordinator coordinator:
                      UIViewControllerTransitionCoordinator) {
  super.willTransitionToTraitCollection(newCollection,
                         withTransitionCoordinator: coordinator)
  if let flowLayout = collectionViewLayout as?
                      UICollectionViewFlowLayout {
    if newCollection.verticalSizeClass == .Compact {
      flowLayout.scrollDirection = .Vertical
    } else {
      flowLayout.scrollDirection = .Horizontal
```

```
      }
    }
  }
```

This method has exactly the same purpose as the one you replaced. However, the new method uses the vertical class size to determine the scroll direction, as opposed to the orientation. This matches the way the layout is determined; that is, decoupling scroll direction from the orientation of the device as well as from the device itself. This makes it easier to reuse the collection view controller.

Build and run. You'll see no visible difference in your app. But that's okay – it's exactly the result you wanted. There's no longer any reliance on deprecated methods, and you've achieved that without any changes to the app's functionality.

Eagle-eyed readers will have noticed that the method you introduced above is passed a transition coordinator; you'll make use of this in the next section to create some amazing transition effects.

The power of transition coordinators

iOS 7 introduced the `UITransitionCoordinator` protocol as a way to customize and control transitions between view controllers. Transition coordinators provide a single point from which to manage concurrent animations; this provides a high level of control over the transitions that was simply non-extent prior to iOS 7. iOS 8 extends this to handle transitions for size and trait collection changes within the same view controller.

As mentioned earlier `willTransitionToTraitCollection(_, withTransitionCoordinator:)` is passed a transition coordinator that you can use to hook into the animations associated with the layout change, and customize them as you wish.

When the iPhone rotates, the view in KhromaLike updates its layout according to the auto layout constraints in the storyboard. When rotated from portrait to landscape – that is, when the vertical size class changes from Regular to Compact – the collection view changes from a horizontal orientation to a vertical one, and the scroll direction is changed from horizontal to vertical.

The following diagram demonstrates this process:

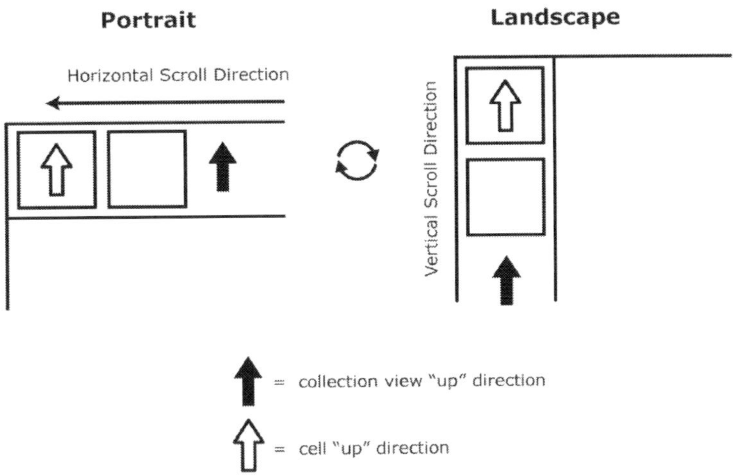

The black arrows represent the upward direction of the collection view, while the white arrows represent the upward direction of the cells.

Your task in this section is to create a cool effect that *rotates* the collection view first and then rotates the contained cells to the correct orientation. Here's a brief description of the process you'll follow:

1. Currently, the effect of rotating the device is to resize and reposition the collection view, as per the storyboard layout, but this requires that you change the scroll direction. To achieve the effect you're after, you can't change the scroll direction, so instead you rotate the collection view so that the scroll direction *appears* correct. Therefore, when the device rotates, you will counter-rotate the collection view. This means the scroll direction will be correct, but the size and position will be incorrect, as demonstrated below:

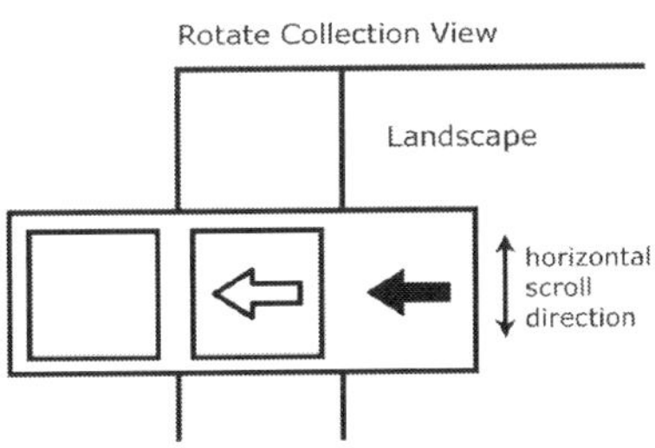

2. Next, resize the collection view so it's pinned to the top, bottom and left edges of the containing view. The collection view will then be in the correct position, but the cells will all be incorrectly oriented – remember that you rotated the entire collection view before? The following shows the resized and repositioned collection view, but with the cells incorrectly oriented:

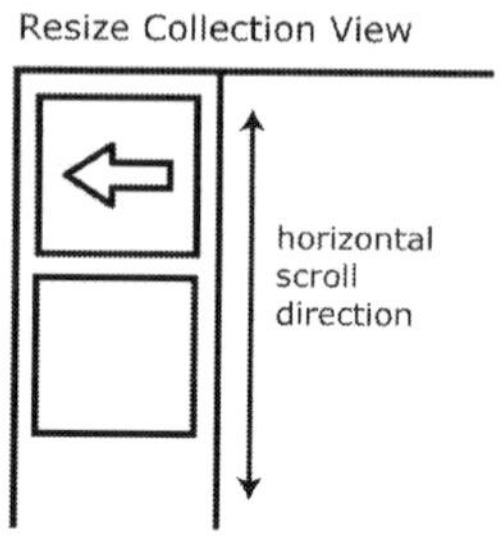

3. Finally, rotate each cell individually so they have the correct orientation:

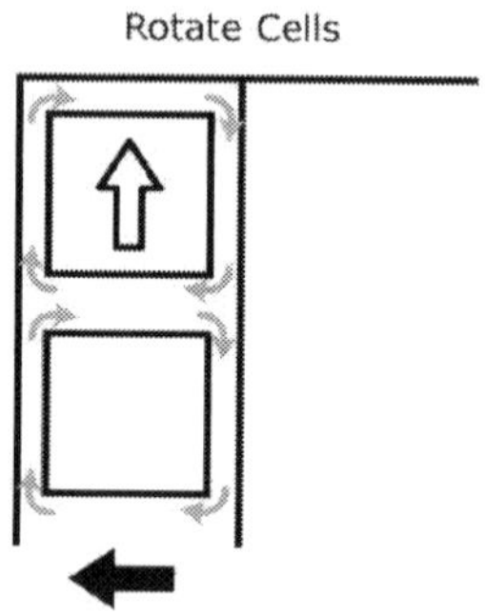

Open **ColorSwatchCollectionViewController.swift** from the **CollectionView** group and add the following property just below the existing ones:

```
var currentCellContentTransform = CGAffineTransformIdentity
```

Now delete the existing implementation of `willTransitionToTraitCollection(withTransitionCoordinator:)` and replace it with the following:

```
override func willTransitionToTraitCollection(newCollection:
UITraitCollection, withTransitionCoordinator
coordinator:UIViewControllerTransitionCoordinator) {
```

```
  super.willTransitionToTraitCollection(newCollection,
withTransitionCoordinator: coordinator)

  // 1
  let targetTForm = coordinator.targetTransform()
  let inverseTForm = CGAffineTransformInvert(targetTForm)
  // 2
  coordinator.animateAlongsideTransition({ _ in
    // Empty
    }, completion: { _ in
      // 3
      self.view.layer.transform =
CATransform3DConcat(self.view.layer.transform,
CATransform3DMakeAffineTransform(inverseTForm))
      // 4
      if abs(atan2(Double(targetTForm.b), Double(targetTForm.a))
/ M_PI) < 0.9 {
        self.view.bounds = CGRect(x: 0,
          y: 0,
          width: self.view.bounds.size.height,
          height: self.view.bounds.size.width)
      }
      // 5
      self.currentCellContentTransform =
CGAffineTransformConcat(self.currentCellContentTransform,
targetTForm)
    UIView.animateWithDuration(0.5, delay: 0,
usingSpringWithDamping: 0.6, initialSpringVelocity: 1, options:
nil, animations: {
      for cell in self.collectionView.visibleCells() as
[UICollectionViewCell] {
          cell.contentView.transform =
self.currentCellContentTransform
      }
    }, completion: nil)
  })
}
```

Taking each numbered comment in turn:

1. Calculate the inverse transform. `targetTransform()` is a new property of `UIViewControllerTransitionCoordinator`; it returns a `CGAffineTransform` that represents the destination transform associated with the current transition.
2. `animateAlongsideTransition:completion:` lets you specify an animation block to perform alongside the existing transition. You're not using the animation block here since you need to wait for Auto Layout to calculate the correct size of the new

layout. Instead, you'll use the completion block that is called once the transition has finished.

3. Apply the inverse transform to the collection views layer. Since you're using Auto Layout, it's not possible to simply use the `transform` property of the view. Luckily, applying a transform to the underlying layer works just fine! :]
4. Update the bounds of the view. If the device rotation is 90 degrees, that is, portrait to landscape or vice versa, then you need to switch the width and the height.
5. The collection view is now in the correct location, is of the correct size and scrolls in the correct direction. However, the orientation of the cells is still incorrect. Iterate through the visible cells and animate each of them to the correct orientation.

What's the purpose of `currentCellContentTransform` above? This is for cell reuse; it's important that you apply the correct transform to the cells as you reuse them.

Add the following method to `ColorSwatchCollectionViewController`:

```
override func collectionView(collectionView: UICollectionView,
  willDisplayCell cell: UICollectionViewCell,
  forItemAtIndexPath indexPath: NSIndexPath) {
    cell.contentView.transform = currentCellContentTransform
}
```

Here you're taking advantage of a `UICollectionViewDelegate` method to apply the correct transform to each cell just before it's displayed on screen.

Build and run using the iPhone simulator; perform a rotation using **cmd+left** or **cmd+right** to see the cool rotation effect in action, as illustrated:

The entire view rotates to the new orientation, and then the cells appear to *catch-up*, each one rotating with a spring-like animation.

Resizing Cells on Rotation

Turning your attention to the iPad now, build and run to see what the state of play currently is. Before you even start thinking about the rotation effects, you'll notice that the cells aren't nearly big enough for the collection view:

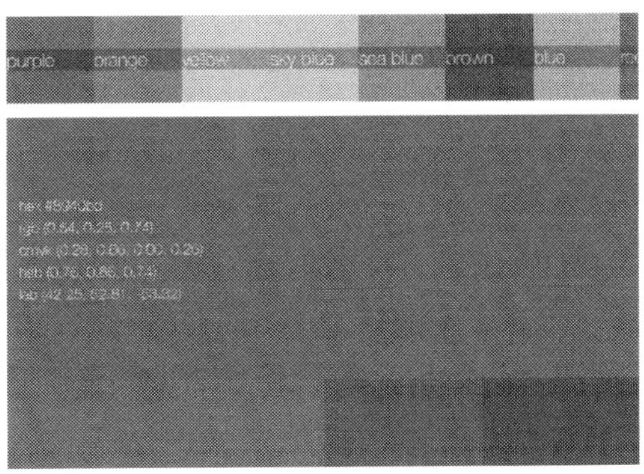

It isn't possible to automatically resize cells based on the bounds of the collection view. The collection view is laid out using Auto Layout, and is constrained to a quarter of the width of the overall view. Instead of manually tweaking cell sizes, it's a much better idea to continue to use Auto Layout to calculate your layout for you.

As the Auto Layout engine calculates the layout, it calls `viewWillLayoutSubviews()` on the collection view controller. Add the following method to the class in **ColorSwatchCollectionViewController.swift**:

```
override func viewWillLayoutSubviews() {
  super.viewWillLayoutSubviews()
  if let flowLayout = collectionViewLayout as?
    UICollectionViewFlowLayout {
    // Find the restrictive dimension
    let minDimension = min(CGRectGetHeight(view.bounds),
      CGRectGetWidth(view.bounds))
    let newItemSize = CGSize(width: minDimension,
      height: minDimension)
    if flowLayout.itemSize != newItemSize {
      flowLayout.itemSize = newItemSize
      flowLayout.invalidateLayout()
    }
  }
}
```

Since you want square cells, you can determine their size using their smallest dimension. Here you determine the smallest dimension, and then use it to create a `CGSize`. If this size is different to the current `itemSize` of the collection view flow layout, the code updates `itemSize` to the new size and invalidates the layout. This forces the collection view to re-layout, and subsequently resizes the cells.

Build and run your app in the iPad simulator; rotate the simulator using **cmd+left** or **cmd+right**. You'll see that the cells now resize as expected, in either orientation:

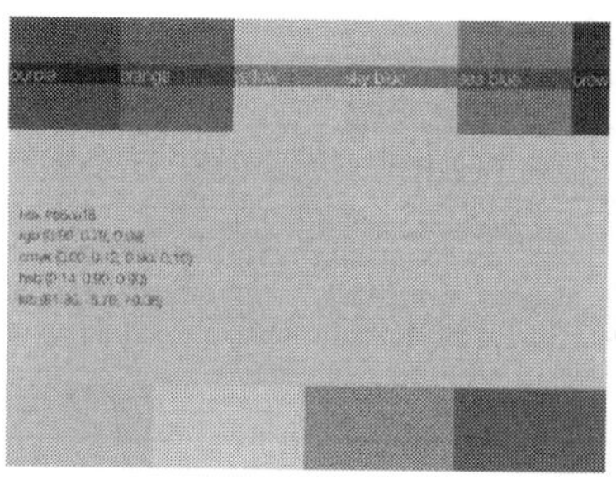

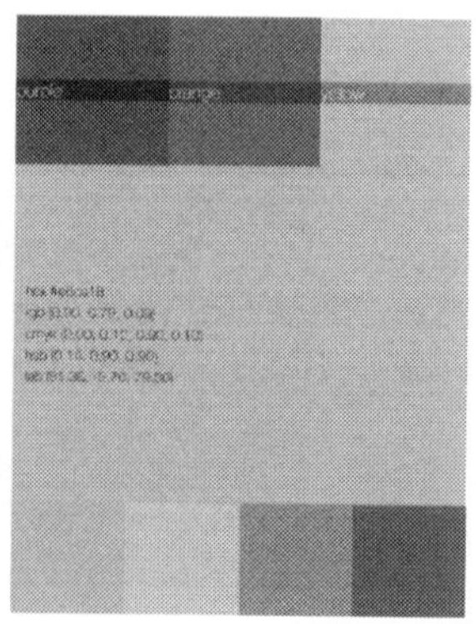

iPad rotation effects

So far you've concentrated just on the iPhone layout because its vertical size class is different for each orientation; in portrait its vertical size class is **Regular** and in landscape it is **Compact**. However, the **Regular** size class represents both dimensions on an iPad.

This means that rotating the iPad neither updates the layout, nor does it call `willTransitionToTraitCollection(withTransitionCoordinator:)`. However, the layout transition you created for the iPhone would look equally as cool on the iPad.

Luckily there's another method declared by in `UIContentContainer` protocol that you can use in this situation: `viewWillTransitionToSize(withTransitionCoordinator:)`. This method is called when the size of the content container changes, so that means when the device is rotated – well, so long as your device isn't square :]

Since rotation doesn't trigger a trait change, it won't be possible to build different layouts for the iPad in Interface Builder. However, you'll see how you can reuse the constraints setup for iPhone for the iPad version of this transition as well.

You're going to create two collections of layout constraints using `IBOutletCollection` – one for landscape and one for portrait.

> **Note:** You have used an `IBOutlet` in the past – but `IBOutletCollection` might be new to you. They are a way to access a *group* of objects that exist in a nib or storyboard from your code, in comparison to an `IBOutlet`, which represents a single object.

Open **Main.storyboard** and in the **Document Outline** expand **View Controller Scene**, then **View**, and finally **Constraints** (see next page):

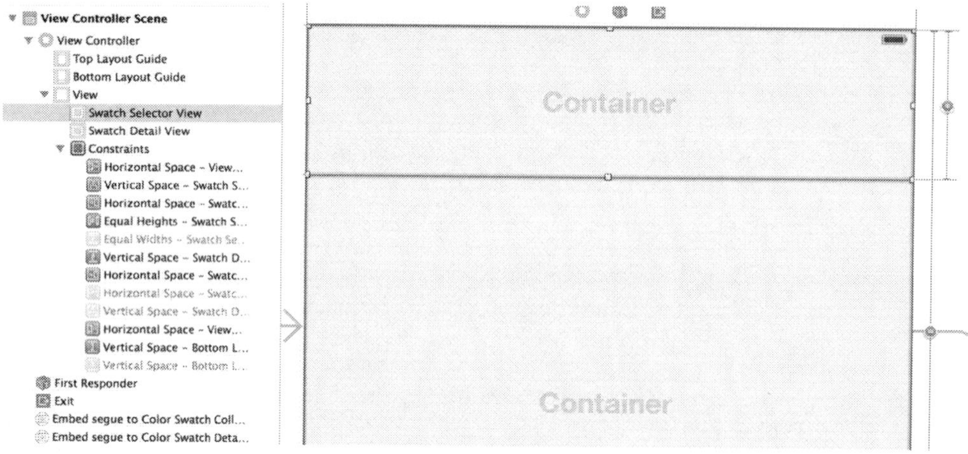

You'll notice that some of the constraints are grayed out, or *uninstalled*. This is because not all the constraints are associated with the current trait collection. The enabled, or *installed*, constraints are relevant to the portrait configuration; to reference them in code you'll need to create an `IBOutletCollection`.

Open the **Assistant Editor** and ensure that it's displaying **ViewController.swift**. Then **ctrl+drag** from one of the installed layout constraints in the **Document Outline** to **ViewController.swift**:

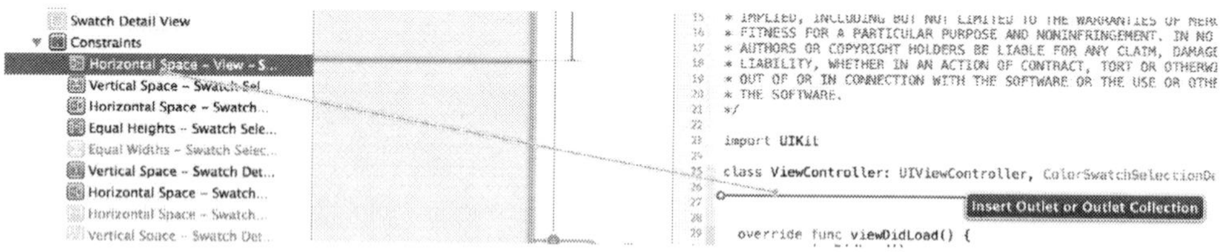

In the popup dialog, set the **Connection** to **Outlet Collection**, its **Name** to `tallLayoutConstraints` and finally its **Type** to `NSLayoutConstraint`, like so:

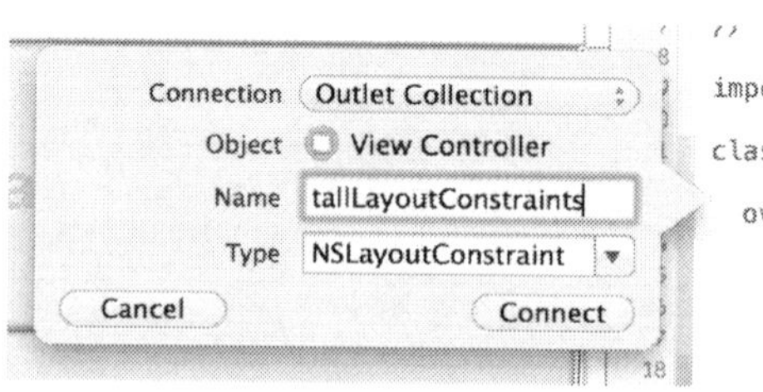

This will add code to **ViewController.swift** that looks like the following:

```
@IBOutlet var tallLayoutConstraints: [NSLayoutConstraint]!
```

This declares an `@IBOutlet` that is an array of `NSLayoutConstraint` objects.

> **Note:** You might wonder why the name is `tallLayoutConstraints` rather than `portraitLayoutConstraints`. This is a personal naming choice – so it could be changed – but the choice of tall/wide as opposed to portrait/landscape re-asserts the independence of the view controller layout from the device orientation. You could re-use the `ViewController` class as a contained view controller instead of full-screen – in which case portrait/landscape are terms that aren't necessarily applicable.

With each of the remaining installed constraints, **ctrl-drag** from the constraint to the outlet you just created in **ViewController.swift**:

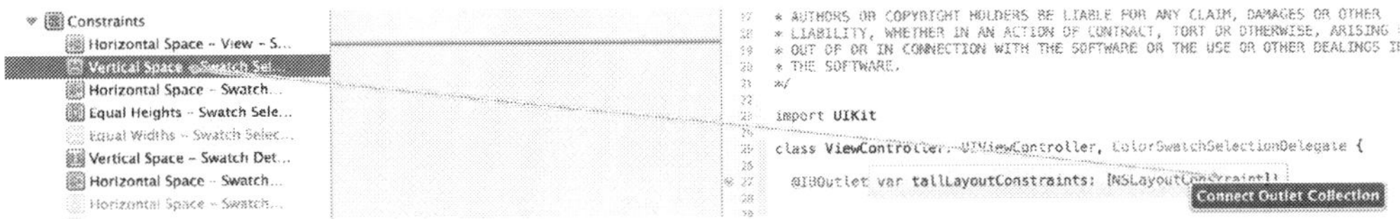

> **Note:** It's incredibly easy to make a mistake during this process. Ensure that you drag carefully from each of the installed constraints to the correct outlet in code.

Now you've created the collection of constraints required for the tall layout, it's time to repeat the same process for the wide layout.

Switch to the **Any Width, Compact Height** layout using the size-class selection popup dialog in **Interface Builder**, as shown on the next page:

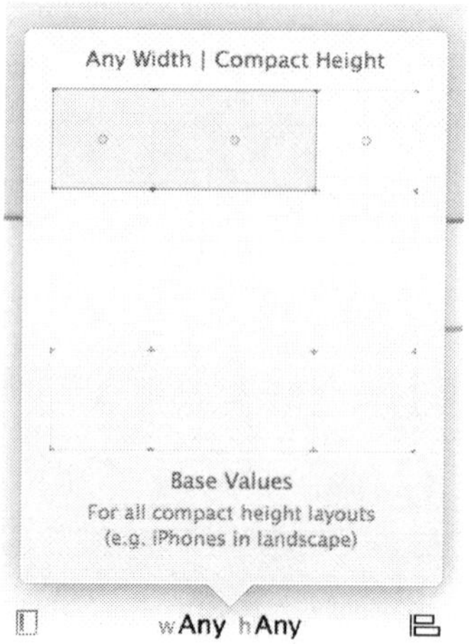

This updates the canvas to a layout more commonly associated with an iPhone in landscape orientation. The Document Outline will now highlight those constraints installed only for this layout:

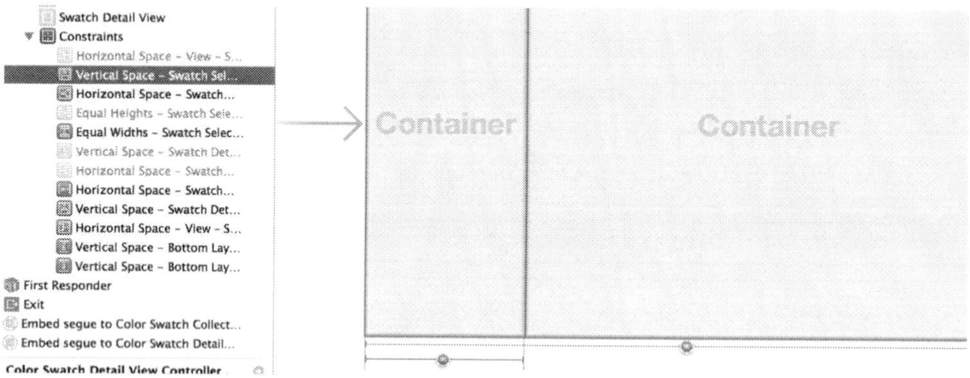

Open the **Assistant Editor** and ensure that it's displaying **ViewController.swift**. Then **ctrl+drag** from any of the installed layout constraints in the **Document Outline** to **ViewController.swift**. In the popup dialog, set the **Connection** to **Outlet Collection**, the **Name** to `wideLayoutConstraints`, and finally the **Type** to `NSLayoutConstraint`. With each of the remaining installed constraints, **ctrl-drag** from the constraint to the outlet you just created in **ViewController.swift**. Make sure to take care with this process, as Xcode *can* be a touch temperamental.

In the **Document Outline**, select **View Controller** from **View Controller Scene** and then open the **Connections Inspector**. Check there are eight constraints connected to `wideLayoutConstraints`, and eight constraints connected to `tallLayoutConstraints`, as shown below:

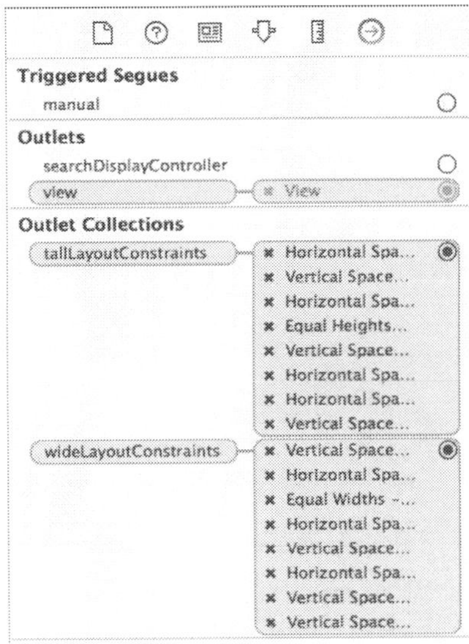

You can now refer to these collections of constraints from code and use them to switch between the two layouts.

Open **ViewController.swift** and add the following method to the class:

```
override func viewWillTransitionToSize(size: CGSize,
  withTransitionCoordinator coordinator:
  UIViewControllerTransitionCoordinator) {

  super.viewWillTransitionToSize(size,
      withTransitionCoordinator: coordinator)

  let transitionToWide = size.width > size.height
  let constraintsToUninstall = transitionToWide ?
      tallLayoutConstraints : wideLayoutConstraints
  let constraintsToInstall = transitionToWide ?
      wideLayoutConstraints : tallLayoutConstraints

  // Ask Auto Layout to commit any outstanding changes
  view.layoutIfNeeded()
  // Animate to the new layout alongside the transition
  coordinator.animateAlongsideTransition({
    _ in
NSLayoutConstraint.deactivateConstraints(constraintsToUninstall)
    NSLayoutConstraint.activateConstraints(constraintsToInstall)
```

```
      self.view.layoutIfNeeded()
    }, completion: nil)
  }
```

Here you check if the content container, in this case the view, is transitioning to a landscape layout. You then determine which set of constraints should be activated and which should be deactivated.

This method is passed a transition coordinator that allows you to provide a custom animation block to run alongside the transition animation. You're using it here to remove one set of constraints and add another.

> **Note:** The process used here for adding and removing constraints may be different to what you have seen or used before. Previously, you would use the `addConstraint(constraint:)` and `removeConstraint(constraint:)` methods on `UIView`, but now you should use the `NSLayoutConstraint` class methods demonstrated above.

Both the `activateConstraints(constraints:)` and `deactivateConstraints(constraints:)` methods take an array of `NSLayoutConstraint` objects. If you wish to toggle the state of an individual constraint, you can use its `active` property. This new approach matches how layout constraints behave in storyboards. It's a much simpler model, and is more in-line with what's happening behind the scenes.

Whenever you manually change any layout constraints you must call `layoutIfNeeded()` on the superview of the views that are affected by constraint change. Since the layout has been performed by this stage, you don't need to do anything else, so you simply pass `nil` for the completion block.

Build and run the app using the iPad simulator; rotate the simulator using **cmd+left** or **cmd+right**. You'll see the layout of the container view controller updates correctly, as shown:

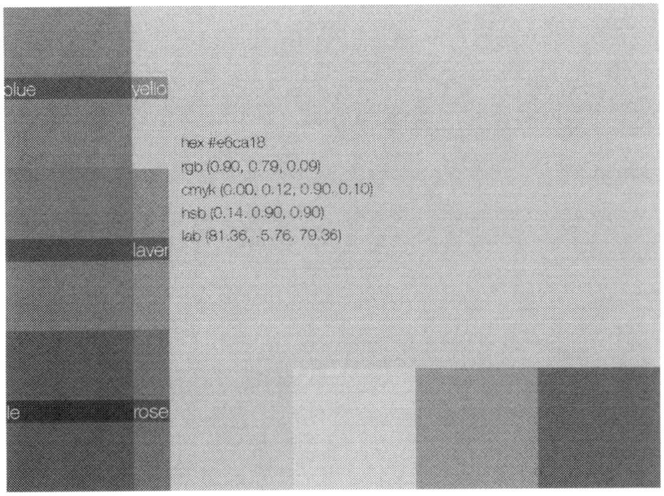

However, the collection view isn't updating to match, and it still scrolls horizontally.

Think back to how you implemented this feature earlier. When you created the custom animation associated with the transition, you implemented it in `willTransitionToTraitCollection(withTransitionCoordinator:)`. However, as stated earlier in this section, this method isn't called when an iPad rotates.

However, `viewWillTransitionToSize(withTransitionCoordinator:)` *is* called on both iPads and iPhones when the device is rotated. Therefore the solution is to simply switch these methods.

Open **ColorSwatchCollectionViewController.swift** and replace the following method signature and `super` call:

```
override func willTransitionToTraitCollection(newCollection:
UITraitCollection,
  withTransitionCoordinator
coordinator:UIViewControllerTransitionCoordinator) {

    super.willTransitionToTraitCollection(newCollection,
withTransitionCoordinator: coordinator)
```

With the following:

```
override func viewWillTransitionToSize(size: CGSize,
  withTransitionCoordinator coordinator:
  UIViewControllerTransitionCoordinator) {
    super.viewWillTransitionToSize(size,
withTransitionCoordinator: coordinator)
```

Since the implementation never referenced the `traitCollection` parameter, nothing else needs to change.

Build and run the app using iPad simulator. Rotate the simulator using **cmd+left** or **cmd+right** and you'll see the layout and rotation transition are now identical to those on the iPhone:

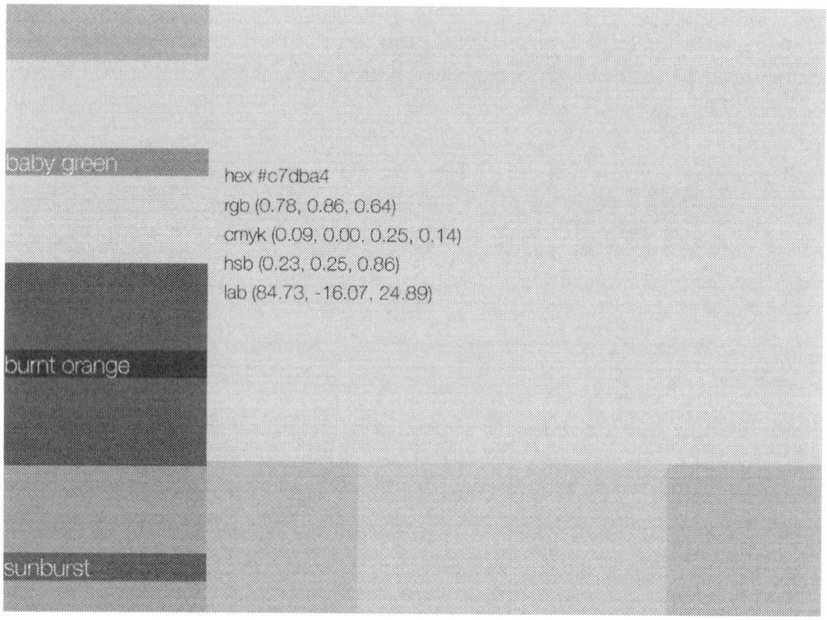

Now that you have the same transition working for both iPad and iPhone – without a single idiom check – you can now give some attention to the appearance of the content.

Creating an adaptive padded label

The cells contain a label that displays the name of the associated color. There isn't any vertical padding on this label; this looks fine on a screen with compact height, but not so much when there's an abundance of vertical space:

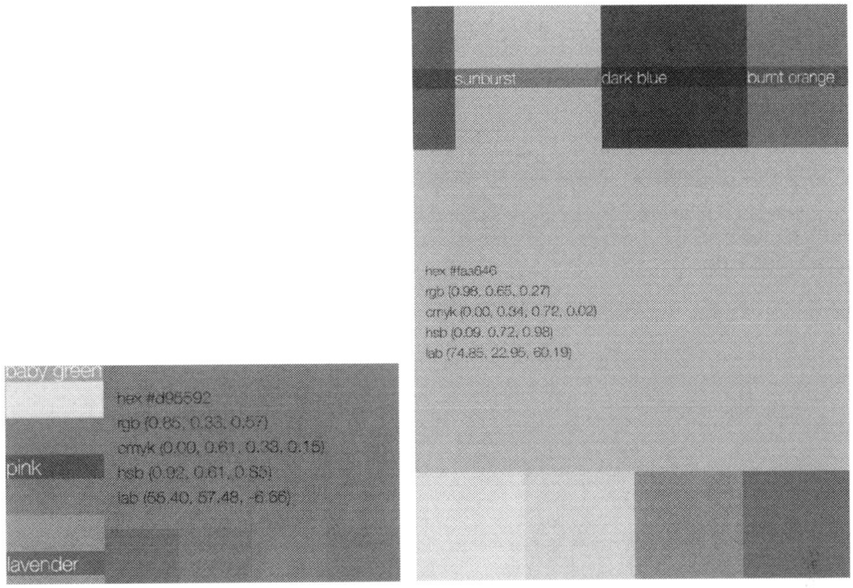

The label in the cells in the iPhone on the left is well proportioned, but the label in the iPad on the right looks a little swamped by the size of the cell.

In this section you'll learn how to create a custom view that responds to changes in its trait collection. You'll use this to create a label that adds vertical padding when displayed within a regular size class, and removes it when displayed in a compact size class.

Previously, you learned how to respond to trait collection changes from within a `UIViewController` subclass using `willTransitionToTraitCollection(_, withTransitionCoordinator:)`. This method belongs to the `UIContentContainer` protocol, which `UIViewController` conforms to. But `UIView` doesn't, therefore you can't use the same approach.

When dealing with trait collections, there is another protocol that you can conform to called `UITraitEnvironment`. It's used to declare an object participates in the trait system and understands how to work with trait collections. It contains just a single property and a single method, shown below:

```
protocol UITraitEnvironment : NSObjectProtocol {
  var traitCollection: UITraitCollection! { get }
  func traitCollectionDidChange(previousTraitCollection:
                                UITraitCollection)
}
```

With this protocol, you can request the current `traitCollection` of the adopting object and override `traitCollectionDidChange(previousTraitCollection:)` in order to respond to the changes in that trait collection.

In Xcode choose **File\New\File...** then **iOS\Source\Cocoa Touch Class** and click **Next**. Name the class **PaddedLabel**, and make it a subclass of `UILabel`. Set the Language to **Swift**. Finally, click **Next** and then **Create**.

This vertical padding of this label will depend on its current vertical size class.

Replace the contents of **PaddedLabel.swift** with the following:

```
class PaddedLabel: UILabel {

  var verticalPadding = 0.0

  override func traitCollectionDidChange(
    previousTraitCollection: UITraitCollection?) {
      // Check the vertical size class
      if traitCollection.verticalSizeClass == .Compact {
        // No padding when vertically compact
        verticalPadding = 0.0
      } else {
        // Padding when have regular size class
        verticalPadding = 20.0
      }
      // Need to update the layout
      invalidateIntrinsicContentSize()
  }
}
```

This defines the variable `verticalPadding` that represents the current padding applied to the label. It also overrides `traitCollectionDidChange(previousTraitCollection:)`; a change in the trait collection affecting this view will result in this method being called, which simply sets the `verticalPadding` property based on the new vertical size class. It then calls `invalidateIntrinsicContentSize()` which instructs Auto Layout to request the intrinsic content size for this view and trigger a new layout pass.

The class doesn't yet make use of the `verticalPadding` property. To rectify this, add the following:

```
override func intrinsicContentSize() -> CGSize {
  var intrinsicSize = super.intrinsicContentSize()
```

```
    // Add the padding
    intrinsicSize.height += CGFloat(verticalPadding)
    return intrinsicSize
  }
```

`intrinsicContentSize()` is part of the Auto Layout system and provides the size of the view it's called on. In the implementation above, you'll see the intrinsic size is actually calculated by the superclass - in this case `UILabel` - and then you modify it by adding the `verticalPadding` to the height.

Now the implementation is complete, you need to use it.

Open **Main.storyboard**, and in the **Document Outline** find **Color Swatch Collection View Controller Scene**. Keep expanding the disclosure triangles until you find the label, and then select it. In the **Identity Inspector**, set the **Class** to **PaddedLabel**, as shown below:

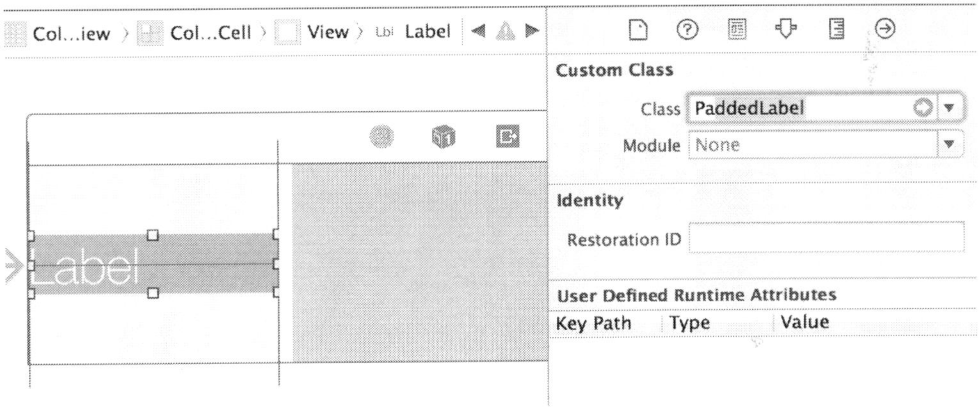

Build and run your app using the iPad simulator. You should see the labels in the cells now have the necessary padding, as shown on the next page:

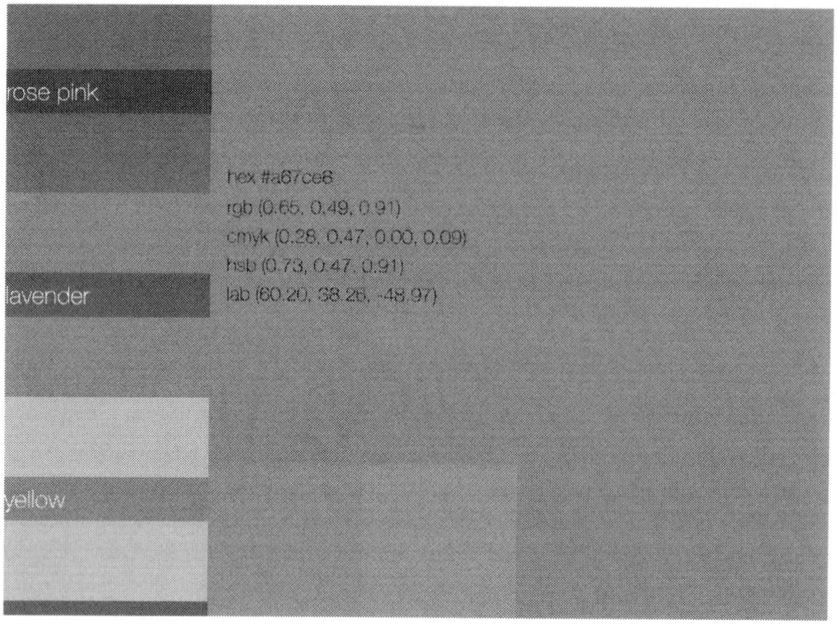

Now build and run the app using the iPhone simulator. Make sure the device is in portrait and then take a look at the labels. As the vertical size class is **Regular** you will see the labels are padded:

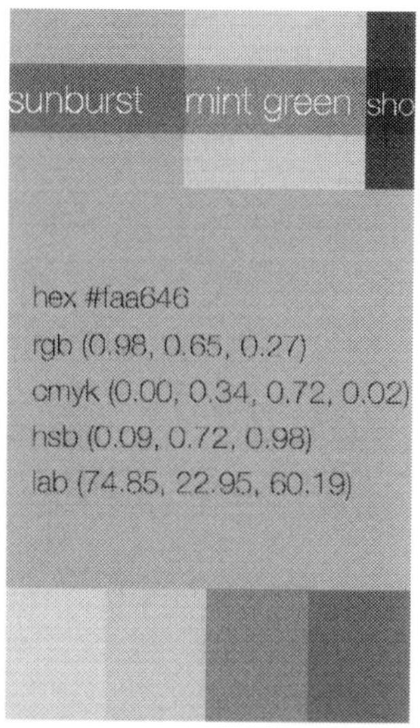

However, if you rotate to landscape, the vertical size class becomes **Compact**, and therefore your adaptively padded label loses the padding and becomes more compact itself, like so:

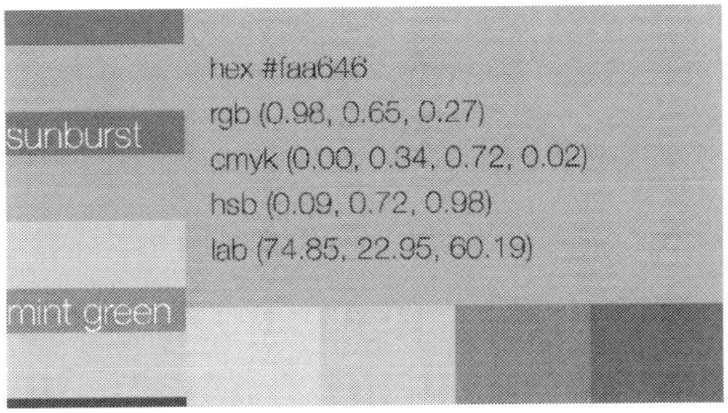

Conclusion

In most cases, the new approach to managing rotation with size classes won't affect your apps. That's because anything that was automatic before will remain automatic.

However, if you want to customize the transition performed during rotation, or to queue up some custom behavior to be run once the transition has completed, then you'll need to utilize the skills you've learnt whilst working with transition coordinators.

Not only has Apple simplified rotation, but they've also aligned it with existing approaches to view controller transitions. You can use the knowledge you've gained in this chapter to create some truly amazing rotation effects.

You likely noticed this chapter relied heavily on Auto Layout and used some rather complex methodologies. This should be taken as a sign that Auto Layout is a key component of Adaptive Layout; learning to work with Auto Layout and create adaptive layouts will pay dividends many times over as you start to build the next generation of iOS apps.

Chapter 6: Introducing Presentation Controllers

By Nicholas Waynik

Prior to iOS 8, it was quite common for your apps to be cluttered with tons of platform-specific cases like this:

```
if UIUserInterfaceIdiom() == UIUserInterfaceIdiom.Pad {
  // Present in popover
} else {
  // Push view controller
}
```

With iOS 8's new Adaptive UI, this kind of code is ancient history! With the advent of a new system called presentation controllers, you can write a single code path that works on all devices.

The way presentation controllers work is that when you present a view controller, you specify a preferred presentation style (such as popover for example). Based on the size class of your device, the OS will either present your view controller in that style or switch to an alternative style. For example, on compact-width devices, a popover will actually be presented full screen by default.

In this chapter, you will learn how to adaptively present content as popovers on regular-width devices, or a full-screen on compact-width devices, in a single adaptive code path. In addition, you will learn about two important new view controllers you can use in your apps: `UIAlertController` and `UISearchController`. These replace `UIAlertView`, `UIActionSheet`, and `UISearchDisplayController` with adaptive alternatives.

Getting started

In this chapter, you'll be working with an iPhone app called **CountryFunFacts**. I've created a starter project for you with the basic user interface built, so you can focus on the new presentation controller code.

Build and run the project, and you'll see a list of countries as shown below:

Now tap on any country's flag and you'll see a small quiz on that country:

Tap on any of the answers listed; you'll notice that nothing happens. Your job is to use the new presentation controllers in iOS 8 to provide the user with some feedback on their answers.

UIAlertController

Prior to iOS 8, you used `UIAlertView` or `UIActionSheet` to present a simple popup with information, or a few buttons of various options to users.

Now in iOS 8, Apple has introduced a new view controller, `UIAlertController`, which replaces `UIAlertView` and `UIActionSheet`. It has a number of advantages over `UIAlertView` and `UIActionSheet`:

- It's incredibly easy to switch between an alert view style and action sheet style (which used to be a pain).
- The API is clean and modern; rather than having to implement delegate methods to respond to button taps, you can use closures!
- `UIAlertController` is adaptive. When running in an action sheet style on the iPad, it can automatically present itself in a popover without you having to write platform-specific code.

You definitely want to start using this in your apps, so let's try it out.

Open **RWTCountryDetailViewController.swift** and replace `quizAnswerButtonPressed()` with the following code:

```
@IBAction func quizAnswerButtonPressed(sender: UIButton) {
  let buttonTitle = sender.titleLabel?.text // 1
  var message = ""
  if buttonTitle == country!.correctAnswer { // 2
    message = "You answered correctly!"
  } else {
    message = "That answer is incorrect, please try again."
  }

  var alert = UIAlertController(title:nil,
    message:message,
    preferredStyle:UIAlertControllerStyle.Alert) // 3

  alert.addAction(UIAlertAction(title: "OK",
    style: UIAlertActionStyle.Default,
    handler: {(alert :UIAlertAction!) in
```

```
        println("You tapped OK")
    })) // 4

    self.presentViewController(alert, animated: true,
        completion: nil) // 5
}
```

Here's what the above method does:

1. Retrieves the title string of the button so you can compare it against the correct answer.
2. Assigns the appropriate response to `message` depending on whether the answer is correct or not.
3. Creates a new instance of `UIAlertController` and presents it to the user. Make note of how you pass in `UIAlertControllerStyle.Alert`; this is a new enumerated type in iOS 8, which lets you modify how the alert controller appears. You'll learn more about this later.
4. Adds a button to close the alert, and a callback closure that is executed when the button is tapped. There's no need to worry about delegates when you use `UIAlertAction` – how nice is that?

Build and run your app; tap on any flag, then tap any answer button to see your new alert:

This is the alert style; let's see how easy it is to switch it over to the action sheet style.

Simply go back to `quizButtonAnswerPressed()` and change the enumerated type from `UIAlertControllerStyle.Alert` to `UIAlertControllerStyle.ActionSheet` like so:

```
var alert = UIAlertController(title:nil,
  message:message,
  preferredStyle:UIAlertControllerStyle.ActionSheet)
```

Build and run your app; this time when you tap on a quiz answer you'll see that the alert has changed to an action sheet as shown below:

If you build and run this on the iPad, you'll notice the app currently crashes. This is because on the iPad, the alert controller presents itself inside a popover controller. For this to work, you need to add two lines of code to instruct the alert controller where to point the popover arrow.

To fix this, add these two lines to the end of `quizButtonAnswerPressed()`, right before the call to `presentViewController()`:

```
alert.popoverPresentationController?.sourceView = view
alert.popoverPresentationController?.sourceRect = sender.frame
```

When you present a view controller in a popover (like you would for this action sheet-style alert controller on the iPad), UIKit automatically creates a property on the view controller called `popoverPresentationController` that manages the display of the popover.

You'll learn more about how this works in the next section, but for now all you need to know is that you need to direct the popopver where to point by setting the `sourceView` to the view containing the popover, and the `sourceRect` to the rectangle inside the `sourceView` where the popover should point. Here, you direct the popover to point on the button that the user tapped.

Build and run on the iPad, and notice that the alert controller now presents itself inside a popover in an adaptive manner:

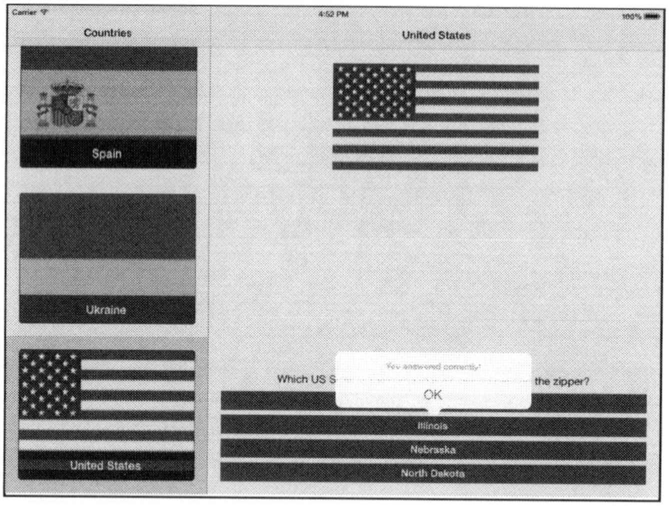

Your app is shaping up nicely, but it would be nice if you displayed some fun facts for each country. Let's do that next!

UIPopoverPresentationController

Currently, your storyboard contains a view controller that can display some fun facts for each country:

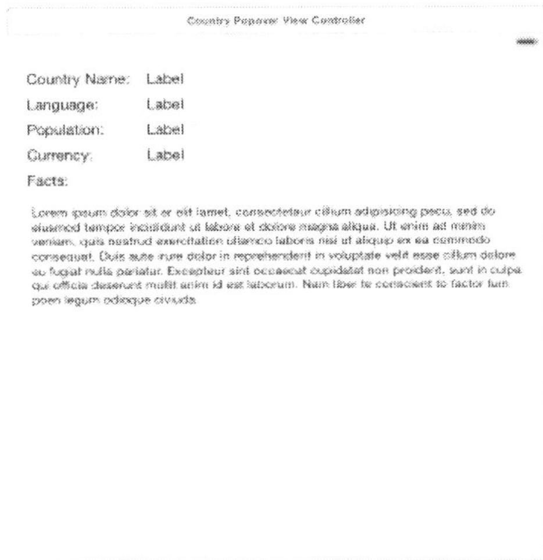

This fact view controller has enough data to fill an entire compact-width screen, but not enough to fill a regular-width screen. Therefore, you'd like to present this fact view controller as a modal view controller on the compact-width screens, but as a popover on regular-width screens.

Prior to iOS 8, doing this would have required a lot of platform specific code. Now, you can do this incredibly simply with a brand new class: `UIPopoverPresentationController`.

To use this, you simply set your view controller's `modalPresentationStyle` to `.Popover`. You don't need to create a `UIPopoverPresentationController` manually; as you learned in the previous section, UIKit automatically creates one of these for you when you present a view controller in a popover style. All you need to do is configure a few parameters on the popover presentation controller, such as the `sourceView` or `sourceRect` properties you set earlier.

Let's try this out. First, you'll need a button the user can tap to present the country fact view. To do this, open **RWTCountryDetailViewController.swift** and add the following code to the bottom of `configureView()`:

```
let detailsButton: UIBarButtonItem =
UIBarButtonItem(title: "Facts",
  style: UIBarButtonItemStyle.Plain,
  target: self, action: "displayFacts:")

navigationItem.rightBarButtonItem = detailsButton
```

This code adds a **Facts** button to the right side of the navigation controller.

Next add the following method to the bottom of the same class, which will be called when the **Facts** button is tapped:

```
func displayFacts(sender: UIBarButtonItem) {

  let storyboard : UIStoryboard =
  UIStoryboard(name: "Main", bundle: nil)

  var contentViewController :
    RWTCountryPopoverViewController =
    storyboard.instantiateViewControllerWithIdentifier(
      "RWTCountryPopoverViewController")
      as RWTCountryPopoverViewController
  contentViewController.country = country  // 1

  contentViewController.modalPresentationStyle =
      UIModalPresentationStyle.Popover  // 2

  var detailPopover: UIPopoverPresentationController =
    contentViewController.popoverPresentationController!

  detailPopover.barButtonItem = sender; // 3
  detailPopover.permittedArrowDirections =
      UIPopoverArrowDirection.Any
  presentViewController(contentViewController,
      animated: true, completion:nil) // 4
}
```

Clicking the **Facts** button calls this method. Here's what it does:

1. First you load `RWTCountryPopoverViewController` from a storyboard, then assign the country that it should display facts for.
2. Then you set the `modalPresentationStyle` property of `contentViewController` to `UIModalPresentationStyle.Popover`. This is the key step to configure the view controller to appear as a popover on regular-width screens.

> **Note:** iOS 8 introduces the three new options to `UIModalPresentationStyle`. You've already seen the first (`.Popover`), but there are two more that you should be aware of:
>
> `.OverFullScreen` displays the presented view over the full screen.

> `.OverCurrentContext` displays the presented view only over the parent view controller's content.
>
> The above two presentation styles let the underlying views show through if the presented view doesn't cover the entire screen.

3. Next you set a variable to point to the `contentViewController's` `popoverPresentationController` property for convenience.
4. Then you configure a few properties on the popover presentation controller. First, you have to tell the popover presentation where to point, You could use the `sourceView` and `sourceRect` properties as before, but alternatively you can set a `barButtonItem` to point to like you do here. You can also configure other properties such as `permittedArrowDirections`, which configures the directions the popover can point to. You set it to `Any` here, for maximum flexibility.
5. Finally you present the fact view controller to the user. Note you use the standard `presentViewController()` API to do this, but thanks to the power of `UIPopoverPresentationController` this now works in an adaptive manner!

Build and run your app in the iPad simulator; you'll see the country's facts displayed in a popover as you'd expect:

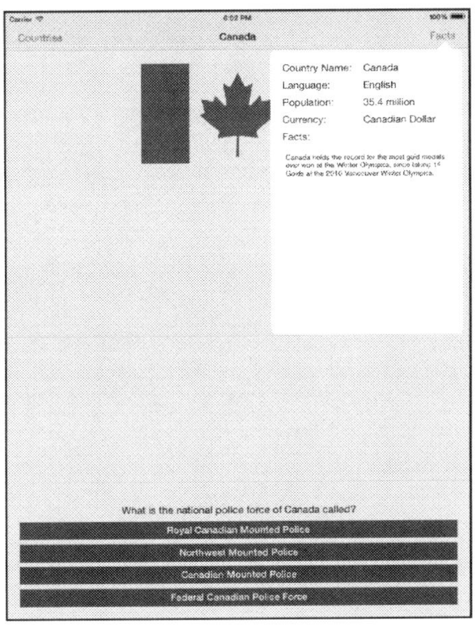

Now launch the app in the Phone 5S simulator and tap the Facts button. It will present the view controller modally instead:

Pretty cool! However, there is currently no way to dismiss the dialog from the screen on fixed-width devices.

What you want to do is display the fact dialog in a navigation controller on compact-width devices. To do this, you need to set your view controller as the delegate of the `UIPopoverPresentationController`, and implement two delegate methods:

1. `adaptivePresentationStyleForPresentationController()`: This method is called when the app presents a view controller on a compact-width device. You should implement this to tell the OS the new presentation style to use in this case. For example, you will tell the OS to present the new view controller as a full screen view controller on compact-width devices.

2. `presentationController(_:viewControllerForAdaptivePresentationStyle)`: This method is called when a view controller is presented in a different presentation style than originally configured. For example, you have configured the fact view controller to have a popover presentation style, but on compact-width devices it will switch to a full screen style.

   Here you have an opportunity to return a modified view controller to use when this style switch occurs. In this case, you will wrap the fact view controller in a navigation controller so that you can add a button the user can tap to dismiss the fact view controller.

Let's try this out. Change the class definition at the top of **RWTCountryDetailViewController.swift** to conform to the `UIPopoverPresentationDelegate` protocol as shown:

```
class RWTCountryDetailViewController: UIViewController,
  UISplitViewControllerDelegate,
  UIPopoverPresentationControllerDelegate {
```

Next, add the following line to `displayFacts()` just before the call to `presentViewController(animated:completion:)`:

```
detailPopover.delegate = self
```

This sets your detail view controller as the delegate of the fact view controller's popover presentation controller.

Finally, add the following two delegate methods to the bottom of the class:

```
// #pragma mark - UIAdaptivePresentationControllerDelegate
func adaptivePresentationStyleForPresentationController(
  controller: UIPresentationController!) ->
    UIModalPresentationStyle {

  return UIModalPresentationStyle.FullScreen
}

func presentationController(controller:
    UIPresentationController!,
    viewControllerForAdaptivePresentationStyle style:
    UIModalPresentationStyle)
    -> UIViewController! {

  let navController =
    UINavigationController(rootViewController:
      controller.presentedViewController)

  return navController
}
```

These are the two delegate methods you have to implement. Note they are actually part of `UIAdaptivePresentationControllerDelegate`, which `UIPopoverPresentationControllerDelegate` derives from.

`adaptivePresentationStyleForPresentationController()` returns `UIModalPresentationStyle.FullScreen` so that the presented view controller's view takes up the full screen.

`presentationController(_:viewControllerForAdaptivePresentationStyle:)` wraps the content view controller in a navigation controller when the app is run on the iPhone and the view is in full screen presentation mode. On the iPad the content view controller displays without the navigation controller since it doesn't use the full screen display.

Build and run the app again in both the iPhone and iPad simulators to see the difference:

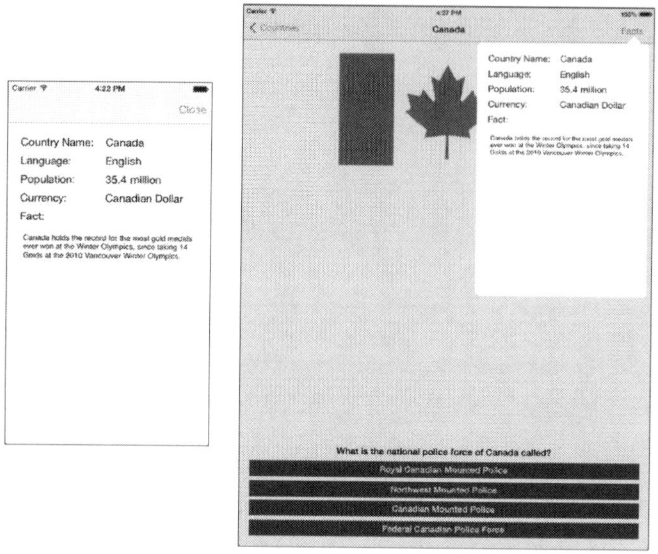

That solves the immediate problem of being able to close the dialog, but wouldn't it be nice if the iPhone app could display a popover just like the iPad does?

It's easier to do that than you think.

Change the return type of `adaptivePresentationStyleForPresentationController(controller:)` in **RWTCountryDetailViewController.swift**, to the following:

```
return UIModalPresentationStyle.None
```

Could it get any simpler? Here you tell the OS not to change the presentation style of the fact view controller on fixed-width devices.

Build and run your app in the iPhone simulator to see the results of this one-line change:

Not only does that look great, it also brings the visual design of your iPhone app in line with that of the iPad.

With 196 countries in the world, it would be a bit tedious to scroll through them all! A search function would be extremely handy to add to your app.

UISearchController

`UISearchController` is a new view controller in iOS 8 that replaces `UISearchDisplayController`. The new `UISearchController` has the advantage of being fully adaptive, and it also lets you use any kind of view controller to present the results (not just table views).

Using a `UISearchController` just takes three steps:

1. Create a view controller to present your search results. Again, this can be any kind of view controller you like: a table view controller, a collection view controller, or something completely custom.
2. Create a `UISearchController`, and pass it your search results view controller.
3. The `UISearchController` will notify its `searchResultsUpdater` (a class that conforms to `UISearchResultsUpdating`) when the search text changes. Typically,

you will make your search results view controller implement this protocol so you can update the filtered results.

In your project, I have created a view controller for you that you'll use to display a filtered list of countries (**RWTCountryResultsController.swift**). Open the file and take a peek; you'll see that it's a simple table view, with a handy `filteredContentForSearchText()` method that you'll use soon. Take a look at this file and make sure you understand how it works.

Now, let's create a `UISearchController` that uses this view controller to display and filter the search results. Open **RWTCountryListViewController.swift** and add this new property:

```
var searchController: UISearchController? = nil
```

This will store a reference to the `UISearchController` you're about to create.

Next, add this new method to create the search controller:

```
func addSearchBar() {
  var resultsController = RWTCountryResultsController()
  resultsController.countries = countries
  resultsController.delegate = self

  searchController = UISearchController(searchResultsController:
    resultsController)

  searchController!.searchResultsUpdater = resultsController

  searchController!.searchBar.frame = CGRect(
    x: searchController!.searchBar.frame.origin.x,
    y: searchController!.searchBar.frame.origin.y,
    width: searchController!.searchBar.frame.size.width,
    height: 44.0)

  tableView.tableHeaderView = searchController!.searchBar
  self.definesPresentationContext = true

}
```

Here you create a new `UISearchController`, and specify `RWTCountryResultsController` as its search results controller and `searchResultsUpdater`. This means the UISearchController will present the `RWTCountryResultsController` when you enter search text, and call a method on the `RWTCountryResultsController` every time the user updates the search text so you can re-filter the results.

You'll notice that there's an error on the line that you set the `RWTCountryResultsController` as the `searchResultsUpdater`. This is because you haven't yet implemented the required protocol (`UISearchResultsUpdating`). Let's do that next.

Open **RWTCountryResultsController.swift** and mark the class as conforming to this protocol:

```
class RWTCountryResultsController: UITableViewController,
UISearchResultsUpdating
```

Then implement the required method as follows:

```
func updateSearchResultsForSearchController(
  searchController: UISearchController) {
  if !searchController.active {
    return
  }
  self.filterContentForSearchText(
    searchController.searchBar.text)
}
```

This is the method that is called whenever the search text changes. Here you simply call the helper method to filter the search results appropriately.

There is one more method to add to RWTCountryResultsController.swift. Add the following toward the end of the class:

```
override func tableView(tableView: UITableView,
  heightForRowAtIndexPath indexPath: NSIndexPath)
  -> CGFloat {
  return 246.0
}
```

This method is overridden to return a specific height for the table view cells. This method is needed to prevent a bug which happens when selecting a flag from the search results, then pressing the back button to show the search results.

There's one last step – you need to call the `addSearchBar()` method you wrote earlier. To do this, switch back to **RWTCountryListViewController.swift** and add this line to the end of `viewDidLoad()`:

```
addSearchBar()
```

Build and run, and scroll up a bit on the country list to reveal the search bar. Enjoy your nice adaptive search results!

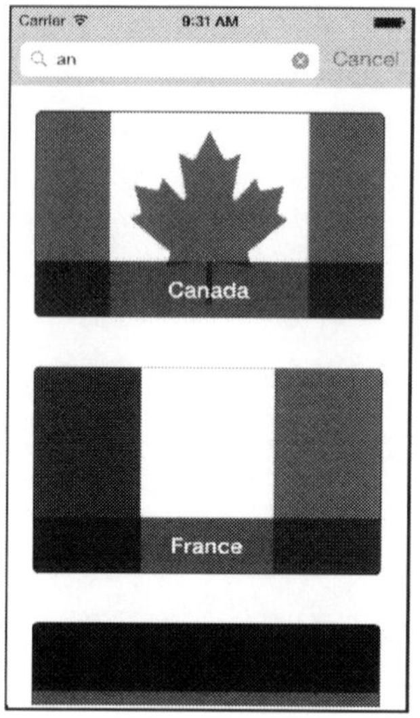

There's one last thing to fix. Currently when you tap a search result, the app does nothing. This is because the `RWTCountryResultsControllerDelegate` isn't implemented.

Open **RWTCountryListViewController.swift** and make the class conform to `RWTCountryResultsControllerDelegate` as shown.

```
class RWTCountryListViewController: UITableViewController,
RWTCountryResultsControllerDelegate {
```

Next add the delegate method to the bottom of this class.

```
// #pragma mark - RWTCountryResultsControllerDelegate

func searchCountrySelected() {
  performSegueWithIdentifier("showDetail", sender: nil)
}
```

This delegate method is called from RWTCountryResultsViewController.swift whenever a user taps on a country listed in the results.

While still in RWTCountryListViewController.swift, update `prepareForSeque()` to handle the additional call from the delegate method you just added.

```
override func prepareForSegue(segue: UIStoryboardSegue,
  sender: AnyObject?) {

  if segue.identifier == "showDetail" {
    var country : RWTCountry? = nil
    if searchController!.active {
      let resultsController =
      searchController!.searchResultsController as
      RWTCountryResultsController
      let indexPath =
      resultsController.tableView.indexPathForSelectedRow()
      country =
        resultsController.filteredCountries[indexPath!.row]
        as? RWTCountry
    } else {
      let indexPath = self.tableView.indexPathForSelectedRow()
      country = countries[indexPath!.row] as? RWTCountry
    }
    let navController = segue.destinationViewController as
UINavigationController
    let topViewController = navController.topViewController as
RWTCountryDetailViewController
    topViewController.country = country
  }
}
```

Build and run, perform a search, and tap a result – everything works!

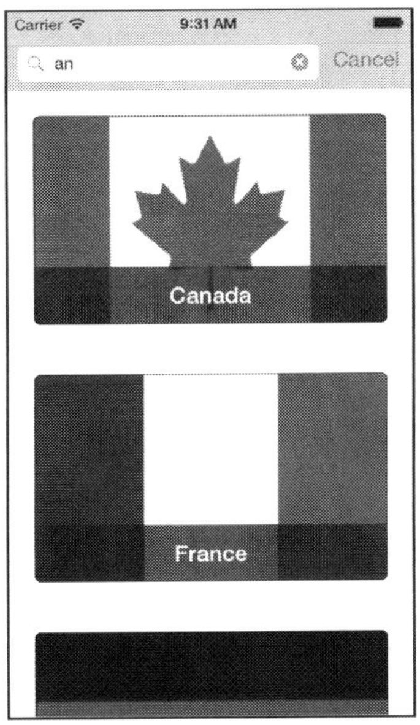

And best of all, with these new view controllers your app is completely adaptive!

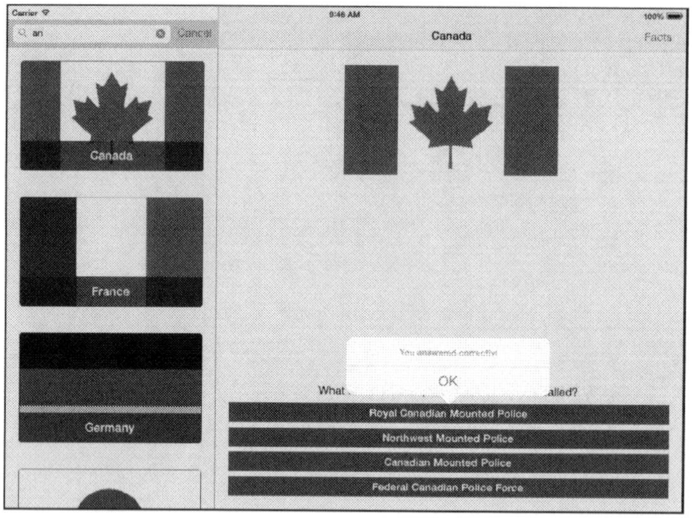

Where to go from here?

Now that you're familiar with `UIAlertController`, `UIPopoverController`, and `UISearchController`, and other adaptive techniques, having to separate code paths in your apps for different devices is a thing of the past.

But what if you want to present your view controllers with a custom animation or look? Keep reading for the next chapter, where I'll show you how!

Chapter 7: Custom Presentations

By Nicholas Waynik

In chapter 6, **Introducing Presentation Controllers**, you saw how to use the new `UIPresentationController` as the foundation for displaying alerts, action sheets, and popovers. If you haven't read that chapter I suggest you do so first, to learn about how Apple replaced `UIAlertView` and `UIActionSheet` with the `UIPresentationController` based `UIAlertController`.

This chapter is all about customization, so you will delve into some advanced uses of presentation controllers. You'll create a simple custom presentation to display content over a dark, semi-transparent background. You'll then learn how to animate your collection view cells off the screen while enlarging the flag image of a tapped cell. In addition to this animation, you will animate the content view of the presented view controller to display just under the enlarged flag image. The following two screenshots display the final states of these two types of presentations.

Before jumping into the coding, there's just a little bit of background knowledge you should have so that you can attack these new presentation controllers like the code ninja you are!

Presented and presenting controllers

Presenting view controllers isn't a new concept; in fact, presenting view controllers has been possible since the original iPhone OS SDK. With the release of iOS 5, Apple added `presentedViewController` and `presentingViewController`, which are still alive and well in the latest iteration of the SDK. As you would expect, they've been improved upon in order to make your life a little easier. Some of these improvements include Adaptive Layout considerations, to help with the sizing of presented view controllers, custom presentations such as a side bar menu sliding in from the left, custom animations through the use of a transition coordinator, and a few others covered in this chapter.

> **Note:** What's the difference between the *presented* view controller and the *presenting* view controller? *Presented* refers to the view controller being displayed, while *presenting* refers to the view controller hosting the presentation.

`UIPresentationController` is new to iOS 8; it holds references to both the presented and presenting view controllers, and provides ways to customize the chrome, animations and trait changes of your views.

No, we're not talking about Google's web browser: *chrome* is typically the semi-transparent dimmed background view that lies between the presenting view controller and the presented view controller, as shown in the following image.

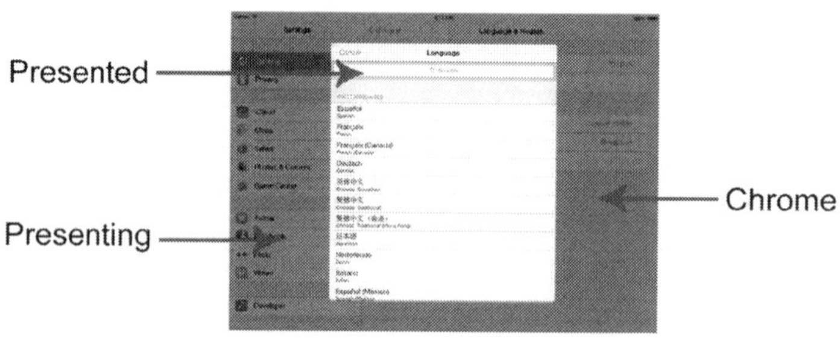

Although the chrome in this image is semi-transparent, it could be anything you can think of. In the second part of this chapter your chrome will be completely transparent to highlight the animation of the collection view cells.

Now that the theory is out of the way, the fun can begin :]

Getting started

Open **CustomPresentation.xcodeproj** in Xcode to get started.

Build and run. You'll see the app adopts the same country-flag theme from the chapter 6. All it does at the moment is display two columns of flags:

Admittedly, it's not terribly exciting. But that's where you come in! Your first task will be to add chrome (a dimmed semi-transparent background) and present a content view controller, which will display some data about the selected country when the user taps on a flag.

The following image highlights the key items as they relate to this app:

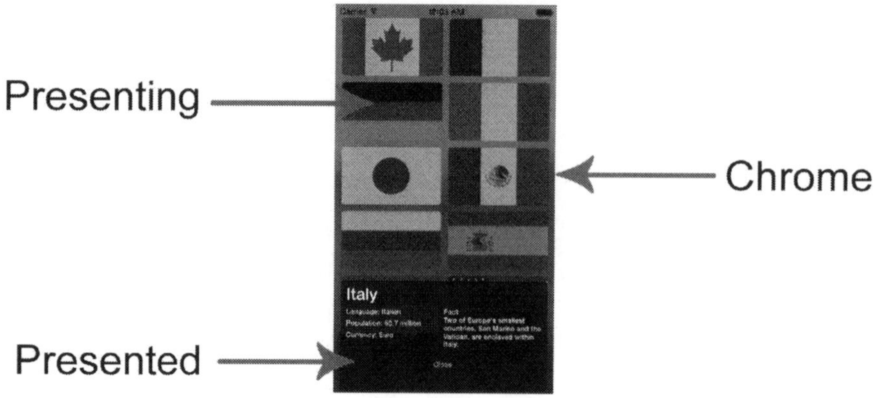

Adding a basic presentation controller

The first step is to add a presentation controller that will do the following:

- Set up the chrome
- Animate the chrome when the content is displayed and dismissed
- Adjust the chrome for layout changes
- Specify the adaptive presentation style to be used

That sounds like a big task, but you'll make short work of it thanks to the new presentation controllers.

Right-click on the **PresentationControllers** group in the **Project Navigator** and select **New File...** then choose **iOS\Source\Cocoa Touch Class** and click **Next**. Name the class `SimplePresentationController` and make it a subclass of `UIPresentationController`. Set **Language** is set to **Swift**, and click **Next**. Finally, click **Create**.

Open SimplePresentationController.swift and replace the contents with the following:

```
import UIKit

// 1
class SimplePresentationController: UIPresentationController,
UIAdaptivePresentationControllerDelegate {
  // 2
  var dimmingView: UIView = UIView()

  override init(presentedViewController: UIViewController!,
    presentingViewController: UIViewController!) {

    super.init(presentedViewController:presentedViewController,
     presentingViewController:presentingViewController)
    // 3
    dimmingView.backgroundColor = UIColor(white:0.0, alpha:0.4)
    dimmingView.alpha = 0.0
  }
}
```

Here's what the code above does:

1. Declares that the view controller adopts the `UIAdaptivePresentationControllerDelegate` protocol. This will allow you to override a method that will return the type of adaptive presentation style to use when presenting this controller.
2. Creates a `UIView` property called `dimmingView` that will be used as the chrome
3. Sets the background color and alpha value of `dimmingView`; the alpha is set to zero so that it won't initially be visible

Next, add the following code to `SimplePresentationController`:

```
override func presentationTransitionWillBegin() {
  // 1
  dimmingView.frame = self.containerView.bounds
  dimmingView.alpha = 0.0
  containerView.insertSubview(dimmingView, atIndex:0)
  // 2
  let coordinator =
presentedViewController.transitionCoordinator()
  if (coordinator != nil) {
    // 3
    coordinator!.animateAlongsideTransition({
```

```
      (context:UIViewControllerTransitionCoordinatorContext!) ->
Void in
      self.dimmingView.alpha = 1.0
      }, completion:nil)
  } else {
    dimmingView.alpha = 1.0
  }
}
```

The method above overrides `presentationTransitionWillBegin()`; here's what it does:

1. You set the frame of `dimmingView` to the bounds of the container view, its alpha to `0.0`, and insert the view into the container view. The container view is the view where the presentation will take place, and is a property of `UIPresentationController`.
2. Next you set the local variable `coordinator` to the presented view controller's transition coordinator. The transition coordinator is in charge of animating both the presentation and dismissal of the content. More on that later.
3. Finally, you call `animateAlongsideTransition(animation:, completion:)` so you can perform additional animations alongside of the presentation animation. Here you simply animate the alpha to `1.0`.

Still working in `SimplePresentationController`, add the following code that handles the dismissal of the view controller:

```
override func dismissalTransitionWillBegin() {
  let coordinator =
presentedViewController.transitionCoordinator()
  if (coordinator != nil) {
    coordinator!.animateAlongsideTransition({
      (context:UIViewControllerTransitionCoordinatorContext!) ->
Void in
      self.dimmingView.alpha = 0.0
    }, completion:nil)
  } else {
    dimmingView.alpha = 0.0
  }
}
```

The code above is almost identical to the presentation code; however, this time you animate the alpha value of `dimmingView` back down to `0.0`.

Add the following method to `SimplePresentationController`:

```
override func containerViewWillLayoutSubviews() {
  dimmingView.frame = containerView.bounds;
  presentedView().frame = containerView.bounds;
}
```

This ensures the frames of both `dimmingView` and `presentedView` are set to the bounds of `containerView`, otherwise they won't resize if the device is rotated. Since `UIPresentationController` is a new class introduced in iOS 8, there are plenty of properties and methods to review. `presentedView()` is one of these methods. It will return a view used in the animation of the view controller presentation. This typically will be the view of the presented view controller.

```
override func shouldPresentInFullscreen() -> Bool {
  return true
}
```

This simply determines whether the presentation will cover the full screen; in this case you want it to so return `true`.

Since you've declared that the class conforms to the `UIAdaptivePresentationControllerDelegate` protocol, add the following optional method to `SimplePresentationController`

```
func adaptivePresentationStyleForPresentationController(
  controller: UIPresentationController!) ->
UIModalPresentationStyle {
    return UIModalPresentationStyle.OverFullScreen
}
```

The returned type of this method is simply indicating that the presented view should cover the full screen.

> **Note**: `adaptivePresentationStyleForPresentationController(_:)` must return `.OverFullScreen` or `.FullScreen`. The only difference between the two is that `.OverFullScreen` will allow the views under the presented view controller to be visible, if the presented view controller's view doesn't cover the underlying content.

Now that the presentation controller is set up, it's time to add the transitioner.

Adding the transitioner

The transitioner file will contain two classes: `SimpleTransitioningDelegate` will implement the `UIViewControllerTransitioningDelegate` protocol that returns the `UIPresentationController` and `UIViewControllerAnimatedTransitioning` objects used when transitioning between presenting and dismissing view controllers. `SimpleAnimatedTransitioning` implements the `UIViewControllerAnimatedTransitioning` protocol and performs the custom animations for transitioning between view controllers.

Right-click on the **Transitioners** group in the **Project Navigator** and select **New File...** then choose **iOS\Source\Cocoa Touch Class** and click **Next**. Name the class **SimpleTransitioner**, make it a subclass of **NSObject**, and ensure you choose **Swift** for the language. Click **Next**, followed by **Create**.

Open **SimpleTransitioner.swift** and replace the contents of the file with the following.

```
import UIKit

class SimpleAnimatedTransitioning: NSObject,
 UIViewControllerAnimatedTransitioning {

  var isPresentation : Bool = false

  func transitionDuration(
   transitionContext: UIViewControllerContextTransitioning)
    -> NSTimeInterval {
    return 0.5
  }
}
```

This creates an animated transitioning class with a `Bool` property that will be used to determine if the presentation animation is presenting. `transitionDuration(transitionContext:)` returns a value for the duration of the transition animation, and is part of the `UIViewControllerAnimatedTransitioning` protocol. Here you return half of a second.

> **Note**: There's quite a lot of code to add in the next step, so I've broken it out into easy-to-digest chunks. Each block needs to be added to the same method, directly below the previous block.

Add the start of `animateTransition(transitionContext:)` just below `transitionDuration(transitionContext:)`. This is another `UIViewControllerAnimatedTransitioning` protocol method you are utilizing to specify the animation for presenting and dismissing a view controller.

```
func animateTransition(transitionContext:
 UIViewControllerContextTransitioning) {

  let fromViewController =
   transitionContext.viewControllerForKey(
    UITransitionContextFromViewControllerKey)
  let fromView = fromViewController!.view
  let toViewController =
   transitionContext.viewControllerForKey(
    UITransitionContextToViewControllerKey)
  let toView = toViewController!.view
```

Here you declare a few view controllers and view variables using `viewControllerForKey(key:)`. You'll use these in the upcoming configuration and animation section to aid with determining which items to make modifications to based on the presentation animation type (presenting or dismissing).

> **Note:** There are two constants defined for use with `viewControllerForKey(key:)`. These are `UITransitionContextFromViewControllerKey`, which is the view controller that's visible at the start of the transition, and `UITransitionContextToViewControllerKey`, which is used to retrieve the view controller which will be visible at the end of the transition. If you are dismissing rather than presenting then the view controllers these keys point to will be reversed.

Add the following to the bottom of `animateTransition(transitionContext:)`:

```
var containerView: UIView =
 transitionContext.containerView()
if isPresentation {
  containerView.addSubview(toView)
}
```

If the transition is a presentation and not a dismissal, then add `toView` as a subview of `containerView`.

Again, add the following to the bottom of `animateTransition(transitionContext:)`:

```
// 1
var animatingViewController = isPresentation ?
 toViewController : fromViewController
var animatingView = animatingViewController!.view
// 2
var appearedFrame =
 transitionContext.finalFrameForViewController(
  animatingViewController!)
var dismissedFrame = appearedFrame
dismissedFrame.origin.y += dismissedFrame.size.height
// 3
let initialFrame = isPresentation ? dismissedFrame :
 appearedFrame
let finalFrame = isPresentation ? appearedFrame : dismissedFrame
animatingView.frame = initialFrame
```

Taking each numbered comment in turn, here's what's happening:

1. Determine which view controller to animate based on the value of `isPresentation`.
2. `appearedFrame` and `dismissedFrame` are the start and end positions of the view, respectively. If the content is being presented then slide the view up; otherwise, slide it down.
3. Set up `initialFrame` and `finalFrame` based on the current value of `isPresentation` . These are the frames that will be used by the animation.

Add the final section of code to the bottom of `animateTransition(transitionContext:)`:

```
UIView.animateWithDuration(
 transitionDuration(transitionContext), delay:0.0,
 usingSpringWithDamping:300.0,
 initialSpringVelocity:5.0,
 options:UIViewAnimationOptions.AllowUserInteraction |
 UIViewAnimationOptions.BeginFromCurrentState, animations:{
    animatingView.frame = finalFrame
  }, completion:{ (value: Bool) in
    if !self.isPresentation {
      fromView.removeFromSuperview()
    }
    transitionContext.completeTransition(true)
  })
}
```

This is where the animation actually takes place. First you set the frame of animatingView to the final frame inside of the animation's closure. If you're presenting the view, it will move up. If you're dismissing the view, it will move it down, off screen. Only remove the presented view if the transition is a dismissal. Finally, complete the transition by calling completeTransition(didComplete:), passing true to indicate the transition animation finished.

Next, add the following code below the SimpleTransitioning class you just added:

```
class SimpleTransitioningDelegate: NSObject,
  UIViewControllerTransitioningDelegate {
}
```

This sets up the SimpleTransitioningDelegate and declares that it conforms to the UIViewControllerTransitioningDelegate protocol.

Add the following method to SimpleTransitioningDelegate:

```
func presentationControllerForPresentedViewController(
 presented: UIViewController!,
 presentingViewController presenting: UIViewController!,
 sourceViewController source: UIViewController!)
 -> UIPresentationController! {
  let presentationController = SimplePresentationController(
   presentedViewController:presented,
    presentingViewController:presenting)
  return presentationController
}
```

This method creates and returns an instance of SimplePresentationController. You use this method to return a presentation controller. The presentation controller manages the presentation process when presenting a view controller.

Now add the following to SimpleTransitioningDelegate:

```
func animationControllerForPresentedController(
 presented: UIViewController!,
 presentingController presenting: UIViewController!,
 sourceController source: UIViewController!)
 -> UIViewControllerAnimatedTransitioning! {
  var animationController = SimpleAnimatedTransitioning()
  animationController.isPresentation = true
  return animationController
}
```

This method creates and returns a `UIViewControllerAnimatedTransitioning` object, or animator for short, that will be used when a view controller is being presented.

The animator is the object in charge of specifying the animation and duration used when presenting and dismissing a view controller.

Take note of `isPresentation` being set to `true`; this determines if the presented controller is being presented or dismissed. In this case it's being presented, since this method deals exclusively with presentation.

Open **SimplePresentationController.swift** and add the following to the `SimplePresentationController` class:

```
func animationControllerForDismissedController(
 dismissed: UIViewController!)
 -> UIViewControllerAnimatedTransitioning! {
  var animationController = SimpleAnimatedTransitioning()
  animationController.isPresentation = false
  return animationController
}
```

This method does almost the same thing as the previous method – it returns an animator object. You return the same animator object since it handles both the presentation and dismissal of a view controller. Notice that `isPresentation` is being set to `false` to indicate the animation is not a presentation, but a dismissal of a view controller.

That wraps up the SimpleTransitioning implementation.

Build and run the app. All of that code and there is still no view controller being presented to display country content on the screen! You'll fix that now.

Open **CountriesViewController.swift** and add the following to the top of the class:

```
let simpleTransitionDelegate = SimpleTransitioningDelegate()
```

This creates a property that holds a reference to the transitioning delegate. This is needed to keep a strong reference to the delegate, because the view controller's `transitioningDelegate` property uses a weak reference.

Now add the following method to the bottom of the class:

```
func showSimpleOverlayForIndexPath(indexPath: NSIndexPath) {
  let country = countries[indexPath.row] as Country

  transitioningDelegate = simpleTransitionDelegate

  var overlay = OverlayViewController(country: country)
  overlay.transitioningDelegate = simpleTransitionDelegate

  presentViewController(overlay, animated: true, completion:
nil)
}
```

This method retrieves a country based on the index path passed in, and assigns `SimpleTransitioningDelegate` as the view controller's `transitioningDelegate`. Next, the method creates the overlay, which is simply the view controller (content) to display. At the very end of the method you finally present the view controller that contains content about the country.

There is one last remaining detail to take care of. You actually have to call this method from somewhere.

Implment `collectionView(_:didSelectItemAtIndexPath)` in `CountriesViewController` as follows:

```
func collectionView(collectionView: UICollectionView!,
 didSelectItemAtIndexPath indexPath: NSIndexPath!) {
  showSimpleOverlayForIndexPath(indexPath)
}
```

Build and run. Tap any flag and you'll see the country details slide up from the bottom of the screen, as the content behind it dims:

Tap the detail view to dismiss it.

That's a good start on your journey through the world of custom presentation controllers, but why stop there? You can add even more flair by animating the collection view cells.

Advanced presentation controllers

> **Note**: Since you've already learned the basics of using custom presentation controllers, the rest of this chapter is optional. If you're trying to get up-to-speed with what's new in iOS 8 quickly, we recommend skipping the rest of this chapter and moving on to the next topic: App Extensions.
>
> But if you specifically want to dive deeper into some more complex animations you can do with presentation controllers, keep reading!
>
> Just be aware that there's another large chunk of code coming up that you'll need to get through before you can build and run again. I realize this is a bit tedious, but bear with it, as the result is well worth the effort.

Right-click on the **CustomPresentation** group in the Project navigator and select **New File...**, then choose **iOS\Source\Cocoa Touch Class** and click **Next**. Name the class **SelectionObject**, make it a subclass of **NSObject**, and then ensure you choose **Swift** for the language. Click **Next**. Finally, click **Create**.

Open **SelectionObject.swift** and replace its contents with the following code:

```
import UIKit

class SelectionObject: NSObject {

  var originalCellPosition: CGRect
  var country: Country
  var selectedCellIndexPath: NSIndexPath

  init(country:Country, selectedCellIndexPath: NSIndexPath,
    originalCellPosition: CGRect) {

    self.country = country
    self.selectedCellIndexPath = selectedCellIndexPath
    self.originalCellPosition = originalCellPosition
  }
}
```

This class simply holds some information required by your presentation controller.

Right-click on the **PresentationControllers** group in the Project navigator and select **New File...**, then choose **iOS\Source\Cocoa Touch Class** and click **Next**. Name the class **AwesomePresentationController**, make it a subclass of **UIPresentationController**, and then ensure you choose **Swift** for the language. Click **Next**, followed by **Create**.

Open **AwesomePresentationController.swift** and replace its contents with the following:

```
import UIKit

class AwesomePresentationController: UIPresentationController,
UIViewControllerTransitioningDelegate {

  var dimmingView: UIView = UIView()
  var flagImageView: UIImageView = UIImageView(
   frame: CGRect(origin: CGPointZero,
   size: CGSize(width: 160.0, height: 93.0)))
  var selectionObject: SelectionObject?
  var isAnimating = false

  override init(presentedViewController: UIViewController!,
   presentingViewController: UIViewController!) {
    super.init(presentedViewController:
     presentedViewController,
      presentingViewController: presentingViewController)

    dimmingView.backgroundColor = UIColor.clearColor()
    flagImageView.contentMode =
     UIViewContentMode.ScaleAspectFill
    flagImageView.clipsToBounds = true
    flagImageView.layer.cornerRadius = 4.0
  }
}
```

The above class contains a `dimmingView` just like the first presentation controller; however, this one includes an image view, a selection object, and a `Bool` used to determine the state of the animation. `init(presentedViewController:, presentingViewController:)` sets the dimming view's background color to clear and configures the image view to scale the flag image appropriately, and round its corners.

Now add the following method to **AwesomePresentationController.swift:**

```
func configureWithSelectionObject(selectionObject:
 SelectionObject) {
  self.selectionObject = selectionObject
```

```
    var image: UIImage =
     UIImage(named: selectionObject.country.imageName)!
    flagImageView.image = image
    flagImageView.frame = selectionObject.originalCellPosition
  }
```

The above method accepts a selection object and uses it to configure the `flagImageView` with the necessary image and position.

Add the following three methods to **AwesomePresentationController.swift**:

```
  func adaptivePresentationStyleForPresentationController(
   controller: UIPresentationController!) ->
   UIModalPresentationStyle {
    return UIModalPresentationStyle.OverFullScreen
  }

  override func frameOfPresentedViewInContainerView() ->
   CGRect {
    return containerView.bounds
  }

  override func containerViewWillLayoutSubviews() {
    dimmingView.frame = containerView.bounds
    presentedView().frame = containerView.bounds
  }
```

These methods should look familiar; you added similar ones to the simple presentation controller example earlier. In this case, the above methods ensure the view controllers' view fits the full screen, and maintains its bounds after orientation changes.

Add the following helper method to **AwesomePresentationController.swift**:

```
  func scaleFlagAndPositionFlag() {
    var flagFrame = flagImageView.frame
    var containerFrame = containerView.frame
    var originYMultiplier: CGFloat = 0.0
    var cellSize = selectionObject!.originalCellPosition.size

    if containerFrame.size.width > containerFrame.size.height {
      // Smaller sized flag
      flagFrame.size.width = cellSize.width * 1.5
      flagFrame.size.height = cellSize.height * 1.5

      originYMultiplier = 0.25
    } else {
```

```
    // Larger sized flag
    flagFrame.size.width = cellSize.width * 1.8
    flagFrame.size.height = cellSize.height * 1.8

    originYMultiplier = 0.333
  }

  flagFrame.origin.x = (containerFrame.size.width / 2)
   - (flagFrame.size.width / 2)
  flagFrame.origin.y = (containerFrame.size.height *
   originYMultiplier) - (flagFrame.size.height / 2)

  flagImageView.frame = flagFrame
}
```

This method scales the flag based on the orientation and the available screen space of the device. You'll only call this method when the `flagImageView` is in its final resting place and the presentation animation has finished.

Add the next method to **AwesomePresentationController.swift**:

```
func moveFlagToPresentedPosition(presentedPosition: Bool) {
  let containerFrame = containerView.frame

  if presentedPosition {
    // Expand flag and center
    scaleFlagAndPositionFlag()
  } else {
    // Move flag back to original position
    var flagFrame = flagImageView.frame
    flagFrame = selectionObject!.originalCellPosition;
    flagImageView.frame = flagFrame
  }
}
```

This method uses `scaleFlagAndPositionFlag()` to adjust the image view if the animation has finished; otherwise it moves the image view back to it's original position within its owning cell in the collection view.

Now add the final helper method to **AwesomePresentationController.swift**:

```
func animateFlagToPresentedPosition(presentedPosition: Bool) {
  let coordinator =
   presentedViewController.transitionCoordinator()

  coordinator!.animateAlongsideTransition({
   (context: UIViewControllerTransitionCoordinatorContext!)
```

```
      -> Void in
      self.moveFlagToPresentedPosition(presentedPosition)
    }, completion: {
     (context: UIViewControllerTransitionCoordinatorContext!)
      -> Void in
      self.isAnimating = false
    })
  }
```

The above method animates the flag from its original position in its owning cell in the collection view to an enlarged, and horizontally centered, position in the chrome.

When you dismiss the content, the method animates the image view back to its original position and size. You've wrapped both animations in `animateAlongsideTransition(animation:, completion:)` so that they animate at the same time.

Once the animation has finished, you set `isAnimating` to `false`.

Now you need to override two methods that are for the presentation and dismissal controllers.

Add the following two methods to **AwesomePresentationController.swift**:

```
override func presentationTransitionWillBegin() {
  super.presentationTransitionWillBegin()
  // 1
  isAnimating = true
  moveFlagToPresentedPosition(false)

  // 2
  dimmingView.addSubview(flagImageView)
  containerView.addSubview(dimmingView)

  animateFlagToPresentedPosition(true)
}

// 3
override func dismissalTransitionWillBegin() {
  super.dismissalTransitionWillBegin()

  isAnimating = true
  animateFlagToPresentedPosition(false)
}
```

The above methods behave as follows:

1. Assign `true` to `isAnimating` and move `flagImageView` to its original position.

2. Add `flagImageView` as a subview of `dimmingView`, and then add `dimmingView` as a subview of `containerView`. Once the views are configured, call `animateFlagToPresentedPosition(_:)` to scale and position the flag alongside the animator's transition.

3. Set `isAnimating` to `true` and animate the flag back to its original position alongside the animator's transition.

Build the app using ⌘b. It should build without errors.

Now you'll need the transitioner file.

Right-click on the **Transitioners** group in the Project navigator and select **New File...**, then choose **iOS\Source\Cocoa Touch Class** and click **Next**. Name the class **AwesomeTransitioner**, make it a subclass of **NSObject**, and then ensure you choose **Swift** for the language. Click **Next**, followed by **Create**.

Open **AwesomeTransitioner.swift** and replace its contents with the following:

```
import UIKit

class AwesomeTransitioningDelegate: NSObject,
UIViewControllerTransitioningDelegate {

  var selectedObject: SelectionObject?

  init(selectedObject: SelectionObject) {
    super.init()
    self.selectedObject = selectedObject
  }
}

class AwesomeAnimatedTransitioning: NSObject,
  UIViewControllerAnimatedTransitioning {

  var isPresentation: Bool = false
  var selectedObject: SelectionObject?

  init(selectedObject: SelectionObject,
    isPresentation: Bool) {
    self.selectedObject = selectedObject
    self.isPresentation = isPresentation
  }
}
```

These two classes should look somewhat familiar; they're similar to the ones you added to the example in the first part of this chapter, with a few new twists.

Since you're using an object to assist with the animation, you need to set some additional properties in `init(selectedObject:)`.

Add the following method to `AwesomeTransitioningDelegate`:

```
func presentationControllerForPresentedViewController(
  presented: UIViewController!,
  presentingViewController presenting: UIViewController!,
  sourceViewController source: UIViewController!)
  -> UIPresentationController! {

  var presentationController =
   AwesomePresentationController(presentedViewController:
    presented, presentingViewController: presenting)

  presentationController.
   configureWithSelectionObject(selectedObject!)
  return presentationController
}
```

This method creates an instance of `AwesomePresentationController`, configures it, and then returns it. You'll use this to manage the presentation.

Now add the following method to `AwesomeTransitioningDelegate`:

```
func animationControllerForPresentedController(
 presented: UIViewController!,
 presentingController presenting: UIViewController!,
 sourceController source: UIViewController!)
 -> UIViewControllerAnimatedTransitioning! {
  var animationController =
   AwesomeAnimatedTransitioning(
    selectedObject: selectedObject!, isPresentation: true)
  return animationController
}
```

The above method returns the animator. Notice the custom `init(selectedObject:)` method; this is a handy way to pass in all values required by the animator object.

Finally add the third and final method to `AwesomeTransitioningDelegate`:

```
func animationControllerForDismissedController(
 dismissed: UIViewController!)
  -> UIViewControllerAnimatedTransitioning! {

  var animationController =
   AwesomeAnimatedTransitioning(selectedObject:
    selectedObject!,isPresentation: false)
```

```
    return animationController
  }
```

The above method returns the animator for the dismissal of a view controller.

Add `transitionDuration(_transitionContext:)` to `AwesomeAnimatedTransitioning`:

```
  func transitionDuration(_transitionContext:
   UIViewControllerContextTransitioning) -> NSTimeInterval {
    return 0.7
  }
```

This returns the duration of the dismissal animation; in this case just over half a second.

Here comes another fairly large method that has been broken into smaller chunks for easy digestion. Buckle up and add the following method to `AwesomeAnimatedTransitioning`:

```
  func animateTransition(transitionContext:
   UIViewControllerContextTransitioning) {

    let fromViewController =
     transitionContext.viewControllerForKey(
      UITransitionContextFromViewControllerKey)
    let fromView = fromViewController!.view
    let toViewController =
     transitionContext.viewControllerForKey(
      UITransitionContextToViewControllerKey)
    let toView = toViewController!.view

    var containerView: UIView = transitionContext.containerView()

    if isPresentation {
      containerView.addSubview(toView)
    }

    let animatingViewController =
     isPresentation ? toViewController : fromViewController
    var animatingView = animatingViewController!.view
```

Just as you did with the simple presentation example, you create several variables to store the *to* and *from* view controllers. If the animator is presenting, then add the `toView` as a subview of `containerView`, and determine the animating view controller.

Add the next block of code just below where the previous one left off:

```
    animatingView.frame =
     transitionContext.finalFrameForViewController(
      animatingViewController!)

    var appearedFrame =
     transitionContext.finalFrameForViewController(
      animatingViewController!)

    var dismissedFrame = appearedFrame
    dismissedFrame.origin.y += dismissedFrame.size.height

    var initialFrame = isPresentation ? dismissedFrame :
     appearedFrame
    var finalFrame = isPresentation ? appearedFrame :
     dismissedFrame

    animatingView.frame = initialFrame
```

In this block you set the animating view's frame and then determine the initial and final frame positions for the content view. Once you have the initial frame, set it on the animating view.

Finally, add the last section of code, just under the last block of code, to wrap this method up.

```
  UIView.animateWithDuration(transitionDuration(
   transitionContext), delay: 0.0, options:
   UIViewAnimationOptions.AllowUserInteraction |
   UIViewAnimationOptions.BeginFromCurrentState, animations: {
    animatingView.frame = finalFrame
  }, completion: { (value: Bool) in
    if !self.isPresentation {
      fromView.removeFromSuperview()
      transitionContext.completeTransition(true)
    } else {
      transitionContext.completeTransition(true)
    }
  })
  }
```

The above code sets the animating view's frame. If the animation is a dismissal, then you remove `fromView` from the view hierarchy. Unlike the simple example, there is no dimming view in the chrome to animate.

This is another good place to build your app, just to verify there are no errors. Press ⌘b to build now.

Open **CountriesViewController.swift** and add the following property just below the other properties at the top of the class:

```
var awesomeTransitionDelegate:AwesomeTransitioningDelegate?
```

This will be used to hold a strong reference to the awesome transitioning delegate, and is very similar to the property you added for the simple transitioning delegate. This time the property isn't being assigned a value up front, so is marked as an optional. You will assign it a value in the next method.

Move to the bottom of **CountriesViewController.swift** and add the following method:

```
func showAwesomeOverlayForIndexPath(indexPath: NSIndexPath) {
  let country = countries[indexPath.row] as Country
  let selectedCell =
   collectionView.cellForItemAtIndexPath(indexPath)
    as CollectionViewCell
  // 1
  var rect = selectedCell.frame
  let origin = view.convertPoint(rect.origin, fromView:
   selectedCell.superview)
  rect.origin = origin
  // 2
  let selectionObject = SelectionObject(country: country,
   selectedCellIndexPath: indexPath,
    originalCellPosition: rect)
  // 3
  awesomeTransitionDelegate = AwesomeTransitioningDelegate(
   selectedObject: selectionObject)
  transitioningDelegate = awesomeTransitionDelegate
  // 4
  var overlay = OverlayViewController(country: country)
  overlay.transitioningDelegate = awesomeTransitionDelegate
  presentViewController(overlay, animated: true,completion: nil)
}
```

This method displays the content as follows:

1. Get the collection view cells' frame for the cell at the index path. Use the value from the cells' `superview` so that you're using the actual position from the view controller and not just the position in the collection view.

2. Create a selection object using the `country`, `indexPath`, and frame of the cell.

3. Next assign `awesomeTransitionDelegate` an instance of `AwesomeTransitionDelegate`, configured with your selection object, and set it as the view controller's `transitioningDelegate`.

4. Finally, create and present the overlay.

Now you just need to call this method from somewhere.

Replace the call to `showSimpleOverlayForIndexPath(indexPath:)` with a call to `showAwesomeOverlayForIndexPath(indexPath:)` in `collectionView(_, didSelectItemAtIndexPath:)`. It should now look like the following:

```
func collectionView(collectionView: UICollectionView!,
 didSelectItemAtIndexPath indexPath: NSIndexPath!) {
  showAwesomeOverlayForIndexPath(indexPath)
}
```

Your patience is soon to pay off! Build and run your app. Select one of the flags and you'll see it expand, and center itself as the content view slides up from the bottom of the screen:

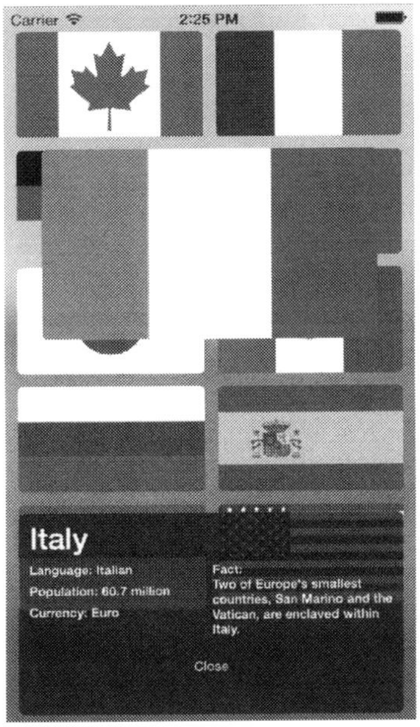

Hmm, that doesn't look quite right. The flag image in the cell remains while a duplicate image expands. That's not what you want.

To fix this open **Country.swift** and add the following property, just under the other properties at the top of the class:

```
var isHidden: Bool = false
```

This tracks which country to hide during the animation.

Open **CountriesViewController.swift** and add the following property to the top of the class:

```
var selectionObject: SelectionObject?
```

This property will be used to keep track of which item the user selected.

Now find `showAwesomeOverlayForIndexPath(indexPath:)` in **CountriesViewController.swift** and update the code as shown below:

```
rect.origin = origin // Existing

// Add the following new code...
selectionObject = SelectionObject(country: country,
 selectedCellIndexPath: indexPath,
  originalCellPosition: rect)
awesomeTransitionDelegate = AwesomeTransitioningDelegate(
 selectedObject: selectionObject!)

transitioningDelegate = awesomeTransitionDelegate // Existing
```

And add the following just before the closing brace:

```
UIView.animateWithDuration(0.1, animations:{
  selectedCell.imageView.alpha = 0.0
}, completion: nil)
```

This simply fades out the cell's image view by animating its `alpha` property to `0.0`.

Add the following helper method at the bottom of **CountriesViewController.swift**:

```
func hideImage(hidden: Bool, indexPath: NSIndexPath) {
  if selectionObject != nil {
    selectionObject!.country.isHidden = hidden
  }

  if indexPath.row < self.countries.count {
    collectionView.reloadItemsAtIndexPaths([indexPath])
  }
}
```

The above method simply hides the selected cell's image view, and then reloads the cell.

Now open **AwesomeTransitioner.swift** and add the following code to `animateTransition(transitionContext:)` just before the first animation block:

```
animatingView.frame = initialFrame // Existing

// Add the following new code...
var countriesViewController: CountriesViewController =
  (isPresentation ? fromViewController : toViewController)
  as CountriesViewController

if !isPresentation {
  countriesViewController.hideImage(true,
    indexPath: selectedObject!.selectedCellIndexPath)
}
```

In the method above, you check if the animator's animation is presenting; if so, set the `countriesViewController` to `fromViewController`, otherwise set it to `toViewController`. Next, if the animation is a dismissal then hide the cell's image view.

Build and run. Tap a flag and the image view fades out in the selected cell, while the second image view expands, and centers in the chrome:

This creates the illusion that the same image is being used for the animation.

Tap on a few flags at random, then dismiss the content view; you'll likely notice some odd behavior, as there are now some flag images missing in the collection view. Why is this happening? In the code you just added, you are making a call to hide the flag image. So after you dismiss the content view the second image view shrinks back to its original size, and then disappears. There is nothing to inform the selected cell to unhide its image view. You'll be happy to know it's just a simple fix.

Open **CountriesViewController.swift** and add the following code to `collectionView(_:cellForItemAtIndexPath:)` just above where you return the cell:

```
// Add the following new code...
if selectionObject != nil &&
  selectionObject?.country.countryName == country.countryName {
    cell.imageView.hidden = selectionObject!.country.isHidden
} else {
    cell.imageView.hidden = false
}

// Existing
return cell
```

This checks to see if there is a `selectionObject`, and that it's not the same as the one being displayed. If so, it uses the value stored in the new property of `Country` to update the visibility of the image view. If there is no `selectionObject`, then the image view is shown.

Build and run the app. You will notice that this fix didn't actually fix anything. Don't worry; you will be animating the cells on and off the screen. This code will then become very important in determining the flag image visibility.

Before you add the cell animation, there are three helper methods that you will need. Add the first of these helper methods to the bottom of **CountriesViewController.swift**:

```
func indexPathsForAllItems() -> NSMutableArray {
  var count = countries.count
  var indexPaths = NSMutableArray()
  for var index = 0; index < count; ++index {
    indexPaths.addObject(NSIndexPath(forItem: index,
     inSection: 0))
  }
  return indexPaths
}
```

This method returns an array of `indexPaths` for all of the country objects being displayed in the collection view.

Next add the second method just below:

```
func changeCellSpacingForPresentation(presentation: Bool) {
  if presentation {
    var indexPaths = indexPathsForAllItems()
    countries = NSArray()
    collectionView.deleteItemsAtIndexPaths(indexPaths)
  } else {
    countries = Country.countries()
    var indexPaths = indexPathsForAllItems()
    collectionView.insertItemsAtIndexPaths(indexPaths)
  }
}
```

This method takes the `indexPaths` returned from the previous method you added and either deletes the objects if the content is being presented, or it inserts the objects if the content is being dismissed.

Adding objects to, or deleting objects from the collection view animates the cells in the left column to and from the left side of the screen, while the cells in the right column move to and from the right side of the screen.

> **Note:** If you're wondering how the collection view knows how to animate the cells on and off the screen, read through **CollectionViewLayout.swift** that was included in the starter project and contains the necessary code to make the animations happen.

Now add the last of the three methods, as shown below:

```
func frameForCellAtIndexPath(indexPath: NSIndexPath) ->
 CGRect {
  var cell = collectionView.cellForItemAtIndexPath(indexPath)
   as CollectionViewCell
  return cell.frame
}
```

This method simply returns the frame of a cell at the given `indexPath`.

Now it's time to make use of these helper methods.

Open **AwesomeTransitioner.swift** and update the animation block inside of `animateTransition(transitionContext:)` with the following:

```
    animatingView.frame = finalFrame // Existing
    // Add the following new code...
    countriesViewController
    .changeCellSpacingForPresentation(self.isPresentation)
  }, completion: { // Existing
```

This inserts or deletes cells in the collection view based on the presentation type.

Staying in the same method, update the code in the completion block as shown below:

```
  }, completion: { (value: Bool) in
      if !self.isPresentation { // Existing

        // Add the following new code...
        countriesViewController.hideImage(false, indexPath:
          self.selectedObject!.selectedCellIndexPath)

        UIView.animateWithDuration(0.3, animations: {
                fromView.alpha = 0.0;
                }, completion: {
                  (value: Bool) in
                  fromView.removeFromSuperview()
                  transitionContext.completeTransition(true)
              })
          } else { // Existing
```

First, the cell's image view is unhidden once the dismissal animation has completed. Then, the content view is faded out, and removed once the fade animation finishes.

Build and run your app; select any flag and watch your new presentation controllers in action:

The animations keep getting better and better, but you're not stopping yet! You'll add a custom bounce animation, as the icing on this particular cake.

Open **AwesomePresentationController.swift** and add the following method:

```
func animateFlagWithBounceToPresentedPosition(
 presentedPosition: Bool) {
  UIView.animateWithDuration(0.7,
   delay: 0.2,
   usingSpringWithDamping: 0.4,
    initialSpringVelocity: 0.0,
    options: UIViewAnimationOptions.CurveEaseOut, {
      self.moveFlagToPresentedPosition(presentedPosition)
  }, completion: { (value: Bool) in
    self.isAnimating = false
  })
}
```

This adds some bounce to the animation when the flag image view moves. This animation will happen separately from that of the transition coordinator's animation. If you had piggybacked the other animation, you wouldn't have been able to set different options on your animation.

Find `presentationTransitionWillBegin()` and comment out the call to `animateFlagToPresentedPosition(_:)`. Now add a call to `animateFlagWithBounceToPresentedPosition(_:)`. Your code should now look like the following:

```
// animateFlagToPresentedPosition(true)
animateFlagWithBounceToPresentedPosition(true)
```

This uses the bounce animation instead of the simple, existing animation.

Find `dismissalTransitionWillBegin()` and make a similar change by commenting out the call to `animateFlagToPresentedPosition(_:)` and adding a call to `animateFlagWithBounceToPresentedPosition(_:)`. It should now look as follows:

```
// animateFlagToPresentedPosition(false)
animateFlagWithBounceToPresentedPosition(false)
```

Here you're passing `false` to signify this is a dismissal.

Build and run your app. When the content displays, the flag bounces into position; when you dismiss the content, the flag bounces back into place.

Where to go from here?

This type of animation effect is quite simple to implement, but it does add that polish to your app that sets it apart from your competitors. For starters, try changing the behavior of the animation that presents the content view controller. Feel free to experiment and improve upon the app you just created. Above all, have fun with these fantastic new API that Apple has provided as part of iOS 8.

Section II: App Extensions

App Extensions are one of the most anticipated features of iOS 8; they let you extend your app's content and functionality throughout the rest of the OS. Such extensions allow you to present custom functionality in other apps and gives users the power of your applications when and where they need it most. Once you've completed the following seven chapters you'll no doubt wonder how you ever survived without App Extensions – both as a developer *and* as a user.

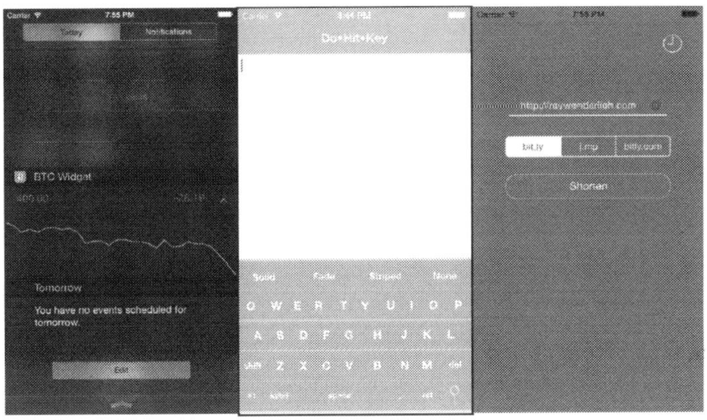

Chapter 8: Introducing Extensions

By Chris Wagner

Imagine the following scenario: Apple has just invited you and your team to Cupertino to write some first-class features for iOS. In the glassed-in boardroom, the Apple execs give you the laundry list of features they need: extend Safari so users can share content easily with your social network; provide custom photo-editing capabilities directly from Photos; let users save and access documents stored in the cloud from any app on their device; and redesign and replace the system keyboard!

Does this sound like an appealing opportunity? Good, because iOS 8 is an open invitation to *all* developers to make big changes to the way that users interact with content on their iOS devices. **App extensions** give developers the power to provide custom functionality in apps they don't own – including the stock Apple apps!

App extensions will have a tremendous impact on how users create, modify, and share the content on their devices. In fact, the implementation of app extensions is so seamless that most end users won't have any idea just how revolutionary this feature really is! :]

App extension types

App extensions are grouped into six distinct types, each which extend functionality from your app to other apps, or to the system itself. Each type is described below and introduces the extensions that you will be creating in the chapters to follow.

Today extensions

More commonly known as "widgets", Today extensions appear in the Today view of Notification Center. These small view controllers make snippets of information available to the user at a glance. You've likely seen these already in the form of the Stocks and Weather widgets, while iOS 7 introduced even more widgets such as Reminders, Calendars and a "Today Summary" along with contextual information such as how long it will take you to get home from your present location.

iOS 8 now lets you add your own widgets. It's *your* turn to decide what shows up in Notification Center!

The left-hand screenshot below shows an app that tracks Bitcoin values, while the right-hand side shows this same information as a Today extension:

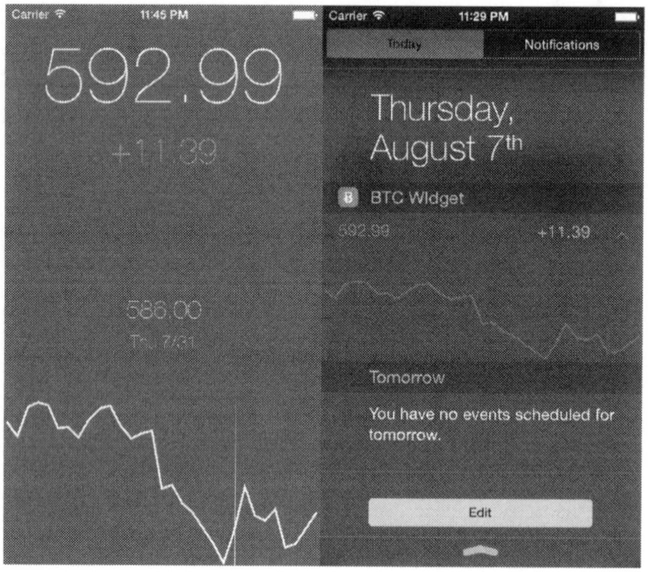

Share extensions

As the name implies, Share extensions let users share content between apps or other services. This functionality was introduced in iOS 5, which made it possible to do things such as tweet images directly from Photos and tweet websites from Safari. iOS 6 added similar sharing features for Facebook users.

Thankfully, the days where you had to wait for Apple to release new service integrations are now a thing of the past. Now *you* can write extensions to share content with your own service, or with any other service that has a consumable API for your app to use. Will you be the developer to write the next big social networking app that's bought up in a billion-dollar acquisition? :]

As an example, users can easily share their photos using imgur.com with the Imgvue app as shown below:

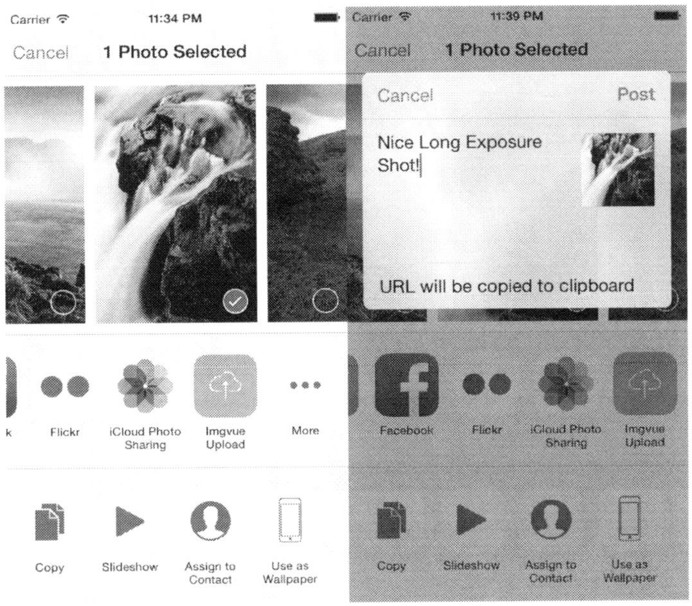

Action extensions

Although they might sound a bit nebulous at first, Action extensions let you view and transform content within the context of another app. For example, Apple demoed an extension that translates the text content of the current web page right in Safari – without ever leaving the browser. 1Password has built an extension that lets you access your password vault right from within Safari, just as if you were using their desktop browser extensions.

Action extensions blow things wide open and redefine the way users work with content on iOS.

The image below shows the Quicker Bit Action extension that shortens URLs without ever leaving Safari:

Photo Editing extensions

Does your app have amazing photo filters or mustache applicators? If so, Photo Editing extensions are right up your alley; they extend the photo-editing capabilities of your application to Apple's Photos app. Users can now use external apps to modify their photos in Edit mode; once the user is happy with the results, they simply tap Save and the changes will be applied to the photo.

Worried about an app ruining all of your users' photos? Fear not! Apple's implementation of Photo Editing extensions always lets the user revert their changes back to the original photo. Your extension can even provide an entire undo stack to let users revert their changes one step at a time between editing sessions.

The screenshots below show how the user can access the filters from the Imgvue app directly from within Photos:

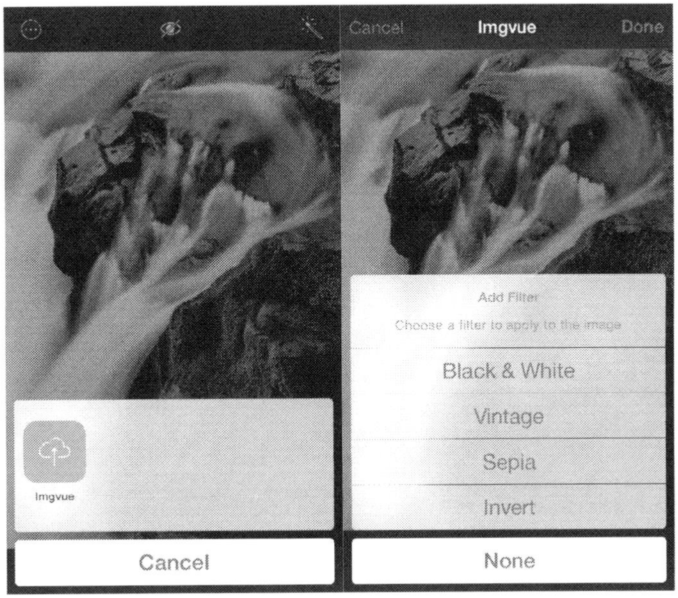

Document Provider extensions

New with iOS 8, Apps can present a document picker view controller. These pickers allow the user to import, export, open external and move local documents. As a developer you may want your app's documents to be available to others. To achieve this you would write a Document Provider extension. Once your extension is installed the user can choose files from your app to interact with or export their files to your storage.

As an example, a journaling app might let users save their journal entries to their Dropbox account. Prior to iOS 8 you needed to leverage the Dropbox API and SDK directly to achieve this functionality; but if Dropbox provides a Document Provider extension then the journaling app could make use of this service without any internal use of the API or SDK. Imagine how much more valuable – and usable – cloud storage services would be if they all implemented a Document Provider extension.

The provider you will be creating as shown in the screenshots below allows the user to upload images Amazon S3, view images already stored in S3 and even import images from other provides like iCloud to be uploaded to S3.

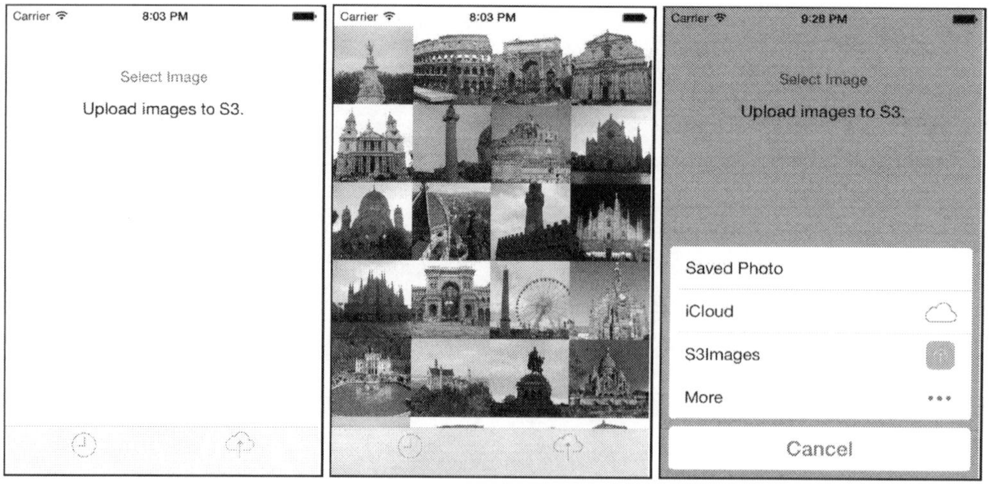

Custom Keyboard extensions

To the surprise and astonishment of many long time iOS users, Apple has quite literally handed over the keys to iOS 8! You can now create system-wide custom keyboards – high up the wish list of many iOS power users. Just as it was possible to select keyboards for different languages or Emoji in previous versions of iOS, you now have the ability in iOS 8 to select third party keyboards.

Brace yourself for major innovations in this area. Other platforms such as Fire OS and Android have seen amazing third party keyboards such as Swype, which completely redefined text entry on touch screens. Now is the time for all those bottled-up frustrations with the iOS keyboard to take root as amazing new Custom Keyboard extensions.

The screenshots below show off the keyboard extension you will be creating, Do-Hit-Key. The custom keyboard provides a standard QWERTY keyboard with additional keys to obtain the user's location and switch between themes.

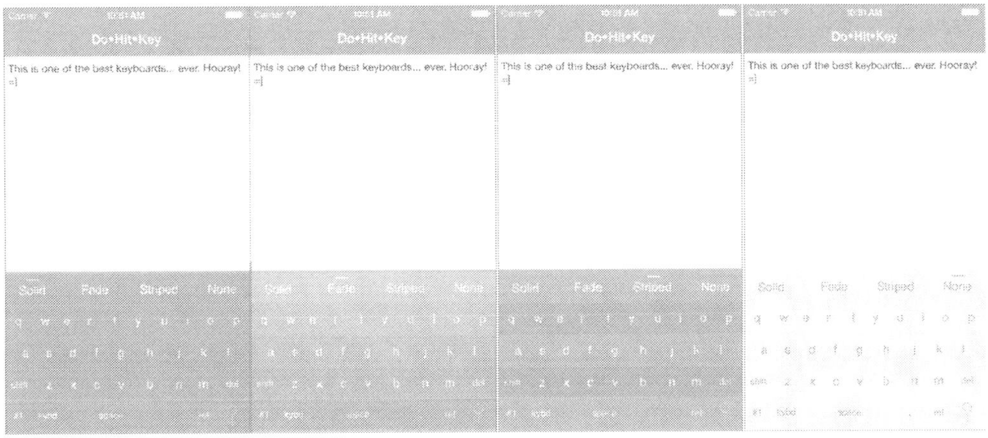

App extensions under the hood

The preceding section covered app extensions from an end-user perspective. But how do they work under the hood? And how are they packaged and delivered?

As the name implies, an app extension is an extension of *your* application's functionality. App extensions are not standalone utilities or plugins that extend other developer's apps. Extensions are delivered via the App Store with your app bundle; they aren't apps of their own. The app with which you bundle your extension is called the **container app**.

You invoke each extension differently, which resulted in Apple creating several new APIs for this feature. This isn't the same old application delegate song and dance; each of the following app extensions chapters covers the new, and importantly, individual APIs for each extension type.

Although app extensions ship with your app, they don't run in the same process as your app. Instead, every single instance of your extension runs as its own process. Contrary to the way apps work on iOS, the same extension can be spawned into multiple processes.

Consider the following scenario: your user is working in Photos and wants to share a photo via your Share extension. The user then switches to Safari and chooses to share different content using the same extension. It's entirely possible that two instances of the extension will be running side-by-side – system resources permitting. iOS guarantees that these instances will be in separate processes so you won't be required to manage states between the two instances.

App extensions are delivered in their own binaries, separate from your app's binary. In Xcode, each app extension for an app is configured as a separate target with its own bundle identifier. Creating an extension target is as simple as adding a new target to your project and picking the type of extension that you want, as shown below:

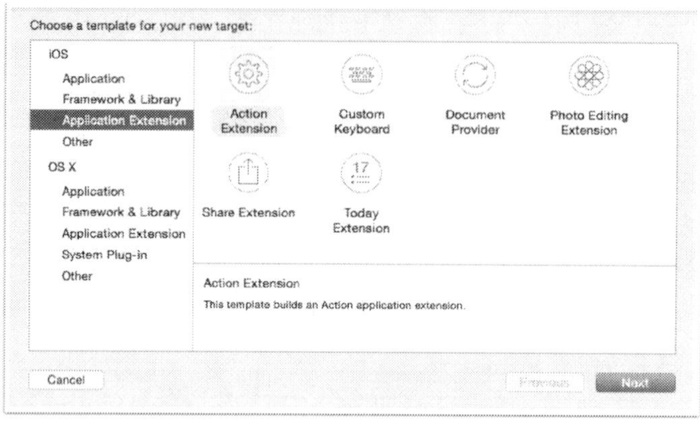

While you may be tempted to create a skeleton app to contain your shiny new extension, beware! Apple is likely to reject any apps taking this route. According to Apple's documentation, any submitted iOS apps must provide some level of functionality. It will be interesting to see how Keyboard Extension container apps handle this constraint! :]

How extensions work

Extensions have their own separate binary and are spawned as separate processes. The lifecycle of an extension is a bit different from that of an app. When a user invokes your extension within another app, the lifecycle of your extension begins at that point. The app in which you invoke an extension is known as the **host app**. After an extension has completed its task, its lifecycle comes to an end. It is possible, however, that artifacts of the extension will still be running on the system, such as background network requests via `NSURLSession` or image processing on a background queue.

While running, an extension can directly communicate only with the host app. Though extensions do have the capability of making network and file-system requests; extensions do **not** provide inter-process communication between apps; nor does the extension create a communication bridge between the host app and the container app. This means that the extension does not – and cannot – communicate directly with its containing app. Quite often the containing app won't even be running when the extension is running. This helps keep extensions as lightweight processes running alongside the host app.

If an extension must communicate with its container app, it can do so indirectly via a shared data container or via `openURL()`. You're probably familiar with the `openURL()` method of `UIApplication`. However, since extensions aren't fully-fledged apps, the `UIApplication` object doesn't exist. Instead, you must call `openURL(_:,completionHandler:)` on an instance of `NSExtensionContext`. If your container app registers its own URL scheme, your extension can launch the container app using this API. This might be useful when the user must configure the container app before using its extension, for instance.

A **shared data container**, on the other hand, is effectively a sandbox where both the extension and container app can read and write data. Typical solutions include storing preferences that apply to both the extension and the container app via new API on `NSUserDefaults`. You can also configure a directory on the file system to be used by both the app and any of its extensions.

As an example, consider a Today extension that shows a daily comic strip; If the container app had downloaded the strip previously, the Today extension could be more network efficient by retrieving the image file saved in the shared container, rather than downloading it again. Some of the sample apps included in the chapters in this section will use shared containers.

The above solutions to extension <-> container app communication are depicted in the following diagram:

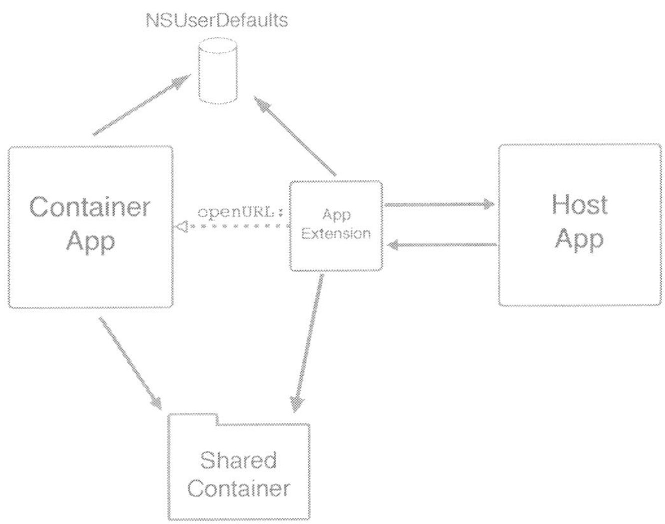

As shown, the host app and container app cannot communicate directly, but the extension can act as a proxy between the two using either the shared user defaults, the shared data container or the `openURL` API.

Shared functionality

With the requirement that each extension be its own target and separate from the container app. How do you go about re-using code? For example, if you've written an application that lets users post pictures to a social networking service, it would be ideal to re-use those mechanisms in a Share extension.

iOS 8 makes it possible to create embedded frameworks that can be used across app and extension targets. For instance, if you design your app to separate out the various functions, such as network requests to social networking services, you can easily reuse that logic in that apps' extensions if it's contained in a framework.

Since the subject of frameworks came up, you should also note that not all of the Cocoa Touch framework APIs are available for use in extensions. You can have the compiler tell you when you've used disallowed APIs by doing the following: select your project in the **Project Navigator** and then select your framework from the list of targets. Click the **General** tab and check **Allow app extension API only**. This is illustrated below:

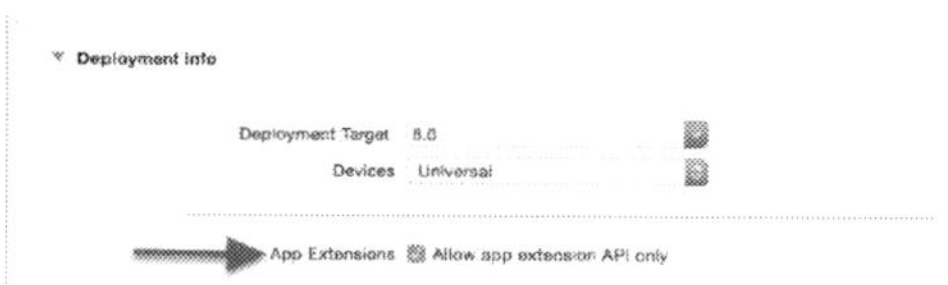

Enabling this causes the compiler to show a warning on any line that uses a prohibited API. You should be verifying that this is enabled for any framework target that is included by an app extension. As of this writing there are not many APIs that are unavailable. They include the following:

- `EventKitUI`, all classes.
- `UIActionSheet` and `UIAlertSheet`. You should use `UIAlertController` instead.
- `UIApplication`
    - `sharedApplication`
    - `beginIgnoringInteractionEvents`
    - `endIgnoringInteractionEvents`
    - `openURL`

The extension's Info.plist

Just like an app, extensions contain an **Info.plist** file, but the content is quite different. The **NSExtension** dictionary is required for all extensions; however, the contents of this dictionary will vary from extension to extension, but they all must include the **NSExtensionPointIdentifier** key, which identifies the type of the extension.

The **NSExtension** dictionary also helps the OS and other apps decide when to make your extension available to users. The **NSExtensionActivationRule** dictionary defines the necessary rules; additionally, there will be many different contexts in which a user will invoke your extension. For example, you can control whether your Photo Editing extension accepts videos or images, or both, and whether it'll accept just one, or multiple files, using the entries in this dictionary.

You also need to declare which storyboard file or class to use as your extensions entry point via the **NSExtensionMainStoryboard** and **NSExtensionPrincipalClass** keys respectively.

The contents of the **NSExtension** dictionary is different for each type of extension. For more in-depth coverage of how to leverage this dictionary in your extension, take a look at Apple's App Extensions Keys (https://developer.apple.com/library/prerelease/ios/documentation/General/Reference/InfoPlistKeyReference/Articles/SystemExtensionKeys.html) page.

Designing app extensions

An app extension should be designed to perform a very specific task. If you have a lot of different features you'd like to provide to your users, it will probably make sense to provide multiple extensions rather than clutter the user interface. You will also need to pick the appropriate extension type for the task you want to perform.

For example, you won't use an Action extension to post content to a social networking site; you'd be better off using a Share extension. Likewise, a Photo Editing extension shouldn't shoulder the task of sharing images. Ultimately, it's Apple's call whether or not you're using an extension type in an appropriate manner. It's your responsibility to apply due diligence when choosing the most relevant type for your extension.

Keep in mind that when you invoke the extension, the user won't leave the host app; instead, the host app presents your extensions' interface to the user. This is your opportunity to differentiate your extension from the host app and show off the functionality you're providing. From a UI perspective, a user chooses your extension either by tapping your container app's icon, or by tapping an icon you explicitly defined for that extension. This provides the user with some context as to which app is providing the extension.

The screenshots below highlight this comparison; the Photo Editing extensions clearly indicate which app is providing the service by displaying its full-color icon, while Action extensions display monochrome icons instead:

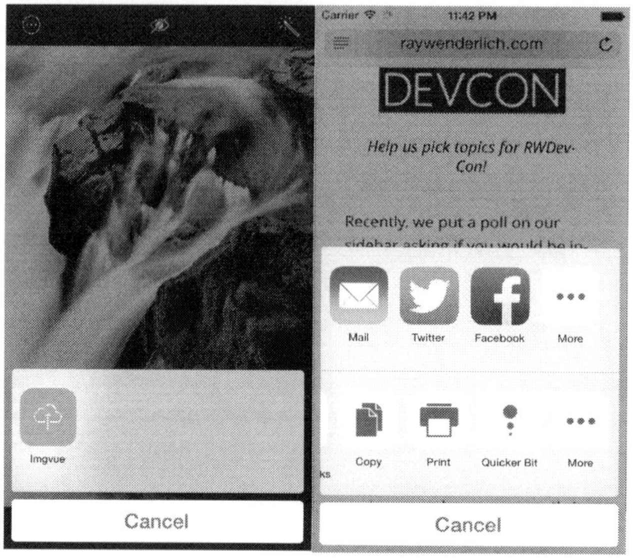

Extensions aren't visible by default; the user must explicitly enable your extensions. Furthermore, the user can then disable it, or reorganize the list of third party extensions providing similar functionality. Be sure to offer useful features in-order to keep your app at the top of their list!

It's likely that many users wont' be aware that your app provides an extension. You will need to decide the best approach for alerting users that your extension is available. This could be achieved through release notes and your description in the App Store, an email-marketing message or even a notice within your app. In any case don't let your extension slip through the cracks!

Show me the code!

The following six chapters each guide you through the creation of an extension; one chapter per extension type. While it's impossible to think up all of the various ways extensions can, and will be used, this section of the book will set you on the path of shaping the future with app extensions on iOS.

We hope that iOS users hungry for new functionality will download your apps and love their extensions in the near future. There's an incredible amount of room to innovate and release creative and useful extensions on the App Store – so what are you waiting for? Dive in!

Chapter 9: Today Extensions

By Chris Wagner

Today Extensions are essentially the iOS equivalent of desktop widgets. Once activated, the user can find them in Notification Center. They're great for providing immediate and up-to-date information that the user is interested in.

Another nice feature is that because they reside in Notification Center, your users can access Today Extensions from the lock screen without the need to first unlock the device. All that's needed is a quick press of the Home button followed by a swipe down and voila; your widget is available for consumption.

Never has it been so easy to deliver valuable information so quickly to your users!

Crypticker

In this chapter, you'll write a Today Extension that renders the current market price of a Bitcoin (https://bitcoin.org/en/) based on the United States Dollar.

If you're not familiar with Bitcoin, the short explanation is that it's a digital cryptocurrency that's still in its infancy. Aside from using it for peer-to-peer exchanges and purchases, Bitcoin trading allows the user to exchange it for a number of other cryptocurrencies like Dogecoin and Litecoin, and flat currency such as the US Dollar and the Euro.

As a relatively new currency, its market value fluctuates by the minute; there have been huge peaks and troughs in its short lifetime. Thus, it's a perfect candidate for a Today Extension.

If someone intends to trade Bitcoin, they want to know the current price at *any given moment*. You're going to build a widget to display the current average price from multiple major exchanges, as provided by https://blockchain.info/charts/market-price.

Since you're writing an extension, you'll first need a host app to extend; meet Crypticker.

Crypticker is a simple app that displays the current Bitcoin price, the difference between yesterdays price and the current price, as well as a price history chart. The chart includes 30 days of history; sliding your finger on the chart reveals the exact price for a specific day in the past.

The extension will contain all of these features, except for touching the chart to see the price for a specific day. There are some limitations within Today Extensions, especially when it comes to swiping. The swipe gesture often triggers swiping between the **Today** and **Notifications** sections within Notification Center, so it doesn't really provide the best or most reliable user experience.

Starter project

Open the Crypticker starter project to get started. The project contains the entire Crypticker app as described above. Please note that the extension chapters don't focus on the development of their container apps, so you may be pleasantly surprised to find them to be rather succinct. After all, you're writing an extension, not an entire app.

Build and run. Please note that you'll need a working Internet connection to pull the real-time prices from a web service.

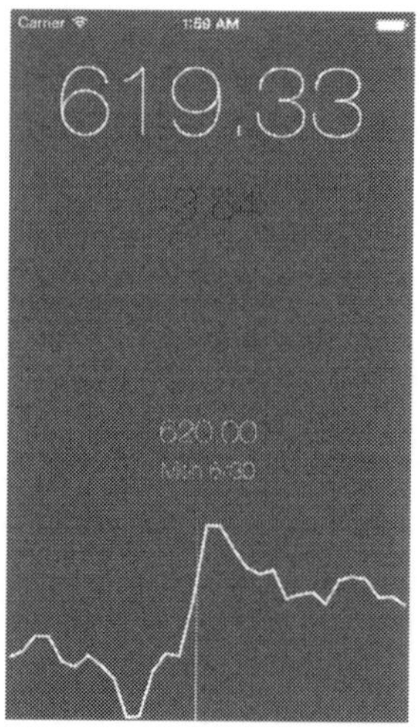

The app looks very similar to the screenshot above; the data displayed will, of course, depend on how the Bitcoin market looks *right now*. Touching the chart near the bottom of the view will draw a line and display the price for the relevant day.

BTC widget

For the unfamiliar, **BTC** is shorthand for **Bitcoin**; much like **USD** stands for **United States Dollar**. The Today Extension will render a scaled down version of Crypticker's primary view.

Theoretically, the Crypticker app has the ability to show pricing for multiple Cryptocurrencies, but your extension is specific to BTC. Therefore, its name shall be **BTC Widget**.

> **Note:** Extensions, by nature, have just one simple purpose. If you wanted to provide information for another cryptocurrency, like Dogecoin, it would be best to package a second widget with the app or design your UI appropriately, perhaps like the Stocks widget.

By the end of the chapter, your Today Extension will look something like this:

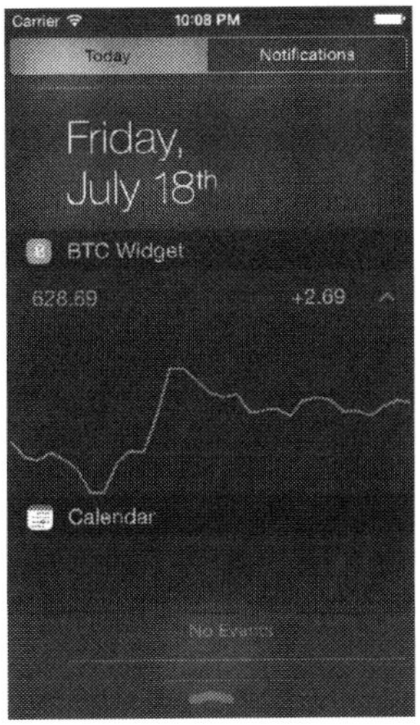

Add a Today Extension target

As discussed in Chapter 8, **Introducing Extensions**, extensions are packaged as a separate binary from their host app. So you'll need to add a Today Extension target to the Crypticker project.

In Xcode's **Project Navigator**, select the **Crypticker** project and add a new target by selecting **Editor\Add Target...** When the template picker appears, choose **iOS\Application Extension**, and then **Today Extension**. Click **Next**.

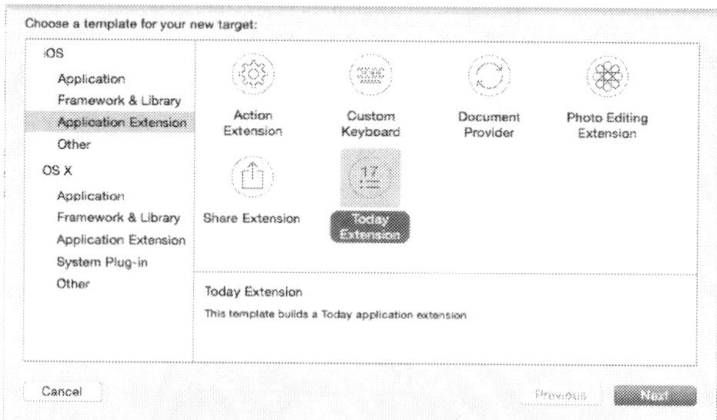

Set the **Product Name** to **BTC Widget,** and verify that the language is **Swift**, the project is **Crypticker** and **Embed in Application** is also **Crypticker**. Click **Finish**.

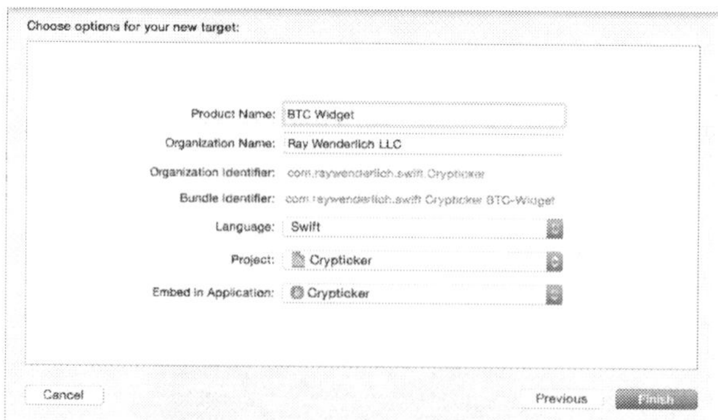

You might see a prompt that asks if you want to "Activate BTC Widget scheme?". As the text indicates, another Xcode scheme will be created for you. Since you're going to edit and build in this target, press **Activate**.

Congratulations! BTC Widget will now appear in your list of targets.

Make sure you select **BTC Widget**, then the **General** tab, and then press the **+ button** under **Linked Frameworks and Libraries**.

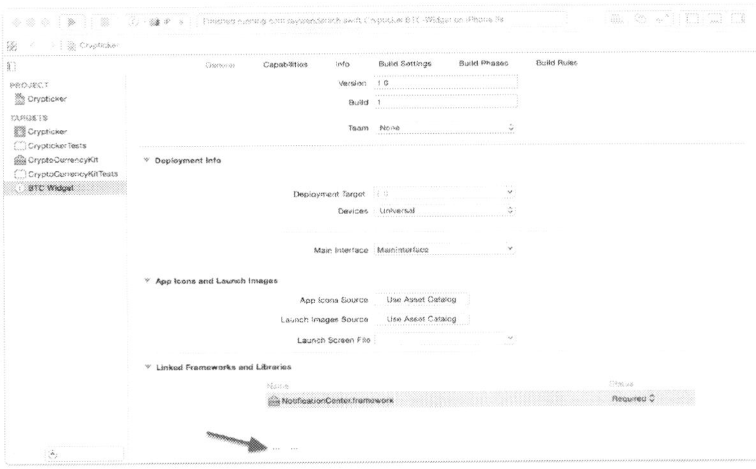

Select **CryptoCurrencyKit.framework** and press **Add**.

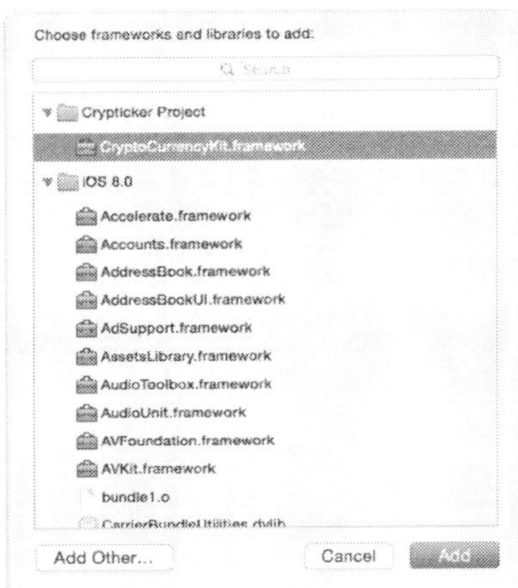

`CryptoCurrencyKit` is a custom framework used by the Crypticker app to retrieve currency prices from the web. Luckily for you, the incredibly kind and thoughtful developer behind Crypticker modularized the code into a framework, so that it can be shared between multiple targets :]

As mentioned in Chapter 8, in order to share code between a host app and its extensions you must use a custom framework. If you don't, you'll find yourself duplicating a lot of code and violating an important rule of software engineering: DRY – or, **D**on't **R**epeat **Y**ourself. I'll say it again: "*Don't repeat yourself*".

At this point, you're ready to begin implementing the extension.

Notice there's now a group in the Project navigator named after your new target, **BTC Widget**. This is where the Today Extension's code is grouped, by default.

Expand the group and you'll see there is a view controller, a storyboard file and an `Info.plist` file. Its target configuration also tells it to load its interface from `MainInterface.storyboard`, which contains a single view controller with the class set to `TodayViewController.swift`.

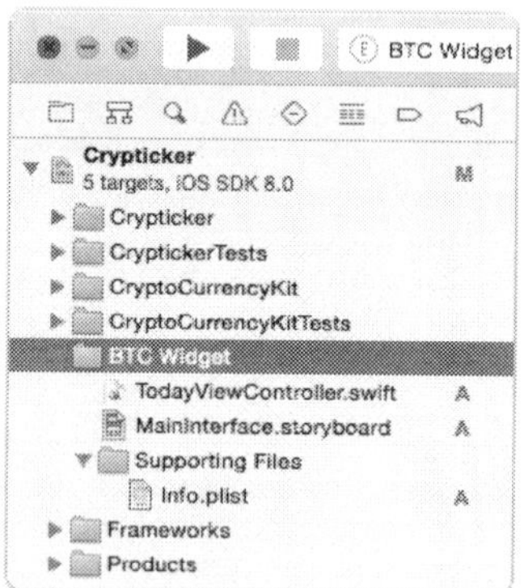

You'll notice some files you might expect to see are missing from the Today Extension template; like an app delegate for instance. Remember that extensions run inside another host app, so they don't go through the traditional app lifecycle.

In essence, the lifecycle of the extension is mapped to the lifecycle of the `TodayViewController`.

Open **MainInterface.storyboard**. You'll see a dark colored view with a light *Hello World* label. Today Extensions are most legible when they have a clear background and light or vibrantly colored text in order to harmonize with the dark, blurred background of Notification Center.

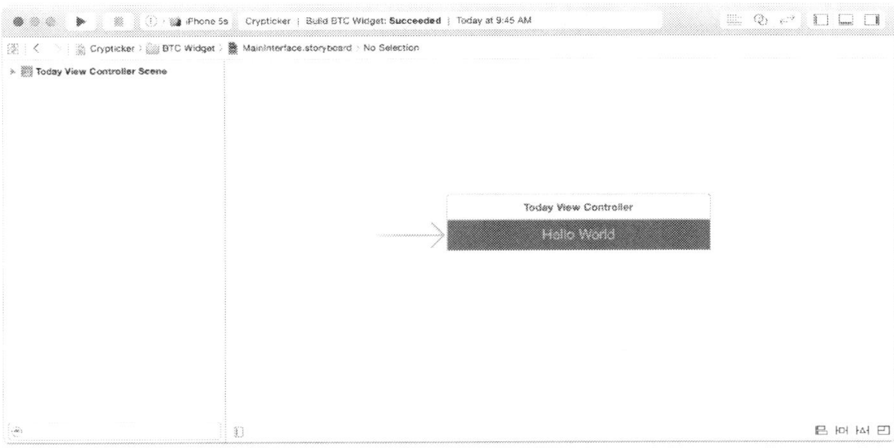

Make sure the **BTC Widget** scheme is selected in Xcode's toolbar and build and run. This will cause a window to appear asking which app to run. Xcode is asking you which *host* app to run. Choose **Today**. This tells iOS to open Notification Center in the Today view, which in turn launches your widget. Notification Center is effectively the host app for Today Extensions.

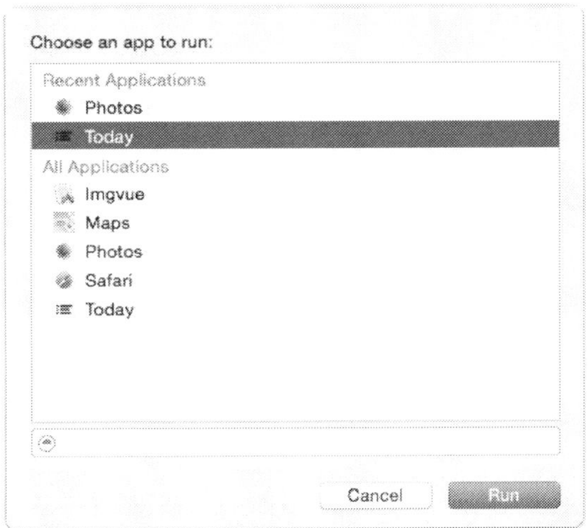

This also causes Xcode to attach its debugger to the widget's process.

Behold your widget. Cool, right? Whilst this is super-exciting stuff, the widget clearly needs a little work. It's time to make it do some interesting things!

> **Note**: You might notice a lot of Auto Layout errors printed to the console when launching the widget. This is an issue with the Xcode template, and will hopefully be resolved by Apple in the future. Don't worry though, since you'll be adding your own interface, including Auto Layout constraints.

Build the Interface

Open **MainInterface.storyboard** and delete the label. Set the view to 150pts tall and 320pts wide in the **Size Inspector**. Drag a **Button**, two **Labels** and a **View** from the **Object Library** onto the view controllers view.

Position one of the labels in the top left corner, and in the **Attributes Inspector** set its **Text** to **$592.12** and its **Color** to **Red: 66**, **Green: 145** and **Blue: 211**. This will display the current market price. Position the other label to the right of the one you've just set up, but leave a margin to the right for the button. In the **Attributes Inspector** set its **Text** to **+1.23** and its **Color** to **Red: 133**, **Green: 191** and **Blue: 37**. This will display the difference between yesterdays price and the current price. Move the button to the upper right of the view, and in the **Attributes Inspector** set its **Image** to **caret-notification-center** and delete its **Title**. Finally, position the empty view below the two labels and the button, stretch it so it's bottom and side edges are touching the containing view and set its **Height** to **98**. In the **Attributes Inspector** set its **Background** to **Clear Color**, and in the **Identity Inspector** set its **Class** to `JBLineChartView`.

> **Note:** There is a class named `JBLineChartDotView` that Xcode may suggest when typing, verify that you chose `JBLineChartView`.

The view and **Document Outline** should now look something like this:

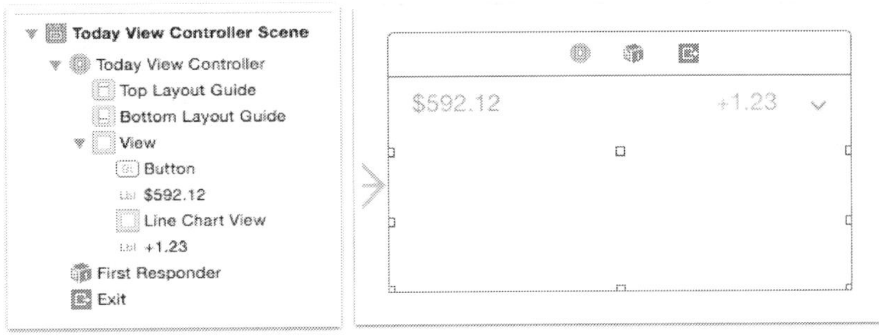

> **Note:** The view shown here has a white background for the purpose of visibility in this book. Your view will actually have a dark grey background that simulates how your view appears within Notification Center.

Don't worry about laying things out *exactly* as shown, as you'll soon be adding Auto Layout constraints to properly define the layout.

Now, expand the **Crypticker** group in the **Project Navigator** and select **Images.xcassets**. In the **File Inspector**, add the asset catalog to the extension's target by checking the box to the left of **BTC Widget**.

This causes Xcode to include the image asset catalog from the Crypticker target in your BTC Widget target; that is where the **caret-notification-center** image that you used for your button resides. If you have an overlap of image assets between your container app and widget it is a good idea to use a dedicated catalog that only contains the assets that will actually be shared. This will reduce bloat in your finalized bundles by not including images that are unused.

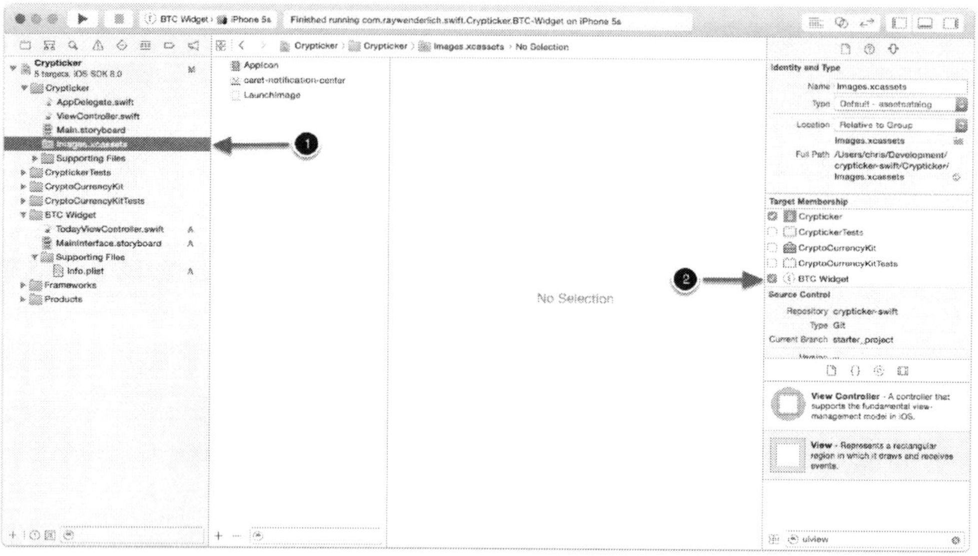

Switch back to **MainInterface.storyboard** and open the **Assistant Editor**. Make sure **TodayViewController.swift** is the active file. Add this at the top of the file:

import CryptoCurrencyKitThis imports the `CryptoCurrencyKit` framework.

Next, you need to update the class declaration, like this:

```
class TodayViewController: CurrencyDataViewController,
NCWidgetProviding {
```

This makes the `TodayViewController` a subclass of `CurrencyDataViewController`, and ensures it conforms to the `NCWidgetProviding` protocol.

`CurrencyDataViewController` is included in `CryptoCurrencyKit` and is also used by the primary view within Crypticker. Since the widget and app will be displaying similar information through a UIViewController, it makes sense to put reusable components in a superclass and then sub-class that as requirements vary.

`NCWidgetProviding` is a protocol specific to widgets; there are two methods from the protocol that you'll be implementing.

Ctrl+drag from the button to the class, just below the class declaration. In the popup dialog make sure the **Connection** is set to **Outlet**, the **Type** is set to `UIButton`, and enter `toggleLineChartButton` for the **Name**. Click **Connect**.

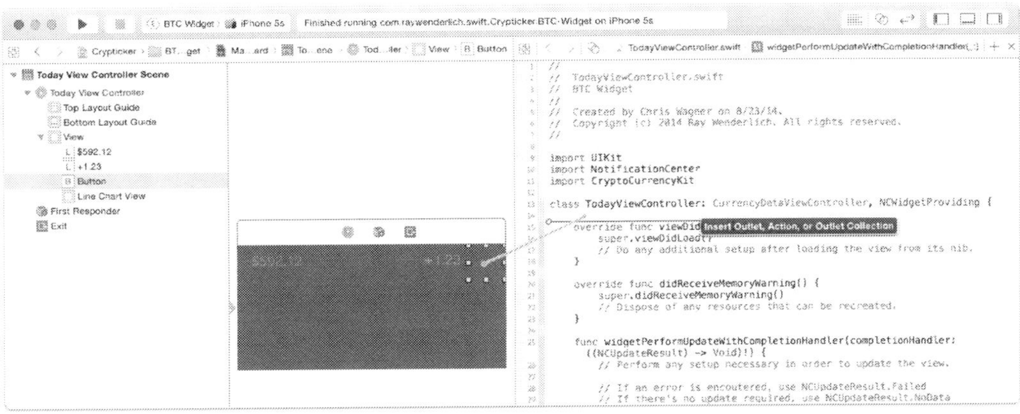

Then **ctrl+drag** from the button to the bottom of the class this time. In the popup dialog change the **Connection** to **Action**, set the **Type** to `UIButton`, and enter `toggleLineChart` for the **Name**. Click **Connect**.

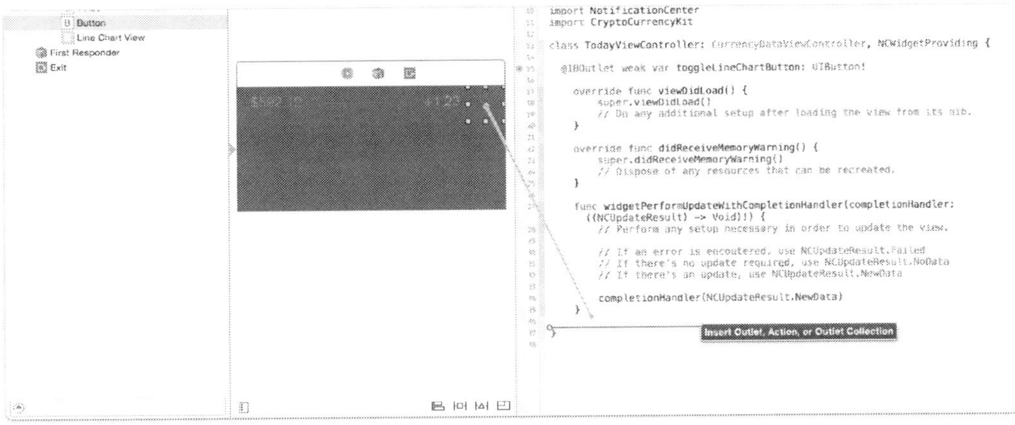

`TodayViewController` subclasses `CurrencyDataViewController`, which has outlets for the price label, price change label and line chart view. You now need to wire these up. In the **Document Outline**, **ctrl+drag** from **Today View Controller** to the **price label** (the one with its text set to $592.12). Select `priceLabel` from the popup to create the connection. Repeat for the other label, selecting `priceChangeLabel` from the popup. Finally, do the same for the **Line Chart View**, selecting `lineChartView` from the popup.

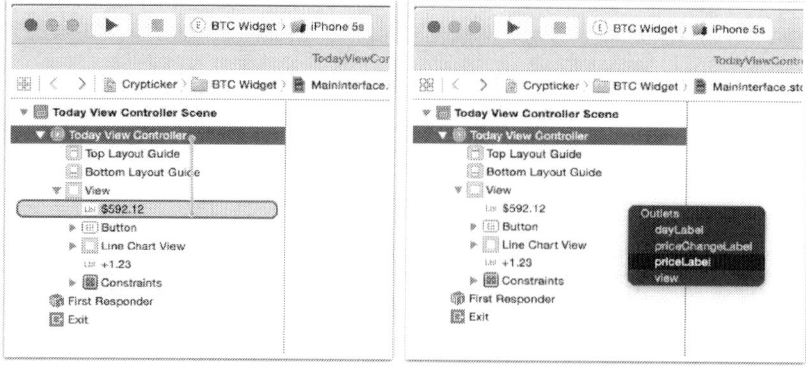

Auto Layout

For your widget to be adaptive, you'll need to set up Auto Layout constraints. New with iOS 8 is the concept of Adaptive Layout. The general idea is that views are designed with a single layout that can work on a variety of screen sizes. The view is considered adaptive when it can adapt to unknown future device metrics. The first chapters of this book explain detail what it takes to be adaptive.

One of the constraints that you will add is to show and hide the chart, and help define the overall height of the widget. Notification Center will rely on you to display your widget with the appropriate height.

Select the **$592.12** label and then select **Editor\Size to Fit Content**. If the **Size to Fit Content** option is disabled in the menu, deselect the label, and then reselect it and try again; sometimes Xcode can be a little temperamental. Next, using the **Pin** button at the bottom of the storyboard canvas, pin the **Top** and **Leading** space to 8 and 16 respectively. Make sure that **Constrain to margins** is turned off.

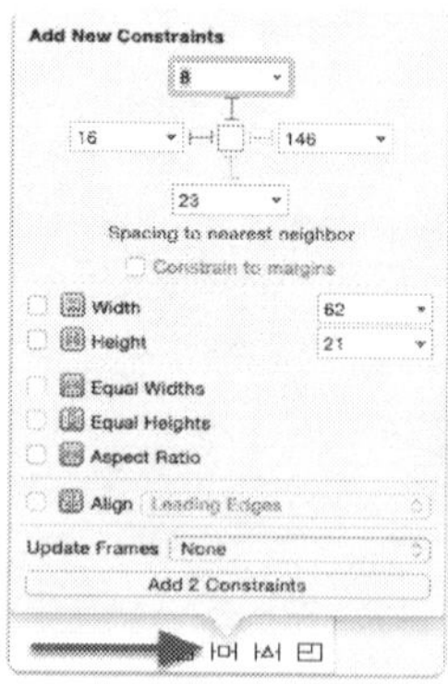

Select the **+1.23** label and again select **Editor\Size to Fit Content**. Then, using the **Pin** button, pin the **Top** and **Trailing** space both to 8.

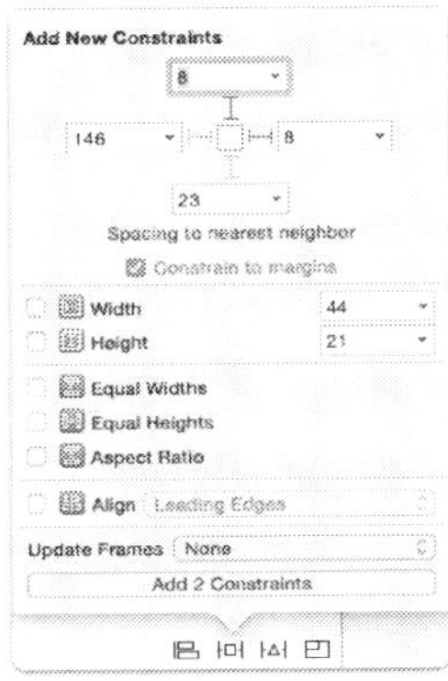

Select the **Button**, and using the **Pin** button, pin its **Top** and **Trailing** space to `0`, and its **Bottom** space to 8. Pin both its **Width** and **Height** to 44. Make sure that **Constrain to margins** is turned off.

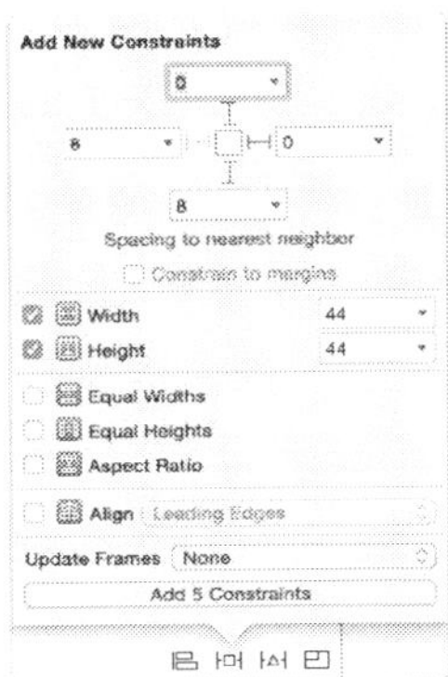

You need to reduce the priority for the bottom spacing constraint of the button. Select the button, and then open the **Size Inspector**. Locate the **Bottom Space to:** constraint in the list of constraints, click **Edit** and change it's **Priority** to `250`.

By lowering the priority you are allowing the Auto Layout system to break this constraint, as it deems necessary. 250 is an arbitrary value that happens to be less than 1,000, which is what the priority is set to for all constraints by default and means required. This constraint needs to be broken when the widget is in its collapsed state. By having varying levels of priorities per constraint you are hinting to the system which constraints to break first or last when a conflict arises.

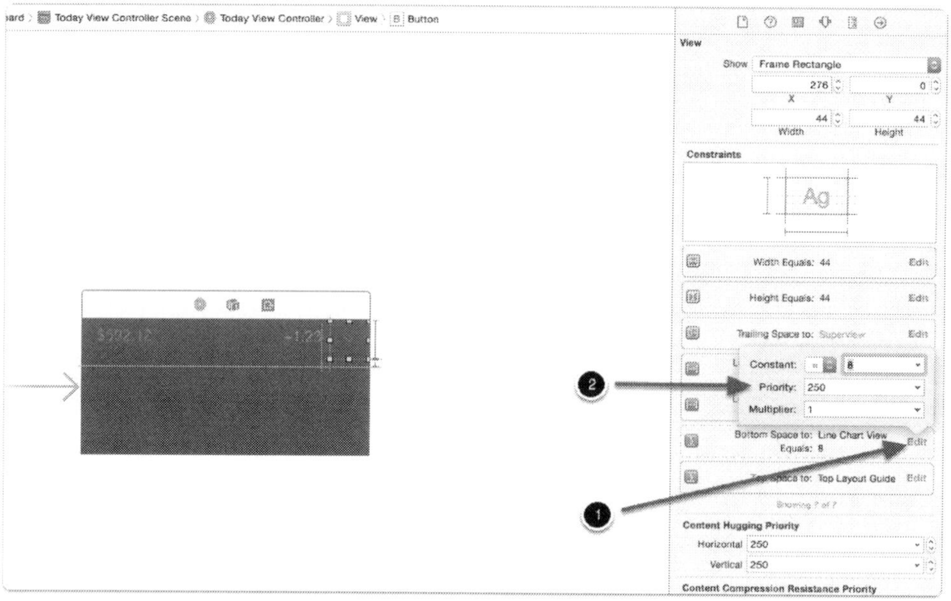

Finally, select the **Line Chart View**. Using the **Pin** button, pin its **Leading**, **Trailing** and **Bottom** space to `0` and its **Height** to 98.

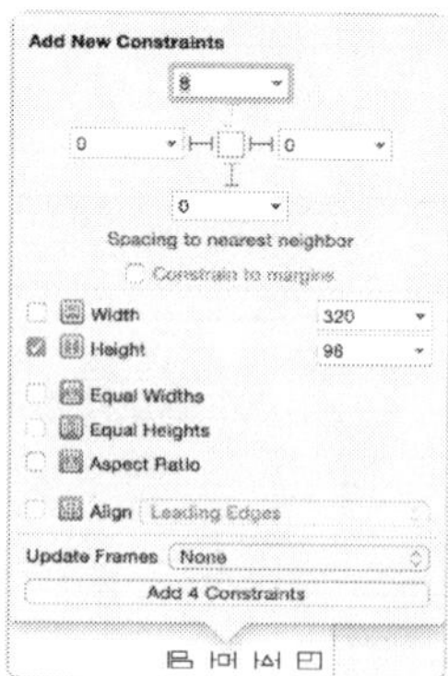

From the **Document Outline** select the view controllers **View**, the choose **Editor\Resolve Auto Layout Issues\All Views\Update Frames**. This will fix any Auto Layout warnings in the canvas by updating the frames of the views to match their constraints. If **Update Frames** is not enabled then you laid everything out perfect and it is unnecessary to run.

With all of your constraints in place, the final step is to create an outlet for the line chart view's height constraint. Find the **Line Chart View** in the **Document Outline** and click the disclosure triangle. Then click the disclosure triangle for the **Constraints** to find the necessary height constraint. Select it, and then **ctrl+drag** into the **Assistant Editor**, releasing just below the other outlet. In the popup, make sure the **Connection** is set to **Outlet** and enter `lineChartHeightConstraint` for the **Name**. Click **Connect**.

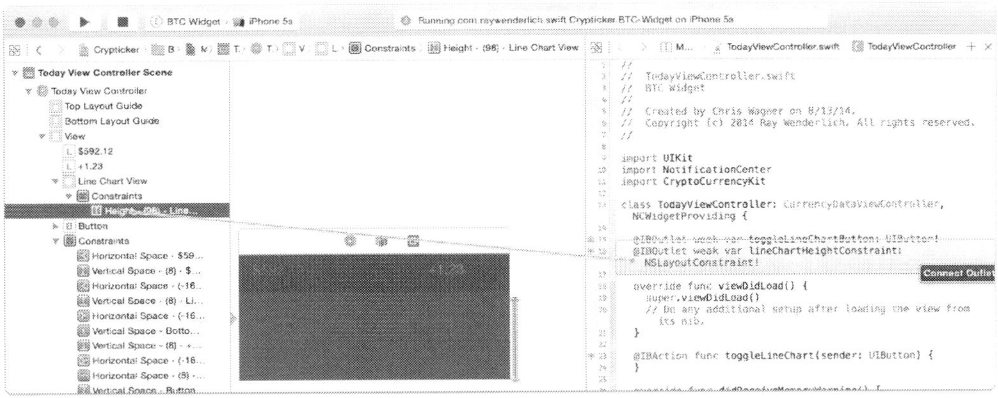

Implementing TodayViewController.swift

Now the interface is in place and everything is wired up, open up **TodayViewController.swift** in the **Standard Editor**.

You'll notice you're working with bog-standard `UIViewController` subclass. Comforting, right? Although later you'll encounter a new method called `widgetPerformUpdateWithCompletionHandler` from the `NCWidgetProviding` protocol. You'll learn more about it towards the end of the chapter.

This view controller is responsible for displaying the current price, price difference, responding to a button press and showing the price history in a line chart.

Define a property at the top of `TodayViewController` that you'll use to track if the line chart is visible or not:

```
var lineChartIsVisible = false
```

Now replace the boilerplate `viewDidLoad()` method with the following implementation:

```
override func viewDidLoad() {
  super.viewDidLoad()
  lineChartHeightConstraint.constant = 0
```

```
    lineChartView.delegate = self;
    lineChartView.dataSource = self;
    priceLabel.text = "--"
    priceChangeLabel.text = "--"
  }
```

This method does the following:

1. Sets the line view charts' height constraints' constant to `0`, so that it's hidden by default.
2. Sets `self` as the data source and delegate for the line chart view.
3. Sets some placeholder text on the two labels.

Still in `TodayViewController`, add the following method:

```
override func viewDidAppear(animated: Bool) {
  super.viewDidAppear(animated)

  fetchPrices { error in
    if error == nil {
      self.updatePriceLabel()
      self.updatePriceChangeLabel()
      self.updatePriceHistoryLineChart()
    }
  }
}
```

The `fetchPrices` method is defined in `CurrencyDataViewController`, and is an asynchronous call that takes a completion block. The method makes a request to the web-service mentioned at the beginning of the chapter to obtain Bitcoin price information.

In the method's completion block update both labels and the line chart. The update methods are also defined for you in the super-class. They simply take the values retrieved by the `fetchPrices` method and format them appropriately for display.

Due to the design of the widget, you'll also need to implement `widgetMarginInsetsForProposedMarginInsets` to provide custom margin insets. Add the following code to `TodayViewController`:

```
func widgetMarginInsetsForProposedMarginInsets
  (defaultMarginInsets: UIEdgeInsets) -> (UIEdgeInsets) {
    return UIEdgeInsetsZero
}
```

By default, widgets have a large left margin, which is evident in many of Apple's default widgets. If you want to fill the entire width of Notification Center, you must implement this method and return `UIEdgeInsetsZero`, which translates to `0` on all sides.

Now it's time to see what you have so far. Select the **BTC Widget** scheme. Build and run. Choose **Today** as the app to run when prompted.

- If Notification Center doesn't appear, swipe down from the top of the screen to activate it.
- If the widget doesn't appear in Notification Center, you'll need to add it via the **Edit** menu. Towards the bottom of the Today's view content you will see an Edit button. Tap the button to reveal a menu of all Today Extensions that are installed on the system. Here you can enable, disable and re-order them as desired. Enable BTC Widget if not already.

> **Note:** If you're not using a physical device you must have the simulator open in order to run the extension and attach the debugger. To open the simulator, select **Xcode\Open Developer Tool\iOS Simulator**.

Cool! Your widget now displays real-time Bitcoin pricing right in Notification Center. But you may have noticed a problem; the button doesn't work and you can't see the line chart.

Next, you'll implement `toggleLineChart` for the button that you added so that it expands the widget's view and exposes the line chart. As the method name implies, this button will behave as a toggle; it will also collapse the view to hide the chart.

Replace the empty `toggleLineChart` method with the following code:

```
@IBAction func toggleLineChart(sender: UIButton) {
  if lineChartIsVisible {
    lineChartHeightConstraint.constant = 0
    let transform = CGAffineTransformMakeRotation(0)
    toggleLineChartButton.transform = transform
    lineChartIsVisible = false
  } else {
    lineChartHeightConstraint.constant = 98
    let transform = CGAffineTransformMakeRotation(CGFloat(180.0
* M_PI/180.0))
    toggleLineChartButton.transform = transform
    lineChartIsVisible = true
  }
}
```

This method manipulates the constant of the Line Chart Views' height constraint to toggle its display. It also applies a rotation transform to the button so it accurately reflects the visibility of the chart.

After updating the constraint, you must reload the chart's data so that it redraws based on the new layout. You'll do this in `viewDidLayoutSubviews`. Add the following to `TodayViewController`:

```
override func viewDidLayoutSubviews() {
  super.viewDidLayoutSubviews()
  updatePriceHistoryLineChart()
}
```

Make sure the **BTC Widget** scheme is selected. Build and run. Choose **Today** as the app to run when prompted.

On the left, you'll see how the widget appears when the chart is hidden. On the right, you'll see how it appears when opened. Not too shabby!

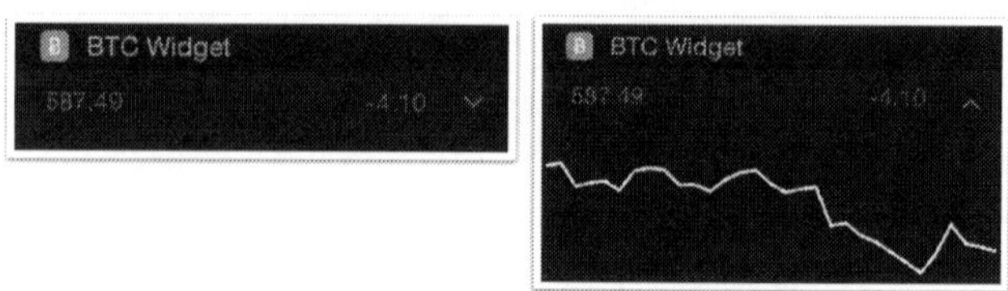

A quick update of the line's color and you'll have one sharp looking widget. Add the following method to `TodayViewController`:

```
override func lineChartView(lineChartView: JBLineChartView!,
  colorForLineAtLineIndex lineIndex: UInt) -> UIColor! {
    return UIColor(red: 0.17, green: 0.49,
      blue: 0.82, alpha: 1.0)
}
```

Make sure the correct scheme is still selected. Build and run. Choose **Today** as the app to run when prompted.

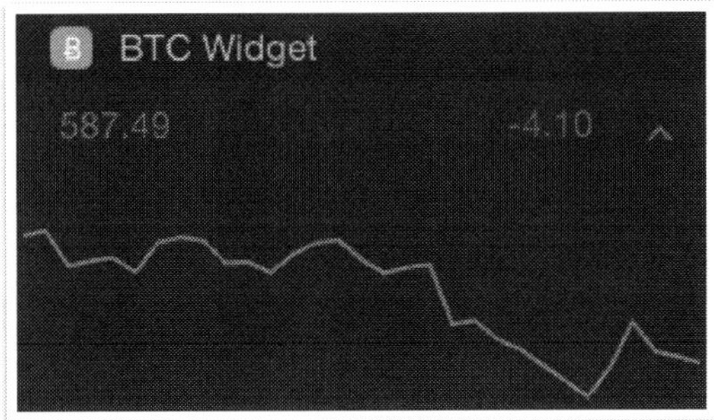

Your last order of business is to add support to your widget to update its view when it's off-screen, by allowing the system to create a snapshot. The system does this periodically to help your widget stay up to date.

Replace the existing implementation of `widgetPerformUpdateWithCompletionHandler` with the following code:

```
func widgetPerformUpdateWithCompletionHandler(completionHandler:
((NCUpdateResult) -> Void)!) {
  fetchPrices { error in
    if error == nil {
      self.updatePriceLabel()
      self.updatePriceChangeLabel()
      self.updatePriceHistoryLineChart()
      completionHandler(.NewData)
    } else {
      completionHandler(.NoData)
    }
  }
}
```

This method does the following:

- It fetches the current price data from the web service by calling `fetchPrices`.
- If there's no error the interface is updated.
- Finally – and as required by the `NCWidgetProviding` protocol – the function calls the system-provided completion block with the `.NewData` enumeration.
- In the event of an error, the completion block is called with the `.Failed` enumeration. This informs the system that no new data is available and the existing snapshot should be used.

And that wraps up your Today Extension!

Diving deeper

This chapter covered the key points of Today Extensions. You were able to get a lot accomplished by using some pretty basic approaches, but there are more things to consider when designing your extensions.

Limitations

When designing an extension, keep in mind that user interaction should be minimal. If there's any level of configuration required, then lean on the container app to handle that. One major reason for this is because the keyboard is not available for Today Extensions. If your user has to type in any information in order to be able to consume your extension, they must do so through the container app.

If your widget is in a state where it must be configured, or you want to allow your user to see more details, it might make sense to launch the container app. You can do so through the `openURL` API of `NSExtensionContext`.

Development options

If you would rather develop your extensions without the use of a storyboard, you can remove the provided storyboard file and tell the system to load a specific view controller instead.

You do this by editing the extension targets' `Info.plist` so that it contains the `NSExtensionPrincipalClass` key set to the name of your view controller's class. Also, be sure to remove the `NSExtensionMainStoryboard` key.

In some scenarios, it won't make sense for your widget to appear. Think about a widget that shows the score of an NFL game. The season runs from September through February, and ends in December for most teams. Thus, it would be silly for your widget to appear in May when there are no games.

Your widget and its containing app can specify when there's content to display. The `setHasContent(forWidgetWithBundleIdentifier:)` of the `NCWidgetController` class allows you to specify if content is available.

Once the system learns that the widget no longer has content available, your container app must call this API again once new data is available. Only then will Notification Center launch your widget.

Enabling Today Extensions

When iOS 8 first rolls out to your users, remember that many won't know about extensions or how to enable them. So, add some information somewhere in your host app to let them know about your shiny new extension and make sure they know to enable it by opening **Notification Center** and tapping the **Edit** button at the bottom of the scroll view.

Where to go from here?

The iOS 8 Notification Center is your own personal playground! Widgets have been available on some other mobile operating systems for years, and Apple has finally provided you the ability to create them.

As an enterprising developer, you might want to take another look at your existing apps and think about how you can update them with widgets. Take it a step further and dream up new app ideas that exploit the possibilities of widgets. The community at Ray Wenderlich can't wait to see what you come up with, and hope to have your Today Extensions at the top of our Notification Centers soon!

Chapter 10: Share Extensions

By Chris Wagner

Have you ever been browsing in Safari and stumbled upon an article you wanted to save to Instapaper? Or, maybe you find a particularly scrumptious Boston crème-peanut-butter-cup-brownie-chocolate-chip-cookie-candied-bacon desert recipe that must pin on Pinterest?

What did you do? You probably copied the URL, switched to the app you wanted to save or share it in, performed the action, and then switched back to Safari to continue on your way. Either that or you used a bookmarklet; and you're still waking up in cold sweats, forever shaken by the nightmare process you had to go through to get that thing installed.

They work, but they're a little cumbersome, right? Well, good news! Share Extensions are here to save the day. It's now possible for your users to share content directly to your service, right from *within* Safari or other apps, even native apps like Photos.

In this chapter, you'll write a Share Extension that allows users to upload an image directly to imgur.com from within the stock Photos and Camera apps.

Imgvue

As with any extension for iOS, you must first provide a container app that offers the functionality to be provided by the extension. For this chapter, you'll work with an app named Imgvue. It allows users to view the current most popular images on imgur.com, a well-liked image sharing website. Users can then choose to save their favorite images, and apply filters to those saved images. Finally, the app lets users upload their own images to the imgur website.

> **Note:** If you jumped ahead and have already completed Chapter 12, **Photo Editing Extensions**, you will have already completed this section. You can either re-use the same project or re-use your imgur Client ID in a new project for this chapter. If not, all of the information that you need is right here.

Register at Imgur.com

In order to proceed, you'll need a Client ID from imgur.com so you can use their API.

1. Start by creating an imgur account at https://imgur.com/register. If you already have an account, sign in with that.
2. Once registered and signed in, click your username at the top right of the screen and then choose **Settings** from the menu.

> **Note:** As websites are ever changing, these instructions or screenshots may not match with the current version of the imgur website. As always, if things do not match, then defer to their own documentation.

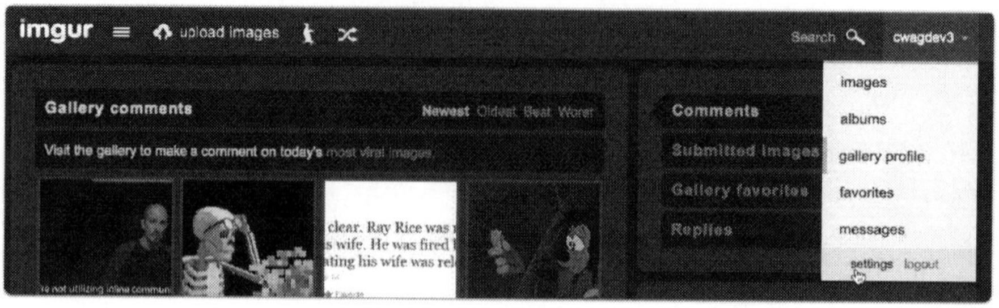

3. Within **Settings**, click **Applications**

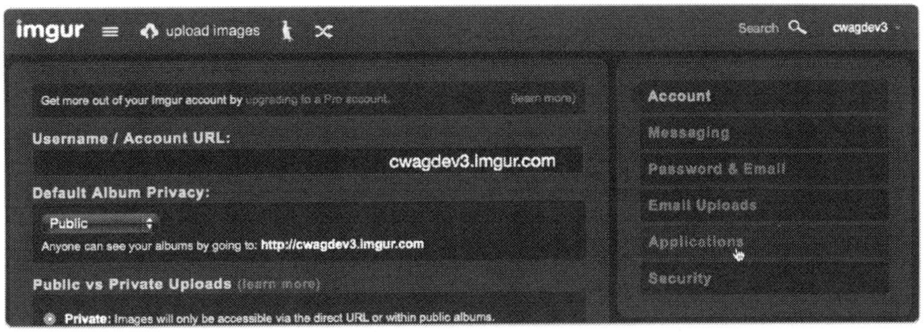

4. Under the **Apps Used** section, click **create your own!**

5. Click **Register an Application** from the menu on the left, and then click the **register their application** link

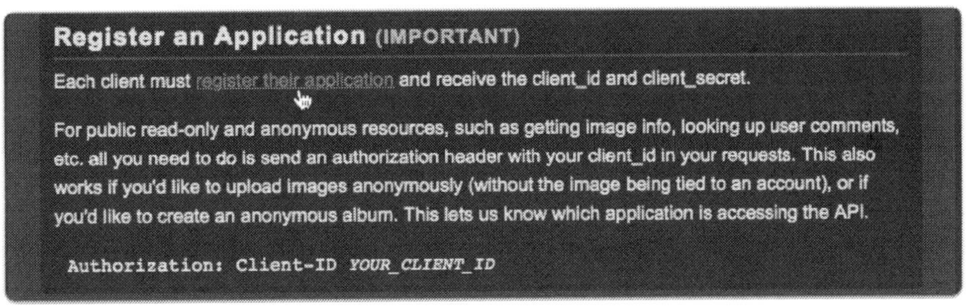

6. Fill out the **Register an Application** form. You can enter anything you like for the **Application Name**, select the second option from the **Authorization type** section, **OAuth 2 authorization with a callback URL**, enter your email address for **Email**, and finally add a sentence or two for the **Description**. Enter the security text into the relevant box and click **submit**.

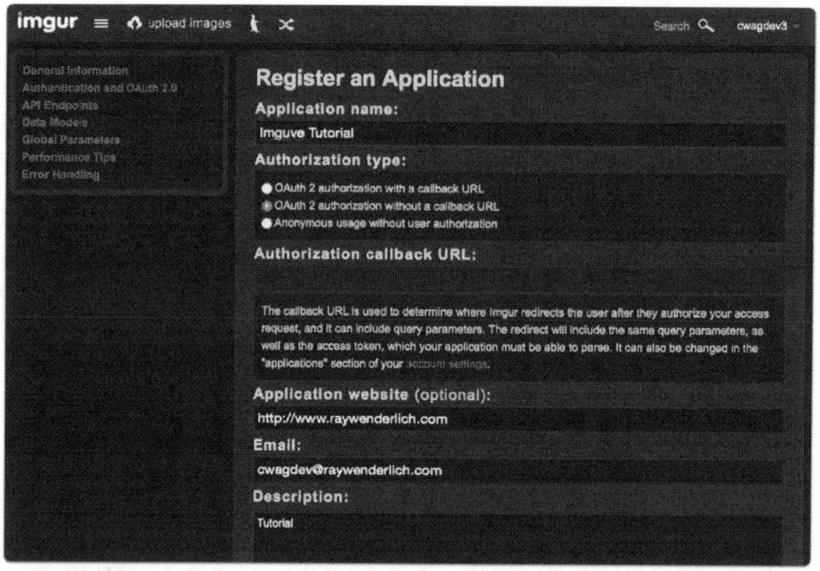

7. Take note of the **Client ID** and **Client secret** as you'll need them both later in the chapter. You'll also receive an email with this information.

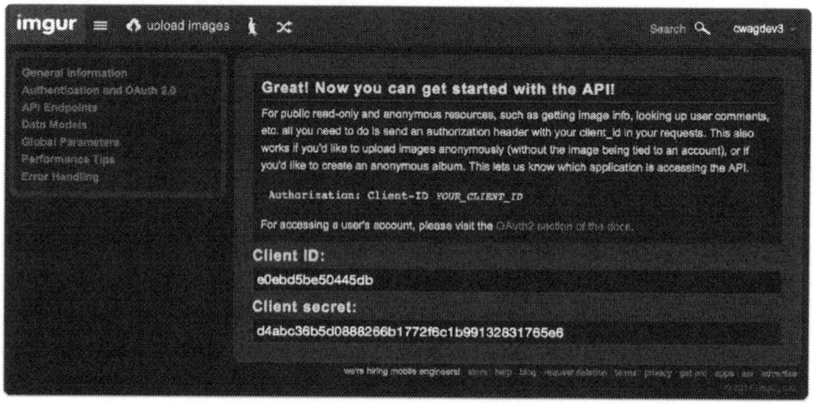

Set Imgur Client ID

Now that you're all setup with an imgur account and have your API credentials, you have everything you need to power **Imgvue**. Open the project in Xcode, and then open **ImgurService.swift** from the **ImgvueKit\Services** group in the **Project Navigator**.

At the top of the class, locate the `imgurClientId` constant and replace `YOUR_CLIENT_ID` with your Client ID.

```
private let imgurClientId = "YOUR_CLIENT_ID"
```

This will be used when creating all imgur.com API requests.

Configure App Group

In order for Imgvue to share content with its extensions, you'll need to set up an **App Group**. App Groups allow access to group containers that are shared amongst related apps, or in this case your container app and extension.

Select the **Imgvue** project in the **Project Navigator**, and then select the **Imgvue** target from the list of targets. On the **General** tab, update the **Bundle Identifier** to **com.<YOUR_DOMAIN>.swift.imgvue**, replacing <YOUR_DOMAIN> with your actual domain. This step is essential as App Groups are intrinsically linked to bundle identifiers.

Now switch to the **Capabilities** tab and enable **App Groups** by flicking the switch. If you're prompted to "select a Development Team" then choose the most appropriate one; usually your personal account. Add a new group by clicking the + button and name it **group.com.<YOUR_DOMAIN>.swift.imgvue**, again replacing <YOUR_DOMAIN> with your actual domain.

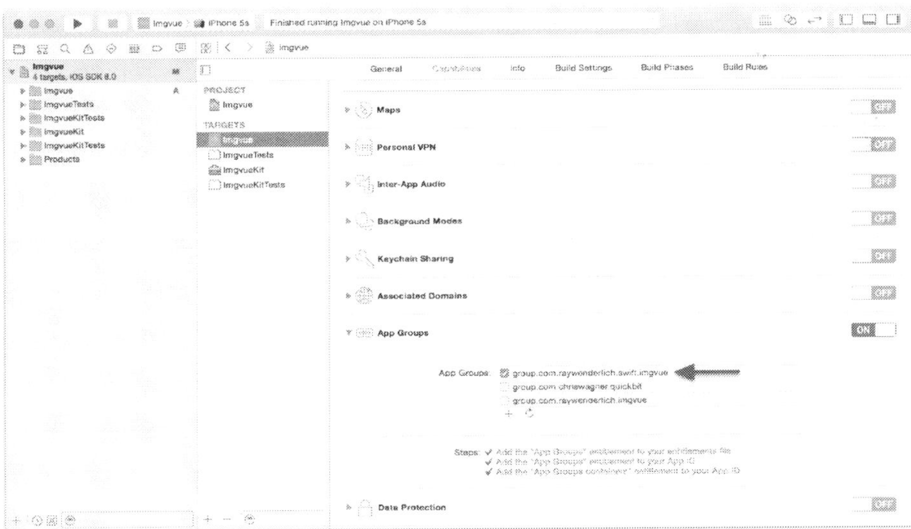

> **Note:** You need an active developer account to enable App Groups. Creating a group in Xcode will also create the entry within your developer portal. Therefore, you may want to remove the group after you complete this tutorial.

Open **SavedImageService.swift** and look for the `urlForDirectoryWithName(name:)` method. The first line sets the appropriate App Group. Change `group.com.raywenderlich.swift.imgvue` to match the group you just created.

Build and run. The app will load the current most popular images from imgur.com.

Tap on any image to view it, and tap **Save** to add the image the favorites tab. You can also upload your own photos from here. Tap the button at the top right to upload a picture to Imgur from your photo library. After selecting a picture the upload begins and upon completion an alert will appear that lets you copy the URL or open it in Safari.

The favorites tab displays all of the images you've saved and uploaded, switch to the favorites tab.

> **NOTE:** If your app crashes here, it means you didn't configure your App Group correctly in the previous section. If that's your case, go back to the previous section and reconfigure your App Group.

In the favorites tab you can tap an image to view it.

For this chapter you will be extending the upload capabilities of the app so that the Apple Photos and Camera apps can upload images to Imgur.

Create the extension

Open **Imgvue** in Xcode. Select the **Imgvue** project in the **Project Navigator**, and then choose **Editor\Add Target...**:

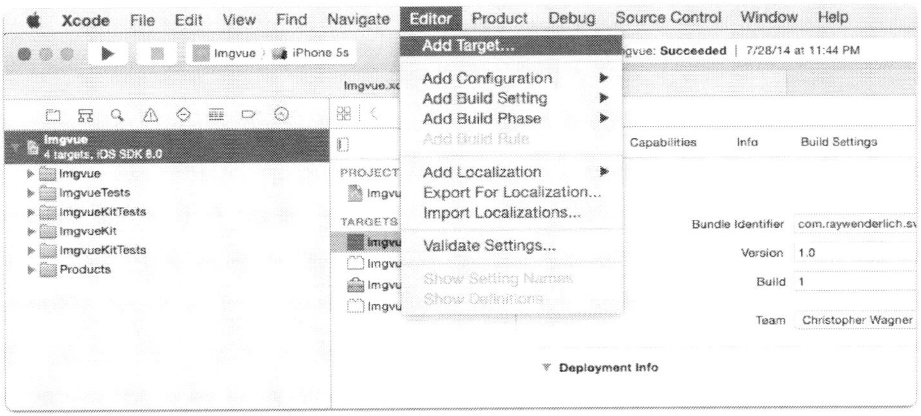

Choose **iOS\Application Extension\Share Extension** and then press **Next**.

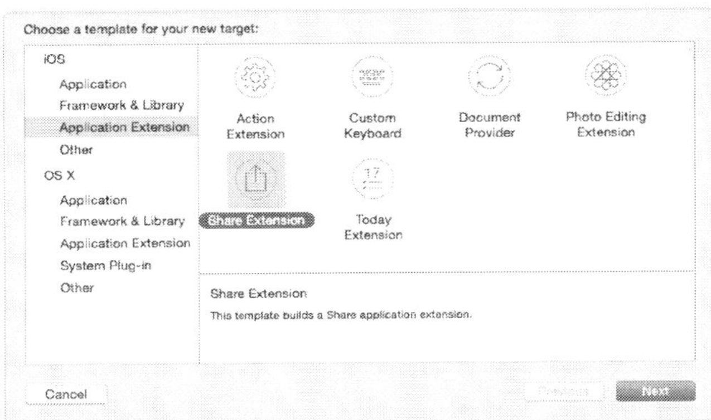

Set the **Product Name** to **Imgvue Upload**, the **Language** to **Swift**, the **Project** to **Imgvue**, and finally **Embed in Application** to **Imgvue**. Click **Finish**.

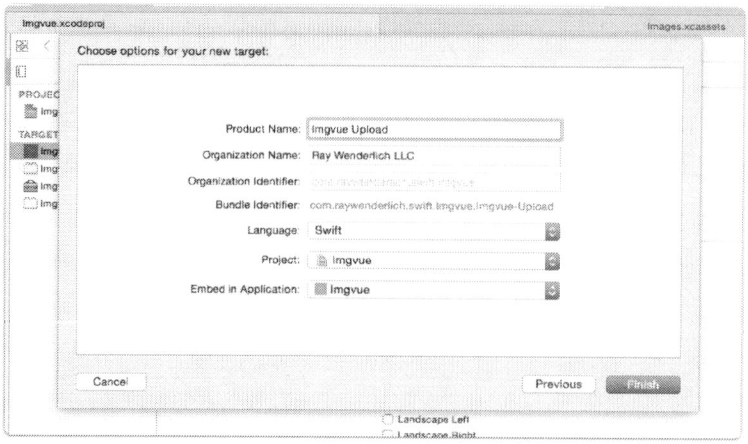

When prompted to **Activate "Imgvue Upload" scheme**, choose **Activate** so that you can select the scheme when you build and run.

You'll now have a new group in the Project Navigator named **Imgvue Upload** that contains **ShareViewController.swift**, **MainInterface.storyboard** and **Info.plist**.

Share Extensions and Action Extensions are similar in that both can utilize a JavaScript file to obtain content from the current web page in Safari.

To achieve this, you need to add the **NSExtensionJavaScriptPreprocessingFile** key to your **Info.plist** file with the value set to the name of your JavaScript file.

The JavaScript file effectively has two required methods: namely "`run`" that runs the moment your extension is invoked in order to pass data to it, and the other "`finalize`" that runs after your extension completes, and receives data back from the extension, so that it can be used in Safari.

This tutorial does not utilize a JavaScript file, but you can try it for yourself in Chapter 11, **Action Extensions**, to see how to use JavaScript to make an awesomely powerful extension.

Configure your App Group

Select the **Imgvue** project in the **Project Navigator** and then select the **Imgvue Upload** target. Open the **Capabilities** tab and enable **App Groups**. Select the group you created when setting up the Imgvue project. The App Group simply allows both the extension and container app to share files.

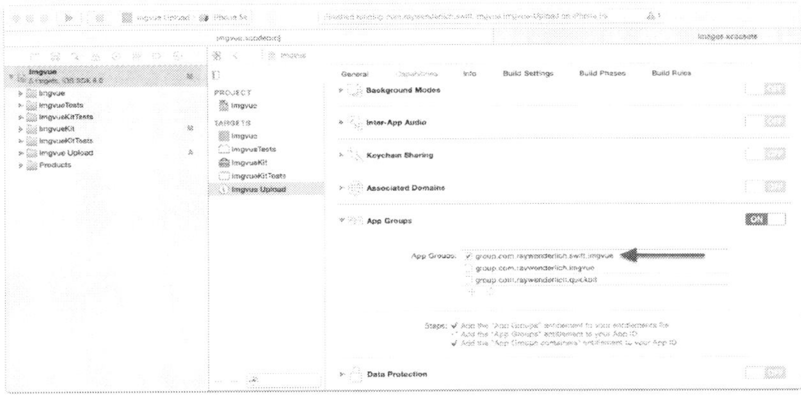

This is important because of the way files are uploaded when using the extension. Before uploading, image files are saved to the shared container. Then, they are scheduled for upload via a background task. Imgvue also saves any files the user chooses to save from Imgur in this same container.

Link ImgvueKit

You need to link the `ImgvueKit` framework to the **Imgvue Upload** target. With the Imgvue Upload target still selected:

1. Select the **General** tab
2. Under **Linked Frameworks and Libraries** click the + button
3. Select **ImgvueKit.framework** and click **Add**

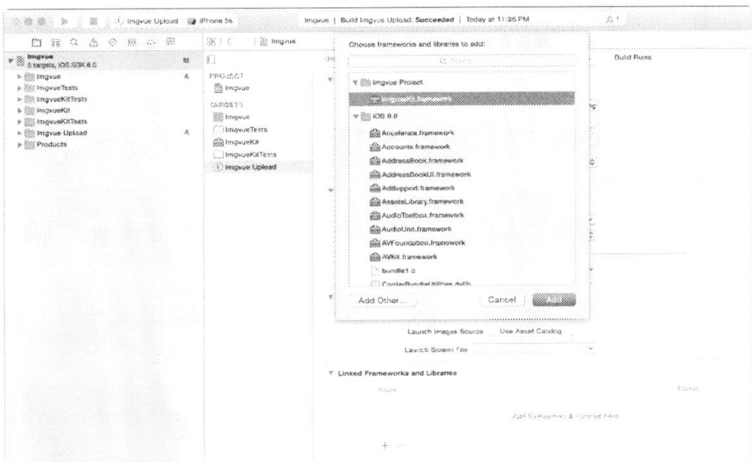

`ImgvueKit` contains some code that is shared by both the container app and the extension. The container app already has the ability to upload files, so it makes sense to re-use that API.

Configure activation rule

In the newly created **Imgvue Upload** group open the **Info.plist** file and locate the `NSExtension` key, twist open the dictionary and you will `NSExtensionActivationRule`. This key tells the system when to show your Share extension as a valid option for the user to choose from. By default the template sets the value of this key as a String of `TRUEPREDICATE`. This means that your extension will always be available. While convenient for development, this would result in a poor user experience if your extension claimed it could handle a situation that it indeed can't.

> **Note:** You must set the activation rule to something explicit before submitting your app to the App Store. If it is set to `TRUEPREDICATE` Apple will reject your app.

The Imgvue app is only capable of uploading a single image, so we need to let the system know. Change the type of `NSExtensionActivationRule` from `String` to `Dictionary`.

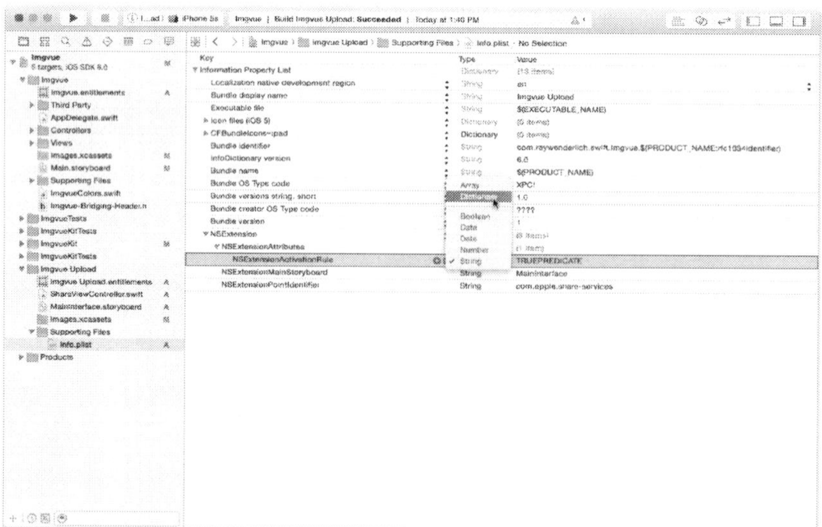

Now add a new key/value pair by pressing the small + button next to `NSExtensionActivationRule`. For the newly added row, set the key name to `NSExtensionActivationSupportsImageWithMaxCount`, the type to Number and value to 1.

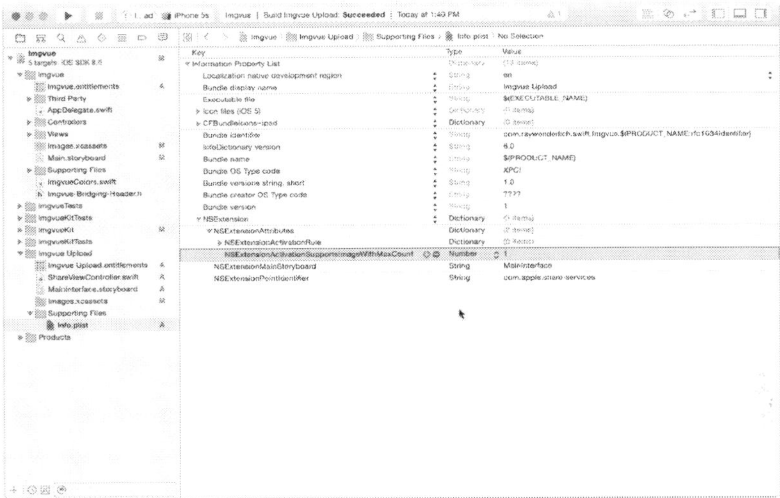

Now your extension is configured to only be available when the user is attempting to share a single image.

Interface

When creating a Share Extension, you have the option to use a custom interface.

Alternatively, you can opt for a standard, system-supplied compose view. Typically, this view is sufficient. The most important thing about the user interface of your Share Extensions is that it should be both simple and uncomplicated.

This tutorial relies on the system-supplied compose view, specifically `SLComposeServiceViewController`. This may look familiar if you've ever shared anything to Facebook or Twitter in iOS 7.

Extension implementation

By default, the Xcode template configures the extension target to use the standard compose view. Open **ShareViewController.swift**; you'll notice that it's a subclass of `SLComposeServiceViewController` as mentioned. The controller contains just three methods.

1. `isContentValid`: In this method, you should inspect the `extensionContext` property to validate any attachments and the value of `contentText`. As with any user-input it is important to validate the user has not done something wrong before allowing them to proceed. If the content is valid, return `true`. Otherwise, return `false`. The **Post** button remains disabled until `true` is returned. This method is called each time user-input changes in the compose view, so that you have a chance to update the return value accordingly.
2. `didSelectPost`: Called after the user taps the **Post** button. Here, you're responsible for actually uploading the content to be shared, which includes `contentText` and any appropriate attachments in `extensionContext`. Once you've scheduled your upload, you must then inform the host app that you're done by calling `completeRequestReturningItems(_:, completionHandler:)` on `extensionContext`. The first parameter is an array of `NSExtensionItem` objects. When the request completes, it calls the completion handler. It's passed an `expired` Boolean value to indicate if the system is terminating any previous invocations of the completion handler earlier than expected.

3. `configurationItems`: The standard compose view allows you to configure what appears at the bottom of the view, using table view cells. You must initialize and return an array of `SLComposeSheetConfigurationItem` objects if you have configurations for the user to set. Return an empty array if this does not apply to you. A configuration item is a strict model that is used behind the scenes to generate table view cells. Typically these are used to allow the user to control aspects of the share action, such as which account they want to share from.

The extension context referenced in the steps above is a new property on `UIViewController`. It represents the context of the host app when the app extension was invoked. Typically its `inputItems` property is the most interesting component and contains attachments that your extension is likely interested in.

Now that you're familiar with these three methods of `SLComposeServiceViewController`, it's time to implement the rest of this view controller.

Open **ShareViewController.swift**. Import `ImgvueKit` and `MobileCoreServices` by adding the following at the top of the file:

```
import ImgvueKit
import MobileCoreServices
```

Inside the class definition, add an optional `UIImage` instance variable named `imageToShare`:

```
var imageToShare: UIImage?
```

This will eventually hold the `UIImage` that will be shared, and will be set in `viewDidLoad()`.

Override `viewDidLoad()` by adding the following to `ShareViewController`:

```
override func viewDidLoad() {
  // 1
  let items = extensionContext?.inputItems
  var itemProvider: NSItemProvider?

  // 2
  if items != nil && items!.isEmpty == false {
    let item = items![0] as NSExtensionItem
    if let attachments = item.attachments {
      if !attachments.isEmpty {
        // 3
        itemProvider = attachments[0] as? NSItemProvider
```

```
      }
    }
  }

  // 4
  let imageType = kUTTypeImage as NSString as String
  if itemProvider?.hasItemConformingToTypeIdentifier(imageType)
== true
  {
    // 5
    itemProvider?.loadItemForTypeIdentifier(imageType,
      options: nil)
      { item, error in
        if error == nil {
          // 6
          let url = item as NSURL
          if let imageData = NSData(contentsOfURL: url) {
            self.imageToShare = UIImage(data: imageData)
          }
        } else {
          // 7
          let title = "Unable to load image"
          let message = "Please try again or choose a different
image."

          let alert = UIAlertController(title: title,
            message: message,
            preferredStyle: .Alert)

          let action = UIAlertAction(title: "Bummer",
            style: .Cancel)
            { _ in
              self.dismissViewControllerAnimated(true,
                completion: nil)
          }

          alert.addAction(action)
          self.presentViewController(alert, animated: true,
            completion: nil)
        }
    }
  }
}
```

When the user chooses to share an image via your extension, an instance is created. The image is bundled with some other metadata described below, which is then passed to your extension via the `extensionContext` object.

Your first job is to extract that information. There's a lot going on here, so take it step-by-step:

1. Capture the `inputItems` from `extensionContext` into the `items` local constant, and create a local variable for `itemProvider`. An `NSItemProvider` is a class that represents an arbitrary object that will be shared, in this case the image to be shared.
2. Determine if `items` is empty. If not, dive deeper and determine if its `attachments` property is empty.
3. Set `itemProvider` to reference the first attachment. Since your extension only supports uploading a single image, you can assume this is the only attachment.
4. Capture the `kUTTypeImage` string definition into a local constant and then use that to ask the `itemProvider`, the attachment, if it has an item that conforming to that type.

> **Note**: `kUTTypeImage` is a system-defined string constant for core uniform type identifiers. These types are defined in the `MobileCoreServices` framework you imported earlier. When working with extensions, these string constants are used to identify the attachment types.

5. You've found an image, but it's wrapped in the `NSItemProvider` class. So, load it asynchronously using `loadItemForTypeIndentifier(_:, options:, completionHandler:)`.
6. If there was no error passed to the completion handler, use the returned `item` parameter. Images, when extracted from an `NSItemProvider`, are saved to the disk. You'll be passed an instance of `NSURL` pointing to the location of where the image was saved; load the `UIImage` from that location into the `imageToShare` instance variable.
7. If there was an error, alert the user that they will need to try again, or use a different image. If this occurs it is likely that something catastrophic has occurred and there are no real recovery options other than the user trying again.
8. Use the new `UIAlertController` class to present the alert to the user.

When an issue occurs, and with the user alerted, it would be best to also disable the **Post** button, since the upload will fail if there is no image to upload.

To disable the **Post** button replace the existing `isContentValid()` implementation with the following:

```
override func isContentValid() -> Bool {
  if imageToShare == nil {
    return false
  }
  return true
}
```

This simply checks if `imageToShare` is `nil`. If it is, return `false` to disable the **Post** button. Otherwise, return `true`.

Build and run. Do a little test by completing the following:

1. Select the **Imgvue Upload** scheme and run the app
2. You'll see the **Choose an app to run:** prompt. If you're running on a device, choose **Photos**.
3. The **Photos** app will launch, select a picture
4. Tap the **Action** button.
5. In the top row of icons, swipe right to find the **Imgvue Upload** button. You will notice that it does not yet have an icon, rest assured you will fix this soon!
6. Finally, tap the **Imgvue Upload** button. A familiar share sheet will appear:

Splendid, absolutely splendid! You're over halfway there and soon will be sharing photos without qualm – or madly switching between apps.

Now, it's time to actually upload the image being shared. Add the following to `ShareViewController`:

```
func shareImage() {
  // 1
  let defaultSession = ImgurService.sharedService.session
  let defaultConfig = defaultSession.configuration
  let defaultHeaders = defaultConfig.HTTPAdditionalHeaders

  // 2
  let sessionId = "com.raywenderlich.imgvue.backgroundsession"
  let config =
NSURLSessionConfiguration.backgroundSessionConfigurationWithIden
tifier(sessionId)

  config.sharedContainerIdentifier =
  "group.com.raywenderlich.swift.imgvue"

  config.HTTPAdditionalHeaders = defaultHeaders

  // 3
  let backgroundSession = NSURLSession(configuration: config,
    delegate: ImgurService.sharedService,
    delegateQueue: NSOperationQueue.mainQueue())

  // 4
  let completion: (ImgurImage?, NSError?) -> () =
  { image, error in
    if error == nil {
      if let imageLink = image?.link {
        UIPasteboard.generalPasteboard().URL = imageLink
        NSLog("Image shared: %@", imageLink.absoluteString!)
      }
    } else {
      NSLog("Error sharing image: %@", error!)
    }

  }

  // 5
  let progressCallback: (Float) -> () = { progress in
    println("Upload progress for extension: \(progress)")
  }

  // 6
```

```
  let title = contentText
  ImgurService.sharedService.uploadImage(imageToShare!,
    title: title,
    session: backgroundSession,
    completion:completion,
    progressCallback:progressCallback)

  // 7
  self.extensionContext?.completeRequestReturningItems([], nil)
}
```

There are a few things happening here, so again take this in step-by-step.

1. Obtain the headers from the session that `ImgurService`'s singleton provides, as you'll need these later. These headers are already populated with the necessary authorization information required by the imgur.com API.
2. Create an `NSURLSessionConfiguration` for background sessions. Use the headers obtained in step 1. A background session is required so that your extension can terminate immediately after the user taps **Post**. The system will process your upload in the background.
3. Create a new `NSURLSession` using the background session configuration you just created.
4. Create the completion block to be passed to `uploadImage(_:, title:, session:, completion:, progressCallback:)`. This completion block is passed an `ImgurImage` model class instance, or an error. The `ImgurImage` model contains the URL for the successfully uploaded image. Copy that URL to the clipboard so that the user can access it. Otherwise, log the error.
5. Create a progress block to log progress of the upload. This is useful for your own debugging purposes; you won't display an upload progress indicator to the user because your interface is immediately dismissed after the user taps Post.
6. Upload the image using `ImgurService`. This method is asynchronous and will return immediately. Your completion and progress blocks will be called when the upload completes or fails, and when the upload progress changes, respectively.
7. Notify the host app that your extension has completed doing what it needs to do by calling `completeRequestReturningItems(_, completionHandler:)`. The host app then dismisses your extensions interface. Your extension may terminate at this point, but the network request it dispatched will continue to run in the background.

> You may have noticed the reference to `config.sharedContainerIdentifier` in the code above. **You must** change the value from `group.com.raywenderlich.swift.imgvue` to the value you used when setting up your shared App Group name. **Note:** At the time of writing, there is currently no clear way to inform the user that the operation completed once your extension terminates. This may or may not change with future versions of iOS or the iOS SDK. Feel free to file a Radar with Apple – many on the RayWenderlich.com team already have!

As this is such a disconnected process, it would be nice to inform the user what happens when the operation finishes. To achieve just that, replace the existing `configurationItems()`in `ShareViewController` with the following:

```
override func configurationItems() -> [AnyObject]! {
  let configItem = SLComposeSheetConfigurationItem()
  configItem.title = "URL will be copied to clipboard"
  return [configItem]
}
```

Generally, you use configuration items to display a small menu of choices, such as a list of recipients to share the photo with. However, you can also use them to display a small line of text. Create a configuration instance that has a title, letting the user know that the URL of the shared image will be copied to the device's clipboard.

Finally, replace the existing `didSelectPost()` with the one below:

```
override func didSelectPost() {
 shareImage()
}
```

That's a simple one! You've already done all of the work; just call `shareImage()`.

Now build and run, making sure the **Imgvue Upload** scheme is selected. Follow the same steps you did previously to test the app. When prompted to choose an app to run, choose Photos.

Once Photos is open, select any photo and tap the **Action** button. With your extension now available, tap its icon, or lack thereof ;]

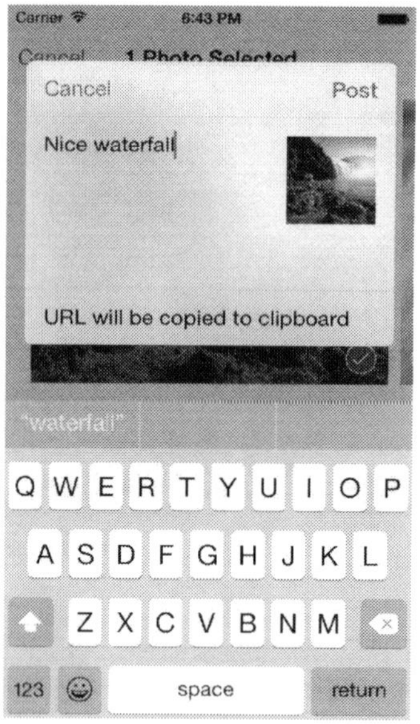

The standard share composer sheet will display with the image, a text area, and your recently added configuration item at the bottom.

Enter some text and tap **Post** and watch the Xcode console.

```
Upload progress for extension: 0.0178081151098013
Upload progress for extension: 0.0356162302196026
Upload progress for extension: 0.0534243434667587
... [Log output trimmed for breavity]
Upload progress for extension: 0.961638212203979
Upload progress for extension: 0.979446351528168
Upload progress for extension: 0.997254431247711
Upload progress for extension: 1.0
2014-08-02 18:49:30.245 Imgvue Upload[6167:390369] Image shared:
http://i.imgur.com/MwOk1BB.jpg
```

You'll see the upload progress, and eventually the URL for your image. The URL will also be copied to your clipboard. Go to Safari and paste the URL into the address bar to view it.

Success! You can now upload images directly to imgur.com from within Photos.

Share Extension Icon

As was pointed out, your extension has the default icon. While it works fine, it's certainly not pretty. Fix that now by doing the following:

1. Select the **Imgvue Upload** target
2. Click **Use Asset Catalog** for **App Icons Source**, found in the **App Icons and Launch Images** section

3. In the dialog that's presented, choose **New Asset Catalog** and uncheck **Also migrate launch images**. Extensions after-all don't have launch screens!
4. Click **Migrate**

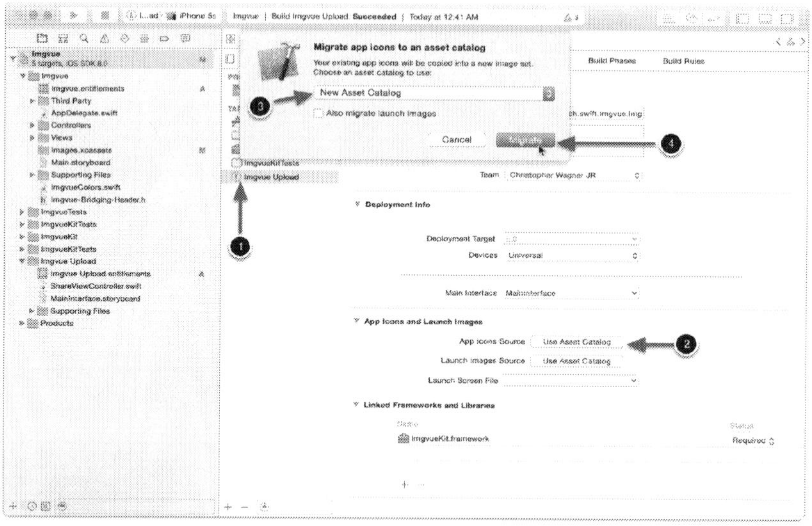

Xcode is a bit misleading here, the action is **Migrate** but nothing actually gets migrated; perhaps this is an Xcode bug. In any case you'll end up with a broken and empty **AppIcon** image set, delete it. Then, click the + and choose **New App Icon** from within the new asset catalog.

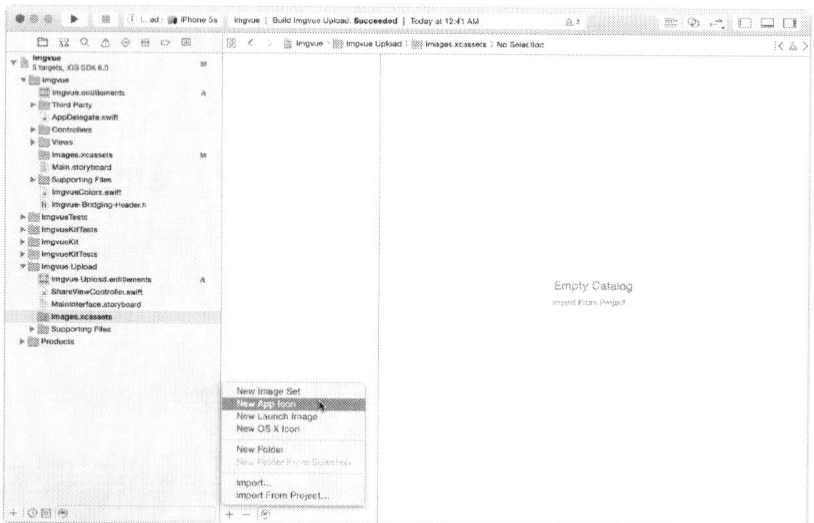

Poach the app icons from the Imguve target's Asset Catalog. Right click on anyone of the icons and click **Show in Finder**. Now drag each one from Finder into their appropriate place.

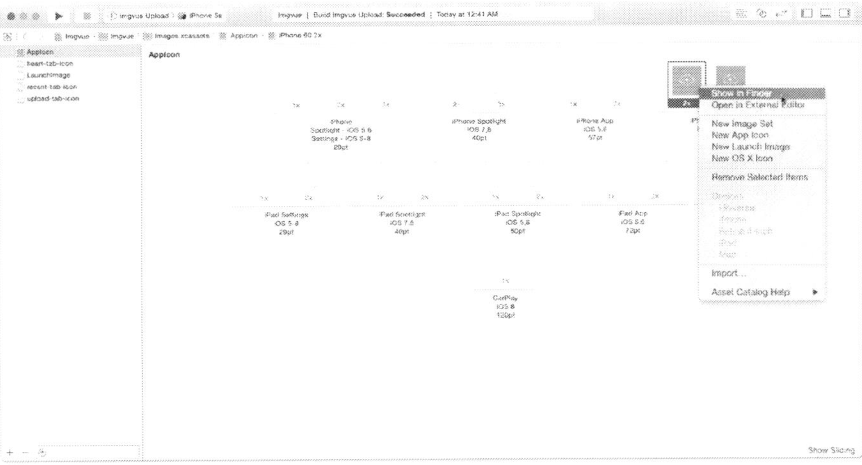

Here is a cheat sheet so that you know which goes where.

- **app-icon-120@2x** - iPhone App iOS 7,8 -- 2x
- **app-icon-120@3x** – iPhone App iOS 7,8 -- 3x
- **app-icon-152** – iPad App iOS 7,8 -- 1x
- **app-icon-152@2x** – iPad App iOS 7,8 -- 2x

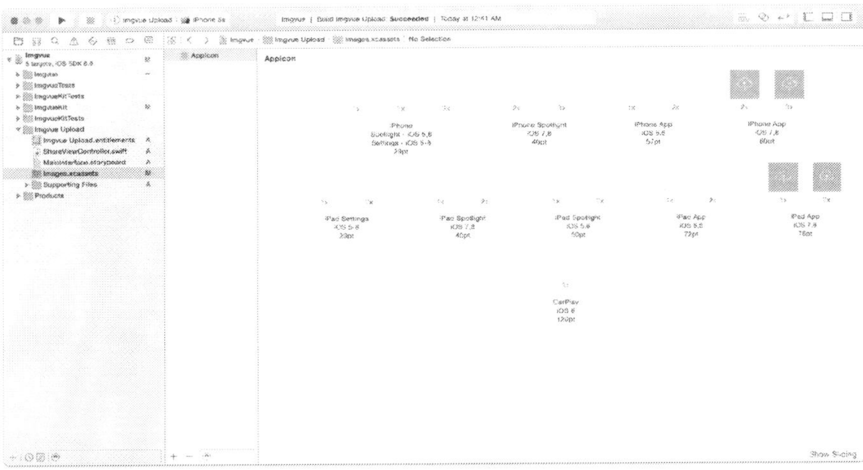

Build and run. You'll now see your icon in place:

Much better! Now your imgur.com extension is all set, and ready to ship :]

Diving deeper

This tutorial offered a look into how Share extensions work. But there are many ways to make your Share extension more interesting and relevant to your user base.

Configuration items

In this tutorial you used a configuration item to give the user some information as to what will happen when the upload finishes. You told the user that the resulting URL would be copied to their clipboard. This worked well but there are far more interesting things that you can do with configuration items. If you are using the standard composer you should consider providing your user with extra options that make sense.

Consider if the Imgvue app also allowed the user to Tweet the link to the picture after it is uploaded. A configuration option in the extension that allows the user to enable or disable the Tweet feature would make perfect sense. Facebook uses configuration items to let the user adjust the audience that can see their post. `SLComposeSheetConfigurationItem` has a `tapHandler` property that takes a block allowing you to perform your own routine when it is tapped. In the example above you could have the block work as a toggle that enables and disables the Tweet feature. Just remember to keep the process simple and quick for your users.

Sharing other things

The tutorial covered how to upload images from within the Photos and Camera apps. For this app a user might also be interested in uploading an image from a website to Imgur. This is actually a feature on imgur.com, you can paste in the URL of any image on the web and they will re-host it.

To adjust what your extension accepts you can modify the `NSExtensionActivationRule` dictionary in the **Info.plist** file for your extension. To accept a URL you would add the `NSExtensionActivationSupportsWebURLWithMaxCount` key with a value of 1. Your extension could then check for an image or a URL and handle them accordingly.

You can even provide complex predicate strings that the system compiles to be evaluated in order to handle other file types such as PDF. Look to Apple's App Extension Programming Guide under the "Handling Common Scenarios" section.

Where to go from here?

You've only scratched the surface with this tutorial. Share Extensions will undoubtedly change the way you use iOS, breaking you free from the shackles of the old and convoluted ways of sharing. You'll no longer have to switch between apps to share content from one service to another. Imagine all the extra time you'll have to share even more of your favorite stuff!

If you currently have an app that allows users to share content to a web service, you should strongly consider adding a Share Extension. The faster users can share their content to your service, the better; and the more they're likely to share. When it's this easy, they'll ultimately do it more often and that will undoubtedly help drive engagement.

Once people discover how easy it is to share a photo of their dinner to social sharing site, your app could be the next billion-dollar acquisition! Okay, okay, that's a lofty goal, but even if it doesn't make it that far, you know that your users will appreciate your Share Extensions, if you build them.

I'll look forward to seeing your cat and dinner pictures on imgur.com in the meantime :]

Chapter 11: Action Extensions

By Chris Wagner

Action Extensions could very well pan out to be the most exciting of all the new Extension types. While on the surface they appear fairly basic, these extensions offer great utility to some of Apple's stock apps, your apps, and third party apps. It's quite possible that by WWDC 2015, you won't remember iOS before Action Extensions; much like cut, copy and paste.

If you recall from Chapter 8, **Introducing Extensions**, Action Extensions allow users to view or transform content from within the context of the host app. Your app's Action Extension can take data passed from another app and allow the user to interact with that data without leaving the host app.

On stage at WWDC, Apple demoed an Action Extension that translated the contents of a web page from one language to another without ever leaving Safari. *Mind. Blown.*

The lines between the extension types are blurry at best, and none more so than with Action Extensions. Apple expresses that you must carefully choose the most appropriate extension point for the functionality you wish to provide. They specifically highlight using Action Extensions to share content to social networking sites or other similar services as a misuse. You could achieve the same result with both Share and Action extensions, but for this example you should opt to use the Share Extension.

There is a similar blurring of lines between Action Extensions and Photo Editing Extensions. You may have an Action Extension that allows the user to perform quick photo editing operations, like applying a watermark. These are likely safe to publish on the App Store.

It's also important to note that Photo Editing Extensions are limited to the Photos app. Therefore, you may be able to justify an Action Extension for other apps to use when editing photos.

Don't take my word for it though, because I'm just doing my best to interpret what seems to be subjective App Store guidelines and policies – at least at the time of this writing. With time, I'm sure there'll be more clarity.

But for now, don't concern yourself with these subtle nuances, because it's time to add a new feature to Mobile Safari!

Quick Bit

In this chapter, you'll extend an app that allows users to create bitly.com links quickly. If you're not familiar with the service, bitly.com allows you to take any URL and compact it into a much shorter one, such as bit.ly/1wOl2zf.

The result is a shorter URL that consumes fewer characters; you can also use a vanity URL to customize exactly how your Bitly looks.

If you need to put URLs in print, it makes sense to use shortened versions that are easier for the readers to manually type into a browser. When sharing a URL on social media, often with a limited character count, you don't want to waste any more than necessary on the URL itself.

Bitly.com also has the added benefit of analytics. When you share a link you can easily analyze it's analytics by appending a + to the end of the URL, such as bit.ly/1wOl2zf+.

Meet the project app, Quick Bit.

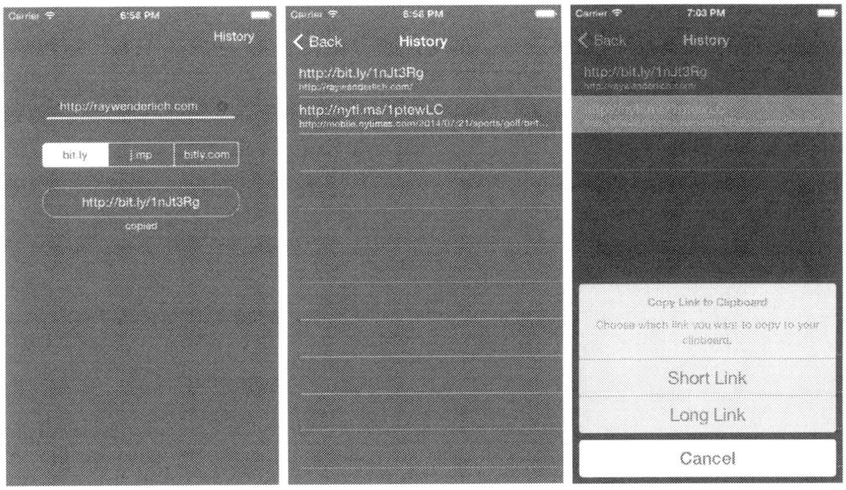

The app provides a choice of domains for use when creating shortened links, and it lets you copy the newly created short link or the original long link to the clipboard. It also detects links on the user's clipboard when the app is launched, offering to shorten them. Finally, it keeps each shortened link in a handy history log for quick reference and access.

Register for Bitly.com account

Before running the app and developing the extension, you'll need an access token for your Bitly.com account so your app can use its services. Follow the steps below to obtain an access token. Keep in mind that websites change – *frequently* – so it may look different than how it does in the following screenshots. Refer to Bitly's documentation as needed to complete this step.

1. Register for an account at https://bitly.com/a/sign_up
2. Verify your email by visiting https://bitly.com/a/settings and clicking the **Click here** link underneath the email address.

3. Check your email and click the provided link. Note that Gmail has a habit of marking this type of email message as spam, so be sure to check you **Spam** folders.
4. Once signed in, visit https://bitly.com/a/oauth_apps
5. Click **Register an application** at the top of the page.

6. Click **Get Registration Code**.

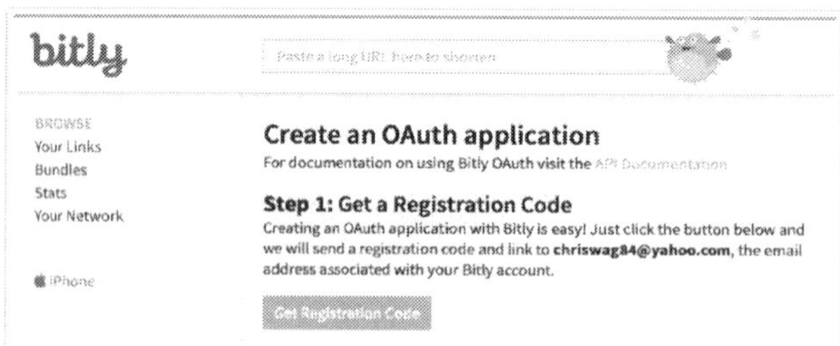

7. Check your email and click on the provided link. Again, be sure to check your **Spam** folders.

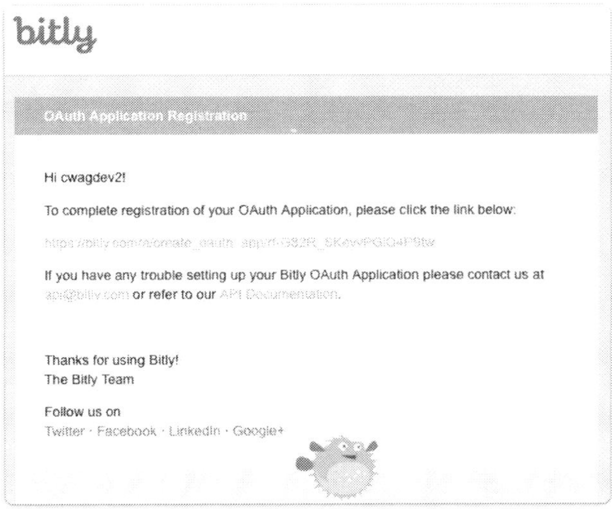

8. Fill out the form as follows: set **Application Name** to **Quick Bit**, **Application Link** to http://raywenderlich.com and **Redirect URIs** to http://raywenderlich.com/auth, and simply enter "**Quick Bit sample app**" for the **Description**. Click **Create Your App**.

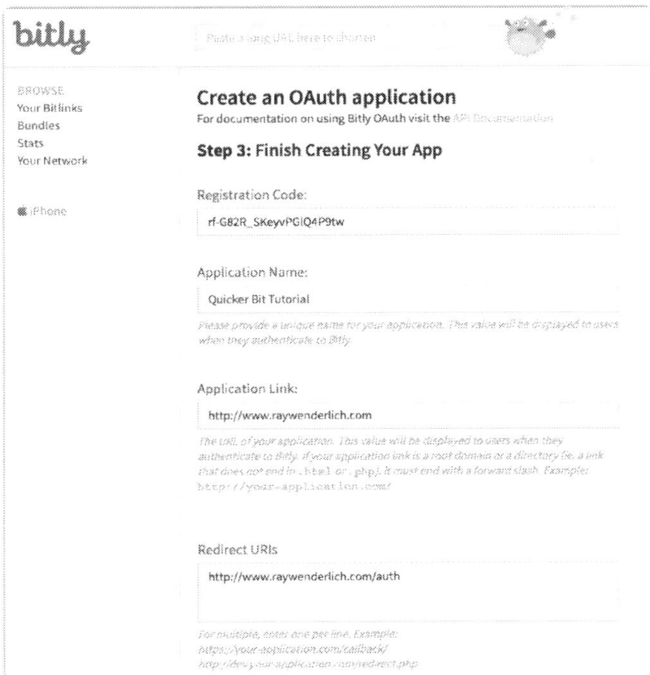

> **Note:** If you come across an error stating "*Application name unavailable*" simply enter another name for the application. It doesn't really matter for the purposes of this chapter, but in the real world you'd want to enter a name that's associated with your app, since it's displayed to any user wanting to authorize your app to use their Bitly account.

9. Enter your password into the **Confirm password** box and click **Generate Token**.

> **Note:** If you haven't verified your account via email, you must do so before you can generate an access token.

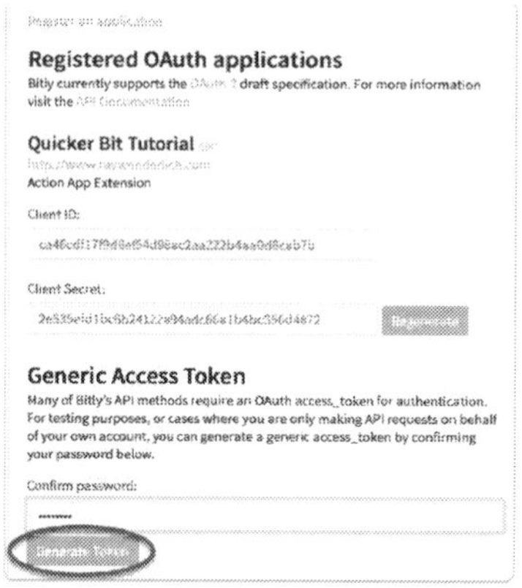

10. Take note of the generated access token.

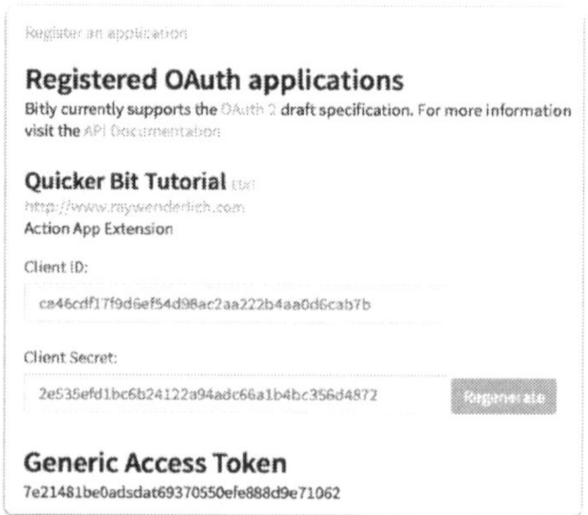

> **Note:** Generating an access token in this manner is suitable for testing purposes. However, if you were to ship an app like Quick Bit you'd need implement the OAuth flow, rather than hard coding your own, so that users can log in to their own account and use their own access tokens.

Now that you have your access token, open the **Quick Bit** project in **Xcode**, and then open **ViewController.swift** from the **Project Navigator**. In the `init(coder:)` method, replace the string `"YOUR_ACCESS_TOKEN"` with the access token you copied from Bitly.

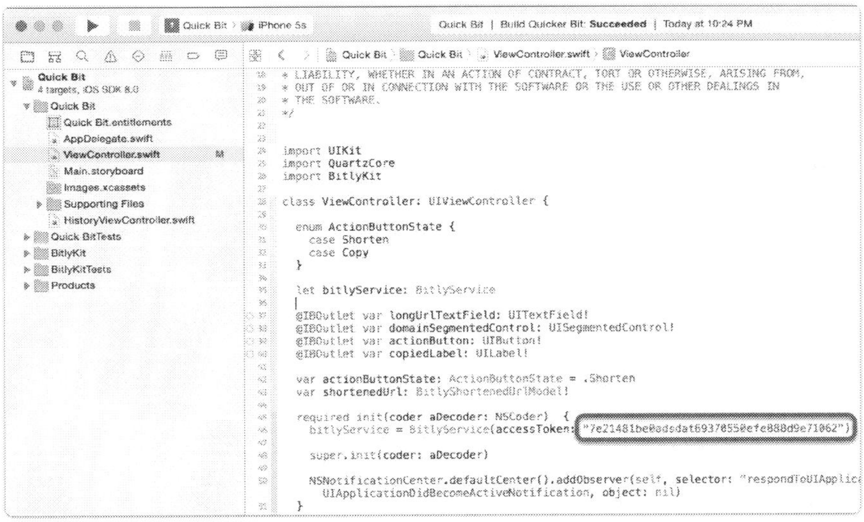

Configure the App Group

As mentioned, the Quick Bit app keeps a history of shortened URLs. Wouldn't it be great if URLs shortened with the Action Extension were also logged to the same history? In order for a container app and its' extensions to share data, you must use App Groups.

An App Group is used to define access to a shared container, which is simply a directory that both the container app and its extensions can access.

Select the **Quick Bit** project in the **Project Navigator**, and then select the **Quick Bit** target. First, you're going to edit the app's **Bundle Identifier** so it's unique to you. Reverse DNS is generally the best way to go. So swap out `raywenderlich` with your own domain.

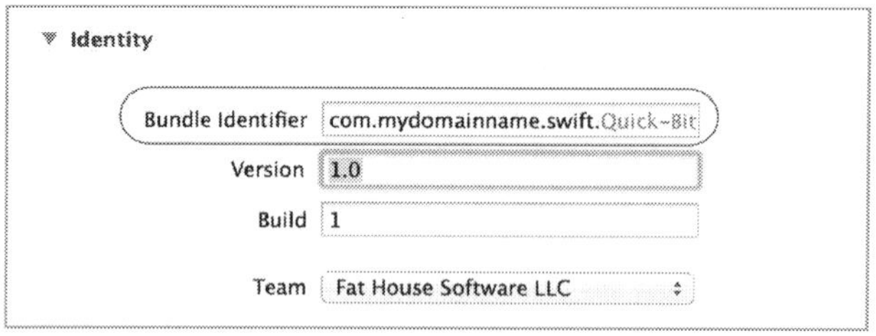

Now, still in the **Quick Bit** target, select the **Capabilities** tab, and click the **App Groups** switch to turn them **On**.

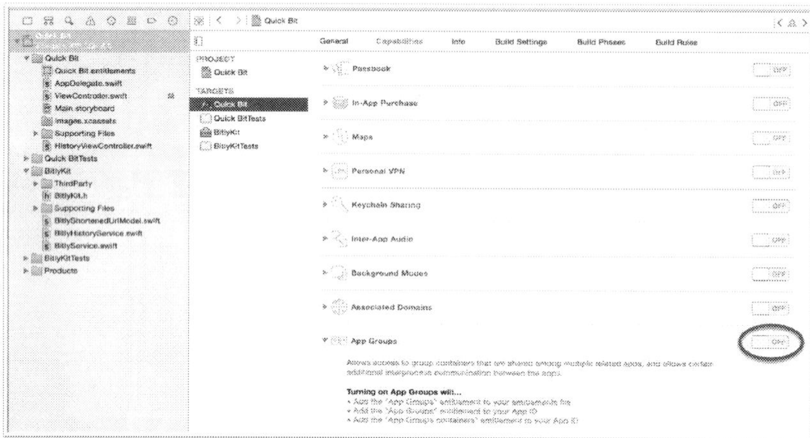

> **Note:** If you are a member of more than one development team, you'll likely see a modal dialog appear asking you to select a team. Choose the one that's most appropriate for you (likely your personal account) and click **Choose** to continue.

Depending on your developer account, you may see existing app groups appear in the list of options. In any case, you'll be creating a new group. Press the + button to add a new group, and give it a unique name. App Group identifiers should start with **group**, use reverse DNS style naming, and should probably include the name of the app family that you're grouping. Something like: `group.com.raywenderlich.swift.quickbit`.

But be careful, App Group identifiers must be unique! So don't use the one above; substitute your own domain for `raywenderlich`.

You'll need to update the reference to this App Group in your code. In the **Project Navigator**, expand the **BitlyKit** group and open **BitlyHistoryService.swift**. Find the `savedItemsFileUrl` method and replace the group identifier string with your own. Based on the example above, it should look something like this:

```
func savedItemsFileUrl() -> NSURL {
  let containerUrl = NSFileManager.defaultManager().
containerURLForSecurityApplicationGroupIdentifier("group.com.ray
wenderlich.swift.quickbit")

  return containerUrl.URLByAppendingPathComponent(
"RWTBitlyHistoryServiceItems.dat")
}
```

Build and run. Open **Safari** and visit a web page. Copy the URL. Open **Quick Bit**, and when you're prompted to shorten the URL, choose **Yes** and tap the **Shorten** button. Then tap the button containing the shortened URL to copy it to your clipboard. Finally, open the shortened link in Safari.

> **Note:** This shortened URL history saves when the app goes into the background. So, make sure you exit to the Home screen occasionally to save the history! If you terminate the app by stopping the debugger your history may not be persisted. In the simulator you can point to the **Hardware > Home** menu option.

Quicker bit

After playing around with Quick Bit, you probably noticed how quick it's to create a short URL. Sure it's quick, but you can make it even faster. Through an Action Extension, you'll be able to shorten the current URL in Safari using just two taps. That's it; *just two taps.* You don't have to leave Safari. Does this sound too good to be true? Well, it's not.

Add Quicker Bit target

The first order of business is to add a new target. Select the **Quick Bit** project in the **Project Navigator**. Then select **Editor\Add Target...** and choose **iOS\Application Extension\Action Extension**. Finally, click **Next**.

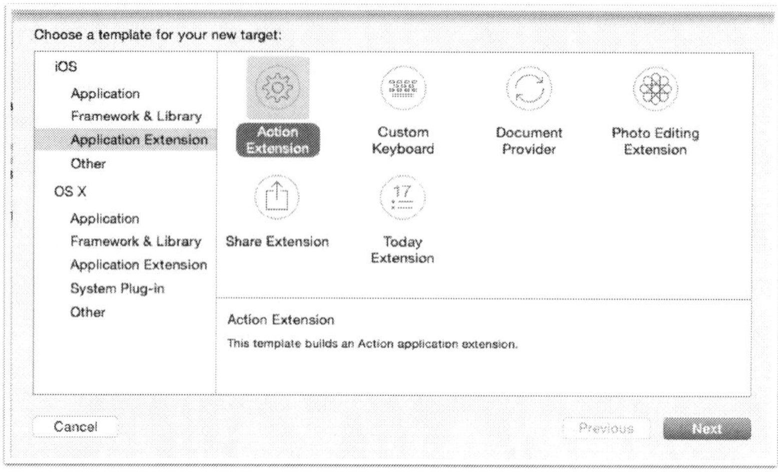

In the next screen, set **Product Name** to **Quicker Bit**, verify the **Language** is set to **Swift**, **Action Type** is set to **No User Interface**, **Project** is **Quick Bit** and **Embed in Application** is **Quick Bit**. Click **Finish**.

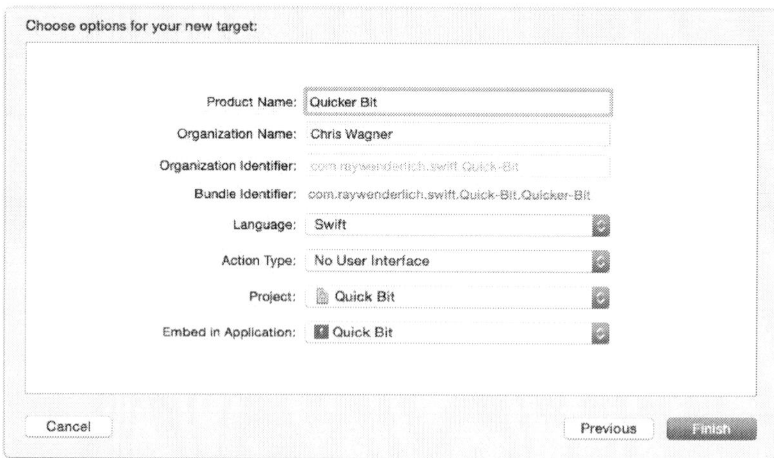

When prompted, click **Activate** to activate the new scheme.

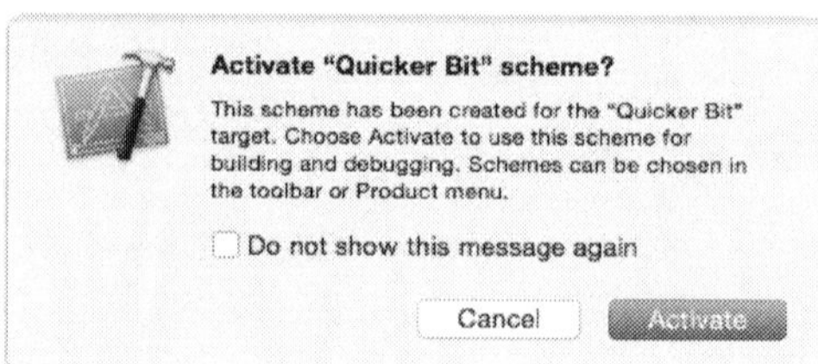

Configure App Groups

The **Quicker Bit** target should be added to your project and selected. If it's not, then select it from the list of targets, and then select the **Capabilities** tab. Just as you did for the Quick Bit target, you need to add Quicker Bit to an App Group. Click the switch next to the **App Groups** section so it changes to **On**.

This time you don't need to add a new App Group, rather you use the same one that you added earlier by simply checking the box next to it.

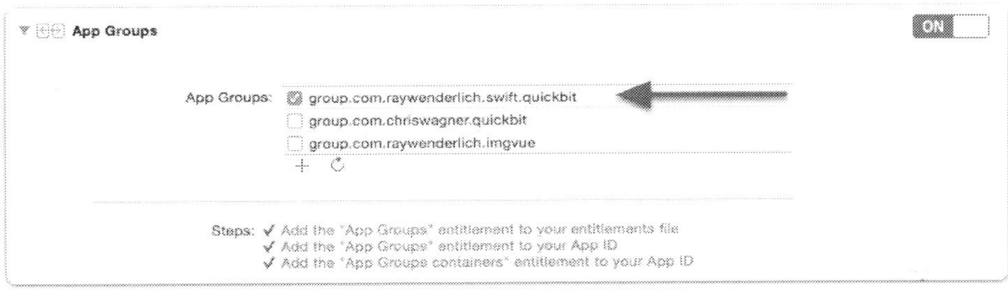

Embed custom framework

Now switch to the **General** tab and under **Linked Frameworks and Libraries**, click the + button.

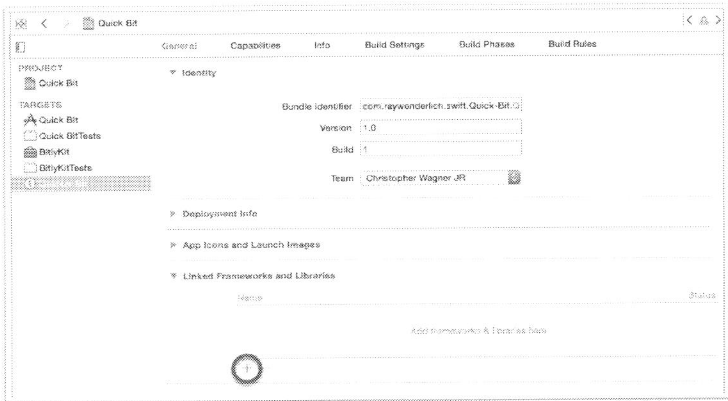

Select **BitlyKit.framework** and click **Add**.

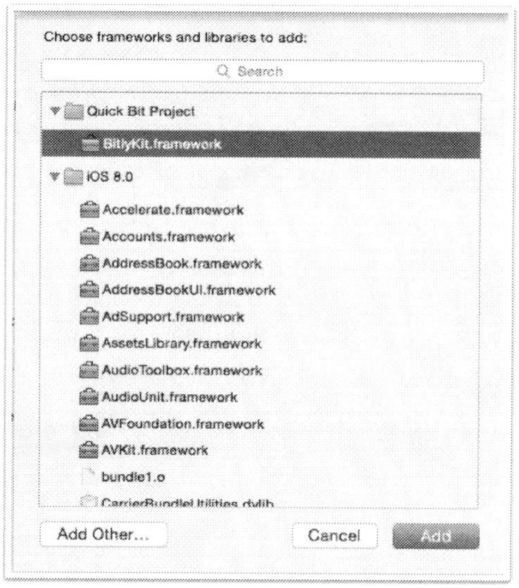

Now the **Quicker Bit** group should look like this in the **Project Navigator**:

> **Note:** You won't see the "A" status next to your files if you aren't using a Git repository.

The entitlements file is used to define the entitlements required by the target. Xcode generated this file when you set up the App Group.

ActionRequestHandler.swift is the class that's called when the action extension is invoked. **Action.js** is used to gain access to the contents of the web page that Safari is rendering. Finally, **Info.plist** configures the extension.

Wait, Safari? What about other apps? If you are building a "No User Interface" action extension you will be limited to Safari as this process is specific to it. However, if you *are* providing a user interface you can do a lot more.

The company Agile Bits has built a library that utilizes Action Extensions that allows users to access their 1Password vault from within your app. They announced on September 3, 2014 that over 100 apps support their extension, http://blog.agilebits.com/2014/09/03/1password-app-extension-developers/. Take a look at the post to see what some of the interactions look like. It is truly amazing what their team has done and this should give you an idea of how powerful Action Extensions are.

Add Action Extension icon

When an Action Extension appears in the system UI, an icon known as a template icon represents it. This differs from the container app icon in that it doesn't have any color and is specific to the action being performed.

If your app contains multiple Action Extensions, you should provide unique icons to distinguish them. There are a few rules to follow when designing icons:

1. Use black and white with the appropriate alpha transparency. The alpha channel is the only channel used when rendering the icon. An appropriate tint color is applied by the system to the values in this channel.
2. Do not include drop shadows.
3. Do use antialiasing.
4. Create your icon design and scale it appropriately for all of the devices you are supporting.
5. Use square images, just like you would with an app icon; the system will mask it to a *superellipse* for you.

For Quicker Bit, the icon is already made for you, and it resembles the container app's icon.

Select the **Quicker Bit** target and click **Use Asset Catalog** for **App Icon Sources**. Choose **New Asset Catalog**, uncheck **Also migrate launch images** and click **Migrate**.

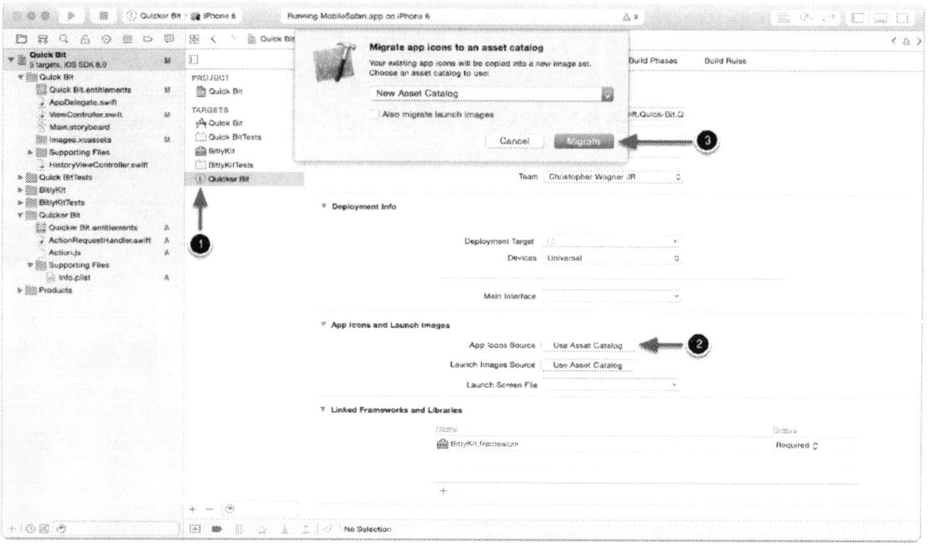

This will create a new asset catalog named Images under the Quicker Bit group, open the new asset catalog file.

As of this writing the Xcode is bugged and this process requires some strange steps. Delete the **AppIcon** set from the new catalog and add a new App Icon to it.

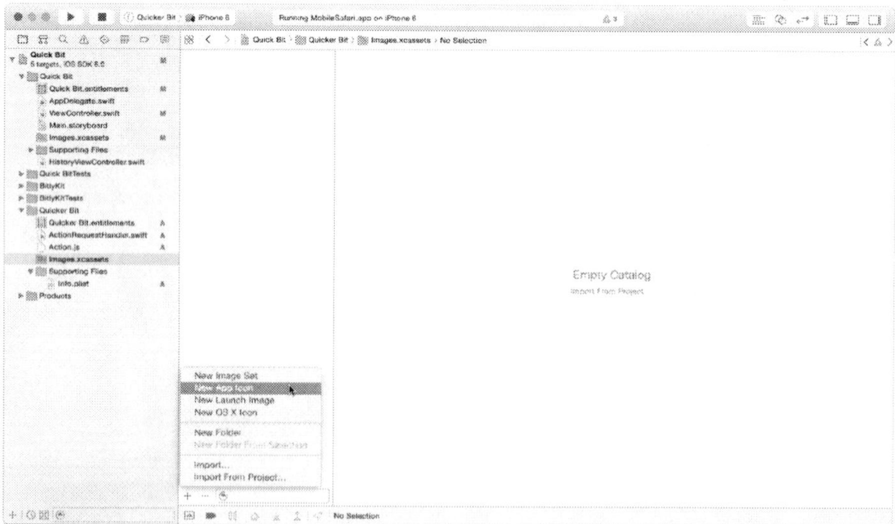

Rename the icon to **QuickerBitIcon** and then drag the respective icon files to their appropriate locations. You will find the icons in the **QuickerBit-Icons** directory bundled with the starter project for this tutorial.

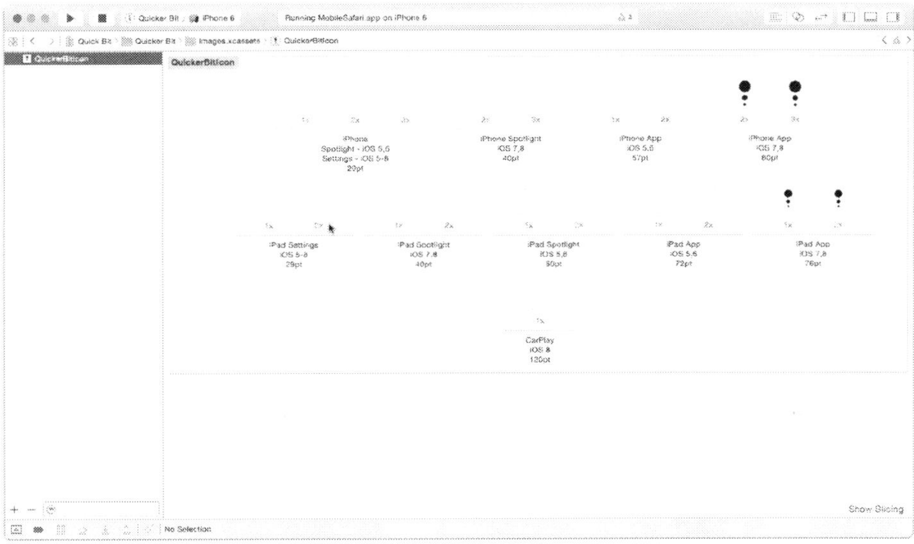

Now go back to the Quicker Bit target and select **QuickerBitIcon** as the **Apps Icon Source**.

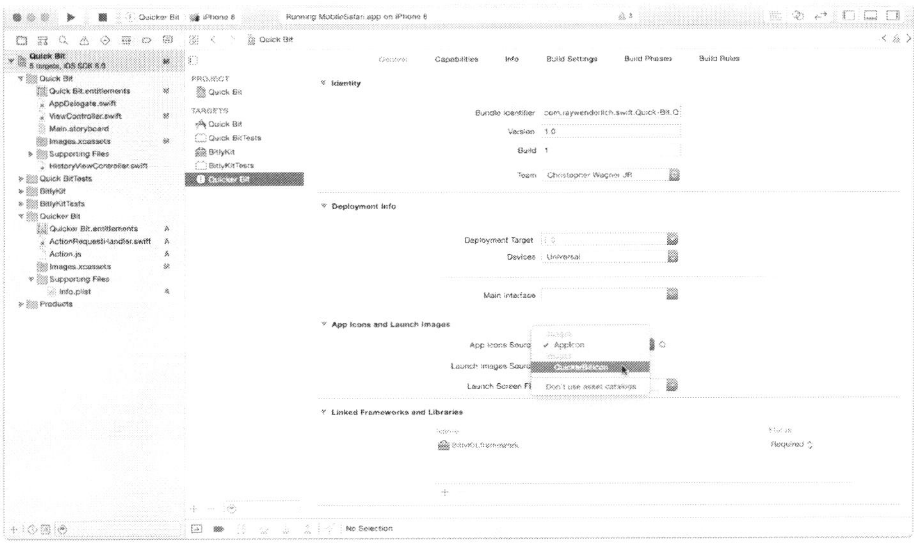

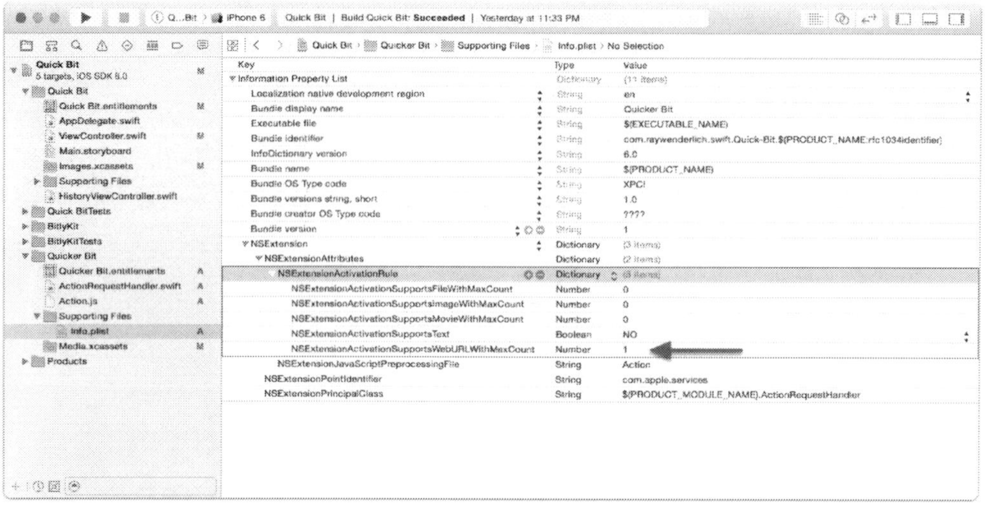

All set! The end goal here is to create a new App Icon set and configure the extensions target to use that set with your specially created template icons.

Declare supported data type

Action Extensions are selected by the system based on the type of content that the host app vends when the user taps the Share button. If the host app is vending an image but your extension works with URLs, it will not be made available to the user.

You achieve this through the **NSExtensionActivationRule** key within the **NSExtensionAttributes** dictionary in **Info.plist**. Your extension must declare what content it supports, and the number of instances of that content it can handle.

Quicker Bit only supports a single URL. Open **Info.plist** for the Quicker Bit extension and then expand the **NSExtension\NSExtensionAttributes\NSExtensionActivationRule** key. You should see a list of keys beginning with **NSExtensionActivationSupports** and their associated values.

Additionally, you should see a key named **NSExtensionActivationSupportsWebURLWithMaxCount** with a value of 1.

> **Note:** If you don't see it, add it now by pressing the + button next to **NSExtensionActivationRule**. You may also see other keys in that group. They should all be set to `0` or `NO`. The definitions in the screenshot are provided by default from Apple's Action Extension Xcode template as of this writing. Depending on how the template changes overtime you may have to manually add the rule.

This configuration tells the OS to offer your extension to the user when an app they're using attempts to share a single URL.

The Action Extension template

Now it's time for a quick tour around the Action Extension template.

When the user invokes your extension, the `run` method found in **Action.js** executes against the content of the current web page in Safari.

Wait, Action.js? JS as in JavaScript? What kind of madness is this?

Yes, you read that correctly. Action Extensions have the ability to define a JavaScript file to run against the content of the current web page in Safari. It's not madness, it's brilliance!

Open the **Action.js** file. The `run` method is responsible for returning a JSON object to a completion handler. The default implementation of the Action Extension template will change the site's background color. If there's no background color it will set it to red, if a background color exists it will set it to green. The `finalize` function here is responsible for modifying the content. You'll learn how and when it's a little later.

Now open **ActionRequestHandler.swift**. Once the `run` function in Action.js completes, the system calls your extension's `beginRequestWithExtensionContext(context:)` method. There's quite a bit to grasp. There are a number of collections being iterated over and looked into. The method receives an `NSExtensionContext` that provides details of the context in which the extension was invoked. It may include input items of the type `NSExtensionItem`, and each item can contain multiple attachments that can be any number of things; URLs, images, videos, etc.

`NSExtensionContext` and its input items, `NSExtensionItem` instances, are provided by the host app. The host app determines what is shared with the extension and that is done so by creating a context and extension items. These are immutable concrete classes that your extension can query in an expected way. Things would get messy real quick if each host app defined their own constructs that app extension developers had to adopt.

The `hasItemConformingToTypeIdentifier` API allows you to query if the attachment contains a specific type of resource. Once it determines that a specific type exists, you can access that resource via the `loadItemForTypeIdentifier` method. At this point, you can interact with the object as you normally would. It's a bit of boilerplate code, but it's good to understand what can come your way when your extension is invoked.

Next is the `itemLoadCompletedWithPreprocessingResults(javaScriptPreprocessingResults:)` method. This method encapsulates the processing logic for the `NSDictionary` passed in by the extension. The dictionary is created by the methods defined within Action.js, you're effectively speaking JSON in and out between Safari and your extension.

Once it has finished doing what it needs to, it calls out to the `doneWithResults` method, which is a method bespoke to the template and not provided by the framework. This method takes the processed results and prepares them to be sent back to the host app. Just like on the way in, `NSExtensionItem` objects are used on the way out.

The `completeRequestReturningItem` method is called to pass results back to the host app. The host app, Safari in this case, will receive the results passed in the `finalize` function defined in **Action.js**.

Implementing Quicker Bit

Now that you understand the flow, it's time to replace much of Apple's code with your own. With some modifications, you'll be shortening URLs directly in Safari in a few moments.

Start by opening **Action.js**. Update the `run` function to the following:

```
run: function(arguments) {
  arguments.completionFunction({ "currentUrl" : document.URL })
},
```

This creates a JSON object with a single property, `currentUrl`. The value of this property is set to the URL of the current web page.

Now open ActionRequestHandler.swift. Replace `beginRequestWithExtensionContext(context:)` with the following:

```
func beginRequestWithExtensionContext (context:
 NSExtensionContext) {
  self.extensionContext = context

  // 1
  let extensionItem = context.inputItems.first as?
NSExtensionItem
  if (extensionItem == nil) {
    self.doneWithResults(nil)
    return
  }

  // 2
  let itemProvider = extensionItem!.attachments?.first
    as? NSItemProvider
  if (itemProvider == nil) {
    self.doneWithResults(nil)
    return
  }

  // 3
  let propertyListType = kUTTypePropertyList as NSString as
String
  if
itemProvider!.hasItemConformingToTypeIdentifier(propertyListType
) {
    itemProvider!.loadItemForTypeIdentifier(propertyListType,
      options: nil)
      { item, error in
        let dictionary = item as NSDictionary
        NSOperationQueue.mainQueue().addOperationWithBlock {
          // 4
          var results =
dictionary[NSExtensionJavaScriptPreprocessingResultsKey]
            as NSDictionary

self.itemLoadCompletedWithPreprocessingResults(results)
        }
    }
  } else {
    self.doneWithResults(nil)
  }
}
```

Since Quicker Bit can only shorten one URL at a time, you can complete the task assuming only one will be present. Rather than iterating over `inputItems` and `attachments`, you'll grab the first object from each array.

1. Get the first object from the `inputItems` array, which can contain instances of `NSExtensionItem`. If there are no objects call `doneWithResults`, passing in `nil`.
2. Get the first object from the `attachments` array, which can contain instances of `NSItemProvider`. If there are no objects call `doneWithResults`, passing in `nil`.
3. See if the `NSItemProvider` from step two has an item conforming to the type `kUTTypePropertyList`. If so, call `loadItemForTypeIdentifier` whose completion handler receives an instance of `NSDictionary` representing the JSON object returned by the `run` JavaScript function within Action.js.
4. On the main queue create extract the `NSExtensionJavaScriptPreprocessingResultsKey` dictionary from the one loaded from step three. This key is what Safari will use, to store the JSON object from your `run` method, as a convention. It is important to do this task on the main queue as the `loadItemForTypeIdentifier` call happens asynchronously.

In the next step, you'll make use of the `BitlyKit` framework provided by the project. Add the following import to the top of `ActionRequestHandler.swift`:

```
import BitlyKit
```

Next you need to shorten the URL, place it on the user's clipboard and log it to the apps history.

> **Note:** As you might recall Quick Bit will detect a URL on the user's clipboard at launch and suggest shortening in. This could get annoying if you are asking the user if they want to shorten an already shortened URL. There are measures in place to ensure that the app does not ask to shorten URLs it knows for a fact are already shortened, but they are not perfect. This is type of situation where you need to weigh the pros and cons of the feature and decide how to proceed.

Moving right along… Replace the existing implementation of `itemLoadCompletedWithPreprocessingResults(javascriptPreprocessingResults:)` with the following:

```
func itemLoadCompletedWithPreprocessingResults
  (javaScriptPreprocessingResults: NSDictionary) {
    // 1
    let currentUrlString =
    javaScriptPreprocessingResults["currentUrl"] as? String
    if currentUrlString != nil &&
```

```
      currentUrlString!.isEmpty == false {
        // 2
        let bitlyService = BitlyService(accessToken:
"YOUR_ACCESS_TOKEN")
        let longUrlOpt: NSURL? = NSURL(string:
currentUrlString!)
        if let longUrl = longUrlOpt {
          //3
          bitlyService.shortenUrl(longUrl, domain: "bit.ly") {
            shortenedUrl, error in
            if let error = error {
              // 4
              self.doneWithResults(["error" :
error.description])
            } else {
              // 5
              if let shortUrl = shortenedUrl?.shortUrl {
                UIPasteboard.generalPasteboard().string =
shortUrl.absoluteString
                let results = ["shortUrl" :
shortUrl.absoluteString ?? ""];
                // 6
                let historyService =
BitlyHistoryService.sharedService
                historyService.addItem(shortenedUrl!)
                historyService.persistItemsArray()
                // 7
                self.doneWithResults(results)
              } else {
                self.doneWithResults(["error" : "Unable to
shorten URL."])
              }
            }
          }
        }
    }
}
```

5. Extract the `currentUrl` value from the passed in dictionary; remember this is the native representation of the JSON object returned from the `run` function in **Action.js**

6. Initialize an instance of `BitlyService`, passing your access token. Then create an `NSURL` instance using the `currentUrlString`.

7. If the URL is valid, shorten it.

8. If the request fails, call `doneWithResults` passing a dictionary containing details of the error.
9. Otherwise, add the shortened URL to the user's clipboard, and wrap it in a dictionary that can then be passed to `doneWithResults`.
10. Add the shortened URL via the `BitlyHistoryService` so that it can be later viewed from the History list. Persist the items.
11. Call `doneWithResults` and pass in the results array.

> **Note:** Make sure you substitute the access token with your own in `itemLoadCompletedWithPreprocessingResults(javascriptPreprocessingResults:)`

In the previous code block you used two classes `BitlyService` and `BitlyHistoryService`. Both of these are defined in the BitlyKit framework. `BitlyService` provides the API and mechanisms for sending requests to the bitly.com API. `BitlyHistoryService` encapsulates the logic required to persist and load shortened URLs to and from the shared container so that they can be viewed later.

Now you need to wrap the shortened URL in an instance of `NSExtensionItem` and pass it back to the host app, which will subsequently be handled by the `finalize` function in **Action.js**.

Replace the existing `doneWithResults` method in **ActionRequestHandler.swift** with the following:

```
func doneWithResults
 (resultsForJavaScriptFinalizeArg: NSDictionary?) {
  if let results = resultsForJavaScriptFinalizeArg {
    // 1
    var resultsDictionary =
[NSExtensionJavaScriptFinalizeArgumentKey: results]

    // 2
    let itemType = kUTTypePropertyList as NSString as String
    var resultsProvider = NSItemProvider(item:
resultsDictionary, typeIdentifier: itemType)

    // 3
    var resultsItem = NSExtensionItem()
    resultsItem.attachments = [resultsProvider]
```

```
    // 4
    extensionContext!.completeRequestReturningItems(
     [resultsItem], completionHandler: nil)
  } else {

      // 5
      extensionContext!.completeRequestReturningItems(nil,
       completionHandler: nil
  }

  // 6
  extensionContext = nil
}
```

12. Build a dictionary with the extension specific `NSExtensionJavaScriptFinalizeArgumentKey` key, setting its value to the dictionary passed in. The host app will look for the result using this key.

13. Create an instance of `NSItemProvider`, passing the dictionary from step 1 and the appropriate item type.

14. Create an instance of `NSExtensionItem`, and set its `attachments` property to an array containing the item provider created in step 2.

15. Notify the host app that you've completed your task via `completeRequestReturningItems`, passing the extension item from step 3.

16. If the method is passed a `nil` dictionary, inform the host app that you have no results by passing `nil` instead of an extension item.

Phew! You're all finished with native code, and that was a fair bit of work, so to recap:

- The host app triggers your Action Extension, which executes some JavaScript that extracts the URL of the current page, wraps it in a JSON object and passes it back to your app.
- Your app pulls the URL out of the supplied dictionary, and uses the `BitlyKit` framework to shorten it via the Bitly.com API.
- If the URL is successfully shorted, it's copied to the users clipboard and appended to the apps history. It's also wrapped in a dictionary and passed back to the containing app.

Now, the final step; Open **Action.js** and replace `finalize` with the following:

```
finalize: function(arguments) {
```

```
    var error = arguments["error"];
    if (error) {
      alert('There was an error creating your bit.ly link');
    } else {
      var shortUrl = arguments["shortUrl"];
      alert('Your bit.ly link is now on your clipboard\n\n' +
shortUrl);
    }
  }
```

This function checks to see if there is an error, and if so, presents a JavaScript alert informing the user. Otherwise, it displays an alert with a success message and the shortened URL string.

As you can see, you have control over what Safari does with your extensions' results via JavaScript. The options are quite possibly, limitless.

At this point, you're ready to run the app and see your Action Extension in, well, action!

Make sure the current scheme is set to **Quicker Bit**. Build and run. This will install the extension and launch **Safari**. Navigate to any page you'd like and tap the **Share** button. Action Extensions appear in the lower section with the monochrome icons, you may need to scroll to the right to see **Quicker Bit**.

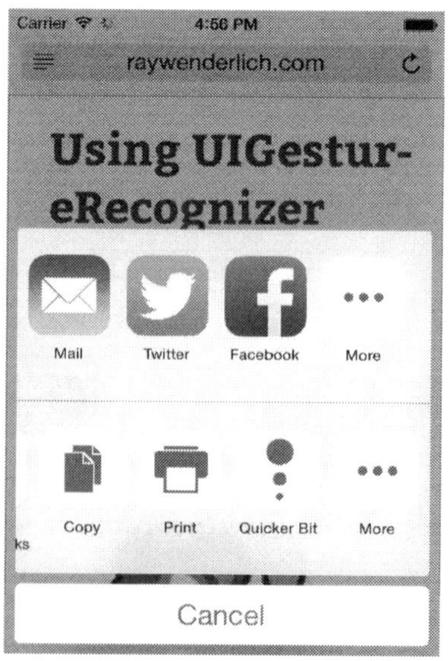

Tap **Quicker Bit**, and within a few moments you'll see a JavaScript alert; if successful the shortened URL will also have been added to your clipboard.

> **Note from the Author**: As of Xcode 6.1 and iOS 8.1 the clipboard feature does **not** work. After some investigation it appears that there is a bug with "No User Interface" Action Extensions interacting with `UIPastebaord`. This issue did not appear until sometime after Xcode 6.0 beta 5.
>
> It was however found that an Action Extension that **does** have user interface can successfully interact with `UIPasteboard`.
>
> While this feature is pivotal to the purpose of this sample app, we feel that the end goal of writing an Action Extension is still achieved. We are tracking this issue as a bug report with Apple, and will address the situation once we hear back from them.
>
> If you happen to have more information or get this working, please do let us know via the forums!

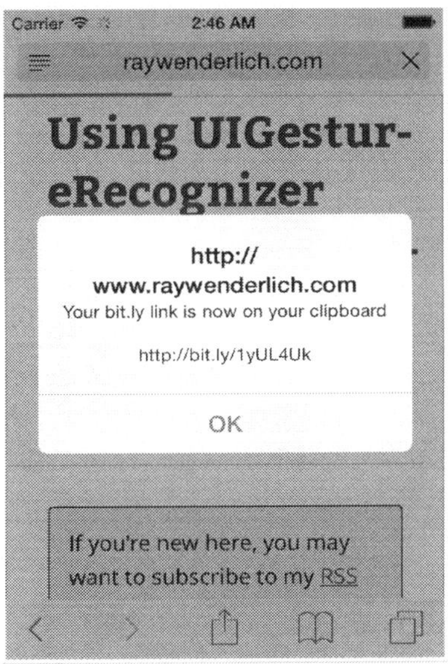

That *was* quicker, right? Feel free to do this a few times and take in just how fast and elegant this extension is.

Your next step is to dream up some Action Extensions of your own! This concludes the tutorial, great work!

What about the UI?

In this tutorial, you wrote an Action Extension with an Action Type of **No User Interface**. In the case of Quicker Bit, it was unnecessary to have a user interface and it would have only slowed down the shortening process.

Depending on what your action does, it may very well make sense to have a user interface. Just like other extension types, you can create an Action Extension that presents a view controller; this is an option when you add the extension target:

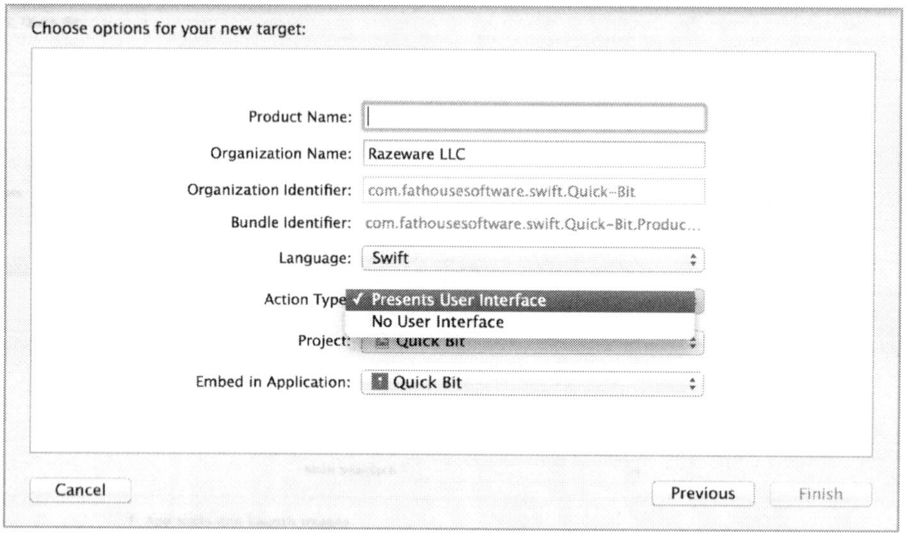

The **Presents User Interface** based Action Extensions work very similarly, except that they don't rely on JavaScript. Rather, the host app determines the `NSExtensionContext`'s input items. Your view controller based extension can tailor its display to your specific needs.

Where to go from here?

Reimagine iOS.

Action Extensions will forever change how users interact with your apps. It's now paramount that you begin to take other developers' apps into consideration when developing your own. If you know of a specific app that allows sharing of data via `UIActivitySheet`, consider how your extensions can provide further functionality to their users.

You've witnessed first hand how a simple app like Quick Bit can literally add new features to a stock app. When was the last time Apple phoned you to ask you to write a feature for Safari? Exactly!

Well, they asked the world to do that during the WWDC 2014 keynote. And in doing so, they asked you to do the same on behalf of *every* third party app developer. Do you feel empowered now? You should!

Chapter 12: Photo Editing Extensions

By Chris Wagner

One of the many charms of the iPhone is its convenient and user-friendly camera, and built-in app for viewing the photos you've taken. Throughout its lifetime, both the camera and photo software have become rather powerful.

For instance, the camera in iPhone 5s captures beautiful images at 8 megapixels, and has a larger aperture to let in even more light. It includes desirable features such as autofocus, image stabilization, burst mode, geotagging, face detection, and many more. These features and its ubiquity have arguably propelled the iPhone to become the most popular camera in the world.

Never before have people been so fascinated by pictures of your dinner, kittens, or seemingly random snapshots.

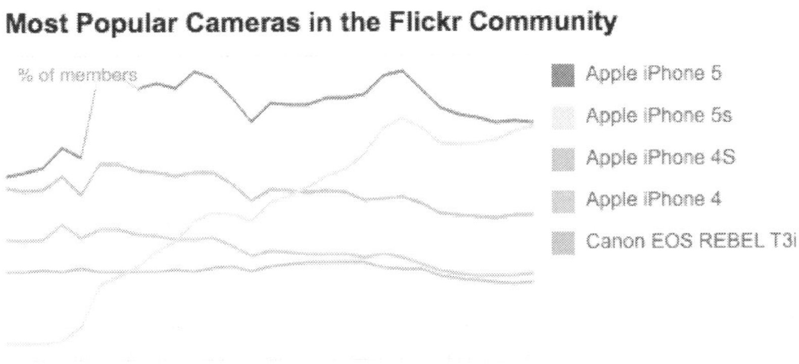

Source: https://www.flickr.com/cameras as of September 2014.

Apple has tightly controlled the software that supports the iPhone camera. Many third party apps that allow users to take and manipulate photos have come and gone. Few have remained popular. As they've never been allowed to hook directly into the OS in the same way Apple's Camera app does, users have often had to go through extra steps in order take a picture and then edit it within said app, or import a picture from their Camera Roll. Of course, don't forget that the iPod Touch and iPad also have cameras!

Well, that all changes *right now*. Apple is opening its doors and inviting you to add your features to their apps, specifically Photos and Camera.

And that's exactly what you'll be doing in this chapter, by creating a Photo Editing Extension.

That's just swell!

Imgvue

As with any extension for iOS, you must first provide a container app that offers the functionality to be provided by the extension. For this chapter, you'll work with an app named Imgvue. It allows users to view the current most popular images on imgur.com, a well-liked image sharing website. Users can then choose to save their favorite images, and apply filters to those saved images. Finally, the app lets users upload their own images to the imgur website.

> **Note:** If you have already completed Chapter 10, **Share Extensions**, you will have already completed this section. You can either re-use the same project or re-use your Imgur Client ID in a new project for this chapter. If not, all of the information that you need is right here.

Register at imgur.com

In order to proceed, you'll need a Client ID from imgur.com so you can use their API.

1. Start by creating an imgur account at https://imgur.com/register. If you already have an account, sign in with that.
2. Once registered and signed in, click your username at the top right of the screen and then choose **Settings** from the menu.

> **Note:** As websites are ever changing, these instructions or screenshots may not match with the current version of the imgur website. As always, if things do not match, then defer to their own documentation.

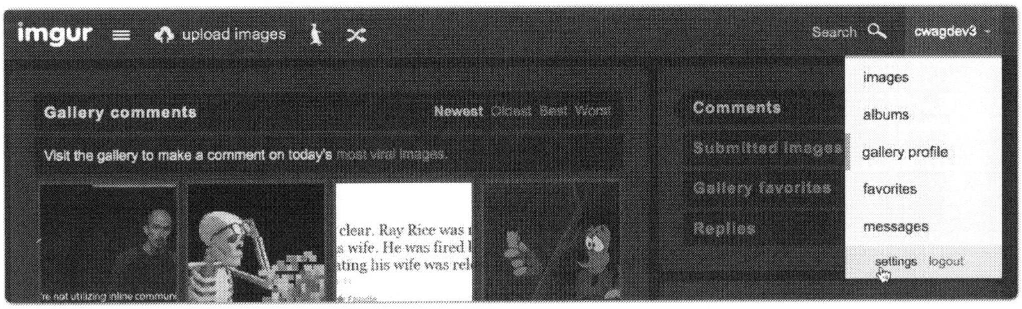

3. Within **Settings**, click **Applications**

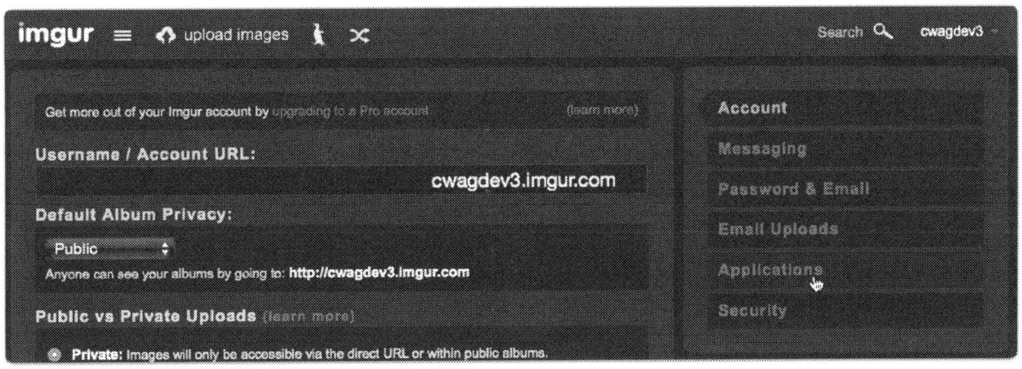

4. Under the **Apps Used** section, click **create your own!**

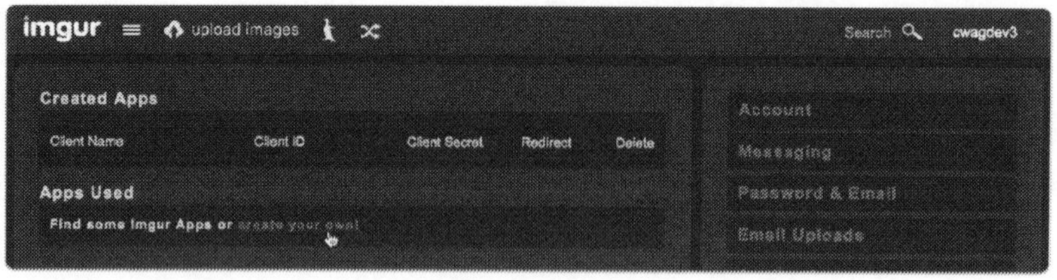

5. Click **Register an Application** from the menu on the left, and then click the **register their application** link

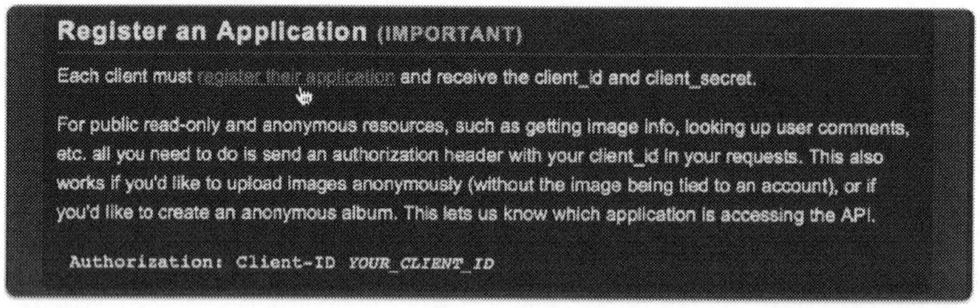

6. Fill out the **Register an Application** form. You can enter anything you like for the **Application Name**, select the second option from the **Authorization type** section, **OAuth 2 authorization with a callback URL**, enter your email address for **Email**, and finally add a sentence or two for the **Description**. Enter the security text into the relevant box and click **submit**.

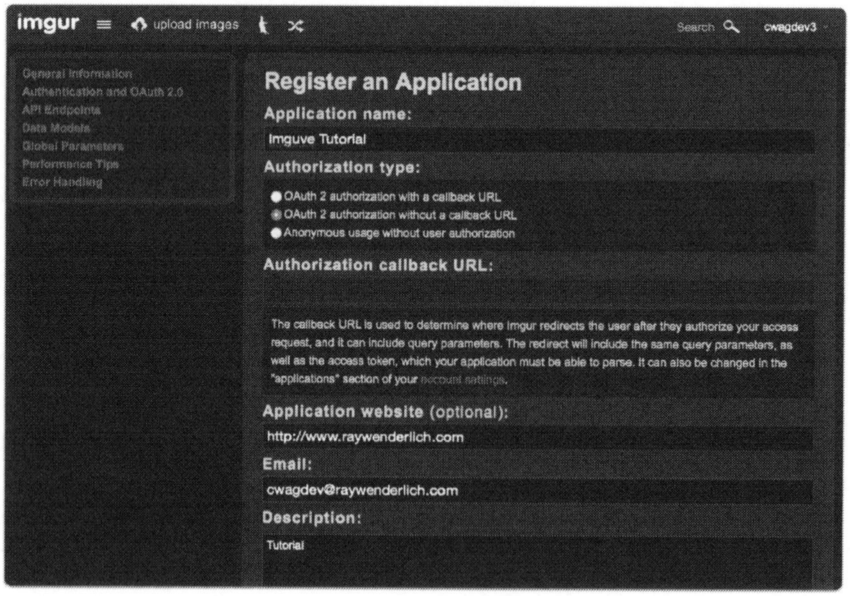

7. Take note of the **Client ID** and **Client secret** as you'll need them both later in the chapter. You'll also receive an email with this information.

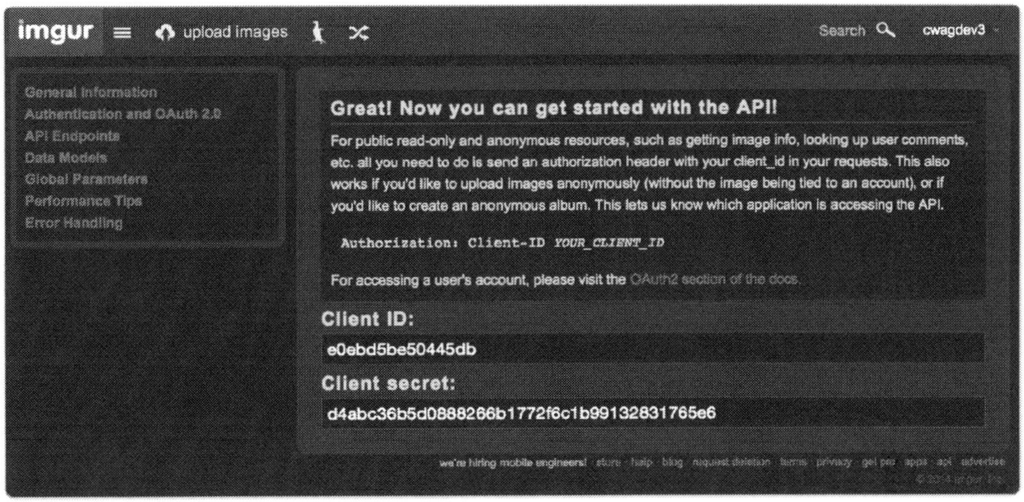

Set Imgur Client ID

Now that you're all setup with an imgur account and have your API credentials, you have everything you need to power **Imgvue**. Open the project in Xcode, and then open **ImgurService.swift** from the **ImgvueKit\Services** group in the **Project Navigator**.

At the top of the class, locate the `imgurClientId` constant and replace `YOUR_CLIENT_ID` with your Client ID.

```
private let imgurClientId = "YOUR_CLIENT_ID"
```

This will be used when creating all imgur.com API requests.

Configure App Group

In order for Imgvue to share content with its extensions, you'll need to set up an **App Group**. App Groups allow access to group containers that are shared amongst related apps, or in this case your container app and extension.

Select the **Imgvue** project in the **Project Navigator**, and then select the **Imgvue** target from the list of targets. On the **General** tab, update the **Bundle Identifier** to **com.<YOUR_DOMAIN>.swift.imgvue**, replacing <YOUR_DOMAIN> with your actual domain. This step is essential as App Groups are intrinsically linked to bundle identifiers.

Now switch to the **Capabilities** tab and enable **App Groups** by flicking the switch. If you're prompted to "select a Development Team" then choose the most appropriate one; usually your personal account. Add a new group by clicking the + button and name it **group.com.<YOUR_DOMAIN>.swift.imgvue**, again replacing <YOUR_DOMAIN> with your actual domain.

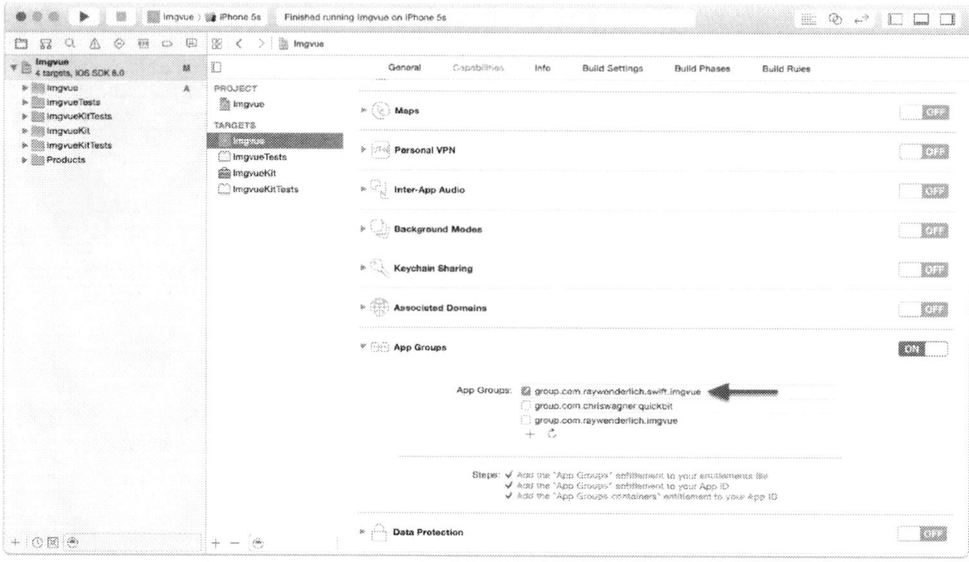

> **Note:** You need an active developer account to enable App Groups. Creating a group in Xcode will also create the entry within your developer portal. Therefore, you may want to remove the group after you complete this tutorial.

Open **SavedImageService.swift** and look for the `urlForDirectoryWithName(name:)` method. The first line sets the appropriate App Group. Change `group.com.raywenderlich.swift.imgvue` to match the group you just created.

Build and run. The app will load the current most popular images from imgur.com.

Tap on any image to view it, and tap **Save** to add the image the favorites tab. You can also upload your own photos from here. The favorites tab displays all of the images you've saved.

> **NOTE:** If your app crashes here, it means you didn't configure your App Group correctly in the previous section. If that's your case, go back to the previous section and reconfigure your App Group.

See what I mean? Food, cats and random photos rule the world. In the favorites tab, tap an image to view it.

Tap **Add Filter** and choose **Vintage**. Neat! The app provides its own implementation of one of the most popular filters of the social photo-sharing service Instagram.

Since photo editing is the focus of this chapter, you'll create an extension that provides the image filtering functionality to Apple's Camera and Photos apps.

Create the extension

Select the **Imgvue** project in the **Project Navigator**, and then choose **Editor\Add Target...**

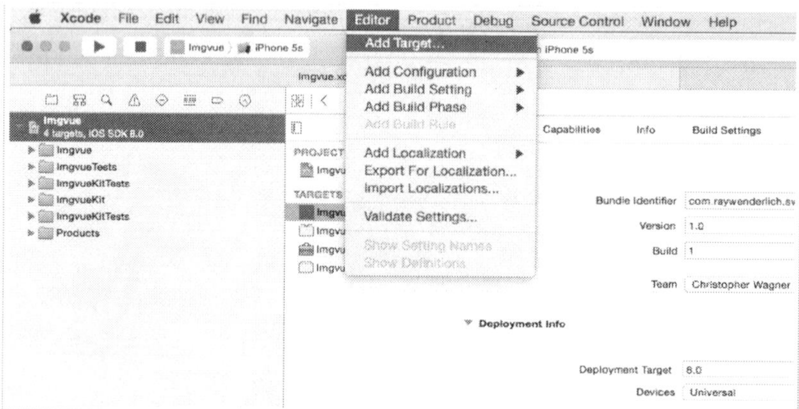

Choose **iOS\Application Extension\Photo Editing Extension** and click **Next**.

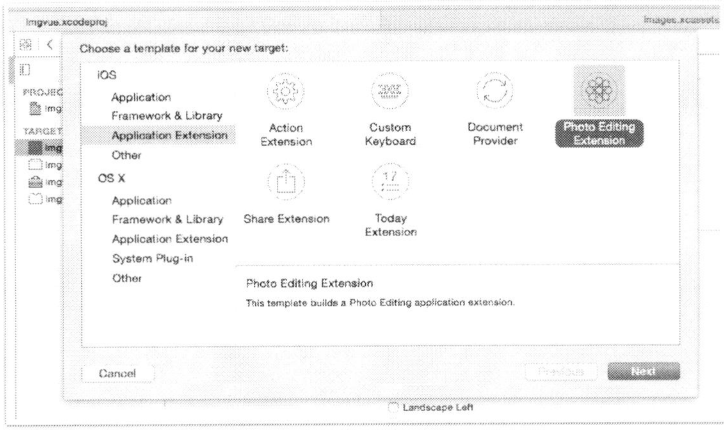

Set **Product Name** to **Imgvue Filters**, **Swift** as the language, **Imgvue** as both **Project** and **Embed in Application**, then click **Finish**.

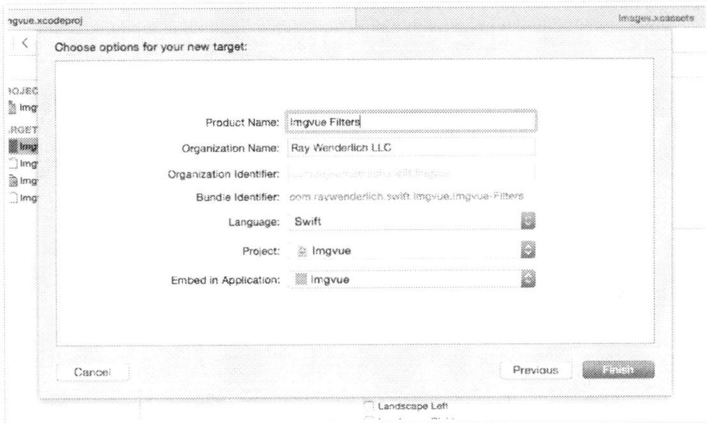

Activate the new scheme when prompted.

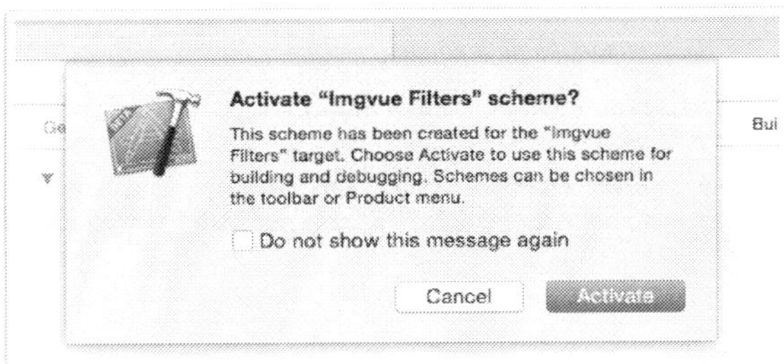

You'll now have a new group in the **Project Navigator** called **Imgvue Filters**. Expand it to see that it contains three files: **PhotoEditingViewController.swift**, **MainInterface.storyboard**, and **Info.plist**.

Open **MainInterface.storyboard** and select the **Photo Editing View Controller** in the **Document Outline**. In the **File Inspector**, enable size classes by checking the **Use Size Classes** checkbox.

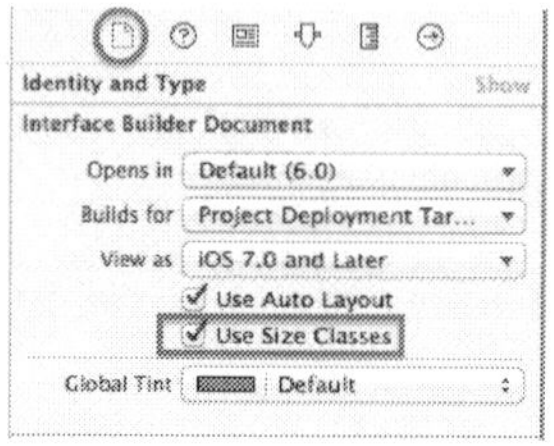

Choose **Enable Size Classes** when prompted. Next, delete the existing view controller from the storyboard, and drag a **View Controller** on from the **Object Library**. This sets up the storyboard so that it is ready for Adaptive Layout. Adaptive Layout allows you to more simply design for varying screen sizes. You can read more about them in the first few chapters of this book. In the **Identity Inspector**, set its class to `PhotoEditingViewController` and then in the **Attributes Inspector**, check **Is Initial View Controller**.

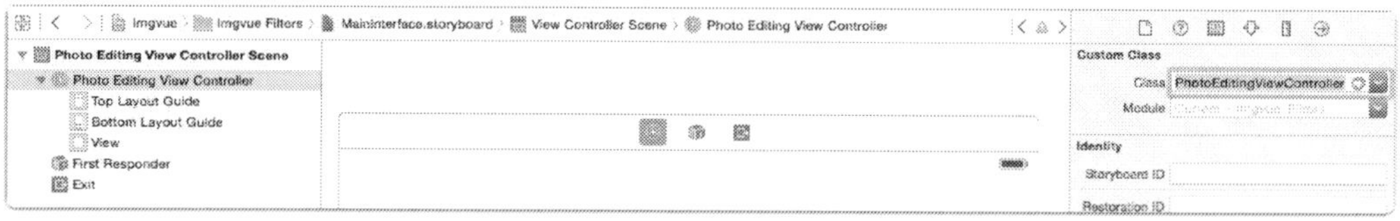

Select the **View** in the **Document Outline** and then switch to the **Attributes Inspector**. Set the **Background** to **View Flipside Background Color**.

Drag two **Buttons** from the **Object Library** onto the view, positioning one in the bottom-left of the view and the other in the bottom-right. Select the left button. In the **Attributes Inspector** set **Text Color** to **White** and **Title** to **Undo**. Do the same for the right button, but set its title to **Add Filter**. With the right button still selected, choose **Editor\Size to Fit Content** and then re-position it so it's comfortably within the bounds of the view.

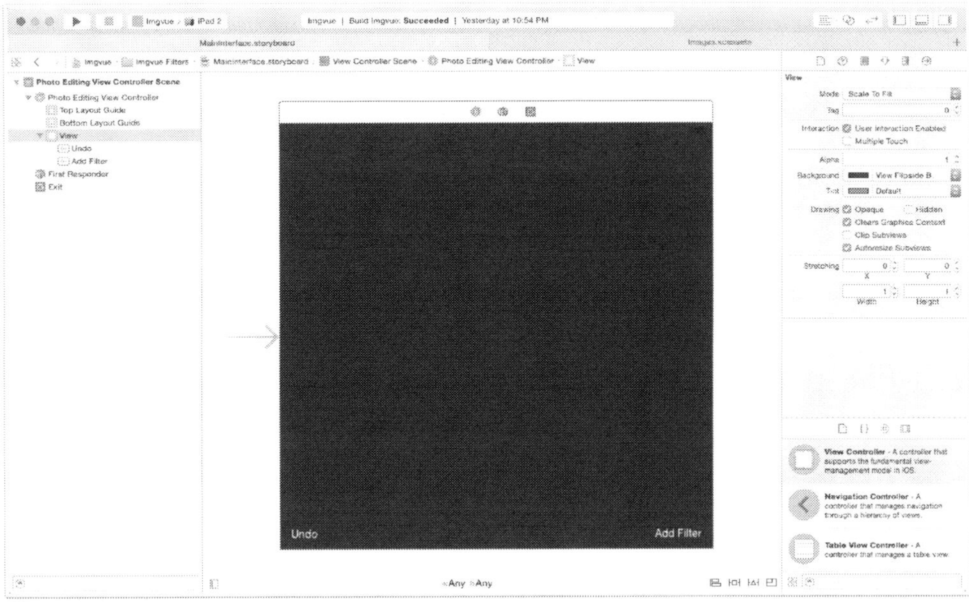

Now drag an **Image View** onto the view from the **Object Library**. Resize the image view so it snaps to the top, left and right sides of the parent view. Drag the bottom edge down until the blue guide appears as you approach the top of the buttons. With the image view selected, open the **Attributes Inspector** and change the **Mode** to **Aspect Fit**.

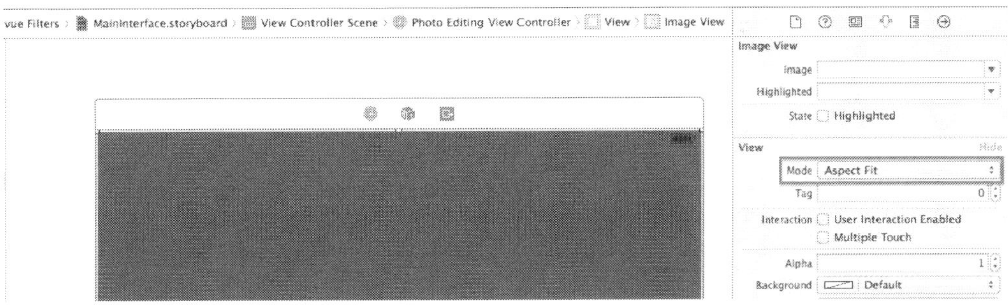

In order for the layout to adapt to all screen sizes and orientations, you need to add some Auto Layout constraints. This is a rather simple interface so you only need to add a few. Select the **Image View** and pin the top, left and right. Then for the bottom pin choose the bottom layout guide by clicking the drop down arrow in the value field.

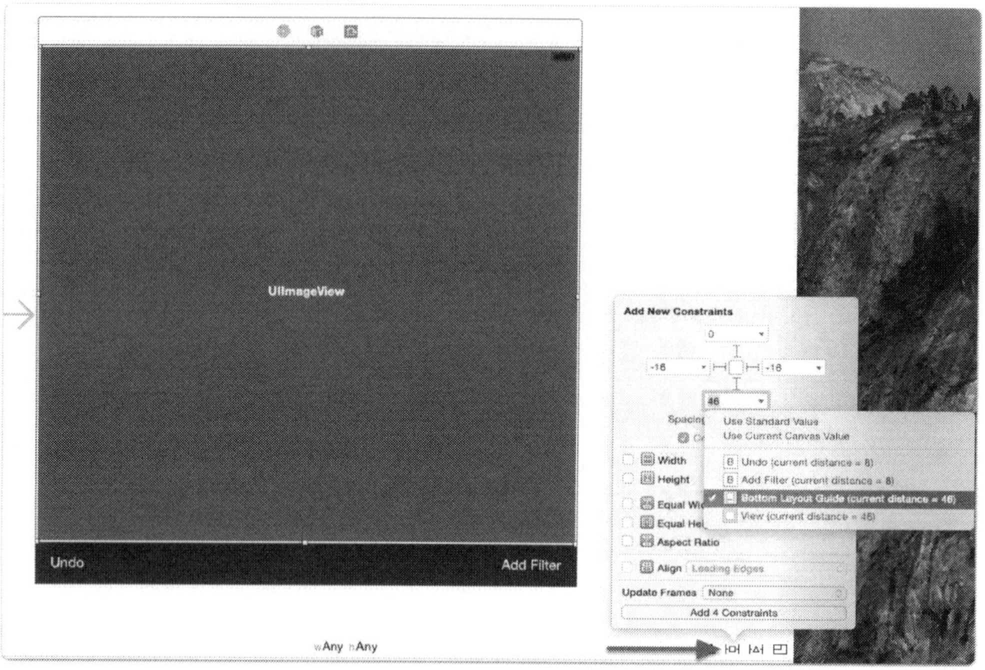

Then select the **Undo** button and pin the left and bottom.

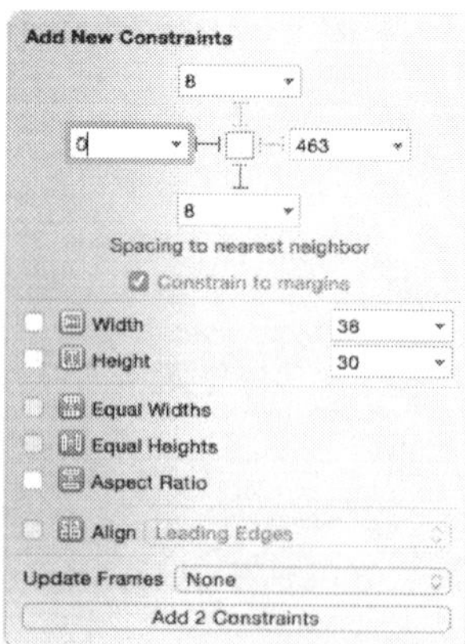

Lastly, pin the right and bottom of the **Add Filter** button.

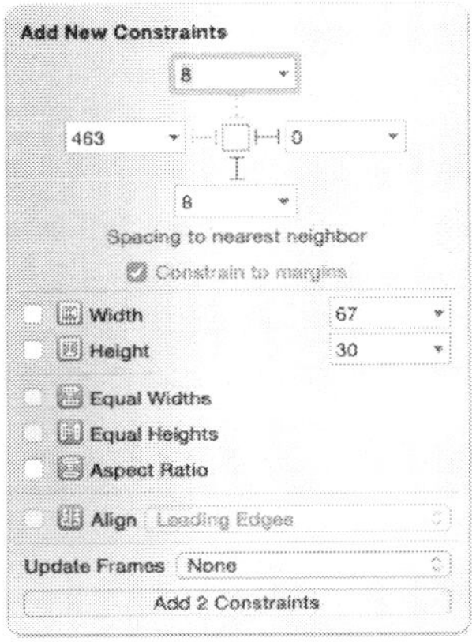

Open the **Assistant Editor** and make sure **PhotoEditingViewController.swift** is the file being edited. **Ctrl+drag** from the image view to the top of the class to create an `IBOutlet`; in the popup dialog set **Name** to `imageView` and click **Connect**. Repeat the process for the **Undo** and **Add Filter** buttons, naming them `undoButton` and `addFilterButton` respectively. The top of the class should now look like the following:

```
@IBOutlet weak var imageView: UIImageView!
@IBOutlet weak var addFilterButton: UIButton!
@IBOutlet weak var undoButton: UIButton!
```

Next, **ctrl+drag** from the **Undo** button to the **Assistant Editor**, just below where the properties are defined. In the popup dialog change **Connection** to **Action**, set **Name** to `undo`, and change **Type** to `UIButton`. Click **Connect**. Repeat for the **Add Filter** button, setting the name to `addFilter`.

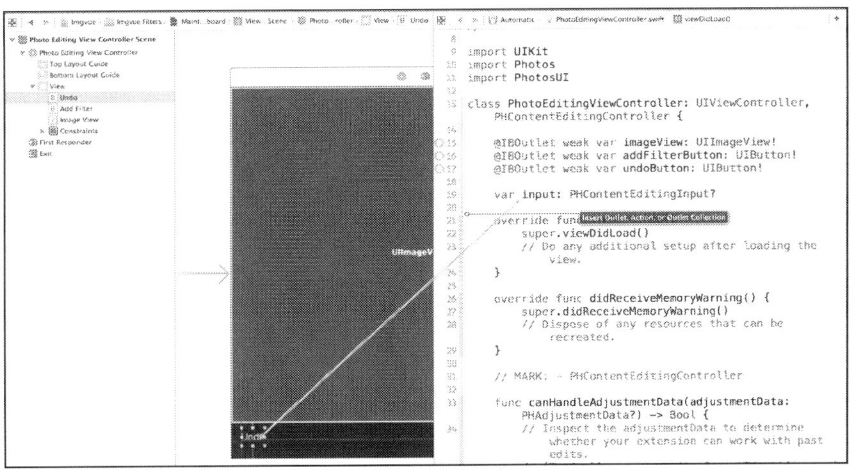

Open **PhotoEditingViewController.swift** in the **Standard Editor** and review the boilerplate code provided by Apple.

Aside from the typical view controller methods, there are four new ones specific to Photo Editing Extensions. You'll also notice that this class conforms to the `PHContentEditingController` protocol, which is where these four methods are declared.

1. `canHandleAdjustmentData(adjustmentData:)` returns a `Bool` to inform the OS if your extension can work with previous edits it made. Information about edits is stored when an app or extension modifies a photo in the Photos Library. If your app is capable of reapplying edits, return `true`. Otherwise return `false`.

   This method is passed an instance of `PHAdjustmentData` representing the past edits, which you should capture if returning `true`.

2. `startContentEditingWithInput(contentEditingInput:, placeholderImage:)` is called when the asset is available for editing, but before your view controller appears. The method is passed two objects. The `PHContentEditingInput` instance describes the asset to be edited. The `UIImage` instance is dependent on what you returned from the method above; if `true` then the image represents the previous version of the asset, otherwise it's a rendered version of the previous edit. The image is scaled down and meant for display purposes only. You'll make any edits on the full-sized image provided by the `contentEditingInput` argument passed in.

3. `finishContentEditingWithCompletionHandler(completionHandler:)` is called when the user ends editing. At that point, you're responsible for disabling your UI to prevent further edits. You create an instance of `PHContentEditingOutput`, using the `PHContentEditingInput` you stored earlier. This stores the final edits, along with the adjustment data describing the edit. Finally, call the `completionHandler`, passing your output item. Once you've called the completion handler you should perform any necessary clean up.

4. `cancelContentEditing`, as its name implies, is called when the user cancels editing. You're responsible for cleaning up any resources that are no longer needed.

Now that you have a good understanding of the protocol methods, it's time to implement them, along with the rest of the class.

Add the following to `PhotoEditingViewController`, just below the existing imports:

```
import ImgvueKit
```

Next, add the following variables, just below the existing ones:

```
let filterService: ImageFilterService = ImageFilterService()
var currentFilterName: String?
var filteredImage: UIImage?
```

Now, add the following to `addFilter`:

```
let alertController =
UIAlertController(title: "Add Filter",
  message: "Choose a filter to apply to the image",
  preferredStyle: .ActionSheet)
for (name, filter) in filterService.availableFilters() {
  let action = UIAlertAction(title: name, style: .Default) {
    _ in
    if let input = self.input {
      self.filteredImage =
        self.filterService.applyFilter(filter, toImage:
          input.displaySizeImage)
      self.imageView.image = self.filteredImage
      self.currentFilterName = filter
    }
  }
  alertController.addAction(action)
}
let noneAction =
UIAlertAction(title: "None", style: .Cancel) { action in
  if let input = self.input {
    self.imageView.image = input.displaySizeImage
    self.currentFilterName = nil
    self.filteredImage = nil
  }
}
alertController.addAction(noneAction)
presentViewController(alertController, animated: true,
  completion: nil)
```

When this method is called, it displays an activity sheet – just like in the Imgvue app – which presents the list of available filter options, including None.

Upon selecting a filter, the filter service applies it, and then the filtered image is displayed in the image view. The name of the chosen filter is also captured.

The filter is only applied to the display image, so the operation takes less time and the filtered image can be displayed sooner. This allows the user to try out multiple filters before deciding which one to use. Later, you'll use the filter name you captured to apply the same filter to the full size asset.

Add the following code to undo:

```
if let input = input {
  imageView.image = input.displaySizeImage
  currentFilterName = nil
  filteredImage = nil
}
```

This sets the image view back to the original image, and sets both the current filter name and filtered image to `nil`.

Add the following to the bottom of `startContentEditingWithInput`:

```
if let input = contentEditingInput {
  imageView.image = input.displaySizeImage
}
```

When your extension is informed that it's about to start editing an asset, capture the input and display it in the image view.

Finally, delete the contents of `finishContentEditingWithCompletionHandler`, replacing them with the following:

```
// 1
if currentFilterName == nil || input == nil {
  self.cancelContentEditing()
  return;
}
// 2
let queuePriority = CLong(DISPATCH_QUEUE_PRIORITY_DEFAULT)
let backgroundQueue = dispatch_get_global_queue(queuePriority,0)
dispatch_async(backgroundQueue) {
  // 3
  let output = PHContentEditingOutput(contentEditingInput:
self.input)
  // 4
  let archiveData =
NSKeyedArchiver.archivedDataWithRootObject(self.currentFilterNam
e!)
  let identifier = "com.raywenderlich.imgvue-imgvue-filters"
  let adjustmentData = PHAdjustmentData(formatIdentifier:
identifier,
    formatVersion: "1.0", data: archiveData)
  output.adjustmentData = adjustmentData
  // 5
  if let path = self.input!.fullSizeImageURL.path {
    var image = UIImage(contentsOfFile: path)!
```

```
      image =
self.filterService.applyFilter(self.currentFilterName!,
        toImage: image)
      // 6
      let jpegData = UIImageJPEGRepresentation(image, 1.0)
      var error: NSError?
      let saveSucceeded =
jpegData.writeToURL(output.renderedContentURL,
        options: .DataWritingAtomic, error: &error)
      if saveSucceeded {
        // 7
        completionHandler(output)
      } else {
        // 8
        println("An error occurred during save: \(error)")
        completionHandler(nil)
      }
    } else {
      println("An error occurred loading the input image")
      completionHandler(nil)
    }
  }
```

`finishContentEditingWithCompletionHandler` is the real workhorse. Here's the breakdown of what's going on here:

1. Check if either `currentFilterName` or `input` are `nil`. If so, there's nothing to do so return. Having this check allows you to implicitly unwrap the variables later in the method without having to account for `nil`.
2. Create a background queue on which to perform the work, and dispatch an asynchronous block to it.
3. Create an instance of `PHContentEditingOutput` using the input captured in `startContentEditingWithInput(contentEditingInput:, placeholderImage:)`.
4. Create adjustment data containing the selected filter's name. The data needs to have an identifier unique to your extension, and a version number. Using reverse domain name notation is considered a best practice. The version number will help if future versions of your extension un-archive data in a different way to the current version. Finally, set the adjustment data on the output item. `NSKeyedArchiver` is used to serialize the filter name string as an `NSData` object. An `NSData` object is required for saving the adjustment data. You can theoretically store any object for the archive data as long as it conforms to `NSCoding` or can be serialized to and form NSData.

5. Load the full size image from disk, and apply the filter.
6. Convert the `UIImage` instance to JPEG data and write it back out to disk, using the `renderedContentURL` as the destination.
7. If the file is written, call the completion handler passing the output item.
8. Otherwise, print the error to console and call the completion handler passing `nil`. Then lastly print a different error if the full sized image path was unattainable.

And that wraps up the code. That wasn't too hard, was it?

With the **Scheme** to **Imgvue Filter**, build and run. A window will appear asking you which app to run, choose Photos.

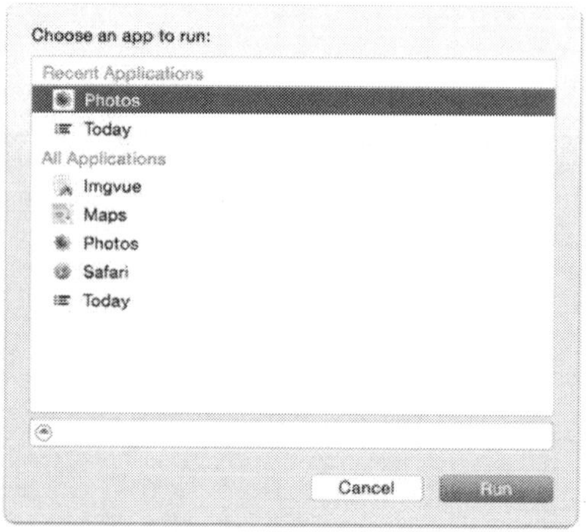

Once the Photos app launches select any picture and tap **Edit**.

In the top left corner, you'll see a new button with three dots. Tap it to reveal any 3rd party Photo Editing Extensions:

Wouldn't you look at that! Imgvue is now available to use as a Photo Editing Extension.

Tap the **Imgvue** icon, and then tap **Add Filter** to present the activity sheet listing the available filters. Choose **Invert** and tap **Done** to apply the filter and exit your extension.

Tap **Done** again to save the changes to your photo library.

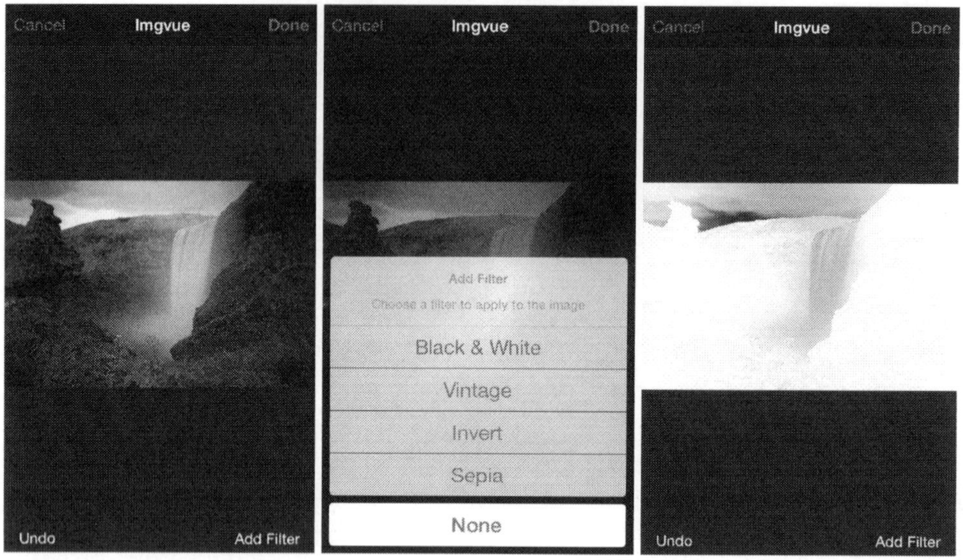

Wait, on second thought, that's pretty darn ugly. Tap **Edit** again and tap **Revert**.

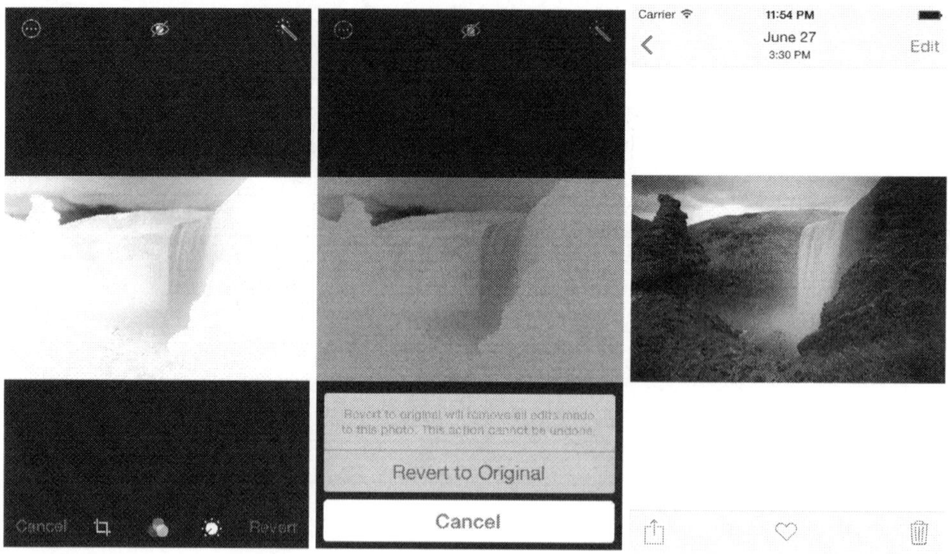

Much better. As mentioned, Photos.app does indeed keep the original copy of the photo around; thank goodness!

> **Note:** You may see some errors about CoreMedia permissions and failure of token consumption. These two errors started appearing with the release of Xcode 6 GM. The extension will work regardless, it seems that it is safe to ignore the messages.

What's next?

Photo Editing Extensions are sure to do two things:

1. Get more people using Apple's Photos.app.
2. Provide more value to 3rd party photo manipulation apps.

This is great news for the users, Apple, and you as a developer. If you have any photo editing features in your app, you should create an extension for it as soon as possible.

What about videos? Great question.

You *can* edit video with Photo Editing Extensions, despite what the name implies. To allow your app to provide support for video editing you must include a value of **Video** in the **PHSupportedMediaTypes** array of the **Info.plist** file.

Keep in mind that you should keep your extensions lightweight and focused. For instance, if your app provides full video editing capabilities, then you should keep the majority of that functionality in your app, and not in the extension. What you want to do is come up with simple use-cases and let you extension focus on those.

Go forth! The Ray Wenderlich team and community are eager to see the Photo Editing Extensions you build – perhaps a good one for the Imgvue app would be a meme generator?

Chapter 13: Document Provider Extensions

By Michael Katz

iOS 8 gives you many ways to share your app's functionality with others, through the power of app extensions. One of the new extensions is the Document Provider extension, which allows apps to send and receive files from other apps.

If you've ever pined for a way to get cloud storage and your apps to seamlessly share files, Document Providers are for you!

To share data between apps, iOS actually uses two separate extensions:

- **Document Picker**: A view controller that can be presented when another app launches an iCloud file picker.
- **File Provider**: A non-UI component that `NSFileCoordinator` hooks into to move file data between the host and extension apps. `NSFileCoordinator`, as the name implies, coordinates read and write access to files. It also allows multiple processes, such as the host and containing app, to access the file simultaneously without clobbering each other.

You also need a containing app to serve as a home base for these extensions, but in reality, another app – the host app – launches them. Additionally, you have to set up a narrowly defined interface for the host app and extensions to share file data.

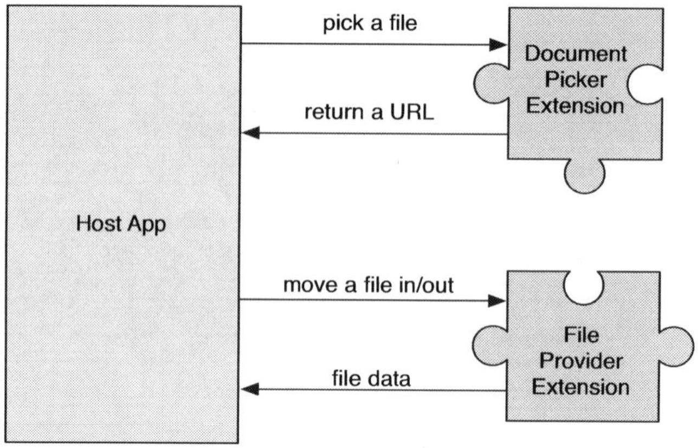

Document Providers use four operations to share data between apps: Import, Open, Export, and Move.

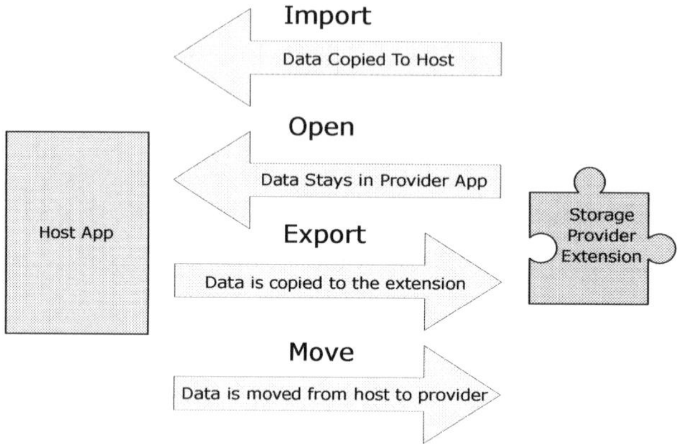

Let's go over these one by one:

1. **Import**: Import gets a file from the provider and copies it into the host app. The classic use case is a content creating app. For example, a presentation-making app like Keynote or PowerPoint would want to import images, movies, and sounds. It wants to keep a copy of that data so it is always available.
2. **Open**: Like import, open also brings data from the provider into the host app. However with open, the file stays in the provider. For example, you might use this in a player app (like for music or movies) or an app that edits files in place, like a photo editor.

3. **Export**: Export allows the host app to save a file to the provider. For example, if the provider is for a generic cloud file system (like a Dropbox or iCloud Drive), this would be how a host app would save the file to the provider's storage. In the presentation editor example, after the user is done editing the presentation, they would Export it in order to later open it in a different app.
4. **Move**: Moving works just like export, except that instead the host does not retain it's own copy of the file after it is moved. This is likely to be the least common action, as most iOS apps aren't built to give up their data.

In this chapter, you will add a document picker and file provider extension to a photo album application. The application uses Amazon S3 for remote storage, and is meant to serve as a model for any file storage you provide, whether that's in the cloud, a corporate data center, or a shoebox of hard drives with an Internet connection.

This tutorial requires Xcode 6 and iOS 8. A **paid developer account** is also a requirement, as you'll need valid iCloud entitlements to launch the Document Picker.

> **Note**: This chapter is on an advanced topic, so is for intermediate to advanced developers only. There are some steps, such as layout out view controllers in a Storyboard, that we will not spell out step by step so you should be familiar with doing such activities.

Getting started

In the resources for this chapter, find the starter project for this chapter. Open the project in Xcode, but don't build and run yet – you have to make a change before it will run, which you'll learn about in a moment.

The starter project (Imgvue) is a simple photo management application backed by Amazon S3 (Simple Storage Service). However, when you develop your own document provider extension, you could use another cloud storage service, like Dropbox, Box, Google, Azure, etc.

Amazon is popular, and provides its own SDK to handle server communication. It also provides the ability to access data globally without a login. So, it's an ideal subject for this chapter.

Imgvue provides a giant, public bucket for storing photos. Obviously, it's not a great candidate to submit to the App Store since there are no enforced limits, nor oversight on the images that could be uploaded and shared. But again, it's a great test subject.

Setting up S3

This version of Imgvue is built on top of Amazon S3. Amazon provides an Objective-C framework to handle its complicated request signing process.

To use this application, you'll need an Amazon Web Services (AWS) Account and an S3 bucket. S3 charges you based on how much storage space you are using in your account (among other things), so note that there will likely be a small charge from S3 to store the images you need for this tutorial (probably in the order of a few cents per month until you remove your S3 bucket). The good news is, if you are signing up for AWS for the first time, you may qualify for their free tier for the first year.

> **Note**: Be careful about the costs of using S3 in a real app. If you use S3 to store images for thousands of users, the costs can really add up – so be careful!

First go to http://aws.amazon.com/, and sign in or create a new account. You'll have to bear through a few verification steps and enter a credit card. However, the couple of images you'll upload to S3 for this tutorial should be very cheap, or even free (if you quality for the free tier).

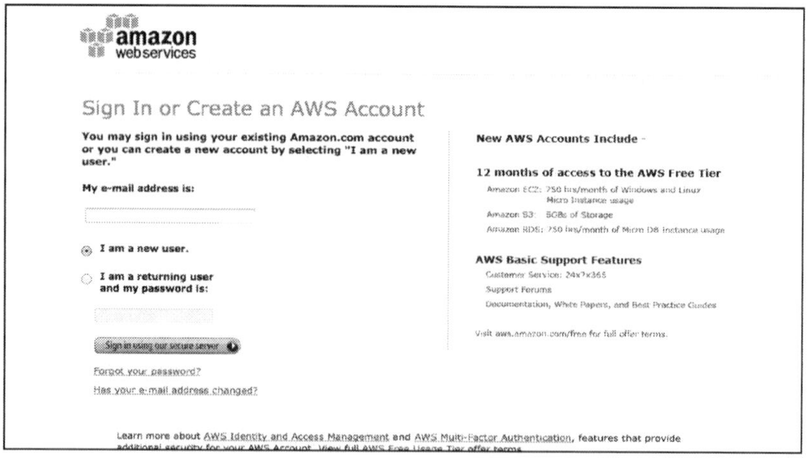

Then in the **console**, open the **S3** dashboard.

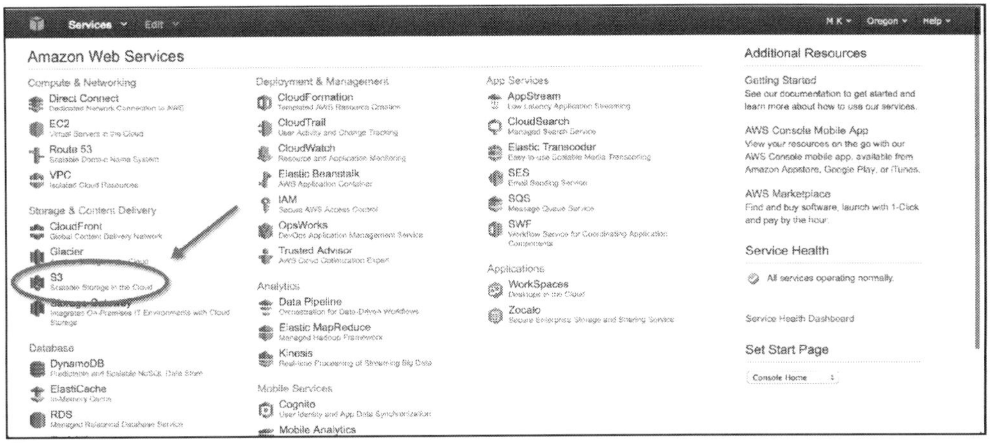

S3 organizes information into **buckets**. Create a new bucket by clicking the **Create Bucket** button. Your project app will place images in this bucket.

> **Note:** It's important to create this ahead of time – without, your app will crash and your efforts to complete this chapter will be futile.

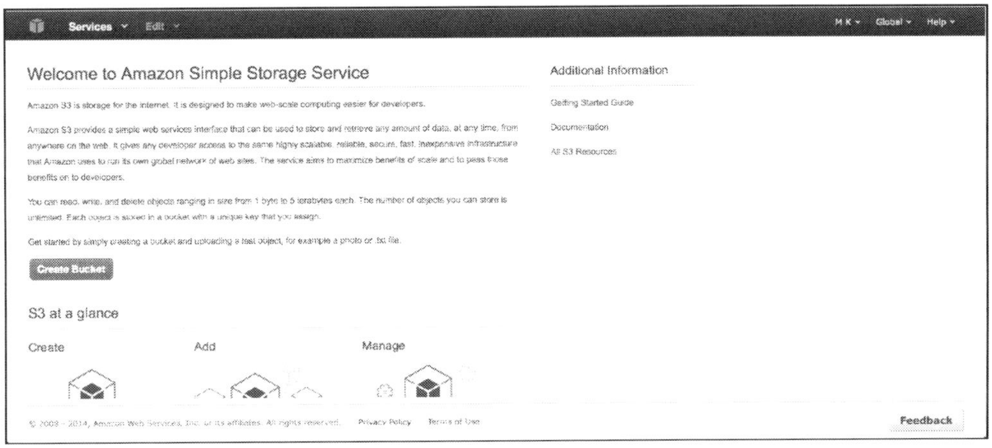

Next, configure your bucket. **Enter a name** and **select a Region near you**. Be creative with your Bucket Name, it must be globally unique. Try using something with your name or domain.

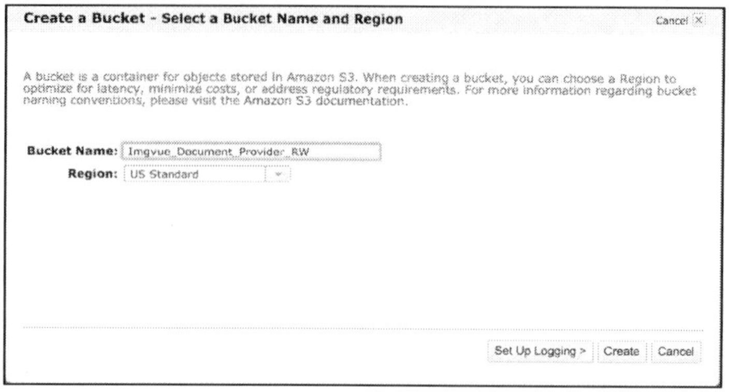

Copy the name you chose for your bucket somewhere safe, as you will need it shortly. Click **Create** when you're done.

Next, you need to create the AWS security credentials that will authenticate the app with AWS servers. To do this, click the **Services** menu in the upper left, and then click **IAM** to open the identity and access management console.

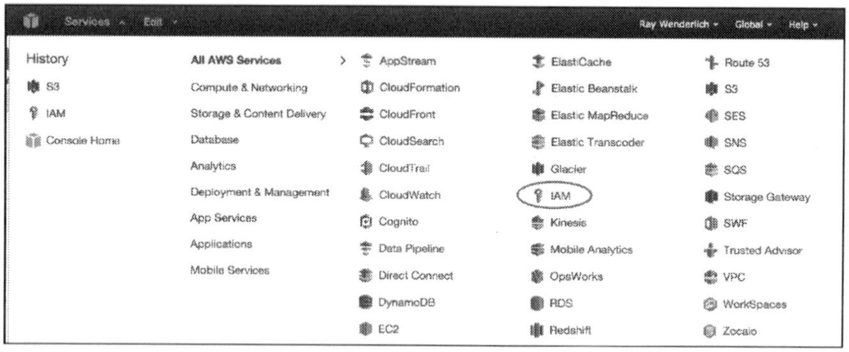

Click the **Users** tab, and click **Create New Users**:

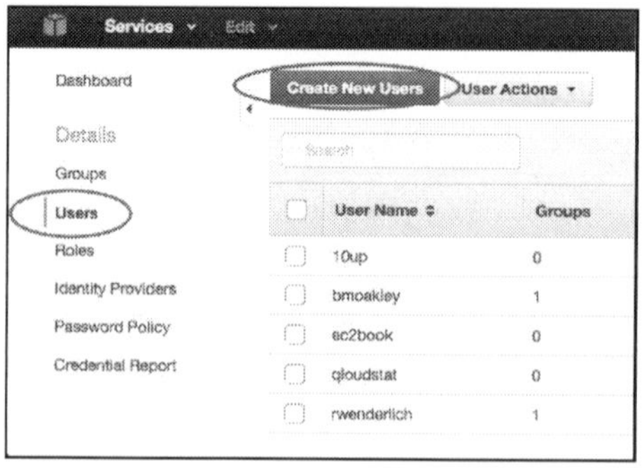

Enter a username of your choice (for example **ImgVue**) and click **Create**.

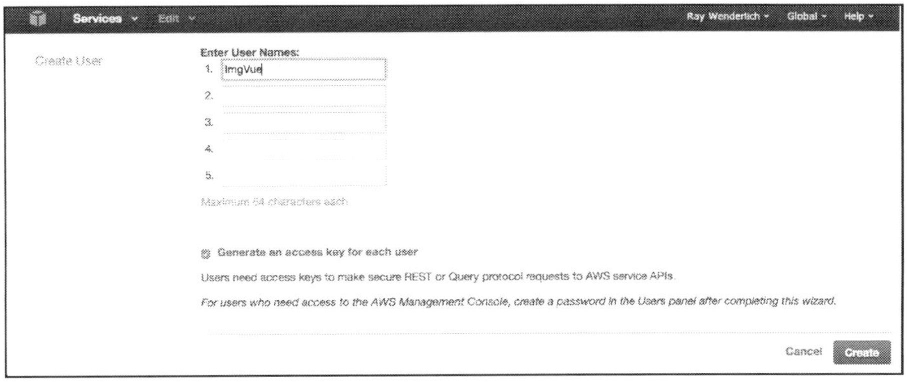

On the next page, click **Show User Security Credentials** to reveal your user's **Access Key ID** and **Secret Access Key**. Copy these down somewhere safe, as you will need them shortly. Click **Close**, and then **Close** again.

There's one last step – you need to give your new user permissions to access your new bucket. Select your new user in the users list, scroll down to the **User Policies** section, and click **Attach User Policy**.

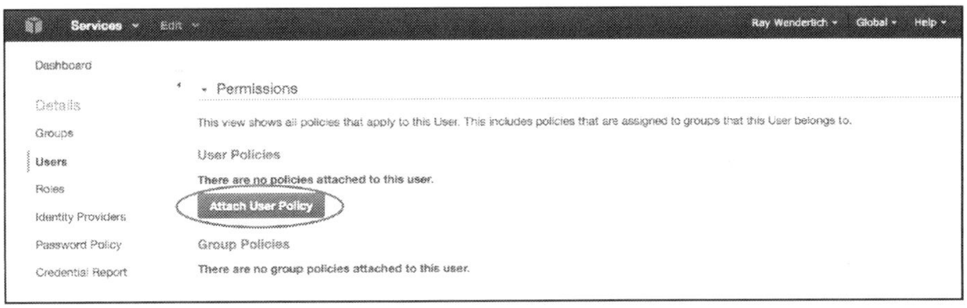

On the next page, choose the **Custom Policy** radio button, and click **Select**.

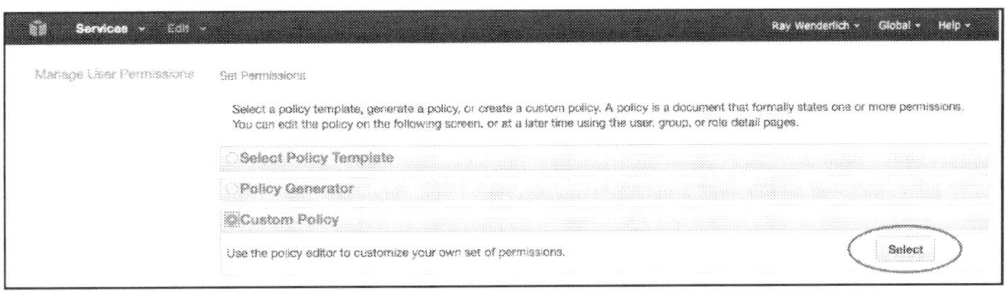

For **Policy Name** enter **ImgVue_Bucket_Access**, and for **Policy Document** enter the following (replacing [BUCKET NAME] with the name you entered for the bucket earlier):

```
{
  "Statement": [
    {
      "Effect": "Allow",
      "Action": ["s3:GetBucketLocation", "s3:ListAllMyBuckets"],
      "Resource": "arn:aws:s3:::*"
    },
    {
      "Effect": "Allow",
      "Action": ["s3:ListBucket" ],
      "Resource": [ "arn:aws:s3:::[BUCKET NAME]"]
    },
    {
      "Effect": "Allow",
      "Action": [ "s3:PutObject", "s3:GetObject",
"s3:DeleteObject"],
      "Resource": [ "arn:aws:s3:::[BUCKET NAME]/*"]
    }
  ]
}
```

This grants your user access to the bucket you created (but gives it no other access). Giving users limited access like this is best practice when working with Amazon Web Services.

Once you're done, click **Apply Policy**. That's it for S3 setup – back to code!

App frameworks

As mentioned earlier in this chapter, app extensions require some shared code between the container app and the extensions. The Imgvue starter app is already broken down into three targets.

1. **Imgvue:** This is your **Container App**. It provides functionality for listing image thumbnails in the S3 bucket, and allows the user to upload photos from the Photos album.
2. **S3Kit** framework: This framework wraps the `AWSS3.framework` provided by Amazon. It's a pre-iOS 8 non-module static framework, so it's not directly usable by Swift code. Hence, the S3Kit framework helps bridge that gap with the `SWrapper` class. It's kind of like the facilitator, providing logic for transferring images between the main Imgvue app, extensions and S3.

3. **UIWidgets**: This framework contains thumbnail collection views and other screens that the Document Picker extension and the main application will share.

> **Note:** The Amazon-provided frameworks are nothing to get excited about. In particular, network calls are synchronous, and they handle errors by throwing exceptions. Of course, this behavior is unacceptable for a production app, but suffices to show how Document Providers work.
>
> S3 request signing is quite complicated, and explaining it would dilute the purpose of this chapter, and add at *least* a bijillion more steps. When building and running, remember the device or simulator MUST have an Internet connection or it will crash.

Select your project, and select the **S3Kit** target. In the **General** tab's **Deployment Info** section, make sure that the **Allow app extension API only** is checked:

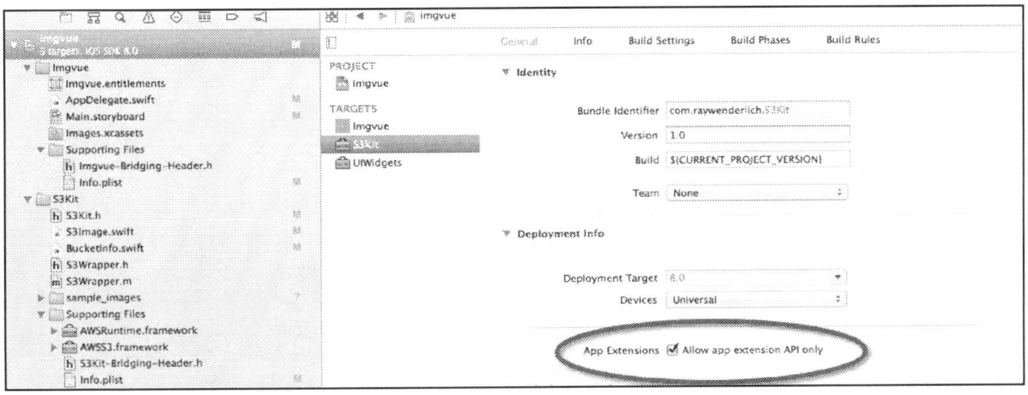

This ensures the framework only uses iOS SDK calls that are available to extensions. For example, an extension does not have access to instances of `UIApplication`. Keep this step in mind when you build frameworks that an extension will use.

Setting up the app

Open **BucketInfo.swift** in the **S3Kit** framework. Replace the `ACCESS_KEY_ID` and `SECRET_KEY` constants with the credentials you obtained from Amazon. Also, set `BUCKET_NAME` to your chosen bucket id.

Since this app uses iCloud, you'll need to configure an App ID and Bundle Identifier using Xcode (or the Apple Provisioning Portal). In the Imgvue target's General tab, set the **Bundle Identifier** to an unique Bundle ID (something like this: com.mydomain.Imgvue). On the **Team** dropdown, select your team with a paid developer account.

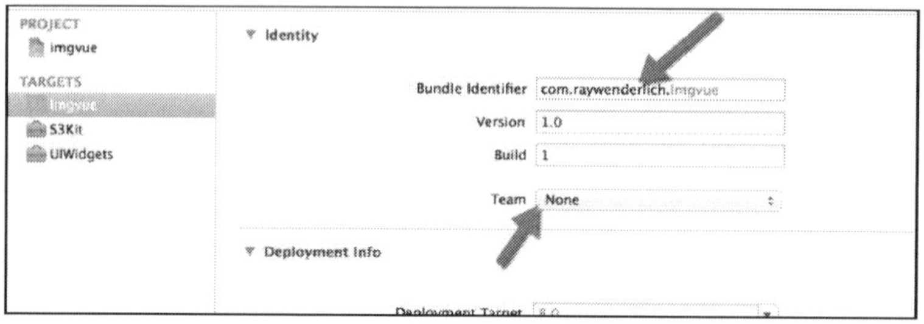

Build and run. You'll see a crisp, clean, plain white screen; there are no images yet. Use the **Upload tab** in the app to upload a few photos.

When you return to the images collection view, your images will be pulled down from S3.

> **Note:** If you get an error about a missing entitlement, try making a provisioning profile manually on iTunes Connect and configure your project to use it in Build Settings\Code Signing\Provisioning Profile.

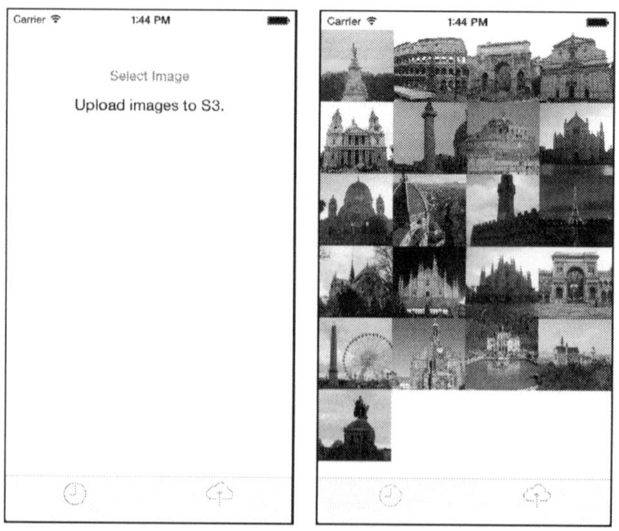

> **Note:** You can also use the S3 console to verify if the images uploaded and to bulk upload other images.

Adding the extension

This is all fine and good, but right now only Imgvue has access to its set of beautiful images, and you want to make those files available to other apps. In comes Document Provider extensions.

Select the **Imgvue Xcode Project file** in the project navigator within Xcode. From the editor menu, choose **Add Target**. Choose **iOS \ Application Extension \ Document Provider**, and click **Next**.

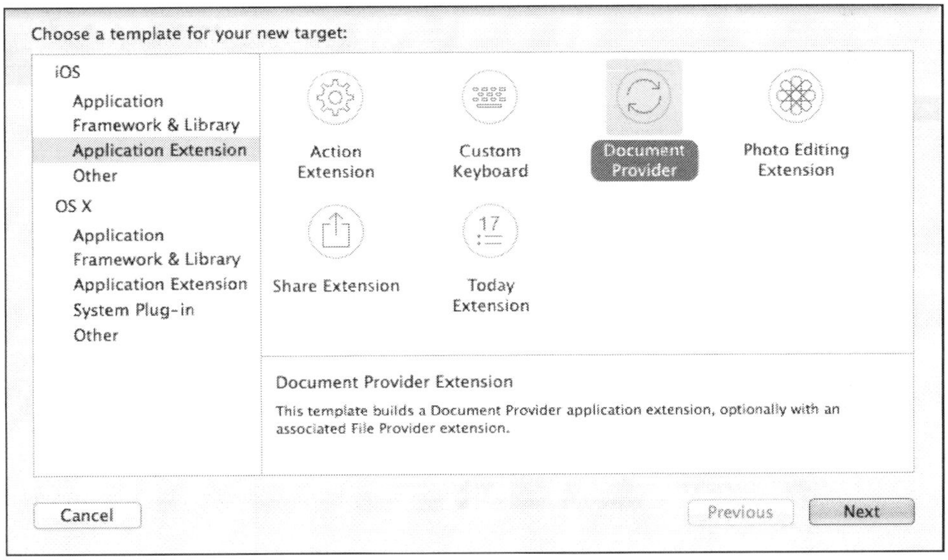

You need a recognizable and *short* **Product Name**, so it's easy for a user to tell that the extension goes with your app when they see it in the host app.

For this tutorial, enter **S3Images**. Check the box next to **Include a File Provider extension**.

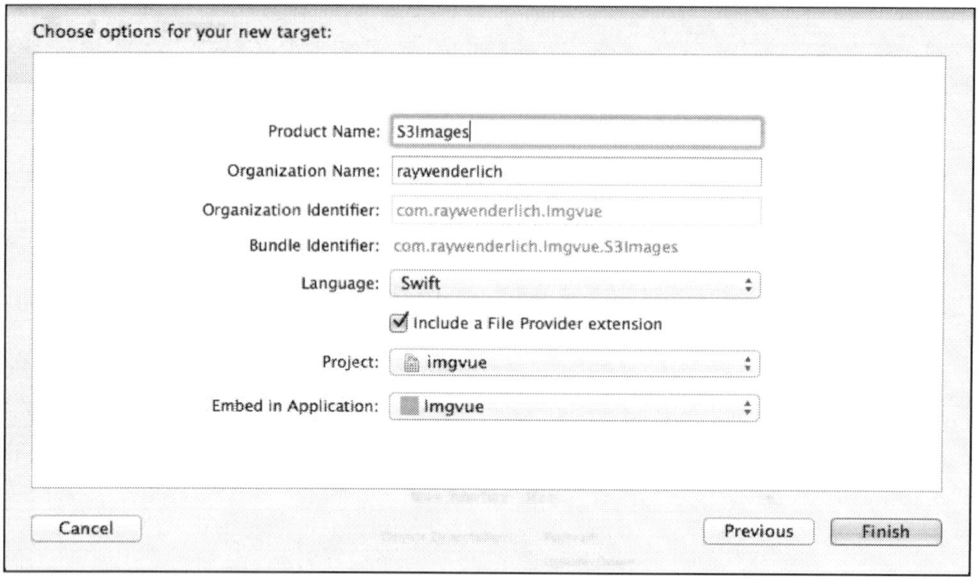

When prompted to activate new schemes, click **Activate**.

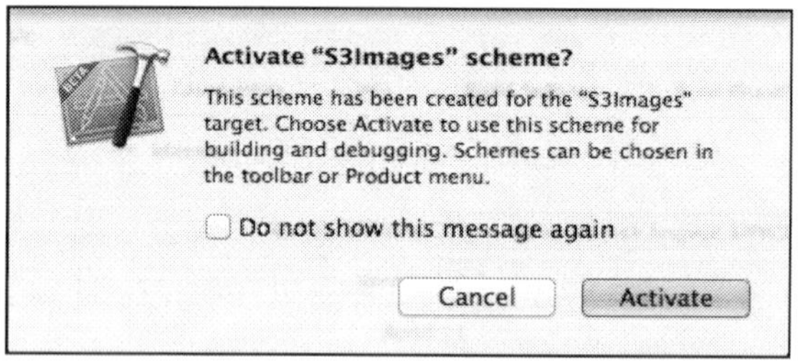

Two new folders, targets and schemes should now be created. The first one, **S3Images**, is the Document Picker extension. The other, **S3ImagesFileProvider**, is the extension used by `NSFileCoordinator` to handle access to your file system. You don't need the Provider extension if you plan to provide only Import or Export options.

Document Picker extension

The Document Picker is a view controller that allows host apps to select files and interact with them. By default, apps that launch a Document Picker can access the iCloud Drive. It allows the user to select your extension from a list of file locations, triggering your Document Picker's UI to load.

The Document Picker extension template starts off with a Storyboard and a `DocumentPickerViewController` class. To load the images from the S3 bucket, you'll wire up the same collection view as the container app.

1. Open the **MainInterface.storyboard** in the **S3Images** folder. You should see something that looks like this:

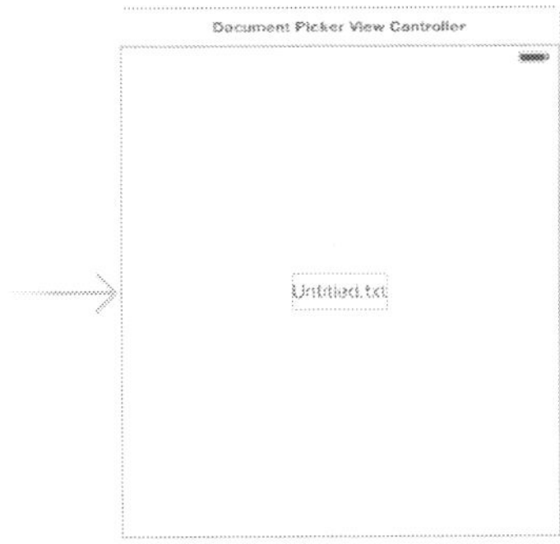

2. Remove the existing untitled.txt button.
3. Drag a **Container View** on to the Document Picker View Controller Scene's view.
4. Set up Auto Layout constraints by making the width and height equal to its parent view, so it takes up the full screen. Center the view in its parent view.
5. Drag a **Navigation Controller** onto the canvas.
6. Control-drag from the Container View to the Navigation controller and select the **Embed** segue. Now the child view of the Document Picker will be a navigation view. (This is how to set up a navigation stack inside a Document Picker.)
7. Delete the extraneous view controller leftover from the original container view.
8. Delete the navigation controller's root table view controller and replace it with a **Collection View Controller**.
9. Make the Collection View Controller the *root view controller* of the navigation view controller. To do this, Control-drag from the navigation controller to the collection view controller, and then select the **Root View Controller** segue.
10. In the **Identity Inspector** of the **collection view controller,** set the class to **ThumbnailCollectionViewController** and the module to **UIWidgets**. This tells the storyboard to set the controller's class to the one coming from the separate module. This class is the same as the one used in the container app.

Okay, stop! This is a good point to come up for air and make sure your storyboard looks something like this:

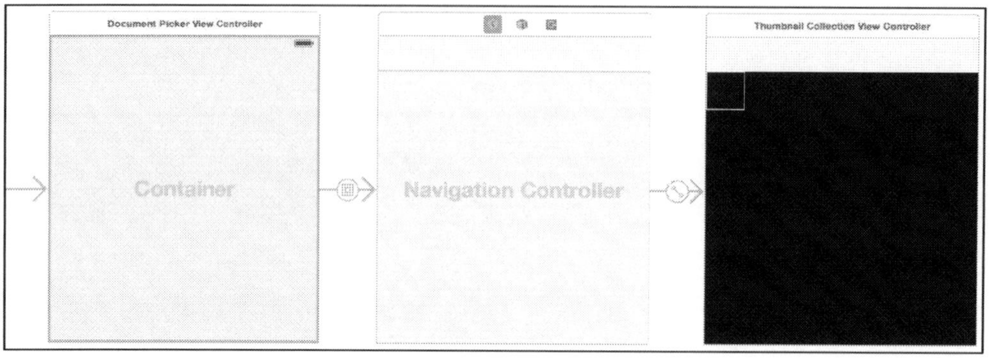

If it does, then take a deep breath and dive back in:

1. Click the **Collection View Cell** prototype in the collection view.
2. In the Identity Inspector, set the custom class to `ThumbnailCell` and the module to `UIWidgets`.
3. In the **Attribute Inspector**, set the **Reuse Identifier** to `ThumbCell`.
4. Drag an **Image View** onto the cell and use constraints to make it take up the full cell size.
5. Go the cell's **Connection Inspector** and drag the `imageView` outlet to the new image view.
6. In the **Size Inspector** for the Collection View, change the width and height for cell size to `80`.
7. Also in the same inspector, change the **Min. Spacing** to `0` for both the cells and lines.

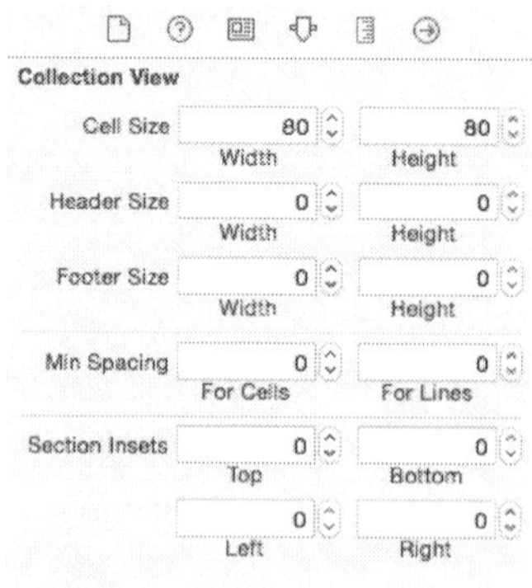

The `ThumbnailViewController` already is wired up to load images from S3, so you're almost ready to test out the view.

To make sure that the extension can access these modules, add the `S3Kit.framework` and `UIWidgets.framework` as dependencies and linked libraries in the S3Images target's **Build Phase**.

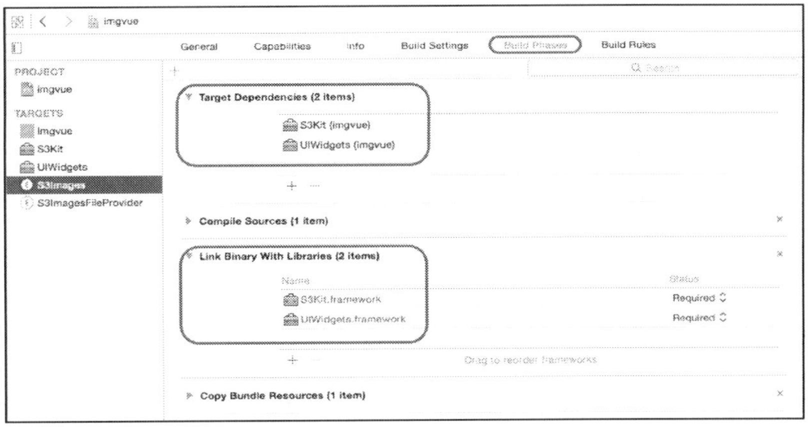

Then, in the main **Imgvue** target and in *both* Document Provider extension targets, go to the **Capabilities** tab. Enable the **App Groups** capability and make sure that all three targets have the same app group.

This required entitlement enables the shared container you need to allow the extension and the container app to share files and pass URLs back to the host app.

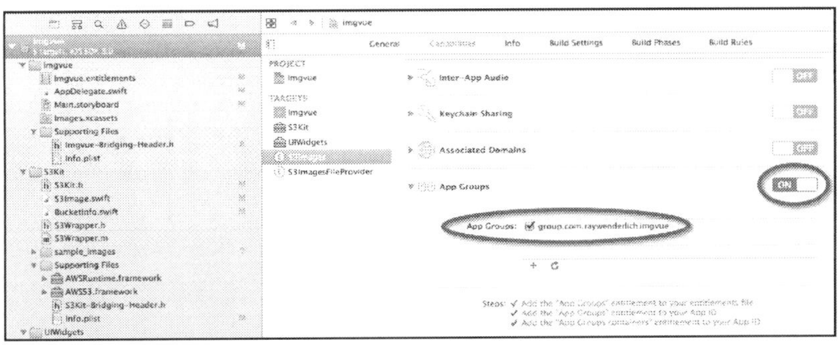

Now the extension is ready to display the S3 thumbnails inside a document picker, though it doesn't do much else. To display this document picker, you need a separate host app.

Build and run to see if everything looks okay. You'll take care of the host app next.

DocTester

The other application included in this chapter's download is called **DocTester,** and it's a bare-bones application that's sole purpose is to be your host app. The *Open* and *Import* actions load an image and display it in the main view. *Export* and *Move* download a random cat image and upload it to the service.

Open **DocTester.xcodeproj** to set up this app.

Because document extensions are meant to extend iCloud documents, a host app needs to enable iCloud entitlements before launching the document picker.

First, in the target's **General** tab, update the **Bundle Identifier** to an app id your account can use, and change **Team** to your team id.

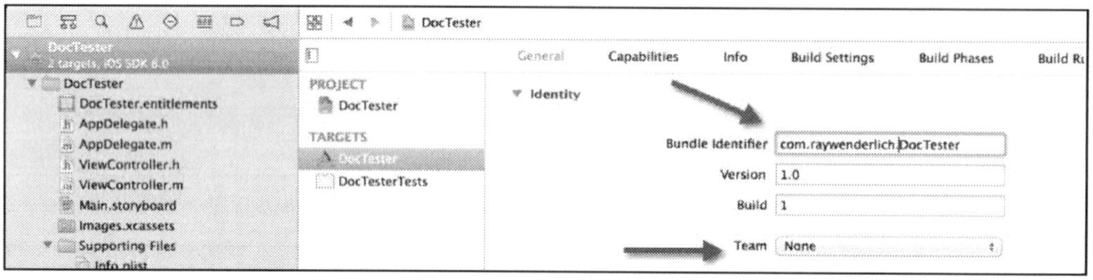

Then, in the **Capabilities** tab enable iCloud and iCloud documents.

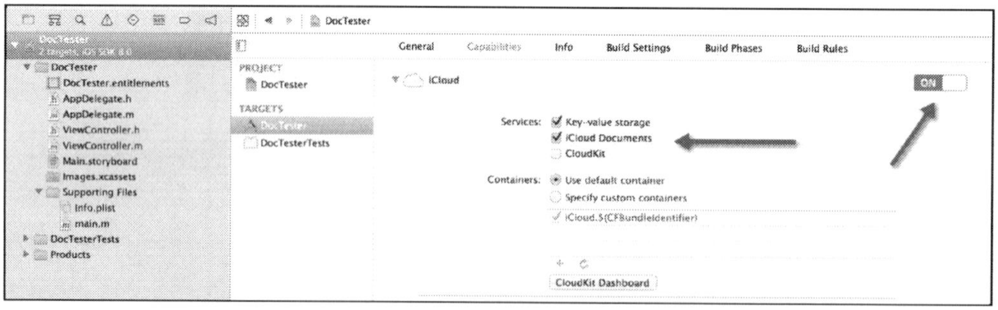

And now for the final step before running the app, I promise!

In **Xcode**, in the **Xcode menu**, select **Open Development Tool\iOS Simulator.** In the Simulator's **Settings** app, sign in to iCloud. At the time of writing this, you need a valid iCloud account with **iCloud Drive** enabled for Document Provider extensions to work properly.

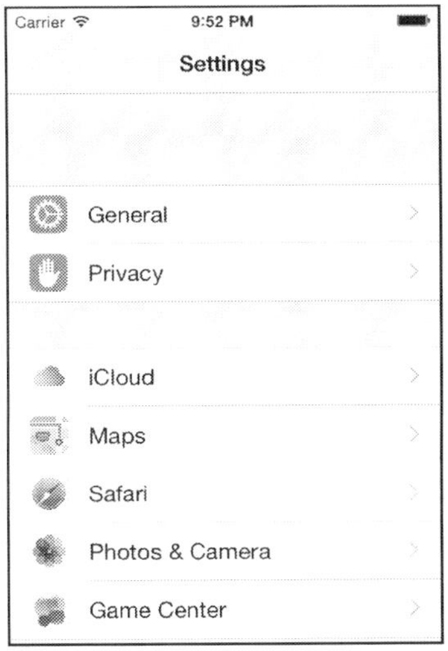

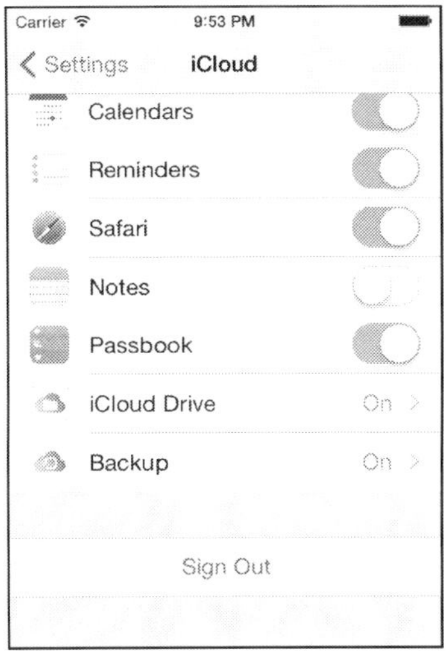

Now, build and run **DocTester**. This will install it on the simulator and make it available to Imgvue. In Xcode, select **Product\Stop** (CMD-Period.) Very good!

With DocTester installed, you can move on to testing the Document Picker.

Using the Document Picker

Next, switch to the **Imgvue** project. Select the **S3Images scheme** and build and run to launch the Simulator and view a list of apps. You don't actually want to run Imgvue, rather you need the host app **DocTester**.

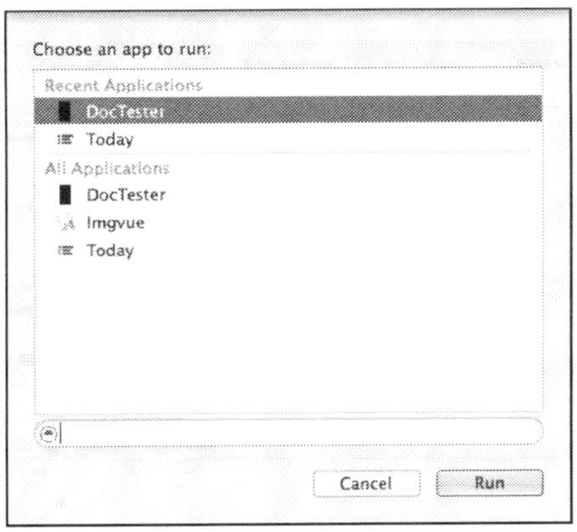

This should launch the app – it's pretty basic!

Tap the **Import** button. If you've set up iCloud Drive properly, the iCloud file chooser will appear. If not, iOS will walk your through the set up steps.

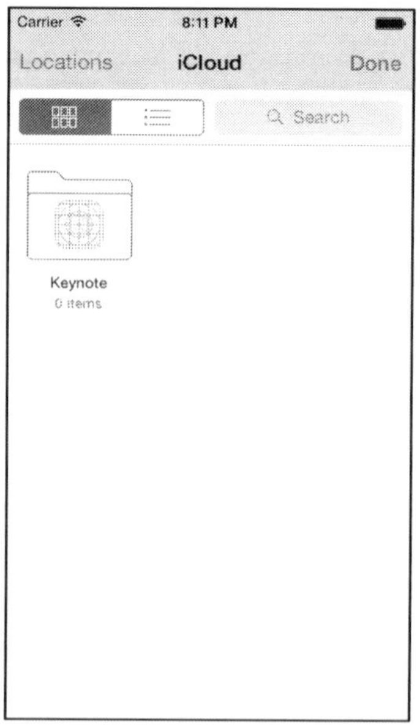

To switch to the Imgvue extension, tap the **Locations** button in the top left to bring up the Document Provider extension menu. Tap **More ...** to enable the extension and add it to the menu.

Then, enable the S3Images switch and tap **Done**.

This cancels the import menu, so tap **Import** again at the top of the screen. Now the *S3Images* extension will show up in the Locations list. Tap it to bring up the Document Picker extension. In the picker view, as shown in the following screenshots, there will be two toolbars at the top of the window. The top one, with buttons for Locations and Done, are supplied by iOS as part of the document picker system and is not configurable. The second one is the navigation bar for the container view's contained nav controller. You'll hide this weird little guy with the code added in the next section.

Tapping an image doesn't do anything – yet. Though you've created the Document Picker extension UI, you've not created file providing. You'll do that soon, starting with building out the import.

Troubleshooting

While everything *should* be working, it's possible that the picker doesn't show up.

There's a few possible causes for this. In particular, if the extension crashes, look at crash logs in the Console app to debug. You can also take a look at the simulator's logs by hitting **Command-/**.

Here is a list of things to check:

- Make sure you have a network connection. If there are unexpected network-related issues, restart the device or simulator.
- Make sure there is an iCloud account with iCloud Drive enabled.

- The App ID and Team settings on all targets need be consistent; the Team specified in the targets must also issue the App ID.
- The DocTester and the Imgvue targets need to have iCloud Documents capabilities enabled. Use the fix issues button if it's available.
- Check your target settings to see if there are any issues listed in the General tab. If so, try **Fix Issue**, or try generating a provisioning profile manually.
- The Imgvue, S3Images, and S3ImagesFileProvider targets should all have a matching app group entitlement. Sometimes the selections in the Capabilities pane don't update in the `.entitlements` or `.plist` files for each extension. Check these manually.
- Sometimes building and running doesn't fully update the host app. If the expected changes seem to be missing, kill and restart the host and container apps and then re-run.

Import

The simplest of the four document provider operations is `Import`, or the "download and copy to my app" function.

To perform the import, the extension returns a file URL that points to a file in a shared container for the host app to access. Subsequently, the host app moves that file to its sandbox once the document picker is dismissed.

To generate the URL, the extension controller needs to be notified when the user chooses a picture. The `ThumbnailCollectionViewController` has a delegate protocol to provide this event.

At the top of the **DocumentPickerViewController.swift** file, import the following modules:

```
import UIWidgets
import S3Kit
```

Then, declare the controller as a `ThumbnailDelegate` and an `NSFileManagerDelegate` by adding the protocols to the class definition:

```
class DocumentPickerViewController:
UIDocumentPickerExtensionViewController, ThumbnailDelegate,
NSFileManagerDelegate {
```

Add the required `didSelectImage` method from the `ThumbnailDelegate` protocol:

```
// MARK: ThumbnailDelegate
func didSelectImage(image: S3Image) {
  let imageUrl = image.url!

  //1
  let filename = imageUrl.pathComponents.last as String

  //2
  let outUrl =
documentStorageURL.URLByAppendingPathComponent(filename)

  // 3
  let coordinator = NSFileCoordinator()
  coordinator.coordinateWritingItemAtURL(outUrl,
    options: .ForReplacing,
    error: nil,
    byAccessor: { newURL in
      //4
      let fm = NSFileManager()
      fm.delegate = self
      fm.copyItemAtURL(imageUrl, toURL: newURL, error: nil)
  })

  // 5
  dismissGrantingAccessToURL(outUrl)
}
```

This method takes the file URL (as an `S3Image`) from the image you download from S3 and creates a new one to send to the host app. Let's go over it step by step:

1. The filename is the last part of the path. The front of the path represents the location of the cached image in the host app's sandbox.
2. The `documentStorageURL` is a special location defined by the `UIDocumentPickerExtensionViewController` class. Both the File Provider extension and host app can access the location. By appending the unique filename for the image, it can serve as an identifier so the file provider extension can retrieve the file later.
3. Create a file coordinator to ensure proper access to the document storage location. The coordinator writes the file to the document storage location, and it also overwrites any existing file in that location.

4. The `accessor` block receives a new URL to use instead of the `outUrl`, in case the coordinator wants to write to a temporary location and move it later. You create a file manager to actually copy the file from the download location to the storage location.

5. Call `dismissGrantingAccessToURL` to close the document picker and return control to the host app.

Next, implement the required `NSFileManagerDelegate` method in `DocumentPickerViewController`:

```
// MARK: NSFileManagerDelegate
func fileManager(fileManager: NSFileManager,
  shouldProceedAfterError error: NSError,
  copyingItemAtURL srcURL: NSURL,
  toURL dstURL: NSURL) -> Bool {

    return true
}
```

This method allows for replacement of the file if an old version exists at the same location.

Finally, replace the template `prepareForPresentationInMode()` method with the following code:

```
override func prepareForPresentationInMode(mode:
UIDocumentPickerMode) {
  super.prepareForPresentationInMode(mode)

  let vc = self.childViewControllers;
  let nav = vc.first
    as UINavigationController

  let thumbController = nav.topViewController
    as ThumbnailCollectionViewController

  thumbController.navigationController?.setNavigationBarHidden(
    true, animated: false)

  thumbController.delegate = self
}
```

You might notice some similarities to `viewDidLoad()`. You're locating a reference to the `ThumbnailCollectionViewController`, so you can set its delegate to the picker.

Use DocTester to build and run the extension again.

Hmmm…seems that selecting an image does absolutely nothing. That is because the File Provider extension template merely provides empty data. You should fix that!

The File Provider extension

The File Provider extension has a few purposes:

- **Provide and satisfy placeholder file URLs**: So even if the file doesn't exist, the file provider can perform the download on demand.
- **Provide file metadata**: Document-based apps interact with a file system primarily through metadata queries (more so on Mac than iOS). The file provider can provide metadata without gathering the file data. If the host app provides a list of documents but the user wants to open just one, this is useful.
- **Handle bookmark URLs**: Bookmarks work with state restoration to create a document URL the user can resume later. If the extension/container app changes the file or cleans up local files as they go out of scope, these ensure the file is available and in the proper state when the user re-launches the host app.

Technically, the last two points are outside the scope of this chapter, but if you're intrigued then review WWDC 2014 session 234, "Building a Document-Based App" for more details.

> **Note:** If the extension provides only Import and Export functionality, then you don't need a File Provider extension. The Document Picker extension can just copy the data to/from storage container directly.

Open to **FileProvider.swift** in the **S3ImagesFileProvider** extension. Import S3Kit at the top of the class:

```
import S3Kit
```

Now, replace `startProvidingItemAtURL` with:

```
override func startProvidingItemAtURL(url: NSURL,
completionHandler: ((error: NSError?) -> Void)?) {
    let fileManager = NSFileManager()
    let path = url.path!
    if fileManager.fileExistsAtPath(path) { //1
      //if the file is already, just return
      completionHandler?(error: nil)
```

```
      return
    }

    //load the file data from Amazon S3
    let key = url.lastPathComponent //2
    let bucket = BucketInfo()
    let fileData = bucket.load(key)! //3

    var error: NSError? = nil
    var fileError: NSError? = nil
    fileCoordinator.coordinateWritingItemAtURL(url,
      options: .ForReplacing,
      error: &error,
      byAccessor: { newURL in //4
      _ = fileData.writeToURL(newURL, options: .AtomicWrite,
error: &fileError)
    })
    if error != nil { //5
      completionHandler?(error: error);
    } else {
      completionHandler?(error: fileError);
    }
  }
```

This method ensures the image data is available at the URL when the host app requests it. Initially, the `documentStorageURL` resides in a shared folder outside the container app's sandbox, so the file has to be there *before* the method returns.

1. If the file already exists at this location, then the method just calls the callback and returns.

2. If the file is not at the expected location, it has to be downloaded. The S3 keys are the same as the file name in this app. Since the URL constructed by the Document Picker extension has that same filename as the last path component, it can be extracted here.

3. Th synchronous `load` method downloads the file data from S3.

4. The file coordinator provides a temporary URL to access to the location so the file data can be written to the URL. File coordination then takes care of moving that data, if the URLs differ. By specifying `ForReplacing,` the file coordinator knows the contents will be completely set.

5. After writing the file, the completion handler is called. If an error occurred during the write, it receives an error object.

Reading the image in the host app

The file provider is accessed with an `NSFileCoordinator`. Note the `importImage` function called by the document picker callback of DocTester's **ViewController.swift**. Here's what it looks like (you don't need to add this, it's already in DocTester):

```
func importImage(url : NSURL) {
  let fileCoordinator = NSFileCoordinator(filePresenter: nil)

  // 1
  fileCoordinator.coordinateReadingItemAtURL(url,
    options: .WithoutChanges,
    error: nil) { newURL in
      // 2
      if let data = NSData(contentsOfURL: newURL) {
        let image = UIImage(data: data)
        self.imageView.image = image
      }
  }
}
```

This reads the Document Picker extension-supplied URL and loads the image in the app's `imageView`. Here's the breakdown:

1. The `coordinateReadingItemAtURL` method accesses the sandboxed URL for reading, and calls the `accessor` block when the file is ready to be read. It supplies a new URL to represent the file, in case it has to copy the data to a different location (for security or multi-access purposes).
2. The supplied URL can be used like a regular file URL inside the `accessor` block.

Now build and run the S3Images target. Select **DocTester** as the app to run. Choose **Import** and select an image.

Voila! The picker should dismiss and display a picture inside the app.

Note: If you have any troubles, try running DocTester from the S3ImagesProvider target.

Export

At this point, the Document Provider extensions transfer an image file to the host app, but it doesn't upload new images. To make uploads possible, the Document Picker needs to provide a view for the user to enter the new file name instead of providing a thumbnail chooser.

To build the view, open **MainInterface.storyboard** in the **S3Images** target.

1. Add a new View Controller to the storyboard.
2. Right-drag a segue from the thumbnail controller to the new controller. Make it a **Push** segue and give it the identifier *upload*.

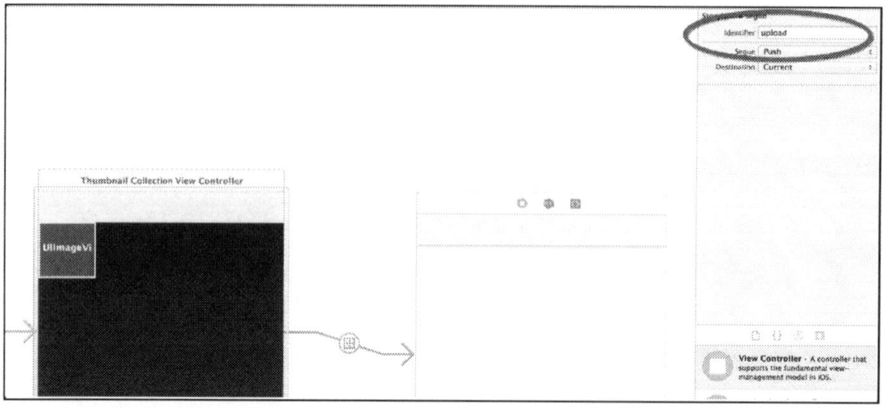

3. Drag a **Text Field** onto the view controller's view. Give it 10pt horizontal space on the leading and trailing edges, as well as on the vertical space between the top and the top layout guide. Supply placeholder text like *Type new filename*.

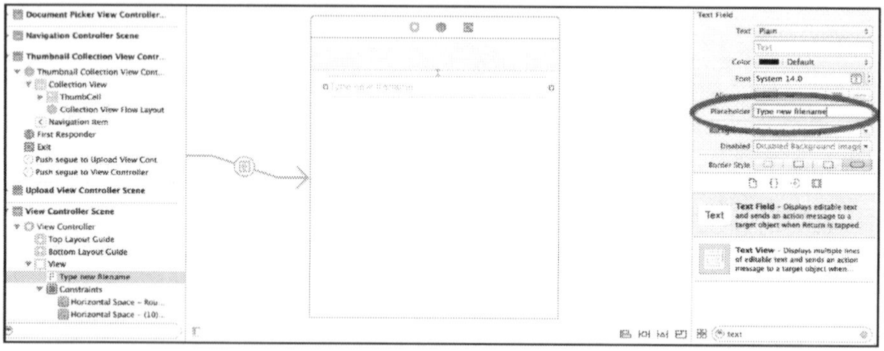

4. Add a **Button** to the view. Set the constraints so the Center X aligns with the text field, and the top space is 8pt to the bottom of the text field. Set the button title to *Upload*.

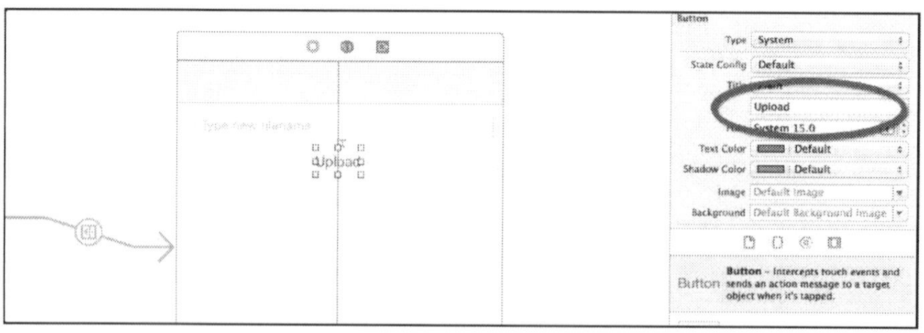

5. Create a new file in the S3Images project. Use the Cocoa Touch Class template. Call it **UploadViewController** and set its superclass to `UIViewController`.

6. Back in the storyboard, set the new view controller's class to `UploadViewController` in the Identity Inspector.

7. Open the Assistant Editor to show **UploadViewController.swift**. Then CTRL-drag outlets for the text field and button called **textField** and **button**, respectively. CTRL-drag from the button to create an `IBAction` named **upload**.

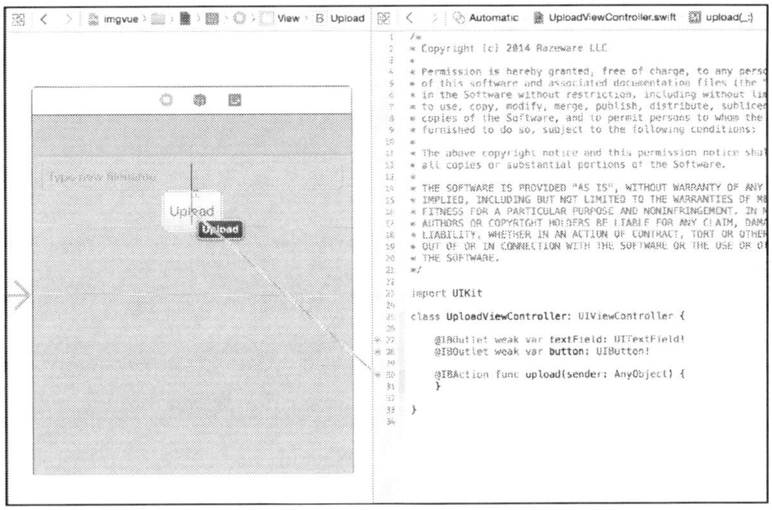

And that's how you set up the UI to allow the user to set a filename and upload the image.

Now you need the code to handle the UI events. Crack those knuckles and put your fingers to the keyboard once again. Oh, and hey, you're almost done!

You need to define a new protocol to notify the Document Picker subclass when the user sets a name. At the top of **UploadViewController.swift** add:

```
protocol UploadControllerDelegate {
  func nameChosen(name:String)
}
```

While passing in entered text, `nameChosen` gets called. Then, this method needs to be called on a delegate object.

Add a new instance variable to `UploadViewController`:

```
var delegate: UploadControllerDelegate?
```

Now set the delegate by overriding `viewWillAppear`:

```
override func viewWillAppear(animated: Bool) {
  super.viewWillAppear(animated)
  let navController = parentViewController
  let docPicker = navController?.parentViewController
  delegate = docPicker as DocumentPickerViewController
}
```

This locates the Document Picker view controller by walking back through the hierarchy. It then sets the picker as its delegate.

Next, add the code to call the delegate in the button's action:

```
@IBAction func upload(sender: AnyObject) {
  let name : NSString = textField.text
  if name.length > 0 {
    delegate?.nameChosen(name)
  }
}
```

This just makes sure the filename has at least one character.

Bring it all together by going back to **DocumentPickerViewController.swift** and adding a new `UploadControllerDelegate` protocol to the long class declaration:

```
class DocumentPickerViewController:
UIDocumentPickerExtensionViewController, ThumbnailDelegate,
NSFileManagerDelegate, UploadControllerDelegate {
```

Implement the delegate method by adding the following:

```
// MARK: UploadControllerDelegate
```

```
func nameChosen(name: String) {
  let justFilename = name.stringByDeletingPathExtension
  let exportURL =
documentStorageURL.URLByAppendingPathComponent(name).URLByAppend
ingPathExtension("jpg")
  upload(name, outURL: exportURL)
}
```

This code receives the new name, formats it and calls a helper method to do the upload. The first line prevents users from adding their own extensions. Then it creates a JPG-based URL. Finally, it calls the aforementioned helper method.

Add the following to implement the `upload` helper method:

```
func upload(name: String, outURL: NSURL) {
    let access =
originalURL!.startAccessingSecurityScopedResource() //1
    if access {
      let fc = NSFileCoordinator()
      var error: NSError?
      fc.coordinateReadingItemAtURL(originalURL!, //2
        options: .ForUploading,
        error: &error) { url in
          let bucket = BucketInfo() //3
          let data = NSData(contentsOfURL: url)!
          bucket.uploadData(data, name: name) { error in //4
            if error != nil {
              println("error uploading: \(error)")
            }
          }
          data.writeToURL(outURL, atomically: true) //5
          self.dismissGrantingAccessToURL(outURL) //6
      }
      originalURL!.stopAccessingSecurityScopedResource()
    }
  }
```

Step by step, here's what makes the helper method tick:

1. First, it ensures the host app has appropriate credentials, since it supplies a URL in its own sandbox.

2. A file coordinator then makes sure the file is ready for read access and can supply it a new URL if needed.

3. `BucketInfo` is the helper class in `S3Kit` that can access the remote storage. You reference it to perform the actual uploads.

4. If the file upload fails, then the error logs. There's no recovery, you just have to try again.
5. Since *Move* and *Export* just copy the data to the container app, this copies the file to the extension sandbox as well. It's up to the host app to handle the *Move* semantics by removing its own copy of the file. The extension requires the data to exist at this location, preventing a crash.
6. This passes the new local copy location back to the host app. Depending on the Document Picker mode semantics, the host app can update the file at this location.

Nice work! How are you holding up? Ready for more? Good, because you still need to call the upload segue to show the upload chooser.

Almost There

Modify `prepareForPresentationInMode` to check the mode and show the upload screen when it's in *Export* or *Move* mode.

The document picker extension has the same entry point regardless of picker mode. `prepareForPresentationInMode` is the mechanism for checking the mode and customizing the views for each. Since the Export and Move modes upload files to S3, the `upload` segue is performed in order to show the "enter file name" view. If it's in Import or Open mode, then the thumbnail chooser is shown with its delegate set.

Find this line in `prepareForPresentationInMode(mode:)`.

```
thumbController.delegate = self
```

And replace it with the following:

```
if mode == .ExportToService || mode == .MoveToService {
  thumbController.performSegueWithIdentifier("upload",
    sender: nil)
} else {
  thumbController.delegate = self
}
```

Build and run the **S3Images** target, and select the DocTester app to run.

Choose **Export** and it will download a random cat image. Choose the **S3Images** location, enter a name in the upload controller and press upload. When the controller dismisses, the image should now be in the S3 bucket. Verify by running the *Imgvue* app. Huzzah!

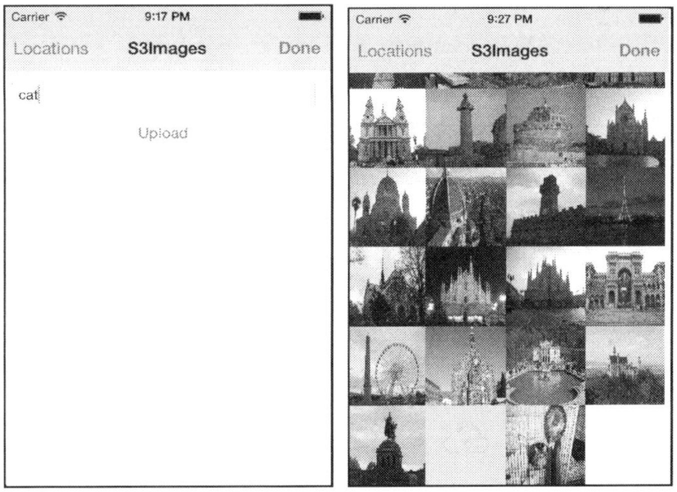

Opening and moving files

Although there are four Document Provider operations: Import, Open, Export and Move, you only implemented two code paths. Because the app's implementation only provides the option to download or upload to S3, Move and Export are treated the same; Import and Open are also treated the same.

The distinction between the methods that transfer and share common access (Open and Move) versus the ones that just transfer (Export and Import) are policy-based and not enforced by the storage provider's semantics.

For example, when opening or importing a file, the file downloads from S3, moves to the shared location and the URL returns to the host app.

If the host app intends to Import the file, it moves it to its sandbox. Or, in DocTester's case, it just loads the data into memory.

If the intention is to open the URL and use it throughout the host app lifecycle, then you use `startAccessingSecurityScopedResource` to hold the URL to obtain a bookmark and regain access to the file across app launches.

For example, in the `openImage` function called by the Document Picker callback in the DocTester **ViewController.swift** it does that, at least long enough to load the image.

```
func openImage(url : NSURL) {
  let accessing = url.startAccessingSecurityScopedResource() //1
  if accessing {
    let fileCoordinator = NSFileCoordinator(filePresenter: nil)
    fileCoordinator.coordinateReadingItemAtURL(url,
      options: .WithoutChanges,
      error: nil) { newURL in
        if let data = NSData(contentsOfURL: newURL) {
          let image = UIImage(data: data)
          self.imageView.image = image
        }
    }
    url.stopAccessingSecurityScopedResource() //2
  }
}
```

If the host app modifies a URL in the shared container, then `itemChangedAtURL` is called. The File Provider extension template comes with a stub for this method.

In the S3ImagesFileProvide group, open **FileProvider.swift**. Replace the template method with the following:

```
override func itemChangedAtURL(url: NSURL) {
  // 1
  let key = url.lastPathComponent
  let bucket = BucketInfo()

  // 2
  fileCoordinator.coordinateReadingItemAtURL(url,
    options: .ForUploading,
    error: nil) { newURL in
      var error: NSError
      let data = NSData(contentsOfURL: newURL)!
      bucket.uploadData(data,
        name: key,
        completion: { error in

          // 3
          if (error != nil) {
            println("error uploading updated file: \(error)")
          }
      })
  }
}
```

1. The extensions consistently use the filename as the S3 key.

2. `NSFileCoordinator` has a handy `ForUploading` option with the read accessor.

3. Uploads the updated file to S3.

This method will be called when the storage is shared between the host and providing apps. That is, in *Import* or *Export* mode, the host app has its own copy of the file and stops interacting with the shared URL after it handles the transfer. But with *Open* and *Move* mode that file remains in the control of the provider, but the host app continues to use it for as long as it needs to.

To try it out; build and run S3Images with DocTester. Open an image into DocTester, and then tap **Modify**.

This will draw a green square on the image and update it in the shared container. The update triggers the File Provider extension to update the copy on S3.

Now run Imgvue to see the modified file from S3. Try again, but instead import a different image. The **Modify** action will still update the in-app image, but it will result in a call to `itemChangedAtURL`, and therefore not update the file on S3.

Summary

Document Provider extensions allow apps to share custom remote storage with other apps on a user's device, usually via a Document Picker extension. A special shared file location is used between the extensions and host apps. Access to the container is controlled with a `NSFileCoordinator`. The File Provider extension allows for monitoring the shared container.

This chapter has just scratched the surface of the raw potential of File Provider extensions – it can also provide placeholder information, file sizes and thumbnails without downloading an entire file's data.

For more information on this, see the 2014 WWDC video, "Building a Document-based App" (https://developer.apple.com/videos/wwdc/2014/#234).

You can also customize the Document Picker extension to only provide certain file types or work with a subset of the four modes. This is controlled by the **info.plist**, under `NSExtension` > `NSExtensionAttributes`.

`UIDocumentPickerModes` is an array of supported modes, and `UIDocumentPickerSupportedFileTypes` is an array of the string UTType supported. This is `public.content` by default, which is pretty much everything.

Another interesting area to note is the `UIDocumentMenuViewController`, which is a menu that lets the user select from the activated Document Picker extensions.

The neat thing about this class is that you can add additional non-document-pickers. For example, the `UploadChooserViewController` in `UIWidgets` module (used by the upload tab in the container app) has a menu item to load images from the photos album in addition the iCloud document pickers.

Of course, extensions have some limitations and aren't good for every app. First, the extra Document Pickers have to be enabled, which requires the user to have an iCloud account with iCloud drive logged in to the device – probably a safe assumption.

Then, the host app needs to be somewhat document-based and have iCloud document entitlements. Finally, the user has to navigate through several non-intuitive screens to enable each extension individually.

This is a lot of work, which may be why Apple only recommends this extension for apps that act as a file repository for other apps like Dropbox, Box, Google Drive, etc.

For those apps where you just want ubiquity for your own documents, you can use iCloud and iTunes directly. Moreover, apps can open other files using URL schemes and supported UTTypes. In this case, an Action, Share, or Photo Editing extension might be more appropriate.

Otherwise, have fun with Document Providers!

Chapter 14: Keyboard Extensions

By Tammy L. Coron

Prior to iOS 8, replacing the system-wide keyboard with one of your own wasn't even an option. If your app utilized `UITextView` or `UITextField` you could present your own input views as alternatives to the system keyboard, but these were only available from within your app.

However, thanks to app extensions, the user can replace the system keyboard with one you provide, bundled with your app.

This chapter will guide you through the process of creating a Custom Keyboard extension.

Understanding "key" custom keyboard concepts

A custom keyboard is one that you design, build, install, and offer to the user as a replacement for the system keyboard. Just like the system keyboard, yours can interact with the user by responding to taps and other input events. The idea is to capture, and then send, an unattributed `NSString` instance to the host app. Use your imagination for this task, but don't go overboard.

More importantly, all custom keyboards must provide a dedicated **Next Keyboard** button so the user can easily switch between keyboards. Without this feature, your app would likely be rejected during review.

Note: It's important to understand the difference between in-app keyboards over which you have total control, and a system-wide keyboard. If you want to develop a supplement to the system keyboard, exclusive to your app, there are better options provided within the SDK, which have existed prior to iOS 8. These include custom input and accessory views. For more information, read Apple's **Text Programming Guide for iOS** http://bit.ly/1zXtUXB - specifically **Custom Views for Data Input** http://bit.ly/1rw0VYt.

Managing user expectations

Managing user expectations is absolutely crucial to your app's success. When you develop a keyboard that affects how users interact with their devices, system-wide, that task becomes even more important.

The best way to understand how to develop a custom keyboard is to first examine the system keyboard and recognize how it behaves and operates.

The system keyboard is quick to respond and simple to use; it doesn't nag the user with unnecessary feedback. *It just works!* When your custom keyboard functions at this level, you'll have happy users.

Another great attribute of the system keyboard is its design is clean and focused. The bar has been set, and a custom keyboard should aim to meet these same high standards. For instance, while it might seem like a stroke of brilliance to skin a keyboard using the entire color spectrum of a rainbow, it's probably best to stick to something a little less gaudy, a little more legible. That is unless you're coding an app for a magical unicorn :]

Expected keyboard features

There are obvious features your custom keyboard will provide, such as having the ability to take user input and send it to the host app. However, one of the most important features - and one that is often overlooked - is providing a mechanism to switch between different keyboards. This has been a long-standing feature of the system keyboard, allowing you change between standard QWERTY style keyboards, foreign language keyboards such as Chinese, and of course, Emoji. In fact, as I mentioned earlier, implementing this feature is mandatory; the `UIInputViewController` class provides a specific method – `advanceToNextInputMode` – to do exactly this.

Additional features a seasoned iOS user would expect include:

- Appropriate layout and features based on keyboard type trait
- Automatic period upon detecting a double space
- Caps lock support
- Dictation
- Keycap artwork
- Multistage input for languages based on ideograms, such as Chinese

All these features are of-course optional, but many are expected. At the time writing, there are no APIs provided to aid their implementation. Manually adding them to any custom keyboard extension will certainly make your keyboard stand out from the rest.

Technology limitations

When building a custom keyboard, there are certain limitations of which to be aware. First and foremost, a custom keyboard can only be drawn within the primary view of its parent `UIInputViewController` object; as a result, you can't draw keycap artwork above the top-row in the same way Apple does. You can, however, increase the overall height of the keyboard by using Auto Layout and changing the necessary height constraints. The width cannot be changed.

Selecting text and manipulating the cursor position also isn't possible; these actions remain tightly under the control of the text input object that's providing the keyboard.

Likewise, editing menu options – such as Cut, Copy and Paste – provided by any text input controls are inaccessible. Since a keyboard has no access to the text input control that summoned it, inline auto-correction at the text insertion point is also not possible.

In addition, custom keyboards don't have access to many of the general keyboard settings found in Settings.app. You can however provide your own settings bundle that can be displayed in Settings.app.

> **Note:** For more information about implementing a settings bundle, refer to Apple's guide, **Implementing an iOS Settings Bundle**
> http://bit.ly/1n5sNzV

Finally, a custom keyboard cannot be used with any of the following text input objects:

- **Secure text input objects:** any object that has its `secureText` property set to `YES`
- **Phone pad objects:** any object that has a keyboard type trait of `UIKeyboardTypePhonePad` or `UIKeyboardTypeNamePhonePad`

When any of these objects receives focus, the system keyboard temporarily replaces your keyboard. When an object not displaying any of the above traits receives focus, your keyboard will automatically return.

Mandatory development requirements

There are two mandatory requirements for all custom keyboards. Actually, only one is mandatory in Apple's eyes. The other, while not *officially* mandatory, is definitely something that should be high up your list of priorities when developing a keyboard.

- **Next Keyboard**

  All custom keyboards must provide an obvious way to display to the next keyboard. This *is* mandatory. Failure to provide such a mechanism will result in your app being rejected.

> **Note:** There is no API available for obtaining a list of installed keyboards; the system is responsible for selecting the *next* keyboard when you invoke the `advanceToNextInputMode` method.

- **Trust**

  Today, users are more aware of the vulnerability of their data than ever before, so it's understandable why they may hesitate to trust developers. Hence, it's crucial that developers remain cognizant of the users' privacy. For helpful tips and best practices, please review the **Best Practices for Maintaining User Privacy** section in Apple's **iOS App Programming Guide**. http://bit.ly/1gmQ0FX

Trustworthy development

Developing with trust and security in-mind isn't something to take lightly, especially when it comes to custom keyboards.

Users expect their keystrokes to be handled safely and accurately. When they tap a key, they expect that tap-event to translate into the appropriate character in the corresponding text input object; they don't expect – or want – it sent to a random server somewhere out in cyberspace without their knowledge. Apple, and your users are putting their trust in you to *do the right thing*; don't abuse that trust.

The same holds true for accessing other private user data, such as location data or address book data. While both may enhance the experience your custom keyboard provides, it's up to you to make a compelling argument for doing so.

Open access/network access keyboard

By default, all custom keyboards have their network access disabled; the **RequestsOpenAccess** key in the **info.plist** file controls this.

Keyboards with their network access disabled allow developers to provide functionality while creating a trustworthy environment. By also restricting a keyboards file system access to just its own sandbox, keystrokes are prevented from *wandering* off.

In stark contrast, network-enabled keyboards offer a variety of possibilities, but increase the developer's overall responsibilities. When building a network-enabled keyboard, remember to adhere to the networked keyboard guidelines found in Apple's **App Extension Programming Guide**.

The following list shows the capabilities available to a network-enabled keyboard. Bare in mind that some of these features will require the user's permission before they can be used:

- Location Services
- Address Book
- Game Center and In-App Purchases, via the container app
- Shared data container with the container app
- Server-side processing of keystrokes and other input events
- iCloud integration

If you intend on supporting any these features, you should strongly consider your responsibilities and the users' privacy concerns before proceeding.

OK, now to build a custom keyboard!

Now that you're empowered with a well-rounded knowledge of custom keyboards, you're ready to get your hands dirty.

In the next two sections, you'll build two custom keyboards:

- The first section aims to familiarize you with the Custom Keyboard template provided by Xcode, walking you through the process of building a simple custom keyboard.
- The second uses a starter project, and dives much deeper into the concepts and APIs behind creating a custom keyboard.

Custom keyboard template (Xcode)

Creating a custom keyboard target is very similar to creating other app extension targets. If you haven't already done so, please read Chapter 8, **Introducing Extensions**; it's ok, I'll wait :]

Creating a new application and target

Open Xcode and select **Editor\File\New Project...** then choose **iOS\Application\Single View Application** and click **Next**.

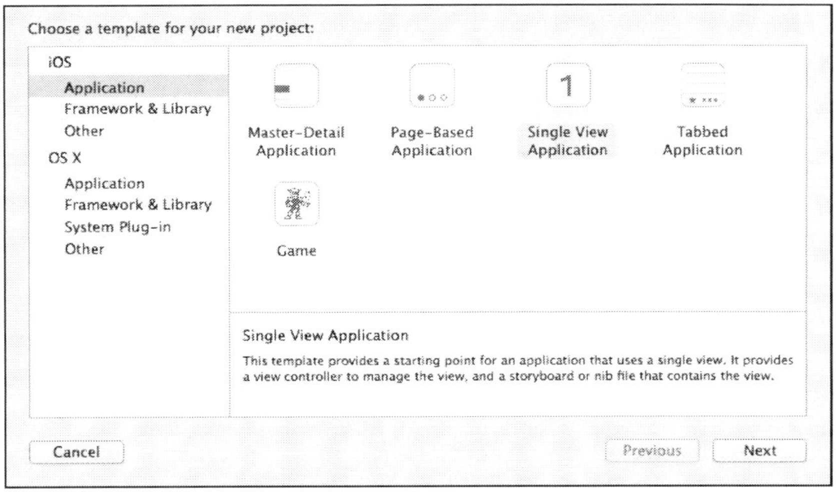

Set **Product Name** to **KeyboardContainingApp**, set the **Language** to **Swift**, and **Devices** to **Universal**. Click **Next**.

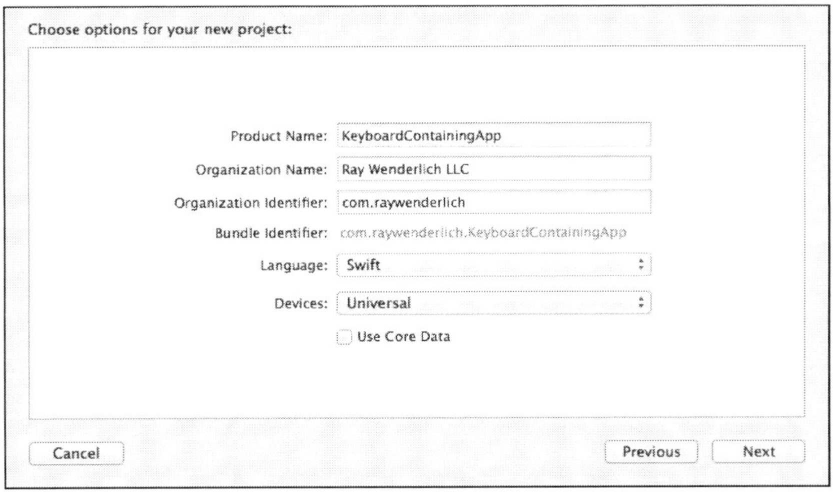

Choose a location to save your project, then click **Create**. You now have a single view application that will act as the containing app for your keyboard extension.

> **Note:** All extensions must be bundled with a containing app. This app **must** provide some functionality, in addition to the extension, in order to make it through the review process. Apple is very clear on this matter; containing apps must not be skeleton apps whose sole purpose is to distribute an extension.

The next step is to add the extension target to your project.

Select **Editor\Add Target...** then **iOS\Application Extension\Custom Keyboard** and click **Next**.

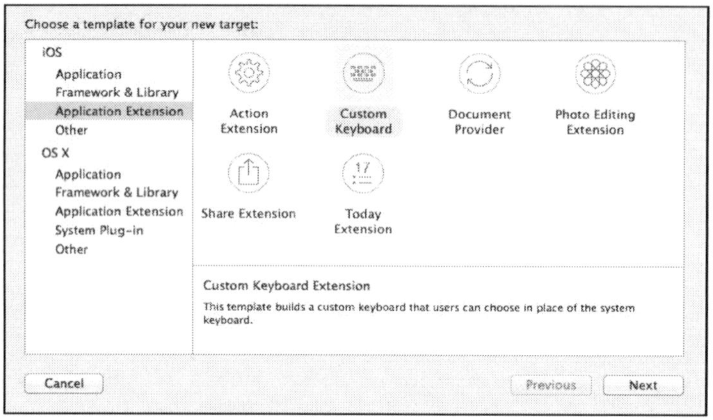

Set the **Product Name** to **CustomKeyboard**. Set the **Language** to **Swift**. Also set both **Project** and **Embed in Application** to **KeyboardContainingApp**. Finally, click **Finish**.

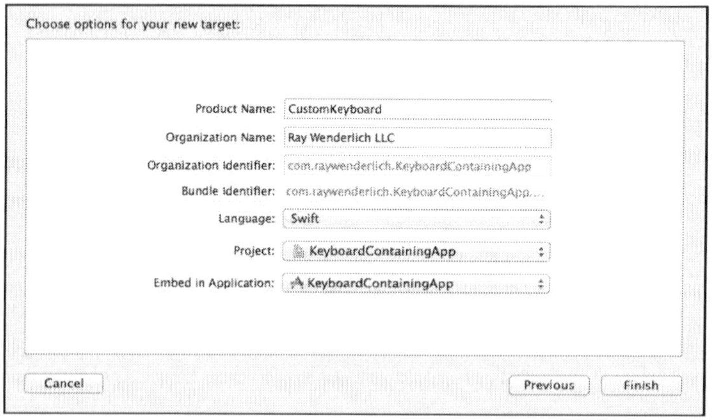

You'll be prompted to activate the new targets' scheme, but in this instance click **Cancel**.

The project and target are now ready for customization.

Customizing the keyboard extension template

In the **Project Navigator**, expand the **CustomKeyboard** group and open **Info.plist**. Of particular interest are the keys within the **NSExtension\NSExtensionAttributes** dictionary. These control certain behaviors of your keyboard.

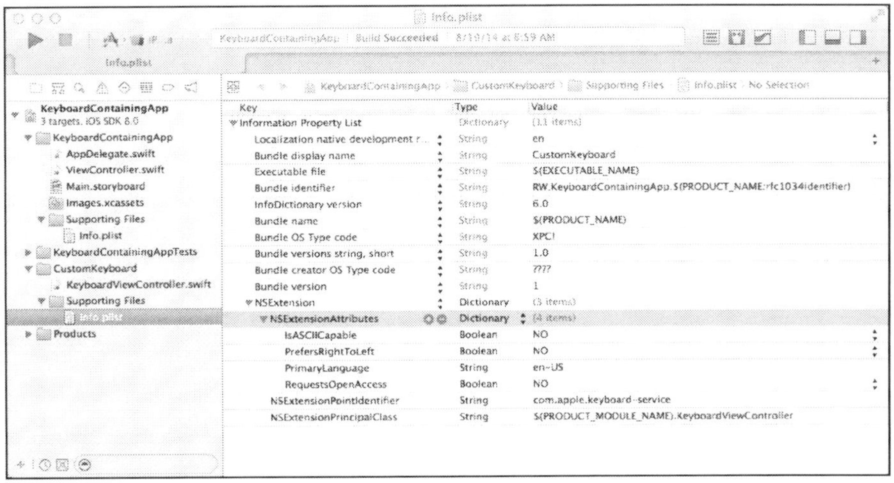

- **isASCIICapable:** Determines if the custom keyboard can support ASCII characters. If your keyboard supports the `UIKeyboardTypeACSIICapable` keyboard trait, set this value to **YES**. The default setting is **NO**. According to Apple's documentation, `UIKeyboardTypeACSIICapable` "displays a keyboard which can enter ASCII characters, non-ASCII keyboards remain active".

- **PrefersRightToLeft**: Specifies the direction of the primary language of the keyboard. The default setting is **NO**.

- **PrimaryLanguage**: The primary language of the keyboard. The default is **en-US**.

- **RequestsOpenAccess**: Determines the network access of the keyboard. Setting this value to **YES** provides all the functionality covered in the **Open Access/Network Access** section above. The default setting is **NO**.

For now, you'll simply use the defaults.

Reviewing The Keyboard Template's Default Code

In the **Project Navigator**, expand the **CustomKeyboard** group if it isn't already, and open **KeyboardViewController.swift**.

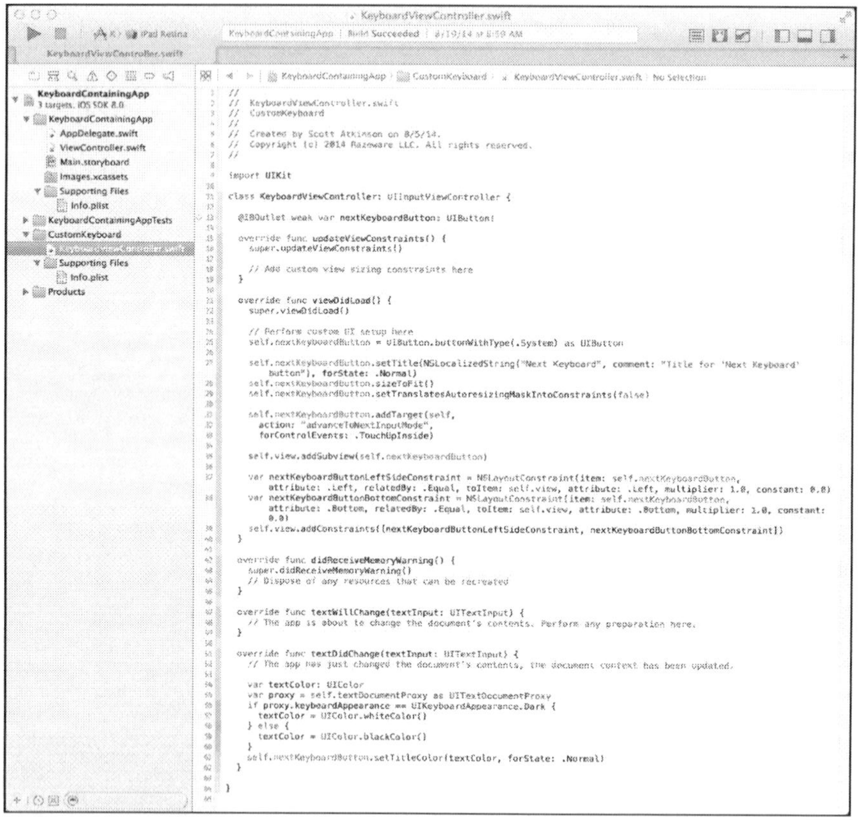

The default template includes the boilerplate code necessary for creating a custom keyboard. Take a look at `viewDidLoad`. Note the inclusion of the mandatory call to `advanceToNextInputMode`.

```
self.nextKeyboardButton.addTarget(self,
  action: "advanceToNextInputMode",
  forControlEvents: .TouchUpInside)
```

The template makes use of `NSLayoutContraint` for laying out its buttons. All custom keyboards should work across all devices, in both orientations. Using Auto Layout makes this a cinch.

Although you're not making changes to this code, it's important to realize what's included with the default template, so take some time to review `KeyboardViewController` in-order to get an understanding of what's going on.

The real work begins in the next section, where you'll be working with a fully functional containing app along with its custom keyboard extension.

But first, one more thing...

Adding a new keyboard in iOS

Change the active scheme to **KeyboardContainingApp**. Build and run. At this point, the simulator displays an empty white screen. This is to be expected, since you're simply running the **Single View Application** template.

From the simulator's menu, select **Hardware\Home** to return to Springboard. Alternatively, use the keyboard shortcut **shift+cmd+h**.

Open **Settings.app** and navigate to **General\Keyboard\Keyboards**.

Next, tap **Add New Keyboard...**, and select **KeyboardContainingApp**. The simulator screen will look like the one shown here on the far right.

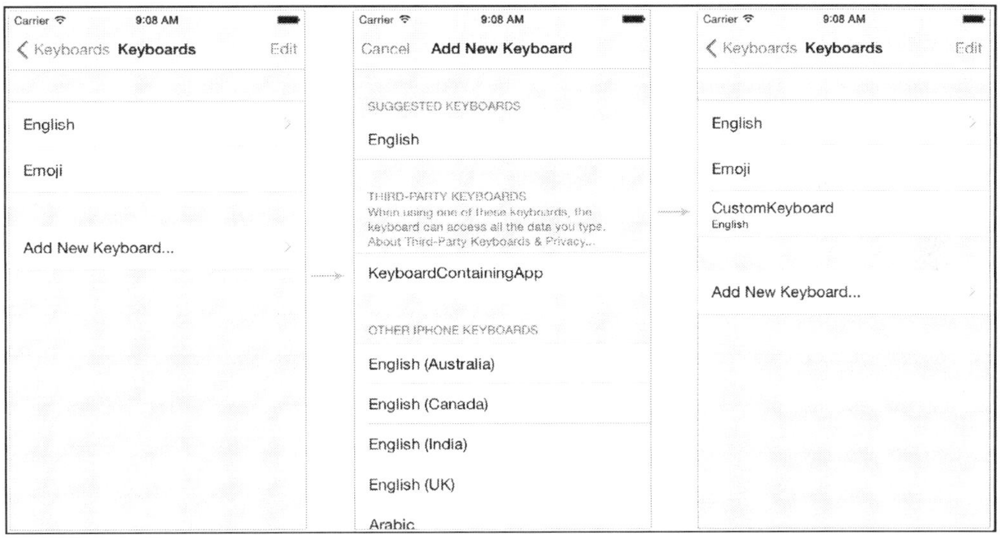

> **Note:** You can use the **Bundle display name** key found in the targets **Info.plist** file to change the display name of your keyboard.

The last thing to do is verify that you've installed the keyboard properly.

Shift+cmd+h back to Springboard and launch **Safari**. Tap the URL field to summon the keyboard. Press the **Next Keyboard** button – represented by a globe or smiley face – to switch to your newly installed, custom keyboard.

> **Note:** You may see an **Alternate Keyboards** alert view. If you do, read the alert and then tap **OK**.

Once again, if everything went according to plan, your simulator should look like the one shown here, on the far right.

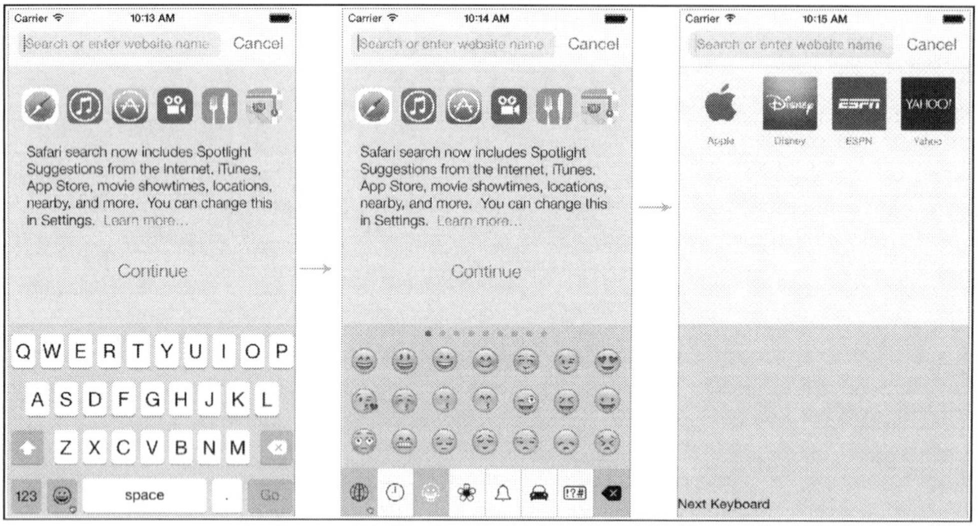

As you can see, a single button has been placed on the custom keyboard, which allows the user to navigate to the next available keyboard.

Okay, now it's time to craft a real keyboard extension. Excited? *You should be!*

Do-hit-key (doo-hick-ey)

So, you have a good understanding of custom keyboard extensions, the template used for creating them and how to enable them in iOS. *What's next?* In this section, you'll build on this knowledge with a simple app titled **Do-Hit-Key**.

For the most part, the project is setup for you. It contains an app target, a custom keyboard target, and a Nib file that represents the primary view of the keyboard. It's also linked to the `CoreLocation` framework, which is used to implement a key that obtains the user's current location.

Furthermore, all `IBOutlet` and `IBAction` objects are already connected to their respective targets, and the necessary `NSLayoutConstraint` objects are defined.

In addition to providing basic keyboard functionality, Do-Hit-Key offers the choice of four different keyboard themes and four alternate top-row key-sets. As an added bonus, Do-Hit-Key implements a swipe-up gesture on the top-row that allows users to input the numbers 0-9. Your task is to add the code that enables all this functionality.

The containing app and custom keyboard extension work on all devices, in both orientations, compliments of Auto Layout.

Meet Do-Hit-Key!

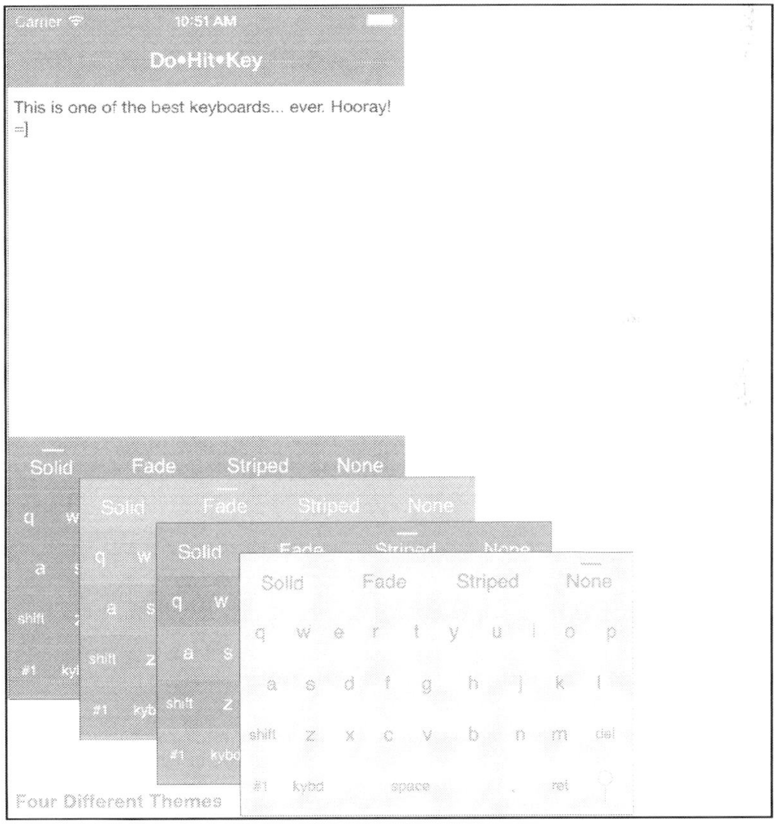

An overview of the theme data

Open the starter project in Xcode, expand the **CustomKeyboard** group in the **Project Navigator** and open **KeyboardThemeData.swift**.

This class defines the keyboard's various themes, including color settings, font settings and other identifiers. You won't be working in this class, but it's helpful to be aware of what's going on in there.

The `configureThemeData` method returns an array containing four objects; each one representing one of the four available themes: solid, fade, striped and none.

```
let themeData = [KeyboardThemeData.solidTheme(),
  KeyboardThemeData.fadeTheme(),
  KeyboardThemeData.stripedTheme(),
  KeyboardThemeData.noneTheme()]
return themeData
```

The objects are created using the class methods: `solidTheme`, `fadeTheme`, `stripedTheme` and `noneTheme`. Since these methods are similar in their implementation, I'll just cover `solidTheme` here:

```
class func solidTheme() -> KeyboardThemeData {
  var theme: KeyboardThemeData = KeyboardThemeData()
  theme.themeID = 0
  theme.themeName = "Solid"

  theme.colorForBackground = UIColor(red: 107.0/255.0,
    green: 205.0/255.0, blue: 159.0/255.0, alpha: 1.0)
  theme.colorForCustomRow = UIColor(red: 69.0/255.0,
    green: 195.0/255.0, blue: 136.0/255.0, alpha: 1.0)
  theme.colorForRow1 = UIColor(red: 69.0/255.0,
    green: 195.0/255.0, blue: 136.0/255.0, alpha: 1.0)
  theme.colorForRow2 = UIColor(red: 69.0/255.0,
    green: 195.0/255.0, blue: 136.0/255.0, alpha: 1.0)
  theme.colorForRow3 = UIColor(red: 69.0/255.0,
    green: 195.0/255.0, blue: 136.0/255.0, alpha: 1.0)
  theme.colorForRow4 = UIColor(red: 69.0/255.0,
    green: 195.0/255.0, blue: 136.0/255.0, alpha: 1.0)

  theme.colorForButtonFont = UIColor.whiteColor()
  theme.keyboardButtonFont = UIFont(name: ButtonFontName,
    size: ButtonFontSize)!

  return theme
}
```

This class method sets up each property for the theme. It sets the id, name, colors and font information. Once configured, the theme object is returned.

As mentioned before, you won't be working in this file, so don't make any changes to it at this time. Just absorb what's going on and keep it in mind as you move forward.

An overview of the containing app

In the **Project Navigator**, expand the **DoHitKey** group and open **RWTViewController.swift**.

This is another file for you to review, but you won't need to make any changes to it during this chapter.

This class is responsible for the containing app. Remember, all app extensions must be bundled with a containing app, and that app must provide some kind of functionality. In this case, the containing app allows the user to jot down a note.

Open **Main.storyboard**. This is the main interface for the containing app, and it contains nothing more than a `UITextField` along with its necessary constraints. The `UIViewController` is also embedded in a `UINavigationController`.

Ok, that's it! Now that you've familiarized yourself with various pieces of the app, it's time to step out of the role of a reviewer and into the role of the developer.

From here on out, *you're* writing the code to make things happen.

Adding the view

From the **CustomKeyboard** group, open **KeyboardViewController.swift**. Locate `viewDidLoad()` and add the following block to the bottom of the method:

```
let nib = UINib(nibName: "KeyboardView", bundle: nil)
let objects = nib.instantiateWithOwner(self, options: nil)
containerView = objects[0] as UIView
view = containerView;
configureGesturesForView(rowCustomAlt1)
configureGesturesForView(rowCustomAlt2)
configureGesturesForView(rowCustomAlt3)
configureGesturesForView(rowCustomAlt4)

themeData = KeyboardThemeData.configureThemeData()
getCurrentAppSettings()
configureCoreLocationManager()
```

Here you load the nib containing the interface for your keyboard and sets it as the primary view for your keyboard extension.

You also call the methods responsible for configuring the swipe-up gestures on the custom top-rows. In addition, you've populated the variable `themeData` with the results from `KeyboardThemeData.configureThemeData()` should you need access to this data elsewhere in your code.

The last two lines load the current settings and configure the location manager. You'll implement these later.

Build and run.

Remember, you'll need to add the Do-Hit-Key keyboard extension in the **Settings.app** before you can actually use it. When you select Do-Hit-Key from the list of available keyboards, this time you'll be taken to a new screen that controls the keyboards' network access. Even though you can *request* network access using the necessary key in the targets' **info.plist** file, the control ultimately lies with the user. If prompted, tap the **Allow Full Access** switch, and tap **Allow** on the subsequent alert:

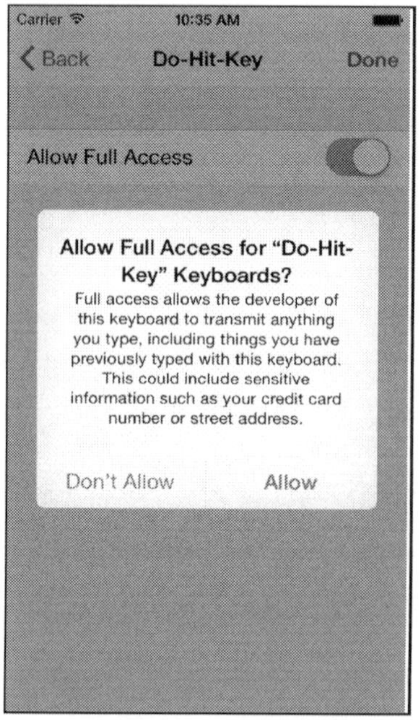

> **Note:** The starter project is preconfigured to request for full access.

Once you've added the keyboard, head back to the containing app, tap anywhere to summon the keyboard, and advance to the next keyboard until you see the Do-Hit-Key keyboard. It should look like this:

Although the buttons are connected to their actions, the methods are currently just stub, since you need to flesh them out. It's a pretty, albeit useless keyboard at this moment.

Time to make the magic happen!

Configuring the gestures

In `KeyboardViewController`, find `configureGesturesForView(view:)` and add the following:

```
for index in 1...10 {
  let button: UIButton? = view.viewWithTag(index) as? UIButton;
  let swipeUp = UISwipeGestureRecognizer(target: self,
    action: "swipeForNumber:")
  swipeUp.direction = .Up
  button?.addGestureRecognizer(swipeUp)
}
```

This method accepts an instance of `UIView` and iterates over its ten `UIButton` subviews. For each iteration, it creates a `UISwipeGestureRecognizer`, assigns the appropriate action and direction, and then adds it to the button.

Now find `swipeForNumber(gesture:)` and add the following code:

```
if gesture.view!.tag == 10 {
  (textDocumentProxy as UIKeyInput).insertText("0")
} else {
  let string = "\(gesture.view!.tag)"
  (textDocumentProxy as UIKeyInput).insertText(string)
}
```

Here you retrieve the tag of the view belonging to the gesture recognizer and insert it at the insertion point of the current text input object, via the `textDocumentProperty`. This is an object conforming to the `UITextDocumentProxy` protocol, which acts as a proxy between your keyboard and the text input object that summoned it. Coincidentally, the tag of each button is the same as the number the button represents, which is why this code is so succinct.

Alternating the top-row on button press

The top row allows the user to choose a keyboard style. It also contains a button that cycles between four different top rows, each having its own keyset. This button calls `btnChangeAltRowTap(button:)`.

Locate `btnChangeAltRowTap(button:)` and add the following code to it:

```
rowCustom.hidden = true

rowCustomAlt1.hidden = true
rowCustomAlt2.hidden = true
rowCustomAlt3.hidden = true
rowCustomAlt4.hidden = true

if button.titleLabel!.text == "#1" {
  rowCustom.hidden = true
  rowCustomAlt1.hidden = false
  button.setTitle("#2", forState: .Normal)
} else if button.titleLabel!.text == "#2" {
  rowCustom.hidden = true
  rowCustomAlt2.hidden = false
  button.setTitle("#3", forState: .Normal)
} else if button.titleLabel!.text == "#3" {
  rowCustom.hidden = true
  rowCustomAlt3.hidden = false
  button.setTitle("#4", forState: .Normal)
} else if button.titleLabel!.text == "#4" {
  rowCustom.hidden = true
  rowCustomAlt4.hidden = false
```

```
    button.setTitle("#0", forState: .Normal)
  } else if button.titleLabel!.text == "#0" {
    rowCustom.hidden = false
    button.setTitle("#1", forState: .Normal)
  }
```

Initially, all views associated with the top row are hidden. Once it's determined which row to display, that row is made visible and the button's title updated accordingly.

Build and run. The first thing you'll notice is that you can use the #1 key to cycle between the four alternate top rows, and the theme-selection row. You should also be able to swipe up on any of those four rows and have the relevant number appear in the text area.

If all is well, you can move on to styling the keyboard.

Styling the keyboard

In `viewDidLoad()` you added a call to `getCurrentAppSettings()`; now you're going to implement it.

Add the following lines to `getCurrentAppSettings()`:

```
let defaults = NSUserDefaults.standardUserDefaults()
currentThemeID = defaults.integerForKey(ThemePreference)
styleKeyboardWithThemeID(currentThemeID)
```

This reads an integer from `NSUserDefaults` and stores it in the `currentThemeID` property. A call is made to `styleKeyboardWithThemeID(theme:)` passing the integer, which represents the theme ID. This method applies the theme.

There are three methods called by `styleKeyboardWithThemeID(theme:)`:

- `styleThemeButton(button:, theme:)`
- `setButtonCase()`
- `setButtonFont(viewWithButtons:, theme:)`

You'll implement these first. Find `styleThemeButton(button:,theme:)` in `KeyboardViewController` and add the following code:

```
let image = UIImage(named:
"whiteLine")?.imageWithRenderingMode(.AlwaysTemplate)
button.selected = false
button.setBackgroundImage(image, forState: .Selected)
button.tintColor = theme.colorForButtonFont
```

Here you create an image and add it as the background image for the selected state of the button. This provides the user with some visual feedback about the selected keyboard theme.

Since one of the themes uses a light background, it makes sense to use the font color from the selected theme as the tint color. In order for image tinting to work, you set the image as a template using `imageWithRenderingMode`.

Next, locate `setButtonCase()` and add the following four lines:

```
setShiftStatus(row1)
setShiftStatus(row2)
setShiftStatus(row3)
setShiftStatus(row4)
```

You'll implement `setShiftStatus(viewWithButtons:)` shortly.

Finally, locate `setButtonFont(viewWithButtons:, theme:)` and add the following:

```
for view in viewWithButtons.subviews {
  if let button = view as? UIButton {
    button.titleLabel!.font = theme.keyboardButtonFont;
    button.setTitleColor(theme.colorForButtonFont,
      forState: .Normal)
    if button.tag == TagForSpecialButtons {
      button.titleLabel!.font = UIFont(name:
button.titleLabel!.font.fontName,
        size: SpecialButtonFontSize)
    }
  }
}
```

Here you iterate over the subviews of the passed in view, specifically looking for instances of `UIButton`. When one is found, the title color and font are set accordingly. You also take into account any utility buttons such as shift, delete, return etc. These buttons have their `tag` property set to `99` in the nib, which is also the value of the `TagForSpecialButtons` constant.

You're finally ready to populate `styleKeyboardWithThemeID(theme:)`. This is the *meat and potatoes* of the implementation! By the way, you're almost done :]

In `KeyboardViewController`, find `styleKeyboardWithThemeID(theme:)` and add the following:

```
var currentTheme = themeData[themeID]
```

```
/* Reset theme buttons */
styleThemeButton(btnTheme1, theme: currentTheme)
styleThemeButton(btnTheme2, theme: currentTheme)
styleThemeButton(btnTheme3, theme: currentTheme)
styleThemeButton(btnTheme4, theme: currentTheme)

/* Set selected theme button */
switch themeID {
case 0:
  btnTheme1.selected = true
case 1:
  btnTheme2.selected = true
case 2:
  btnTheme3.selected = true
case 3:
  btnTheme4.selected = true
default:
  btnTheme1.selected = true
}

/* Handle Tint Color for Location Button */
let image = UIImage(named:
"pin")?.imageWithRenderingMode(.AlwaysTemplate)
btnLocation.setImage(image, forState: .Normal)
btnLocation.tintColor = currentTheme.colorForButtonFont

/* Set Colors */
containerView.backgroundColor = currentTheme.colorForBackground;

rowCustom.backgroundColor = currentTheme.colorForCustomRow;
row1.backgroundColor = currentTheme.colorForRow1;
row2.backgroundColor = currentTheme.colorForRow2;
row3.backgroundColor = currentTheme.colorForRow3;
row4.backgroundColor = currentTheme.colorForRow4;

rowCustomAlt1.backgroundColor = currentTheme.colorForCustomRow;
rowCustomAlt2.backgroundColor = currentTheme.colorForCustomRow;
rowCustomAlt3.backgroundColor = currentTheme.colorForCustomRow;
rowCustomAlt4.backgroundColor = currentTheme.colorForCustomRow;

/* Set Button Case */
setButtonCase();

/* Set Button Fonts */
setButtonFont(rowCustom , theme: currentTheme)
setButtonFont(rowCustomAlt1 , theme: currentTheme)
setButtonFont(rowCustomAlt2 , theme: currentTheme)
setButtonFont(rowCustomAlt3 , theme: currentTheme)
```

```
setButtonFont(rowCustomAlt4 , theme: currentTheme)

setButtonFont(row1 , theme: currentTheme)
setButtonFont(row2 , theme: currentTheme)
setButtonFont(row3 , theme: currentTheme)
setButtonFont(row4 , theme: currentTheme)
```

Whoa! That's quite the block of code, isn't it? Please don't be intimidated; it's simply bringing the whole thing together, calling methods that you've already explored or added yourself.

Essentially, user's chosen theme is being used to style the interface.

The final step to get those styles working is to populate `btnChangeThemeTap(button:)`. This `IBAction`, just like the others, is already connected up in Interface Builder.

Locate `btnChangeThemeTap(button:)` in **KeyboardViewController.swift** and add:

```
button.selected = true

let defaults = NSUserDefaults.standardUserDefaults()
defaults.setInteger(button.tag, forKey: ThemePreference)
defaults.synchronize()
currentThemeID = defaults.integerForKey(ThemePreference)
styleKeyboardWithThemeID(currentThemeID)
```

The method reads the `tag` property of the button responsible for calling it, and stores it in `NSUserDefaults`. This is how the theme is persisted across launches of the keyboard.

Build and run. You should now be able to use the appropriate buttons to cycle through the four different themes.

Adding the standard input keys

You have a great looking keyboard, nice! Unfortunately, it's form over function in its current state. Luckily for you, it's a relatively easy fix.

The keys on the keyboard are connected to one of five methods, depending on their purpose. Their names are pretty self-explanatory.

For now, you'll just implement the first four.

First, add the following to `btnKeyPressedTap`:

```
var string = button.titleLabel!.text
(textDocumentProxy as UIKeyInput).insertText("\(string!)")
```

Then, add the following to `btnBackspaceKeyTap`:

```
(textDocumentProxy as UIKeyInput).deleteBackward()
```

Next up, find `btnSpacebarKeyTap` and add:

```
(textDocumentProxy as UIKeyInput).insertText(" ")
```

Finally add the following to `btnReturnKeyTap`:

```
(textDocumentProxy as UIKeyInput).insertText("\n")
```

Using `insertText`, which is defined in the `UIKeyInput` protocol, each method inserts the relevant text into the current text input object, at its insertion point.

The exception to this is the delete key; that uses the `deleteBackward` method.

Build and run. Tap each key and it should place the corresponding character inside the text view. Hang on a minute, why only capital letters?

Why u make me shout?

> **Note:** The `UIKeyInput` protocol is the heart and soul of creating a custom keyboard. Its primary focus is inserting and deleting text. Any subclass of `UIResponder` can adopt this protocol. For more information, please refer to the `UIKeyInput` Protocol Reference. http://bit.ly/1ucMZkv

Adding the shift key

First, locate `setShiftStatus(viewWithButtons:)` and add the following:

```
for view in viewWithButtons.subviews {
  if let button = view as? UIButton {
    let buttonText = button.titleLabel!.text
    if shiftOn {
      if button.tag != TagForSpecialButtons {
        let text = buttonText!.uppercaseString
        button.setTitle("\(text)", forState: .Normal)
      }
    } else {
      let text = buttonText!.lowercaseString
      button.setTitle("\(text)", forState: .Normal)
    }
  }
}
```

This method uses `shiftOn` to determine the current shift state, and sets each buttons' text to either the uppercase or lowercase equivalent.

Next, locate `btnShiftKeyTap(button:)` and add the following:

```
shiftOn = !shiftOn
setButtonCase()
```

Here you toggle the shift state, and then update the case of each button by calling `setButtonCase`.

Finally, back in `btnKeyPressedTap(button:)`,add the following at the very end:

```
if (ShiftAutoOff) {
  shiftOn = false
  setButtonCase()
}
```

This simply turns shift off after each key press unless you're using caps-lock.

Build and run. You should now see the keys alternate between upper and lower case each time you press the shift key.

Adding the current location key

There are two custom methods and one protocol method you'll use to capture the user's current location:

- `configureCoreLocationManager()`
- `btnLocationTap(button:)`
- `locationManager(manager:, didUpdateLocations locations:)`

First, find `configureCoreLocationManager()` in `KeyboardViewController` and add the following:

```
locationManager = CLLocationManager()
locationManager.delegate = self
locationManager.desiredAccuracy = kCLLocationAccuracyBest
locationManager.distanceFilter = 30
locationManager.requestWhenInUseAuthorization()
locationManager.startUpdatingLocation()
btnLocation.enabled = false
```

Here you create an instance of `CLLocationManager`, set up its properties as necessary, and then ask it to start updating its location. You also disable the location button to prevent users attempting to insert a location when one isn't available.

Next, locate `btnLocationTap(button:)` and add:

```
if (currentLocation != nil) {
  let string = "\(currentLocation.coordinate.latitude),
\(currentLocation.coordinate.longitude)"
  (textDocumentProxy as UIKeyInput).insertText(string)
}
```

This retrieves the `latitude` and `longitude` values from the `currentLocation` property, and inserts them into the text view using the familiar `insertText:` method.

Finally add the following to `locationManager(manager:, didUpdateLocations locations:)`:

```
currentLocation = locations.first as CLLocation
btnLocation.enabled = true
```

This is the one protocol method from `CLLocationManagerDelegate`. Once a location is received, it's stored in the view controller's `currentLocation` property.

> **Note**: For more information about the Core Location Framework, please refer to Apple's Core Location Framework Reference (http://bit.ly/1txhb9x).

Build and run. On launch you'll be prompted to allow access to your location; tap **Allow**. When your location becomes available, you can tap the location key to enter your current latitude and longitude into the text view.

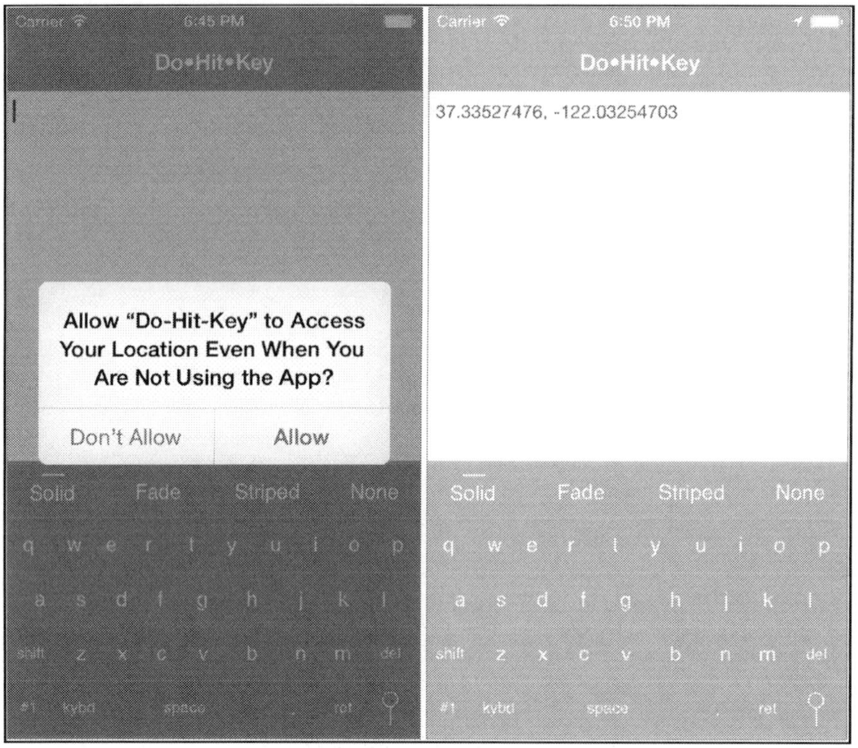

> **Note:** In order to simulate a location within the simulator, select **Debug\Location** and choose **Apple**.

Adding keyboard feedback

At present, there's no visual feedback that a button has been tapped. In this final section, you'll add a subtle animation that increases the buttons size when it's tapped, and then returns it to normal after a short delay.

Locate the `animateButtonTapForButton(button:)` and add the following lines:

```
UIView.animateWithDuration(ScaleSpeedOnTap, animations: {
  button.transform =
CGAffineTransformScale(CGAffineTransformIdentity,
    ScaleSizeOnTap,
    ScaleSizeOnTap)
  }, completion: {(_) -> Void in
    button.transform =
CGAffineTransformScale(CGAffineTransformIdentity, 1, 1)
})
```

Finally, add the following to the bottom of `btnKeyPressedTap(button:)` to actually call the method:

```
animateButtonTapForButton(button)
```

And that's it, you're all done! Build and run. Tap some buttons. You'll see the keys expand and shrink with every tap. Now that's much more satisfying, isn't it?

Where to go from here?

Custom Keyboards are new to iOS 8. This is a feature that power users have been keen on for quite some time. As a developer, you should definitely be thinking of ways to expand on the ideas presented here.

Make sure to review the Expected Keyboard Features section (at the beginning of this chapter) to discover additional capabilities that you can implement in your own keyboard.

The custom keyboard market is wide open for you to explore your creative and technical talents. Apple has given you an opportunity to shape and mold the users' experience.

This tutorial showed you how you could access the user's location. Maybe in your keyboard you could create a "quick access" button to input a user's contact email. Personally, I would love to see that! I'm also sending articles to myself from my device, and having to type my address (25 times a day) gets old. =]

Section III: Major New Features

In this section, you'll learn about the biggest and most important new features and frameworks in iOS 8 not already covered in this book. You'll cover Apple's entry into the BaaS (Backend as a Service) sector, a new and highly performant way to render 3D content in your app, a much improved way to access and manipulate users' photos, how to render your custom views and controls in Interface Builder and much, *much* more. Sit yourself down, grab a cup of your favorite coffee, and read on!

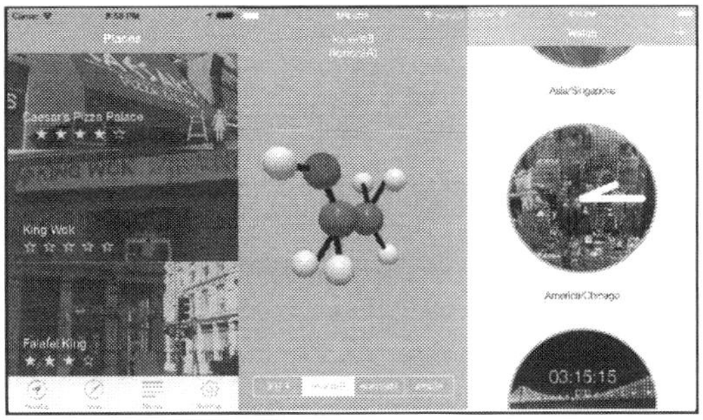

Chapter 15: Beginning CloudKit
Chapter 16: Intermediate CloudKit
Chapter 17: Beginning Scene Kit
Chapter 18: Intermediate Scene Kit
Chapter 19: Beginning Photos
Chapter 20: Intermediate Photos
Chapter 21: Beginning Live Rendering
Chapter 22: Intermediate Live Rendering
Chapter 23: Handoff
Chapter 24: Beginning WebKit
Chapter 25: Intermediate WebKit

Chapter 15: Beginning CloudKit

By Michael Katz

CloudKit, Apple's new remote data storage service for apps based on iCloud, provides a low-cost option to store and share app data using users' iCloud accounts as a back-end storage service. There are two parts to CloudKit: a web dashboard to manage the record types along with any public data, and a set of APIs to transfer data between iCloud and the device. It's secure as well; users' private data is completely protected, as developers can only access their own private database and aren't able to look at any users' private data.

CloudKit is a good option for iOS-only applications that use a lot of data but don't require a great deal of server-side logic. It's not the same as using Core Data with iCloud, as apps based on CloudKit have direct control over data transfer as well as the aforementioned concept of public and private databases. Unlike Core Data, CloudKit has no built-in local data persistence, so caching has to be performed by the app.

Why you should choose CloudKit

So why would you choose CloudKit over Core Data, other commercial BaaS (Back end as a Service) offerings, or even rolling your own server? The answers are simplicity, trust, and cost.

Unlike other backend solutions, CloudKit requires little setup. You don't have to choose, configure, or install servers and worry about scaling and security. Registering for the iOS Developer Program makes you eligible to use CloudKit – you don't have to register for additional services or create new accounts. As part of turning on the CloudKit capabilities, all the necessary setup magic on the servers happens automatically.

Finally there's no need to download additional libraries and configure them – CloudKit is imported like any other iOS framework. The CloudKit framework itself also provides a level of simplicity by offering convenience APIs for common operations. These abstract lower-level operations and return results in a single completion block. This chapter uses these APIs and the Intermediate CloudKit chapter introduces the lower-level ones.

There's also simplicity for users. Since CloudKit uses the iCloud credentials already entered when the device is set up (or through the Settings app), there's no need for building complicated login screens with their insane rules for what's a "valid" password, laying out long forms for creating accounts, and dealing with forgotten passwords or usernames. As long as they are logged in, users can seamlessly start using your app!

Another benefit to CloudKit is that users can trust the privacy and security of their data by trusting Apple, rather than app developers. CloudKit insulates the users' data from you. While this lack of access can be frustrating during development (for debugging) it is a net plus since you don't have to worry about security or convince users their data is secure. Even if an app user isn't aware of CloudKit's nuances, if they trust iCloud they can trust you.

Finally, for any developer the cost of running a service is a huge deal. Even the cheapest server hosts do not care if your app is free or cheap, and so it will cost even a little bit to run an app. With CloudKit, you get a reasonable amount of storage and data transfer for public data for free. See https://developer.apple.com/icloud/documentation/cloudkit-storage/ for details.

These strengths make the CloudKit service a low-hassle no-brainer for Mac and iOS apps.

> **Note:** To work with the sample app in this chapter you'll need an active iOS developer account. Without one you won't be able to enable the iCloud entitlements or access the CloudKit dashboard.

Introducing BabiFüd

The sample app for this chapter, **BabiFüd**, is the freshest take on the standard "rate a location" style of app. However, instead of reviewing locations based upon food quality, speed of service, or price, users rate locations in terms of child-friendliness. This includes availability of changing facilities, booster seats, and healthy food options.

The app contains four tabs: a list of nearby locations, a map showing nearby locations, user-generated notes, and settings. You can get a glimpse of the app in action from the two screenshots below:

A model class backs these views and wraps the calls to CloudKit. CloudKit objects are termed **records**; the main record type in your model is an `Establishment`, which represents the various locations in your app. Along the way you'll add `Rating` and `Note` records to your database as well.

You'll have to change the Bundle Identifier and Team of your app before you can start coding. You need a team set in order to get the necessary entitlements from Apple, and having a unique bundle identifier makes the process a whole lot easier.

Open **BabiFud.xcodeproj** in Xcode 6. Select the **BabiFud** project in the **Project Navigator**, and then select the BabiFud target. With the **General** tab selected, replace the **Bundle Identifier** with something unique; I recommend using reverse domain name notation, and include the project name. Next, select the appropriate **Team**:

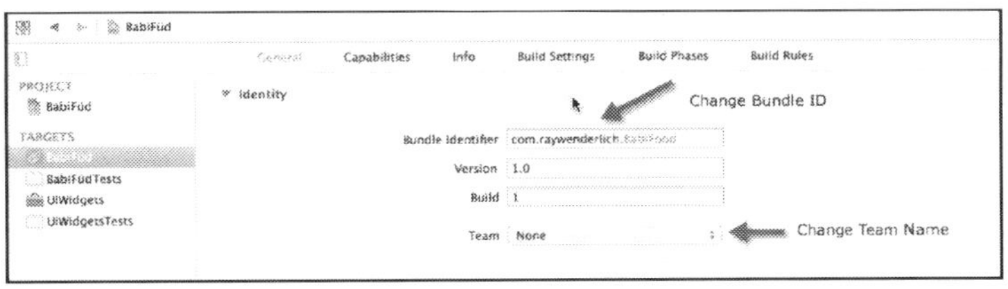

That takes care of the Bundle Identifier and Team. Now you'll need to get your app set up for CloudKit, and create some containers to hold your data.

Entitlements and containers

You'll need a container to hold the app's records before you can add any via your app. A container is the term for the conceptual location of all the app's data on the server—it is the grouping of public and private databases. To create a container you first need to enable the iCloud entitlements for your app.

To do so, select the **Capabilities** tab in the target editor, and then flip the switch in the **iCloud** section to **ON**, as shown in the screenshot below:

At this point, Xcode might prompt you to enter the Apple ID associated with your iOS developer account; if so, type it in as requested. Finally, enable **CloudKit** by checking the **CloudKit** checkbox in the **Services** group.

This creates a default container named **iCloud.<your app's bundle id>**, as illustrated in the screenshot below:

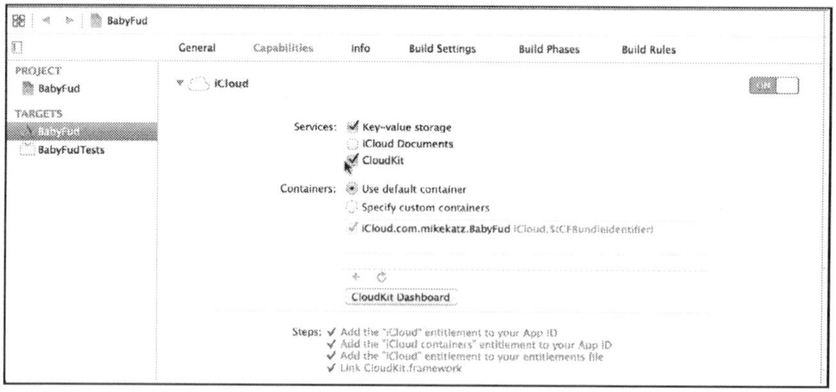

If you see any warnings or errors when creating entitlements, when building the project, or when running the app, and it's complaining about the container ID, here are some troubleshooting tips:

- If there are any warnings or errors shown in **Steps** group in the **iCloud** section, try pressing the **Fix Issue** button. This might need to be done a few times.

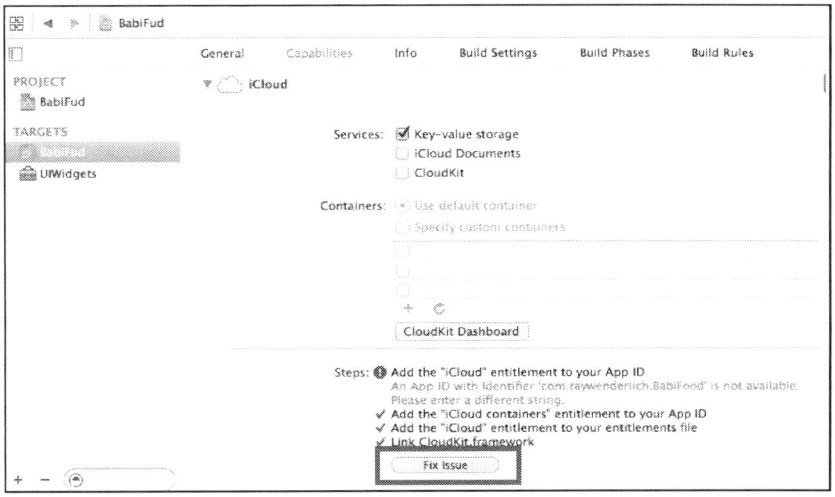

- It's important that the app's bundle id and iCloud containers match, and exist in the developer account. For example, if the bundle identifier is "com. <your domain>.BabiFud", then the iCloud container name should be "iCloud." plus the bundle bundle id: "iCloud.com. <your domain>.BabiFud".

- The iCloud container name must be unique because this is the global identifier used by CloudKit to access the data. Since the iCloud container name contains the bundle id, this means that the bundle id must also be unique (which is why it has to be changed from com.raywendrelich.BabiFud).

- In order for the entitlements piece to work, the app/bundle id has to be listed in the App IDs portion of Certificates, Identifiers, and Profiles portal. This means that that the certificate used to sign the app has to be from the set team id, and has to list the app id, which also implies the iCloud container id. Normally Xcode does all of this automatically for you, if you are signed in to a valid developer account. Unfortunately sometimes this gets out of sync. It can help to start with a fresh ID, and then change the CloudKit container ID to match, using the iCloud capabilities pane. Otherwise, to fix it you may have to edit the info.plist or in BabiFud.entitlements files to make sure the id values there reflect what you set for the bundle id.

Introducing the CloudKit Dashboard

After setting up the necessary entitlements, the next step when implementing CloudKit is to create some record types that define the data used by your app, and you can do this using the CloudKit dashboard. Click **CloudKit Dashboard**, found in the target's **Capabilities** pane, under **iCloud**, as shown below:

> **Note:** You can also launch the CloudKit dashboard by opening the URL https://icloud.developer.apple.com/dashboard/ in your browser.

You'll see the dashboard appear, like so:

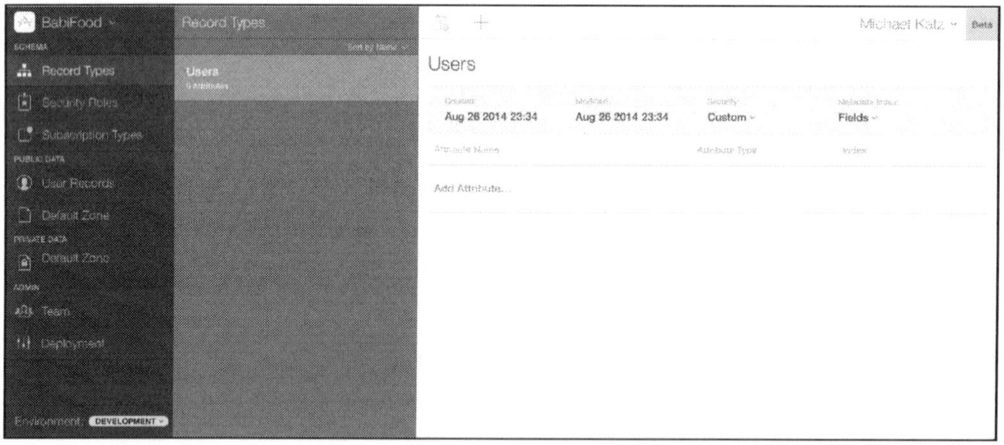

Here's a basic overview of what you'll see in the CloudKit dashboard, for the purposes of this chapter:

The **SCHEMA** section of the left-hand pane represents the high level objects of a CloudKit container: **Record Types**, **Security Roles**, and **Subscription Types**. You'll only be concerned with **Record Types** in this chapter. The Intermediate CloudKit chapter will cover subscriptions, but security roles are outside the scope of this book.

A **Record Type** is a set of attributes that define individual records. In terms of object orientated programming, a Record Type is like a class template for individual objects. A record can be considered an *instance* of a particular Record Type. It represents structured data in the container, much like a typical row in a database, and encapsulates a series of key/value pairs.

The **PUBLIC DATA** and **PRIVATE DATA** sections let you add data to, or search for data, in the databases you have access to; remember, as a developer you access all public data, but only your own private data. The **User Records** store data about the current iCloud user such as name and email. A **Record Zone** (here noted as the **Default Zone**) is used to provide a logical organization to a private database, by grouping records together. Custom zones support atomic transactions by allowing multiple records to be saved at the same time before processing other operations. Custom zones are outside the scope of this book.

The **ADMIN** section provides a means to configure the dashboard permissions available to your team members. If you have multiple people on your development team, you can restrict their ability to edit data here. This too is out-of-scope for this book.

Adding the Establishment record type

With **Record Types** selected, click the + icon in the top left of the detail pane to add a new record type, as shown below:

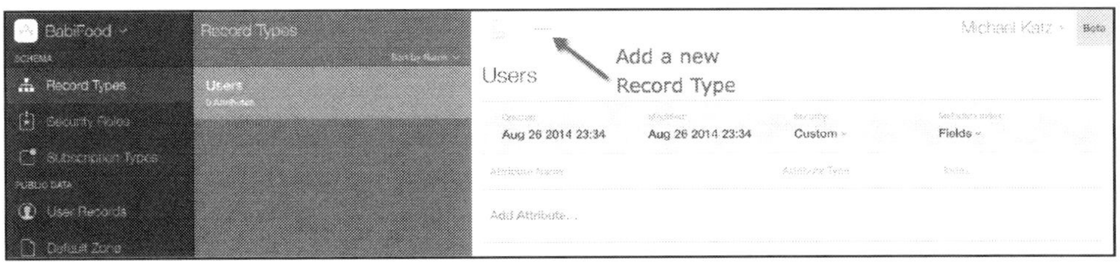

Name your new record type **Establishment**.

Think about the design of your app for a moment. Each establishment you'll want to track has lots of data: a name, a location, and whether or not various child-friendly options are available. Record types use **attributes** to define the various pieces of data contained in each record.

You'll see a row of fields where you can define the **Name**, **Attribute Type**, and **Index**, as shown below. A template StringAttribute has been automatically created for you.

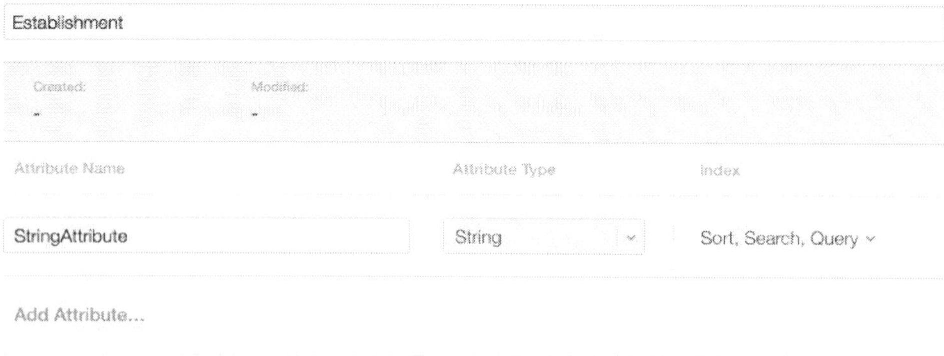

Replace StringAttribute and then add the following attributes one at a time. Click **Add Attribute...** to add new attributes as required:

Attribute Name	Attribute Type	Index
Name	String	Sort, Search and Query
Location	Location	Sort, Query
ChangingTable	Int(64)	Sort, Query
CoverPhoto	Asset	None
SeatingType	Int(64)	Sort, Query
HealthyOption	Int(64)	Sort, Query
KidsMenu	Int(64)	Sort, Query

When you're done, your list of attributes should look like the following:

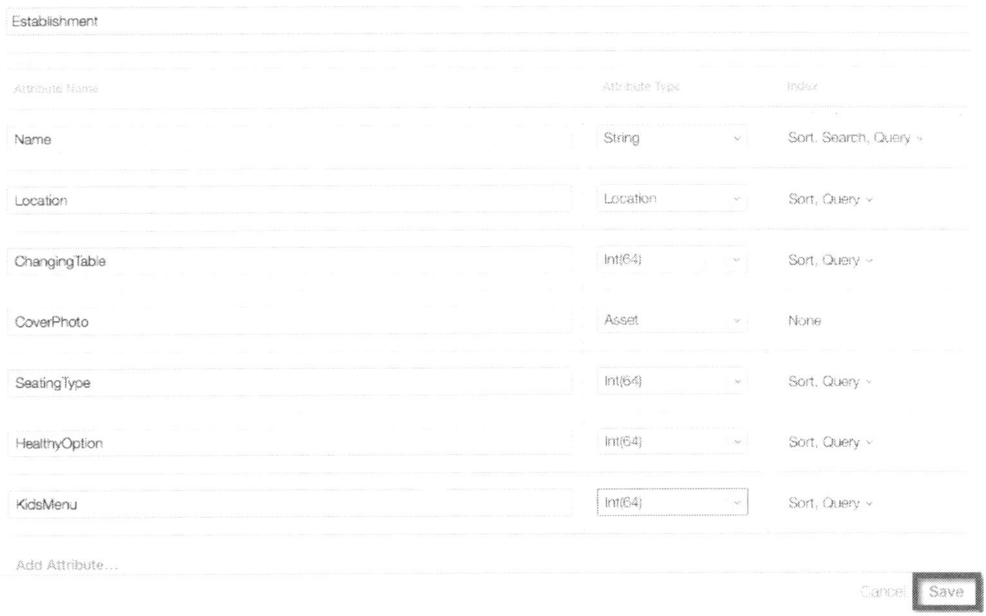

Click **Save** at the bottom of the page to save your new record type.

You're now ready to add some sample establishment records to your database.

Select **Default Zone** under the **PUBLIC DATA** section in the navigation pane on the left; this zone will contain the public records for your app. Select the **Establishment** record type from the dropdown list in the center pane if it's not already selected, then click the **+** icon in the right detail pane, as shown in the screenshot below:

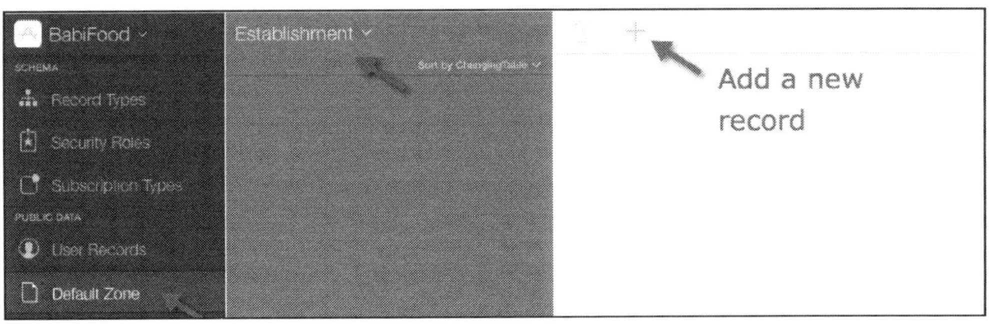

This will create a new, empty Establishment record as shown below:

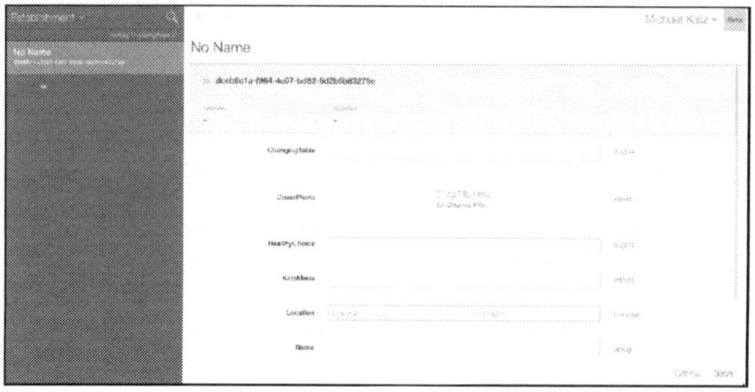

At this point you're ready to enter some test data for your app.

The following sample establishment data is fictional; the data has them located near Apple's headquarters so they're easy to find in the simulator.

Enter each record as described below:

> **Note:** The image for each **CoverPhoto** element is included in the **Supporting Files\Sample Images** folder in the Xcode project. To add the image to the establishment record, simply drag it to the **CoverPhoto** field. The image uploads automatically when the record is saved.

Attribute	Record 1	Record 2	Record 3
ChangingTable	2	0	3
CoverPhoto	pizza.jpg	chinese.jpg	steak.jpg
HealthyOption	0	1	1
KidsMenu	1	0	1
Location	37.322, -122.03	37.1,-122.1	37.4, -122.03
Name	Caesar's Pizza Palace	King Wok	The Back Deck
SeatingType	2	0	3

Once all three records have been saved, the dashboard should look like:

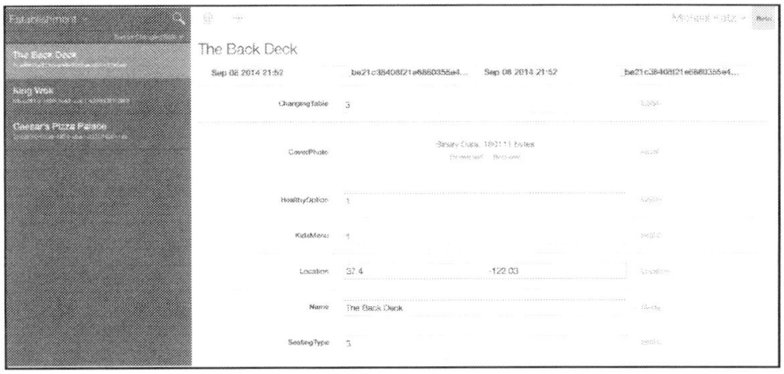

For each record, the values entered are the database representation of the data. On the app side, the data types are different. For example SeatingType and ChangingTable are an enum, so the specified Int value corresponds to the of the enumeration values. For HealthyOption and KidsMenu, the Int values represent Boolean types: a 0 means that establishment doesn't have that option and a 1 means that it does.

Return to Xcode. It's time to start integrating this data into your app.

Querying Establishment records

`CKQuery` objects are used to select records from a database. A `CKQuery` describes how to find all records of a specified record type that match certain criteria. These criteria can be something like "all records with a Name attribute that starts with 'M'", or "all records that have booster seats", or "all records within 3km." These types of expressions are coded in Cocoa with `NSPredicate` objects. A `NSPredicate` evaluates objects to see if they match the specified criteria. Predicates are also used a lot in Core Data and are a natural fit for CloudKit, because predicates commonly are defined as a comparison on an attribute.

CloudKit supports only a subset of available `NSPredicate` functions. These include mathematical comparisons, some string and set operations (such as "attribute matches one of the items in a list"), and new special distance function. The method `distanceToLocation:FromLocation:` was added to `NSPredicate` for CloudKit to match records with a location field within a specified radius for a known location. This type of predicate is covered in detail below. For other types of queries, the CKQuery class reference has a detailed list of the supported functions and how to use them.

> **Note**: CloudKit includes support for `CLLocation` objects; these are Core Location Framework objects that contain geospatial coordinates. This makes it quite easy to run a query for finding establishments inside of a geographic region – without doing all of the messy coordinate math yourself.

Open **Model\Model.swift**; this contains stubs for all server calls.

Replace `fetchEstablishments(location:, radiusInMeters:)` with the following:

```
func fetchEstablishments(location:CLLocation,
                         radiusInMeters:CLLocationDistance) {
  // 1
  let radiusInKilometers = radiusInMeters / 1000.0
  // 2
  let locationPredicate = NSPredicate(format:
"distanceToLocation:fromLocation:(%K,%@) < %f",
    "Location",
    location,
    radiusInKilometers)
  // 3
  let query = CKQuery(recordType: EstablishmentType,
                      predicate:  locationPredicate)
  // 4
  publicDB.performQuery(query, inZoneWithID: nil) {
    results, error in
    if error != nil {
      dispatch_async(dispatch_get_main_queue()) {
        self.delegate?.errorUpdating(error)
        return
      }
    } else {
      self.items.removeAll(keepCapacity: true)
      for record in results{
        let establishment = Establishment(record: record as
CKRecord, database: self.publicDB)
        self.items.append(establishment)
      }
      dispatch_async(dispatch_get_main_queue()) {
        self.delegate?.modelUpdated()
        return
      }
    }
  }
}
```

Taking each numbered comment in turn:

1. CloudKit uses kilometers in its distance predicates; this line simply converts `radiusInMeters` to kilometers.
2. The predicate filters establishments based on their distance in kilometers from the current location. This statement finds all establishments with a `location` value that puts them within the specified distance from the user's current location.
3. `CKQuery` objects are created using a predicate and a record type. Both will be used when performing the query.
4. Finally, `performQuery(_:, inZoneWithID:, completionHandler:)` sends your query up to iCloud, returning any matching results. In this case, you're running the query against your default zone; that is, your public database. This is because you passed `nil` as the `inZoneWithID` parameter. If you want to retrieve records from both public *and* private databases, you have to query each database using a separate call.

This is all fine and good, but you're probably wondering where the `CKDatabase` instance `publicDB` comes from. Take a look the top of `Model`:

```
let container : CKContainer
let publicDB : CKDatabase
let privateDB : CKDatabase

init() {
  // 1
  container = CKContainer.defaultContainer()
  // 2
  publicDB = container.publicCloudDatabase
  // 3
  privateDB = container.privateCloudDatabase
}
```

Here you define your databases:

1. The default container represents the one you specified in the iCloud capabilities pane.
2. The public database is the one shared among all users of your app.
3. The private database contains only the data belonging to the currently logged-in user; in this case, you.

This code will retrieve some local establishments from the public database, but it has to be wired up to a view controller in order to see anything in the app.

Setting up the requisite callbacks

You can take care of notifications with the familiar delegate pattern. Here's the protocol from the top of **Model.swift** that you'll implement in your view controller:

```
protocol ModelDelegate {
  func errorUpdating(error: NSError)
  func modelUpdated()
}
```

Open **MasterViewController.swift** and replace `modelUpdated()` with the following:

```
func modelUpdated() {
  refreshControl?.endRefreshing()
  tableView.reloadData()
}
```

This executes when new data is available. All the wiring up of the table view cells to CloudKit objects has already been taken care of in `tableView(_: cellForRowAtIndexPath:)`. Feel free to take a look.

Now replace `errorUpdating(error:)` with the following:

```
func errorUpdating(error: NSError) {
  let message = error.localizedDescription
  let alert = UIAlertView(title: "Error Loading Establishments",
   message: message, delegate: nil, cancelButtonTitle: "OK")
  alert.show()
}
```

Any errors produced by query result in this method being called. Errors can occur from poor networking conditions, or CloudKit specific issues such as missing or incorrect user credentials, or when the record you requested wasn't found.

> **Note**: Good error handling is essential when dealing with any kind of remote server. For now, you'll just display a popup informing the user that there has been an issue. Chapter 16, **Intermediate CloudKit**, demonstrates how to properly handle error conditions resulting from remote requests.

Build and run using the simulator. You should see list of nearby establishments, as shown below:

You can see the establishment name, and the services the establishments offer, but none of the images are being displayed. *What gives?*

When you retrieved the establishment records, you automatically retrieved the images as well. However, you still need to perform the necessary steps to load the images into your app.

Troubleshooting steps

If the list doesn't populate, make sure you have the correct location set by selecting **Debug\Location\Apple**. If you needed to change the location, pull the table down to force a refresh, instead of waiting for a location trigger.

If you're using an iPhone or iPad, location services are enabled, and the list *still* isn't populating, it'll be because the establishments aren't close enough in to your current location. You have two options here: either change the coordinates of the sample data to be closer to your current location, or use the simulator to run the app. There is a third option, but it's not terribly practical as you'd have to travel to Cupertino and hang around the Apple campus :]

If the data isn't appearing properly – or isn't appearing at all – inspect the sample data using the CloudKit dashboard. Make sure all of the records are present, and that you've added them to the default zone and they have the correct values. If you need to re-enter the data, you can delete records by clicking the trash icon as shown below:

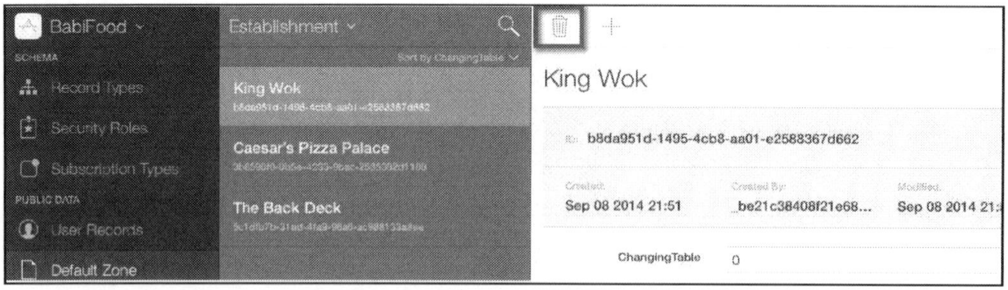

Debugging CloudKit errors can be tricky at times. As of writing, CloudKit error messages don't contain a tremendous amount of information, so to determine the cause of the error you'll need to look at the error code and what particular database operation you're attempting. Using the numerical error code, look up the matching CKErrorCode enum. The name and description in the documentation will help narrow down the cause of the issue. See below for some examples.

> **Note**: For a good primer on CloudKit errors, read the official Apple documentation on the `CKErrorCode` enum under CloudKit constants.

Here are some common error enums, and suggestions on how to address them:

- `.BadContainer` and `.MissingEntitlement`
  - Check that you have specified a container in the iCloud entitlements section, that it matches the `CKContainer` object, and that the container exists in the CloudKit dashboard.
- `.NotAuthenticated, .RequestRateLimited` and `.PermissionFailure`
  - Check that you've correctly entered your iCloud credentials in Settings.app and that iCloud is enabled.
- `.UnknownItem`
  - Check that your `RecordType` string matches the record type name in the CloudKit dashboard.

Working with binary assets

An asset is binary data, such as an image, that you associate with a record. In your case, your app's assets are the establishment photos shown in the **Nearby** table view.

In this section you'll add the logic to load the assets that were downloaded when you retrieved the establishment records.Open **Model\Establishment.swift** and replace `loadCoverPhoto(completion:)` with the following code:

```
func loadCoverPhoto(completion:(photo: UIImage!) -> ()) {
  // 1
  dispatch_async(
   dispatch_get_global_queue(
    DISPATCH_QUEUE_PRIORITY_BACKGROUND, 0)){
    var image: UIImage!
    // 2
    let coverPhoto = self.record.objectForKey("CoverPhoto") as
CKAsset!
    if let asset = coverPhoto {
      // 3
      if let url = asset.fileURL {
        if let imageData = NSData(contentsOfFile: url.path!) {
          // 4
          image = UIImage(data: imageData)
        }
      }
    }
    // 5
    completion(photo: image)
  }
}
```

This method loads the image from the asset attribute as follows:

1. Although you download the asset at the same time that you retrieve the rest of the record, you want to load the image asynchronously, so wrap everything in a `dispatch_async` block.
2. Assets are stored in `CKRecord` as instances of `CKAsset`, so cast appropriately.
3. Load the image data from the local file URL provided by the asset.
4. Use the image data to create an instance of `UIImage`.
5. Execute the completion callback with the retrieved image.

Build and run. The establishment images should now appear:

There are two gotchas with CloudKit assets:

1. Assets can only exist in CloudKit as attributes on records; you can't store them on their own. Deleting a record will also delete any associated assets.
2. Retrieving assets can negatively impact performance because the assets are downloaded at the same time the rest of the record data is. If your app makes heavy use of assets, you should store references to a different type of record that holds just the asset. This strategy is covered later in this chapter.

> **Note:** At the time of writing, there are still a few bugs in the iCloud dashboard that affect assets. If you don't see any images in the app, delete all of your Establishment records using the dashboard, then uncomment `doWorkaround()` in **AppDelegate.swift**. Run the application once, which will upload the seed data, and then comment out that line again. This will populate your public database with the same data you added manually, but using the APIs rather than the dashboard.

Your next task is to let the users add their own ratings to the establishments. You'll want to maintain multiple ratings per establishment, so you'll need some way to link the individual ratings to their establishments.

Enter CloudKit References!

Creating references between records

References let you link CloudKit records together. In concept, it's similar to how relationships are handled in CoreData – just a lot more straightforward!

The star ratings will be stored as separate records with two attributes: the numerical rating, and a `CKReference`, which is a back reference to the Establishment record.

CloudKit prefers back references – that is, references from the child object to the parent object – for efficiency. When CloudKit retrieves a record, it also retrieves all directly referenced objects at the same time. If your parent Establishment record contained many references to the child Rating objects, it would be an incredibly expensive operation to retrieve the parent object, as all Rating objects would be retrieved at the same time.

Back references avoid this, as a parent has no knowledge of their children, but all children know who their parent is. *There's a Jerry Springer show in there somewhere!* :]

In addition to being more efficient, having a separate record for the rating makes it easy to modify ratings in the future, and to calculate an average rating for an establishment.

Head back to the CloudKit dashboard to create your new Rating record type, and to add a few ratings.

Under the **SCHEMA** navigation item, create a new record type and name it **Rating**. Create two new attributes for your new record type as follows:

Attribute Name	Attribute Type	Index
Establishment	Reference	Query
Rating	Int(64)	Sort, Query

When you're done, your dashboard should look like the following:

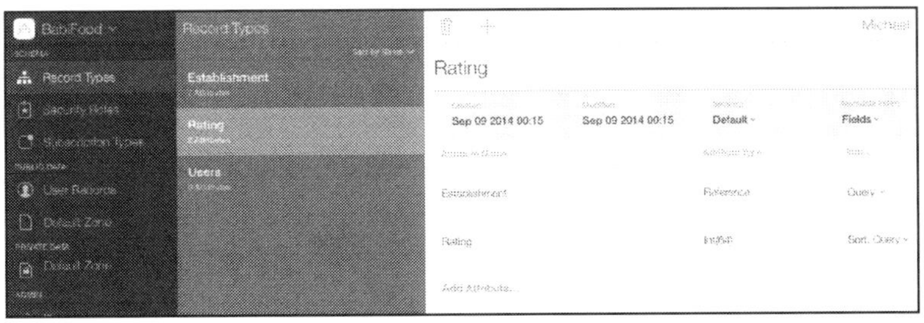

Save your changes, then click **Default Zone**, select the **Establishment** record type then select any one of the Establishment records. Copy the **UUID** from the ID field, as shown below:

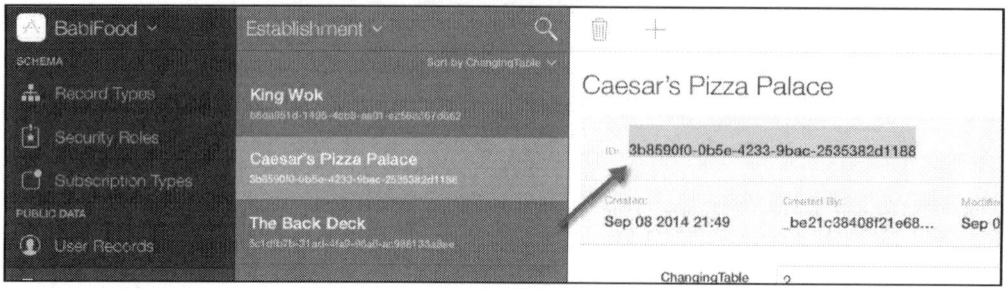

You'll use this UUID to manually create a reference to this record from your Rating records.

Change the dropdown at the top of the page from **Establishment** to **Rating**. Add a new Rating record, pasting the UUID you copied into the Establishment field, then check **DeleteSelf**.

> **Note: DeleteSelf** allows you to cascade deletes so that child records are deleted with the parent record. If you delete an Establishment from the application, there's no need to keep the associated Rating records around, so you might as well let CloudKit delete those for you automatically.

Enter a number from 1 to 5 in the **Rating** field; when you're all done, your record should look like the screenshot below:

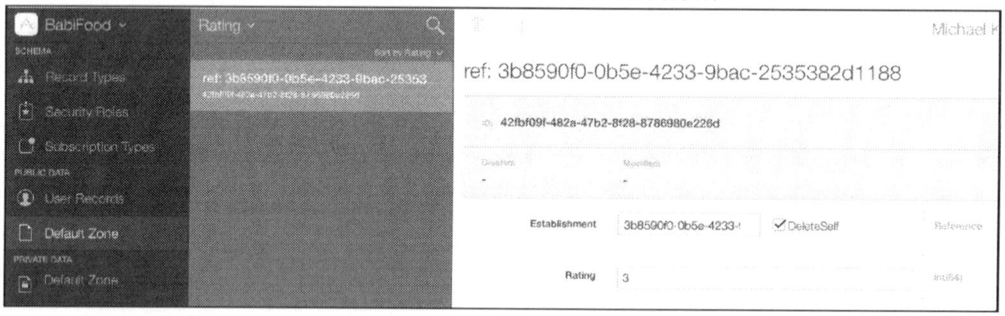

Save this record. Create a few more ratings for this, or any other Establishment, so you can see how the app averages ratings.

Retrieving all the ratings for an Establishment is simply a matter of querying all Ratings whose Establishment ID is that of the parent Establishment record.

Open **Model\Establishment.swift** and replace `fetchRating(userRecord:, completion:)` with the following:

```
func fetchRating(userRecord: CKRecordID!,
 completion: (rating: Double, isUser: Bool) -> ()) {
  // 1
  let predicate = NSPredicate(format: "Establishment == %@",
record)
  // 2
  let query = CKQuery(recordType: "Rating", predicate:
predicate)
  database.performQuery(query, inZoneWithID: nil) {
    results, error in
    if error != nil {
      completion(rating: 0, isUser: false)
    } else {
      let resultsArray = results as NSArray
      // 3
      let rating = resultsArray.valueForKeyPath("@avg.Rating")
as Double?
      if (rating != nil) {
        completion(rating: rating!, isUser: false)
      } else {
         completion(rating: 0, isUser: false)
      }
    }
  }
}
```

Here you retrieve all of the ratings for an Establishment, and then average them. Since you can't run server-side code in CloudKit, you're stuck with having to retrieve all the ratings and do the math yourself.

Taking each numbered comment in turn:

1. Set up the predicate to query for all Ratings for the current Establishment.
2. Create in instance of `CKQuery`, specifying that you want Rating records, and to use the predicate from step 1. Then perform the query.
3. You can access attributes of a `CKRecord` using key paths, just like other KVC compliant Cocoa classes. Calling `valueForKeyPath:"@avg.Rating"` on an `NSArray` containing instances of `CKRecord`, like you have here, computes the average of the Rating field.

Build and run. You should see that the stars are now populated with the average rating, as shown below:

If the ratings don't appear, make sure that the Establishment IDs in the Rating records are correct. You can quickly check this using search in the CloudKit dashboard.

To search for a record in the dashboard, click the magnifying class at the top of the center panel. Press the + button, select **Establishment** from the left drop down and paste an **Establishment ID** in the right-hand text box, as shown below:

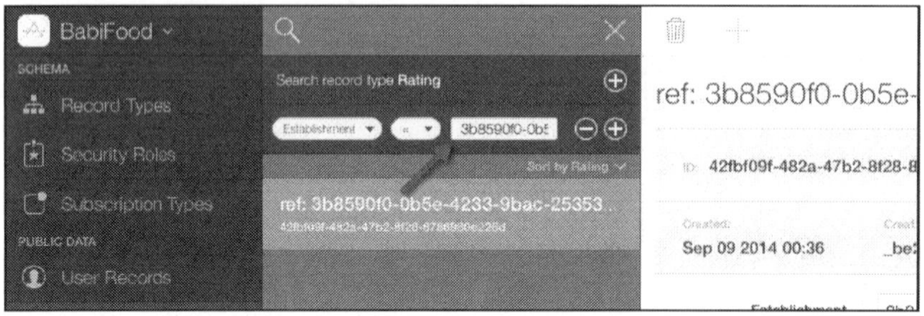

The list of matching records updates automatically as changes are made to the search criteria. If no results are found, then the search terms do not match any records. In that case, check that the id string exactly matches one of the Establishment records' id and try again.

Updating existing records

So far you've manually seeded the public database for the app, but wouldn't it be nice to let users add their own photos, notes and ratings via the app itself? Fortunately, it's a relatively simple process to post a record to CloudKit.

Add the following to the bottom of `viewDidLoad()` in **DetailViewController.swift**:

```
starRating.editingChangedBlock = { rating in
  self.saveRating(rating)
}
```

This block is called when the user taps a star to choose or update a rating. The new value is then saved in a record with a reference to the selected Establishment.

Next, replace `saveRating(rating:)` with the following:

```
func saveRating(rating: NSNumber) {
  // 1
  let ratingRecord = CKRecord(recordType: "Rating")
  // 2
  ratingRecord.setObject(rating, forKey: "Rating")
  // 3
  let ref = CKReference(record: self.detailItem.record,
    action: .DeleteSelf)
  // 4
  ratingRecord.setObject(ref, forKey: "Establishment")

  // 5
  Model.sharedInstance().userInfo.userID() {
    userID, error in
    if let userRecord = userID {
      //6
      let userRef = CKReference(recordID: userRecord,
        action: .None)
      ratingRecord.setObject(userRef, forKey: "User")
      // 7
      self.detailItem.database.saveRecord(ratingRecord) {
        record, error in
        if error != nil {
          println("error saving rating: (\rating)")
        } else {
          dispatch_async(dispatch_get_main_queue()) {
            self.starRating.emptyColor = UIColor.yellowColor()
            self.starRating.solidColor = UIColor.yellowColor()
```

```
            self.starRating.setNeedsDisplay()
          }
        }
      }
    }
  }
}
```

Taking each numbered comment in turn:

1. Create an instance of `CKRecord` making sure to set its record type to `Rating`.
2. Assign the actual rating to the new record. Only a few types are supported for attribute values. These are limited to `NSNumber`, `NSString`, `NSDate`, `NSData`, `CLLocation`, and `NSArrays` of those. Also supported are CloudKit types `CKReference` and `CKAsset`.
3. Create an instance of `CKReference`, pointing to the Establishment and enabling the proper cascade delete behavior.
4. Set the reference on the new rating record.
5. Call a helper method to obtain the current user's User record ID. This method is asynchronous, relying on a secondary call to `CKContainer`, hence the callback.
6. Set a reference to the current user's record on the new rating record.
7. Finally, save the new rating record in the public database. This is another asynchronous network call so errors should be handled appropriately. If the save is successful, the color of the star rating control is updated to signify the user has rated this Establishment.

You'll need to be logged in to iCloud via Settings.app in order for the star ratings to work. Build and run. Select an establishment and then tap the stars at the top of the detail pane to create and save a new rating record.

Going back to the CloudKit dashboard, you'll see new records listed under Rating (you may have to refresh the page first). To find a particular one of the new ratings, search by matching the Establishment id.

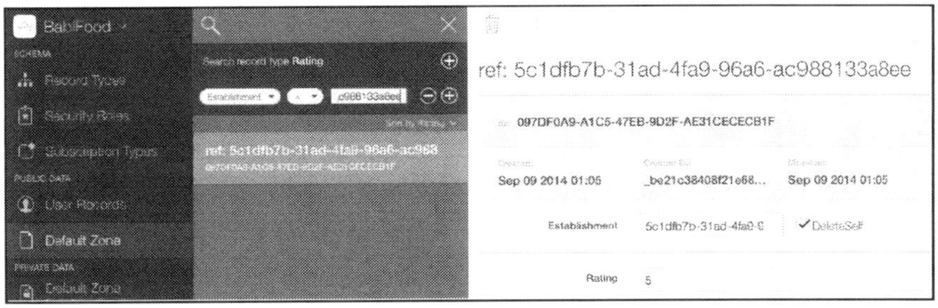

Adding an asset

Under the hood, CloudKit represents an asset using `CKAsset`, which has a `fileURL` property that resolves to the asset's physical location on disk. CloudKit manages asset data independently from record data in order to optimize data transfer and caching.

Your app already has a +button in the detail view controller, shown below, that's hooked up to an image picker that lets the user choose a photo to upload.

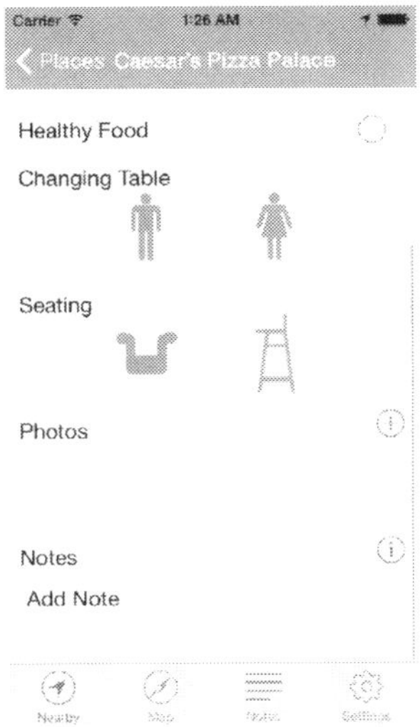

Your task is to upload the photo as an instance of `CKAsset` and associate it with the correct Establishment record. You can avoid needlessly downloading assets when retrieving Establishment records by storing them as separate records and using references to link the asset record to the parent Establishment record.

Recall that each Establishment record has a **CoverPhoto** attribute which doesn't change. All user-submitted photos will instead be stored in their own **EstablishmentPhoto** record type.

Open **DetailViewController.swift** and replace `addPhotoToEstablishment(photo:)` with the following:

```
func addPhotoToEstablishment(photo: UIImage) {
  // 1
  let fileURL = generateFileURL()
  let data = UIImageJPEGRepresentation(photo, 0.9)
  var error : NSError?
  let wrote = data.writeToURL(fileURL, options: .AtomicWrite,
error: &error)

  if (error != nil) {
    UIAlertView(title: "Error Saving Photo",
     message: error?.localizedDescription, delegate: nil,
      cancelButtonTitle: "OK").show()
    return
  }
  // 2
  let asset = CKAsset(fileURL: fileURL)
  // 3
  let ref = CKReference(record: self.detailItem.record,
   action: .DeleteSelf)
  // 4
  Model.sharedInstance().userInfo.userID() {
    userID, error in
    if let userRecordID = userID {
      let userRef = CKReference(recordID: userRecordID, action:
.None)
      // 5
      let record = CKRecord(recordType: "EstablishmentPhoto")
      record.setObject(asset, forKey: "Photo")
      // 6
      record.setObject(ref, forKey: "Establishment")
      record.setObject(userRef, forKey: "User")
      // 7
      self.detailItem.database.saveRecord(record) {record, error
in
        if error == nil {
          // 8
          self.addNewPhotoToScrollView(photo)
        }
        NSFileManager.defaultManager().removeItemAtURL(fileURL,
error: nil)
      }
    }
  }
}
```

Taking each numbered comment in turn:

1. Use `generateFileURL()` to generate a unique URL for the cache directory, and use it to cache the selected photo.
2. Create an instance of `CKAsset` pointing to photo you cached in step 1.
3. Create a reference to the current Establishment record. Since there's no point in keeping the user submitted photos if the parent record is deleted, set the appropriate cascade delete rules.
4. Grab the ID of the current user. Remember this method is asynchronous.
5. Create a new record of type `EstablishmentPhoto`, and set the asset from step 2 as the `Photo` attribute.
6. Set the references to both the user and the Establishment on the new record.
7. Save the record to CloudKit.
8. If the record is saved successfully, add the image to the list of user-submitted photos in the app.

Build and run. Select an establishment and then tap the + icon for **Photos**. Select an photo to upload. Once uploaded, you'll see the photo in the user-submitted photos section, as shown below:

Wait a minute... this function uploads a new record of type **EstablishmentPhoto**, but this type hasn't been defined in the iCloud dashboard yet. How can that be?

Record types can be added dynamically just by saving an object! Additionally, new attributes can be added to an existing record type this way as well. This is because CloudKit will re-compute the schema when a new attribute or record type is added. If you look at the record type in the dashboard, you'll see the new attributes, with their attribute type already figured out:

Private versus public databases

Up to this point, all of the data used by your app resides in the public database. However, BabiFüd lets users enter their own private notes about the various establishments; you'll need to store those in a separate record, and you don't want to store them in the public database. You can make records private by saving them to the user's private database, as illustrated below:

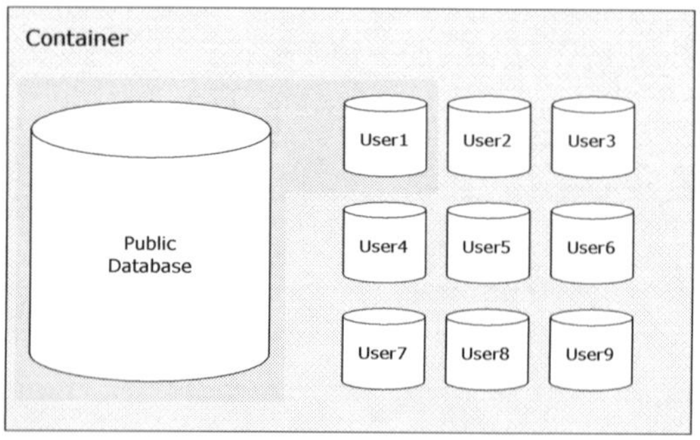

Each container you define in the CloudKit dashboard has only a single public database, but provides many private databases – one for each user of your app. CloudKit apps only ever has access to the public database, and the private database of the current user. You can access the user's private database via `privateCloudDatabase` on any instance of `CKContainer`.

The code to add and load Note records is already part of **DetailViewController.swift**, so you'll only need to update the model.

Open **Model\Model.swift** and replace `addNote(note:, establishment:, completion:)` with the following:

```
func addNote(note: String, establishment: Establishment!,
 completion: (error : NSError!)->()) {
  if establishment == nil {
   return
  }
  // 1
  let noteRecord = CKRecord(recordType: "Note")
  noteRecord.setObject(note, forKey: "Note")
  // 2
  let ref = CKReference(record: establishment.record,
   action: .DeleteSelf)
  noteRecord.setObject(ref, forKey: "Establishment")
  // 3
  privateDB.saveRecord(noteRecord) { record, error in
    dispatch_async(dispatch_get_main_queue()) {
      completion(error: error)
    }
  }
}
```

Here's what's going on in the code above:

1. Create a new instance of `CKRecord`, setting its record type to Note.
2. Create a reference to the parent Establishment in the public database, and store it on the new record.
3. Save the Note record, but this time to the user's private database.

Querying a private database works almost identically to querying a public database.

Replace `fetchNote(establishment:, completion:)` with the following:

```
func fetchNote(establishment: Establishment,
 completion:(note: String!, error: NSError!) ->()) {
  // 1
  let predicate = NSPredicate(format: "Establishment == %@",
establishment.record)
```

```
    let query = CKQuery(recordType: "Note", predicate: predicate)
    // 2
    privateDB.performQuery(query, inZoneWithID: nil) {
      results, error in
      var note: String!
      if results.count > 0 {
        // 3
        note = results[0].objectForKey("Note") as String!
      }
      completion(note: note, error: error)
    }
  }
```

Here you retrieve a Note record in the following manner:

1. Specify the current Establishment as the reference on which to filter Note records.
2. Query the users' private database for the matching Note records.
3. If any records are found, pass the Note attribute of the first record to the completion handler. To keep the UI simple, it is a limitation that only the first note is displayed. Any additional notes will not appear in the view.

Build and run. Select an establishment and then tap the **i** icon for **Notes** to add a note. Add some text and then click **Save**. Your note will upload and subsequently appear both at the bottom of the detail view controller and on the Notes tab, as shown below:

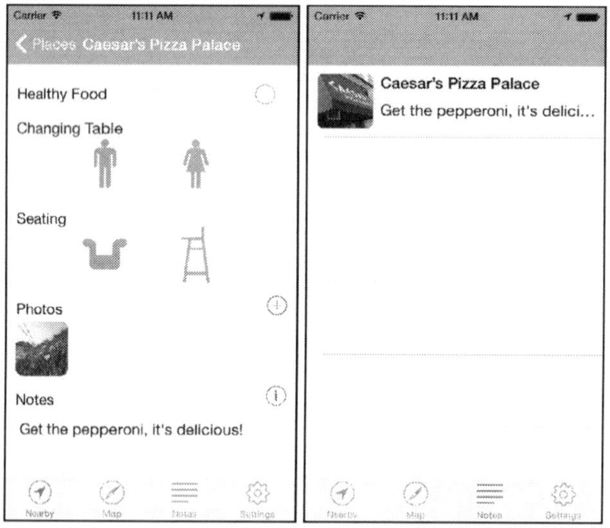

Since notes are saved to the users' private database, you can only view your own notes – not the notes of any other users. To view *your* **Note** records in the CloudKit dashboard, click **Default Zone** under **PRIVATE DATA**, then select **Note** from the dropdown in the center panel. Your **Note** records will appear below:

So where are the **User** records stored? The next section answers that very question! :]

Exploring the User record type

User records represent the logged-in iCloud user; by default, the attributes of this record are private, but users can opt-in to be discoverable by email address. If the user makes their record discoverable, then other users of the app can find that record given only the email address, either as a contact or by entering it in the app (not part of this this tutorial). The default fields of this record are the users' first and last name, but additional attributes can be added as needed.

> **Note**: Sensitive information should **never** be added to a user record, as these records reside in the public database.

You interact with User records via `CKContainer`. All operations on the User record data are asynchronous, including: obtaining permissions, requesting the User record ID or user info, or finding other users. This makes things a little more difficult for a developer, as programs have to be coded as a series of asynchronous callbacks, rather than a straightforward series of function calls.

The Settings view in the app loads information about the current user. It will display their account status and if available, name. This is shown on the next page:

There are three steps to obtaining a users' information:

1. Check there is a currently logged-in user. CloudKit requires a user to be logged-in when accessing data.
2. Get that users' User records' ID.
3. Using the record ID, request the rest of the user's info from the CKContainer using `fetchUserRecordIDWithCompletionHandler`.

All the donkeywork has been implemented for you in **SettingsViewController.swift**. Feel free to open this file and take a look at `updateLogin()` for the implementation.

Right now the Settings view just displays "Not logged in to iCloud" regardless of the actual account status. To get this working, add the code below to retrieve the account status and get permission to look up the users' name.

Open **Model\UserInfo.swift**; this contains all of the `CKContainer` related user management logic for your app.

Replace `loggedInToICloud(completion:)` method with the following:

```
func loggedInToICloud(completion : (accountStatus :
CKAccountStatus, error : NSError!) -> ()) {
  container.accountStatusWithCompletionHandler() { (status :
CKAccountStatus, error : NSError!) in
    completion(accountStatus: status, error: error)
  }
}
```

This asks the container to get the account status, which happens asynchronously, and passes the result back to the view controller.

The rest of `UserInfo` is concerned with obtaining the user record. A `CKContainer` has several useful functions for handling the user record. One is `fetchUserRecordIDWithCompletionHandler(_:)`. This is called by `userID(completion:)` to obtain the current user's record id.

This method has already been implemented, since it was needed earlier to link the user to photos and ratings, and is explained below:

```
func userID(completion: (userRecordID: CKRecordID!, error:
NSError!)->()) {
  // 1
  if userRecordID != nil {
    completion(userRecordID: userRecordID, error: nil)
  } else {
    // 2
    container.fetchUserRecordIDWithCompletionHandler() {
      recordID, error in
      // 3
      if recordID != nil {
        // 4
        self.userRecordID = recordID
      }
      completion(userRecordID: recordID, error: error)
    }
  }
}
```

This function caches the record ID for a faster response since it is called often.

1. If the `userRecordID` has been previously fetched and cached, call the completion block with it right away.
2. Fetch the user record id.
3. If there is no iCloud user or access has been restricted, there will be an error, otherwise a record id non-nil.
4. Store the record id for easy retrieval later.

Another useful `CKContainer` function is `discoverUserInfoWithUserRecordID(_:, completionHandler:)`. This is called by `userInfo(recordID:, completion:)` to get information about the user. Right now the returned information is limited to first and last name. If the user has granted permission to share identifying information, the returned `CKDiscoveredUserInfo` will have that user's name.

Replace `userInfo(recordID:, completion:)` with the following:

```
func userInfo(recordID: CKRecordID!,
  completion:(userInfo: CKDiscoveredUserInfo!, error: NSError!)-
>()) {
    container.discoverUserInfoWithUserRecordID(recordID,
      completionHandler:completion)
}
```

`discoverUserInfoWithUserRecordID` can also be used to find information about any other user in the app, given the record id. This record id could come from a public app data record, such as another user's rating or photo for an establishment. There is also `discoverUserInfoWithEmailAddress(_:, completionHandler:)` to get the same information by email address instead.

If you build and run now, the Settings view will just display whether the user is logged in to iCloud or not.

To get the user's name, that user must grant discoverability permissions to the app through a permission dialog launched by calling `CKContainer requestApplicationPermission(_:completionHandler:)`.

To show that dialog, replace `requestDiscoverability(completion:)` with the following:

```
func requestDiscoverability(completion: (discoverable: Bool) ->
()) {
  // 1

container.statusForApplicationPermission(
    .PermissionUserDiscoverability) {
      status, error in
    // 2
    if error != nil || status ==
CKApplicationPermissionStatus.Denied {
      completion(discoverable: false)
    } else {
    // 3
    self.container.requestApplicationPermission(
     .PermissionUserDiscoverability) { status, error in
        // 4
        completion(discoverable: status == .Granted)
      }
    }
  }
}
```

This asks the user for discoverability permission if it hasn't before, otherwise uses the previous permission status. Right now, user discoverability is the only permission type in CloudKit.

1. Check to see if there is already a permission status set for discoverability.
2. If there was an error or the user previously denied permission, then stop here and call the completion.
3. Ask the container to request discoverability permission for the user. If the user previously granted permission, the dialog won't be shown and the `Granted` status is automatically returned.
4. Call the completion block and check that permission was granted.

If you build and re-launch the app you'll be greeted with a permission dialog right away. This is because the user information is requested along with the establishments to match up the user's own contributions.

If you select **OK**, the settings tab will list your name (as shown earlier). If you instead select **Don't Allow**, then you'll just see "Logged in to iCloud", as before. If you regret your decision, you have to re-install the app or reset the device to change permission.

Where to go from here?

Your app is now fully capable of downloading curated establishments from CloudKit and allowing users to add notes and photos to the app.

There are a number of features that you can add to improve their experience:

- Let the user create new Establishment records using the map. The functions added to your Model class can serve as an example for saving the record to either the public or private databases.
- Add filtering and searching. The Model class constructs a `CKQuery` with a distance predicate, but this can be modified to be a more complex predicate. CloudKit supports text searching of string attributes as well.
- Improve the performance of the app and the data loading experience. This tutorial used the available convenience methods to invoke the necessary completion handlers when everything is ready. Instances of `CKDatabase` also have `NSOperation`-based methods that provide more control over how the API is executed, such the ability to

receive data during the operation instead of all at the same time, once the operation is complete.

- Provide caching and synchronization so the app remains responsive offline and keeps the content up to date when it reconnects to a network.

You'll cover the last two points when you work through Chapter 16, **Intermediate CloudKit**, adding this functionality to the BabiFüd app.

Chapter 16: Intermediate CloudKit

By Michael Katz

The **Beginning CloudKit** chapter showed you how to remotely store and retrieve your app's data, which lives in a server-side container made up of public and private databases. CloudKit provides simple convenience methods for accessing this remote data.

Sometimes those convenience methods aren't quite enough in terms of performance or flexibility for a large-scale production app. CloudKit offers more advanced APIs to receive records as they are downloaded (even if all records haven't been retrieved yet), fetch partial data, and receive automatic updates when data changes. This chapter builds on top of the BabiFüd restaurant-rating app that was introduced in the previous chapter by adding additional features, performance improvements, and improving stability.

> **Note:** You require a paid iOS developer account in order to add the CloudKit entitlements to an app, and access the CloudKit dashboard used in this tutorial.
>
> Before running BabiFüd, make sure you update the Bundle Identifier to something of your own, such as `com.mydomain.BabiFüd`. If have entitlement issues while running the sample project, read through the beginning of chapter 15, **Beginning CloudKit**, for some help on how to resolve such issues.

Getting started

In a simple application, fetching a handful of records doesn't require too much thought. But when you start getting into hundreds or even thousands of records, the data transfer requirements become a real concern. Large transfers of data mean you have to worry about connection speeds, connection stability, memory usage, battery life, and potential service provider imposed data caps.

Extract the sample application included with this chapter and open it in Xcode.

> **Note:** The sample project provide for this chapter is based on the one from the previous chapter, but has been updated with new classes and methods. To follow along, please use the sample application provided for this chapter rather than re-using the one from the previous chapter.

Fetching in Batches

`CKOperation` subclasses such as `CKQueryOperation` let you control the way data is sent to, and received from, CloudKit; they can help you minimize the use of limited resources but still provide your user with the rich experience they desire. This is done by requesting only a subset of attributes, or only changed records.

Open **Model\NearbyLocationsResultsController.swift** and take a look at the code that's been provided:

```
class NearbyLocationsResultsController {
  // 1
  let db: CKDatabase
  // 2
  var predicate: NSPredicate?
  // 3
  let delegate: NearbyLocationsResultsControllerDelegate
  // 4
  var results = [Establishment]()
  // 5
  init(delegate: NearbyLocationsResultsControllerDelegate) {
    self.delegate = delegate
    db = CKContainer.defaultContainer().publicCloudDatabase
  }
}
```

This class will be responsible for fetching batches of records from the database and updating the table view as records are loaded. Taking each comment in turn:

1. Create a constant that will hold a reference to the public database.
2. Create a variable that will eventually hold a reference to the predicate you'll use to select the necessary records.
3. The delegate will handle the results of your search as they're changed or updated.
4. Create a variable in which to store the search results; in this case it's an array of `Establishment` objects.
5. This is the class' initializer where you setup the delegate and database reference.

Add the following protocol declaration to the top of **NearbyLocationsResultsController.swift**:

```
protocol NearbyLocationsResultsControllerDelegate {
  func willBeginUpdating()
  func establishmentAdded(establishment: Establishment, index:
Int)
  func establishmentUpdated(establishment: Establishment, index:
Int)
  func didEndUpdating(error: NSError!)
}
```

These delegate methods will be called at various points during the download lifecycle of the search results. The following breakdown illustrates this more thoroughly:

1. The results controller submits the operation to the database.
2. `recordFetchedBlock`, a property on `CKQueryOperation`, is called for each record retrieved from the server.
3. The results controller's delegate will be told to start updating its view when the first record is fetched. This is so `beginUpdates()` is called on the table view before the rows change.
4. As you fetch a record, check if it's already associated with an `Establishment` in the list of results. If so, then update that existing object with the new record and call `establishmentUpdated(establishment:, index:)`. If not, create a new `Establishment` with this record, add it to the results list, and then call `establishmentAdded(establishment:, index:)` on the delegate.
5. Once all records have been retrieved, `queryCompletionBlock` is called on the instance of `CKQueryOperation` performing the query.

6. If there are additional records beyond the results' limit (as an optionally specified `resultsLimit` on the operation), you'll get an instance of `CKQueryCursor` in the query operation's completion block. Use the cursor to initialize a new `CKQueryOperation` that picks up where the previous operation left off.

Add the following to the top of `NearbyLocationsResultsController`, just below where the other variables are declared:

```
var resultLimit = 30
var cursor: CKQueryCursor!
var startedGettingResults = false
let RecordType = "Establishment"
var inProgress = false
```

Here you declare a handful of variables, including one used to set the queries' record limit to 30. The 30 record limit was chosen as a starting point to balance download speed with the number of requests sent. A smaller limit means fewer records fetched, resulting in the completion called sooner. However that results in more requests needed to fetch all the records, increasing the chance of a network error and draining battery.

Next, add the following to the bottom of `NearbyLocationsResultsController`:

```
func start() {
  // 1
  if inProgress {
    return
  }
  inProgress = true
  // 2
  let query = CKQuery(recordType: RecordType, predicate:
predicate)
  let queryOp = CKQueryOperation(query: query)
}
```

This code is responsible for starting the fetch operation. Taking each numbered comment in turn:

1. Check that you aren't sending multiple queries to the database at the same time. For example, if the user tries to refresh the nearby places list or updates their location before an in-flight fetch has completed then return immediately.

2. The predicate is used to construct the query, and the query is used to construct the query operation. The query operation will eventually be passed to the database to execute, but you're yet to write that code. :]

Now you need to write the query code.

Add the following method to `NearbyLocationsResultsController`:

```
func recordFetched(record:CKRecord!) {
  // 1
  if !startedGettingResults {
    startedGettingResults = true
    dispatch_async(dispatch_get_main_queue()) {
      self.delegate.willBeginUpdating()
    }
  }
  var index = NSNotFound
  var e: Establishment!
  var newItem = true
  // 2
  for (idx, value) in enumerate(results) {
    if value.record.recordID == record.recordID {
      index = idx
      e = value
      e.record = record
      newItem = false
      break
    }
  }
  // 3
  if index == NSNotFound {
    e = Establishment(record: record, database: db)
    results.append(e)
    index = results.count - 1
  }
  dispatch_async(dispatch_get_main_queue()) {
    // 4
    if newItem {
      self.delegate.establishmentAdded(e, index: index)
    } else {
      self.delegate.establishmentUpdated(e, index: index)
    }
  }
}
```

Note the two `dispatch_async` blocks: these ensure all the delegate methods are called on the main queue so the delegate can update its table view directly.

Looking at the code a little more closely, you'll see the following:

1. Since there's no callback on `CKQueryOperation` for when data first arrives, this checks to see if this record is the first record downloaded, and if so notifies the delegate to begin updating.
2. Enumerates over the existing records and determine if an Establishment record with a matching `recordID` already exists locally.
3. If it's a new record add it to the `results` array.
4. Finally, call the appropriate delegate method depending on whether this record was new, or simply updated.

Next, add the following to `NearbyLocationsResultsController`:

```
func queryCompleted(cursor: CKQueryCursor!, error: NSError!) {
  startedGettingResults = false
  dispatch_async(dispatch_get_main_queue()) {
    self.delegate.didEndUpdating(error)
  }
}
```

Here you're resetting `startedGettingResults` and informing the delegate it should finish updating.

Now add the following to `NearbyLocationsResultsController`:

```
func fetchNextResults(cursor: CKQueryCursor) {
  let queryOp = CKQueryOperation(cursor: cursor)
  sendOperation(queryOp)
}
```

In order to fetch the next batch of results, you create a new `CKQueryOperation`, but instead of constructing it with a query object, you can use a `CKQueryCursor`. This object acts as in index into the result-set so that the new operation starts where the last one left off. For example, if there are 100 records on the server that match the query, but only 30 were previously fetched, the cursor will indicate to fetch items starting at number 31.

Finally, wrap things up by implementing `sendOperation(queryOp:)` in `NearbyLocationsResultsController`. Add the following:

```
func sendOperation(queryOp: CKQueryOperation) {
  // 1
```

```
    queryOp.queryCompletionBlock = {
      cursor, error in
        // 2
        self.queryCompleted(cursor, error: error)
        if (cursor != nil) {
          // 3
          self.fetchNextResults(cursor)
        } else {
          // 4
          self.inProgress = false
        }
    }
    queryOp.recordFetchedBlock = { record in
      // 5
      self.recordFetched(record)
    }
    queryOp.resultsLimit = resultLimit
    // 6
    startedGettingResults = false
    // 7
    db.addOperation(queryOp)
  }
```

This method sets up the necessary callbacks on the `CKQueryOperation` instance that's passed in, imposes the record limit, and then submits the operation to the queue:

1. The `queryCompletionBlock` is called when all records have been fetched, the record limit was reached, or an error cancelled the operation.
2. Call the internal method that handles notifying the delegate to finish updating.
3. If the operation returns a cursor, then there is still more data to fetch from the server. A call to `fetchNextResults(cursor:)` kicks off an additional query operation.
4. If no cursor is returned, then all the records have been retrieved and the operation is finished.
5. Call the internal method used to create an instance of `Establishment` from the fetched record.
6. Reset the tracking state for the operation you're about to execute.
7. Kick off the query operation.

Add the following line to the very bottom of `start()`:

```
sendOperation(queryOp)
```

This is the final piece of the jigsaw, and passes the query operation so it can be properly set up and executed.

> **Note:** If you encounter any build errors, ensure the bundle ID and team are set correctly in the target's General pane, and that your bundle ID matches the container ID in the iCloud section of the Capabilities pane. Refer to Chapter 15, **Beginning CloudKit**, for more information on setting up the necessary bundle IDs and teams.

Using the Controller

Open **MasterViewController.swift** and replace `refresh()` with the following:

```
func refresh() {
  var location = locationManager.location
  // 1
  if location == nil{
    // Using Apple as our default location
    location = CLLocation(latitude: 182,
     longitude: -122.03118)
  }
  // 2
  let predicate =
   Model.sharedInstance().createLocationPredicate(location,
    radiusInMeters:FilterDistance)
  controller.predicate = predicate
  // 3
  controller.start()
}
```

You call this method at various points during the view controller lifecycle, such as when a new location is found, or when the user wants to refresh the table view. This starts off the following series of events that ultimately sends the query to iCloud:

1. The location predicate filters locations by distance. If the location manager doesn't have a location, or is unable to get one due to issues such as being denied the necessary permissions, then set the default location to Apple's headquarters in Cupertino – this is also the location around which the sample data is based.

2. This helper method creates the necessary `NSPredicate` object using the location.

3. Calls the `start()` on the results controller, which will eventually execute the delegate callbacks.

Replace the `NearbyLocationsResultsControllerDelegate` stubs with the following code; these are the delegate methods responsible for updating the table view as data is retrieved:

```
func willBeginUpdating() {
  // 1
  tableView.beginUpdates()
}

func establishmentUpdated(establishment: Establishment, index:
Int) {
  // 2
  let indexPath = NSIndexPath(forRow: index, inSection: 0)
  tableView.reloadRowsAtIndexPaths([indexPath],
   withRowAnimation: .Automatic)
}

func establishmentAdded(establishment: Establishment, index:
Int) {
  // 3
  let indexPath = NSIndexPath(forRow: index, inSection: 0)
  tableView.insertRowsAtIndexPaths([indexPath],
   withRowAnimation: .Automatic)
}

func didEndUpdating(error: NSError!) {
  // 4
  tableView.endUpdates()
  refreshControl?.endRefreshing()
```

}Each call to `refresh()` may result in the delegate being called multiple times if the number of matching records on the server exceeds the self-imposed batch size. This lets the table view show the records that *have* been downloaded and lets the user interact with the app while data is still being transferred.

One tricky downside to using `CKQueryOperation` is that there's no way to get a count of matching records ahead of time, so you'll only know how many matching records you have once there are no more records left to fetch.

> **Note:** The suggested values for the batch size, maximum results, and the initial count are all just reasonable guesses. Tuning these parameters is more best guess than exact science, and the process is complicated by the ever-changing landscape of mobile network capacities.
>
> Experiment with the batch size until you find something that works for you. You could also try to use the timing of previous fetches to adjust your batch size dynamically, but that's left as an exercise for you, the reader.

Setting Sample Data

Build and run. You'll likely see no data in your app, or receive an error stating "no entity of that type". To resolve this you'll have to create some new Establishment records. You can either manually enter these via the app, or simply run `uploadSampleData()` once to upload some initial seed data. Simply uncomment `uploadSampleData()` at the top of `application(_:, didFinishLaunchingWithOptions:)` in **AppDelegate.swift**, run the app and then re-comment out the same statement.

> **Note:** Make sure to log into your iCloud account on the simulator before running the app. You can do this in Settings.app.

To verify that batch loading is working, change `resultLimit` in `NearbyLocationsResultsController` to a lesser value, such as `2`, and then restart the app. You should now see the view update as the rows animate in, two at a time. The following screenshots show an example of before and after a batch.

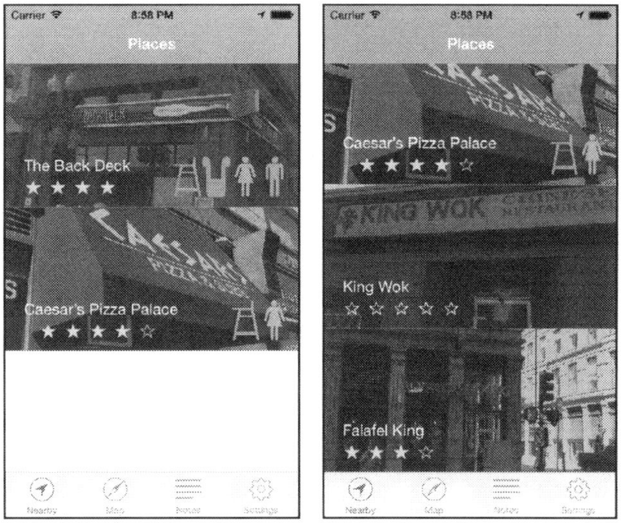

You may experience some transitory errors when refreshing the list. For cases such as a "Network Failure" error, restarting the device or simulator can often help. If you don't receive an error, but only a few Establishments (*or none at all!*) show up in the list, this might be due to the way the distance to the locations are being calculated.

If you need to work around this for the sake of the tutorial, replace the query predicate in `refresh()`, found in `MasterViewController`, with a predicate that shows all records, as shown below:

```
let predicate = NSPredicate(value: true)
```

If you made the change, build and run now to verify it's working.

Syncing With Subscriptions

One of the most powerful features of CloudKit is the ability to subscribe to changes on the server through a feature called **Subscriptions**. Your app will receive a push notification when the data matching the subscription, which is based on a predicate, changes. Using a push model like this let's your app update based on external activities and makes your synchronization activities fairly lightweight.

What makes CloudKit stand out against other BaaS providers is that you don't need any additional push configuration, including wrangling with certificates and device tokens.

Plus, since subscriptions don't require user-facing notifications, there's no permission dialogs to worry about.

Subscriptions can be either **zone-based**, where your app monitors all records in a particular zone, or they can be based on a specific query. You can set up query subscriptions to notify your app when records are added, deleted, or updated.

For BabiFüd, you'll use a query subscription to keep the list of establishments up-to-date since it's already backed by a query.

> **Note: Record Zones** haven't been covered yet since they aren't used in BabiFüd. Zones are a way of grouping records, which let you easily monitor them for changes.

Subscribing to updates

Subscribing to a query and responding to a notification requires a Subscription to be saved to a container, and for your app to be set up to receive remote notifications.

Open **NearbyLocationsResultsController.swift**. Since this class is already managing the list of Establishments and has delegate callbacks to update that list, it's a good place to add the subscription functionality.

First add the following instance variables to the top of the class:

```
var subscriptionID = "subscription_id"
var subscribed = false
```

Then, add the following method to `NearbyLocationsResultsController`:

```
func subscribe() {
  // 1
  if subscribed {
    return
  }
  // 2
  let options = CKSubscriptionOptions.FiresOnRecordCreation |
   CKSubscriptionOptions.FiresOnRecordDeletion |
    CKSubscriptionOptions.FiresOnRecordUpdate
  // 3
  let subscription = CKSubscription(recordType: RecordType,
   predicate: predicate, subscriptionID: subscriptionID,
    options: options)
```

```
    // 4
    subscription.notificationInfo = CKNotificationInfo()
    subscription.notificationInfo.alertBody = ""
    // 5
    db.saveSubscription(subscription, completionHandler: {
      subscription, error in
      if (error != nil) {
        println("error subscribing: \(error)")
      } else {
        self.subscribed = true
        println("subscribed!")
      }
    })
}
```

This method is responsible for creating the subscription and pushing it up to the container in iCloud.

1. Before attempting to subscribe, check that the user isn't already subscribed. Duplicate subscriptions won't result in duplicate notifications, but they do have the cost of extra network requests to the server and your users will thank you for being responsible with their data allowance.

2. Subscribe to all three different types of notification in order to keep the list synchronized.

3. Create a subscription object with the appropriate record type, predicate, subscription ID, and which types of notification your interested in.

4. Create a `CKNotificationInfo`. This is saved to CloudKit and sent back as part of each remote notification for the subscription. This sets up information about the alert displayed to the user. Although no alert is shown in this case, a notification info object must be set on the subscription for a remote notification to be sent. This is just one of the quirks of CloudKit.

5. Save the subscription.

Add the following statement to the very bottom of `start()`:

```
subscribe()
```

This simply calls the method you added above, making sure the app subscribes to the relevant notifications.

Before your app can receive push notifications, it needs to register for them.

Add the following line to `application(_:, didFinishLaunchingWithOptions:)` in **AppDelegate.swift**:

```
application.registerForRemoteNotifications()
```

This is a new method on `UIApplication` introduced in iOS 8. When an app wants to receive push notifications for remote events, but doesn't want to spam the user with lock-screen messages or in-app popups, this method requests the push token without needing to ask the user for permission.

The `UIApplicationDelegate` methods for push token management need to be implemented as well.

Add the following two methods to `AppDelegate`:

```
func application(application: UIApplication!,
 didRegisterForRemoteNotificationsWithDeviceToken deviceToken:
  NSData!) {
  println("Registered for Push notifications with token:
\(deviceToken)")
}

func application(application: UIApplication!,
 didFailToRegisterForRemoteNotificationsWithError error:
  NSError!) {
  println("Push subscription failed: \(error)")
}
```

CloudKit is able to submit the token through the subscription mechanism, so you don't need to do anything with it here. The code above simply prints a message to the console for illustrative purposes. There is no mechanism right now to resubmit the request, but logic could be added to the `subscribe()` method to check for one each time the master list view is loaded until there is a valid token and saved subscription.

There is one final step to getting a subscription up and running: the **Remote notifications** capability needs to be enabled. Select the project in the **Project Navigator**, and then select the **BabiFüd** target. Click the **Capabilities** tab, and then flip the switch to enable **Background Modes**. Finally, check the box for **Remote notifications**.

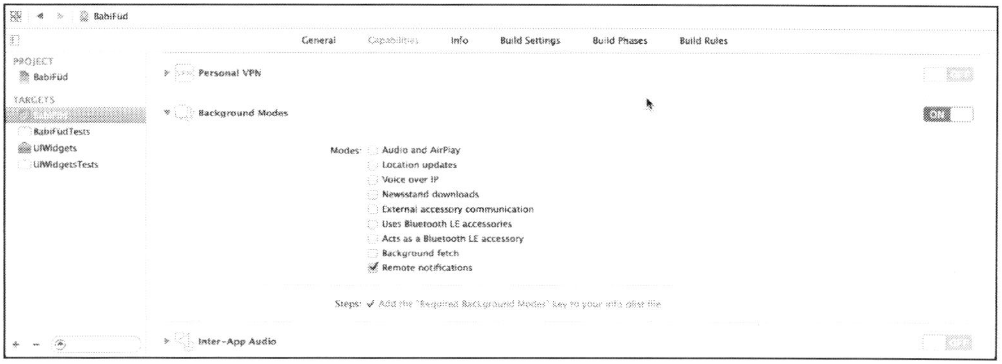

Plug in an iOS device and build and run the app. An actual iOS device is needed to test out subscriptions since push notifications cannot be simulated. If the token request is successful, you'll see console output like below:

```
Registered for Push notifications with token: <c72ee6b8 a138fc39
5a570185 39022bfd 6b009225 89059599 6628ae64 f3c63398>
subscribed!
```

Fielding notifications

`CKQueryNotification` is a subclass of `CKNotification` that represents the information pushed from the server; you construct an instance of `CKNotification` from the `userInfo` dictionary. Although `userInfo` is just a regular `NSDictionary`, you should treat it as an opaque object, as the keys and values are not publically define and likely to change in future releases.

Interaction with the userInfo happens through the `CKNotification` object, which exposes the notification values in a supported API. You then hand off the notification to the results controller object. This will get the ids of the records that triggered the notification, fetch the records from the server, update the appropriate Establishments, and tell the results controller delegate to update its views.

Because the subscription was set to notify for record removals as well as additions and updates, the results controller will need to handle record removal. Open **NearbyLocationsResultsController.swift** and add the following line to the protocol definition for `NearbyLocationsResultsControllerDelegate`:

```
func establishmentRemovedAtIndex(index:Int)
```

Next, add the following method to NearbyLocationsResultsController:

```
func itemMatching(recordID: CKRecordID) -> (item:
 Establishment!, index: Int) {
  var index = NSNotFound
  var e: Establishment!
  for (idx, value) in enumerate(results) {
    if value.record.recordID == recordID {
      index = idx
      e = value
      break
    }
  }
  return (e, index: index)
}
```

This is just a convenience method to determine if the item passed into it is already stored in the array of establishments. After all, you can't remove an object that doesn't exist.

To remove the local copy of any records that are removed from the server, add the following to NearbyLocationsResultsController:

```
func remove(recordID: CKRecordID) {
  dispatch_async(dispatch_get_main_queue()) {
    // 1
    var (e, index) = self.itemMatching(recordID)
    // 2
    if index == NSNotFound {
      return
    }
    self.delegate.willBeginUpdating()
    // 3
    self.results.removeAtIndex(index)
    self.delegate.establishmentRemovedAtIndex(index)
    self.delegate.didEndUpdating(nil)
  }
}
```

Removing an item is relatively straightforward:

1. Use the method you just added to find the index of the establishment with the matching record ID.
2. If no matching establishment is found then return immediately.
3. Remove the establishment from the array and then notify the delegate.

To update the view to remove rows from the table when a record is removed, in **MasterViewController.swift** replace the stub `establishmentRemovedAtIndex(_:)` with the following:

```
func establishmentRemovedAtIndex(index: Int)  {
  let indexPath = NSIndexPath(forRow: index, inSection: 0)
  tableView.deleteRowsAtIndexPaths([indexPath],
withRowAnimation: .Automatic)
}
```

Next, to add new or to update existing records, go back to `NearbyLocationsResultsController` and add the following method:

```
func fetchAndUpdateOrAdd(recordID: CKRecordID) {
  db.fetchRecordWithID(recordID) { record, error in
    if error == nil  {
      var (e, index) = self.itemMatching(recordID)
      if index == NSNotFound {
        e = Establishment(record: record, database: self.db)
        dispatch_async(dispatch_get_main_queue()) {
          self.delegate.willBeginUpdating()
          self.results.append(e)
          self.delegate.establishmentAdded(e, index:
           self.results.count - 1)
          self.delegate.didEndUpdating(nil)
        }
      } else {
        dispatch_async(dispatch_get_main_queue()) {
          self.delegate.willBeginUpdating()
          e.record = record
          self.delegate.establishmentUpdated(e, index: index)
          self.delegate.didEndUpdating(nil)
        }
      }
    }
  }
}
```

Since `CKQueryNotification` only contains the `recordID` relating to the record of interest, you'll have to fetch the entire record to get the rest of the data. If it's a new record, then add it to the list of establishments via the delegate; if it's an existing record then just update the Establishment object to reflect the new data, and again, notify the delegate.

Both updating a record and creating a record are handled in the same way. A create notification can be sent out of order, or even be a duplicate. Therefore, the code has to take into account that the record the notification represents might already be in the list of establishments, an updated record could have been previously removed from the list, or that an update notification could be received before a create notification. It's a lot of logic to manage!

Add the following method to NearbyLocationsResultsController:

```
func handleNotification(note: CKQueryNotification) {
  let recordID = note.recordID
  switch note.queryNotificationReason {
    case .RecordDeleted:
      remove(note.recordID)
    case .RecordCreated:
      fetchAndUpdateOrAdd(note.recordID)
    case .RecordUpdated:
      fetchAndUpdateOrAdd(note.recordID)
    }
  markNotificationAsRead([note.notificationID])
}
```

The app subscribes to notifications for record creation, deletion and update. To keep the local list in sync with the server, the results list needs to update by adding, removing, or updating its records. Since CKQueryNotification is used for all three operations, this method switches on queryNotificationReason to invoke the appropriate action.

Add the following method to NearbyLocationsResultsController:

```
func markNotificationAsRead(notes:[CKNotificationID]) {
  let markOp = CKMarkNotificationsReadOperation(
   notificationIDsToMarkRead: notes)
  CKContainer.defaultContainer().addOperation(markOp)
}
```

Subscription notifications are normally sent soon after their trigger. If the device is offline and unable to receive push notifications, and multiple notifications are triggered, only the last one will be sent to the device when it is back online. The rest are queued up on the server and have to be fetched manually. Notifications marked as read aren't sent back to the client in a notification fetch. CKMarkNotificationsReadOperation is a CKOperation subclass that marks notifications as read, so subsequent fetches don't include these.

Add the following method to **AppDelegate.swift**:

```
func application(application: UIApplication!,
 didReceiveRemoteNotification userInfo: [NSObject :
  AnyObject]!) {
```

```
    let note = CKQueryNotification(
     fromRemoteNotificationDictionary: userInfo)
    masterViewController.controller.handleNotification(note)
  }
```

This application delegate method is called when a remote notification comes in. A `CKQueryNotification` is constructed from the notification info and then passed to the results controller to update the list, as seen above. `CKQueryNotification` is a subclass of `CKNotification` that has additional information for queries, such as the notification reason. There is also a separate subclass for zone notifications, but that is outside the scope of this chapter.

Build and run on your device, as push notifications won't work in the simulator.

Open the CloudKit dashboard (https://developer.icloud.com/dashboard) and add, update, or delete an Establishment record to trigger a notification. For example, rename one of the Establishments visible in your list. This will trigger the notification, and start off the action cascade, resulting in the view automatically updating to reflect the new name.

Using the Notification Collection

There is a good reason for being cautious about the ordering of notifications: there is no guarantee that your notifications will be delivered, and the push notification server only stores the most recent push notification. That means if the device is turned off, or is in airplane mode for example, the device only receives the latest notification when it's back online.

To solve this problem, CloudKit provides a way to retrieve missed notifications through a Notification Collection in the container. You fetch the backlog of notifications through a `CKFetchNotificationChangesOperation`.

For now, you'll make this call to fetch the outstanding notifications when you first start fetching records with the results controller, or when the app resumes from being in the background.

Add the following method to **NearbyLocationsResultsController.swift**:

```
  func getOutstandingNotifications() {
    // 1
    let op = CKFetchNotificationChangesOperation(
     previousServerChangeToken: nil)
    // 2
```

```
    op.notificationChangedBlock = {
      notification in
      if let ckNotification = notification as?
        CKQueryNotification {
        self.handleNotification(ckNotification)
      }
    }
    op.fetchNotificationChangesCompletionBlock = {
      serverChangeToken, error in
      // 3
      if error != nil {
        println("error fetching notifications \(error)")
      }
    }
    // 4
    CKContainer.defaultContainer().addOperation(op)
  }
```

4. This operation fetches all unread notifications from the server. The optional change token allows the app to ask for notifications after a specific date and time, which works well for fetching in batches, or to prevent applying duplicate or out-of-date changes.

5. `CKFetchNotificationChangesOperation` only fetches unread notifications. Since you mark received notifications as read, it's not necessary to track the change token. This functionality is more important when using app icon badges or other methods of indicating the read status to the user.

6. `notificationChangedBlock` is called for each notification. Here you simply hand off the notification to `handleNotification(:note)`.

7. When the fetch has completed, `fetchNotificationChangesCompletionBlock` is called. There's not much else to do here; if the operation fails, leave the unread notifications as unread and they'll be included the next time you fetch all notifications.

8. Unlike previous query operations, this is a container-wide call, so you pass the operation to the container object instead of the database object.

The next step is to make sure you call this new method. Add the following to the bottom of `start()`:

```
getOutstandingNotifications()
```

This simply calls the methods you've just implemented.

Add the following method to the same class:

```
func listenForBecomeActive() {
  NSNotificationCenter.defaultCenter()
   .addObserverForName(
     UIApplicationDidBecomeActiveNotification as NSString,
      object: nil, queue: NSOperationQueue.mainQueue()) {
       notification in
        self.getOutstandingNotifications()
  }
}
```

This adds an observer so you're notified when the application becomes active, which when received triggers the download of any unread notifications.

Add the following call to the existing `db.saveSubscription` callback in `subscribe()`:

```
db.saveSubscription(subscription, completionHandler:  {
  subscription, error in
    if (error != nil) {
      println("error subscribing: \(error)")
    } else {
      self.subscribed = true
      self.listenForBecomeActive() // ← Add this
    }
})
```

If the subscription is successful, this will call the previous method to listen for the application becoming active, in order to fetch the unread notifications.

Build and run on a device. Once the app has launched, put it into the background by pressing the home button. Head over to the CloudKit dashboard and modify a few Establishment records. Bring the app back to the foreground, and you'll see that the list updates to reflect your new changes.

The following screenshots show a before and after changing two of the establishment's names:

Take a look at the left-hand side of the CloudKit dashboard; under the SCHEMA sections you'll see **Subscription Types**. Selecting it will list the one active subscription for the app - **Establishment: Location**

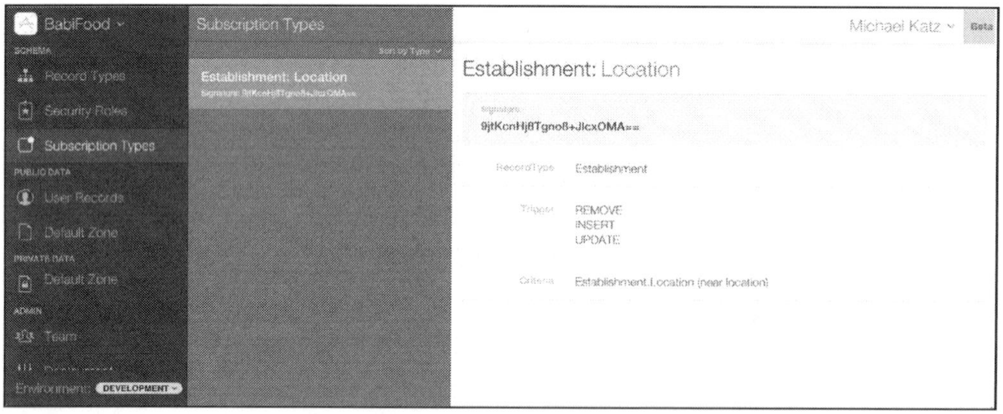

It's named this way because the subscription has a predicate on the Location attribute of the Establishment record type.

Handling errors

Apple's advice for error handling when working with CloudKit is to simply "*Handle your errors.*" Of course you should, but it begs the question, how?

The unfortunate reality is that dealing with errors is hard. There are many ways to mess up, from network issues, server problems, user mistakes, to simple programmer errors. Each situation requires a different response, and the response for each depends on the type of request. For instance, failing to update a photo of a meeting location has less impact than failing to update the physical location or time of the meeting!

Implementing proper error handling could probably fill a book all on its own, but there are a few things specific to CloudKit that you can do to improve your users' experience.

Retrying requests

One easy solution is to add is automatic retries when a request fails. CloudKit has two conditions under which you could attempt a retry: when the service is unavailable, and when a client is rate-limited. Rate-limiting in this is case means that the CloudKit server is receiving too many requests within a short amount of time, and is asking clients to back off in order to protect resources (and possibly prevent a denial-of-service attack). In this case, CloudKit suggests a retry time, probably based on server conditions, such as amount of free memory and ability to spin up new servers.

Add the following method to **NearbyLocationsResultsController.swift**; since the method doesn't depend on any class-specific state, place it outside the of class definition as a static method:

```
func isRetryableCKError(error:NSError?) -> Bool {
  var isRetryable = false
  // 1
  if let err = error {
    // 2
    let isErrorDomain = err.domain == CKErrorDomain
    let errorCode: Int = err.code
    // 3
    let isUnavailable = errorCode ==
CKErrorCode.ServiceUnavailable.rawValue
    let isRateLimited = errorCode ==
CKErrorCode.RequestRateLimited.rawValue
    let errorCodeIsRetryable = isUnavailable || isRateLimited
    isRetryable = error != nil && isErrorDomain &&
     errorCodeIsRetryable
```

```
  }
  return isRetryable
}
```

9. Check if there's a valid error object.

10. Check if the error belongs to the `CKErrorDomain`, so you know it's a CloudKit related error.

11. Check if the error code is either `.ServiceUnavailable` or `.RequestRateLimited.` In either case, it's safe to retry your request.

You can call the above method inside any `CKOperation` completion block to retry an operation if it failed.

Add the following code to the very top of `queryOp.queryCompletionBlock(cursor:, error:)` in `sendOperation(queryOp:)`:

```
// 1
if isRetryableCKError(error) {
  let userInfo : NSDictionary = error.userInfo!
  // 2
  if let retryAfter = userInfo[CKErrorRetryAfterKey] as?
NSNumber {
    let delay = retryAfter.doubleValue * Double(NSEC_PER_SEC)
    let time = dispatch_time(DISPATCH_TIME_NOW, Int64(delay))
    // 3
    dispatch_after(time, dispatch_get_main_queue()) {
      self.sendOperation(queryOp)
    }
    return
  }
}
```

This code executes in the completion callback for the Establishment query.

1. If you're able to retry the request based on the error, then do so.

2. Only retry the request if a delay time is available in the `userInfo` dictionary under `CKErrorRetryAfterKey`.

3. After waiting the specified amount of time, retry the operation.

There are a few downsides to this approach; the client might retry indefinitely, or the user could stare at a progress spinner for what feels like forever until the operation does succeed.

To solve the first issue, you could add a retry limit and then bail when that limit is reached. The second issue could be solved by tracking the total amount of time the user has been waiting and exiting the retry loop after a specified amount of time.

There is no way to reliably reproduce these errors, so building and running your app won't necessarily show anything different, unless you're unlucky – or lucky, as the case may be – and you hit one of these conditions as you're developing.

Caching data

If the network can't be reached, you could always serve data cached locally until a network connection is re-established. CloudKit has some optimizations built-in to prevent downloading redundant data by caching results and tracking changes – it won't help in all scenarios, but it's a good solution in most cases.

To demonstrate caching, you'll add a persistence layer to BabiFüd through `NearbyLocationsResultsController`. This will cache results between app launches so if the query fails, the view will still populate. As an added benefit, you'll add image caching for the Establishment cover photos, which will improve load times and scroll speed.

The first thing to do is update `Establishment` so instances can be written to disk. There are many ways to persist objects in Cocoa, but one common way is to use `NSCoding`. `NSCoding` is a Cocoa protocol that is used to serialize objects to p-lists, as shown below.

Add the `NSCoding` protocol to the `Establishment` class declaration, as follows:

```
class Establishment : NSObject, MKAnnotation, Equatable,
NSCoding {
```

The moment you add the protocol to the class, you'll receive a compile error since you won't have added the required methods; you'll add these in just a moment.

Next add `init(aDecoder:)` and `encodeWithCoder(aCoder:)` to `Establishment`, as follows:

```
required init(coder aDecoder: NSCoder) {
  super.init()
  // 1
```

```
    let recordName = aDecoder.decodeObjectForKey("recordName")
      as String
    // 2
    let recordID = CKRecordID(recordName: recordName)
    // 3
    self.record = CKRecord(recordType: "Establishment",
     recordID: recordID)
    self.database = Model.sharedInstance().publicDB

    let kidsMenu = aDecoder.decodeBoolForKey("KidsMenu")
    self.record.setObject(kidsMenu, forKey: "KidsMenu")

    let healthyOption = aDecoder.decodeBoolForKey("HealthyOption")
    self.record.setObject(healthyOption, forKey: "HealthyOption")

    // 4
    let lat = aDecoder.decodeDoubleForKey("latitude")
    let lon = aDecoder.decodeDoubleForKey("longitude")
    // 5
    let decodedLocation = CLLocation(latitude: lat,
     longitude: lon)
    self.record.setObject(decodedLocation, forKey: "Location")
    self.location = decodedLocation

    self.name = aDecoder.decodeObjectForKey("name") as String
    self.record.setObject(name, forKey: "Name")
}
```

1. Extract the `recordName` from the decoder.

2. Use `recordName` to create an instance of `CKRecordID`.

3. Create an instance of `CKRecord` using the `CKRecordID`. You don't need to supply the zone in this case since the app uses the default zone.

4. `CLLocation` isn't `NSCoding` compliant, so the latitude and longitude values have to be saved separately, and therefore restored separately.

5. Finally, reconstruct the location object from the latitude and longitude values.

Since `Establishment` is mostly a wrapper around `CKRecord`, it also needs to recreate the record object in `init(aDecoder:)`. The above method simply extracts objects from the coder – the tricky part is the record property itself, because it is a complex object that is not NSCoding-compliant. This means, the properties of concern have to be coded and decoded separately. In this instance, it's perfectly fine to create a fresh `CKRecord` object instead of fetching one.

A `CKRecord` without a `recordID` will automatically receive one when it's saved. However, in order for caching to work, the `recordID` of a restored record should match the record stored on the server. `recordID` is not simply a string, but an object that includes information about the record name and record zone.

Next add `encode(aCoder:)` method to `Establishment`:

```
func encodeWithCoder(aCoder: NSCoder) {
  aCoder.encodeObject(record.recordID.recordName,
   forKey: "recordName")

  aCoder.encodeBool(kidsMenu, forKey: "KidsMenu")
  aCoder.encodeBool(kidsMenu, forKey: "HealthyOption")

  aCoder.encodeDouble(location.coordinate.latitude,
    forKey: "latitude")
  aCoder.encodeDouble(location.coordinate.longitude,
    forKey: "longitude")

  aCoder.encodeObject(name, forKey:"name")
}
```

This is pretty much the reverse of the initialization method. It takes the data in an instance of `Establishment` and serializes it into the encoder.

To make use of this serialization, you'll need to create some methods to load and save the `Establishment` objects.

Open **NearbyLocationsResultsController.swift** and add the following methods to the end of the class:

```
// 1
func cachePath() -> String {
  let paths = NSSearchPathForDirectoriesInDomains(
   .CachesDirectory, .UserDomainMask, true)
  let path = paths[0]
   .stringByAppendingPathComponent("establishments.cache")
  return path
}

func persist() {
  let data = NSMutableData()
  // 2
  let archiver = NSKeyedArchiver(forWritingWithMutableData:
data)
  // 3
  archiver.encodeRootObject(results)
```

```
  archiver.finishEncoding()
  // 4
  data.writeToFile(cachePath(), atomically: true)
}
```

Here's how you persist the local data:

1. The path to the cache file will be in the cache directory for the app; you'll save it as a property list file called **establishments.cache**.
2. Create an instance of `NSKeyedArchiver`. This knows how to organize the data added in the encodeRootObject step in to plist-format. This means that data can be written to disk and then later restored to recreate the encoded object hierarchy.
3. Encode the array of `Establishment` objects. The array will be traversed by the encoder, and each item will be encoded using `encodeWithCoder(aCoder:)`.
4. Write the encoded data to the local file in the cache directory.

Restoring the array of `Establishment` objects from the cache is just the inverse process. Before building up that logic, add a new delegate method to the results controller. This will be used by the restoration method to notify the delegate once the data has been loaded from disk.

At the top of **NearbyLocationsResultsController.swift**, add the following method declaration to **NearbyLocationsResultsControllerDelegate:**

```
func controllerUpdated()
```

Next, go to **MasterViewController.swift** and implement the new method as follows:

```
func controllerUpdated() {
  tableView.reloadData()
  refreshControl?.endRefreshing()
}
```

Now, open **NearbyLocationsResultsController.swift** and add the following method:

```
func loadCache() {
  let path = cachePath()
  // 1
  let data = NSData(contentsOfFile: path)!
```

```
    if data.length > 0 {
      let decoder = NSKeyedUnarchiver(forReadingWithData: data)
      // 2
      let object: AnyObject! = decoder.decodeObject()
      if object != nil {
        // 3
        self.results = object as [Establishment]
        dispatch_async(dispatch_get_main_queue()) {
          // 4
          self.delegate.controllerUpdated()
        }
      }
    }
  }
```

Here you perform the following steps to load the array of objects:

1. Load the local data from the cache directory.
2. Decode the array using `NSKeyedUnarchiver`.
3. If the array decodes successfully, set it as the `results` property.
4. Call the new delegate method, which should in-turn refresh the interface.

You've now added the necessary methods to persist a local cache of records. The code will compile, but you still need to add the calls that trigger the loading and persisting your Establishment records.

Still working in **MasterViewController**, add the following to `viewDidLoad()` just after you set up the controller:

```
controller.loadCache()
```

The app will now use the cached data until the first update from the server. This way, if the app is launched in poor network conditions, the user will still have access to any previous Establishment data. This is very handy when you're on the move!

You now need to save the data at an appropriate time; a good choice would be once all the data has been loaded after a fetch operation.

Open **NearbyLocationsResultsController.swift** and add the following line to `queryOp.queryCompletionBlock(cursor:, error:)` inside `sendOperation(queryOp:)`:

```
if (cursor != nil) {
```

```
    self.fetchNextResults(cursor)
  } else {
    self.inProgress = false
    self.persist() // ← Add this call to persist()
  }
```

Build and run, this time on a device. Wait for the list of Establishments to populate, then stop the app. Enable Airplane Mode on the device to prevent network access, then re-launch the app. The list of establishments will now populate from the local cache instead of the network:

You've probably noticed the photos aren't loaded. In order to cache the images and provide them along with the rest of the Establishment data, the app will need to take over managing the images. This will involve fetching the photo's asset attribute separately from the rest of the Establishment record.

Fetching partial records

CloudKit provides a feature for loading just a subset of a record's attributes. Fetching only the needed data makes fetches faster when the records are large (such as a lot of attributes or assets). Large data, such as assets can then be downloaded separately as needed, making the app more responsive. As a bonus, in BabiFüd's case,Open **Establishment.swift** and add the following method to `Establishment`:

```
  func imageCachePath() -> String {
```

```
    let paths = NSSearchPathForDirectoriesInDomains(
      .CachesDirectory, .UserDomainMask, true)
    let path = paths[0].stringByAppendingPathComponent(
      record.recordID.recordName)
    return path
  }
```

The path to where images will be cached will be in the system-provided cache directory for the app.

Next, add the following method to `Establishment`:

```
func processAsset(records: [NSObject : AnyObject]!,
 error: NSError!, completion:(photo: UIImage!) -> ()) {
  // 1
  if error != nil {
    completion(photo: nil)
    return
  }
  // 2
  let updatedRecord = records[self.record.recordID]
   as CKRecord
  // 3
  if let asset = updatedRecord.objectForKey("CoverPhoto")
   as? CKAsset {
    // 4
    let url = asset.fileURL
    let im = UIImage(contentsOfFile: url.path!)
    // 5
    NSFileManager.defaultManager().copyItemAtPath(url.path!,
     toPath: self.imageCachePath(), error: nil)
    // 6
    dispatch_async(dispatch_get_main_queue()) {
      completion(photo: im)
    }
  } else {
    dispatch_async(dispatch_get_main_queue()) {
      completion(photo: nil)
    }
  }
}
```

This does the following processing the asset:

1. If there is an error (such as a network timeout), call the completion block passing `nil`. This will result in no photo for the row.

2. The fetch operation returns a dictionary, which will be passed in to this method. This dictionary maps requested `recordIDs` to the fetched `CKRecords`. From this dictionary, extract the one corresponding to the current object.

3. Check to see if the **CoverPhoto** key returns an instance of `CKAsset`.

4. If so, get the local URL and use it to load the photo into an instance of `UIImage`.

5. CloudKit usually manages the local `CKAsset` cache, but because the app is implementing it's own caching, it needs to copy the photos somewhere under the app's control, such as its cache directory. This has a side effect of temporarily increasing the app's local data usage since two copies of each image will exist on disk.

6. Finally, pass the photo to the completion block.

Replace the existing `loadCoverPhoto(completion:)` with the following:

```
func loadCoverPhoto(completion:(photo: UIImage!) -> ()) {
  let backgroundQueue = dispatch_get_global_queue(
   DISPATCH_QUEUE_PRIORITY_BACKGROUND, 0)
  // 1
  dispatch_async(backgroundQueue) {
    // 2
    let imagePath = self.imageCachePath()
    // 3
    if NSFileManager.defaultManager()
     .fileExistsAtPath(imagePath) {
      // 4
      let image = UIImage(contentsOfFile: imagePath)
      // 5
      dispatch_async(dispatch_get_main_queue()) {
        completion(photo: image)
      }
    } else {
      // 6
      let fetchOp = CKFetchRecordsOperation(recordIDs:
       [self.record.recordID])
      // 7
      fetchOp.desiredKeys = ["CoverPhoto"]
      fetchOp.fetchRecordsCompletionBlock = {
       records, error in
        // 8
        self.processAsset(records, error: error,
         completion: completion)
      }
      // 9
```

```
        self.database.addOperation(fetchOp)
      }
    }
  }
```

This code loads a photo from the local cache, and if it isn't available, fetches it from the server:

1. Let the processing happen on a background queue so you don't tie up the main queue with file I/O or network requests.
2. Use the helper method to get the necessary path to the cache directory.
3. Make sure the photo actually exists on disk before attempting to load it.
4. If it does, load it into an instance of `UIImage`.
5. Pass the photo to the completion block, which is called on the main queue.
6. If the photo doesn't exist, fetch the record again from the server.
7. But this time only request the `CoverPhoto` attribute.
8. Call `processAsset(records:, error:, completion:)` to handle the response.
9. Start the fetch operation.

This method introduces another type of database operation: `CKFetchRecordsOperation`. This fetches records by record ID rather than using a predicate. This can be used to update an existing record, but when you combine it with `desiredKeys`, it can download just the asset instead of a full record. If `desiredKeys` is set to an array of attribute names, then only those attributes will be downloaded, instead of all of them.

As you download records, the associated image assets are placed in the caches directory.

Build and run using a device. Let the app check for updates, and then stop it. Re-launch the app after enabling Airplane Mode and you'll now see photos displayed along with the data.

Right now, the assets are being downloaded twice: once at record query time, and then again when the app requests just the cover photo. To improve the performance of the app, you'll need to modify the original record query operation.

Open **NearbyLocationsResultsController.swift** file and add the following statement to `start()`:

```
let queryOp = CKQueryOperation(query: query)
queryOp.desiredKeys =
  ["Name","Location","HealthyOption","KidsMenu"] // ← Add this
```

This modifies the query to only download the non-asset keys. Unfortunately there is no such thing as an *exclude these keys* property; so `desiredkeys` will need to be kept up to date if you add any new attributes later.

Build and run again on the device. You should see that the list of Establishments loads much faster and still includes the photos! If your connection is slow enough, you'll be able to see the row data appear first, and the photos appear a touch later if they haven't been cached. To see this in action under regular conditions, just throw a `NSThread.sleepForTimeInterval(3)` inside the background dispatch block of `loadCoverPhoto(_:)` in Establishment.swift.

Where to go from here?

There is a lot more to CloudKit than simply saving and fetching records. The convenience API makes it easy to get started, but its performance isn't what you require for a real world application, as seen above with the separate loading of photo assets. Fortunately, CloudKit has a rich API with its database operations and subscriptions, which makes it possible to tune the behavior and performance of your app.

The caching strategy shown here works well for data and assets, but doesn't cover any reference records, such as the ones that store the ratings and user-generated photos and notes. You can use a similar strategy to persist these records to the caches directory and make this data available as well when you're offline. Using `desiredKeys` lets the app fetch the most important data quickly and then selectively load other data later – if at all.

With subscriptions and notifications, you can keep the app's data up to date without polling or manually refreshing. Since CloudKit is integrated with the rest of the iOS SDK, there's little overhead to set up remote notifications, which is a big advantage over other third-party solutions.

It's critical that you handle errors as best you can; the two strategies you covered here – automatic retries and the use of cached data – take place without the user knowing. With a little more code, you can let the user manually retry a lost connection.

Finally, CloudKit can provide fine control over when and how much data is fetched from the server. This is done by specifying the desired attribute keys on both query and fetch-by-record-id operations.

So far, BabiFüd is a pretty good starting off point for a restaurant ratings app. And there are several additional powers and features to take advantage of.

CloudKit provides limited social interaction, by allowing for the discovery of users through the current user's contact list. With this, the list could be organized not just by nearby places, but by those recommended by family and friends. Tapping into a social network makes apps spread quickly, and users are more likely to return when their peer group also uses it.

CloudKit also has additional functionality for handling conflicts when data on the server is changed and the app tries to save different changes. For example, image if users were able to edit establishment details, and one person updated the restroom type and another wanted to update the seating type at the same time. In this case there will be a conflict because the two resulting records will be out of sync with each other. CloudKit uses time-stamp change tokens to help resolve conflicts. In this case the records could merge since different attributes were modified. But if both changed the seating type, then the first saved change would win.

There's a lot more to discover with CloudKit. The documentation is pretty thorough, and the 2014 WWDC Session "Advanced CloudKit" is a tremendous resource.

See you at Caesar's Pizza Palace!

Chapter 17: Beginning Scene Kit

By Ricardo Rendon Cepeda

With iOS 7, Apple made a huge push in the casual, mobile gaming space by introducing Sprite Kit, an incredible 2D-graphics framework. Developers had plenty to chew on for a whole year, and Sprite Kit gave everyone the capability to make simple iOS games with relative ease. However, the 3D space continued to be largely inaccessible, requiring expert knowledge of computer graphics (OpenGL ES), or a sizeable wallet (Unity Pro).

Well, not anymore. :]

At WWDC 2012, Apple introduced Scene Kit to Mac OS X developers, and iOS-only devs like myself felt a little jealous that we weren't invited to the party. Fortunately, it was just a short matter of time before Scene Kit joined the mobile space, and it's very exciting to have it available to us in iOS 8!

While the focus of Scene Kit is 3D games, the fact of the matter is that it's a powerful, easy to access, general-purpose 3D-graphics framework that has marvelous potential for non-gaming apps too.

Scene Kit: The Mac OS X warrior finally comes to iOS!

In this chapter, you'll learn how to build a simple app of that type by developing a 3D Carbon Visualizer, using Scene Kit. 3D visualization is a great option for explaining complex concepts – like chemical compounds, in this case – in a fun, playful, and easily digestible format. Words and diagrams are essential, but Scene Kit can definitely elevate your work to a new level!

Scene Kit Quick Start

By providing a built-in project template, Xcode 6 makes it very easy to get started with Scene Kit. Unlike Xcode 5's *OpenGL Game* template, the new version of Scene Kit is a great introduction to the framework, and a solid starting point for a new project. In this section, you'll take a quick look at this template and familiarize yourself with a basic Scene Kit scene.

Open Xcode and create a new project. Choose the **iOS/Application/Game** template and click **Next**.

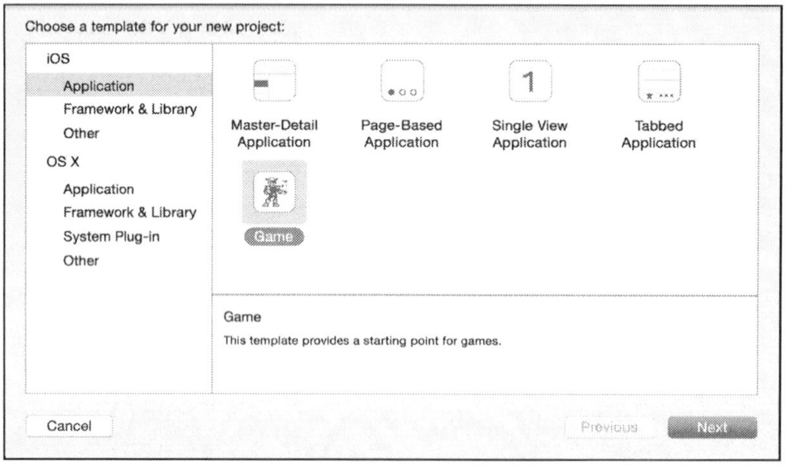

Type in **QuickStart** for **Product Name**, select **Swift** for **Language** and select **SceneKit** for **Game Technology**. Leave everything else as-is, and click **Next**. Select a directory of your choice and click **Create**.

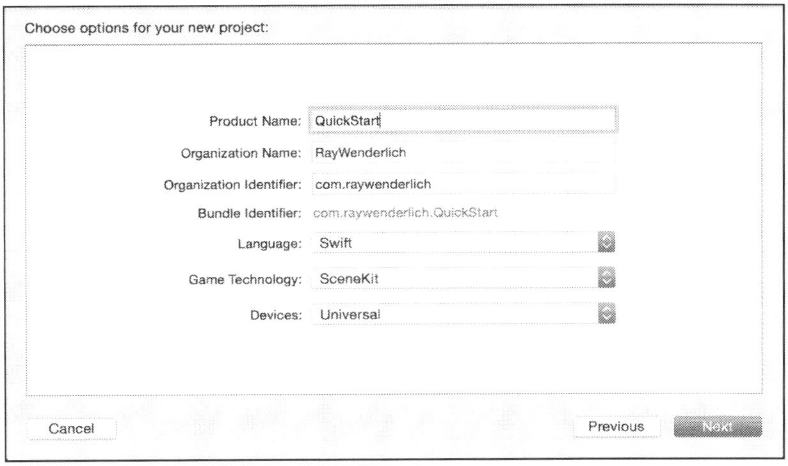

There is no need to examine or modify any code right now, just build and run! You'll see a simple, rotating 3D plane, similar to the following screenshot:

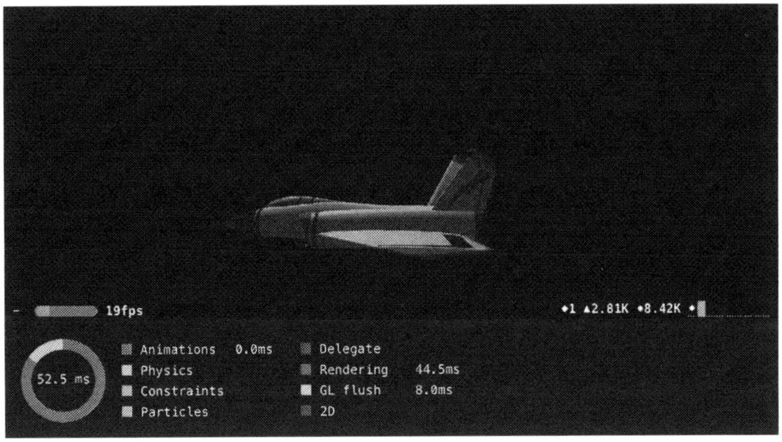

Feel free to explore the scene using the available gestures (pinch, rotate, pan, tap). Also, be sure to take note of the scene statistics (excluding the advanced stats dropdown) at the bottom of the view, defined by the following symbols:

- **fps**: frames per second
- ◆: draw calls per frame
- Δ: number of polygons
- *: number of vertices

This particular scene, with all the included functionality, is the result of a single file and about 100 lines of code. That's how powerful Scene Kit is. :]

Close your **QuickStart** project now, because you're going to build a new one from scratch!

Getting Started

Locate the starter pack for this tutorial, unzip the contents and open the Xcode project titled **CarbonVisualizer.xcodeproject**. Build and run the project to see this screen:

Simple enough. At this stage, the project is very lightweight and takes care of the bulk of the setup steps for you, without writing any significant Scene Kit code just yet. The project contains all the Swift files you need, which you'll develop incrementally as you work through this chapter. Furthermore, **Main.storyboard** contains a single view controller with two standard UI components, already linked to **ViewController.swift**. There's also a new component, a SceneKit View; open up **Main.storyboard** so you can learn about it a bit more.

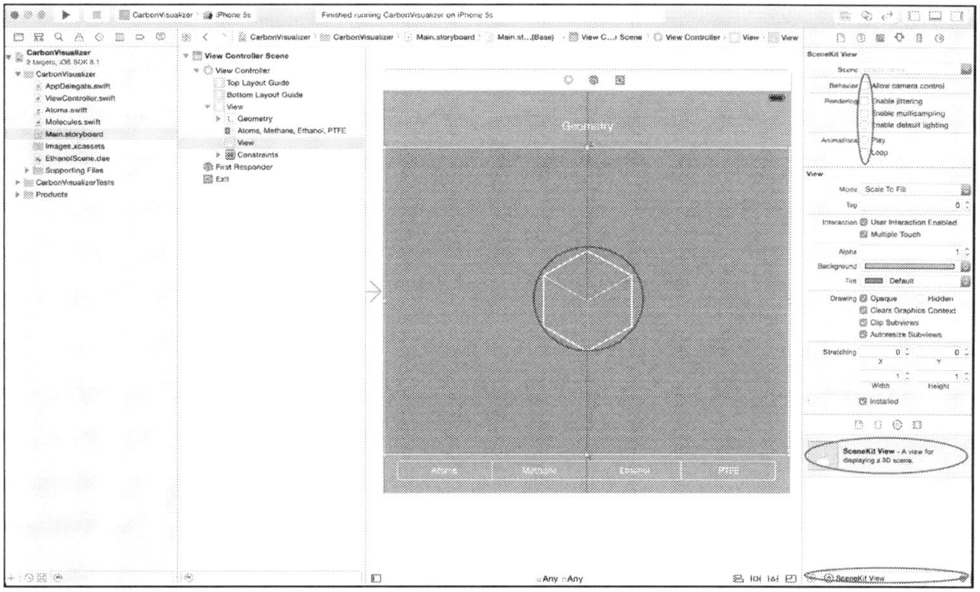

SceneKit View is a great *out-of-the-box* component available from the *Object library* of Interface Builder. SceneKit View is built for 3D graphics rendering – much like GLKit View – and allows you and/or your designer to set up many defining attributes of a scene quickly. For now though, you'll be doing most of the work programmatically so you can switch between different solutions with ease.

Let's get started with Scene Kit!

Your First Scene

With a SCNView already set up, your first step is to create an actual scene to display; but first, a primer on Scene Kit…

Scene Kit is a *node-based framework* that allows for uncomplicated construction and rendering of powerful *scene graphs*. The `SCNScene` object you'll create and manipulate in this chapter contains a `rootNode` property to which you can add several other `SCNNode` objects as child nodes, thus forming a tree structure like so:

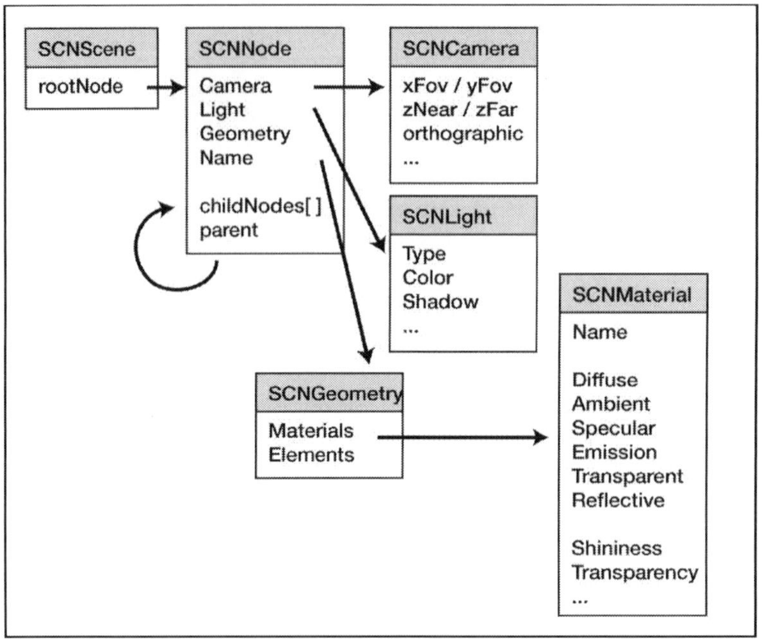

SceneGraph from Apple's *Scene Kit Programming Guide*

One major advantage of this system – especially in relation to this chapter – is that any transformations applied to a node's geometry also apply to that node's children. For example, if a 3D Ferrari lunges forward 10ft, then all of its parts, like the seats and tires, move forward 10ft too – simulating real-world physics. Additionally, every component's relative position to the car remains unchanged and independent e.g. a seat may tilt back without the car tilting back too.

Scene graph systems are very common in 3D graphics applications and you can read more about them here: http://en.wikipedia.org/wiki/Scene_graph

Now it's time to sit in the director's chair and create your first scene! After a quick conference with your casting scouts, you've decided to cast a *box* as the lead actor of your pilot show!

You need to set up a quick test scene first to make sure the box looks good, so add the following function to **ViewController.swift**, just below `viewDidAppear(animated:)`:

```
// MARK: Scene
func sceneSetup() {
```

```
  // 1
  let scene = SCNScene()

  // 2
  let boxGeometry = SCNBox(width: 10.0, height: 10.0, length:
10.0, chamferRadius: 1.0)
  let boxNode = SCNNode(geometry: boxGeometry)
  scene.rootNode.addChildNode(boxNode)

  // 3
  sceneView.scene = scene
}
```

Here's what this code snippet does:

1. You simply instantiate an empty scene (`SCNScene`), which will soon evolve into a more complex scene graph with lights, camera and geometry.
2. You create a box by defining a geometry instance (`SCNBox`) and attaching it to a node (`SCNNode`), which is then appended to your scene's root node.
3. Finally, your scene is attached to your `sceneView`.

Next, add the following line inside `viewDidAppear(animated:)` just below the call to `super`:

```
sceneSetup()
```

Build and run!

While it's not too exciting just yet, you should be happy you could render an object to your screen in just a few simple steps. However, you can't tell whether your starring actor is a box or a flat square. How about you add some lighting to help here?

Lighting plays a critical role in any 3D scene and defines the "look and feel" of your work, and can be a bit of work to get perfect. Sometimes – like right now – you just need the bare minimum to get a glimpse of what's going on. Thankfully, `SCNView` has a property to accomplish this task by enabling default lighting. Add the following line to your code, just below `sceneView.scene = scene` in `sceneSetup`:

```
sceneView.autoenablesDefaultLighting = true
```

Build and run to see an improved rendering of your scene!

After shining a little light on the subject, it's easier to infer depth and see a box taking shape on your screen. `SCNView` has several powerful built-in features and default lighting is just the touching the surface (pun totally intended).

At the moment, your box is taking up far too much space in your scene, so it would be a good idea to zoom out of the object. The next `SCNView` property you'll enable is a helpful debugging feature that allows you to navigate your scene easily. Add the following line to the bottom of `sceneSetup` to enable camera controls:

```
sceneView.allowsCameraControl = true
```

Build and run, then use the following gestures to your interact with your scene:

- *Pan (one finger)* or *rotation*: rotates the camera around the scene.
- *Pan (two fingers)*: pans the camera across the scene.
- *Pinch*: zooms in/out of the scene.

If you're developing this chapter on the iOS Simulator, please take a look at the *iOS Simulator User Guide* if you need help performing the gestures: https://developer.apple.com/library/ios/documentation/IDEs/Conceptual/iOS_Simulator_Guide/InteractingwiththeiOSSimulator/InteractingwiththeiOSSimulator.html

Lights, Camera, Action!

The built-in `SCNView` features are very useful, but also rather limited. In order to fully customize and control your scene, you must learn how to create and add multiple nodes to your scene graph, of various different types.

As film directors would say, "Lights, camera, action!" :]

Add the following lines to `sceneSetup`, just below `let scene = SCNScene()`:

```
let ambientLightNode = SCNNode()
ambientLightNode.light = SCNLight()
ambientLightNode.light!.type = SCNLightTypeAmbient
ambientLightNode.light!.color = UIColor(white: 0.67, alpha: 1.0)
scene.rootNode.addChildNode(ambientLightNode)
```

Here, you're creating a new ambient light node with a 67% white color, then adding it to your scene. Ambient light is a basic form of lighting that illuminates all objects in a scene evenly, with a constant intensity from all directions, much like cloud-filtered sunlight. It's a great addition to most scenes when you want a more natural look. Otherwise, objects in shadow would be pure black and that's not the desired effect in most cases – especially when you build a model-viewer type of app, like the one in this chapter.

Although ambient light is part of the lighting equation, it's not very useful on its own because it does little to illuminate surface details. So, add one more light to your scene with the following lines, just after your previous addition:

```
let omniLightNode = SCNNode()
omniLightNode.light = SCNLight()
omniLightNode.light!.type = SCNLightTypeOmni
omniLightNode.light!.color = UIColor(white: 0.75, alpha: 1.0)
omniLightNode.position = SCNVector3Make(0, 50, 50)
scene.rootNode.addChildNode(omniLightNode)
```

This new type of light is called an omnidirectional light, or point light. It's similar to ambient light in that it has constant intensity, but differs because it has a direction. The light's position relative to other objects in your scene determines its direction. Your box node's default position is (0, 0, 0), so positioning your new light node at (0, 50, 50) means that it's above and in front of your box.

> **Note:** Don't worry too much about units at this point. All units are relative to the scene and defined by your own set of rules. A position of (0, 50, 50) doesn't mean 50 meters, miles, or light years; it's simply *50 units*. You'll define a proper unit of measurement shortly.

Now that you've set up some lights, delete the following line from `sceneSetup`:

```
sceneView.autoenablesDefaultLighting = true
```

Build and run! Pinch to zoom out, and you'll find your box properly illuminated:

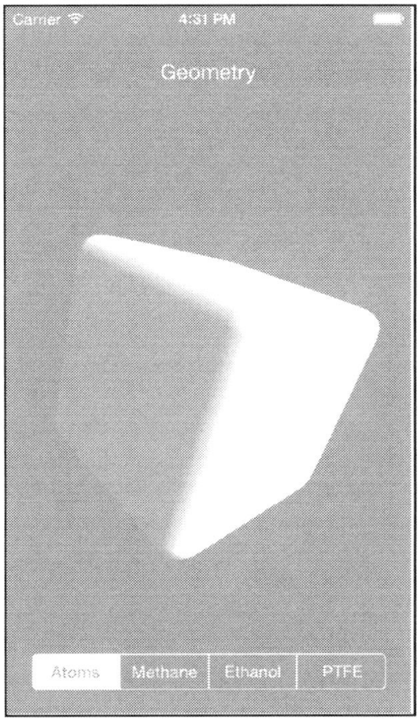

Behold your amazing and talented box! For this chapter, these two sources will do just fine, but be sure to experiment with directional (`SCNLightTypeDirectional`) and spot (`SCNLightTypeSpot`) lights in future projects.

Next, set up a camera by adding the following lines just below where you setup the lights in `sceneSetup`:

```
let cameraNode = SCNNode()
cameraNode.camera = SCNCamera()
cameraNode.position = SCNVector3Make(0, 0, 25)
scene.rootNode.addChildNode(cameraNode)
```

Just like the light nodes, a camera node is just as easy – if not easier – to set up. The default projection settings are spot-on for a basic scene, so you don't have to modify the camera's field of view, focal range or other properties, The only thing you need to define is its position, conveniently set right in front of your box at (0, 0, 25). Build and run to "get behind the lens."

> **Note:** The default projection type of a `SCNCamera` is perspective, but you can easily change this to orthographic projection by enabling `usesOrthographicProjection` and setting an appropriate `orthographicScale` value.

Now, if you navigate your scene with the default camera controls (rotation, specifically), you'll notice an odd effect: you might expect the box to rotate and the lighting to stay in place but, in fact, it's actually the *camera* rotating around the scene. That's why you see the box from different points of view.

The default camera controls are very powerful, but not customizable. In order to gain total control, you'll create your own. First, add the following variables to **ViewController.swift**, just above `viewDidLoad`:

```
// Geometry
var geometryNode: SCNNode = SCNNode()

// Gestures
var currentAngle: Float = 0.0
```

Dealing with a single box is simple enough, but once you have more complex models with multiple geometry sources, it'll be much easier to manage them as a single node –

hence the addition of `geometryNode`. Furthermore, `currentAngle` will help modify the y-axis rotation of `geometryNode` exclusively, leaving the rest of your scene nodes untouched.

Next up, add the following function below `sceneSetup`:

```
func panGesture(sender: UIPanGestureRecognizer) {
  let translation = sender.translationInView(sender.view!)
  var newAngle = (Float)(translation.x)*(Float)(M_PI)/180.0
  newAngle += currentAngle

  geometryNode.transform = SCNMatrix4MakeRotation(newAngle, 0,
1, 0)

  if(sender.state == UIGestureRecognizerState.Ended) {
    currentAngle = newAngle
  }
}
```

Whenever `sceneView` detects a pan gesture, this function will be called, and it transforms the gesture's x-axis translation to a y-axis rotation on the geometry node (1 pixel = 1 degree).

In this implementation, you modify the `transform` property of `geometryNode` by creating a new rotation *matrix*, but you could also modify its `rotation` property with a rotation *vector*. A transformation matrix is better because you can easily expand it to include translation and scale.

Next, add the following lines to `sceneSetup`, just above `sceneView.scene = scene`:

```
geometryNode = boxNode

let panRecognizer = UIPanGestureRecognizer(target: self, action:
"panGesture:")
sceneView.addGestureRecognizer(panRecognizer)
```

These lines finalize the setup by connecting your new functions and variables. Finally, remove the default camera controls by deleting the following line:

```
sceneView.allowsCameraControl = true
```

Build, run, *action*! Now try rotating your cube with a one-finger pan.

Much better :]

> **Note:** A full 3D transformation engine with gestures is far too complex for this chapter, but definitely worth a look. Luckily, for you, it's something we've covered on our site before! Check out "**OpenGL ES Transformations with Gestures**" for the implementation details:
> http://www.raywenderlich.com/50398/opengl-es-transformations-gestures

Atoms

Your box has been a fine star for the scene so far, and did its job in helping you create a pilot app, but now it's time to kick it to the curb. Since you're going to build an app with a purpose, you're going to recast your actors and develop a 3D visualizer starring the common carbon compounds: natural gas, alcohol and Teflon.

These compounds will display as ball-and-stick models (molecules) made of bonded *atoms*. Atoms are quite complex, but for this chapter a single sphere will represent each one, as it's an easy way to depict a basic unit of matter. This model is a simple, but useful way to represent molecular structures in chemistry, and you can learn more about it here: http://en.wikipedia.org/wiki/Ball-and-stick_model

The first atom you'll create is, of course, carbon (http://en.wikipedia.org/wiki/Carbon). Open up **Atoms.swift** and add the following class function inside the `Atoms` class:

```
class func carbonAtom() -> SCNGeometry {
  // 1
  let carbonAtom = SCNSphere(radius: 1.70)

  // 2
  carbonAtom.firstMaterial!.diffuse.contents =
UIColor.darkGrayColor()

  // 3
  carbonAtom.firstMaterial!.specular.contents =
UIColor.whiteColor()

  // 4
  return carbonAtom
}
```

> **Note:** If you're just getting to know Swift, a class function (otherwise, known as type function), is a function that is called directly on a class, rather than on an instance of that class.
>
> In Objective-C, these methods are indicated by the use of plus sign before for the actual method name. For example: `+ (SCNGeometry *)carbonAtom;`

This is a very compact function, but each line is worth understanding completely:

1. As previously mentioned, atoms will be modeled as spheres. 1.70 is the *van der Waals radius* (http://en.wikipedia.org/wiki/Van_der_Waals_radius) of carbon, which corresponds to the radius of an atom, in angstroms (10^{-10}m), if it were a perfect sphere. Now that you've assigned a unit of measurement to your atom, the rest of your scene will be relative to this unit.

2. `firstMaterial` is a property of type `SCNMaterial`, which defines your atom's material. Think of diffused shading as the intrinsic/base color of a surface. In Scene Kit, you can define this by a color, texture, or other source. For additional information, please refer to "**How to Export Blender Models to OpenGL ES: Part 2/3**" for more information: http://www.raywenderlich.com/48297/export-blender-models-opengl-es-part-2

3. Specular shading is another material property, which is the reflective color of a surface. For most materials, this is usually pure white.
4. All atom models in this chapter will be declared as type methods, following a factory method pattern. This will be especially useful when creating molecules with many different atoms of the same type, with these methods returning a fully modeled geometry object.

Now that you understand how to create a type method for a carbon atom, the rest of the atoms in this chapter will be just as easy to model. Add the following code to the `Atoms` class:

```
class func hydrogenAtom() -> SCNGeometry {
  let hydrogenAtom = SCNSphere(radius: 1.20)
  hydrogenAtom.firstMaterial!.diffuse.contents =
UIColor.lightGrayColor()
  hydrogenAtom.firstMaterial!.specular.contents =
UIColor.whiteColor()
  return hydrogenAtom
}

class func oxygenAtom() -> SCNGeometry {
  let oxygenAtom = SCNSphere(radius: 1.52)
  oxygenAtom.firstMaterial!.diffuse.contents =
UIColor.redColor()
  oxygenAtom.firstMaterial!.specular.contents =
UIColor.whiteColor()
  return oxygenAtom
}

class func fluorineAtom() -> SCNGeometry {
  let fluorineAtom = SCNSphere(radius: 1.47)
  fluorineAtom.firstMaterial!.diffuse.contents =
UIColor.yellowColor()
  fluorineAtom.firstMaterial!.specular.contents =
UIColor.whiteColor()
  return fluorineAtom
}
```

There you have it: hydrogen (http://en.wikipedia.org/wiki/Hydrogen), oxygen (http://en.wikipedia.org/wiki/Oxygen), and fluorine (http://en.wikipedia.org/wiki/Fluorine).

All atoms have the same method template and simply differ in sphere radius and diffuse color. In order to display all these atoms together, you'll add them to a single node. To do so, add the following type method to the `Atoms` class, at the bottom of the file (just before the closing brace):

```
class func allAtoms() -> SCNNode {
  let atomsNode = SCNNode()

  let carbonNode = SCNNode(geometry: carbonAtom())
  carbonNode.position = SCNVector3Make(-6, 0, 0)
  atomsNode.addChildNode(carbonNode)

  let hydrogenNode = SCNNode(geometry: hydrogenAtom())
  hydrogenNode.position = SCNVector3Make(-2, 0, 0)
  atomsNode.addChildNode(hydrogenNode)

  let oxygenNode = SCNNode(geometry: oxygenAtom())
  oxygenNode.position = SCNVector3Make(+2, 0, 0)
  atomsNode.addChildNode(oxygenNode)

  let fluorineNode = SCNNode(geometry: fluorineAtom())
  fluorineNode.position = SCNVector3Make(+6, 0, 0)
  atomsNode.addChildNode(fluorineNode)

  return atomsNode
}
```

This is a rather lengthy function, but it's also easy to digest. It simply creates and returns a new node that contains four children, one for each atom, nicely positioned along the x-axis. To see them in your scene, open up **ViewController.swift** and add the following lines to `viewDidAppear(animated:)`, just below the call to `sceneSetup`:

```
geometryLabel.text = "Atoms\n"
geometryNode = Atoms.allAtoms()
sceneView.scene!.rootNode.addChildNode(geometryNode)
```

Finally, remove your previous box object by deleting these lines from inside `sceneSetup`:

```
let boxGeometry = SCNBox(width: 10.0, height: 10.0, length:
10.0, chamferRadius: 1.0)
let boxNode = SCNNode(geometry: boxGeometry)
scene.rootNode.addChildNode(boxNode)
geometryNode = boxNode
```

Build and run! (Or, as *Radioactive Man* would say: "Up and atom!"). You should see four nicely rendered atoms:

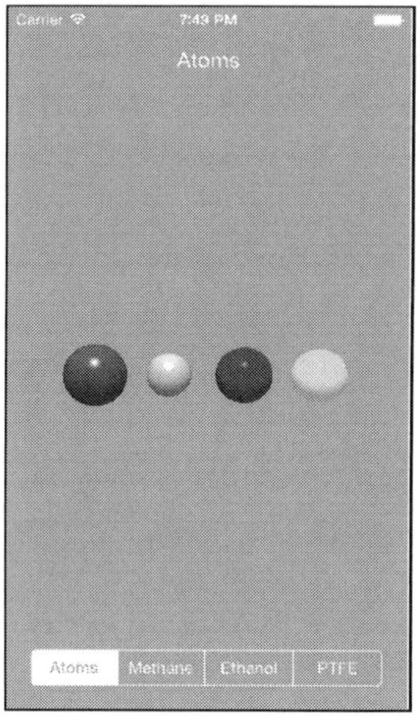

Awesome job so far! The scene is coming together, and now is a good time to take a quick break if you need to.

Molecules

As you may remember from science class, molecules are groups of two or more atoms held together by chemical bonds. All carbon compounds comprise of molecules of varying complexity. In this section of the chapter, you'll build 3D models for various molecules, using your new atoms as building blocks.

You'll learn about and build each molecule separately, but they'll all follow a similar pattern. Your first task is to lay the foundation of your molecules, so open up **Molecules.swift** and add the following lines inside the `Molecules` class:

```
class func methaneMolecule() -> SCNNode {
  var methaneMolecule = SCNNode()
  return methaneMolecule
}
class func ethanolMolecule() -> SCNNode {
```

```
    var ethanolMolecule = SCNNode()
    return ethanolMolecule
  }

  class func ptfeMolecule() -> SCNNode {
    var ptfeMolecule = SCNNode()
    return ptfeMolecule
  }
```

Just like your atoms, you develop your molecules as type methods, which return nodes that you can plug directly into your scene.

Next, open up **ViewController.swift** and add the following lines inside `segmentValueChanged(sender:)`:

```
// 1
geometryNode.removeFromParentNode()
currentAngle = 0.0

// 2
switch sender.selectedSegmentIndex {
case 0:
  geometryLabel.text = "Atoms\n"
  geometryNode = Atoms.allAtoms()
case 1:
  geometryLabel.text = "Methane\n(Natural Gas)"
  geometryNode = Molecules.methaneMolecule()
case 2:
  geometryLabel.text = "Ethanol\n(Alcohol)"
  geometryNode = Molecules.ethanolMolecule()
case 3:
  geometryLabel.text = "Polytetrafluoroethylene\n(Teflon)"
  geometryNode = Molecules.ptfeMolecule()
default:
  break
}

// 3
sceneView.scene!.rootNode.addChildNode(geometryNode)
```

Here's the breakdown for the code:

1. Whenever you select a new segment, your scene changes to display a new model. To clean up the previous model, it must be removed from its parent node (i.e. the scene's root node) and have its rotation angle reset.

2. A new model is assigned to `geometryNode`, and `geometryLabel` is updated accordingly with the model's name.

3. Finally, the new model is added to the scene.

Build and run! Try selecting different segments, and you'll notice an empty scene for *Methane*, *Ethanol* and *PTFE,* since you haven't created the molecules yet. Make sure the label's text changes for each segment. Also, note that *Atoms* will always display with its default starting position upon selection.

Methane

Methane (http://en.wikipedia.org/wiki/Methane) is the main component of *natural gas*. It's composed of one carbon atom and four hydrogen atoms, with the molecular formula CH_4. This molecule is very easy to convert into a 3D model, with carbon in the middle and hydrogen evenly spaced around it, so jump right in!

Open up **Molecules.swift** and add the following function inside the `Molecules` class, at the very end:

```
class func nodeWithAtom(atom: SCNGeometry, molecule: SCNNode,
position: SCNVector3) -> SCNNode {
  let node = SCNNode(geometry: atom)
  node.position = position
  molecule.addChildNode(node)
  return node
}
```

All atoms added to a molecule follow a generic procedure, where they:

1. Initialize a new node

2. Are given a position

3. Are added as a child to the molecule node

The previous function does just that and will be put to use for every atom of a molecule.

Next, replace your `methaneMolecule` stub with the following:

```
class func methaneMolecule() -> SCNNode {
  var methaneMolecule = SCNNode()

  // 1 Carbon
  let carbonNode1 = nodeWithAtom(Atoms.carbonAtom(), molecule:
methaneMolecule, position: SCNVector3Make(0, 0, 0))
```

```
    // 4 Hydrogen
    let hydrogenNode1 = nodeWithAtom(Atoms.hydrogenAtom(),
molecule: methaneMolecule, position: SCNVector3Make(-4, 0, 0))
    let hydrogenNode2 = nodeWithAtom(Atoms.hydrogenAtom(),
molecule: methaneMolecule, position: SCNVector3Make(+4, 0, 0))
    let hydrogenNode3 = nodeWithAtom(Atoms.hydrogenAtom(),
molecule: methaneMolecule, position: SCNVector3Make(0, -4, 0))
    let hydrogenNode4 = nodeWithAtom(Atoms.hydrogenAtom(),
molecule: methaneMolecule, position: SCNVector3Make(0, +4, 0))

    return methaneMolecule
}
```

It's a large block of code, but still pretty straightforward. Here, you're adding one carbon atom at the center of your molecule (0, 0, 0) and four hydrogen atoms around it (think north, east, south, west).

Build and run! Switch to the *Methane* segment to see the beginnings of your new molecule:

Awesome! Your atoms are in place and the next step is to create bonds between them. In a ball-and-stick model, *sticks* act as the bonds that hold the atoms together. Their inclusion is highly important because it really shows the full makeup of a molecule.

Add the following function at the end of your `Molecules` class:

```
class func lineBetweenNodeA(nodeA: SCNNode, nodeB: SCNNode) ->
SCNNode {
  // 1
  // Positions
  let positions: [Float32] = [nodeA.position.x,
nodeA.position.y, nodeA.position.z, nodeB.position.x,
nodeB.position.y, nodeB.position.z]
  let positionData = NSData(bytes: positions, length:
sizeof(Float32)*positions.count)

  // 2
  // Indices
  let indices: [Int32] = [0, 1]
  let indexData = NSData(bytes: indices, length:
sizeof(Int32)*indices.count)

  // 3
  // SCNGeometry
  let source = SCNGeometrySource(data: positionData, semantic:
SCNGeometrySourceSemanticVertex, vectorCount: indices.count,
floatComponents: true, componentsPerVector: 3,
bytesPerComponent: sizeof(Float32), dataOffset: 0, dataStride:
sizeof(Float32)*3)
    let element = SCNGeometryElement(data: indexData,
primitiveType: SCNGeometryPrimitiveType.Line, primitiveCount:
indices.count, bytesPerIndex: sizeof(Int32))

  // 4
  // Line
  let line = SCNGeometry(sources: [source], elements: [element])
  return SCNNode(geometry: line)
  }
```

This is a lengthy function with several steps worth explaining, so here goes:

1. Each bond is simply a line primitive drawn in 3D space, with a start (`nodeA`) and end (`nodeB`) position (i.e. vertices). These positions will be processed as raw data (`positionData`) generated from a float array (`positions`). They are specifically type-annotated as `Float32` due to a few graphics bugs in 64-bit architecture, and that will be explained later. :]
2. The previous positions/vertices also need a set of indices to render properly. For a line primitive, this is just an index of two.
3. A `SCNGeometrySource` object specifies geometry as a set of per-vertex data. A `SCNGeometryElement` further specifies how these vertices connect to a geometric shape (in this case, a line). The parameters of the `SCNGeometrySource` initializer –

very similar to `glVertexAttribPointer()` in OpenGL ES, by the way – are as follows:

a. `data`: the geometry data (see point 1)

b. `semantic`: the semantic/type of the geometry source (vertices/positions)

c. `vectorCount`: the number of geometry source vectors (two: start, end)

d. `floatComponents`: all vertices are float components

e. `componentsPerVector`: the number of scalar components in a vector (three: x, y, z)

f. `bytesPerComponent`: the number of bytes that represent a vector component (byte size of `Float32`)

g. `dataOffset`: the offset from the beginning of the data (zero, because the data just contains positions)

h. `dataStride`: the number of bytes from one vector to the next in the data (three values of size `Float32`)

4. Finally, a new `SCNGeometry` object is created as a simple line from `SCNGeometrySource` and `SCNGeometryElement`, and then returned as a new node.

All these vertex, data, and array concepts might be quite a bit to digest if you're unfamiliar with 3D graphics, but with this function you're essentially telling Scene Kit where your points are and how to use them to draw shapes.

To learn about vertices in detail, check out **"How to Export Blender Models to OpenGL ES: Part 1/3"** for more information http://www.raywenderlich.com/48293/how-to-export-blender-models-to-opengl-es-part-1

One last thing! Add the following lines to `methaneMolecule` just above `return methaneMolecule` to see your new bonds:

```
// Bonds
methaneMolecule.addChildNode(lineBetweenNodeA(carbonNode1,
nodeB: hydrogenNode1))
methaneMolecule.addChildNode(lineBetweenNodeA(carbonNode1,
nodeB: hydrogenNode2))
methaneMolecule.addChildNode(lineBetweenNodeA(carbonNode1,
nodeB: hydrogenNode3))
methaneMolecule.addChildNode(lineBetweenNodeA(carbonNode1,
nodeB: hydrogenNode4))
```

Build and run! *Now* you have a molecule!

Note: Ok then, now to explain the reason for explicitly using `Float32` and `Int32`...

It seems that 64-bit architecture doesn't play well with the GPU and there are two errors to avoid when assembling primitives on your own, so keep these in mind:

```
SceneKit: error,
C3DRendererContextSetupResidentMeshSourceAtLocation - double not
supported
```

This error arises when you use the short-form initializer `SCNGeometrySource(vertices: count:)`. While more convenient, it'll complain that an array of `SCNVector3` (actually treated as `Doubles`) is an unsupported type.

```
SceneKit: error, C3DRendererContextBindMeshElement unsupported
byte per index (8)
```

> On 64-bit architecture, `Int` has a byte size of 8 instead of 4 and is thus incompatible.
>
> Hopefully Apple provides a fix soon…

Ethanol

Your next molecule is ethanol (http://en.wikipedia.org/wiki/Ethanol), also known as *alcohol.*

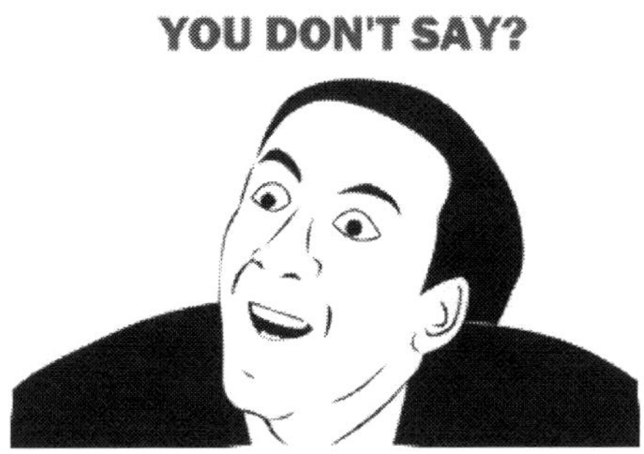

It's composed of two carbon atoms, six hydrogen atoms, and one oxygen atom. Its molecular formula is C_2H_6O and it looks something like this when laid out flat:

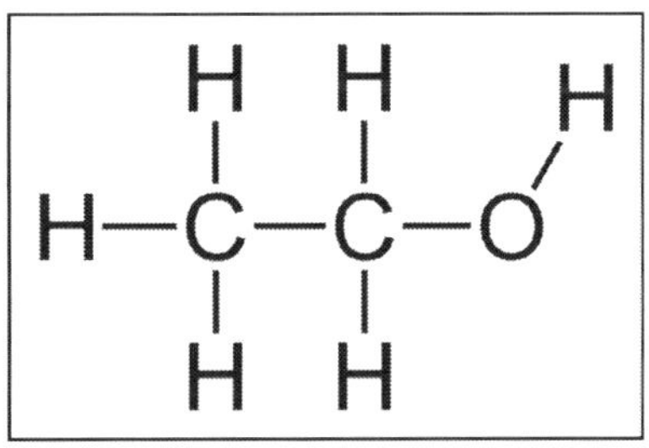

Compared to methane, the atoms and bonds of an ethanol molecule are a bit harder to arrange, so you're going to cheat a little bit and bring in a model from Blender.

Blenders and alcohol, huh? Sounds like things are about to get interesting.

Inside Xcode, in your **Project navigator**, you'll find a file named **EthanolScene.dae**. Click on it to bring up the **Scene Kit Editor**, which will look like the following screenshot:

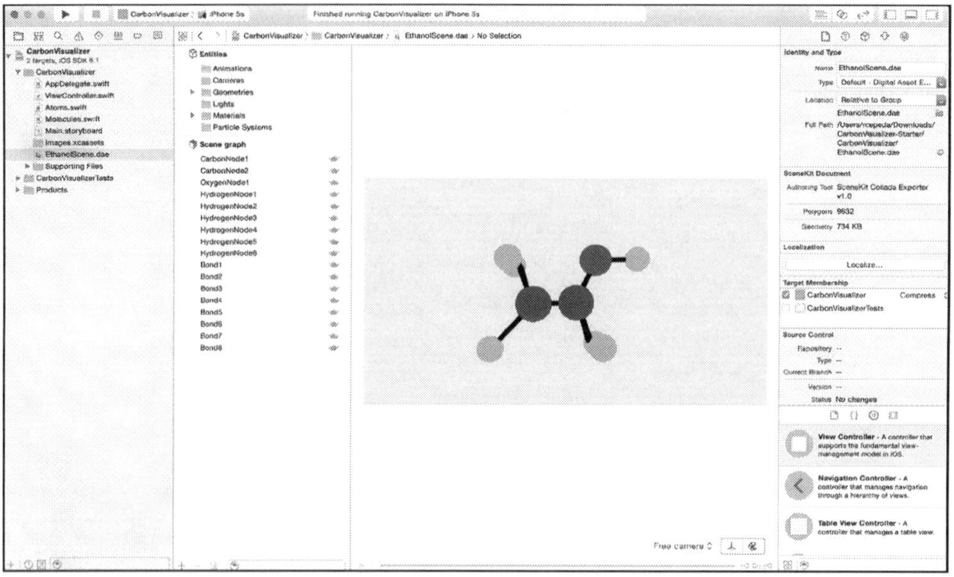

COLLADA .dae (https://www.khronos.org/collada/) is an interchange file format for interactive 3D applications – constituting a scene graph – and many 3D graphics software programs support it, including Blender, Xcode and even Preview and Photoshop. Xcode's built-in Scene Kit Editor (https://developer.apple.com/library/mac/recipes/xcode_help-scene_kit_editor/Articles/AboutSceneKitEditor.html) is a convenient way to preview .dae files and make minor modifications to your 3D models/scenes. The editor is not in scope for this chapter, but feel free to play around with it afterwards.

In order to import this COLLADA scene into your code, open up **Molecules.swift** and replace the `ethanolMolecule` stub with the following:

```
class func ethanolMolecule() -> SCNNode {
  var ethanolMolecule = SCNNode()

  let scene = SCNScene(named: "EthanolScene")!
  for child : AnyObject in scene.rootNode.childNodes {
    ethanolMolecule.addChildNode(child as SCNNode)
  }

  return ethanolMolecule
}
```

In this function, you're iterating through all the objects in your ethanol scene graph and adding them as children to a new node. Very simple, very powerful.

Build and run! How about that pretty little ethanol molecule model, eh? And no, you can't drink it.

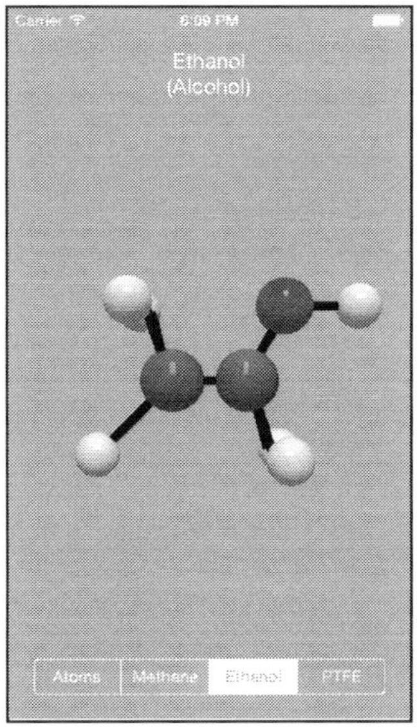

The default spheres in Blender have fewer polygons than the default spheres in Scene Kit, hence why this model looks a bit rougher. Nonetheless, hopefully you can appreciate how easy it is to import and render 3D scenes with Scene Kit. :]

Polytetrafluoroethylene

After a first-hand experience of creating your own model (methane) vs. importing a pre-fabricated model (ethanol), you might ask yourself, "*Why would I ever choose the former?*"

Well, in some cases – especially in data or structure visualization – it's wiser and more flexible to procedurally generate geometry. This is the case for polytetrafluoroethylene (PTFE), better known as *Teflon* (http://en.wikipedia.org/wiki/Teflon).

PTFE comprises two carbon atoms and four fluorine atoms, with the molecular formula $(C_2F_4)n$. It's the *n* part that indicates a new type of molecule, and it's one that can extend its bonds n-times in either direction. When laid out flat, with three molecules, PTFE looks like this:

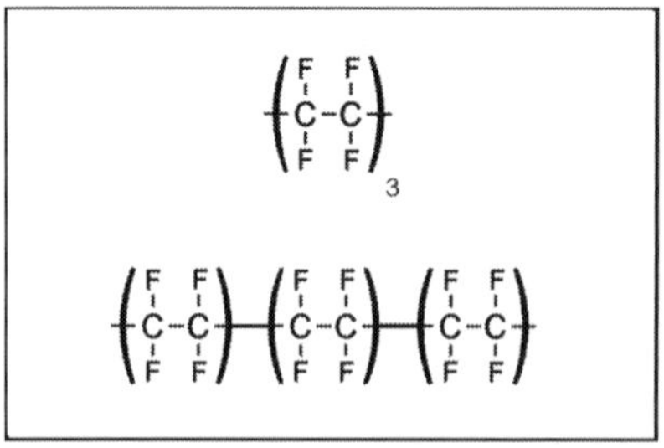

Because of this property, a procedurally generated model is a superior choice to a model built by hand, because creating a million bonded molecules is much harder in a 3D-modeling application, and it comes with a much larger file size.

Open up **Molecules.swift** and replace the `ptfeMolecule` stub with the following:

```
class func ptfeMolecule() -> SCNNode {
  var ptfeMolecule = SCNNode()

  // 1
  var carbonNode2Previous: SCNNode?

  // 2
  for i in -1...1 {
    // 3
    let fi = Float(i)

    // 4
    // 2 Carbon
    let carbonNode1 = nodeWithAtom(Atoms.carbonAtom(), molecule:
ptfeMolecule, position: SCNVector3Make(-2+(fi*8), +2, 0))
    let carbonNode2 = nodeWithAtom(Atoms.carbonAtom(), molecule:
ptfeMolecule, position: SCNVector3Make(+2+(fi*8), -2, 0))

    // 4 Fluorine
    let fluorineNode1 = nodeWithAtom(Atoms.fluorineAtom(),
molecule: ptfeMolecule, position: SCNVector3Make(-2+(fi*8), -4,
+2))
    let fluorineNode2 = nodeWithAtom(Atoms.fluorineAtom(),
molecule: ptfeMolecule, position: SCNVector3Make(-2+(fi*8), -4,
-2))
    let fluorineNode3 = nodeWithAtom(Atoms.fluorineAtom(),
molecule: ptfeMolecule, position: SCNVector3Make(+2+(fi*8), +4,
+2))
    let fluorineNode4 = nodeWithAtom(Atoms.fluorineAtom(),
molecule: ptfeMolecule, position: SCNVector3Make(+2+(fi*8), +4,
-2))
```

```
    // Bonds
    ptfeMolecule.addChildNode(lineBetweenNodeA(carbonNode1,
nodeB: carbonNode2))
    ptfeMolecule.addChildNode(lineBetweenNodeA(carbonNode1,
nodeB: fluorineNode1))
    ptfeMolecule.addChildNode(lineBetweenNodeA(carbonNode1,
nodeB: fluorineNode2))
    ptfeMolecule.addChildNode(lineBetweenNodeA(carbonNode2,
nodeB: fluorineNode3))
    ptfeMolecule.addChildNode(lineBetweenNodeA(carbonNode2,
nodeB: fluorineNode4))

    // 5
    if(carbonNode2Previous != nil) {
      ptfeMolecule.addChildNode(lineBetweenNodeA(carbonNode1,
nodeB: carbonNode2Previous!))
    }
    carbonNode2Previous = (carbonNode2.copy() as SCNNode)
  }

  return ptfeMolecule
}
```

Yes, it's another long chunk of code, but I swear most of it will be familiar by now. :]

1. Since PTFE is a chain of molecules, each iteration after the first needs to bond onto the previous one, specifically, onto the second carbon atom. `carbonNode2Previous` is declared as optional because it's non-existent for the first molecule.
2. The `for` loop has to be balanced (equally negative and positive) so that the iteration at `i=0` is positioned at the center of the scene.
3. i is an `Int`, but it will be used in `Float` calculations. Here, you create a new type-cast variable to facilitate all position calculations.
4. Just like the methane molecule, you create your new model by adding atom nodes to a molecule node and then forming bonds between them.
5. Finally, for every molecule iteration after the first, add an extra bond to the previous molecule.

See, that wasn't too much code, now was it?

Build and run! Check out your multi-molecule Teflon model, WOW!

Conclusion

Congratulations on completing this Beginning Scene Kit chapter! You've entered a completely new world of 3D graphics by learning about one of the most exciting APIs in iOS 8. This chapter is simply a quick introduction and there is far more to explore, but hopefully you've found out how easy yet powerful Scene Kit can be.

One of my favorite apps of all time is "Molecules" by Brad Larson: https://itunes.apple.com/app/molecules/id284943090. Can you imagine building something similar with SceneKit now? Perhaps, an app for carbon allotropes like *graphite* or *diamond*? It's sure easier than it used to be.

`SCNBox` and `SCNSphere` are just two of the many `SCNGeometry` objects available, so why not explore some more? For instance, you could change the molecule bonds from lines to `SCNTube` objects (warning: not as easy as it sounds!).

But if you simply want to keep exploring Scene Kit and try something a bit different, then keep on reading! In the next chapter, you'll work with cool new penguin and ice models, and you'll learn more about the COLLADA editor, brand new physics engine, the all-too-important render cycle, and much more :]

Chapter 18: Intermediate Scene Kit

By Jake Gundersen

While Scene Kit isn't new to OS X, it's an exciting new addition to iOS 8, especially since it now has a built-in physics engine. This evolution offers you the ability to add complex and dynamic interactions to both games and apps alike. Modeling gravity, collisions, forces and even hinges is easy with Scene Kit's physics engine.

In this chapter you'll learn how to import and manipulate a scene from a file, in code.

Knowing the basics of modeling simple physics behaviors means you can create effects that look and feel more realistic.

When you use Scene Kit for you own apps or games, you'll start with a specialized 3D modeling tool like Blender, Maya, 3DS Max because it's much easier to create complex models with these tools.

How often do you see an artist hand-mixing paint or hand-weaving a canvas? Not so much. Both tasks are a lot of work and things can go terribly, terribly wrong. It's why most artists purchase tools, paint and canvasses at an art supplies store.

Similarly, when working with 3D models, you want to work with the right tools. Tasks like animating, modeling and applying textures are easier to do in a dedicated 3D modeling app, so you can focus on the building the model rather than having to code every detail by hand

In this tutorial, you'll dive deeper into Scene Kit and learn the following things:

- Xcode's integrated Collada viewer
- How to incorporate physics with Scene Kit scenes
- How to rotate and apply forces to your objects

- The concept of a physics joint and how to use one
- How to incorporate particle systems into your scene

By the end of this tutorial you'll be armed with the knowledge you need to create your own 3D game.

Xcode's Collada viewer

Xcode has a variety of built-in tools that allow you to work with 3D assets. One of these is a way to view and make modifications to a 3D data file. Though you can't create models and animations in Xcode, you can, amongst other things

- View your scene graph
- Change the position of assets
- View animations
- Alter materials

Scene Kit supports an open 3D data format called Collada. The format can hold information about the position and types of lights, models, materials, animations and even morphs.

The scene you'll use for this chapter is the brainchild of the lovely and talented Vicki Wenderlich, and it features a very brave little penguin.

First, open the starter project for this chapter, and then click on the **SceneIceRotated.dae** file found inside of the **Supporting Files** group to take a look at the scene:

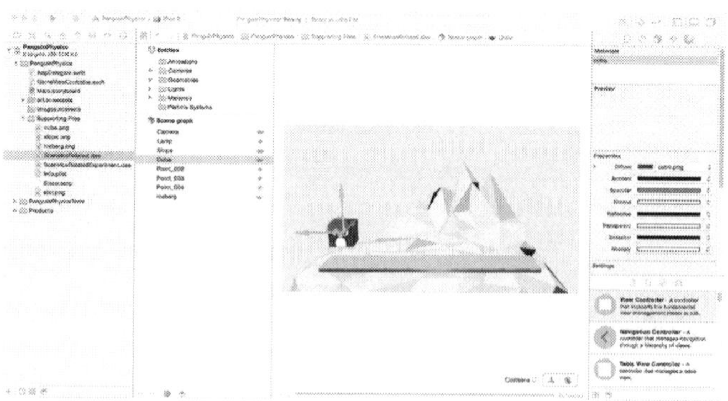

Click around the file to explore its various elements, which include a camera, multiple lights and some models.

> **Note:** The icons next to the names of the elements in the scene graph indicate whether they are lights, models, or the camera.

The names listed in the scene graph are the names you'll use to load the individual elements within a scene.

Since you don't have animations or particle systems in this scene, you'll notice those folders lack a disclosure indicator.

Now, you'll learn how to navigate around the starter project.

You can rotate the scene around using **click+drag**, and **alt+scrolling** zooms in and out. The **cmd+click+drag** combination pans the scene.

To select an individual element, simply click on it and you'll see a purple bounding box around it.

Another way to select specific elements is to select their entries in the **Scene graph** list to the left side of the scene.

You'll see them activate in the scene, and then you can move, rotate and scale them by using the three-arrowed control that appears. The **Node Inspector** tab in the inspector pane provides the same functionality.

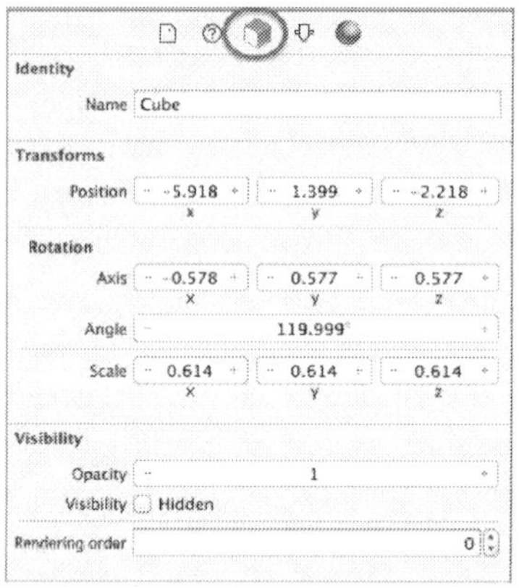

From the **Attribute Inspector**, you can change the color and type of the lighting. This is also where you can change the camera's perspective – another nifty little trick.

If you select a model and view its attributes, you can see its name, number of vertices and polygons, and a list of geometry elements and sources. The attributes provide some insight into the structure and complexity of your models.

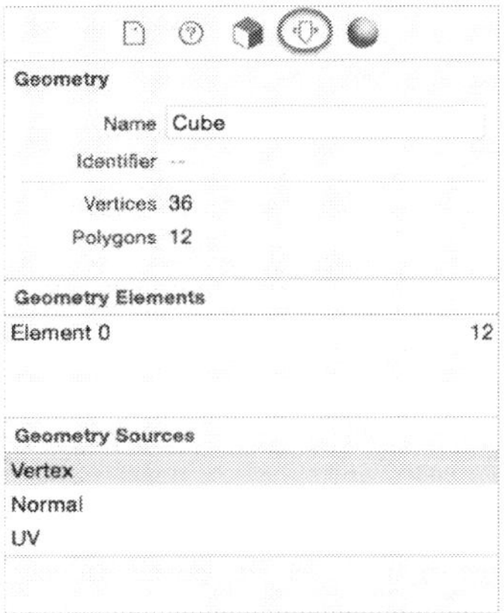

If you select a model and select the **Materials Inspector**, you can view and edit each object's materials properties. This is a quick and powerful way to experiment.

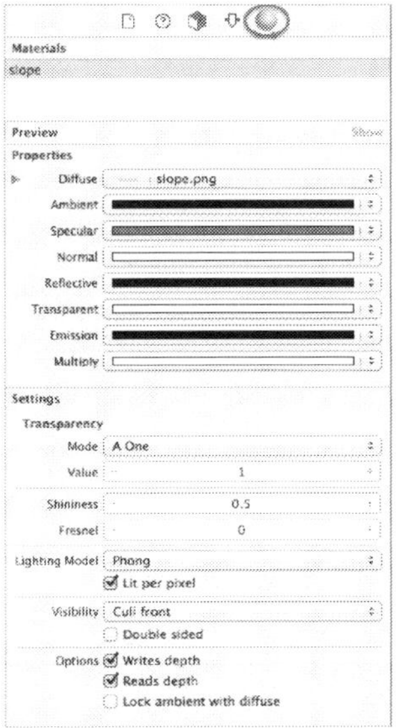

There's an extra copy of the model in the starter project called **SceneIceRotatedExperiment.dae.** Use that version as your sandbox; play around with the settings – especially those in the **Materials Inspector**.

Most importantly, work with the different values for the material lighting properties – now is the time to get comfortable. There are near-limitless appearances to create with materials, and Xcode makes it easy to experiment and see your results.

Load a scene

Loading a scene is pretty easy and you can do it with just a single line of code. Open **GameViewController.swift** and after this line:

```
@IBOutlet var scnView: SCNView!
```

Add this code:

```
let scene = SCNScene(named: "SceneIceRotated.dae")!
```

Then, in `viewDidLoad()` add this line after the call to `super.viewDidLoad()`

```
scnView.scene = scene
```

Build and run.

You'll see the entire scene loads into the scene view.

Pretty easy, right? Well, that's because Vicki did all the hard work for you: modeling the assets, setting up the lighting, positioning the camera – all of that data lives in the Collada file.

Next, add these two lines of code immediately below the code you just added to `viewDidLoad()`:

```
scnView.allowsCameraControl = true
scnView.showsStatistics = true
```

As you learned in chapter 17, **Beginning Scene Kit**, these lines enable some of Scene Kit's debugging tools. Use them to learn more about your scene, navigate through the 3D environment and get a handle on the performance of the current environment.

Next, you'll dive into Scene Kit's physics engine.

Physics Engine

A physics engine is an easy way to create a realistic environment where your game objects interact with each other in complex, dynamic ways without the need to write code accounting for every physical reaction between them.

The physics properties and rules for your scene are simple; the penguin will have a physics body, as will the slope where he plays. The bodies will prevent the penguin from moving through the slope. You will then apply gravity and a physical force to the Cube. The force applied and gravity will compete to cause the penguin to slide up or down the slope. As you work through this section, you'll learn the principles of physics engine integration.

Even though the penguin is already loaded as part of the scene, you still need to get a reference to him so you can set up his physics properties, and control him in your code.

If you go back to the scene viewer, you'll see the penguin is named **Cube** in the scene graph. *Hey, Cube!*

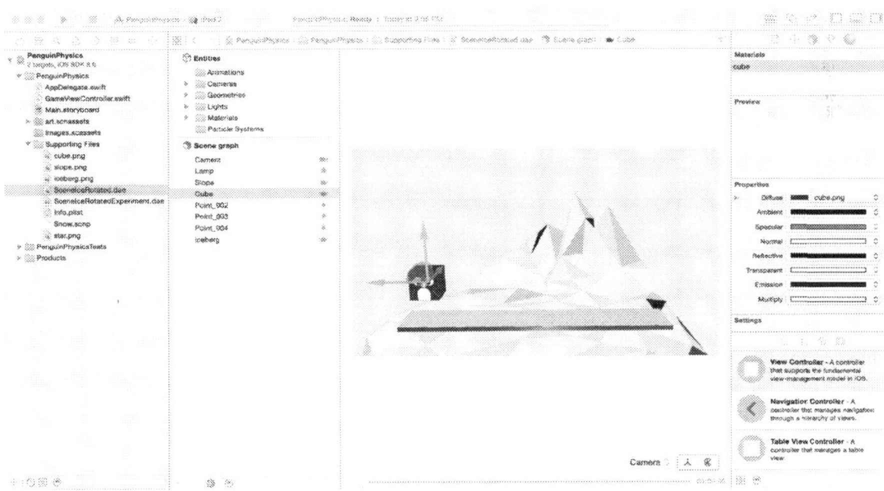

Add the following property and `init()` method to **GameViewController.swift**, just beneath the `scene` variable you just created earlier.

```
let cube:SCNNode

required init(coder aDecoder: NSCoder) {
  cube = scene.rootNode.childNodeWithName("Cube", recursively:
false)!
  super.init(coder: aDecoder)
}
```

The `UIViewController` class provides an `init(coder aDecoder: NSCoder)` initializer. You'll use this method to set up objects that aren't optional types.

Every `SCNScene` object has a `rootNode` property that represents the root (*or parent*) node of every object contained in the scene.

The `SCNNode` class has a `childNodeWithName(name: String!, recursively: Bool)` method that can be used to look up a child nodes by name. Setting `recursively` to `true` looks through all the child nodes of the given node object, no matter how many levels deep the hierarchy may be. Running this search recursively will take more time than if set to `false`. You know that this object is only one level deep in the hierarchy, so there's no need for the extra work.

> **Note:** You could have made these variables optionals, or implicitly unwrapped optionals, but using this technique will just make it easier to reference them without the need to unwrap them every time. You know that the cube object will always exist, so the optional apparatus just isn't helpful in this case.

It's time to create your first physics object.

Basics of physics bodies

If you're familiar with physics engines integrated into other 3D engines or frameworks, the physics properties will look familiar. If you're not, then it's good to know some of the theory behind a physics engine.

A physics engine models physics properties – like bounciness, collisions, forces and gravity – basically, the literal reality and consequences of physical movement.

Physics bodies need volumetric geometry to model collisions. The shapes of the two bodies determine when they touch each other.

In Scene Kit when you create a physics body, it will:

- Either create a geometric shape based on the model's own geometry

  Or...

- You can provide a custom set of vertices that define a geometric shape.

If you opt to create the body automatically, it will create a convex hull to use as the physics shape.

A convex hull works just like wrapping a potato in foil; the wrapper makes the eyes, holes and bumps are far less pronounced. Physics shapes work in a similar way; they cover holes and smooth concave angles, much like the foil-wrapped potato.

Scene Kit has a number of built in primitives that already have defined physics bodies: **spheres**, **boxes**, **planes** and **tori**.

In this app, both of your bodies are just simple cubes, so you'll simply allow Scene Kit to create the physics body automatically.

A couple of reasons you might want to define your own bodies are:

1. Simpler geometry requires fewer resources to perform collision detection.
2. Sometimes you'll want collisions to be more forgiving than the appearance of the on-screen geometry.

Of course, you're sure to run across many other occasions where defining geometry is desirable, hence Apple providing the functionality.

Aside from the shape of an object, there are several other properties that determine how bodies react when colliding.

There are three main types of physics bodies:

Static Body: As the name implies, a static body doesn't move in a physics simulation; it is unaffected by gravity or any other forces. It does, however, collide with other bodies. Use static bodies for floors, walls, or other things that are fixed in your scene.

Dynamic Body: A dynamic body is a free-moving body that is affected by gravity, forces, collisions, etc.

Kinematic Body: A kinematic body isn't affected by forces or gravity, but does move around the scene and collides with other bodies. Use kinematic bodies if you want to move something around your scene programmatically.

I mentioned that a physics body has properties that affect how the physics simulation is modeled. Here's a list of some of the more important properties:

Mass: When two bodies collide, the body with the larger mass transfers more of its inertia to the body with the smaller mass, so the force of gravity will be greater on a body with a greater mass.

Restitution: Think of this as *bounciness*. A restitution of `1.0`, means that a body will bounce off static bodies whilst maintaining its velocity. A restitution of `0.0` will not bounce.

Friction: When two bodies slide past each other, friction applies against the linear force of a body.

Damping: Think of damping as *air friction*. This value reduces the body's velocity in each frame.

Charge: This property controls how much magnetic and electrical fields affect a body. For example, you can apply a force field to a space and bodies with charges will react to it.

Angular Damping: This property affects how much an angular (rotational) force diminishes in each frame.

Now that you have a reference to the penguin, and you know a bit about physics bodies, you can set up the physics properties for it. In `GameViewController`, add this code to the bottom `viewDidLoad()`:

```
// 1
scene.physicsWorld.gravity = SCNVector3Make(0.0, -9.8, 0.0);
// 2
cube.physicsBody = SCNPhysicsBody.dynamicBody()
// 3
cube.physicsBody!.mass = 5.0
cube.physicsBody!.restitution = 0.01
```

1. The first thing to do is turn on gravity, and to do this you'll use the `physicsWorld` object, an instance of `SCNPhysicsWorld`.

   Every `SCNScene` has a single physics world object that simulates physics if it has children with physics bodies.

The `SCNVector3` data type represents gravity. It consists of 3 floats that define a force in the x, y, and z axes. This force is applied to all dynamic bodies each frame. Setting the gravity vector to `-9.8` in the `y` component means that in each frame, a dynamic body accelerates towards the negative direction in the y-axis.

> **Note:** Unlike a 2D game projected on a screen, in a 3D world, there's no real meaning to the idea of *up* or *left* – just like in space! The position and orientation of the camera node determine which side is up when the world displays on a screen.
>
> So, it's up to you to decide how you want to model your scene. In this game, the scene is oriented so that the y-axis is up and down (based on point of view of the camera), the x-axis is left and right, and the z-axis is the depth.
>
> Why? Because it's similar to how 2D game engines work, so it's a familiar look.
>
> When the scene was created in Blender, the default Blender scene had the z and y axes switched. The scene was rotated around in Blender so that it was easier to set things intuitively, like gravity and impulse force.

2. Next, you create a dynamic physics body type and set it to the `physicsBody` property of the cube object. The `dynamicBody()` initializer creates an automatic physics body that is the dynamic type, and it's based on the geometry of the object. If you want to define the shape of the physics body, use the `init(type:shape)` initializer.

3. Finally, you set a couple of properties to control how the penguin reacts. Later, you'll apply an impulse force to the penguin. The amount of force applied needs to overcome the force of gravity to allow the penguin to slide up the slope. The penguin's mass affects how the force of gravity pulls down on him, and therefore, the amount of force required to overcome gravity. You'll set it at `5.0` and leave it there.

   You don't want Cube to bounce much when he lands on the slope, so the restitution is `0.01`.

Build and run. You should see the doomed penguin fall into oblivion, sliding right through the slope and iceberg. *Nooooo!*

The next step is to give the slope physics body properties. Still in **GameViewController.swift**, add this code to the foot of `viewDidLoad()`:

```
if let slope = scene.rootNode.childNodeWithName("Slope",
                                                recursively: false) {
  slope.physicsBody = SCNPhysicsBody.kinematicBody()
}
```

First, you get a reference to the slope object from the Collada file.

Then you set its `physicsBody` property to a kinematic physics body, because it doesn't need to calculate the effect of gravity and the user directly manipulates it.

Build and run. This time Cube has some respite, and should collide with the slope instead.

Physics forces

In addition to gravity, a physics engine allows you to apply forces to dynamic bodies – even allowing you to throw them across a world you create.

Besides gravity, you can apply two kinds of forces to a physics body. One is a linear impulse and the other is torque. You'll apply force to the penguin by tapping the **Apply Force** button in the interface.

Open the **Main.storyboard** and open the **Assistant Editor** to bring up **GameViewController.swift**. **Ctrl+click+drag** from the button to the code editor.

Pick a place where you can create a new method. Choose **action** from the drop down and name the method `applyForceTapped`.

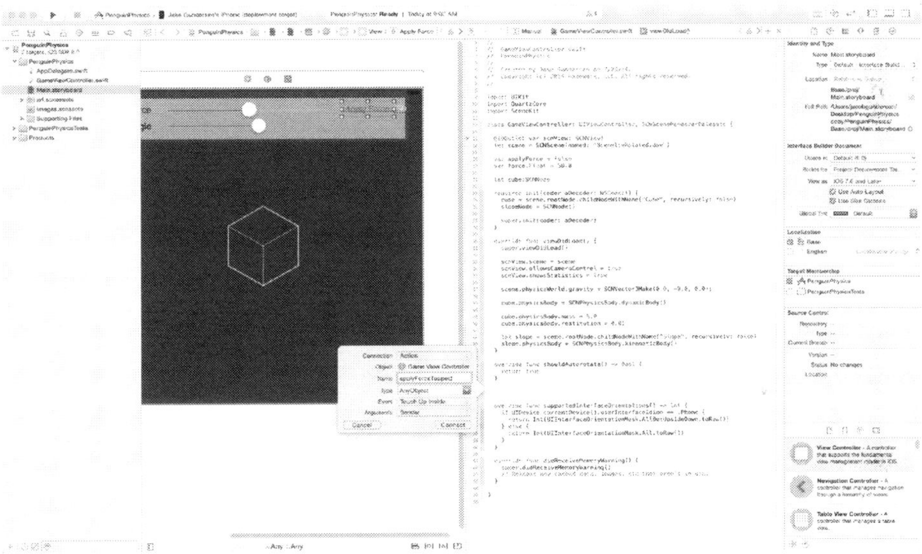

Add the following code to the method you just created:

```
cube.physicsBody!.applyForce(SCNVector3Make(30.0, 0.0, 0.0),
 impulse: true)
```

This method takes a directional vector that defines the amplitude and direction of the force and a `Boolean` that indicates whether or not the force is an impulse. If it is, the body will immediately be set to the full velocity of the force in a single frame. Otherwise force is applied to the body continuously without the initial boost. In this case, the force needs to be applied each frame in order to see the effect.

> **Note:** This method applies the force to the body's center of gravity. But, there's an alternate version of this method that includes another parameter; `SCNVector3 position` defines the location of where the force should apply. If you apply a force to a body in a location that isn't the center of its mass, it causes that body to rotate and move.

Build and run.

You should see Cube slide right and slowly come to a stop with a single tap of the button. Experiment with the impulse parameter. For instance, if you set it to `false`, try increasing the force constant to `300.0`.

Rendering cycle

The simulation you're designing demonstrates the principle that a mass sliding up a plane requires less force to move upwards than a mass that is lifted – which is precisely what makes a simple incline machine useful.

So, you'll be applying a force continuously instead of just applying a single impulse.

First, you need a way to call `applyForce()` for each frame instead of just calling it when the user taps the button. For that you need a property to indicate whether or not to apply the force to the penguin.

In **GameViewController.swift**, add this line of code to the properties section of your class:

```
var applyForce = false
```

Next, change the implementation of `applyForceTapped()` to the following:

```
@IBAction func applyForceTapped(sender: AnyObject) {
  let button = sender as UIButton
  if (applyForce) {
    button.setTitle("Apply Force", forState: .Normal)
    applyForce = false
  } else {
    button.setTitle("Stop", forState: .Normal)
    applyForce = true
  }
}
```

The button now simply changes the state of the property you just added and updates its title to indicate what will happen the next time you tap it.

Next, you need a way to execute some code for each frame. Like Sprite Kit, Scene Kit has a number of callback methods that happen at different points in the rendering cycle.

Here's a graphic that shows what happens every time a frame renders:

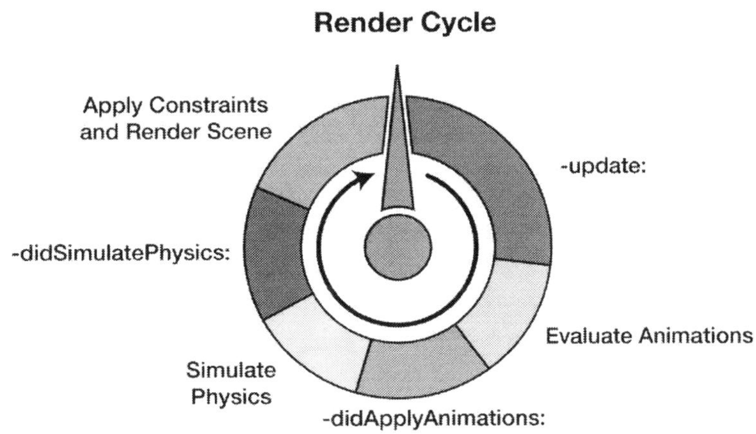

Several different callbacks may be used to execute your code.

Sometimes you'll want the physics engine to update the state of the simulation. For example, knowing the latest state of your bodies can be crucial to understanding what you need to do to make your app function according to your vision.

The `SCNSceneRendererDelegate` protocol defines five optional methods that allow you to run your code at various points in the rendering cycle.

The names clearly indicate the point in the rendering cycle when they execute:

`renderer(_ aRenderer: SCNSceneRenderer!, updateAtTime time: NSTimeInterval)` This callback is the most basic, and the one you'll use for Cube.

`renderer(_ aRenderer: SCNSceneRenderer!, didApplyAnimationsAtTime time: NSTimeInterval)` After the animation code executes, this is called.

`renderer(_ aRenderer: SCNSceneRenderer!, didSimulatePhysicsAtTime time: NSTimeInterval)` After the physics simulation updates, this is called.

`renderer(_ aRenderer: SCNSceneRenderer!, willRenderScene scene: SCNScene!, atTime time: NSTimeInterval)` After the OpenGL context and render buffer are bound, this is called. It's primarily used for custom OpenGL rendering.

`renderer(_ aRenderer: SCNSceneRenderer!, didRenderScene scene: SCNScene!, atTime time: NSTimeInterval)` This is called after rendering finishes.

> Note: Scene Kit has a built in diagnostics tool (enabled by setting the `showsStatistics` property to `true`). This will give you feedback on each stage of the rendering cycle, so you can better determine which piece of your scene it drawing the most GPU resources and make improvements.
>
> To see these details, tap the **Plus** button next to the fps graph on the bottom left of the screen:
>
> 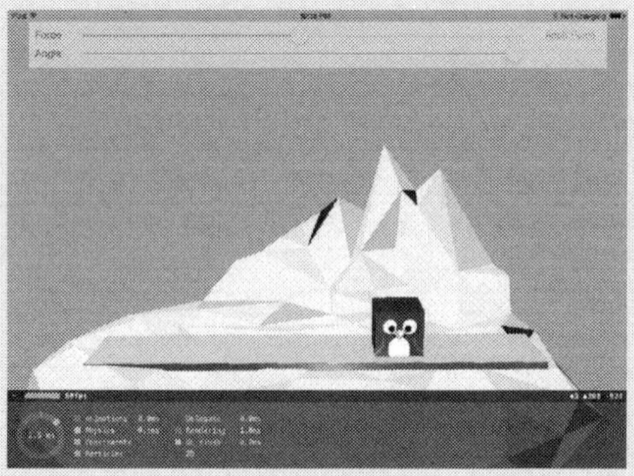

You'll use the first callback to apply a force to the penguin – or not – for each frame. Add the following method to your `GameViewController` class:

```
func renderer(aRenderer: SCNSceneRenderer,
     updateAtTime time: NSTimeInterval) {
  if applyForce {
    cube.physicsBody!.applyForce(SCNVector3Make(50.0, 0.0, 0.0),
```

```
        impulse: false)
    }
}
```

You have the callback function, but you need to set your `GameViewController` class as the delegate so the function will be called.

Go to the line that declares the class and change this:

```
class GameViewController: UIViewController {
```

To this:

```
class GameViewController: UIViewController,
                          SCNSceneRendererDelegate {
```

Also, you need to set the delegate of the `SCNView` class. Right after the line that sets `scnView.showsStatistics` to `true`, add this line:

```
scnView.delegate = self
```

Build and run. Tap **Apply Force** to – as its name implies – apply force to the penguin in each frame. Of course, you're accelerating Cube towards his peril, and now you see why he's such a brave little bird!

Connecting UI to physics simulation

Next, you'll set up the connection between the sliders and the slope. The first task is to control the amount of force that applies when you move the force slider.

Create a new variable to track it; in **GameViewController.swift**, add this line to the class properties:

```
var force:Float = 50.0
```

The default floating-point type in swift is Double. However, you need this variable to be type Float, because you are going to use it in a function that requires a Float input, `SCNVector3Make`. So, in this case you specify the type (`:Float`).

Now, jump back to the storyboard. Open the **Assistant Editor** and **ctrl+drag** from the top slider control to the class body.

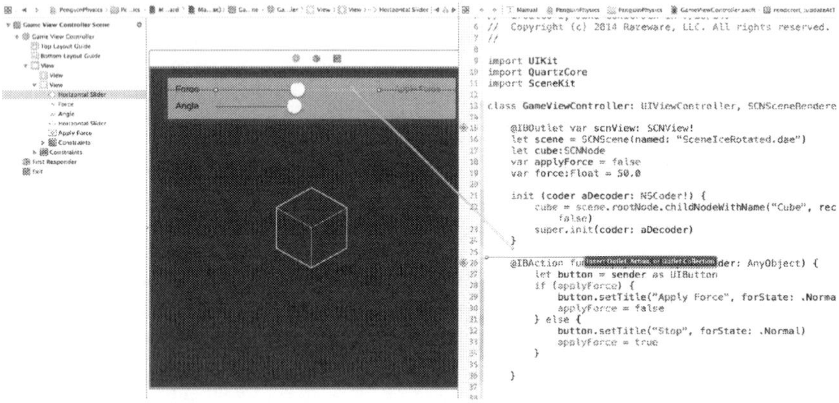

Change the **Connection** to be an **Action** and name the new method `forceSliderMoved`. For the Event, select **Value Changed**.

Add the following to the method:

```
force = sender.value * 300.0
```

Finally, change the `SCNVector3` parameter passed into the `applyImpulse` call in the `renderer(:updateAtTime:)` callback so it looks like the following:

```
cube.physicsBody.applyForce(SCNVector3Make(force, 0.0, 0.0),
 impulse: false)
```

Build and run. If you tap **Apply Force** and move the slider around, you can control Cube's acceleration.

Rotations in 3D space

Now it's time to tweak the angle of the slope based on the **Angle** slider.

You'll create a new `SCNNode` and insert it into the hierarchy between the root node and the slope. Then you'll modify the rotation of this node to affect the rotation of the slope.

> **Note:** You may wonder why you're creating this intermediate node and using it to affect rotation instead of directly rotating the slope. The slope was created using Blender, and it already has rotation and position properties. So, when you apply a new rotation, the response is rather unpredictable. By applying rotation to this new node, it rotates along the axis that you expect.

The first step is to add a new class property that will contain the new node. In **GameViewController.swift**, add the following variable below the other instance variables:

```
let slopeNode: SCNNode
```

Next, add this line to `init()` above the call to `super`:

```
slopeNode = SCNNode()
```

Add these lines to `viewDidLoad()`, inside the `if let` block at the end:

```
slopeNode.addChildNode(slope)
scene.rootNode.addChildNode(slopeNode)
```

You first add the slope to the new node, and then you add the new node to the root node.

Next, you'll connect the value of the **Angle** slider with the rotation of the node that has the slope as its child. As you did with the other slider, create a new method and connect it to the **Angle** slider.

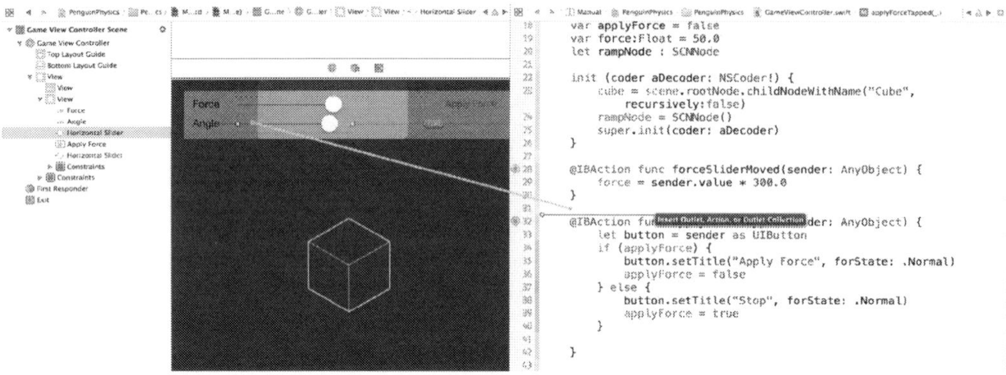

Call this method `angleSliderMoved` and add the following lines to it:

```
var angle:Float = (1.0 - sender.value) * Float(M_PI_4)
slopeNode.eulerAngles = SCNVector3Make(0.0, 0.0, angle)
```

The slider has a `value` between `0.0` and `1.0`. The first line converts it to an angle in radians.

The second line sets the `eulerAngles` property on the slope node.

> **Note:** There are many ways to set the rotation on an `SCNNode`.
>
> The first is to set the `transform` property. Transform is an `SCNMatrix4` struct, or a matrix, that contains the translation, rotation and scale of a node. It's very powerful, but not all that intuitive.
>
> A more intuitive way to set rotation is to use euler angles.

There are certain applications where using euler angle leads to something called *gimbal lock*.

Gimbal lock is the loss of a degree of freedom when two of the three gimbals are in a parallel orientation. What this means is that if you orient two of the axes in a certain way – no matter how you rotate the axis – you can't rotate in certain ways until you move the first two out of a parallel alignment.

Another way to manage rotation is quaternions. This method isn't susceptible to gimbal lock, but is a little more complicated to execute. You can learn more about it here: http://www.raywenderlich.com/12667/how-to-rotate-a-3d-object-using-touches-with-opengl

Because you're only rotating the plane 45 degrees in a single axis, gimbal lock isn't an issue. Hence, euler angles are the best option because they are easy to understand.

Build and run.

Moving the slider rotates the slope to the correct direction, within a 45-degree angle. But it's not right because you want the slope to rotate like it's hinged to the far left edge, and not from the center.

You will fix that by changing the origin point the node uses to calculate rotation. In a 2D drawing system, there is a concept of an anchor point. It serves as the basis to calculate position, rotation and scale.

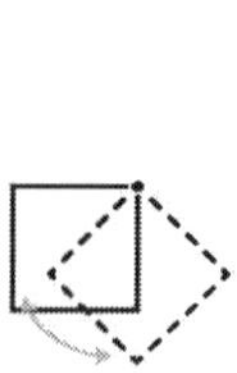

In Scene Kit, a node has a `pivot` property that essentially does the same thing. By default, it's the center of the object. However, if you set it to the far left side, the object will rotate around that point instead of around the center.

What's interesting is that changing the pivot point also changes the position of the node.

Add this line of code to `viewDidLoad()`, right after the line that set the kinematic physics body on the slope object:

```
slopeNode.pivot = SCNMatrix4MakeTranslation(-7.0, 0.0, 0.0)
```

In this case, you just want to move the pivot point to the left edge of the slope. So you move the pivot point `-7.0` units along the x-axis.

> **Note:** Units can mean whatever *you* want them to mean. You can define them to correlate to some real world units and measures, define them in terms of some in game size or leave them undefined.
>
> In the case of the penguin game, the unit is an arbitrary length. It's the result of jumping into Blender and using the default grid as a basis for the size of the scene.

Build and run.

You'll notice a couple things. First, the slope is now ascending to the sky to the right. Also, the rotation now happens from the left side of the slope.

Now you need to change the position of the slope to put it back in the middle of the iceberg. Of course, without the slope in the proper position, Cube is lost to the ether.

Add this line of code after the line that sets the pivot property in `viewDidLoad()`:

```
slopeNode.position = SCNVector3Make(-7.0, 0.0, 0.0)
```

Build and run. Ah-ha! There's your brave little penguin. You can change the angle, tap to apply force and launch Cube into the air!

While launching penguins in the air is always an entertaining pastime, the purpose of this tutorial is to demonstrate the use of an incline. The penguin falling off the plane is a huge inconvenience – and not so much fun for him!

You need to do something to keep Cube on the plane, while allowing him to slide up and down.

Physics behaviors: Hinges and joints

The Scene Kit physics engine has another feature to keep that penguin in place. It's called a joint and it connects two physics bodies together, or one body to a point in space.

Here are the available joints:

SCNPhysicsBallSocketJoint: This joint allows a body to pivot around another. It can rotate in three axes.

SCNPhysicsHingeJoint: This joint allows a body to rotate around another in a single axis.

SCNPhysicsSliderJoint: This joint allows two bodies to slide against each other and rotate around their connecting point.

SCNPhysicsVehicle: This is a special type that allows you to build wheeled vehicles, like cars and motorcycles.

You may have guessed already, but you'll be using the slider joint to constrain the penguin to slide along the top of the plane.

In **GameViewController.swift**, add a new property to the class:

```
var sliderJoint:SCNPhysicsSliderJoint!
```

Next, add this code to the end of `viewDidLoad()`, inside the `if let` block:

```
// 1
sliderJoint = SCNPhysicsSliderJoint(
                          bodyA: cube.physicsBody,
                          axisA: SCNVector3Make(0.0, -1.0, 0.0),
                        anchorA: SCNVector3Make(0.0, 0.0, -1.0),
                          bodyB: slope.physicsBody,
                          axisB: SCNVector3Make(0.0, -1.0, 0.0),
                        anchorB: SCNVector3Make(0.0, 0.0, -0.20))
// 2
sliderJoint.maximumLinearLimit = 4.0
sliderJoint.minimumLinearLimit = -5.5
// 3
sliderJoint.maximumAngularLimit = 0.0
sliderJoint.minimumAngularLimit = 0.0
// 4
scene.physicsWorld.addBehavior(sliderJoint)
```

1. This sets up the slider joint. You specify two bodies to connect by the joint.

   In a hinge joint, each body has an axis that defines the direction the joint can move. Think of the axis as an invisible rod that both runs through the body and allows the object to slide up and down. In this case, you're defining the same axis for both. The slope won't move, but if it did, it would slide along the same axis.

2. Next, you define an anchor point that dictates where the bodies connect, and in this case, the bottom of the cube connects with the top of the slope. Along the other axes, x and y, you want the two bodies to be centered.

3. Here, you define the range of motion for the joint. These values allow the penguin to slide from one end of the slope to the other. If you decrease these limits to `0.0`, you'd see the cube is halfway up the slope.

4. You define the allowed rotation of the bodies. You don't want the penguin to rotate; rather, he should remain flat on the slope. You zero both rotation limits so that there is no allowance for rotation.

5. Finally, when you create a joint, you add it to the physics world so it takes effect. There is an opposite method, `removeBehavior`, which removes a physics behavior when you no longer want it to have an effect.

> **Note:** Joints are technically behaviors. Each one is a subclass of `SCNPhysicBehavior`.

Build and run.

Now Cube is just kind of sitting in one place, perhaps even dancing around a bit. What's going on?

The physics engine is calculating a variety of things and is working with some conflicting data. The collision resolution part of the physics engine keeps the two bodies from intersecting, but the joint is holding them together.

As you've seen, this results in some weird behaviors.

To fix this, you need to make it so the slope and penguin no longer collide. Don't worry about Cube falling into oblivion again; this time the slider joint prevents his demise.

Add the following lines of code at the end of `viewDidLoad()`, still in the `if let` block:

```
cube.physicsBody!.categoryBitMask = 1
cube.physicsBody!.collisionBitMask = 1
slope.physicsBody!.categoryBitMask = 2
slope.physicsBody!.collisionBitMask = 2
```

Each physics body has a bitmask for category and a bitmask for collision. You're assigning the penguin body a category of 1, and you only want it to register collisions with other bodies that are in the same category.

You do the same with the slope, but you assign it a category of 2. This means there aren't any bodies in the world that can collide with either object. That's OK; you still need the bodies to define the action of the hinge.

Build and run.

Now this is kind of funny. When you launch the scene, Cube does this kamikaze-like move before landing on the slope.

Why? When he starts, he's not within a valid position according to the constraint imposed by the hinge.

To prevent this from happening, open the **Scene Editor** and move the penguin by selecting him and dragging the appropriate arrows so he's just above the slope and centered. Build and run. Now you'll see that he finds a valid hinge position much faster and doesn't need to fly around to find it.

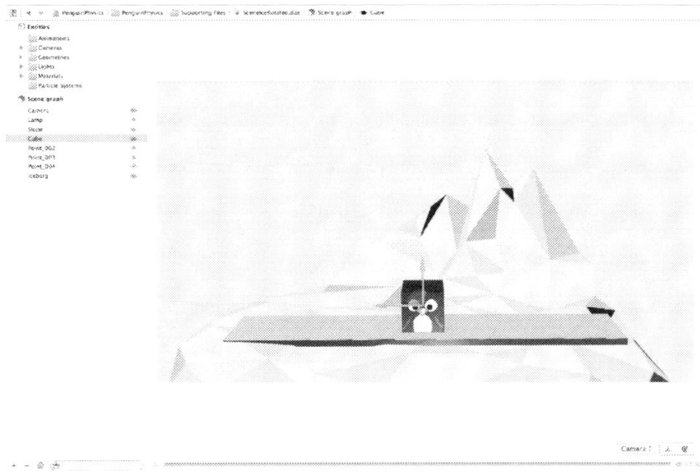

You'll see that Cube still rotates and moves a little to find a position that he is comfortable with. This shouldn't be necessary (since he starts in a valid position), but at the time of writing it appears that the physics engine takes several frames to move bodies into position when a hinge is imposed.

Bonus time: Particles

That's pretty much it for the penguin game. You can see that the higher the angle, the more force required to move Cube up the incline.

Now to add a little polish – snow!

I've included a particle system file in the starter, **Snow.scnp**. Select it in the **Project Navigator** to bring up the **Particle Editor**.

The 3D particle editor in Xcode allows you to move the camera around to see your particle engine in 3D.

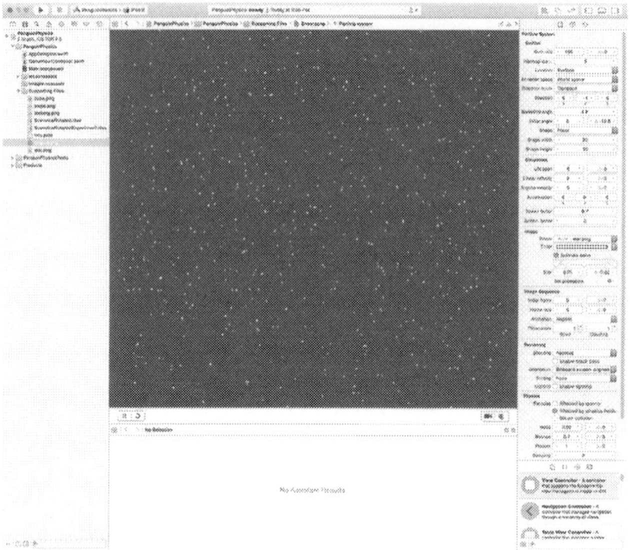

When you add a particle system to your scene, it needs its own node so you can move it around. If you assign it to the root, or any other node, then you must use the editor to define the particle system to get it into the right position

It's much easier to set it on a dedicated node and move that node around.

In **GameViewController.swift**, create a new property for the particle system:

```
let snow = SCNParticleSystem(named: "Snow", inDirectory: nil)
```

Next, add this code to the bottom of `viewDidLoad()`:

```
let particleEmitterNode = SCNNode()
particleEmitterNode.addParticleSystem(snow)
particleEmitterNode.position = SCNVector3(x: 0.0, y: 10.0,
                                          z: 0.0)
scene.rootNode.addChildNode(particleEmitterNode)
```

Each node has an `addParticleSystem()` method that adds a particle system to that node. Here you're just moving the snow up a little so that it starts falling above the visible portion of the scene.

Build and run.

Now Cube looks quite at home, don't you think?

Scene Kit is a huge framework and you've barely scratched the surface. That said, now you know how much easier it is to render 3D scenes and use 3D in your own applications with this innovative framework.

Scene Kit still has a bunch of features for you to explore. The physics engine can apply to particle systems as well as physics bodies. You can apply a 'Physics Field', a set of rules that apply forces to bodies in space, to a node (like making the snow swirl in a vortex pattern). You can set up callback blocks that allow you to execute your own code when two bodies collide (like what happens in Angry Birds).

Scene Kit has the ability to animate geometry. These animations can be set up using Core Animation, your own code in the update blocks, or you can import complex animations created in your 3D modeling tool.

Scene Kit also has some advanced features that let you go into the lower levels of OpenGL. You can supply custom geometry (vertices, texture coordinates, etc), you can add custom shaders, or you can get a callback and write your own OpenGL code.

Chapter 19: Beginning Photos

By Jack Wu

In iOS 8, we – meaning all us developers – welcome the new Photos framework, a framework that provides all the functionality of Assets Library and much more through a brand new, clean set of APIs. It comes with all the features you'll ever need for interacting with the user's photo library.

If you don't believe me, consider this: Apple built the new iOS 8 Photos app exclusively using the Photos framework. *Talk about dogfooding!*

The Photos framework includes a plethora of neat features that allow you to access and edit everything from single photos to entire albums. It also provides a cool API to respond to changes in the photo library made from inside *or* outside of your app. On top of all that, the absolute best feature of the Photos framework is that it does all this while handling all memory and network operations for you. The Photos framework definitely opens up many possibilities for new and unique photo-based apps.

In this chapter, you're going to delve straight into the Photos framework by creating a multiple asset picker. Later on, in Chapter 20, **Intermediate Photos**, you'll build on this project app to implement a hip collage-making app named **Stitch**.

Fetching objects and loading content

The multiple asset picker in this chapter mostly fetches the model objects in the Photos framework and loads their content for display. Here's an overview of the types of model objects in the Photos framework and a quick look at how to fetch them.

Model objects

Model objects in the Photo framework all inherit from the abstract base class `PHObject`. They're lightweight objects containing only the metadata describing the object, and not the content itself. The concrete model objects are:

1. `PHAsset`: Represents a single asset, which can be an image or video. It contains metadata such as favorite, hidden and media type.
2. `PHAssetCollection`: Represents an ordered list of assets.
3. `PHCollectionList`: Represents an ordered list of either `PHAssetCollections` or other `PHCollectionLists`.

Fetching

Fetching is a key feature in the Photos framework. You can fetch for any of the model objects by using class methods on the corresponding model object. Additionally, you can supply `PHFetchOptions` when fetching. `PHFetchOptions` allow you to specify which objects you want, how those objects are arranged in the result, and how Photos should notify you about changes to the result. This is done by setting the `predicate`, `sortDescriptors`, `includeAllBurstAssets`, `includeHiddenAssets` and `wantsIncrementalChangeDetails` properties in an instance of `PHFetchOptions` and passing it to the fetch method.

Fetching always returns a `PHFetchResult`. A `PHFetchResult` is an ordered list of the model objects, and it has an interface similar to that of `NSArray`. The key difference here should get you off your seat and on your feet, cheering – `PHFetchResult` manages memory and performs lazy loading of objects *on your behalf*. This means that fetching and iterating through a thousand assets will, in theory, use no more memory than that of a hundred assets. Simply amazing.

Remember that model objects don't hold any content. If you want to retrieve all the assets in an asset collection, you'll have to fetch them. Similarly, if you want to display the image associated with an asset, you'll have to load it.

Loading content

When you want to display the image or video content belonging to an asset, you'll need to load it using an instance of `PHImageManager`. The default image manager works asynchronously and handles loading, caching and resizing of assets. A subclass called `PHCachingImageManager` can pre-cache assets' contents into memory, making sure they're available when you need to use them.

That's all you need to know to build the multiple asset picker!

Getting started

The multiple asset picker must allow users to select images from a grid and keep track of the selected files. Its interface is somewhat similar to that of `UIImagePickerController`.

As an app component, there's a delegate protocol to return the selected items, as well as Cancel and Done buttons in the navigation bar. You can ignore these for now, they become extra-important in the next chapter and, of course, your own app :]

Open **MultipleAssetPicker.xcodeproj** in Xcode. There are two main classes in this project:

1. `AssetCollectionsViewController`: This is the initial view controller of the asset picker. It displays a table that organizes the users' assets collections so that they're easier to pick from.
2. `AssetsViewController`: After the user selects a row in the table view, the corresponding assets populate this collection view controller. This is where the user *actually* selects Photo assets.

There are also three small, helper classes:

1. `CheckMark`: A `UIView` subclass that draws a checkmark to indicate an asset is selected.

2. `AssetCell`: A simple collection view cell that contains an image view and reuse identifier that you'll use later to ensure you assign the correct image to the view.
3. `SelectedAssets`: A wrapper around an array of `PHAssets`. This is required because the *asset collections view controller* needs to know when an asset has been selected or deselected in the *assets view controller*. Having a wrapper allows you to pass down a reference to the underlying assets array.

Ok. If you're ready, its time to code!

The asset collections view controller

The asset collections view controller is the initial view controller of the picker. Its table view has three sections:

1. **Selected Items:** This has a single cell that takes the user to the collection of assets (s)he selected.
2. **All Photos and Favorites:** This section has two cells that navigate to views of either all the user's photos or their favorite photos. This will surely be convenient for the user!
3. **Albums:** This section contains a list of all the albums (`PHAssetCollections`) the user has on their device.

That does sound rather, um, fetching, doesn't it? Before you start fetching away, there's one last thing to consider – permissions.

Requesting permissions

Like any feature on iOS that touches the users private data, you must obtain permission from the user to access their photo library. On that same note, you also need to fail gracefully if they deny permission. This will be implemented in `viewDidLoad()`, so that you can update the interface accordingly.

To get started, open **AssetCollectionsViewController.swift** and locate `viewDidLoad()`. Add the following to the bottom of the method:

```
// 1
PHPhotoLibrary.requestAuthorization { status in
  dispatch_async(dispatch_get_main_queue()) {
    switch status {
      case .Authorized:
        // 2
        self.fetchCollections()
```

```
            self.tableView.reloadData()
          default:
            // 3
            self.showNoAccessAlertAndCancel()
        }
      }
    }
```

That's quite a short snippet, yet it's positively brimming with functionality! (That's a theme you'll notice when using the Photos framework) Now, here's what's going on:

1. `PHPhotoLibrary` represents the actual photo library, as its name implies. It is where you request any changes and register for change notifications. Here you're simply requesting authorization to access the photo library.
2. The handler block is called immediately if the app is authorized. If not, it displays an alert for the user. If you're now authorized, you can move on to fetching your collections by calling `fetchCollections`, which is currently empty. You'll need to reload the table view because the view controller might have loaded while the user was deciding whether to allow your app.
3. If the user denies permissions, you show an alert and cancel the picker. If you're curious, and you should be, feel free to peruse the implementation of `showNoAccessAlertAndCancel`, which can be found towards the bottom of the class.

Fetching your first objects

For the sake of moving ahead, assume for the moment the user is okay with you accessing their photos; now, it's time to do some fetching! Add the following to `fetchCollections`:

```
userAlbums =
PHCollectionList.fetchTopLevelUserCollectionsWithOptions(nil)
userFavorites =
PHAssetCollection.fetchAssetCollectionsWithType(.SmartAlbum,
  subtype:.SmartAlbumFavorites,
  options: nil)
```

Again, not a lot of code for a ton of function! As you can see, fetching is extremely straightforward. `userAlbums` is a collection of asset collections, represented by `PHCollectionList`. `userFavorites` is a collection of assets, so you can fetch it using `PHAssetCollection`.

That was pretty fun, and easy, right? Next, you'll use these collections to populate the table view!

Populating the table view

To populate a table view, you need to implement the necessary `UITableViewDataSource` protocol methods. Start by finding `tableView(_:, numberOfRowsInSection:)` and update it so it matches the following:

```
switch(section) {
  case 0: // Selected Section
    return 1
  case 1: // All Photos + Favorites
    return 1 + (userFavorites?.count ?? 0)
  case 2: // Albums
    return userAlbums?.count ?? 0
  default:
    return 0
}
```

You've updated the **second case statement** to return the number of favorites, and the **third case statement** to return the total number of albums. Note that these may be `nil` if the user hasn't granted you permissions. You can use the ?? operator to handle this scenario.

The other important method to implement is `tableView(_:, cellForRowAtIndexPath:)`. You can use a `switch` statement, just like the previous method, to implement this. Add a bare switch statement to `tableView(_:, cellForRowAtIndexPath:)` after the comment, like the following:

```
// Populate the table cell
switch(indexPath.section) {
case 0:
  // Selected
```

```
    break
  case 1:
    if (indexPath.row == 0) {
      // All Photos
    } else {
      // Favorites
    }
  case 2:
    // Albums
    break
  default:
    break
  }
```

Now to fill in those `case` statements – this should be a piece of cake! For each section, set the `textLabel` of the cell to the name of the collection and the `detailTextLabel` to the number of assets in that collection.

In the `Selected` section, replace `break` with the following code:

```
// Selected
cell.textLabel.text = "Selected"
cell.detailTextLabel!.text = "\(selectedAssets!.assets.count)"
```

Here you set the title of the cell to "selected" and the detail label to the number of assets that are selected. Easy enough.

Since you haven't fetched them yet, for the `All Photos` section you'll leave the `detailTextLabel` blank. Add the following:

```
// All Photos
cell.textLabel.text = "All Photos"
```

That was another easy one.

The `Favorites` section is a bit more involved than the previous two. Add the following:

```
// Favorites
let favorites = userFavorites[indexPath.row - 1]
  as PHAssetCollection
cell.textLabel.text = favorites.localizedTitle
if (favorites.estimatedAssetCount != NSNotFound) {
  cell.detailTextLabel!.text =
"\(favorites.estimatedAssetCount)"
}
```

Here you get the PHAssetCollection for the current indexPath, use it to set the text property of the cells textLabel, and finally check to see if estimatedAssetCount is available to use by comparing it to NSNotFound. If it is, use it as the text for the detailTextLabel. Since you placed the table cell for favorites after all photos in the same section, remember to subtract one from row to access the correct collection.

> **Note:** estimatedAssetCount does not always accurately match the number of assets represented by a PHAssetCollection. It is provided as a convenient, high performance guess of the actual number of assets.
>
> To obtain the accurate asset count, you need to perform a fetch with fetchAssetsInAssetCollection and use the count of the returned fetch result.

Finally the Albums section; replace break with the following:

```
// Albums
let album = userAlbums[indexPath.row]
  as PHAssetCollection
cell.textLabel.text = album.localizedTitle
if (album.estimatedAssetCount != NSNotFound) {
  cell.detailTextLabel!.text = "\(album.estimatedAssetCount)"
}
```

This behaves almost identically to the Favorites section; get the PHAssetCollection for the current indexPath and use it to populate the textLabel and detailTextLabel properties of the cell.

Build and run. You should see the table view being populated:

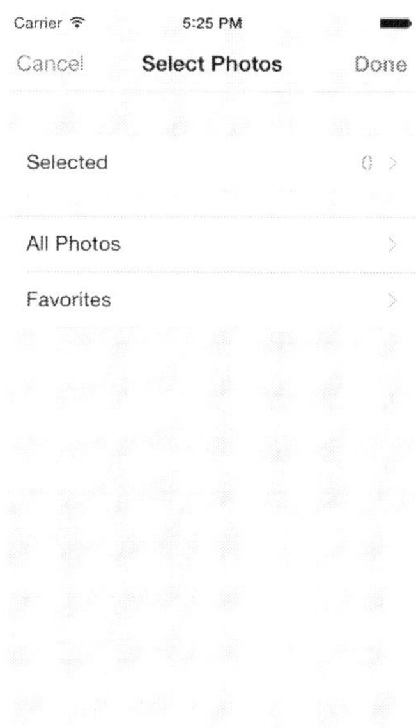

Not bad! No photos to see yet, but that's fine because need somewhere to display them. You just need to implement one last thing before you move on to the collection view – you need to let the collection view controller know what collection the user selected.

Preparing for the assets view

Still in **AssetCollectionsViewController.swift**, find `prepareForSegue` and add the following to the bottom of the method:

```
// 1
destination.selectedAssets = selectedAssets
// 2
let cell = sender as UITableViewCell
destination.title = cell.textLabel.text
// 3
let options = PHFetchOptions()
options.sortDescriptors =
  [NSSortDescriptor(key: "creationDate", ascending: true)]
let indexPath = tableView.indexPathForCell(cell)!
switch (indexPath.section) {
case 0:
  // Selected
  break
case 1:
  if indexPath.row == 0 {
    // All Photos
```

```
  } else {
    // Favorites
  }
case 2:
  // Albums
  break
default:
  break
}
```

There are three things happening here:

1. The `selectedAssets` need to be passed to destination controller, so they can be updated when the user (de)selects assets.
2. The title of the destination view is set to the title of the selected cell.
3. Create an instance of `PHFetchOptions` to sort your results by `creationDate`, just like Photos.app. After that, the familiar `switch` statement is back, so that you can populate the collection view with the correct assets.

Now, you need to fill in those `case` statements. Update the `Selected` section to match:

```
// Selected
destination.assetsFetchResults = nil
```

Here, you just need to set `assetsFetchResults` to `nil` to inform the collection view to only display the selected assets. Since `case` statements always break in Swift, you can also remove the `break` here.

The other three cases look very similar to last time, except this time around, you get to fetch *everything*, oh yeah.

Change the second and third `case` statements to match the following:

```
case 1:
  if indexPath.row == 0 {
```

```
      // All Photos
      destination.assetsFetchResults =
        PHAsset.fetchAssetsWithOptions(options)
    } else {
      // Favorites
      let favorites = userFavorites[indexPath.row - 1]
        as PHAssetCollection
      destination.assetsFetchResults =
        PHAsset.fetchAssetsInAssetCollection(favorites,
          options: options)
    }
  case 2:
    // Albums
    let album = userAlbums[indexPath.row] as PHAssetCollection
    destination.assetsFetchResults =
      PHAsset.fetchAssetsInAssetCollection(album,
        options: options)
```

Again, this is very similar to the last `switch` statement. For the `All Photos` section, you simply fetch every single asset. For the `Favorites` section you use a class method on `PHAsset` – `fetchAssetsInAssetCollection` – to fetch all the favorite assets. The `Albums` section behaves similarly, but the selected `PHAssetCollection` is used to limit the fetch. The Photos framework does the heavy lifting and manages the memory. Remember to pass in your fetch options to sort the assets by date.

You'll notice that for albums, including Favorites, you need to grab the correct asset collection first, and then fetch all the assets in that collection – again, passing in your options to sort the assets.

Now the collection view controller knows exactly what to display, what are you waiting for?

The assets view controller

The assets view controller has just two jobs – to display all the assets in the collection, and to allow the user to select or deselect them. When an asset is (de)selected, it simply updates the asset array in the `selectedAssets` property.

The collection view can operate in two different modes. When `assetsFetchResults` is `nil`, the selected assets display. Otherwise, the assets in `assetsFetchResults` are displayed. Most of this is handled by the `currentAssetAtIndex` helper function, which returns the correct asset for the current mode.

Loading asset content

Open **AssetsViewController.swift** and locate `collectionView(_:, cellForItemAtIndexPath:)` and add this code just above where you return the cell:

```
// 1
let reuseCount = ++cell.reuseCount
let asset = currentAssetAtIndex(indexPath.item)
// 2
let options = PHImageRequestOptions()
options.networkAccessAllowed = true
// 3
PHImageManager.defaultManager().requestImageForAsset(asset,
  targetSize: assetThumbnailSize,
  contentMode: .AspectFill, options: options)
  { result, info in
    if reuseCount == cell.reuseCount {
      cell.imageView.image = result
    }
}
```

That's looks new; here's what's happening:

1. Due to the asynchronous API for loading content, you need to make sure a cell has not been reused before updating the image. You accomplish this by having a reuse counter on each cell that you increment to keep track of the number of times it's been reused.
2. Since network access is off by default, you won't be able to load assets that reside in iCloud. Create an instance of `PHImageRequestOptions` and set the appropriate method to `true` to address this.
3. The actual content loading is performed by the default, shared instance of `PHImageManager`. Check if the cell has been reused inside the completion handler for `requestImageForAsset`, and if it hasn't, update its image.

> **Note:** It's important to note that the completion handler for `requestImageForAsset` may be called multiple times. The Photos Framework provides a low quality version of the asset if it's immediately available, and then may provide a higher quality version later. Keep this in mind when using `requestImageForAsset`.

Build and run. Select an album and you should see a beautiful grid of all the photos on the device:

You even get a pretty checkmark when you tap a photo to infer its been selected. But you don't have the complete *picture* just yet, because you're not persisting the selection. Don't worry though; it's an easy fix and a useful skill to learn.

Selecting and deselecting assets

Still in **AssetsViewController.swift**, find `collectionView(_:didSelectItemAtIndexPath:)` and add the following:

```
let asset = currentAssetAtIndex(indexPath.item)
selectedAssets.assets.append(asset)
```

Very straightforward; just grab the asset for the selected `indexPath` and add it to `selectedAssets` array. As mentioned in the beginning of this section, `currentAssetAtIndex` is just a small helper that returns the asset from either `assetFetchResults` or `selectedAssets`, depending on the current mode.

Now find `collectionView(_:didDeselectItemAtIndexPath:)` and add the following:

```
// 1
let assetToDelete = currentAssetAtIndex(indexPath.item)
selectedAssets.assets = selectedAssets.assets.filter { asset in
  !(asset == assetToDelete)
}
// 2
if assetsFetchResults == nil {
  collectionView.deleteItemsAtIndexPaths([indexPath])
}
```

Also pretty straightforward, the two steps here are:

1. Remove the asset from the array. Calling `filter` on the array is an easy way to accomplish this. Simply replace the assets array with a new array containing everything but `assetToDelete`.
2. Remove the asset from the collection view if you're displaying selected assets.

You're almost done with selecting assets! One last case to consider is when the user has already selected some assets, either from the current collection or another collection that shares assets with the current one. Thus, you will need to pre-select all the user's selected assets when the view appears.

You'll implement this in `updateSelectedItems`, which is already called when the view appears or rotates. Add the following to `updateSelectedItems`:

```
if let fetchResult = assetsFetchResults {
  // 1
  for asset in selectedAssets.assets {
    let index = fetchResult.indexOfObject(asset)
```

```
      if index != NSNotFound {
        let indexPath = NSIndexPath(forItem: index, inSection: 0)
        collectionView.selectItemAtIndexPath(indexPath,
          animated: false, scrollPosition: .None)
      }
    }
  } else {
    // 2
    for i in 0..<selectedAssets.assets.count {
      let indexPath = NSIndexPath(forItem: i, inSection: 0)
      collectionView.selectItemAtIndexPath(indexPath,
        animated: false, scrollPosition: .None)
    }
  }
```

Again, something different happens depending on whether you're displaying albums or selected assets:

1. If you're an album, you find the selected assets by iterating through every one and check if they exist in the displayed fetch result. If an asset is selected, you select it using `selectItemAtIndexPath(_:, animated:, scrollPosition:)`.
2. The second case is much simpler; select every single asset that's being displayed.

Build and run. Now the selection is persisted. You can even select assets from different asset collections. Awesome!

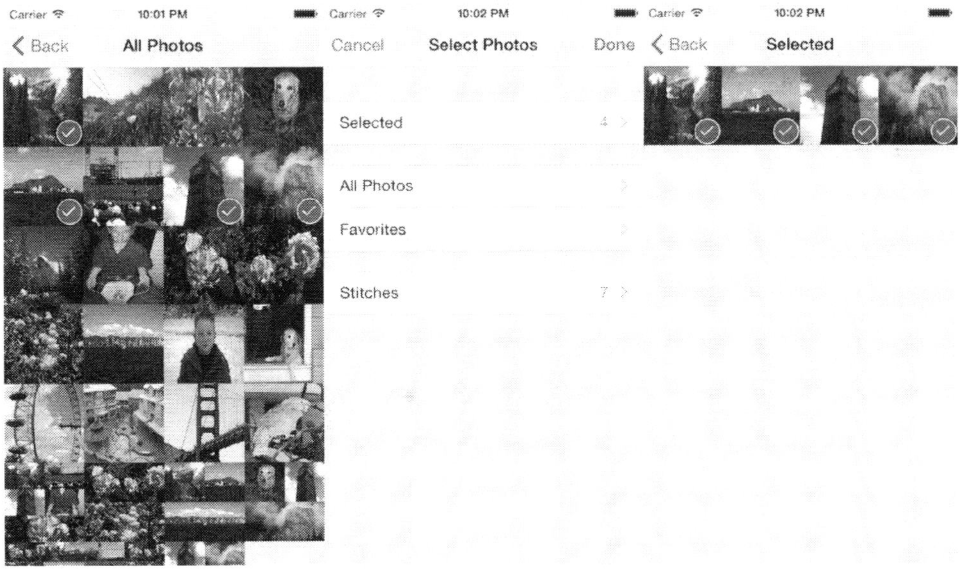

Buttery smooth scrolling

Fetching and displaying assets isn't cool. You know what's really cool? Fetching, and displaying, *thousands* of assets. Also, having them scroll smoothly. Like butter. Okay, fetching and displaying assets is a *little* cool too.

To make sure the scrolling remains buttery smooth when moving through hundreds or even thousands of photos, you need to start loading images *before* they come into view.

Luckily, the Photos framework has you covered; `PHCachingImageManager` provides exactly the functionality you need.

In this section, you'll implement a simple, yet effective caching mechanism. You'll simply cache 60 assets that are off-screen – the 30 above the currently displayed assets, and the 30 below.

To do so, you need to keep track of the current assets being cached, as well as the latest scroll position. In `AssetsViewController`, the variables `cachingIndexes` and `lastCacheFrameCenter` will take care of this for you.

Since `PHCachingImageManager` handles the caching, you'll not be using the default image manager to load the images anymore. Instead, you'll create one of your own.

The first step is to declare the necessary variables. At the top of `AssetsViewController`, add the following variables just below `assetThumbnailSize`:

```
private let imageManager: PHCachingImageManager =
  PHCachingImageManager()
private var cachingIndexes: [NSIndexPath] = []
private var lastCacheFrameCenter: CGFloat = 0
private var cacheQueue =
  dispatch_queue_create("cache_queue", DISPATCH_QUEUE_SERIAL)
```

Here, after you declare the variables, you can simply initialize them to default or empty values. The serial dispatch queue will allow you to calculate which assets to cache without blocking the main thread.

You'll also need to request images from the new caching image manager. Find `collectionView(_:, cellForItemAtIndexPath:)` and replace `PHImageManager.defaultManager()` with `imageManager`.

Now, add the following method to the bottom of `AssetsViewController`:

```
// MARK: Caching
func resetCache() {
  imageManager.stopCachingImagesForAllAssets()
  cachingIndexes.removeAll(keepCapacity: true)
  lastCacheFrameCenter = 0
}
```

Here, you call `stopCachingImagesForAllAssets` to halt all current caching activity and reset `cachingIndexes` and `lastCacheFrameCenter` to their default values.

Calculating which assets to cache

The steps you're going to take to implement the caching are:

1. Determine whether or not you want to cache.
2. Get all the visible indexes, sorted from top to bottom.
3. Calculate the range of indexes you want to cache.
4. Stop caching items that were previously cached but are now out-of-range.
5. Start caching any new items that have entered the caching range.

You're going to add a new method stub, and then update it fives time, once for each step in the list above. This will make it easier to follow what's going on.

To start, add the following `updateCache` method below `resetCache`:

```
func updateCache() {
  let currentFrameCenter = CGRectGetMidY(collectionView.bounds)
  if abs(currentFrameCenter - lastCacheFrameCenter) <
    CGRectGetHeight(collectionView.bounds) / 3 {
    return
  }
  lastCacheFrameCenter = currentFrameCenter
  let numOffscreenAssetsToCache = 60
}
```

There's just a little bit of action in this block, and that's because you don't want to recalculate the caching assets every time the user scrolls a tiny little bit. Hence, you only recalculate if the user scrolls more than one-third of the screen height.

Moving down the list to step two, you now need to obtain the visible indexes. Add the following code to the bottom of `updateCache`:

```
var visibleIndexes = collectionView.indexPathsForVisibleItems()
  as [NSIndexPath]
visibleIndexes.sort { a, b in
  a.item < b.item
}
if visibleIndexes.count == 0 {
  return
}
```

`UICollectionView` provides a handy method for obtaining the index paths of all the visible items, aptly named `indexPathsForVisibleItems`, which perfectly suits your needs. You then sort the array of index paths. If the array is empty, you return.

Now you want to calculate the entire range of assets to cache. Add the following code to the bottom of `updateCache`:

```
var totalItemCount = selectedAssets.assets.count
if let fetchResults = assetsFetchResults {
  totalItemCount = fetchResults.count
}
let lastItemToCache =
min(totalItemCount,visibleIndexes[visibleIndexes.count-1].item +
numOffscreenAssetsToCache/2)
let firstItemToCache = max(0, visibleIndexes[0].item -
numOffscreenAssetsToCache/2)
```

First, you get the total number of items, and then calculate the indexes of the first and last item to cache. `lastItemToCache` equals the last visible index path plus `30`, capped to the total number of items. Similarly, `firstItemToCache` equals the first visible index path minus `30`, capped to `0`. You use the `min` and `max` macros to make sure the calculated index paths don't end up being out-of-bounds.

You now need to add a small helper method. Add the following just below `updateCache`:

```
func assetsAtIndexPaths(indexPaths:[NSIndexPath]) -> [PHAsset] {
  return indexPaths.map { indexPath in
    return self.currentAssetAtIndex(indexPath.item)
  }
}
```

This method returns an array of assets corresponding to the index paths passed in.

Phew! Only two steps remain.

Now, you just need to find the index paths that are no longer within the caching range and stop caching them. Add the following to the bottom of `updateCache`:

```
let options = PHImageRequestOptions()
options.networkAccessAllowed = true
// 1
var indexesToStopCaching: [NSIndexPath] = []
cachingIndexes = cachingIndexes.filter { index in
  if index.item < firstItemToCache || index.item >
lastItemToCache {
    indexesToStopCaching.append(index)
    return false
  }
  return true
}
// 2
imageManager.stopCachingImagesForAssets(assetsAtIndexPaths(index
esToStopCaching),
  targetSize: assetThumbnailSize,
  contentMode: .AspectFill,
  options: options)
```

There are two steps to this:

1. You use `filter` again to determine the index paths of the items for which caching needs to be stopped.
2. Call `stopCachingImagesForAssets` passing in the assets related to the index paths from step 1. The target size, content mode and options must match exactly what you pass to `requestImageForAsset` when actually requesting the contents. The Photos framework handles the rest!

> **Note:** When using `startCachingImagesForAssets` and `stopCachingImagesForAssets`, Photos caches images for the *exact* size, content mode and options that you pass in. If you later request for an image with different properties than the cached ones, Photos disregards the cache altogether and fetches a new version of that image instead.
>
> Thus, to take full advantage of caching, you need to make sure you always request and cache images with the same properties.

The code to begin caching the assets that have scrolled into range is very similar to the code to stop caching. Add the following to the bottom of `updateCache`:

```
// 1
var indexesToStartCaching: [NSIndexPath] = []
for i in firstItemToCache..<lastItemToCache {
  let indexPath = NSIndexPath(forItem: i, inSection: 0)
  if !contains(cachingIndexes, indexPath) {
    indexesToStartCaching.append(indexPath)
  }
}
cachingIndexes += indexesToStartCaching
// 2
imageManager.startCachingImagesForAssets(
  assetsAtIndexPaths(indexesToStartCaching),
  targetSize: assetThumbnailSize, contentMode: .AspectFill,
  options: options)
```

The same two steps are taken here:

1. To find which assets you want to start caching, iterate over all the indices you want to cache and check if they are already contained in `cachingIndexes`. If not, create a new index path and add it to `indexesToStartCaching`. Finally, add all the new index paths to `cachingIndexes`.
2. This time, call startCachingImagesForAssets and pass in the indices for all the new assets you want to start caching. The helper function Remember the importance of passing in the exact `targetSize`, `contentMode` and `options` that you will use to request the image later!

Now make sure you call the methods to facilitate caching.

Find `collectionView(_: cellForItemAtIndexPath: indexPath:) and replace the default image manager with your own caching image manager:`

```
imageManager.requestImageForAsset(asset,
  targetSize: assetThumbnailSize,
  contentMode: .AspectFill, options: options)
{ result, info in
  if reuseCount == cell.reuseCount {
    cell.imageView.image = result
  }
}
```

Add the following to the bottom of `viewDidLoad`:

```
resetCache()
```

Add the following to the bottom of `viewWillAppear`:

```
resetCache()
```

And finally add the following to the bottom of `AssetsViewController`:

```
override func scrollViewDidScroll(scrollView: UIScrollView) {
  dispatch_async(cacheQueue) {
    self.updateCache()
  }
}
```

Build and run. The app will look exactly the same, but if you have lots of photos in any of your albums, the collection view should scroll as smoothly as a hot knife through butter. Or should that be *buddah*? Whatever. It's smooth, and you made it that way.

The caching you just implemented here works, and that's awesome. However, it can still be improved in many ways. Here are some ways you can improve on it. Feel free to tackle these and achieve true *buddah*:

1. Cache in the direction the user is scrolling.
2. Call `updateCache()` more cleverly.
3. Calculate the number of assets to cache based on how many are on the screen.
4. Stop caching when the scroll velocity reaches a certain threshold.

Where to go from here?

In this chapter, you got your feet wet with the Photos framework by fetching assets, asset collections and collection lists. You also implemented caching of assets, which is awe-inspiring!

You've no doubt noticed how clean and simple all this was, thanks to the elegance of the new Photos framework.

It still has a lot more to offer, including, but not limited to:

1. Requesting changes to albums and assets.

2. Editing asset content and providing adjustment data.

3. Observing changes in the library so you can update your interface accordingly.

In Chapter 20, **Intermediate Photos**, you'll implement all of the above, and even more! You'll create a fully blown collage-making app called Stitch. You'll dive deep into the Photos framework, leaving no stone unturned!

Of course, the ultimate goal is always to take this knowledge and apply it to your own app. Go make use of the Photos framework and most importantly, have fun!

Chapter 20: Intermediate Photos

By Jack Wu

In Chapter 19, **Beginning Photos**, you created a simple photos picker using the fetching features of the new Photos framework. In this chapter, you'll go far beyond this, exploring all four corners of the Photos framework. But before you do, you need a foundation to build on – a good understanding of the entire framework.

Building the photos picker gave you a sense of how the Photos framework operates. What it didn't reveal is the grandiose and complete nature of the framework.

This chapter will start with a complete overview of the Photos framework and its API. Hold on tight, and be prepared to have your mind blown :]

Here are the key features of the Photos framework:

- **Fetch Objects**: You can fetch objects that represent assets, collections or collection lists, whilst maintaining performance and privacy.
- **Load and Cache Asset Content**: The Photos framework makes it extremely easy to load image and video assets. It handles all the downloading and caching for you and provides a way to preload assets in bulk, making populating table views and collection views as easy as a walk in the park.
- **Request Changes**: You can request changes to assets, collections or collection lists that will be reflected immediately in the user's photo library.
- **Edit Asset Content**: You can edit an asset by requesting its contents and then committing your edits directly to the photo library. You can also allow the user to change or revert previous edits via adjustment data that you provide when performing edits.

- **Observe Changes**: Register for notifications for whenever a change occurs in the user's photo library. Use these notifications to update your interface, when changes happen both within, and outside of your app.
- **Use Advanced Photos App Features**: You have access to everything the Photos app does, including smart albums, moments, iCloud photo streams, and the ability to identify burst shots, panoramic images and slo-mo videos.

API overview

This tasty API is the delicious icing on the feature-filled cake that is the Photos framework. It carefully and elegantly abstracts away all the loading, caching and resizing that usually tows along when the user accesses photos, leaving you with a clean, well-structured set of APIs.

Here's a list of the main classes that make up the Photos framework, organized by task.

Fetching objects and loading content

These classes handle the **fetching** of assets and collections, as well as **loading** their content:

1. `PHObject`: This object is the abstract base class for all the model objects fetched from the photos library. It contains only the metadata describing the object and not the content itself. All `PHObjects` are **immutable**, so you must create a change request to modify them. `PHObject` has a few subclasses:
   a. `PHAsset`: This concrete subclass represents a single user asset. It can be an image or a video, and can reside locally or in iCloud.
   b. `PHCollection`: This abstract class contains two concrete subclasses: `PHAssetCollection` and `PHCollectionList`. These represent a collection of assets and a collection of collections, respectively. You can also create **transient** collections in your app to temporarily keep track of a set of objects.
   c. `PHObjectPlaceholder`: After the creation of a new object, but *before* it's actually committed to the photo library, you obtain an object placeholder. Then you use the placeholder to fetch the newly created object.

2. `PHFetchResult`: All fetches return a fetch result that contains an ordered list of objects. Its interface is similar to that of `NSArray`. Unlike a typical array, `PHFetchResult` performs lazy loading and manages memory for you.

3. `PHImageManager`: The image manager handles the actual loading of the image or video associated with an asset. It works asynchronously and handles network requests, as well as caching and the resizing of assets. Its direct subclass, `PHCachingImageManager`, can preload many assets into memory to make them available before they're needed.

4. `PHFetchOptions`: Use this to filter, and sort fetch results.

5. `PHImageRequestOptions` and `PHVideoRequestOptions`: Use these to provide options when loading asset content. You can specify quality, delivery priority, a crop area, and whether or not to allow network access. If needed, you can also obtain a progress handler to monitor download progress.

Requesting changes and editing content

These classes deal with making **changes** to the photo library and **editing** assets:

1. `PHPhotoLibrary`: The photo library is a global, shared object that represents the user's photo library. This is where you make requests for any changes to the library, and register for change notifications. All changes to the photo library are handled **asynchronously** and must take place in a photo library change block.

2. `PHAssetChangeRequest`: You create an asset change request in order to create, edit or delete assets. When editing, you can modify properties such as location, whether it's a favorite, and whether or not it's hidden.

3. `PHAssetCollectionChangeRequest` and `PHCollectionListChangeRequest`: You create the corresponding change request to create, edit or delete collections and collection lists. These allow you to create and delete folders (a.k.a albums) and move assets between them.

4. `PHContentEditingInput`: When you want to edit the content of an asset, this becomes available. It describes the asset and provides the adjustment data, as well as the original content. After you're done editing, you must create a...

5. `PHContentEditingOutput`: A content editing output describes the result of your edit. You must supply adjustment data to the output content. To commit the edit, you must assign the content editing output to an asset change request inside a photo library change block.

6. `PHAdjustmentData`: This contains an application-defined *recipe* for the most recent edit to the asset. It contains a format identifier and version for you to verify that your app understands this format. If your app supports the format, you can allow the user to revert or modify the edit.

Observing changes

These classes provide you with details to **respond** to changes in the photo library:

1. `PHChange`: If you have registered for changes, you get a change object whenever a change occurs. You use its instance methods on your objects or fetch results to obtain the corresponding change details.
2. `PHObjectChangeDetails`: This provides you with the object before and after the change occurred. You can also see whether or not the asset contents have changed or if they were deleted.
3. `PHFetchResultChangeDetails`: This provides you with details of the change(s) to your fetch result. You can get the new fetch result object before and after any changes. In the case of incremental changes, it provides details about the objects added, changed, removed or moved, so you can easily update your interface to reflect those changes.

API summary

The Photos framework provides all the flexibility you need along with amazing performance, all whilst respecting the users privacy settings.

Fetching objects and loading content always returns immutable results, which allows you to work with them safely across threads, or even across extensions. On top of that, `PHImageManager` and `PHFetchResult` abstract away all network and memory-related management. You can query and iterate over content and objects without having to worry about fetching from iCloud or caching to disk – *it just works*.

When changes do occur, the change observer API provides you with new objects or fetch results to replace your current ones. You only need to re-fetch data if the content of an asset has changed. This results in little-to-no overhead when responding to changes and updating your interface.

Requesting changes to the photo library must always happen within a photo library change block. The block-based API for requesting changes allows the system to handle prompting the user for permissions and maintaining the integrity of the library, and the adjustment data opens the possibility for different apps and extensions to modify or revert each other's edits.

But enough talk about this lovely API, it's time to get your hands dirty!

Introducing Stitch

Everybody enjoys sharing photos to their favorite social networks, be it GitHub or Stack Overflow ;] Wouldn't it be great if you could share more than one photo *per photo?*

Meet **Stitch**, the magical app that combines up to six photos into a single image – called a stitch – allowing you to share **600 percent** more photos per photo! The catch? It's not quite finished yet; it's waiting for someone who's just read an overview of the Photos framework API to venture in and finish it up.

It's waiting for *you.*

Getting started

Locate and open `Stitch.xcodeproj`. Before jumping in and changing any code, take this quick tour through the existing files and structure of the app.

Open **main.storyboard** and you'll see it's all set up for you. The main structure of Stitch looks like the image on the following page:

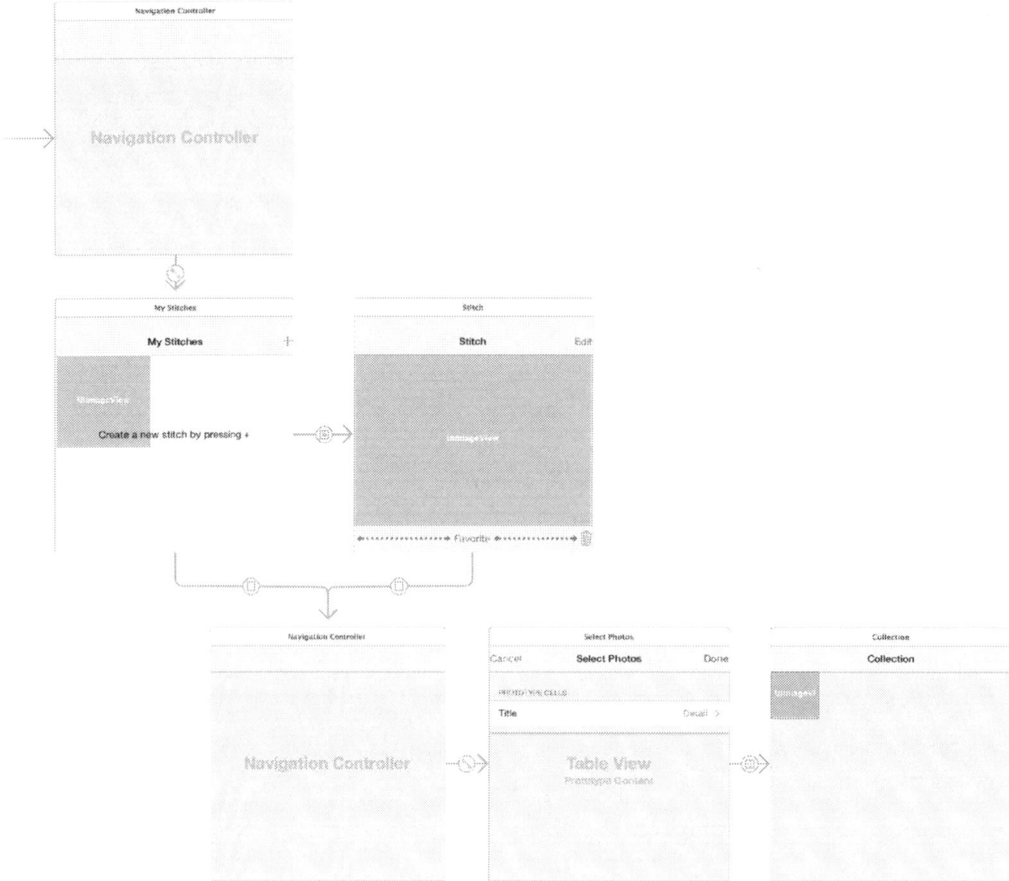

As you can see, Stitch comprises of three main view controllers. Ignore the navigation controllers, and start from the top left:

- The first controller displays all the user's existing stitches
- The second controller displays a single stitch, and allows the user to edit or delete it
- The third one is the photos picker you created in Chapter 19, **Beginning Photos**. *You did read chapter 19, right?* This version of the project already contains the same buttery-smooth scrolling, photo-picking beast, err, ...picker.

Additionally, there are two new view controllers that have the following responsibilities:

1. `StitchesViewController`: Displays all existing stitches using a collection view. It allows users to create new stitches, and view existing ones.

2. `StitchDetailViewController`: Displays a single stitch. It has buttons to allow the user to favorite, delete, or edit it.

`StitchHelper`, a very important helper class, is already declared, and it contains the code that actually creates the stitched images. It also contains function stubs that will help you create new stitches. You will implement these later.

It also implements the actual creation of a stitch, and it's all done for you. It would be a good idea to at least give `StitchHelper.swift` a glance. You can find it in the **Helpers & Categories** group in the **Project Navigator**.

The asset picker is almost identical to the one you implemented in the previous chapter. A few function stubs have been added, that you'll use to implement change observing later on.

Now that you're all familiar and perhaps even cozy with the app, it's time to embark on your journey to complete **Stitch**.

You're going to start with `StitchesViewController`.

Displaying stitches

Stitch saves all the user's stitches into an album conveniently named **Stitches**. `StitchesViewController` needs to load the Stitches album and display all the stitches in a collection view.

Requesting permissions

First things first, you need to obtain permission to access the users library, and fail gracefully if the user denies Stitch their permission. You'll implement this in `viewDidLoad()` so you can update the interface *before it appears* if the user decides to deny permission.

Open `StitchesViewController.swift` and add the following to `viewDidLoad()` below the call to `super`:

```
PHPhotoLibrary.requestAuthorization { status in
  dispatch_async(dispatch_get_main_queue()) {
    // Check Status
  }
}
```

You call `requestAuthorization` to request permission to access the users photo library. Since this is an asynchronous process, you pass in a completion block. Then, you immediately dispatch to the main queue since you're going to update the interface.

To check the status, replace the comment inside the `dispatch_async()` block with the following:

```
switch status {
case .Authorized:
  break // To suppress error
  // Register observer
  // Fetch stitches album
default:
  self.noStitchView.text = "Please grant Stitch photo access in
Settings -> Privacy"
  self.noStitchView.hidden = false
  self.newStitchButton.enabled = false

  self.showNoAccessAlert()
}
```

Here, you check to see if the user granted permission. If not, you disable the buttons and update the interface to show a label that informs the user of Stitch's requirement for them to grant permission.

Just to be safe, Stitch also shows an alert to the user to make sure they grant you the necessary permissions :]

Now that the permissions are out of the way, it's time to fetch some objects.

The stitches album

The first thing you need to do after the user grants you permission is to either:

- Fetch the stitches album, or…
- Create it if it doesn't yet exist

Find the `.Authorized` case statement in the block of code you just added to `StitchesViewController.swift`, and replace `break` with the following:

```
// Fetch stitches album
// 1
let options = PHFetchOptions()
options.predicate = NSPredicate(format: "title = %@",
StitchesAlbumTitle)
```

```
let collections =
PHAssetCollection.fetchAssetCollectionsWithType(.Album,
  subtype: .AlbumRegular, options: options)
// 2
if collections.count > 0 {
  // Album exists
  self.stitchesCollection = collections[0] as PHAssetCollection
  // 3
  self.stitches =
PHAsset.fetchAssetsInAssetCollection(self.stitchesCollection,
      options: nil)
  self.collectionView.reloadData()
  // Hide or Show the label to the user.
  self.updateNoStitchView()
} else {
  // Create the album
}
```

Here's what's going on, step by step:

1. Make use of the `predicate` property on `PHFetchOptions` to filter the results for just collections where the title equals **Stitches**.
2. If at least one album exists, cast and assign the first collection to the `stitchesCollection` property.
3. To fetch the actual stitches themselves, use `fetchAssetsInAssetCollection(_:, options:)` on `PHAsset`. Then assign the returned `PHFetchResult` to the `stitches` property.

But what if the album doesn't exist? Not a problem, you can simply create it. Add the following to the `else` branch of the `if` statement in the code you just added:

```
//Create the album
// 1
var assetPlaceholder: PHObjectPlaceholder?
// 2
PHPhotoLibrary.sharedPhotoLibrary().performChanges({
  // 3
  let changeRequest =
PHAssetCollectionChangeRequest.creationRequestForAssetCollection
WithTitle(StitchesAlbumTitle)
  assetPlaceholder =
    changeRequest.placeholderForCreatedAssetCollection
  }, completionHandler: { success, error in
    // 4
    if !success {
```

```
      println("Failed to create album")
      println(error)
      return
    }
    // 5
    let collections =
PHAssetCollection.fetchAssetCollectionsWithLocalIdentifiers(
      [assetPlaceholder!.localIdentifier], options: nil)
    if collections.count > 0 {
      self.stitchesCollection =
       collections[0] as PHAssetCollection
      self.stitches = PHAsset.fetchAssetsInAssetCollection(
       self.stitchesCollection, options: nil)
    }
  })
```

This code first requests a new album called **Stitches** be created, and then fetches that album inside the completion block. Here's the breakdown:

1. Declare `assetPlaceholder` to hold a reference to the placeholder object. You can fetch the created object using the placeholder later.
2. Begin a photos library change block. Remember that all changes to the photos library *must* happen in a change block. This allows all the following changes to be done in one atomic update, and also give Photos a chance to confirm with the user that they want this change to happen.
3. Create a `PHAssetCollectionChangeRequest` to create the album, and store the returned placeholder object from the change request for use in the completion block.
4. Inside the completion block, you make sure the album was created successfully by checking `success`. If the creation failed, the error is logged and the method returns.
5. This is where `assetPlaceholder` comes into play; you fetch the newly created asset collection (*or album*) by using its local identifier, which uniquely and persistently identifies any object. Lastly, assign `stitches` and `stitchesCollection` just like in the previous section.

Displaying stitches in a collection view

Now that the Stitches album is all set up, you can tackle the more exciting stuff – loading and displaying the images. Remain in **StitchesViewController.swift** and locate `collectionView(_:, cellForItemAtIndexPath:)` and add the following just below the comment:

```
// Configure the Cell
let reuseCount = ++cell.reuseCount

let options = PHImageRequestOptions()
options.networkAccessAllowed = true

let asset = stitches[indexPath.item] as PHAsset
PHImageManager.defaultManager().requestImageForAsset(asset,
 targetSize: assetThumbnailSize,
 contentMode: .AspectFill, options: options) { result, info in
  if reuseCount == cell.reuseCount {
    cell.imageView.image = result
  }
}
```

This code might look familiar; it's almost identical to `AssetsViewController` from the **Beginning Photos** chapter. Here you're requesting from the default image manager rather than the caching manage. I'll leave it up to you to exercise the knowledge garnered in the previous chapter to implement caching :]

Build and run. Note there are no stitches yet, so the app looks pretty much the same as before, but it's a good exercise to make sure everything compiles:

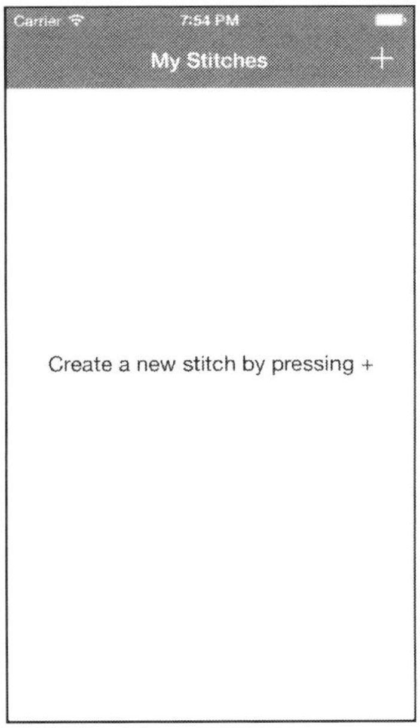

Looks like it's time to make use of the returned assets from the photos picker to create some stitches!

Creating stitches

When the user finishes selecting assets in the photos picker, the delegate method `assetPickerDidFinishPickingAssets` is called in `StitchesViewController`. Let the fun begin!

Locate `assetPickerDidFinishPickingAssets` in **StitchesViewController.swift** and add the following to the bottom of the method:

```
if (selectedAssets.count > 0) {
  // Create new Stitch
  StitchHelper.createNewStitchWith(selectedAssets,
    inCollection: stitchesCollection)
}
```

This simply passes the selected assets to a helper method responsible for creating the actual stitch. You'll implement that now.

Open **StitchHelper.swift** and locate the barren `createNewStitchWith(assets:inCollection:)`. Flesh it out now by adding the following:

```
// Create a new asset for the new stitch
// 1
let stitchImage = self.createStitchImageWithAssets(assets)

// 2
var stitchPlaceholder: PHObjectPlaceholder!
PHPhotoLibrary.sharedPhotoLibrary().performChanges({
  // 3
  let assetChangeRequest =
   PHAssetChangeRequest.creationRequestForAssetFromImage(
    stitchImage)
  stitchPlaceholder =
   assetChangeRequest.placeholderForCreatedAsset

  // 4
  let assetCollectionChangeRequest =
   PHAssetCollectionChangeRequest(
    forAssetCollection: collection, assets: nil)
  assetCollectionChangeRequest.addAssets(
    [stitchPlaceholder])
}, completionHandler: { _, _ in
      // Fetch the asset and add modification data to it
})
```

Creating a new asset is quite similar to creating a new asset collection, much as you did at the very beginning for the Stitches album. Here are the steps:

1. Use the helper method `createStitchImageWithAssets(assets:)` defined on `StitchHelper` to create the actual stitch image.
2. Declare a variable to keep track of the placeholder object, and then begin a photos library change block.
3. Create a `PHAssetChangeRequest` for your new stitch and grab the placeholder object.
4. Add the new stitch asset to your Stitches album by first creating a `PHAssetCollectionChangeRequest` and then adding the placeholder object. Ignore the completion block for now; you don't need it just yet.

And that's it! Build and run. Go to create a new stitch and select a few photos. Tap **Done** and...*hey, where's your stitch?*

Don't worry! You haven't done anything wrong; you've just encountered your first issue. Kill and re-run the app. You'll see it now:

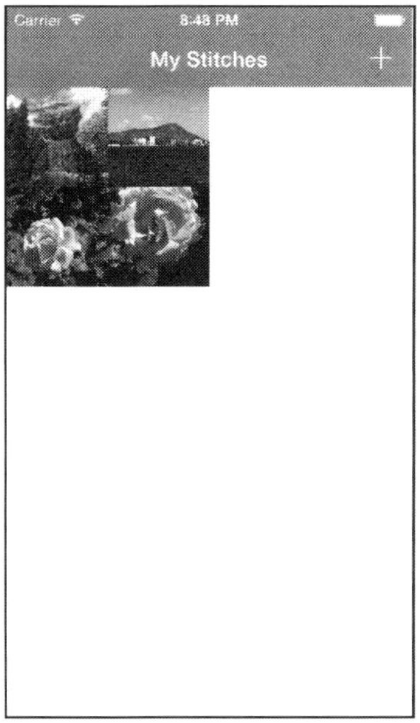

So what happened the first time? Your stitch *was* created, but your view controller didn't know about it and so never updated its interface to display the new stitch. Remember all the cool **change observing** features in the Photos framework that you learned about earlier? You can use them to fix this issue. But first, you're going to set up the last view controller – `StitchDetailViewController`.

Modifying and editing assets

The `StitchDetailViewController` displays a single stitch image and presents the user with a handful of options; the user can favorite, delete or edit the stitch. Editing the stitch takes them back to the photos picker to modify their selected assets.

You might be wondering, "But *how* do you know which assets are in a stitch?" If so, you're getting ahead of yourself. You'll know when you get there :]

First, the stitch image needs to be displayed. Open **StitchDetailViewController.swift** and find `displayImage()`. As the name suggests, this is where you load and display the image.

The difference between loading the image here versus those used by the collection views is that you want to make sure you get an image of the highest quality. It's okay if it takes a touch longer; you want the user to see the most crisp, high-quality version available.

With that in mind, add the following to `displayImage()`:

```
// Load a high quality image to display
// 1
let scale = UIScreen.mainScreen().scale
let targetSize = CGSize(
  width: CGRectGetWidth(imageView.bounds) * scale,
  height: CGRectGetHeight(imageView.bounds) * scale)

// 2
let options = PHImageRequestOptions()
options.deliveryMode = .HighQualityFormat
options.networkAccessAllowed = true;

// 3
PHImageManager.defaultManager().requestImageForAsset(asset,
 targetSize: targetSize,
 contentMode: .AspectFill, options: options) { result, info in
  if (result != nil) {
    self.imageView.image = result
  }
}
```

That looks quite familiar doesn't it? You're already starting to feel the benefit of this elegant new framework. Here's the breakdown:

1. Since quality is the goal, you make sure you're taking advantage of Retina displays. If the screen *is* Retina, you ask for an image that's twice the size.
2. This is new. You're creating an instance of `PHImageRequestOptions` to let the image manager know you want a high quality image. Just like when working with the collection views, you also want to allow the photos library to fetch from the network, if needed.
3. You request the image from the default image manager. Once you get the result you assign it to the image view.

It's a great time to build and run. Select the stitch you created earlier to see it in all its glory:

Simply stunning! Now you can easily show off up to 600 percent more image, per image. Don't run off to show your friends just yet though, there's more to do!

Favoriting, and deleting an asset

That stitch is so gorgeous that you must be itching to mark it as a **favorite** in your photos library. Before you start jumping into such a modification, first make sure it's okay to do so.

Not all assets can be edited, and some can only be edited with certain operations. You'll want to check for this every time this detail view is displayed.

Still in **StitchDetailViewController.swift**, find `viewWillAppear(animated:)` and add the following just below the call to `displayImage()`:

```
// Update the interface buttons
editButton.enabled = asset.canPerformEditOperation(.Content)
favoriteButton.enabled =
 asset.canPerformEditOperation(.Properties)
deleteButton.enabled = asset.canPerformEditOperation(.Delete)
updateFavoriteButton()
```

The Photos framework makes it extremely easy to determine if you can edit an asset. Simply call `canPerformEditOperation` passing the type of operation you want to perform, and then update the interface accordingly. You can also test asset collections and collection lists in this manner.

`updateFavoriteButton()` simply updates the favorite button to display either **Favorite** or **Unfavorite**, depending on the state of asset.

Now its time to favorite that stitch! Find `favoritePressed(sender:)` and add the following:

```
PHPhotoLibrary.sharedPhotoLibrary().performChanges ({
  let request = PHAssetChangeRequest(forAsset: self.asset)
  request.favorite = !self.asset.favorite
}, completionHandler: nil)
```

Short and sweet! See? Photos framework really does make your life easier! Here you simply toggle the favorite state of the current asset. Deleting an asset is just as easy.

Find `deletePressed` and add the following:

```
PHPhotoLibrary.sharedPhotoLibrary().performChanges({
  PHAssetChangeRequest.deleteAssets([self.asset])
}, completionHandler: nil)
```

Here you create a change request for deleting the current asset, which is passed to `deleteAssets` wrapped in an array.

Build and run. Have some fun trying out all the buttons. Again, you'll notice that the interface does not update until you kill and restart the app. You'll remedy that soon, but there's just *one more thing* to do before you fix it.

Editing an existing asset

Now to tackle the burning question, "*How do you know which assets are in a stitch?*"

The answer lies within the **adjustment data**. Remember that when editing an asset, you can supply adjustment data to describe the edits you performed. This adjustment data is stored as an `NSData`, so you can define the format of the adjustment data to be whatever you like! In Stitches, you will simply save the unique asset identifiers for each of its assets.

You may remember that when you created the stitch, you didn't attach any adjustment data to it. Well that's about change.

Go back to `createNewStitchWith(assets:, inCollection:)` in **StitchHelper.swift**. After creating the stitch, you're going to immediately modify it, attaching the adjustment data.

Add the following to the empty completion handler of the call to `performChanges(_:, completionHandler:)`:

```
// Fetch the asset and add modification data to it
let fetchResult = PHAsset.fetchAssetsWithLocalIdentifiers(
  [stitchPlaceholder.localIdentifier], options: nil)
let stitchAsset = fetchResult[0] as PHAsset

self.editStitchContentWith(stitchAsset,
  image: stitchImage, assets: assets)
```

Here you make use of an asset placeholder again to fetch the newly created stitch. Once you have it, you call `editStitchContentWith(stitch:, image:, assets:)`, which is also part of `StitchHelper`, to edit the stitch.

Even though you just want to attach adjustment data here, you need to go through the entire asset editing process. Locate `editStitchContentWith(stitch:, image:, assets:)` and add the following:

```
// Update the stitch with the new assets
//1
let stitchJPEG = UIImageJPEGRepresentation(image, 0.9)
let assetIDs = assets.map { asset in
  (asset as PHAsset).localIdentifier
```

```
}
let assetsData =
 NSKeyedArchiver.archivedDataWithRootObject(assetIDs)
// 2
stitch.requestContentEditingInputWithOptions(nil)
{ contentEditingInput, _ in
  // 3
  let adjustmentData = PHAdjustmentData(formatIdentifier:
    StitchAdjustmentFormatIdentifier, formatVersion: "1.0",
    data: assetsData)
  // 4
  let contentEditingOutput = PHContentEditingOutput(
    contentEditingInput: contentEditingInput)
  stitchJPEG.writeToURL(
    contentEditingOutput.renderedContentURL, atomically: true)
  contentEditingOutput.adjustmentData = adjustmentData
  // 5
  PHPhotoLibrary.sharedPhotoLibrary().performChanges({
    let request = PHAssetChangeRequest(forAsset: stitch)
    request.contentEditingOutput = contentEditingOutput
  }, completionHandler: nil)
}
```

That's a long one. Here's what's going on:

1. Create all the data you need. This includes an array of local identifiers from all the assets in the stitch, and the JPEG data of the new stitch image.

2. To start editing an asset, you request an instance of `PHContentEditingInput`. This input gives you access to a scaled-down version of the image, the URL to access the full image, the adjustment data and some other metadata that you can use to edit the asset. You don't provide any options here, since you won't need to use the previous adjustment data. Later on, you *will* need to use these options to make sure your app can understand the existing adjustment data.

3. Create the adjustment data and provide a format identifier and version number, along with the asset data created earlier in step 1. Stitch uses the format identifier and version number together to confirm that it can understand the adjustment data.

4. Create a `PHContentEditingOutput`. This object holds the output of the edit. You write the JPEG data and assign `adjustmentData`.

5. Finally, like every other change request, you need to begin a new change block. This time you only need to assign the `contentEditingOutput` property of your `PHAssetChangeRequest` to the output created in step 4.

Now all your stitches will have their adjustment data set up at the time of creation. *Great work!*

Loading the existing adjustment data

Now that the data sets are all accounted for, you can allow the user to add or remove images from existing stitches. Before you take them to the photo picker, you'll need to grab the details of all the assets in the stitch, load the images, and pre-select them.

Good thing you stored the necessary information in the adjustment data :]

To do this, you will set it up so that when the user presses the **Edit** button, you'll see if the associated adjustment data is in a format the app can handle. If it is, you fetch the assets and pass them along to the photo picker in `prepareForSegue(_:, sender:)`.

Sounds straightforward, right? Find `editPressed(sender:)` in **StitchDetailViewController.swift** and add the following:

```
StitchHelper.loadAssetsInStitch(asset) { stitchAssets in
  self.stitchAssets = stitchAssets
  dispatch_async(dispatch_get_main_queue()) {
    self.performSegueWithIdentifier(StitchEditSegueID,
     sender: self)
  }
}
```

`StitchHelper` is going to do the heavy lifting here – what a great little helper! As the name implies `loadAssetsInStitch(_:, completion:)` loads all the assets referenced in the adjustment data, and calls the completion handler, passing back the assets.

Once you get the assets back, you save them into a property so you can pass them to the photo picker in `prepareForSegue(_:, sender:)`. When that's all done, manually trigger the segue to the photo picker.

Open **StitchHelper.swift** and locate `loadAssetsInStitch(stitch:, completion:)`. Add the following:

```
// 1
let options = PHContentEditingInputRequestOptions()
options.canHandleAdjustmentData = { adjustmentData in
  (adjustmentData.formatIdentifier ==
    StitchAdjustmentFormatIdentifier) &&
     (adjustmentData.formatVersion == "1.0")
}
// 2
```

```
stitch.requestContentEditingInputWithOptions(options)
 { contentEditingInput, _ in
  if let adjustmentData = contentEditingInput.adjustmentData {
    // 3
    let stitchAssetsID =
    NSKeyedUnarchiver.unarchiveObjectWithData(
     adjustmentData.data) as [String]
    let stitchAssetsFetchResult =
     PHAsset.fetchAssetsWithLocalIdentifiers(
      stitchAssetsID, options: nil)
    // 4
    var stitchAssets: [PHAsset] = []
    stitchAssetsFetchResult.enumerateObjectsUsingBlock
      { obj, _, _ in
        stitchAssets.append(obj as PHAsset)
    }
    completion(stitchAssets)
  } else {
    // 5
    completion([])
  }
}
```

That looks like quite a lot, but you've seen most of it before. Here's the breakdown:

1. You tell the Photos framework what adjustment data format you support by setting the `canHandleAdjustmentData` property on an instance of `PHContentEditingInputRequestOptions`. Here, you return `true` only if *both* the format identifier and version match the ones the app can deal with.

2. Pass the options into the request. If you can handle the adjustment data format, the Photos framework provides you with the *original* image along with the adjustment data. If not, the Photos framework simply provides you with the most recent *modified* image and no adjustment data.

3. If the adjustment data exists, you un-archive it into an array of asset identifiers. You can then use `fetchAssetsWithLocalIdentifiers(identifiers:, options:)` to fetch the corresponding assets.

4. Use `enumerateObjectsUsingBlock` to iterate through the assets in the fetch result and create a new array of assets. Finally, call the completion block and pass in `stitchAssets`.

5. If there is no adjustment data or the app doesn't support its format, you can pass an empty array to the completion handler.

So far so good; now go back to **StitchDetailViewController.swift**. Before presenting the photo picker, you want to pass it those assets you've just loaded using the adjustment data. Find `prepareForSegue(sender:)` and add the following code after the comment at the bottom of the `if` statement:

```
// Set up AssetCollectionsViewController
if let assets = stitchAssets {
  dest.selectedAssets = SelectedAssets(assets: assets)
} else {
  dest.selectedAssets = nil
}
```

Here you set `selectedAssets` to the assets you just fetched. If there are no selected assets, you can assign it to `nil`.

Build and run. Delete any previous stitches and create some new ones so they will have the necessary adjustment data. Now edit any one of these stitches and you'll see the photo picker has the selected the relevant assets right off the bat. *Neat!*

Nothing happens when you tap **Done** in the asset picker though. That's not a problem, as you've already written the code to edit an asset, you just haven't called it here. In order to update the existing asset, you can use `editStitchContentWith` in `StitchHelper`.

Find `assetPickerDidFinishPickingAssets(selectedAssets:)` and add the following code after the comment:

```
// Update stitch with new assets
let stitchImage =
 StitchHelper.createStitchImageWithAssets(selectedAssets)
StitchHelper.editStitchContentWith(self.asset,
 image: stitchImage, assets: selectedAssets)
```

And that's it! You can build and run now, but you'll not see any changes until you restart the app, because the app still doesn't know when something has changed to update its interface.

Observing changes

At the very beginning of this chapter, **change observing** probably didn't seem like the most useful or exciting feature of the Photos framework. By now, it's looking more and more appealing, don't you think?

Imagine if you had to update the interface yourself after *every* change your user makes in the app. Now imagine this: what if you had to update your interface whenever the user deleted a photo in iCloud from their MacBook? Oh my, that sounds like a ton of work. Thank goodness the Photos framework has your back!

In this section, you'll add change observing to all four of your view controllers. You'll start with the easiest – `StitchDetailViewController`.

Open **StitchDetailViewController.swift**. Replace the existing `deinit` implementation with the following:

```
deinit {
  PHPhotoLibrary.sharedPhotoLibrary().unregisterChangeObserver(
   self)
}
```

And the existing implementation of `viewDidLoad()` with the following

```
override func viewDidLoad() {
  super.viewDidLoad()
  PHPhotoLibrary.sharedPhotoLibrary().registerChangeObserver(
   self)
}
```

When you register yourself as a change observer, the Photos framework doesn't spam you with notifications whenever something changes in the photo library. You implicitly declare interest whenever a **fetch** method is used. This makes it so that the Photos framework only notifies you when an object of interest is changed.

For these reasons, always register yourself as a change observer *before* you start fetching any objects.

Your class must also conform to the `PHPhotoLibraryChangeObserver` protocol. This has been done for you, for the relevant classes in Stitch.

Responding to changes in an asset

When an object of interest changes, the protocol method `photoLibraryDidChange(changeInstance:)` gets called, passing you a `PHChange` object. This object represents everything you need in-order to respond to that particular change.

Still in **StitchDetailViewController.swift**, find `photoLibraryDidChange(changeInstance:)` at the very bottom of the file, and add the following:

```
// 1
dispatch_async(dispatch_get_main_queue()) {
  // 2
  if let changeDetails =
changeInstance.changeDetailsForObject(self.asset) {
    // 3
    if changeDetails.objectWasDeleted {
      self.navigationController?.popViewControllerAnimated(true)
      return
    }
    // 4
    self.asset = changeDetails.objectAfterChanges as PHAsset
    if changeDetails.assetContentChanged {
      self.displayImage()
    }
    self.updateFavoriteButton()
  }
}
```

The PHChange object provides change details for any asset or fetch result you previously obtained. You can then use the properties of these change details to update your assets and interface. Here's the step-by-step:

1. Dispatch to the main queue because you'll be modifying the interface, and the callback could be called on a background queue
2. Ask for the change details of your asset. Then check if the change details exist for your object. This is because you might be interested in multiple objects and not all of them have necessarily changed.
3. If the object was deleted, you can just pop to view controller to return back to the Stitches view controller.
4. Update your asset by assigning it to `objectAfterChanges,` from the change detail. Remember that `PHObjects` are all immutable, so if any changes happen, Photos will simply present you with the new object. Next, check if the content of the asset has changed and re-load the image for display if needed. Finally, update the favorite button in case the assets favorite state changed.

That's it! Build and run. Go to view an existing stitch and try editing, favoriting or deleting it. The interface will update almost immediately.

Responding to changes in the table view

Open **AssetCollectionsViewController.swift** and start by registering for notifications. Add the following to `viewDidLoad()`, just below the call to `super`:

```
PHPhotoLibrary.sharedPhotoLibrary().registerChangeObserver(self)
```

And replace the existing implementation of `deinit` with the following:

```
deinit {
  PHPhotoLibrary.sharedPhotoLibrary().unregisterChangeObserver(
   self)
}
```

Okay, with that done, head back to `photoLibraryDidChange(changeInstance:)`. Add the following code:

```
// Respond to changes
dispatch_async(dispatch_get_main_queue()) {
  var updatedFetchResults = false
  // 1
  var changeDetails: PHFetchResultChangeDetails? =
  changeInstance.changeDetailsForFetchResult(self.userAlbums)
```

```
    if let changes = changeDetails {
      self.userAlbums = changes.fetchResultAfterChanges!
      updatedFetchResults = true
    }

    changeDetails = changeInstance.changeDetailsForFetchResult(
     self.userFavorites)
    if let changes = changeDetails {
      self.userFavorites = changes.fetchResultAfterChanges!
      updatedFetchResults = true
    }
    // 2
    if updatedFetchResults {
      self.tableView.reloadData()
    }
  }
```

This code performs the same steps as in the previous section:

1. Ask whether or not there are changes in your objects. In this case, your objects are fetch results and not individual asset objects
2. If there are any changes, simply reload the table

In most cases, any updates will simply cause the asset count to change for a particular cell. For this reason, you can simply reload the entire table. In the next section on collection views, you'll want to animate the addition and removal of assets.

Responding to changes in collection views

The last two view controllers that you need to update are both collection views, so the code will be almost identical for the two.

Switch to **StitchesViewController.swift** to get started. Again, the first step is to register for the change notifications. This time around, `registerChangeObserver(observer:)` should be called once you obtain permission to access the photos library. Add the call to the very beginning of the `.Authorized` case statement in `viewDidLoad()`:

```
  case .Authorized:
    // Register observer
    PHPhotoLibrary.sharedPhotoLibrary().registerChangeObserver(
      self)
```

You can still safely unregister in `deinit`. Add the following:

```
deinit {
  // Unregister observer
  PHPhotoLibrary.sharedPhotoLibrary().unregisterChangeObserver(
    self)
}
```

Jump again to `photoLibraryDidChange(changeInstance:)` near the very bottom. Add the following:

```
// Respond to changes
dispatch_async(dispatch_get_main_queue()) {
  if let collectionChanges =
   changeInstance.changeDetailsForFetchResult(self.stitches)
  {
    self.stitches = collectionChanges.fetchResultAfterChanges

    if collectionChanges.hasMoves ||
      !collectionChanges.hasIncrementalChanges {
        self.collectionView.reloadData()
    } else {
      // perform incremental updates
    }
  }
}
```

This is the same code you've been writing for the other view controllers.

First, you check if the change details exist. Then, you can check what *types* of changes exist. The property `hasIncrementalChanges` lets you know if the changes can be described incrementally. If this is true, the change details will contain information describing the objects that were added, removed, modified or rearranged. In this case, if the changes cannot be described incrementally, or if they have been rearranged, you can directly reload the collection view to reflect the changes.

If there incremental changes do exist, you can then insert and delete the corresponding cells with animation.

The Photos framework makes this extremely easy, by providing you with everything you need in the change details. You'll see it in action when you add the following code after the comment `// perform incremental updates` in the block you added in the previous step:

```
// perform incremental updates
self.collectionView.performBatchUpdates({
```

```
let removedIndexes = collectionChanges.removedIndexes
if removedIndexes?.count > 0 {
  self.collectionView.deleteItemsAtIndexPaths(
   self.indexPathsFromIndexSet(removedIndexes!, section: 0))
}
let insertedIndexes = collectionChanges.insertedIndexes
if insertedIndexes?.count > 0 {
  self.collectionView.insertItemsAtIndexPaths(
   self.indexPathsFromIndexSet(insertedIndexes!, section: 0))
}
let changedIndexes = collectionChanges.changedIndexes
if changedIndexes?.count > 0 {
  self.collectionView.reloadItemsAtIndexPaths(
   self.indexPathsFromIndexSet(changedIndexes!, section: 0))
}
}, completion: nil)
```

The change details conveniently provide `removedIndexes`, `insertedIndexes` and `changedIndexes` that you can use to update your collection view.

The helper function, `indexPathsFromIndexSet(_:, section:)`, creates an array of index paths from the index set provided by the change details. This array can then be passed directly to the relevant update function of a collection view. The Photos framework really does make this easy for you!

Three down, one to go! Luckily, this next one is almost identical to the previous one. And since I've walked you through the previous three, this one's all on you :]

Switch to **AssetsViewController.swift** and add the code to register and unregister for change notifications, to `viewDidLoad()` and `deinit` respectively.

Once you're done with that, replace `photoLibraryDidChange(changeInstance:)` with a copy of the same method from **StitchesViewController.swift**. Fix the compiler errors by replacing the two instances of `self.stitches` with `self.assetsFetchResults`.

That's all there is! I'll trust that you got it right :]

The sweet taste of victory

Congratulations, you did it! Build and run. Watch as the app beautifully updates itself as you add, edit and delete stitches.

Then go to Photos.app and modify some photos – the changes will be reflected in Stitch right away. Keep making stitches; in fact, go ahead and make stitches of stitches of stitches! Don't stop until you've filled the screen:

Where to go from here?

Congratulations! You now have the fundamental knowledge you need to master the Photos framework. If you haven't done so already, go check out Chapter 12, **Photo Editing Extensions** for more photo-based goodness.

If you've already done that, the why not create an extension for Stitch?

To remind you of how far you've come since you cracked open this chapter, here's a recap of your accomplishments. You learned how to:

1. Request permission to access the users photos library, and fail gracefully if they deny access

2. Create a new album called Stitches, and fetch all its assets
3. Load all stitch images and display them in a collection view
4. Create a new stitch asset and add it the Stitches album. Fetch that asset immediately after it's created and attach the relevant adjustment data to it
5. Load and display a high-resolution version of a stitch in the detail view
6. Favorite, delete and edit existing stitch-based assets
7. Implement photos library change observing throughout the entire app

That's a one mammoth list; you must've exercised almost every API in the Photos framework! Thanks to you, everybody can now share *up to 600 percent more photo, per photo!* That never gets old :]

The real next step is to keep on learning. With the release of iOS 8, developers now have more access and control the user's photo library than ever before. Combined with the other amazing libraries and frameworks on iOS, some truly useful and amazing apps that could've never existed before are now possible. Happy Coding!

Chapter 21: Beginning Live Rendering

By Vincent Ngo

iOS developers can create some incredibly useful and beautiful apps with custom controls. However, prior to Xcode 6 there was one major problem with working with custom controls – you couldn't preview your custom controls in Interface Builder!

I don't know about you, but I'm tired of constantly having to use the simulator to see my custom controls in action – or even just to check the results of small changes like the line weights, colors, image positions, scaling, size, or layout. Wouldn't it be great if you could write code and see things change in real-time?

Your wait is over; you can accomplish all this – and more – with Live Rendering in Xcode 6! Seeing your controls update live in Interface Builder will save you untold amounts of time since you don't have to continually run up the simulator to see your UI changes. Coding custom controls in Xcode 6 will make you feel like you're an artist painting on a canvas. :]

In this chapter you'll learn the following:

- How to set up Live Rendering in Interface Builder
- How to expose your custom control's properties to Interface Builder
- How to create a custom control using `CALayers`

You'll create a custom watch control in this chapter, with customizable backgrounds, timezones, and other neat-looking display features. And as a bonus, you'll see how to build this control without launching the simulator even once!

Understanding custom properties

Before you dive into designing your own control, take a moment to see how Live Rendering works in Interface Builder for a built-in control. The following screenshot shows a simple `UIButton`:

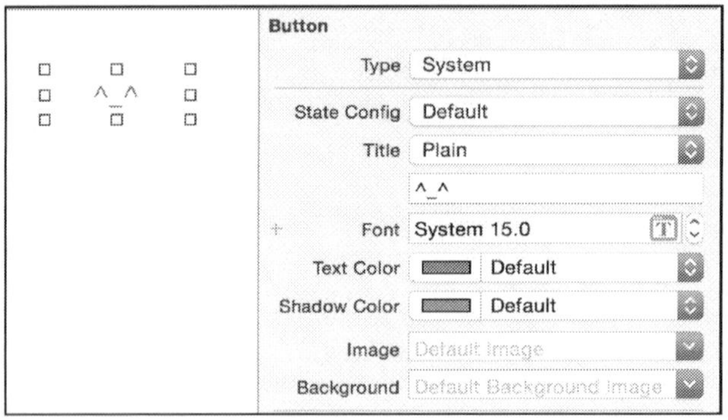

Changing the title of the button in the Attributes Inspector automatically updates the button on the screen. You can also change things such as the button Type, State, Font, Text color, Background and many other elements and have the changes show immediately in Interface Builder.

This feature is great not only for developers, but for designers as well. Instead of telling the developer the font type, size, color and other properties of each UI button, the designer can change the properties directly in Interface Builder without writing any code.

In this chapter you'll learn how to create a similar editing interface for your own custom control. You'll be able to preview your control in Interface Builder as you develop the drawing code step-by-step, and best of all you won't have to build and run the app until the very end of the chapter! Think it can't be done? Read on!

Getting started

Open the starter project included with this chapter; build and run the project to see what you have to work with:

Right now your control is nothing but a grey square. It's hard to imagine, but you're going to build a great looking control on top of this. Before you start designing, take a minute and review the design of the control below. Designing the watch control

Here is a diagram showing how the watch control will be constructed:

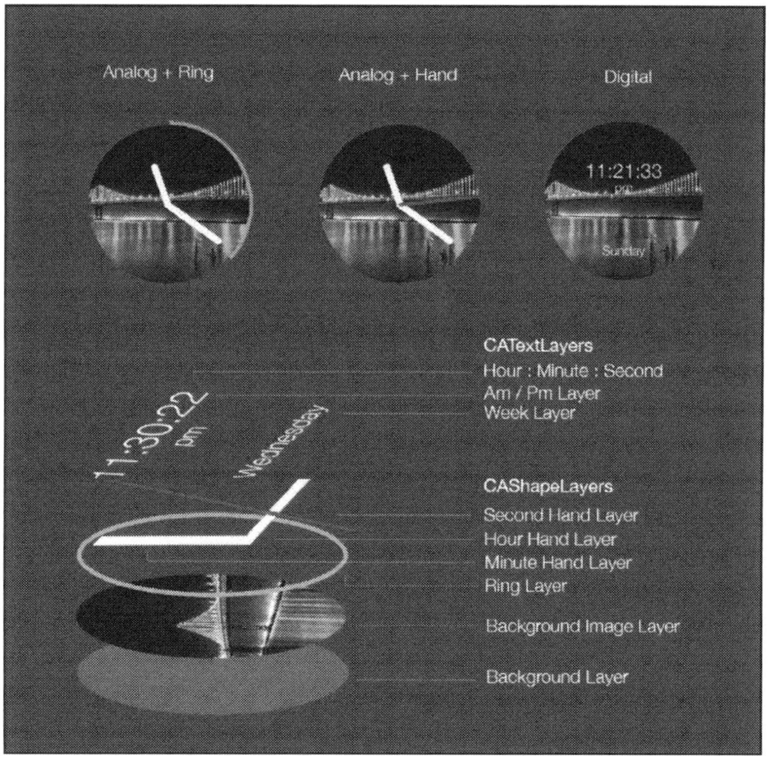

The diagram above shows all nine layers of the watch control, from the background layer right to the text layers that will be superimposed on the watch. You'll add these text layers in the next chapter; for now you'll focus on adding the analog controls.

You'll first create the background layer of the control and add an image layer to that. Next you'll create your ring layer on top of the background image layer. After that, you will create the hour, minute and second hand on top of the ring layer. The ring and watch hands will be composed of `CAShapeLayer` objects.

Setting up Live Rendering

Before you can experience Live Rendering in Interface Builder, you'll need to designate your app as designable. Open **WatchView.swift** and add the `@IBDesignable` attribute as shown below:

```
import UIKit
import QuartzCore

@IBDesignable
class WatchView: UIView {
```

The attribute `@IBDesignable` lets Interface Builder perform live updates on a particular view. Any code change related to your view will be reflected in real time within Interface Builder.

Next open **Main.storyboard;** within the **Watch scene**, click the `UIView` to use the Identity Inspector to change the **Custom Class** to **WatchView** as shown:

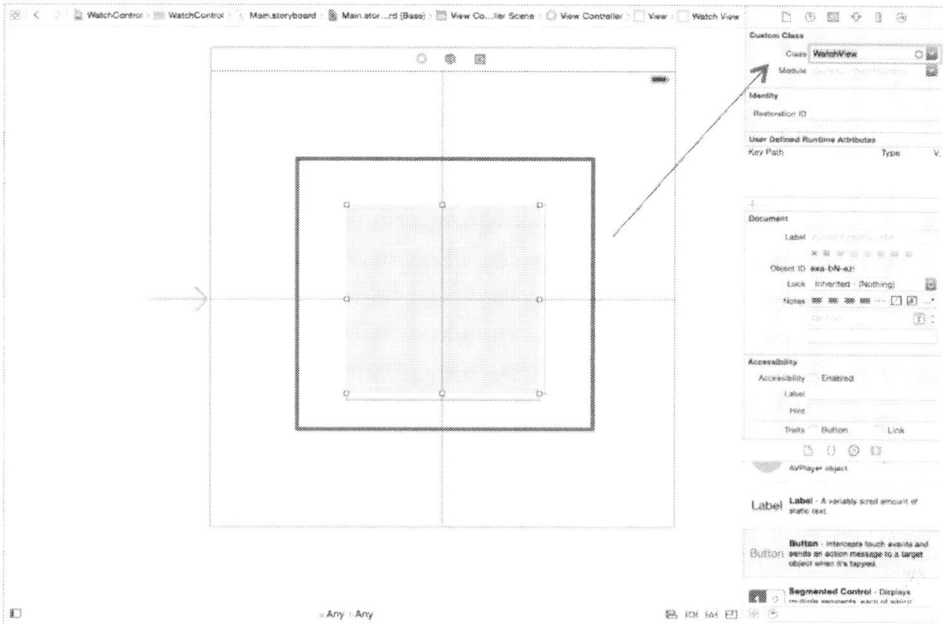

That's all you need to do to enable Live Rendering of your control! Interface Builder recognizes that your control is capable of Live Rendering `WatchView` due to the `@IBDesignable` property.

You likely noticed that when you set the Custom Class to `WatchView`, a **Designables** status indicator appeared as illustrated below:

Up to date status indicator means that your view compiled and rendered properly. **Build failed** status indicator means an error occurred when Xcode tried to render your view, like so:

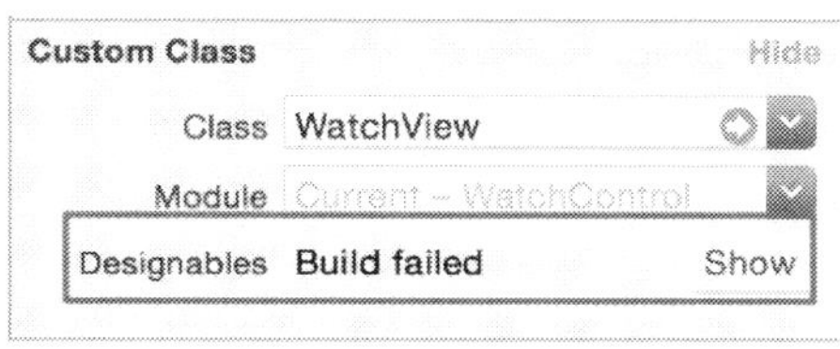

In this situation, Xcode also complains that the Designables agent crashed as you can see above. To debug this kind of issue, click on the **Show** button in the Custom Class section and Xcode will open a debugging session for you and jump right to the statement that caused the crash.

In **Main.Storyboard,** ensure the `WatchView` is still selected and use the Attributes Inspector to set the Background color to **Default.** You don't want the ugly gray background showing while you render your beautiful watch. :]

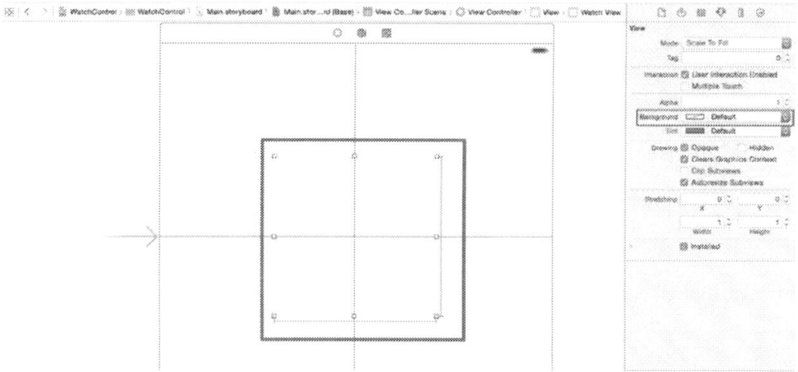

> **Note:** When you're using a control that displays data, like a graphing or charting object, it could be useful to show some dummy data so the designer knows how data in this object will look at runtime. You can override `prepareForInterfaceBuilder()` in your code and put your dummy-data generator inside. This method is only called at design time and has no effect on your app at runtime. You won't need this feature in your watch design, but it's handy to know it's there!

Exposing properties

Applying the `@IBInspectable` attribute to any property of your control exposes it in the attributes inspector. You apply `@IBInspectable` to a class property as follows:

```
@IBInspectable var variableName : variableType = value
```

> **Note**: Valid property types for `@IBInspectable` are `Int`, `CGFloat`, `Double`, `String`, `Bool`, `CGRect`, `CGSize`, `CGPoint`, `UIImage` and `UIColor`.

Open **WatchView.swift** and add `@IBInspectable` to the following two variable declarations:

```
@IBInspectable var enableClockSecondHand: Bool = false {
  didSet { updateLayerProperties() } //1
}

@IBInspectable  var enableColorBackground: Bool = false {
  didSet { updateLayerProperties() } //2
}
```

Here's what's going on in the code above:

1. `enableClockSecondHand` toggles between seconds displayed as a ring or as a second hand. Modifying this variable calls `updateLayerProperties`.
2. `enableColorBackground` toggles between a colored background and an image background. Modifying this variable also calls `updateLayerProperties`.

> **Note**: Declaring a stored variable with `willSet` or `didSet` is known as **property observing**. According to Apple:
>
> "The `willSet` and `didSet` observers provide a way to observe (and to respond appropriately) when the value of a variable or property is being set. The observers are not called when the variable or property is first initialized. Instead, they are called only when the value is set outside of an initialization context."
>
> https://developer.apple.com/library/prerelease/ios/documentation/Swift/Conceptual/Swift_Programming_Language/Declarations.html

Head back to **Main.Storyboard** and you'll see that your properties have appeared in the Attributes Inspector:

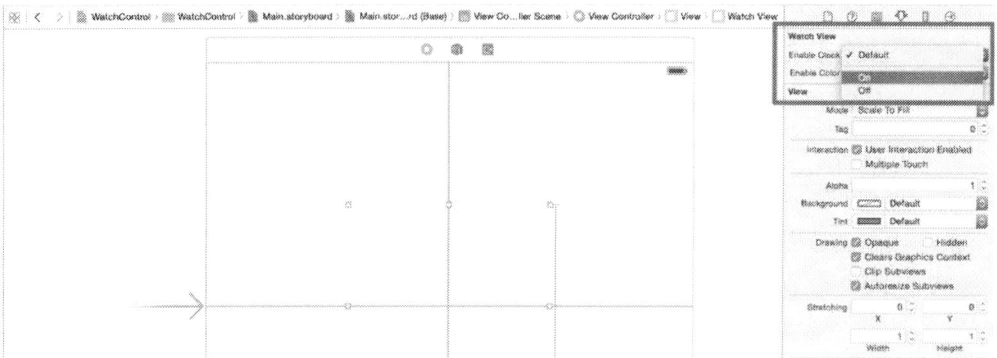

And just like that, you've exposed some properties in the Attributes Inspector – and you still haven't built and run your project. Time to get your watch control designed!

Creating your watch control

Head back to **WatchView.swift**; you'll notice a slew of empty methods waiting to be filled in. It's a good idea to break up the logic of your control into smaller methods which makes debugging much easier – which also leads to code re-use.

Return to **Main.Storyboard**, bring up the Assistant Editor and ensure that the class in the right-hand pane is set to **WatchView.swift** (select **Manual\WatchControl\WatchControl\WatchControl\WatchView.swift**):

This way, as you add your drawing code you can see it update live in Interface Builder. With that set, you're now ready to add some elements to your control.

Creating the background layer

Add the following properties to `WatchView` just after the `enableColorBackground` statement:

```
//Base color background layer
var backgroundLayer: CAShapeLayer! // 1
@IBInspectable var backgroundLayerColor: UIColor =
UIColor.darkGrayColor() { didSet { updateLayerProperties() }
} // 2
@IBInspectable var lineWidth: CGFloat = 1.0 // 3
```

3. `backgroundLayer` is the base layer of your watch; it's declared as a `CAShapeLayer`.
4. This statement exposes the `backgroundLayer's` color attribute. This lets you change the color of the background from within the Attributes Inspector. Also note the observer here; whenever the color is changed, this calls `updateLayerProperties` to update the watch's background color.
5. This exposes the `lineWidth` property in the Attributes Inspector; it's used to increase and decrease the inserts of the circular frame.

You can see that the new properties show up immediately in Attributes Inspector like so:

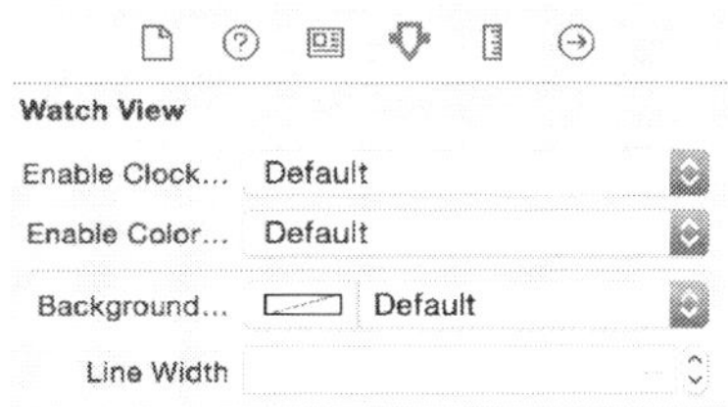

Now you can set your new properties; set **Enable Clock...** to **Off** and **Enable Color...** to **Off** as shown below:

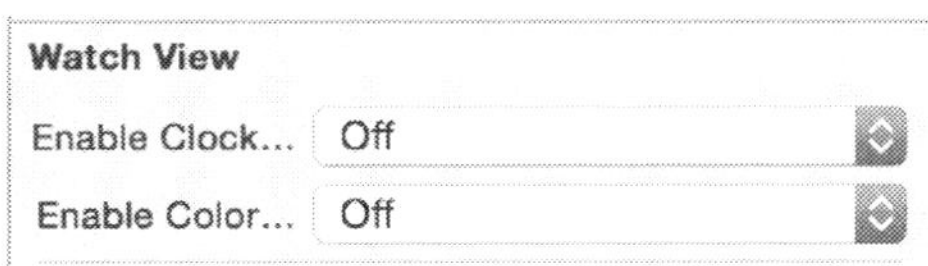

Setting Enable Clock Second Hand to off will let you see the ring layer, which you'll build in just a moment. As well, setting `enableColorBackground` to False lets you see the background layer you're going to add later.

Replace `layoutBackgroundLayer` in `WatchView` with the following code:

```
func layoutBackgroundLayer() {
  if backgroundLayer == nil { //1
    backgroundLayer = CAShapeLayer() //2
    layer.addSublayer(backgroundLayer) //3

    let rect = CGRectInset(bounds, lineWidth / 2.0,
                                   lineWidth / 2.0) //4
    let path = UIBezierPath(ovalInRect: rect) //5

    backgroundLayer.path = path.CGPath //6
    backgroundLayer.fillColor = backgroundLayerColor.CGColor //7
    backgroundLayer.lineWidth = lineWidth //8
  }
  backgroundLayer.frame = layer.bounds //9
}
```

Taking each numbered comment in turn:

1. Check to see if the `backgroundLayer` has already been created. If so, there is no need to recreate the background layer.
2. If the background layer does not exist, the code allocates memory for a `CAShapeLayer` object.
3. Add the `backgroundLayer` to the view's sublayer.
4. Create a `CGRect` variable with insets; this ensures your circle won't clip the view.
5. Create a circular `UIBezierPath`.
6. Apply the circular path to the `backgroundLayer's` path, so the background layer is now circular instead of rectangular.
7. `backgroundLayerColor` is an `@IBInspectable` property; here you set the color of the background to grey. This will be reflected in the object in Interface Builder.
8. Set the layer's `lineWidth.` This is another `@IBInspectable` that you set as 1.
9. This makes sure that the `backgroundLayer's` frame is always within the super view's layer's bounds.

If you check out Interface builder, you'll see that you now have a nice clean circular object on which to draw your watch:

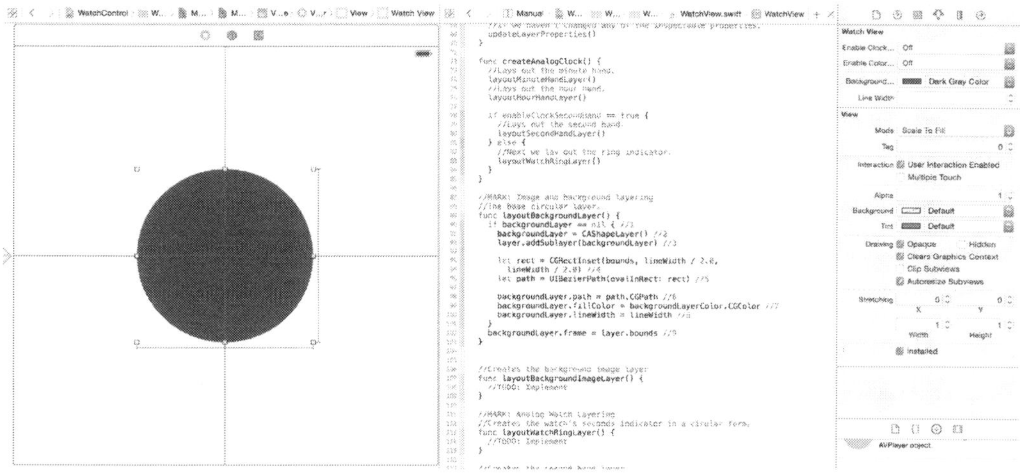

At this point, you've created the grey bottom layer of the control as shown in the diagram below:

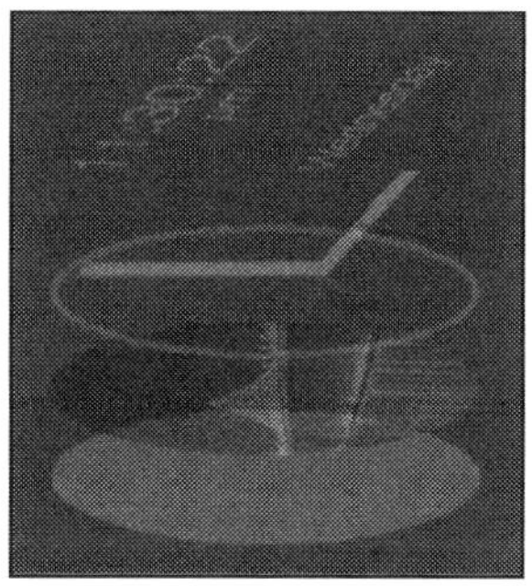

Add the following code to `updateLayerProperties()`:

```
func updateLayerProperties() {
  if backgroundLayer != nil {
    backgroundLayer.fillColor = backgroundLayerColor.CGColor
  }
}
```

Recall that `backgroundLayerColor` is an `@IBInspectable`, with a `didSet` observer. Setting `backgroundLayerColor` calls `updateLayerProperties()`; the code checks that `backgroundLayer` exists, and if so, updates the color of the `backgroundLayer`.

To test this out, try changing the background color in Interface Builder to a different color. You'll see it update your controls look dynamically!

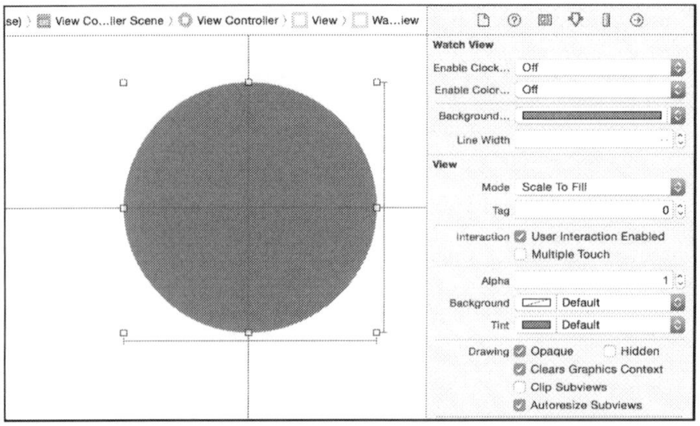

Undo your change so the background is back to gray before you continue.

Creating the image layer

The next step is to add the `backgroundImageLayer`. Add the following properties below the `backgroundLayerColor` property of **WatchView.swift**.

```
var backgroundImageLayer: CALayer!
@IBInspectable var backgroundImage: UIImage? {
  didSet  { updateLayerProperties() }
}
```

Here you expose `backgroundImage` to the Attributes Inspector. This should be old hat to you by now! :]

Next locate `layoutBackgroundImageLayer()` and replace the code with the following:

```
func layoutBackgroundImageLayer() {
  if backgroundImageLayer == nil {
    let maskLayer = CAShapeLayer() //1
    let dx = lineWidth + 3.0
    let insetBounds = CGRectInset(self.bounds, dx, dx)
    let innerPath = UIBezierPath(ovalInRect: insetBounds)
    maskLayer.path = innerPath.CGPath
    maskLayer.fillColor = UIColor.blackColor().CGColor
    maskLayer.frame = self.bounds
    layer.addSublayer(maskLayer)

    backgroundImageLayer = CAShapeLayer()
    backgroundImageLayer.mask = maskLayer //2
    backgroundImageLayer.frame = self.bounds
```

```
    backgroundImageLayer.contentsGravity =
kCAGravityResizeAspectFill
    layer.addSublayer(backgroundImageLayer)
  }
}
```

Here's the explanation of the above code:

1. The `CAShapeLayer` object `maskLayer` creates a circle just like the previous layer.
2. This creates a `backgroundImageLayer` and sets its mask to `maskLayer`. Remember that when you mask a layer, it means that the layer is transparent where the mask is transparent. Since you're using a circular mask, this means that the `backgroundImageLayer` that was previously rectangular shaped is now circular.

Now add the following code before the end of `updateLayerProperties`():

```
//Updates the image layer.
if backgroundImageLayer != nil {
  if let image = backgroundImage {
    backgroundImageLayer.contents = image.CGImage
  }
}
```

Again, remember that you call `updateLayerProperties()` every time a property changes. Here you update the background image layer's contents based on the image the user sets.

Switch over to **Main.Storyboard**, select the `WatchView`, bring up the Attributes Inspector and set the `backgroundImage` property to **test3.jpg**. Your control in Interface Builder should now look like the following:

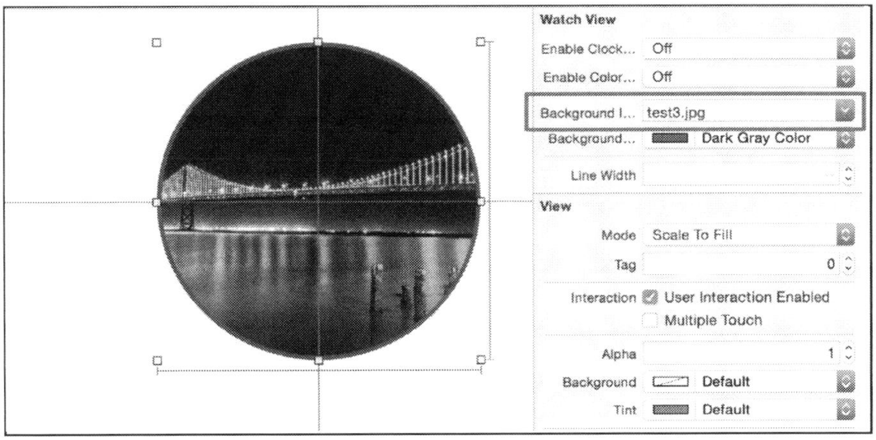

After setting backgroundImage in the Attributes Inspector, you now have a sharp-looking circular background image in Interface Builder.

At this point, you've build the bottom two layers of your control, as shown below:

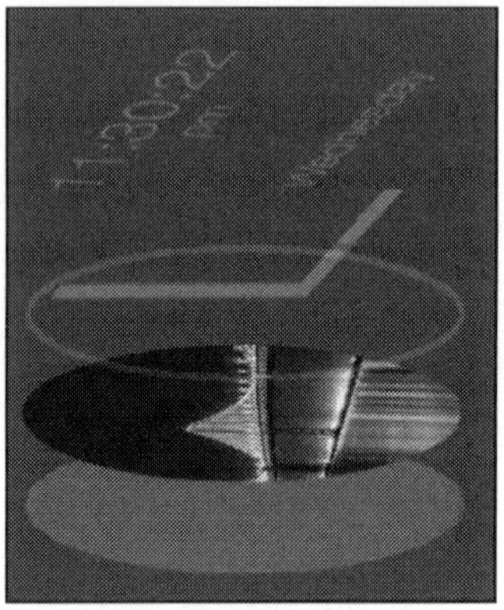

Creating the ring layer

It's time to create the ringLayer. Return to **WatchView.swift** and add the following properties above the lineWidth property:

```
// Ring Layer - Circular style progress bar that ticks
clockwise.
var ringLayer: CAShapeLayer! // 1
@IBInspectable var ringThickness: CGFloat = 2.0 // 2
@IBInspectable var ringColor: UIColor = UIColor.blueColor()
@IBInspectable var ringProgress: CGFloat = 45.0/60 {
  didSet { updateLayerProperties() } // 3
}
```

Here's what this code does:

1. Declares a ringLayer to be a CAShapeLayer object. The ring layer is a circular progress-type indicator to keep track of seconds.
2. Declares three @IBInspectable properties. ringThickness controls the thickness of the ring. ringColor changes the color of the ring. ringProgress keeps track of the indicator's location on the circular path.
3. Declares a setter observer for ringProgress to update the ring's starting and ending position as the seconds tick by.

Next, replace layoutWatchRingLayer in **WatchView.swift** with the following code:

```
func layoutWatchRingLayer() {
  if ringProgress == 0 { //1
    if ringLayer != nil {
      ringLayer.strokeEnd = 0.0
    }
  }

  if ringLayer == nil { //2
    ringLayer = CAShapeLayer()
    layer.addSublayer(ringLayer)
    let dx = ringThickness / 2.0
    let rect = CGRectInset(bounds, dx, dx)
    let path = UIBezierPath(ovalInRect: rect)
    ringLayer.transform = CATransform3DMakeRotation(CGFloat(-
(M_PI/2)), 0, 0, 1) //3
    ringLayer.strokeColor = ringColor.CGColor
    ringLayer.path = path.CGPath
    ringLayer.fillColor = nil
    ringLayer.lineWidth = ringThickness
    ringLayer.strokeStart = 0.0
  }
  ringLayer.strokeEnd = ringProgress / 60.0  //4
  ringLayer.frame = layer.bounds
}
```

Here's what the above method does:

1. Checks to see if the ring progress is equal to zero. If so, it sets the `ringLayer's` stroke to zero. This animates the stroke of the circular layer counter-clockwise all the way back to the 12 o'clock mark.
2. Checks to see if a layer already exists. If it doesn't exist, it creates a circular `CAShapeLayer`.
3. This transforms the layer so the starting position will be at the 12 o'clock mark instead of the 3 o'clock mark.
4. This kicks off the animation. Since `strokeEnd` is an animation property, changing its value causes `CAShapeLayer` to animate the progress indicator.

Add the following code to the very top of `updateLayerProperties()`:

```
// Updates the ring progress.
if ringLayer != nil {
  ringLayer.strokeEnd = ringProgress / 60.0
}
```

This should be familiar territory: here you invoke `updateLayerProperties` each time `ringProgress` changes.

Head back to Interface Builder. Select **WatchView** then use Attributes Inspector to update the new properties as follows:

- **Ring Thickness**: 5
- **Ring Color**: Light blue
- **Ring Progress**: 31

Your new properties should look like the following once you're done:

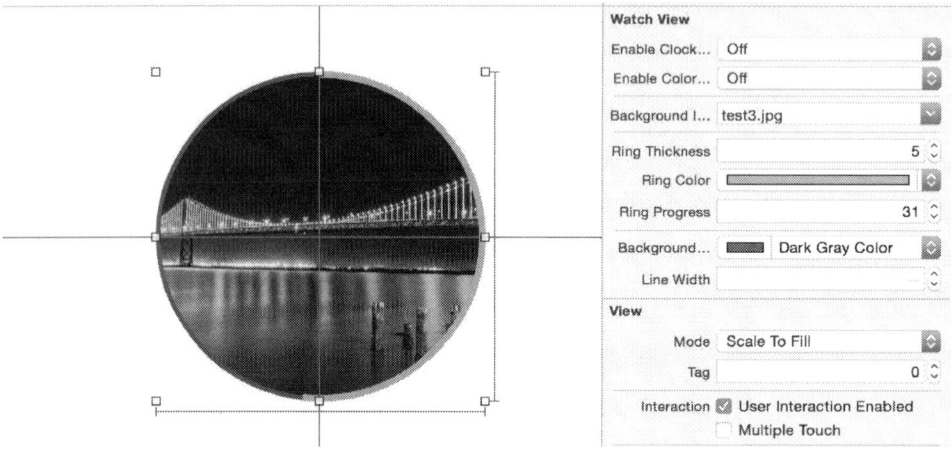

If you'd prefer to see the various properties together in a list view, you can view and set the properties via the Identity Inspector like so:

To see how the ring progress renders on your control, update the `ringProgress` property using the spin control as shown below; the indicator should inch forward and back depending on the value of the property.

You've now completed the first three layers of your control as shown below:

You don't have much further to go!

Creating the clock hand layers

Now you need to create the layers for the hour, minute and second hands. Add the following properties to **WatchView.swift** just above the property `lineWidth`:

```
//Watch second "hand"
var secondHandLayer: CAShapeLayer!
@IBInspectable var secondHandColor: UIColor = UIColor.redColor()

//Watch minute "hand"
var minuteHandLayer: CAShapeLayer!
@IBInspectable var minuteHandColor: UIColor =
UIColor.whiteColor()

//Watch hour "hand"
var hourHandLayer: CAShapeLayer!
@IBInspectable var hourHandColor: UIColor = UIColor.whiteColor()
```

The code snippet above simply declares the hour, minute and second `CAShapeLayers` and three `@IBInspectable` properties to change the color of the clock hands.

Notice all three hands are similar in shape; you can definitely make use of a helper method to render the hands instead of writing the same code three times.

Add the following code under the comment that reads: `//MARK: Helper Methods`

```
//Helper function that creates clock hands of different length
and sizes or what not!
func createClockHand(anchorPoint: CGPoint, handLength: CGFloat,
handWidth: CGFloat, handAlpha: CGFloat, handColor: UIColor) ->
CAShapeLayer {
  let handLayer = CAShapeLayer()
  let path = UIBezierPath()
  path.moveToPoint(CGPointMake(1.0, handLength))
  path.addLineToPoint(CGPointMake(1.0, bounds.size.height /
2.0))
  handLayer.bounds = CGRectMake(0.0, 0.0, 1.0,
bounds.size.height / 2.0)
  handLayer.anchorPoint = anchorPoint
  handLayer.position = CGPointMake(CGRectGetMidX(bounds),
CGRectGetMidY(bounds))
  handLayer.lineWidth = handWidth
  handLayer.opacity = Float(handAlpha)
  handLayer.strokeColor = handColor.CGColor
  handLayer.path = path.CGPath
  handLayer.lineCap = kCALineCapRound
  return handLayer
}
```

This code is similar to the other two layers. However, instead of a circular path, this creates two points (one at the center of the clock face, and the other at `handLength` distance from that point) and draws a line between them.

With your helper method in place, you can use it to create the clock hands. Replace the stub of `layoutSecondHandLayer` in **WatchView.swift** with the code below:

```
//Creates the second hand layer
func layoutSecondHandLayer() {
  if secondHandLayer == nil {
  secondHandLayer = createClockHand(CGPointMake(0.5, 1.0),
handLength: 20.0, handWidth: 4.0, handAlpha: 1.0, handColor:
secondHandColor)
  layer.addSublayer(secondHandLayer)
  }
}
```

Here you call the `createClockHand` method you just wrote with some hardcoded values representing the second hand.

Once you've added this implementation, set `Enable Clock Second Hand` to **On** and set the `Second Hand Color` to red, and you should see the second hand appear as in the screenshot below:

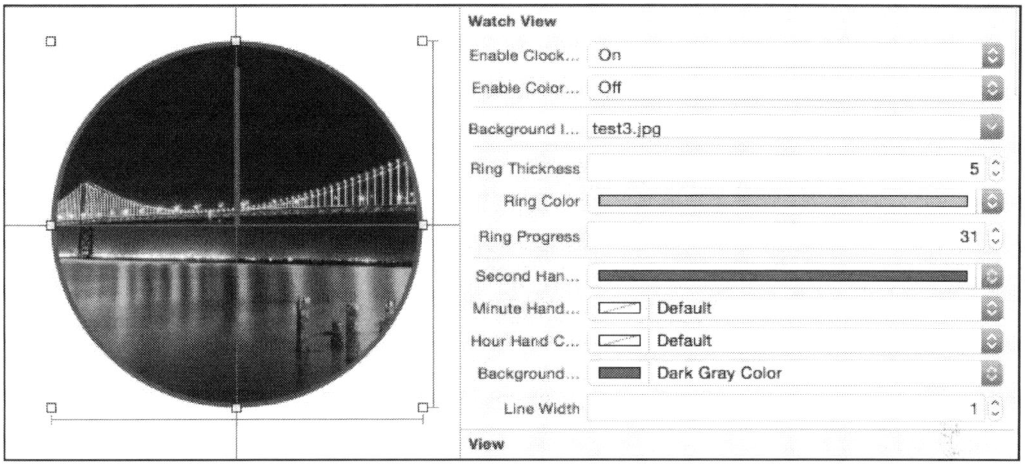

Now replace the stub `layoutMinuteHandLayer` with the following code:

```
func layoutMinuteHandLayer() {
  if minuteHandLayer == nil {
    minuteHandLayer = createClockHand(CGPointMake(0.5, 1.0),
handLength: 26.0, handWidth: 7.0, handAlpha: 1.0, handColor:
minuteHandColor)
    layer.addSublayer(minuteHandLayer)
  }
}
```

This calls the `createClockHand` method you wrote earlier with some different values for the minute hand.

Finally, replace the stub `layoutHourHandLayer` with the code below:

```
func layoutHourHandLayer() {
  if hourHandLayer == nil {
    hourHandLayer = createClockHand(CGPointMake(0.5, 1.0),
handLength: 52.0, handWidth:7.0, handAlpha: 1.0, handColor:
hourHandColor)
    layer.addSublayer(hourHandLayer)
  }
}
```

Set the minute hand to white and the hour hand to blue. You'll then see all three hands (drawn on top of each other) in Interface Builder:

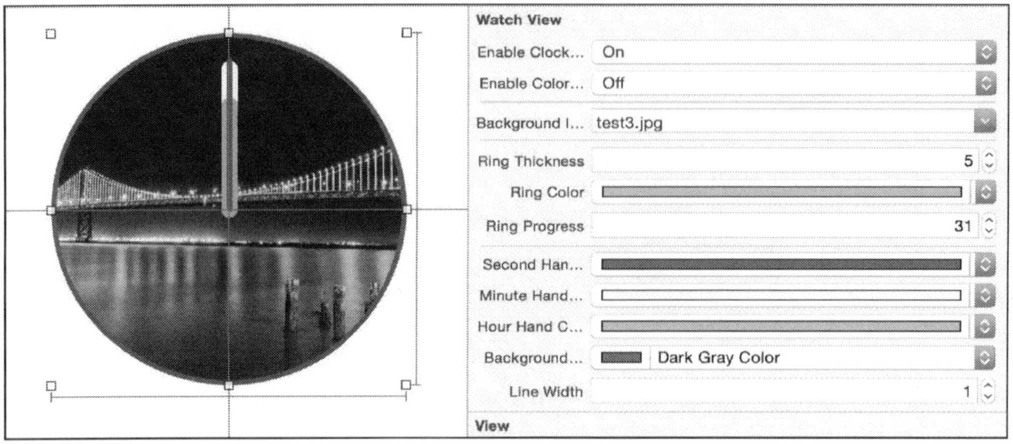

You've completed the entire analog layer stack for your watch as shown below:

There's just a few things left to take care of. Since you have two ways to represent the seconds on your watch, you'll need some mechanism to toggle between them.

Hiding watch layers selectively

Recall the two `@IBInspectable Bool` variables you added at the start of this chapter: `enableClockSecondHand` and `enableColorBackground`, each of which have property observers that call `updateLayerProperties`. `enableClockSecondHand` should hide the ring layer and show the second hand if set to True, and vice versa if the value is set to False. Finally, `enableColorBackground` should show the colored background layer when set to True, or show the image background layer when set to False.

Replace the stub methods in **WatchView.swift** found below the comment: `//MARK: Hide components of the watch`:

```
//Hides image background layer
func setHideImageBackground(willHide: Bool) {
  if backgroundImageLayer != nil {
  backgroundImageLayer.hidden = willHide
  }
}
//Hides the clock second hand
func setHideSecondClockHand(willHide: Bool) {
  if secondHandLayer != nil {
    secondHandLayer.hidden = willHide
  }
}
//Hides the ring layer
func setHideRingLayer(willHide: Bool) {
  if ringLayer != nil {
    ringLayer.hidden = willHide
  }
}
```

The code snippet above is pretty straightforward. Since a `CALayer` has a `hidden` property, you use it to hide or show the various components of the watch.

Now you need to execute these methods in `updateLayerProperties`. Whenever `enableClockSecondHand` or `enableColorBackground` is set, the property observer in Swift makes note of this and executes `updateLayerProperties()`.

Add the following code to `updateLayerProperties`(), immediately following the `if ringLayer` condition.

```
// If user toggles between second hand and ring progress
indicator
if enableClockSecondHand == true {
  setHideSecondClockHand(false)
  setHideRingLayer(true)
} else if enableClockSecondHand == false {
  setHideSecondClockHand(true)
  setHideRingLayer(false)
} else {
  setHideRingLayer(true)
  setHideSecondClockHand(true)
```

```
}
//Handles toggling between color background and image
background.
if enableColorBackground == true {
  setHideImageBackground(true)
} else {
  setHideImageBackground(false)
}
```

Here you simply call the methods to hide or show the appropriate layers based on the values set by the user.

Head back to Interface Builder and change `enableSecondClockHand` to Off; you'll see the second hand disappear and the circular indicator take its place.

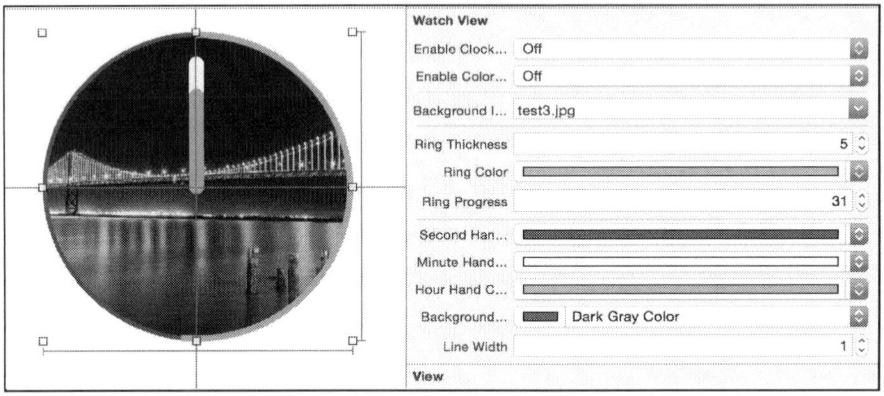

Set **Enable Color Background** to On and the background image will disappear and show the background color of the control instead.

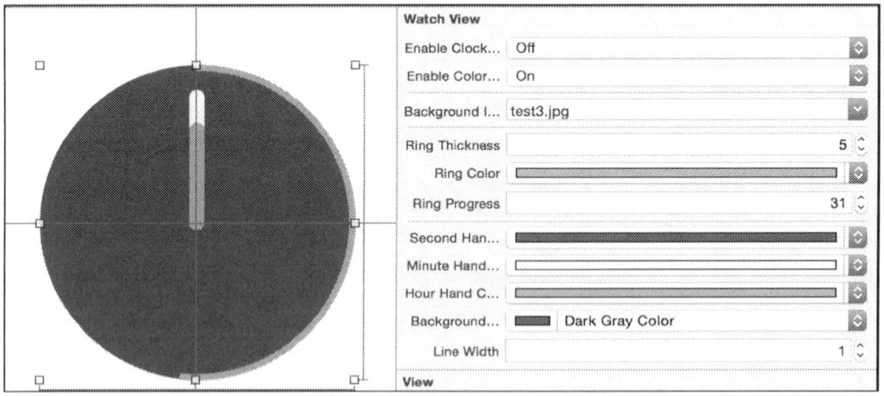

Now that you have finished creating all the components of your control, beautify your watch by changing a few properties in the attributes inspector to the ones shown below:

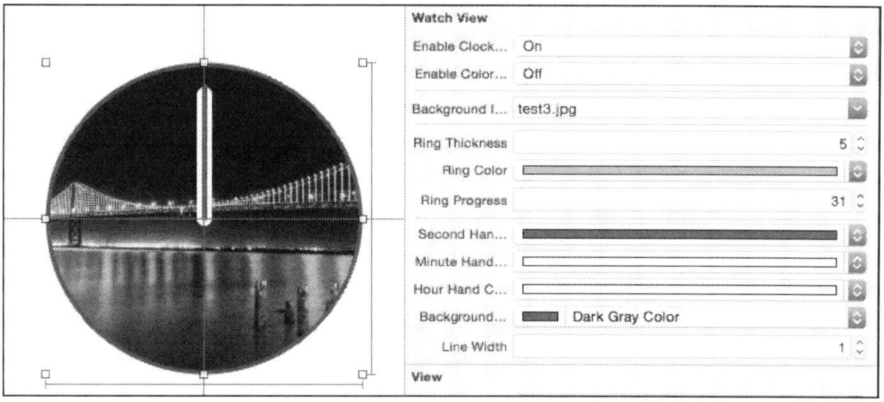

Showing the current time

You have everything ready for your custom watch control; you can customize the color, toggle between various design options, and set an image background to make your watch beautiful. But how useful is a watch that can't tell the time? Time to make this puppy tick.

Add the following properties after the `lineWidth` property:

```
//What makes the clock ticky tick :]
var timer = NSTimer()
var currentTimeZone: String = "Asia/Singapore"
```

You're using an instance of `NSTimer` to operate the clock. It's also a good idea to keep track of the timezone for this watch control; this way you can have multiple watch controls showing the time in various global timezones.

Replace the stub `startTimeWithTimeZone(timezone:)` in **WatchView.swift** with the code below:

```
//Start and Stop Time Controls
func startTimeWithTimeZone(timezone: String) {
  //Set the current time zone selected
  endTime()                          //1
  currentTimeZone = timezone         //2
```

```
    timer = NSTimer.scheduledTimerWithTimeInterval(1.0, target:
self, selector: "animateAnalogClock", userInfo: nil, repeats:
true) //3
}
```

Here's what above code does:

1. Ends the previous time in case anything is running.
2. Sets the time zone to the passed-in time zone.
3. Starts a timer to perform animations related to analog design components. This includes hour, minute, second, and ring layers.

All you need to do to make the clock tick is call `startTimeWithTimeZone(timezone:)`.

Replace the stub `endTime` in **WatchView.swift** with the following code:

```
func endTime() {
  timer.invalidate()
}
```

All this code snippet does is remove the timer from the current run loop.

Next add the code snippet below after `//MARK: Helper Methods` in **WatchView.swift**:

```
func grabDateComponents(dateString: String) -> [String] {
  let dateArray = dateString.componentsSeparatedByString(":")
  return dateArray
}
```

This returns an array of date strings separated by the ":" component.

Replace the `animateAnalogClock()` in **WatchView.swift** with the following:

```
//The stuff that makes the clock just tick
func animateAnalogClock() {
  //Get today's time
  let now = NSDate() //1
  //Createa a date formatter, and set the time zone selected by
the user.
  let dateFormatter = NSDateFormatter() //2
  dateFormatter.timeZone = NSTimeZone(name: currentTimeZone) //3
  dateFormatter.dateFormat = "hh:mm:ss" //4
  //Extract the hour, minute, and second from the date string
```

```
  let dateComponents =
grabDateComponents(dateFormatter.stringFromDate(now)) //5
  //Convert string to integers
  //6
  let hours = dateComponents[0].toInt()
  let minutes = dateComponents[1].toInt()
  let seconds = dateComponents[2].toInt()
  //7
  //Calculate percentage to rotate clock hands by.
  let minutesIntoDay = CGFloat(hours!) * 60.0 +
CGFloat(minutes!)
  let pminutesIntoDay = CGFloat(minutesIntoDay) / (12.0 * 60.0)
  let minutesIntoHour = CGFloat(minutes!) / 60.0
  let secondsIntoMinute = CGFloat(seconds!) / 60.0
  //8
  if enableClockSecondHand == true {
    if secondHandLayer != nil {
      secondHandLayer.transform =
CATransform3DMakeRotation(CGFloat(M_PI * 2.0) *
secondsIntoMinute, 0, 0, 1)
    }
  } else {
  //9
    if ringLayer != nil {
      ringProgress = CGFloat(seconds!)
    }
  }
  //10
  if minuteHandLayer != nil {
    minuteHandLayer.transform =
CATransform3DMakeRotation(CGFloat(M_PI * 2) * minutesIntoHour,
0, 0, 1)
  }
  //11
  if hourHandLayer != nil {
    hourHandLayer.transform =
CATransform3DMakeRotation(CGFloat(M_PI * 2) * pminutesIntoDay,
0, 0, 1)
    }
}
```

Here's how the code breaks down:

1. Create a date object.
2. Create a date formatter.
3. Set the current time zone so the date formatter can get the correct time.

4. Specify the date format. You are only interested in the hour, minutes, and seconds.
5. Break up the date into hours, minutes, and seconds and returns it into an array.
6. Convert hour, minute, and second string into integers.
7. Convert the different time components in order to calculate the rotation of your hour, minute and second hands.
8. Check to see if the user has configured the control to show the ring progress indicator or the standard second hand. If the second hand is in use, rotate the rendered second hand once a second.
9. If the ring progress indicator is selected, update the `ringProgress` variable. Since this variable has a property observer, it calls `updateLayoutProperties` to update the `ringLayer's endStroke`.
10. Rotate the minute hand based on the percentage conversions.
11. Rotate the hour hand based on the percentage conversions.

Now that you are done with the analog watch control, hook it all up and see if it ticks!

Open **Main.storyboard**; ensure the Assistant Editor is open and that **ViewController** is selected in the right hand side like so:

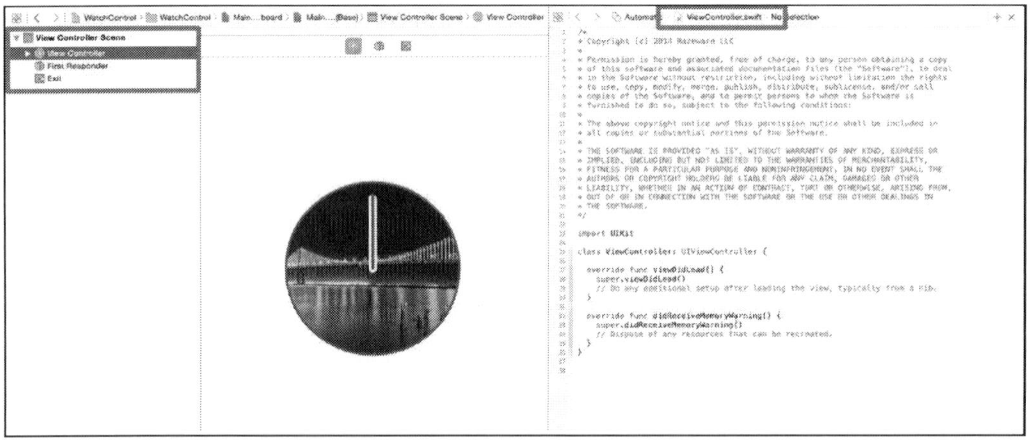

Ctrl-drag from the `WatchView` to `ViewController` class and name the resulting `IBOutlet` property **watchView**, as shown:

Once you have created an outlet, add the following code just under `super.viewDidLoad`:

```
watchView.startTimeWithTimeZone("Asia/Singapore")
```

The code above starts the `watchView's` timer and shows the current time in Singapore.

Now it's time for the one and only reason to launch the simulator. :]

Configure your clock settings however you like and build and run your app. You should see a ticking watch, reminding you that time flies when you're having fun with Live Rendering:

Where to go from here?

Live Rendering is one of the best features of Xcode 6. You can see your changes immediately, easily expose your custom control's properties and load sample data on the fly to build controls in a fraction of the time. Building custom controls will never be the same again. Hopefully this will bring developers and designers just a little bit closer than they were before.

In the next chapter, you'll further enhance your Watch Control and learn how to customize this control further by creating a full-blown World Watch application that the end user can customize to their heart's content.

Chapter 22: Intermediate Live Rendering

By Vincent Ngo

In Chapter 21, "Beginning Live Rendering", you created a great looking analog watch control using Live Rendering techniques and designable properties exposed through Interface Builder. It's time to take your control to the next level.

In this chapter, you'll gain more experience with Live Rendering as you enhance your watch control to support digital displays in addition to your current analog displays. You'll learn how to use existing UIKit controls to control the design of your watch as you create a full-blown application that displays multiple watches for time zones around the world – where each watch has its own custom design.

Finally, you can't let developers have all the fun with customization. You'll extend your control to let users configure the appearance of the watch themselves.

> **Note:** If you followed along with the previous chapter, you already know everything you need to know about Live Rendering to use it in your own controls.
>
> Therefore, this is an optional chapter. It contains a lot of review of Live Rendering and additional examples of working with a custom control, but not a lot of new information.
>
> If you don't feel like you need any review, feel free to skip forward to another chapter in the book. But if you want to see some more examples of Live Rendering, making custom controls, or how to make your watch control even more kick-ass, keep reading!

Getting started

I've provided you with a new starter project for this chapter. It includes the watch control you built in the previous chapter, along with a new user interface to allow users to create watch variants.

Open the starter project and build and run. You'll see the following:

The application isn't much to look at right now; it's just a blank collection view displaying a white background. Tap the + (Add) button in the top right hand corner to reveal your watch control, along with some settings buttons:

The settings buttons don't do anything yet. That's your job in this chapter – starting with the digital display of your watch.

At this point, please take a look at the starter project, and get familiar with what's inside. You'll find the watch control you built in the previous chapter in **Custom Control\WatchView.swift**. Once you're ready, get ready to get digital!

The digital watch display

Some people prefer digital style clocks, while others prefer analog faces. In this section, you'll update the app to accommodate both factions by creating an option to show the time in digital format.

The design of the analog and digital faces is shown below:

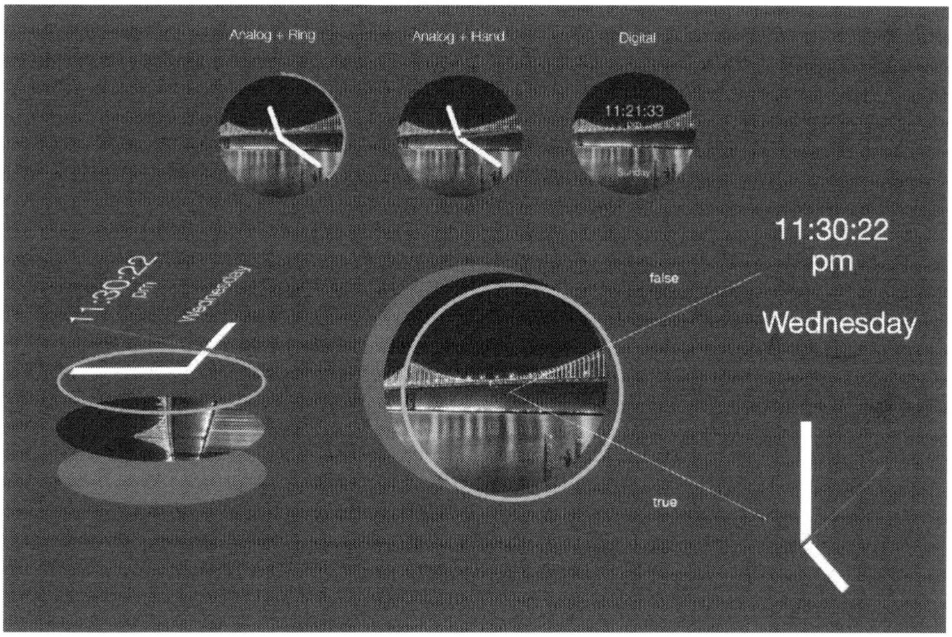

In the previous chapter, you built up the analog watch face in Interface Builder; You added the base, image, ring, and different clock hand layers step by step, layer-by-layer, stacking one upon each other.

You'll place the digital text layer on top of the analog clock hands. You'll use some Boolean properties to toggle the analog and digital displays.

Although tempting, it's not a great idea to create the `CALayers` for your view over and over again as the user toggles between analog and digital mode, as this is inefficient. Instead, you can simply hide the various `CALayers` or `CATextLayers` as required and avoid the overhead of continuous allocations.

Time's a-wasting; you should get coding!

Toggling between digital and analog modes

Open up **Main.Storyboard** in the left hand pane; on the right-hand side, open the Assistant Editor and select **WatchView.swift** as shown below:

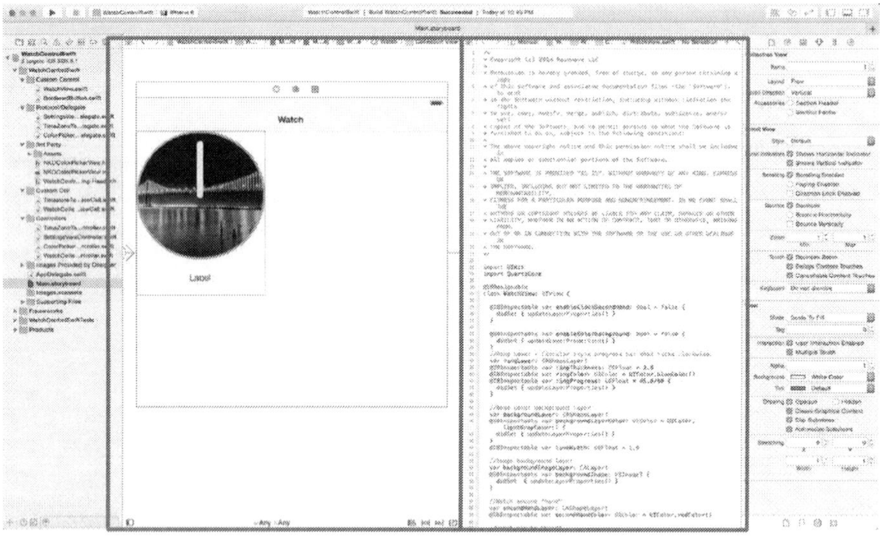

You'll continue building your watch control within the collection view controller's scene as shown above.

In **WatchView.swift**, place the following code above `enableClockSecondHand:`

```
//Toggles between analog or digital clock design
@IBInspectable var enableAnalogDesign: Bool = true {
  didSet { updateLayerProperties() }
}
```

This Boolean property will toggle between the analog and digital interfaces. You should see the property appear in the Attributes Inspector; set the **Enable Analog**, **Enable Clock Hands** and **Enable Color** all to **Default**, as shown:

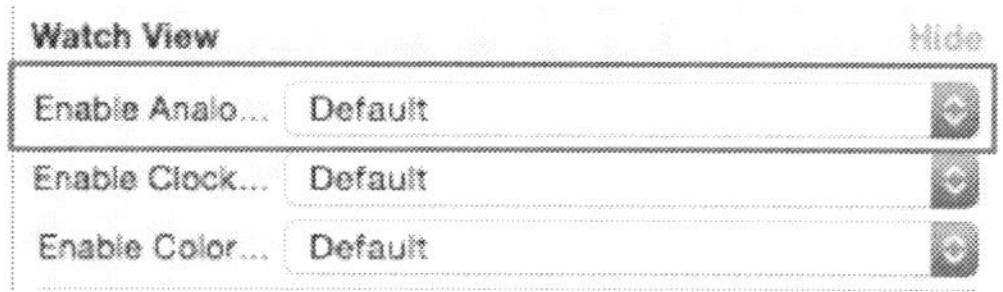

This sets each property to the default value set in code (true, false, and false, respectively).

Next, add the following method directly after `createAnalogClock()`:

```
func createDigitalClock() {
  layoutHourMinuteSecondText()
  layoutAmPmText()
  layoutWeekDayText()
}
```

`createDigitalClock()` creates the different digital watch components. Note that `layoutHourMinuteSecondText`, `layoutAmPmText`, and `layoutWeekDayText` have not been implemented yet; they are just placeholder methods that you will soon fill out with code.

It's always a good idea to break up methods into separate components; this makes the code easy to maintain and keeps it highly reusable. The separation of methods within `createDigitalClock` makes good design sense and the logic is organized and decoupled.

Still in the same file, locate `createClockFace()`, and replace the `createAnalogClock()` statement with the following code:

```
if enableAnalogDesign == true {
  createAnalogClock()
} else {
  createDigitalClock()
}
```

The code above simply checks the property `enableAnalogDesign` to see whether you should create the analog or digital clock face at startup.

Notice that when you change the **Enable Analog Design** property in the Attributes Inspector to **Off**, the clock hands disappear as shown on the following page:

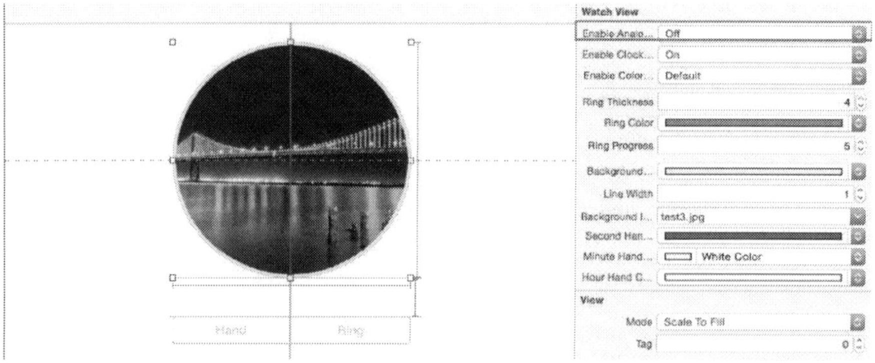

You don't see any digital components yet because the digital display methods are still stubs. Time to correct that.

Creating the text layers

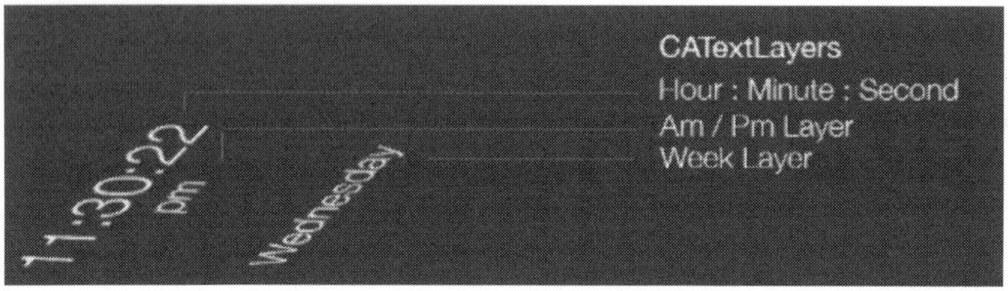

In **WatchView.swift**, add the following code after the `lineWidth` property:

```
var hourMinuteSecondLayer: CATextLayer!
var ampmLayer: CATextLayer!
var weekdayLayer: CATextLayer!
```

Just as you created the clock hands with a helper method, you'll use a helper method to create the various text components of your digital display.

Add the following code after `createClockHand()` in **WatchView.swift**:

```
func createTextLayer(string: String, fontSize: CGFloat,
  offset: CGFloat) -> CATextLayer {
    let layer = CATextLayer() // 1
    layer.font =
      UIFont(name: "HelveticaNeue-Light", size: fontSize) // 2
    layer.fontSize = fontSize // 3
    layer.frame = CGRectMake(0.0, 0.0,
```

```
      bounds.size.width/2.0,   bounds.size.height/2.0) // 4
    layer.position =
      CGPointMake(CGRectGetMidX(bounds), offset) // 5
    layer.string = string // 6
    layer.alignmentMode = kCAAlignmentCenter // 7
    layer.foregroundColor = UIColor.whiteColor().CGColor // 8
    layer.contentsScale = UIScreen.mainScreen().scale // 9
    return layer
}
```

Here's what the above method does:

1. Creates a `CATextLayer`.
2. Specifies the text layer's font.
3. Sets the font size.
4. Sets the layer's frame.
5. Sets the layer's position given the y-axis offset. This is so you can position each text element without overlapping.
6. Sets the text layer's string.
7. Centers the text.
8. Sets the color of text.
9. Sets the text layer scale to the scale of the device. If you don't scale the text layers yourself, the text may be a bit blurry, as iOS will stretch the text instead of scaling it.

Now you are ready to create each text component with your handy helper method.

Creating the hour/minute/second text layer

Replace the empty implementation of `layoutHourMinuteSecondText()` with the following code:

```
func layoutHourMinuteSecondText() {
  if hourMinuteSecondLayer == nil {
    hourMinuteSecondLayer = createTextLayer("00:00:00",
fontSize: bounds.size.height/8.5, offset:
bounds.size.height/2.0)
    layer.addSublayer(hourMinuteSecondLayer)
  }
}
```

Here you call the helper method you just wrote to create a text layer for the digital time, and add it as a sublayer.

Since you already added code to call this method from `createDigitalClock()`, Interface Builder happily renders your `hourMinuteSecondLayer` as shown below:

Now you need to layout the text of the AM/PM designator.

Creating the AM/PM designator layer

Replace the empty implementation of `layoutAmPmText()` with the following:

```
func layoutAmPmText() {
  if ampmLayer == nil {
    ampmLayer = createTextLayer("am", fontSize:
(bounds.size.height/13.0), offset: bounds.size.height/1.6)
   layer.addSublayer(ampmLayer)
  }
}
```

This creates another text layer for the AM/PM designator and adds it as a sublayer.

Once you've added the above code, Interface Builder updates your control with the AM/PM layer in place:

Your control is really coming together; your next task is to add the day of the week to the display.

Creating the weekday text layer

Replace the empty implementation of `layoutWeekDayText()` with the code below:

```
func layoutWeekDayText() {
  if weekdayLayer == nil {
    weekdayLayer = createTextLayer("Thursday", fontSize:
(bounds.size.height/13.0), offset: bounds.size.height)
    layer.addSublayer(weekdayLayer)
  }
}
```

Last but not least, you use your helper method to create a text layer for the day of the week, and add it as a subview.

As promised, the day of the week now shows up nestled at the bottom of the control:

That's the last element of your watch control. Toggle Enable Analog Design on and off using the Attributes Inspector and you'll see the control display change from analog to digital and back.

Now that you've constructed the digital portion of the watch control, it would be nice to hook it up to the button in the Settings screen so the user can toggle between analog and digital themselves.

As a developer, you can use the Attributes Inspector to change the `enableAnalogDesign` property's value at design time. But how could a user modify these properties at runtime?

Recall that enableAnalogDesign is a property observer; this means that setting enableAnalogDesign calls updateLayerProperties where you can handle state changes in your control at runtime. That should do the trick.

Hiding analog and digital components

Locate updateLayerProperties() in **WatchView.swift** and find these lines:

```
if enableClockSecondHand == true {
  setHideSecondClockHand(false)
  setHideRingLayer(true)
} else if enableClockSecondHand == false {
  setHideSecondClockHand(true)
  setHideRingLayer(false)
} else {
  setHideRingLayer(true)
  setHideSecondClockHand(true)
}
```

Replace those lines with the following:

```
// If user toggles between analog and digital, we want to hide
the components
if enableAnalogDesign == true { // 1
  setHideAnalogDesign(false) // 2
  setHideDigitalDesign(true) // 3

  // If user toggles between second hand and ring progress
indicator
  if enableClockSecondHand == true { // 4
    setHideSecondClockHand(false)
    setHideRingLayer(true)
  } else if enableClockSecondHand == false {
    setHideSecondClockHand(true)
    setHideRingLayer(false)
  } else {
    setHideRingLayer(true)
    setHideSecondClockHand(true)
  }
} else { // 5
  //Show digital design
  setHideDigitalDesign(false)
  setHideAnalogDesign(true)
}
```

Taking each numbered comment in turn:

1. Check to see if the user has selected analog design mode.
2. If so, show all of the analog clock components.
3. Hide the text layers as well.
4. This `if` statement switches between the second hand and the ring progress indicator.
5. If the user hasn't selected analog design mode, then hide all of the analog components and show the digital ones instead.

The methods to show and hide the digital and analog watch designs aren't implemented yet – that's your next job.

Replace `setHideAnalogDesign()` with the following code:

```
func setHideAnalogDesign(willHide: Bool) {
  if secondHandLayer != nil {
    secondHandLayer.hidden = willHide
  }
  if hourHandLayer != nil {
    hourHandLayer.hidden = willHide
  }
  if minuteHandLayer != nil {
    minuteHandLayer.hidden = willHide
  }
  if ringLayer != nil {
    ringLayer.hidden = willHide
  }
}
```

The method above simply hides every analog clock component.

Next replace the `setHideDigitalDesign()` with the following code:

```
func setHideDigitalDesign(willHide: Bool) {
  if hourMinuteSecondLayer != nil {
    hourMinuteSecondLayer.hidden = willHide
  }
  if ampmLayer != nil {
    ampmLayer.hidden = willHide
  }
  if weekdayLayer != nil {
    weekdayLayer.hidden = willHide
  }
}
```

The above method is the exact reverse of the previous one; it hides every text component of the digital watch design.

Back in Interface Builder, try turning **Enable Analog Design** on and off. You'll see the new text layers you created properly appear and disappear.

Now that you've taken care of the visual components of your digital watch, you now need to make this thing tick!

Animating the digital text layers

Your task is to incrementally update your text layers using a timer just as you did in your analog watch layers. However, you'll have to check whether the analog or digital display is selected in order to run the correct animation.

Replace `startTimeWithTimeZone(timezone:)` in **WatchView.swift** with the following:

```
//MARK: Start and Stop Time Controls
func startTimeWithTimeZone(timezone: String) {
  //Set the current time zone selected
  endTime()
  currentTimeZone = timezone
  if enableAnalogDesign == true {
    timer = NSTimer.scheduledTimerWithTimeInterval(1.0, target:
self, selector: "animateAnalogClock", userInfo: nil, repeats:
true)
  } else {
    timer = NSTimer.scheduledTimerWithTimeInterval(1.0, target:
self, selector: "animateDigitalClock", userInfo: nil, repeats:
true)
  }
}
```

The code above calls different timer methods: if the user chooses the analog design, an `NSTimer` kicks off a `runloop` and continually calls `animateAnalogClock`. However, if the user chooses the digital design, then you'll call `animateDigitalClock` instead.

Replace `animateDigitalClock()` with the following:

```
func animateDigitalClock() {
  //Get today's time.
  let now = NSDate() // 1
  //Create a date formatter, and set the time zone selected by
the user.
  let dateFormatter = NSDateFormatter() //2
  dateFormatter.timeZone = NSTimeZone(name: currentTimeZone) //3
  dateFormatter.dateFormat = "hh:mm:ss:a:EEEE" //4
  //Extract the hour, minute, and second from the date string
```

```
    let dateComponents =
grabDateComponents(dateFormatter.stringFromDate(now)) //5
    //Convert string to integers
    let hours = dateComponents[0].toInt() //6
    let minutes = dateComponents[1].toInt()
    let seconds = dateComponents[2].toInt()
    let ampm = dateComponents[3].lowercaseString
    let weekday = dateComponents[4]

    let hourminutesecondString = NSString(format:
"%02ld:%02ld:%02ld", hours!, minutes!, seconds!) //7
    if let hmsLayer = hourMinuteSecondLayer { //8
      hmsLayer.string = hourminutesecondString
    }
    if let amPm = ampmLayer { //9
      amPm.string = ampm
    }
    if let week = weekdayLayer { //10
      week.string = weekday
    }
}
```

The above method uses a run loop to update the text layers of the digital watch. Here's what the code does:

1. Creates an `NSDateFormatter` to format the `dateString` as you'd like it to appear.
2. Sets the current time zone for the given date.
3. Sets the date format.
4. Grabs the different components separated by a colon using your helper method.
5. Extracts the date components into different variables and grabs the current hour, minutes, seconds, AM/PM value and day of the week.
6. Combines the different time elements into one single colon delimited string.
7. Checks to see if the `hourMinuteSecondLayer` is `nil`. If not, it's safe to set the string of the layer.
8. Checks to see if the `ampmLayer` is `nil`. If not, it's safe to set the string of the layer.
9. Checks to see if `weekdayLayer` is `nil`. If not, it's safe to set the string of the layer.

Recreating the watch view when you pass data back from different view controllers or when you use reusable cells is not the best approach, since you'd have the overhead of recreating views.

Instead, you can just copy the state of the watch and let updateLayerProperties do its thing!

Copying the watch state

Replace copyClockSettings(clock:) in **WatchView.swift** with the following code:

```
func copyClockSettings(clock: WatchView) {
  enableAnalogDesign = clock.enableAnalogDesign
  enableClockSecondHand = clock.enableClockSecondHand
  enableColorBackground = clock.enableColorBackground

  ringThickness = clock.ringThickness
  ringColor = clock.ringColor
  ringProgress = clock.ringProgress
  hourHandColor = clock.hourHandColor
  minuteHandColor = clock.minuteHandColor
  secondHandColor = clock.secondHandColor
  backgroundImage = clock.backgroundImage
  lineWidth = clock.lineWidth
  backgroundLayerColor = clock.backgroundLayerColor
  currentTimeZone = clock.currentTimeZone
}
```

Here you simply update the current clock settings based on another clock view. This will be useful when you want to make one clock look like another, like you will do shortly.

Fleshing out the world clock app

You may have noticed that on the launch of your app, there's not much to look at besides a white screen.

You're going to change this by providing some sample watches for the user on first run.

The main view controller can display a collection of watches, each with their own time zones and analog or digital displays. The Add button in the top right hand corner will eventually add new watches to the display once you add the supporting code.

Pre-populating sample watches

Open **WatchCollectionViewController.swift** and add the following code after `prepareForSegue`:

```
//We are going to create 3 watch faces to show when the app
first launches
func createDefaultWatches() -> [WatchView] {
  let watch1 = WatchView(frame: CGRectZero)
  watch1.enableAnalogDesign = true
  watch1.enableClockSecondHand = true
  watch1.ringThickness = 2.0
  watch1.ringColor = UIColor(red: 97.0/255.0, green:
171.0/255.0, blue: 250.0/255.0, alpha: 1.0)
  watch1.ringProgress = 45.0
  watch1.hourHandColor = UIColor.whiteColor()
  watch1.minuteHandColor = UIColor.whiteColor()
  watch1.secondHandColor = UIColor.redColor()
  watch1.backgroundImage = UIImage(named: "test2.jpg")
  watch1.currentTimeZone = "Asia/Singapore"
  watch1.lineWidth = 1.0
  watch1.ringThickness = 4.0

  let watch2 = WatchView(frame: CGRectZero)
  watch2.copyClockSettings(watch1)
  watch2.currentTimeZone = "America/Chicago"
  watch2.backgroundImage = UIImage(named: "test1.jpg")
  watch2.enableClockSecondHand = false

  let watch3 = WatchView(frame: CGRectZero)
  watch3.copyClockSettings(watch1)
  watch3.currentTimeZone = "America/New_York"
  watch3.backgroundImage = UIImage(named: "test3.jpg")
  watch3.enableAnalogDesign = false

  let listOfWatches = [watch1, watch2, watch3]
  return listOfWatches
}
```

This code snippet creates three different `WatchViews`; the second and third watches copy the state of the first watch and modify some of the copied properties to make the watches look different. Once you've created the watches, bundle them up in an array and return that to the caller.

`listOfClocks` in `WatchTableViewController` is currently initialized as an empty array. Add the following code to `viewDidLoad()` as shown below:

```
override func viewDidLoad() {
  super.viewDidLoad()
  self.listOfClocks = self.createDefaultWatches()
}
```

This view controller already contains code to present the clocks inside the `listOfClocks` array inside a collection view. Build and run your app; it should look like the following screenshot:

Ready for the final stretch? You just need to implement the code that adds new watches to the table view. Fortunately, `SettingsViewController` does just that!

Customizing the watch view

`SettingsViewController` gives you the opportunity to customize your watch with beautiful image backgrounds and colors, or switch between analog and digital displays. Here's what the view controller looks like in your Storyboard:

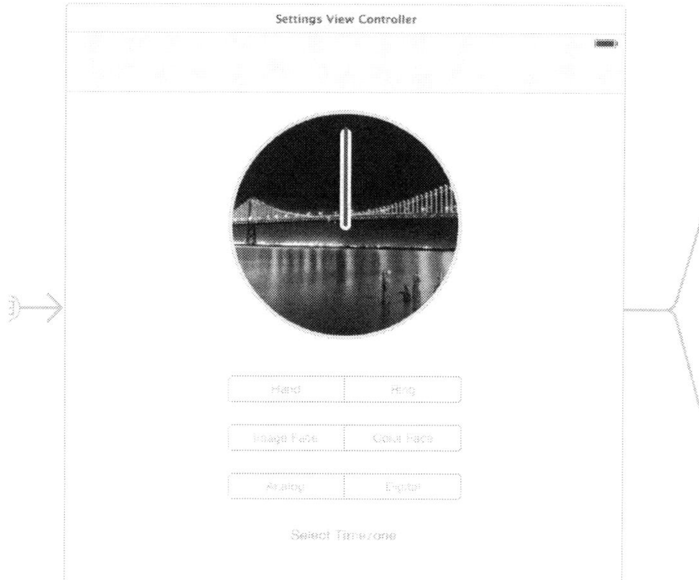

Currently, nothing in the `SettingsViewController` works except for the **Select Timezone** button, which takes you to a list of time zones. Your next task is to flesh out the methods behind each configuration setting.

Implementing user configurable backgrounds

The first item to implement is a user-configurable background. Replace the stub `selectedClockBackground()` in **SettingsViewController.swift** with the following code:

```
@IBAction func selectedClockBackground(sender: AnyObject) {
  let segmentedControler: UISegmentedControl = sender as
UISegmentedControl
  let selectedSegment = segmentedControler.selectedSegmentIndex
  if selectedSegment == 0 {
  if
!UIImagePickerController.isSourceTypeAvailable(UIImagePickerCont
rollerSourceType.SavedPhotosAlbum) {
UIAlertView(title: "Error", message: "Cannot access Saved Photos
on device :[", delegate: nil, cancelButtonTitle: "OK").show()
  } else {
```

```
    let photoPicker: UIImagePickerController =
UIImagePickerController()
                    photoPicker.delegate = self
                  photoPicker.allowsEditing = true
                     photoPicker.sourceType =
UIImagePickerControllerSourceType.PhotoLibrary
        self.showDetailViewController(photoPicker, sender: self)
    }
  } else { //segment = 1
  performSegueWithIdentifier("showColorPicker", sender: self)
  faceTypeSegmentedControl.selectedSegmentIndex = 0
  }
}
```

The code above first checks that one of the segments in the "image face" and "colored face" segmented control is selected.

If the "image face" segment is selected, the `UIImagePickerViewController` appears so the user can select the photo they wish to use for the background.

If the "color face" segment is selected, `ColorPickerViewController` appears instead. This view controller has already been included in your starter project.

How do you know when a user selects a color or picks an image? Delegate methods, of course! Selecting an image calls `UIImagePickerViewControllerDelegate`, while `ColorPickerViewController` calls its own delegate methods. Let's implement these.

First, you'll add the color picker view's delegate. In **SettingsViewController.swift**, replace `didSelectColor(color:)` with the following:

```
//ColorPicker Controller Delegate
func didSelectColor(color: UIColor!) {
  //Enable color background
  if color != nil {
    watchView.backgroundLayerColor = color
    selectedColor = color
    watchView.setNeedsLayout()
    watchView.layoutIfNeeded()
    watchView.enableColorBackground = true
    faceTypeSegmentedControl.selectedSegmentIndex = 1
  } else {
    faceTypeSegmentedControl.selectedSegmentIndex = 0
  }
}
```

The above code checks to see if the color is `nil`, which means the user didn't select a color, but hit the Back button instead. In this case, set the segmented control back to the image face.

If the color is not `nil`, then set `enableColorBackground` to `true` which in turn triggers `updateLayoutProperties()` in `WatchView` due to the property observer. This has the end result of hiding the background image layer.

Next, add the image picker's delegate. Replace `imagePickerController:didFinishPickingMediaWithInfo` in **SettingsViewController.swift** with the following:

```
//Invoked to open UIImagePicker to select an image.
func imagePickerController(picker: UIImagePickerController!,
didFinishPickingMediaWithInfo info: [NSObject : AnyObject]!) {
  picker.dismissViewControllerAnimated(true, completion: {
  self.watchView.backgroundImage =
info[UIImagePickerControllerEditedImage] as? UIImage
  self.selectedImage = info[UIImagePickerControllerEditedImage]
as? UIImage
  self.watchView.enableColorBackground = false

  //Update settings clock to show correct results
  self.watchView.setNeedsLayout()
  })
}
```

The above method executes once the user selects an image; the selected image then becomes `watchView's backgroundImage`. You then disable the color background by setting `enableColorBackground` to `false`. Once again, the property observer calls `updateLayoutProperties` to hide the color background layer.

Build and run your project; navigate to the Settings view controller and try selecting an image or a solid background color for the watch face. The screenshot on the next page shows the included `ColorPickerViewController`:

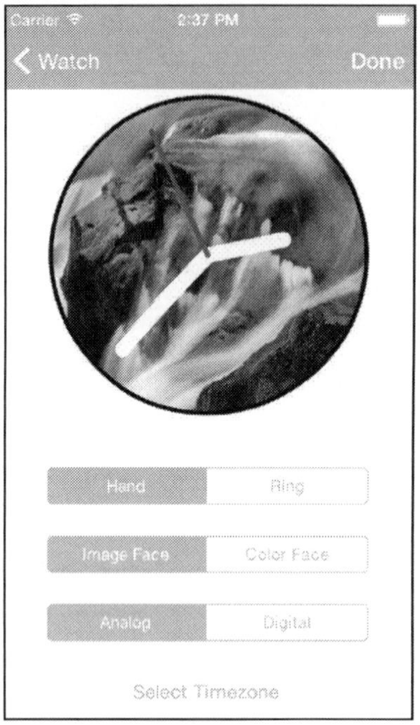

Implementing user configurable displays

Next you'll need to implement some functionality that will let the user switch between analog and digital displays.

Replace `selectClockDesign` in **SettingsViewController.swift** with the following:

```
@IBAction func selectClockDesign(sender: AnyObject) {
  let segmentedControler: UISegmentedControl = sender as
UISegmentedControl
  let selectedSegment = segmentedControler.selectedSegmentIndex
  if selectedSegment == 0 {
    watchView.enableAnalogDesign = true
  } else {
    watchView.enableAnalogDesign = false
  }

watchView.startTimeWithTimeZone(NSTimeZone.localTimeZone().name)
  watchView.setNeedsLayout()
  watchView.layoutIfNeeded()
}
```

Selecting index 0 – analog – sets `enableAnalogDesign` in `watchView` to `true`. Once again, the observer on this property calls `updateLayerProperties()` which hides all of the digital clock components and shows the analog components. However, if the user selects index 1 – digital – then you set `enableAnalogDesign` to `false` which triggers a call to `updateLayerProperties()` which hides the analog components and shows the digital ones instead.

Build and run your app; toggle between the Analog and Digital settings and you'll see the display change accordingly as shown below:

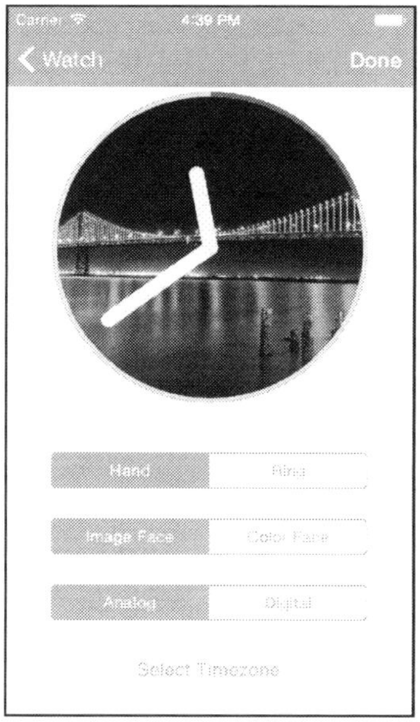

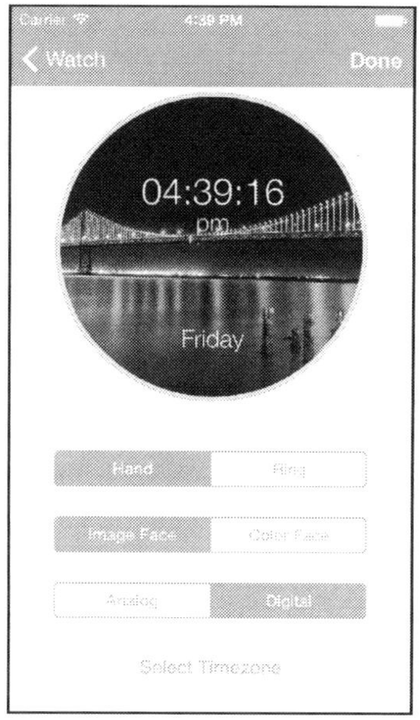

Implementing user configurable seconds indicators

Finally, you need a mechanism to let the user choose between the ring progress indicator and the standard second hand.

Replace the contents of `selectClockSecondsType(sender:)` in **SettingsViewController.swift** with the following:

```
@IBAction func selectClockSecondsType(sender: AnyObject) {
  let segmentedControler: UISegmentedControl = sender as
UISegmentedControl
  let selectedSegment = segmentedControler.selectedSegmentIndex

  if selectedSegment == 0 {
    watchView.enableClockSecondHand = true
```

```
    } else {
      self.watchView.enableClockSecondHand = false
    }
    watchView.setNeedsLayout()
    watchView.layoutIfNeeded()
  }
```

Here you set `enableClockSecondHand` to true or false, depending on the selection made by the user.

Build and run your app; toggle between the ring indicator and second hand to see each one in action as shown below:

Implementing user configurable time zones

The **Select Timezone** button appears operational, but it won't actually pass through the time zone selection until you implement the necessary delegate methods.

Replace `didSelectATimeZone(timezone:)` in **SettingsViewController.swift** with the following:

```
  func didSelectATimeZone(timezone: String) {
    selectedTimeZone = timezone
    watchView.currentTimeZone = timezone
    navigationController!.popViewControllerAnimated(true)
    watchView.startTimeWithTimeZone(timezone)
  }
```

The above method sets the time zone of `watchView` to the user's selection, then pops the `TableViewController` off the navigation controller's stack. It then calls `startTimeWithTimeZone(timezone:)` to display the new time for the selected time zone.

Build and run your project; tap Select Timezone and select any entry in the list:

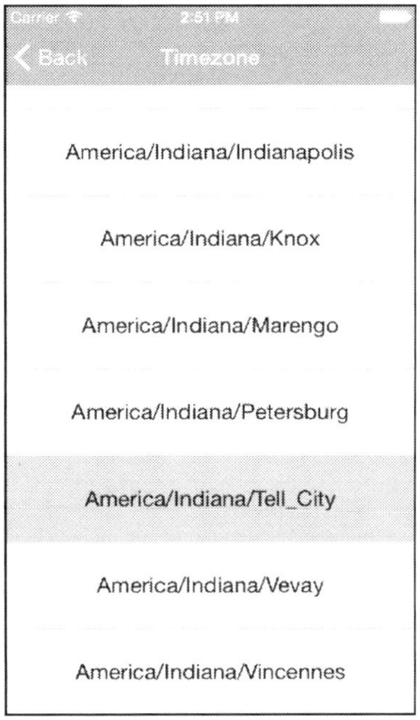

Upon selecting a time zone, you should see the watch control animate all the way to the correct time.

Adding new watches to the list view

You've done all of the heavy lifting to make your watch control fully configurable, but there's one critical piece missing: you need to implement the Done button logic to actually add the watch control to your list!

Replace `addWatchToList()` in **SettingsViewController.swift** with the following:

```
func addWatchToList() {
  watchView.endTime()
  delegate?.didCreateNewClockSettings(watchView)
  navigationController!.popViewControllerAnimated(true)
}
```

The code above ends the current time counter; this is because you don't want to have multiple timers running in the background. After you stop the time you then invoke the protocol `didCreateNewClockSettings()` which notifies `WatchTableViewController` that you've created a new watch. Finally, pop `SettingsViewController` off the navigation stack to return to the list view of watches.

Build and run your app; click the Add button, use the segmented controllers and pickers to create the customized watch of you choice, then click Done. Your watch should appear in the list as shown in the example screenshot below:

Where to go from here?

Live Rendering is a tremendous improvement for custom control designers, as you never feel like you're designing with a blindfold on – and not having to launch the simulator means you can spend more building awesome controls and less time waiting for the simulator to spin up. As well, being able to expose your control's properties right in Interface Builder makes it easy for other developers to customize your control to fit their app.

If you're looking to experiment with Live Rendering and adding designable properties to existing controls, check out the following tutorials on custom controls that could use your special Live Rendering touch:

http://www.raywenderlich.com/56885/custom-control-for-ios-tutorial-a-reusable-knob

http://www.raywenderlich.com/36288/how-to-make-a-custom-control

As another next step, take a look at other great controls people have created on Github that weren't created with Live Rendering in mind and expose their properties through Interface Builder. What kinds of customization can you dream up for these controls?

Chapter 23: Handoff

By Soheil Moayedi Azarpour

Consider the following scenario: you're having your coffee in the morning while scrolling through your mail on your iPhone. You see an important email from your developer friend, so you open it and read it.

You quickly realize that you'll need do a bit of research on your Mac and respond as soon as you can to the email. You stroll to your laptop, open Mail, and start scrolling through the pile of emails in your inbox trying to find the correct one...

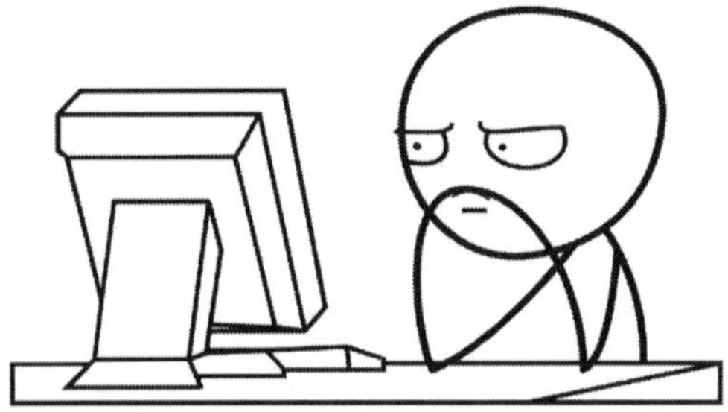

I could swear that email was here somewhere...

It takes a frustrating amount of time to find that email and get back to where you were on your iOS device. Sadly, this kind of problem was all-to-common for iOS and OS X users – until now, with a new technology called Handoff!

Handoff is designed to facilitate the transfer of user activities between multiple devices. Handoff lets you continue an activity uninterrupted when you switch from one device to another – without the need to reconfigure either device.

In this example, Handoff would keep your iOS and OSX devices in synch so that when you switch to your laptop you can pick right up with the email you were just reading!

Jumping Jobs on a pogo stick! Is it really true?

No, it isn't something from The Twilight Zone – you too can add this feature to your iOS and OS X apps in iOS 8 and Yosemite, using the new Handoff APIs.

In this chapter you'll learn the basic workings of Handoff and how to use it on iOS with a non-document-based app.

Handoff overview

Before you dive into the code, it's important to get a high level overview of some important Handoff concepts. In this section, you will learn about the following concepts:

1. **Getting started**: Learn if your devices are Handoff-compatible and run a basic test to make sure things are working.
2. **User activities**: Learn about the core unit of work with Handoff: user activities.
3. **Activity types**: Learn how you can set an "activity type" on a user activity and what that means.

Getting started

Not only can Handoff transfer your current activity from an iOS to an OS X device, but it can also transfer your current activity between iOS devices. For example, if you are reading an email on your iPhone and want to continue reading it on your iPad, Handoff can help with that.

In this chapter, you will get started by implementing Handoff between two iOS apps.

At the time of writing this chapter, Handoff does not work on the iOS simulator. Therefore, to follow along with this chapter, you will need two Handoff-compatible iOS devices. Before you begin coding, you should run a quick test to make sure that your devices are Handoff-compatible, and that Handoff is working OK.

Device compatibility: iOS

To check whether your iOS device is Handoff compatible, go to **Settings** and select **General** from the list. If you see **Handoff & Suggested Apps** in the list, your device is Handoff compatible. The following screenshots show General settings menu of an iPhone 5s (Handoff compatible) and an iPad 3rd Gen (not Handoff compatible), respectively.

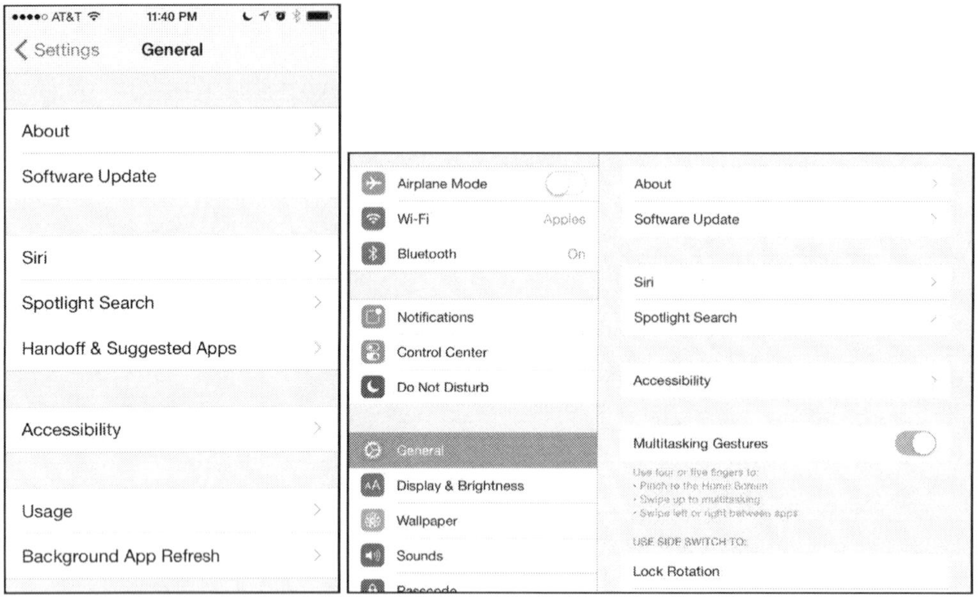

Handoff functionality depends on few things:

1. **An iCloud account**: You must be logged in to the same iCloud account on each device you wish to use Handoff.
2. **Bluetooth LE 4.0**: Handoff broadcasts activities via Bluetooth LE signals, so both the broadcasting and receiving devices must have Bluetooth LE 4.0 support.
3. **iCloud paired**: Devices should have been already paired through iCloud. When you sign into your iCloud account on Handoff compatible devices, each device is paired with other Handoff compatible devices. This is where the magic happens.

At this time, make sure that you have two Handoff compatible devices running iOS 8 or later that are logged onto the same iCloud account.

Handoff test: iOS

Next, let's run a quick test to make sure that Handoff is working between your two devices.

1. Put the first device to sleep by pressing the Power button.
2. Open **Safari** app on the second device and navigate to one of your favorite websites, like www.raywenderlich.com.

3. Press the **Home** button on the first device. In about 2 seconds or so Safari's icon appears on the bottom left corner of the screen:

Swipe up on Safari's icon. If your device has a passcode, you are prompted to enter the passcode. Once you enter your passcode, Safari app is launched and you are navigated to the same website.

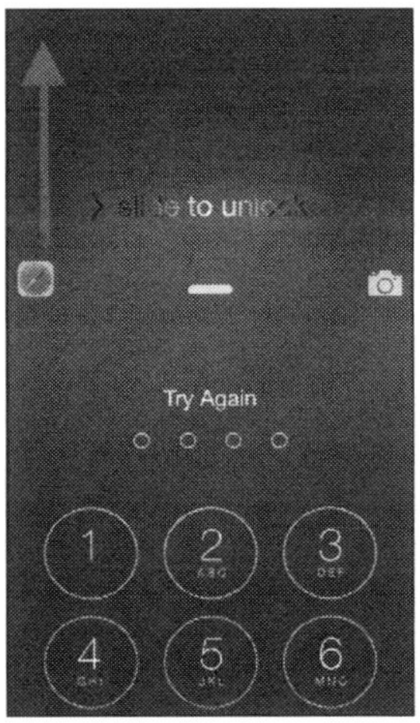

If the quick test above didn't work and you are sure that your devices are Handoff compatible, chances are the devices are not iCloud paired. Unfortunately, there is no way to tell if two devices are paired through iCloud.

But there are a few things you can try to force the devices to sync with iCloud, and hopefully they will be paired:

1. Make sure they are both signed into the same iCloud account.
2. Make sure they are reliably connected to the Internet.
3. Turn the devices off and then turn them back on.

If that didn't work, try signing off from iCloud on both devices, then sign back on to the same iCloud account on both devices.

Once you've verified that Handoff is working on your iOS devices, you are almost ready to dive into the code. But first, you should learn about some important high-level Handoff concepts.

User activities

Handoff is based on the concept of a **user activity**, which is a stand-alone collective unit of information that can be handed off without any dependencies on any other information.

Consider the task of writing an email. To continue the email on another device, the activity must include the recipient, subject, message body, any attachments and possibly even the insertion point of the cursor at the time the email is handed off.

The `NSUserActivity` class represents an instance of a user activity. It encapsulates the state of the application in a way that can be continued on other devices in a related application.

There are three ways to interact with `NSUserActivity` objects:

1. **Create user activity**: The originating app creates an `NSUserActivity` and calls `becomeCurrent()` on it to start the broadcasting process. Here's a quick example:

```
let activity =
```

```
  NSUserActivity(activityType: "com.razeware.shopsnap.view")
activity.title = "Viewing"
activity.userInfo =
  ["shopsnap.item.key": ["Apple", "Orange", "Banana"]]
self.userActivity = activity;
self.userActivity?.becomeCurrent()
```

You can use the `userInfo` dictionary of `NSUserActivity` to pass native data types or `NSCoding`-compliant custom objects to the receiving device. Native data types include `NSArray`, `NSData`, `NSDate`, `NSDictionary`, `NSNull`, `NSNumber`, `NSSet`, `NSString`, `NSUUID`, and `NSURL`. Passing `NSURL` can be a bit tricky; check out the **Best Practices** section of this chapter before using `NSURL` with Handoff.

2. **Update user activity**: Once an instance of `NSUserActivity` becomes current, the OS periodically invokes `updateUserActivityState(activity:)` on your topmost view controller to give you a chance to update the user activity. Here's an example:

```
override func updateUserActivityState(activity: NSUserActivity)
{
  let activityListItems = // ... get updated list of items
  activity.addUserInfoEntriesFromDictionary(
      ["shopsnap.item.key": activityListItems])
  super.updateUserActivityState(activity)
}
```

Notice that you don't set `userInfo` to a new dictionary or update it directly. Instead, you should use the convenience method `addUserInfoEntriesFromDictionary()`.

Later in this chapter, you'll learn how to force the user activity to refresh on demand, or how to get a similar callback at the app delegate level.

3. **Receive user activity**: When your receiving app launches with a user activity from Handoff, the app delegate calls `application(:willContinueUserActivityWithType:)`. Note this method is not passed an instance of `NSUserActivity`, because it takes a while until Handoff downloads and transfers the `NSUserActivity` data to your app.

Later on, the following delegate callback invokes once the user activity has been downloaded:

```
func application(application: UIApplication!,
  continueUserActivity userActivity: NSUserActivity!,
  restorationHandler: (([AnyObject]!) -> Void)!) -> Bool {
    // Do some checks to make sure you can proceed
    if let window = self.window {
```

```
window.rootViewController?.restoreUserActivityState(userActivity
)
    }
    return true
}
```

You can then use the data stored in the `NSUserActivity` object to re-create the user's activity. This is where you will update your app so that it can continue the associated activity.

Activity types

In the example of creating a user activity, you may have noticed when you create a user activity, you must specify an activity type for the activity. An activity type is simply a unique string, usually in reverse DNS notation, like `com.razeware.shopsnap.view`.

Each app that is capable of receiving a user activity must declare the activity types that it will accept. This is much like declaring the URL schemes your app supports. For non-document based apps, activity types are listed under the `NSUserActivityTypes` key at the top level of Info.plist as shown below:

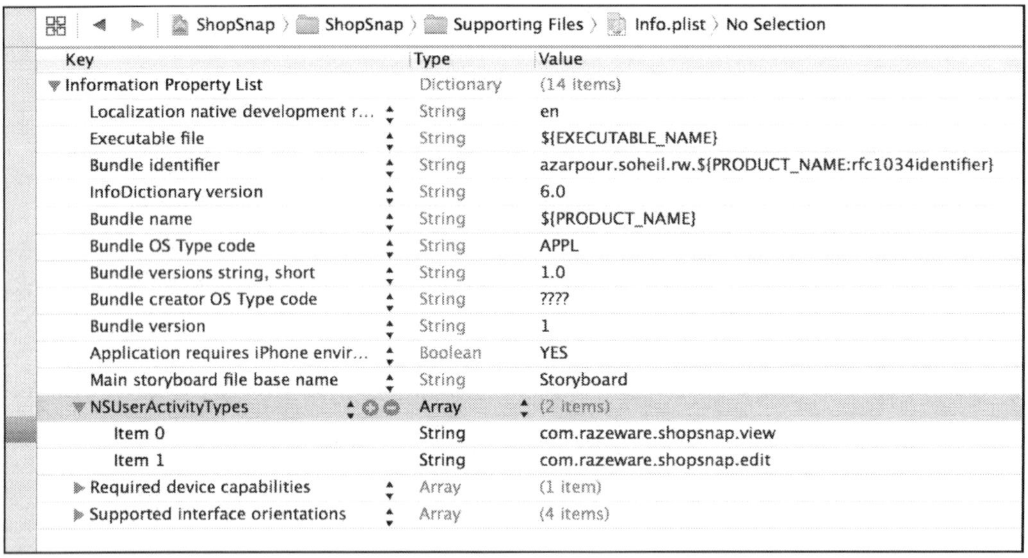

For an app to support a given activity, there are three requirements:

1. **Same team**. Both apps must originate from the same developer with the same developer Team ID.

2. **Same activity type**. The receiving app must have a `NSUserActivityTypes` entry for the activity type created by the sending app.

3. **Be signed**. Both apps must be distributed through the App Store or be signed with a Developer certificate.

Now that you've learned about the basics of user activities and activity types, let's dive in to an example!

The starter project

The starter project you'll use for the remainder of this chapter is called **ShopSnap**. Open the project file in Xcode and build and run in an iPhone simulator. You'll see the following screens:

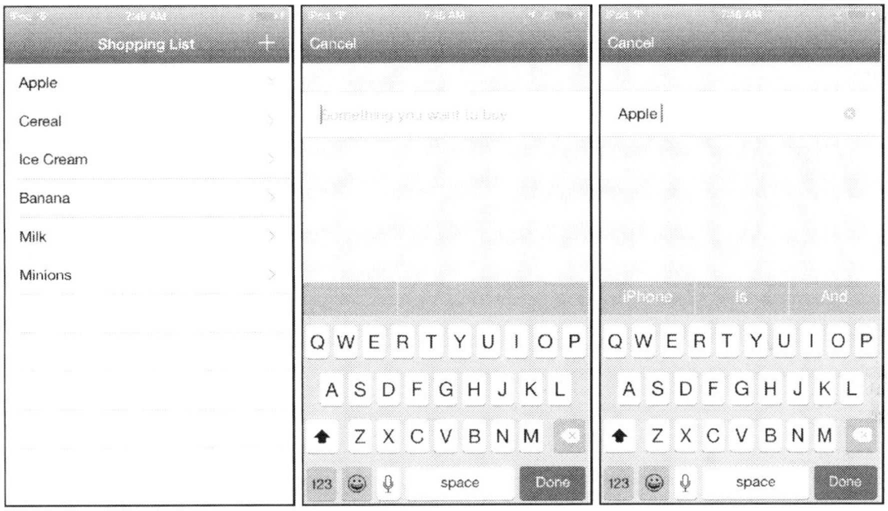

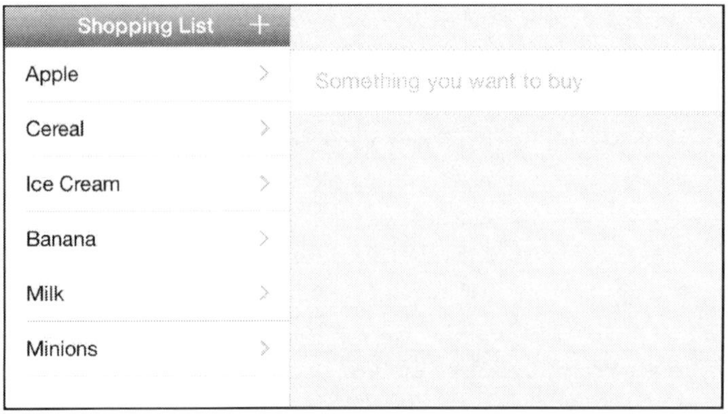

You can build a simple shopping list in this app. A shopping item is represented by a `String` and you store the shopping list as an Array of strings. Tapping the + button adds a new item to the list and swiping removes an item. To delete an entry while editing, tap the x button in the text field then tap **Done**.

You'll define two distinct user activities for this app:

1. **Viewing the list**. If the user is currently viewing the list, you'll Handoff the entire array of items.
2. **Adding or editing an item**. If the user is currently adding a new item, you'll Handoff an "edit" activity for a single item instead.

Setting your team

For Handoff to work, both the sending and receiving app must be signed by the same team. Since this app is both the sender and the receiver, this is simple!

Select your ShopSnap project, and in the general tab, switch the **Team** to your team:

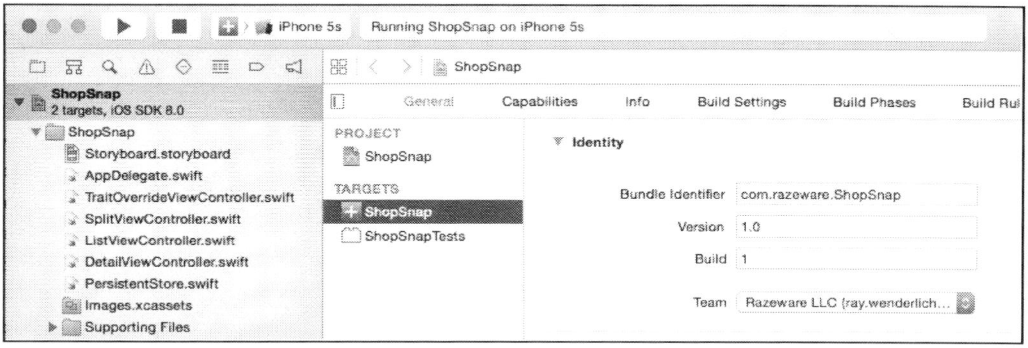

Build and run on one of your Handoff-compatible iOS devices to make sure it runs OK, then continue on.

Configuring activity types

The next step is to configure the activity types your app supports. Open **Supporting Files\Info.plist** and click on the + button that appears next to **Information Property List** to add a new item under the Information Property List dictionary like so:

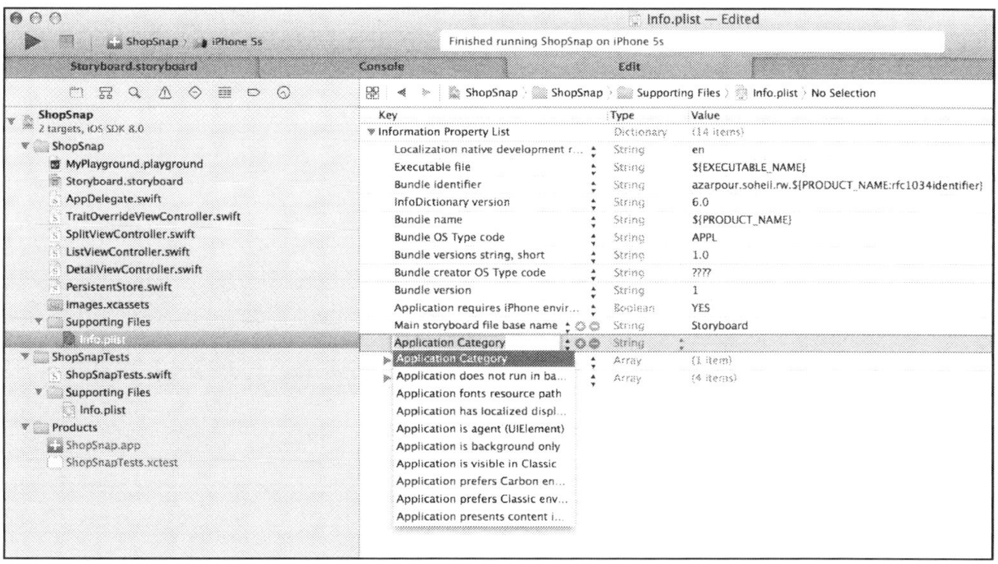

Enter NSUserActivityTypes for the key name and make it an Array type. When you're done, your new entry should appear as shown below:

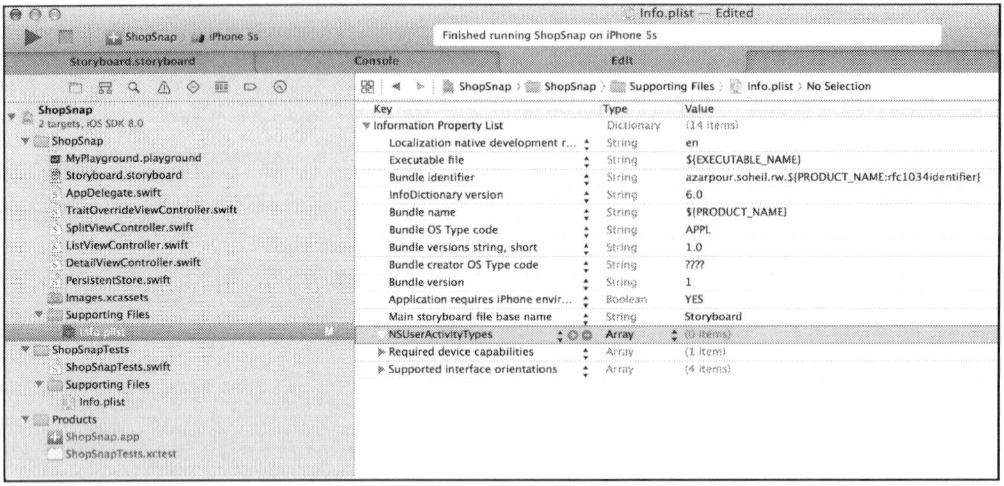

Add two items under NSUserActivityTypes (**Item 0** and **Item 1**) and set their types to String. Enter **com.razeware.shopsnap.view** for **Item 0**, and **com.razeware.shopsnap.edit** for **Item 1**.

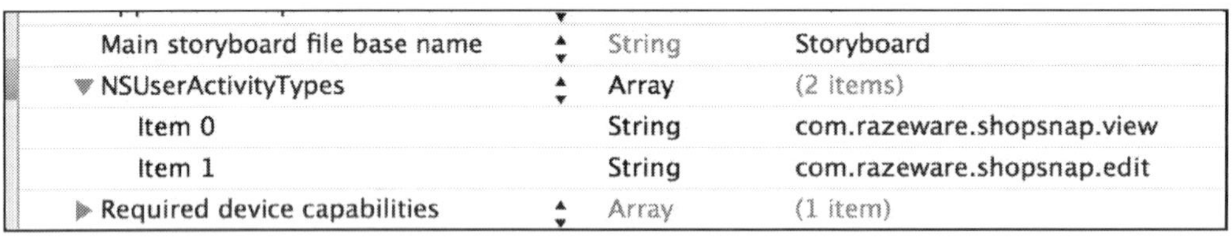

These are arbitrary activity types specific and unique to your app. Since you'll refer to them from multiple places in the app, it's good practice to add them as constants in a separate file.

Right-click on the **ShopSnap** group in the project navigator, select **New File \ iOS \ Source \ Swift File**. Name the class **Constants.swift** and ensure your new class is added to the **ShopSnap** target.

Add the following code to your class:

```
let ActivityTypeView = "com.razeware.shopsnap.view"
let ActivityTypeEdit = "com.razeware.shopsnap.edit"

let ActivityItemsKey = "shopsnap.items.key"
```

```
let ActivityItemKey  = "shopsnap.item.key"
```

Now you can use these constants for the two different activity types. You've also defined some constants for the keys you'll be using in the user activity's `userInfo` dictionary for convenience.

Quick end-to-end test

Now that you've registered your activity types, let's run a quick end-to-end test to make sure that your devices can communicate properly.

Open **ListViewController.swift** and add the following two functions:

```
// 1.
func startUserActivity() {
  let activity = NSUserActivity(activityType: ActivityTypeView)
  activity.title = "Viewing Shopping List"
  activity.userInfo = [ActivityItemsKey: ["Ice cream", "Apple",
"Nuts"]]
  userActivity = activity
  userActivity?.becomeCurrent()
}

// 2.
override func updateUserActivityState(activity: NSUserActivity)
{
  activity.addUserInfoEntriesFromDictionary([ActivityItemsKey:
["Ice cream", "Apple", "Nuts"]])
  super.updateUserActivityState(activity)
}
```

This is just a quick test where you hard code a user activity, to make sure that you can receive it OK on the other end.

Here is what the code above does:

1. `startUserActivity()` is a helper function that creates an instance of `NSUserActivity` with a hardcoded shopping list. Then it starts broadcasting that activity by calling `becomeCurrent()`.

2. After you call `becomeCurrent()`, OS will periodically call `updateUserActivityState()`. `UIViewController` inherits this method from `UIResponder`, and you should override this to update the state of your `userActivity` here.

Here you update the shopping list with the same hardcoded values as before, since this is just a test. Note that `addUserInfoEntriesFromDictionary` is the preferred way of mutating `userInfo` dictionary of `NSUserActivity`. You should always call `super.updateUserActivityState()` at the end.

Now you just need to start this method. Add the following line to the beginning of `viewDidLoad()`:

```
startUserActivity()
```

That's the minimum you need to start broadcasting – let's move on to receiving. Open **AppDelegate.swift** and add the following code:

```
func application(application: UIApplication!,
continueUserActivity userActivity: NSUserActivity!,
restorationHandler: (([AnyObject]!) -> Void)!) -> Bool {
  let userInfo = userActivity.userInfo as NSDictionary
  println("Received a payload via handoff: \(userInfo)")
  return true
}
```

This method on AppDelegate is called when everything goes well and a `userActivity` is successfully transferred. Here you log a message with the `userInfo` dictionary of the `userActivity`. You return `true` to indicate you handled the user activity. You will learn more about this in a bit.

That's it for a quick end-to-end test – let's try this out! There's a little bit of coordination required to get this working on two devices, so follow along carefully.

1. Install and run the app on your first device.
2. Install and run the app on your second device. Make sure that you are debugging the app in Xcode so you can see your `println()` output.

> **Note:** It is also useful to have the console logs open in this step so you can see any output from iOS, in case there is an issue with the connection. To see the console logs, go to **Window\Devices**, select your device, and select the icon in the lower left to expand the console area.

3. Put the second device to sleep by pressing the power button. On the same device, press the Home button. If everything works fine, you should see the ShopSnap app icon appear at the left bottom corner of the screen. From there you should be able to launch the app, and see the log message in Xcode's console:

```
Received a payload via handoff: {
    "shopsnap.items.key" =     (
        "Ice cream",
        Apple,
        Nuts
    );
}
```

If you don't see the app icon on the lock screen, close and re-open the app on the originating device. This forces the OS to restart broadcasting again. Also check the device console to see if there are any error messages from Handoff.

Creating the view activity

Now that you have a basic working Handoff app, it is time to extend it. Open **ListViewController.swift** and update `startUserActivity()` by passing the actual array of items instead of hardcoded values. Update the method to the following:

```
func startUserActivity() {
  let activity = NSUserActivity(activityType: ActivityTypeView)
  activity.title = "Viewing Shopping List"
  activity.userInfo = [ActivityItemsKey: items]
  userActivity = activity
  userActivity?.becomeCurrent()
}
```

Similarly, update `updateUserActivityState(activity:)` in **ListViewController.swift** to pass the array of `items` instead of hardcoded values:

```
override func updateUserActivityState(activity: NSUserActivity)
{
  activity.addUserInfoEntriesFromDictionary([ActivityItemsKey:
items])
  super.updateUserActivityState(activity)
}
```

Note: Whenever `updateUserActivityState(activity:)` is called, the `userInfo` dictionary is usually empty. You don't have to empty the dictionary, just update it with appropriate values.

Now, update `viewDidLoad()` in **ListViewController.swift** to start the `userActivity` after successfully retrieving items from previous session (and only if it's not empty), as follows:

```
override func viewDidLoad() {
  title = "Shopping List"
  weak var weakSelf = self
  PersistentStore.defaultStore().fetchItems({ (items:[String])
in
    if let unwrapped = weakSelf {
      unwrapped.items = items
      unwrapped.tableView.reloadData()
      if items.isEmpty == false {
        unwrapped.startUserActivity()
      }
    }
  })
  super.viewDidLoad()
}
```

Of course, if the app starts with an empty list of items, now the app will never start broadcasting the user activity. You need to fix this by starting the user activity once the user adds an item to the list for the first time.

To do this, update the implementation of the delegate callback `detailViewController(controller:didFinishWithUpdatedItem:)` in **ListViewController.swift** as follows:

```
func detailViewController(#controller: DetailViewController,
  didFinishWithUpdatedItem item: String) {
    // ... some code
    if !items.isEmpty {
      startUserActivity()
    }
}
```

There are three possibilities here:

1. The user has updated an existing item.

2. The user has deleted an existing item.

3. The user has added a new item.

The existing code handles all possibilities; you only need to add the check to start an activity if there is a non-empty list of items.

Build and run on both devices again. At this point you should be able to add a new item on one device and then hand it over to the other device!

Finishing touches

When user starts adding a new item or editing an existing item, the user is not technically viewing the list of items. So you want to stop broadcasting current activity. Similarly, there is no reason to continue broadcasting it all the items in the list are deleted. Add the following helper method in **ListViewController.swift**:

```
func stopUserActivity() {
  userActivity?.invalidate()
}
```

In `stopUserActivity()`, you invalidate the existing `NSUserActivity`. This makes Handoff stop broadcasting the user activity to other devices.

With `stopUserActivity()` in place, it is time to call it from appropriate places.

Update implementation of `prepareForSegue(segue:, sender:)` in **ListViewController.swift** and as follows:

```
override func prepareForSegue(segue: UIStoryboardSegue,
  sender: AnyObject!) {
    // ... some code
    stopUserActivity()
}
```

When the user selects a row or taps the **Add** button, `ListViewController` prepares to segue to detail view. You invalidate the current list-viewing activity.

Still in the same file, update the implementation of `tableView(_:commitEditingStyle:forRowAtIndexPath:)` as follows:

```
override func tableView(tableView: UITableView,
  commitEditingStyle editingStyle: UITableViewCellEditingStyle,
  forRowAtIndexPath indexPath: NSIndexPath) {
    // ... some code
    if items.isEmpty {
```

```
        stopUserActivity()
      } else {
        userActivity?.needsSave = true
      }
  }
```

When the user deletes an item from the list you need to update the user activity accordingly. If all the items have been removed from the list, you stop broadcasting. Otherwise you set `needsSave` to `true` on the `userActivity`. When you do that, the OS immediately calls back on `updateUserActivityState(activity:)`, where you update `userActivity` with the most recent list of items.

To wrap up this section, there is a situation where the user has just returned from `DetailViewController` by tapping the **Cancel** button. This triggers an exit segue. You need to re-start the `userActivity`. Update the implementation of `unwindDetailViewController(unwindSegue:)` as follows:

```
@IBAction func unwindDetailViewController(unwindSegue:
UIStoryboardSegue) {
  // ... some code

  startUserActivity()
}
```

Build and run and verify that everything works fine so far. Try adding a few items to the list and verify they pass between devices.

Creating the edit activity

Now you need to take care of `DetailViewController` in a similar fashion. This time, however, you'll broadcast a different activity type.

Open **DetailViewController.swift** and modify `textFieldDidBeginEditing(textField:)` as follows:

```
func textFieldDidBeginEditing(textField: UITextField!) {
  // Broadcast what we have, if there is anything!
  let activity = NSUserActivity(activityType: ActivityTypeEdit)
  activity.title = "Editing Shopping List Item"
  let activityItem = (countElements(textField.text!) > 0) ?
    textField.text : ""
  activity.userInfo = [ActivityItemKey: activityItem]
  userActivity = activity
```

```
  userActivity?.becomeCurrent()
}
```

Much like the List View activity type, the above method creates an "Editing" activity with the current contents of the item's string.

As user continues editing the item you need to update the user activity accordingly. Still in **DetailViewController.swift**, update the implementation of `textFieldTextDidChange(notification:)` as shown below:

```
func textFieldTextDidChange(notification: NSNotification) {
  if let text = textField!.text  {
    item = text
  }

  userActivity?.needsSave = true
}
```

Now that you have indicated the activity needs to be updated, implement `restoreUserActivityState(activity:)` to update it whenever the OS asks for it:

```
override func updateUserActivityState(activity: NSUserActivity)
{
  let activityListItem = (countElements(textField!.text!) > 0) ?
    textField!.text : ""
  activity.addUserInfoEntriesFromDictionary(
    [ActivityItemKey: activityListItem])
  super.updateUserActivityState(activity)
}
```

Remember, this is the callback method that you learned about earlier that Handoff calls periodically to update your user activity (or whenever you set `needsSave`). Here you simply update the current item to the text in the text field.

Build and run. At this point if you start adding a new item or editing an existing item on one device, you can hand over the edit process to another device.

```
Received a payload via handoff: {
    "shopsnap.item.key" = "This Is A New Item";
}
```

Finishing touches

In the code above you continuously update `userInfo` while the user is typing and interacting with the edit field. `needsSave` is a lightweight operation and you can set it as often as you like. In this case, you set it with each keypress.

There is one small design detail you may have picked up on. The view controllers are laid out as a split view on the iPad and in landscape mode on the iPhone. It's possible to switch between items in the list without resigning the keyboard. If that happens, `textFieldDidBeginEditing(textField:)` won't be called, resulting in your user activity never being updated to the new text.

To fix this, update `item`'s `didSet` observer in **DetailViewController.swift** as shown below:

```
var item: String? {
  didSet {
    if let textField = self.textField {
      textField.text = item
    }
    if let activity = userActivity {
      activity.needsSave = true
    }
  }
}
```

The `DetailViewController`'s `item` property is set when the user taps an item in the `ListViewController`. A simple fix for this situation is to let the view controller know that it has to update the activity when the item changes.

Finally, you'll need to invalidate `userActivity` when the user leaves the `DetailViewController` so the edit activity is no longer broadcasted.

Simply add this line to the beginning of `textFieldShouldReturn(_:)`in **DetailViewController.swift**:

```
userActivity?.invalidate()
```

Build and run your project to make sure the app still works as usual.

That takes care of creating and broadcasting your activity. Now you need to put the bits in place that will handle the incoming activity.

Receiving the activities

So far you have been logging in the Console whenever an activity was handed over from one device to another. In this section you will be wiring up the view controllers so that you can see the results in the app itself!

When the user launches your app through Handoff, the app delegate does most of the processing of the incoming `NSUserActivity`.

Assuming that everything goes well and the data transfers successfully, iOS then calls `application(_:continueUserActivity:restorationHandler:)`. This is your first chance to interact with the `NSUserActivity` instance.

You already have an implementation in place from previous sections. Update it as follows:

```
func application(application: UIApplication!,
  continueUserActivity userActivity: NSUserActivity!,
  restorationHandler: (([AnyObject]!) -> Void)!) -> Bool {
    if let window = self.window {

window.rootViewController?.restoreUserActivityState(userActivity
)
    }
    return true
}
```

You pass the `userActivity` to the `rootViewController` of the app's window and return `true`. This tells the OS you handled the Handoff action successfully. From this point on, you are on your own to forward calls and restore the activity.

The method you call on the `rootViewController` is `restoreUserActivityState(activity:)`. This is a standard mehod that is decalred at `UIResponder` level. The OS uses this method to tell a receiver to restore an instance of `NSUserActivivty`. It is OK for you to call this method and pass on the `userActivity`.

Your task now is to walk down the view controller hierarchy and pass the activity from the parent to child view controllers until reach the point where the activity is consumed. To see how this works, take a moment to review the hierarchy of the view controllers as illustrated below:

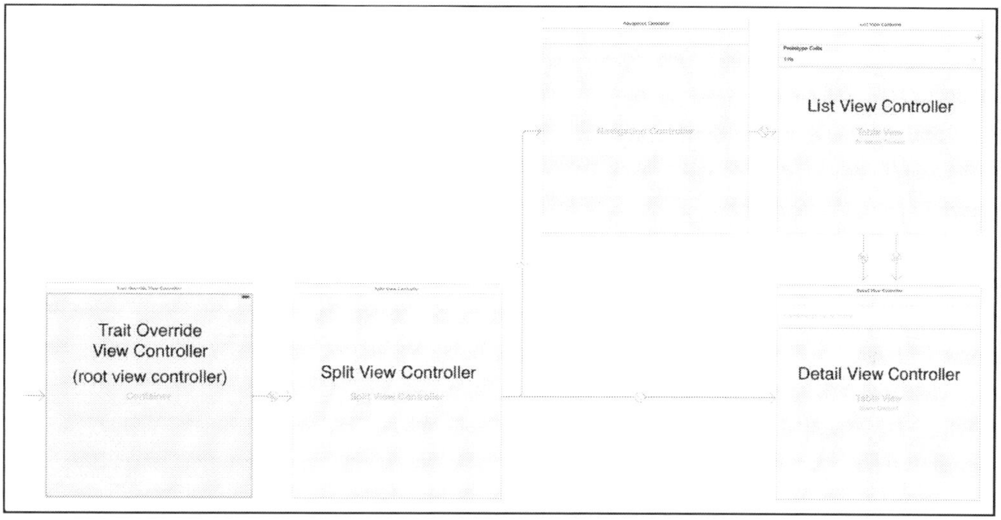

The root view controller is a `TraitOverrideViewController`. A `TraitViewController`'s job is to manage the size classes of the application, so it won't be interested in your user activity

Open **TraitOverrideViewController.swift** and add the following:

```
override func restoreUserActivityState(activity: NSUserActivity)
{
  let nextViewController = childViewControllers.first
    as UIViewController
  nextViewController.restoreUserActivityState(activity)
  super.restoreUserActivityState(activity)
}
```

Here you simply grab the first child view controller contained by the `TraitOverrideViewController`. It's safe to do this, since you know your app's view controller will only contain one child. Once you have the one and only child view controller in your app, pass the activity down to it.

The next view controller in the hierarchy is a SplitViewController, where things get a little more interesting.

Open **SplitViewController.swift** and add the following:

```
override func restoreUserActivityState(activity: NSUserActivity)
{
  // What type of activity is it?
  let activityType = activity.activityType

  // This is an activity for ListViewController.
  if activityType == ActivityTypeView {
    let controller = viewControllerForViewing()
    controller.restoreUserActivityState(activity)

  } else if activityType == ActivityTypeEdit {
    // This is an activity for DetailViewController.
    let controller = viewControllerForEditing()
      controller.restoreUserActivityState(activity)
    }

    super.restoreUserActivityState(activity)
}
```

SplitViewController knows about both ListViewController and DetailViewController. If the NSUserActivity is a List Viewing activity type, you'll pass it to ListViewController. However, if it's an Editing activity type you'll pass it to DetailViewController.

You've passed the activities to all the correct places – now it's time to get some data from those activities.

Open **ListViewController.swift** and implement restoreUserActivityState(activity:) as follows:

```
override func restoreUserActivityState(activity: NSUserActivity)
{
  // Get the list of items.
  if let userInfo = activity.userInfo {
    if let importedItems = userInfo[ActivityItemsKey] as?
NSArray {
      // Merge it with what we have locally and update UI.
      for anItem in importedItems {
        addItemToItemsIfUnique(anItem as String)
      }
      PersistentStore.defaultStore().updateStoreWithItems(items)
      PersistentStore.defaultStore().commit()
```

```
            tableView.reloadData()
        }
    }
    super.restoreUserActivityState(activity)
}
```

In the above method you finally get to continue a viewing activity. Since you want to maintain a unique list of shopping items, you only add those items that are unique to your local list, then save and update the UI once you're done.

Build and run. At this point you should be able to see the list of items that are received from another device via Handoff.

Just one activity type left – editing. Editing activities are handled in a very similar manner. Open **DetailViewController.swift** and implement `restoreUserActivityState(activity:)` as follows:

```
override func restoreUserActivityState(activity: NSUserActivity)
{
  if let userInfo = activity.userInfo {
      var activityItem: AnyObject? = userInfo[ActivityItemKey]
      if let itemToRestore = activityItem as? String {
        item = itemToRestore
        textField?.text = item
      }
    }
  super.restoreUserActivityState(activity)
}
```

This retrieves the information about the edit activity and updates the text field appropriately.

Build and run again to see it in action! Now you can start editing an item on once device, hand it over to another device and see it appear in the detail view of the other device, seamlessly!

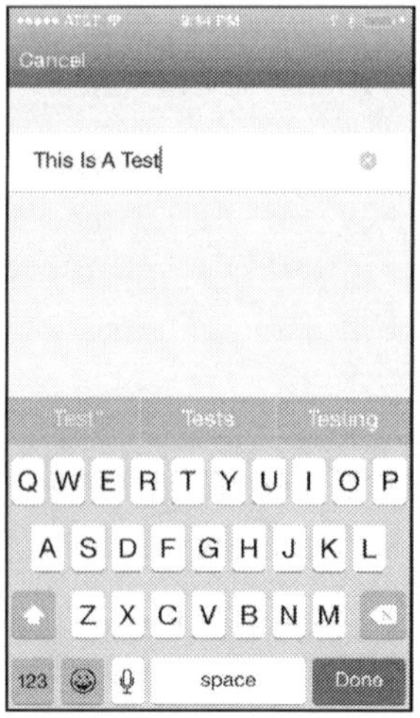

Finishing touches

Even though the app seems to work fine, there are a few things that you need to implement to ensure everything is handled properly.

When the user indicates that they want to continue a user activity on another device by swiping up on the app icon, the OS launches the corresponding app. Once the app is launched, the OS calls on `application(_, willContinueUserActivityWithType:)`.
Open **AppDelegate.swift** and add the following method:

```
func application(application: UIApplication,
  willContinueUserActivityWithType userActivityType: String!) ->
Bool {
  return true
}
```

At this point your app hasn't yet downloaded the `NSUserActivity` instance and its `userInfo` payload. For now, you'll simply return `true`. This forces the app to accept the activity each time the user initiates the Handoff process. If you want to alert your user that the activity is on its way, this is the place to do it.

At this point the OS has started transferring data from one device to another. You have already covered the case where everything goes well. But it is conceivable that the Handoff activity will fail at some point.

Add the following method to **AppDelegate.swift** to handle this case:

```
func application(application: UIApplication!,
  didFailToContinueUserActivityWithType userActivityType:
String!,
  error: NSError!) {
    if error.code != NSUserCancelledError {
      let message = "The connection to your other device may
have been interrupted. Please try again.
\(error.localizedDescription)"
      let alertView = UIAlertView(title: "Handoff Error",
message: message, delegate: nil, cancelButtonTitle: "Dismiss")
      alertView.show()
    }
}
```

If you receive anything *except* `NSUserCancelledError`, then something went wrong along the way and you won't be able to restore the activity. In this case, you display an appropriate message to the user. However, if the user explicitly canceled the Handoff action, then there's nothing else for you to do here but abort the operation.

Versioning support

One of the best practices when working with Handoff is versioning. You might add new data formats or remove values entirely from your `userInfo` dictionary in future versions of the app, so what happens if an old version of your app receives a handoff from a pervious version?

One strategy to deal with this is to add a version number to each handoff that you send, and only accept handoffs from your version number (or potentially earlier). Let's try this.

Open **Constants.swift** and add the following constants:

```
let ActivityVersionKey = "shopsnap.version.key"
let ActivityVersionValue = "1.0"
```

The above version key and value are arbitrary key-value you picked for this version of the app. It gives you a basic versioning system. You can extend this in the future for your own purposes.

If you recall from the previous section, the OS periodically and automatically calls `restoreUserActivityState(activity:)`. If you have noticed, the implementations of this method were very focused and were limited to the scope of the object that implemented it. For example, `ListViewController` overrode this method to update `userActivity` with list of all items, whereas `DetailViewController` overrode to update with the current item that was being edited.

When it comes to something that is generic to your `userActivity` and applies to all of your user activities regardless, like versioning, the best place to do that is in the AppDelegate.

Whenever `restoreUserActivityState(activity:)` is called, the OS calls `application(application:, didUpdateUserActivity userActivity:)` in the app delegate right after that. You'll use this method to add versioning support to your Handoff.

Open **AppDelegate.swift** and add the following:

```
func application(application: UIApplication,
  didUpdateUserActivity userActivity: NSUserActivity) {
    userActivity.addUserInfoEntriesFromDictionary(
      [ActivityVersionKey: ActivityVersionValue])
}
```

Here you simply update the `userInfo` dictionary with the version of your app.

Still in **AppDelegate.swift**, update the implementation of `application(_:, continueUserActivity: restorationHandler:)` as follows:

```
func application(application: UIApplication!,
    continueUserActivity userActivity: NSUserActivity!,
    restorationHandler: (([AnyObject]!) -> Void)!) -> Bool {
      if let userInfo: NSDictionary = userActivity.userInfo {
        if let version = userInfo[ActivityVersionKey] as? String
{
          // Pass it on.
          if let window = self.window {

window.rootViewController?.restoreUserActivityState(userActivity
)
          }
          return true
        }
      }
    return false
  }
```

Here you do a sanity check on the version of the `userAcitivty` and pass it on only if it matches the version you know about. Build and run your app once again to ensure the app runs as usual (but now, a little bit safer).

Handoff best practices

Before you go, I thought I'd leave you with a few thoughts on Handoff best practices.

- **NSURL**: Using `NSURL` in an `NSUserActivity` `userInfo` dictionary can be tricky. The only `NSURLs` you can pass safely in Handoff are web site URLs that use HTTP or HTTPS and iCloud documents. You can't pass local file URLs as the receiver won't translate and map the URL properly at the receiver's end. The best way to achieve file links is to pass a relative path and re-construct your URL on the receiving side.
- **Platform specific values**: Avoid using platform specific values like the content offset of a scroll view; it's always better to use relative landmarks. For example, if your user is viewing some items in a table view, pass the index path of the top most visible item in the table view in your user activity object instead of passing the content offset or visible rect of the table view.
- **Versioning**: Think about using versioning and future-proofing updates of your app. You could add new data formats or remove values entirely from your `userInfo` dictionary in future versions of the app. Versioning gives you more control over how user activities are actioned in current and future versions of your app.

Where to go from here?

This chapter has given you a good insight into basics of Handoff. Handoff makes it easier than ever to provide a seamless experience between your apps on multiple devices.

If you're curious to learn more about Handoff, streaming, and document based Handoff, be sure to check out Apple's **Handoff Programming Guide** for more information now that you know the basics (https://developer.apple.com/library/prerelease/ios/documentation/UserExperience/Conceptual/Handoff/HandoffFundamentals/HandoffFundamentals.html).

Chapter 24: Beginning WebKit

By Cesare Rocchi

Developers around the world celebrated in the streets, joining hands and yelling *Finally!* at the top of their lungs upon hearing about the release of the WebKit framework in iOS 8; the long overdue replacement to `UIWebView`.

Okay, so I may have embellished just a touch, but if you're one of the developers who has ever wrangled with `UIWebView` and its limited functionality, then you'll surely agree that *Finally!* is an expression fit for the occasion.

JavaScript, the workhorse behind many web applications, has historically been difficult to use in native mobile applications since its performance was not comparable to that of the default Safari app.

All developers yearned for was a web view component on par with the performance of the built-in Safari app. It didn't seem too much to ask, but was looking more and more likely that it would never happen.

Well people, the wait is over and your dreams of a performant web view are about to come true! The new WebKit framework enables an entirely new class of web enabled native applications that can exploit the power and speed of Nitro[1], the same JavaScript engine that powers Safari. Here is a list of the new features introduced in iOS8:

1. **Smooth Scrolling**: finally, there is a fix to ease the biggest pain point of all. Previously, the scrolling performance was sub-par at best. Now WebKit exploits Core Animation and hardware acceleration to provide a great performance when you scroll a web page.

---

[1] Nitro is the JavaScript engine that powers Safari, and has done since the first

2. **Gestures**: this is good news, especially for OS X developers. Now web views support track-pad gestures such as swipe to go back, and pinch to zoom.
3. **KVO**: this allows you to monitor the progress of loading a webpage. Progress, title and URL are now observable properties of `WKWebView`, so you can determine the exact status of the web view at any given time, and update your UI accordingly.
4. **Native Communication**: this is the most notable new feature. When iOS7 came out, JavaScriptCore was available to enable the communication between JavaScript and Objective-C[2]. It was a step in the right direction, but it mostly focused on bridging the gap between the two programming languages. In iOS8 there are two new APIs: User Scripts and Script Messages. User Scripts allow you to inject JavaScript code into a webpage, and then run it on a specific part of a page. Script Messages enable native code to receive callbacks from the User Scripts injected into the page – think of them as `NSNotifications`, but from a web page. This opens up endless possibilities, like tweaking a page using native code or parsing web content so it can be displayed in native components like table views.

In this chapter, you're going to learn the basics of `WKWebView` – how to instantiate and configure it, how to load a URL, observe the loading progress, and enable back and forward actions so you can navigate through the web views' history.

You're going to build **EyeBrowse**, a basic application that includes the following features:

- Loading web pages via their URL
- Displaying the progress of loading a web page
- *Back* and *Forward* buttons that update their display according to the history status of the web view
- Cancel the loading of a web page
- Reload a web page
- An adaptive layout so it runs equally as well on both iPhone and iPad

Want to see what you'll be building? Check it out:

---

[2] See Chapter 19 in iOS7 by Tutorials

You're going to build the whole thing from scratch; there's no starter project. Ready?

Getting Started

Open Xcode and select **File\New\Project ...** then select the **iOS\Application\Single View Application** template. Select **Swift** for the language and **Universal** for the device, and name your application **EyeBrowse**.

Open **Main.storyboard** from the Project Navigator. Select the only view controller in the storyboard, and then **Editor\Embed In\Navigation Controller**.

Next, drag a `UIView` onto the navigation bar in the view controller and stretch it to be as wide as the bar. Set the background color to red to make it easy to see.

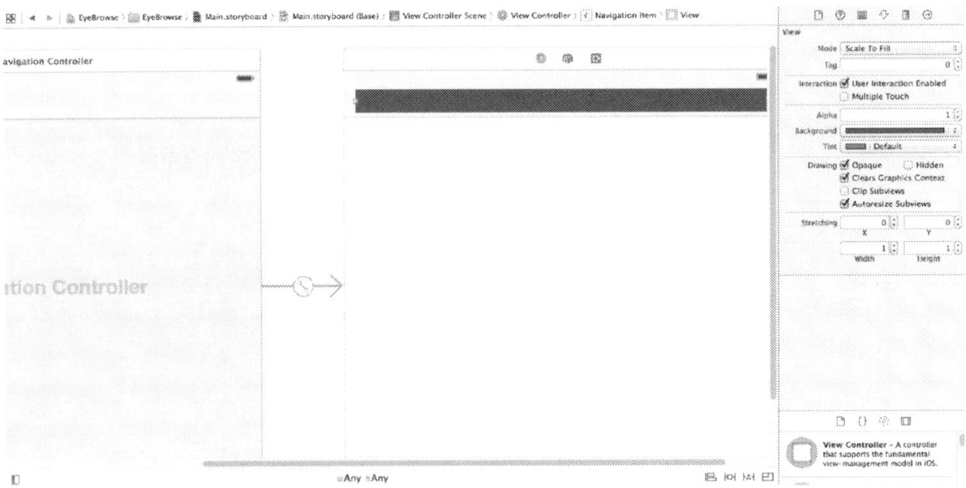

This will become the background of the text field where the user can enter a URL.

But wait, there's a problem! You can't apply Auto Layout constraints within a navigation bar, so to make it adapt to any orientation you'll need to resort to `viewWillTransitionToSize(size:, withTransitionCoordinator:)`. This notifies you when the size of a view controller's view is about to change, and provides the perfect opportunity to adjust the frame of this view.

Create an `IBOutlet` for the red `UIView` by opening the **Assistant Editor** and **ctrl+dragging** from the view to the top of the `ViewController` class. Name it `barBackgroundView`.

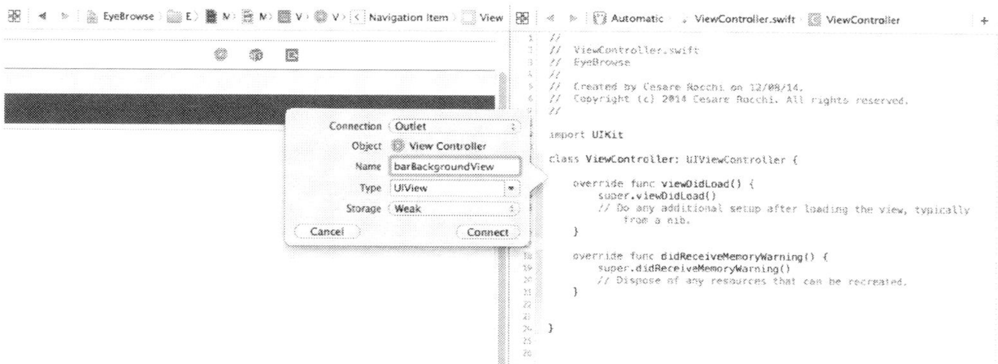

Now add the following line to the bottom of `viewDidLoad` to set the width of the background view .

```
barBackgroundView.frame = CGRect(x:0, y: 0, width:
view.frame.width, height: 30)
```

Next, add the following method to `ViewController`:

```
override func viewWillTransitionToSize(size: CGSize,
withTransitionCoordinator coordinator:
UIViewControllerTransitionCoordinator) {
  barBackgroundView.frame = CGRect(x:0, y: 0, width: size.width,
height: 30)
}
```

Now build and run. Check that the red view you added adapts to any orientation, on both iPhone and iPad.

Now that you've got the foundation in place, it's time for the main event.

Show Them the Web

The first step is to import the new `WebKit` framework. Add the following to the very top of `ViewController`:

```
import WebKit
```

Next add the following variable just below the `IBOutlet` you created:

```
var webView: WKWebView
```

Then add the following `init(coder:)` method.

```
required init(coder aDecoder: NSCoder) {
  self.webView = WKWebView(frame: CGRectZero)
  super.init(coder: aDecoder)
}
```

This initializes the web view with a zero-sized frame.

Later, you'll make the web view grow and shrink with its container view, using some Auto Layout constraints.

Wait, what's this about a web view? You don't have one? That just means you're going to have to make one by adding the following to the bottom of `viewDidLoad`:

```
view.addSubview(webView)
```

That one line is all you need to make the web view. Now, time to add some constraints.

Open the storyboard and select the **View Controller** (not its view). In the **Attributes Inspector**, uncheck the **Under Top Bars** option in the **Extend Edges** group.

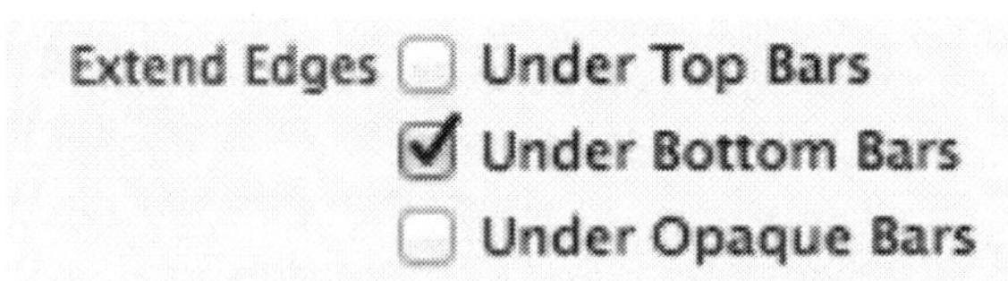

You do this because `WKWebView` is a descendent of `UIScrollView`, and you don't want its `contentInset` to be managed by the navigation controller.

Now, in **ViewController.swift** add the following constraints at the bottom of `viewDidLoad()`:

```
webView.setTranslatesAutoresizingMaskIntoConstraints(false)
let widthConstraint = NSLayoutConstraint(item: webView,
attribute: .Width, relatedBy: .Equal, toItem: view, attribute:
.Width, multiplier: 1, constant: 0)
view.addConstraint(widthConstraint)
let heightConstraint = NSLayoutConstraint(item: webView,
attribute: .Height, relatedBy: .Equal, toItem: view, attribute:
.Height, multiplier: 1, constant: 0)
view.addConstraint(heightConstraint)
```

The first line of code disables auto-generated constraints so that you can create your own.

The second section adds two constraints:

- The first makes sure the web view height equals its superview height.
- The second makes sure that web view width equals its superview width.

Does it work yet? In order to find out you'll need to load a URL. The pattern to follow is exactly the same as when using `UIWebView`:

- Create an instance of `NSURL`
- Create an instance of `NSURLRequest`, using the `NSURL` instance
- Call `loadRequest:` on your `WKWebView`, passing the `NSURLRequest` instance

Add the following to the foot of `viewDidLoad()`, just before the closing brace:

```
let URL = NSURL(string:"http://www.raywenderlich.com")
let request = NSURLRequest(URL:URL!)
webView.loadRequest(request)
```

Build and run. Make sure to try it on both iPhone and iPad. Rotate the simulator, see how the web view adapts its size in all orientations.

Now it's time to access another URL, and make it more user-friendly.

Let Them Type a URL

Open the storyboard and drag a **Text Field** from the **Object Library** onto the red view. It should look like the following:

Next, select the text field and click the **Pin** button in the layout bar at the bottom of the canvas. In the dialog that pops up, add the following four constraints, making sure to use `0` for each one:

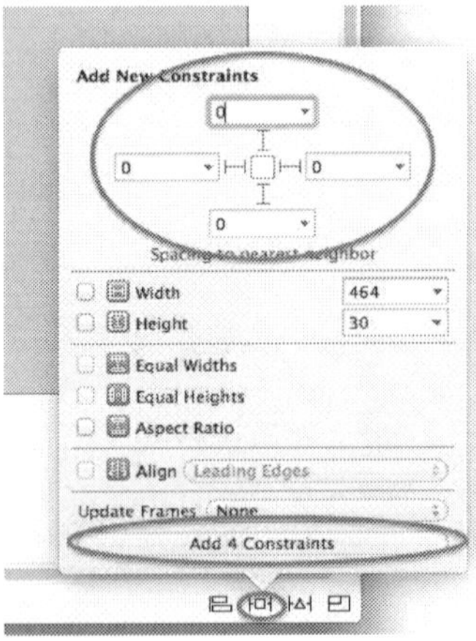

You'll probably see an Auto Layout warning, and to fix it just select the text field, then click **Editor\Resolve Auto Layout Issues\Selected View\Update Frames**. This updates the dimensions of the text field match those expected by the constraints.

Next, create an `IBOutlet` for the text field using the Assistant Editor. Name it `inputURLField`.

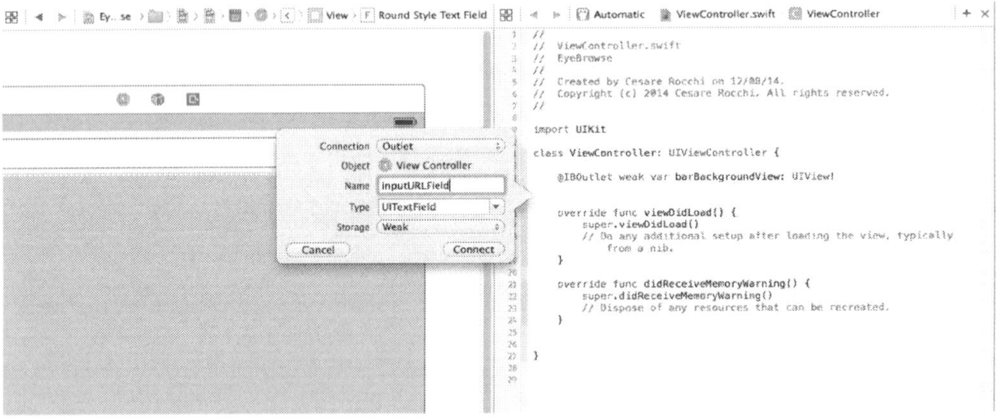

In the **Document Outline**, **ctrl-drag** from the text field to the view controller, and select **delegate** from the popup.

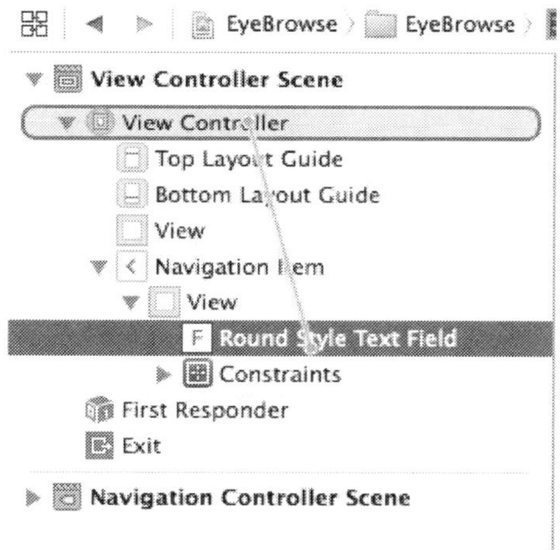

This ensures that the view controller receives the `UITextFieldDelegate` protocol methods.

Finally, with the text field still selected, set the following properties in the **Attributes Inspector**:

- **Clear Button**: Appears while editing
- **Correction**: No
- **Keyboard Type**: URL
- **Return Key**: Go

Select the red view, click **Background** in the attribute inspector to show the color selector. Click the lens in the popup and then click anywhere on the navigation bar. This will make the background view the same color of the navigation bar.

Open **ViewController.swift** and declare the class conforms to the `UITextFieldDelegate` protocol by updating the class declaration to the following:

```
class ViewController: UIViewController, UITextFieldDelegate {
    ...
}
```

Next, in `viewDidLoad()`, replace the last three lines of the function with these:

```
inputURLField.text = "http://raywenderlich.com"
let URL = NSURL(string:inputURLField.text)
let request = NSURLRequest(URL:URL!)
webView.loadRequest(request)
```

Here you've given the text field a default URL, which is subsequently used to form the request loaded by the web view.

Build and run. Check that http://raywenderlich.com loads as it did before.

Now you need to solve a subtle interface issue; the user may tap the text field by mistake and has no way of getting out of it. Time to be a considerate developer and provide a way for a user to dismiss the keyboard without triggering a request.

Add the following function to **ViewController.swift**:

```
func textFieldDidBeginEditing(textField: UITextField!) {
  let cancelButton = UIBarButtonItem(title: "Cancel", style:
.Plain, target: self, action: "cancel")
  navigationItem.rightBarButtonItem = cancelButton
}
```

This adds a cancel button to the navigation bar when text field receives focus.

Now add the method that's called when the cancel button is tapped:

```
func cancel () {
  inputURLField.resignFirstResponder()
  navigationItem.rightBarButtonItem = nil
  barBackgroundView.frame = CGRect(x:0, y: 0, width:
view.frame.width, height: 30)
}
```

By asking the text field to resign its first responder status, the keyboard is automatically dismissed. The rest of this method just performs some clean up.

Build and run. Tap on the text field, then tap on the **Cancel** button. You should see both the keyboard and cancel button vanish from view.

Okay, add a way for a user to enter a URL – check. Cancel button – check. What's missing here? Ah yes, a way to actually load the URL. So the next step is to make sure the **Go** button on the keyboard starts a new request when the user taps it. Add this `UITextFieldDelegate` protocol method to `viewController`:

```
func textFieldShouldReturn(textField: UITextField!) -> Bool {
  inputURLField.resignFirstResponder()
  navigationItem.rightBarButtonItem = nil
  barBackgroundView.frame = CGRect(x:0, y: 0, width:
view.frame.width, height: 30)
webView.loadRequest(NSURLRequest(URL:NSURL(string:inputURLField.
text)))
  return false
}
```

This dismisses the keyboard, hides the cancel button and loads a new request based on the URL provided by the user.

Build and run. Wait for the initial page to load, type in a valid URL, and tap **Go**. The URL will load in the web view. Great work!

Now enter a malformed or incorrect URL such as **http://raywenderlich.awesome**. What loads? Nothing. Huh?

Next up, handling errors.

Oops I did it again

This may come as a shock, but almost any user will mistype a URLs at some point in their life, and for many people, it happens on daily basis. So you need to make sure your app knows what to do when the user types *.con* instead of *.com*.

The new `WKWebView` component has a property named `navigationDelegate`, which expects an object conforming to the `WKNavigationDelgate` protocol. Utilizing this protocol is handy way of dealing with navigation events, including errors related to loading URLs.

Here's a list of the relevant methods:

- `webView(_:, didCommitNavigation:)` called when the loading begins
- `webView(_:, didFailProvisionalNavigation:, withError:)` called when there's an error loading a URL
- `webView(_:, didFinishNavigation:)` called when the page load completes
- `webView(_:, didReceiveServerRedirectForProvisionalNavigation:)` called when the server issues a redirect
- `webView(_:, didFailProvisionalNavigation:, withError:)` called when there's an error loading a web page

To show an error message when encountering an invalid URL, adopt the `WKNavigationDelegate` protocol by updating the class declaration in **ViewController.swift**:

```
class ViewController: UIViewController, UITextFieldDelegate,
WKNavigationDelegate {
    ...
}
```

Then add the following statement to `init`, just below the call to `super`:

```
self.webView.navigationDelegate = self
```

This ensures your class is the navigation delegate of the web view.

Next, add the appropriate delegate method for handling the error:

```
func webView(webView: WKWebView!,didFailProvisionalNavigation
             navigation: WKNavigation!, withError error:
             NSError!) {

  let alert = UIAlertController(title: "Error", message:
error.localizedDescription, preferredStyle: .Alert)
  alert.addAction(UIAlertAction(title: "Ok", style: .Default,
handler: nil))
  presentViewController(alert, animated: true, completion: nil)
}
```

This method simply presents alert drawing the users attention to the error.

Build and run. Type another incorrect URL, and see how the user is now made aware of the issue.

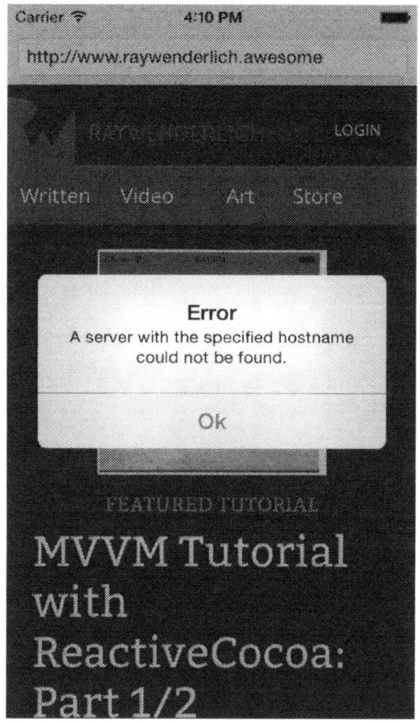

Great work! EyeBrowse can now load URLs entered by the user, show and hide the keyboard, and display a cancel button. It can even tell you when and why a request fails. Now that's progress.

Speaking of progress, remember one of the goals was to monitor the progress of pages as they load? Well, now it's time to add that feature.

Show me Progress

Loading a URL is an asynchronous operation that takes an indeterminate amount of time, and you need some way to convey this to the user.

Until now, the property `estimatedProgress` was exclusive to the Mac OS X SDK. Thanks to the new WebKit framework, it's now available on iOS, and it's observable!

You'll exploit KVO to monitor loading while it's in progress. Aside from that, there are some other interesting observable properties of `WKWebView`:

- `loading`: a `Boolean` that tells whether the web view is currently loading
- `title`: a string that represents the title of the web page
- `URL`: the URL of the request loaded by the web view

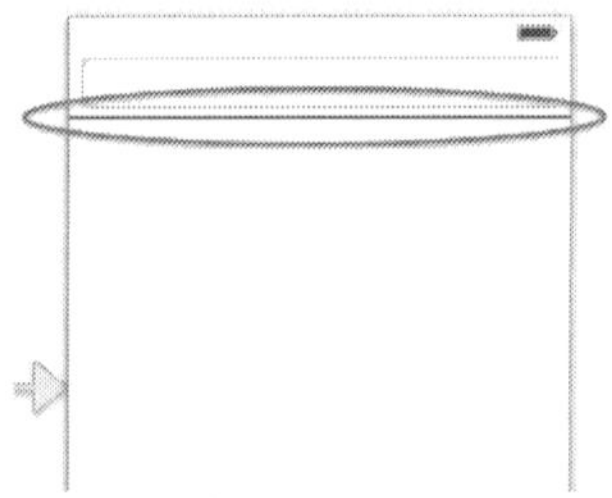

The app will observe both `loading` and `estimatedProgress`. The former will be used to show or hide an activity indicator, and the latter to update a progress view.

Open the storyboard and drag a **Progress View** from the **Object Library** on to the view, just below the navigation bar, like so:

Select it and click the **Pin** button at the bottom of the canvas. Add the following constraints, making sure to change the **Update Frames** drop down to **Items of New Constraints**:

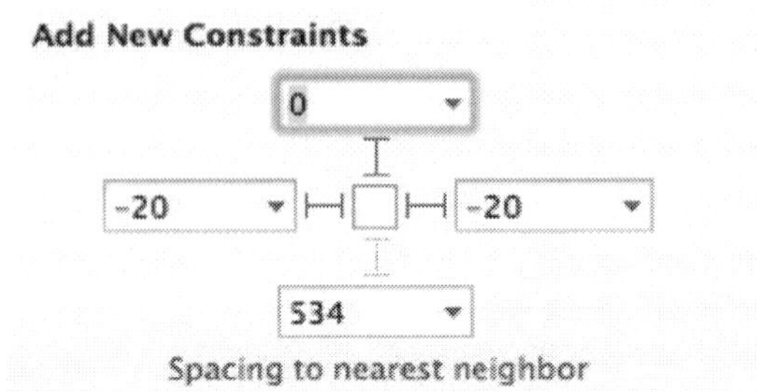

In the **Attributes Inspector** set the **Progress Tint** to **Red: 0**, **Green: 123**, **Blue: 65** - a.k.a. *Ray Wenderlich Green* :]

Your storyboard will now look like this.

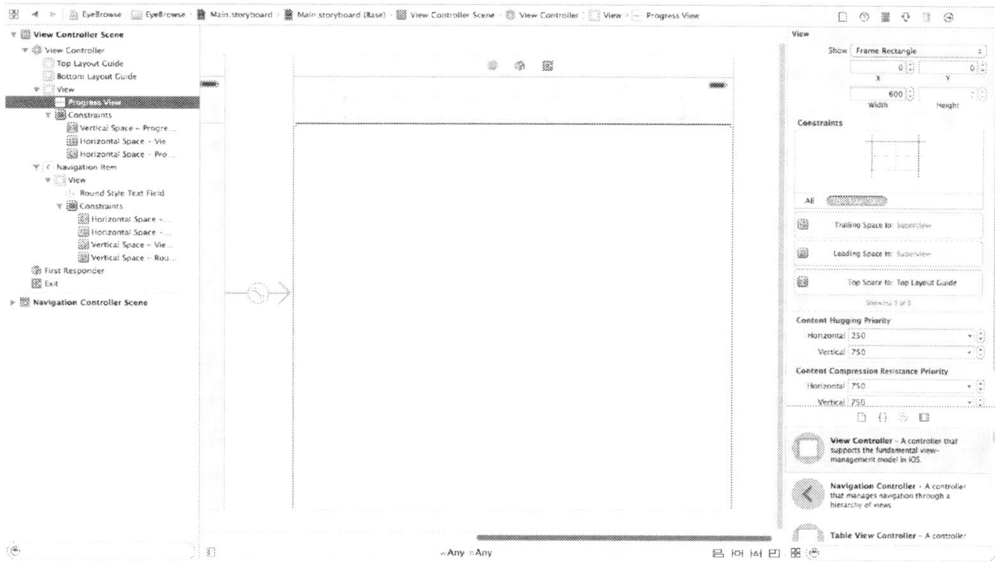

Now create an `IBOutlet` for the Progress View in **ViewController.swift** and name it `progressView`. Locate the following line in `viewDidLoad()`:

```
view.addSubview(webView)
```

And replace it with this line:

```
view.insertSubview(webView, belowSubview: progressView)
```

Which makes sure the progress view can be seen, as it's placed above the web view in the view stack.

And add the following lines to `viewDidLoad()`, just above where you ask the web view to load the request:

```
webView.addObserver(self, forKeyPath: "loading", options: .New,
context: nil)
webView.addObserver(self, forKeyPath: "estimatedProgress",
options: .New, context: nil)
progressView.setProgress(0.0, animated: false)
```

Here you're adding the class as an observer of the `loading` and `estimatedProgress` properties, and resetting the progress view right before a new request is issued.

Now add the following method to your class, which will be called whenever those properties change:

```
override func observeValueForKeyPath(keyPath: String, ofObject
object: AnyObject, change: [NSObject : AnyObject], context:
UnsafeMutablePointer<()>) {
  if (keyPath == "loading") {
UIApplication.sharedApplication().networkActivityIndicatorVisibl
e = webView.loading
    if (webView.loading == false) {
      inputURLField.text = webView.URL!.absoluteString
    }
  } else if (keyPath == "estimatedProgress") {
    progressView.hidden = webView.estimatedProgress == 1
    progressView.setProgress(Float(webView.estimatedProgress),
animated: true)
  }
}
```

A change in the value for `loading` determines whether or not the network activity indicator is visible in the status bar. In case the server issues a redirect or when loading is `false`, the value of the text field shows the actual URL.

A change in the value for `estimatedProgress` updates the progress view or hides it if loading is finished.

Finally add the following method to `viewController`:

```
func webView(webView: WKWebView!, didFinishNavigation
navigation: WKNavigation!) {
  progressView.setProgress(0.0, animated: false)
}
```

This is another method of the `WKNavigationDelegate` protocol, and is used here to reset the value of the progress view when loading is complete.

Build and run. Notice how the progress view fills as the page loads.

What kind of a web browser would this be without any back, forward or reload buttons? A useless one, right? EyeBrowse is currently missing these, and you know how the users will feel about that.

In the next section, you'll add these essential navigation tools.

Back and Forth

Open **Main.storyboard** and select **View Controller** in the **Document Outline**. In the **Attributes Inspector** find the **Simulated Metrics** section and change the **Bottom Bar** from Inferred to **None**.

Next, drag a **Toolbar** from the **Object Library** onto the view, and place it at the bottom like so:

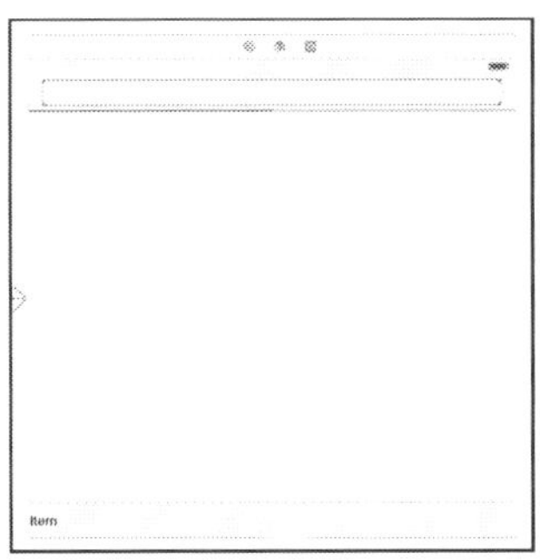

With the toolbar selected, click the **Pin** button and add the following constraints, making sure **Constrain to margins** is unchecked:

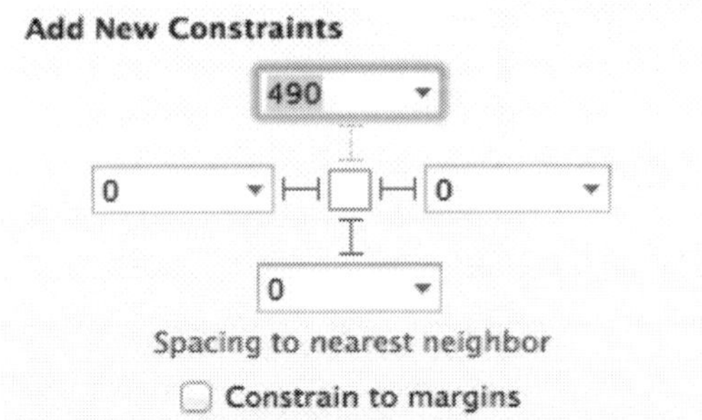

These constraints pin the toolbar to the bottom of the view, whilst making sure its width resizes with its superview.

Open **ViewController.swift** and in `viewDidLoad()`, replace the existing `heightConstraint` definition with the following:

```
let heightConstraint = NSLayoutConstraint(item: webView,
attribute: .Height, relatedBy: .Equal, toItem: view, attribute:
.Height, multiplier: 1, constant: -44)
```

This allows the frame of the web view to take the height of the toolbar into account.

Build and run. Make sure that in all orientations, the toolbar is pinned to the bottom of the view, while the web view fits snug between the navigation bar and the toolbar.

Now open **Main.storyboard**, remove any existing button items from the toolbar and then drag the following, from the **Object Library**, on to it in this order:

1. A **Bar Button Item** for the back button
2. A **Fixed Space Bar Button Item**, to create some padding between button items
3. A **Bar Button Item** for the forward button
4. A **Flexible Space Bar Button Item**, to push the next button over to the right
5. A **Bar Button Item** for the stop & reload button

At this point, your storyboard should look like this:

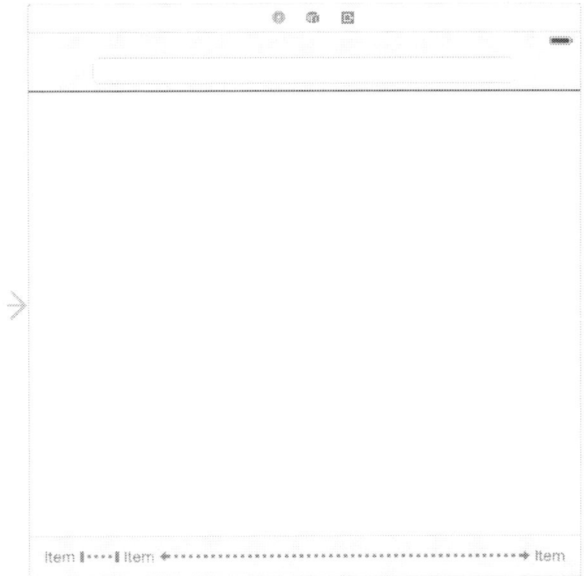

Now, using the **Assistant Editor**, create an `IBOutlet` in `ViewController` for each of the three buttons, from left-to-right, and name them respectively:

1. `backButton`
2. `forwardButton`
3. `stopReloadButton`

Then, again using the **Assistant Editor**, create an `IBAction` in `ViewController` for each of the three buttons, in the same order, and name them:

4. `goBack`
5. `goForward`
6. `stopReload`

For each `IBAction`, make sure you change the **Type** to **UIBarButtonItem** in the popup dialog.

> **Note:** There is an **Assets** folder for this chapter containing the four images needed for the buttons. Locate it, and then import them into Xcode using **File\Add Files to "EyeBrowse"...**, selecting the four images, checking **Copy items if needed** and finally clicking **Add**.

Add the following to the bottom of `viewDidLoad()` in **ViewController.swift**:

```
backButton.image = UIImage(named: "icon_back")
forwardButton.image = UIImage(named: "icon_forward")
stopReloadButton.image = UIImage(named: "icon_stop")
backButton.enabled = false
forwardButton.enabled = false
```

This sets up the images and initial states of the buttons you just added to the toolbar.

Next, add the following to `observeValueForKeyPath(_:, ofObject:, change:, context:)`, just inside the first `if` statement:

```
backButton.enabled = webView.canGoBack
forwardButton.enabled = webView.canGoForward
stopReloadButton.image = webView.loading ?
  UIImage(named: "icon_stop") : UIImage(named: "icon_refresh")
```

This code sets whether or not the back and forward buttons are enabled according to the current state of the web view, and also changes the image for the `stopReloadButton` based on the value of `loading`.

Now it's time to flesh out the three `IBActions` you added earlier. First, add the following line to `goBack`:

```
webView.goBack()
```

And this line to `goForward`:

```
webView.goForward()
```

And finally, add the following to `stopReload`:

```
if (webView.loading) {
  webView.stopLoading()
} else {
  let request = NSURLRequest(URL:webView.URL!)
  webView.loadRequest(request)
```

```
}
```

The methods belonging to the back and forward buttons are pretty straightforward. The `stopReload` method cancels the current request if it's in process, or generates a new request with the current URL thereby reloading the current page.

Build and run. See how the three buttons update their state or display according to the history of the web view and the status of the `loading` property.

In particular, check to see that you're seeing the following behaviour:

- The back button is disabled on launch, and when you go back to the first web page you visited
- Whenever you press the back button the forward button becomes enabled
- The `stopReload` button changes it image according to the progress of the current request
- The progress view hides when loading is complete

Well, that's the basics of WebKit, and you can now install EyeBrowse on any device you like and freely browse around the web.

One more Thing

Just for fun, launch EyeBrowse and once the default page has loaded, tap on the **Art** tab at the top of the site. Hmmm? Nothing loads, right? It looks like there's more you can do to improve EyeBrowse.

Open www.raywenderlich.com in your desktop browser and see what happens when you click that link. It opens the http://www.gameartguppy.com website in a new tab. You've not heard of it before? Well, Game Art Guppy is a website that sells reasonably priced game art to aspiring game developers.

Why didn't it work in EyeBrowse, though?

It's elementary my dear Watson – EyeBrowse doesn't have tabs so it has no idea how to how to open one and display Game Art Guppy! It's time to look at how URLs are loaded in WebKit.

`WKWebView` begins loading a page as soon as you call `loadRequest`, or when a user taps on a link.

A web page can be a complex beast that includes HTML content, JavaScript files, CSS files, images, videos, etc. The flow moves from action to request to response, then it finally renders:

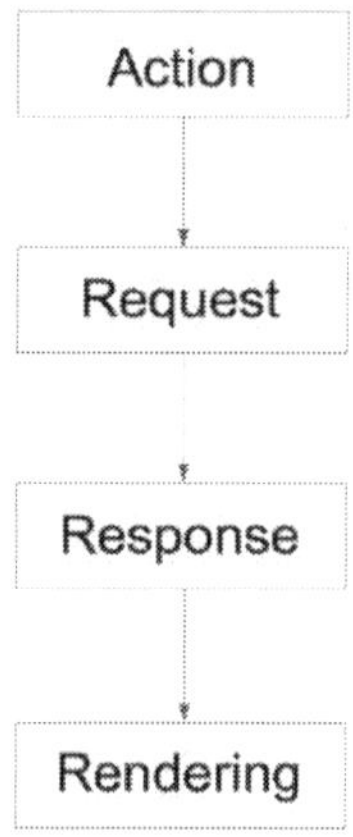

Everything starts with an action, which could be:

- The user taps a link in the web page
- A form was submitted, but not necessarily triggered by the user
- Somebody or something triggers a reload of the page, either the user or a script that periodically refreshes the page to show new content
- The user taps the back or forward button
- Some JavaScript asynchronously loads some external content

After an action is triggered, but before the request is issued to the server, the app is given a chance to intervene.

For example, as you'll see in the **Intermediate WebKit** chapter, you can inject some JavaScript in a web page as soon as the document starts loading. You can also manipulate the response before it's handed off to the rendering phase.

The former is exactly what's needed to resolve the current issue. If the URL doesn't match raywenderlich.com, it will be handed off to Safari.

One of the methods offered by the `WKNavigationDelegate` protocol is `webView(_:, decidePolicyForNavigationAction:, decisionHandler:)` which is called multiple times throughout the loading of a web page. One of its parameters is a

`WKNavigationAction`, which models the action mentioned above and includes two key properties: `navigationType` and `request`.

Add the following function to **ViewController.swift**:

```
func webView(webView: WKWebView!,
decidePolicyForNavigationAction navigationAction:
WKNavigationAction!, decisionHandler:
((WKNavigationActionPolicy) -> Void)!) {
  println("Request \(navigationAction.request)")
  decisionHandler(.Allow)
}
```

This simply prints each request made by the web view to the console, and then allows it to continue. Build and run. Watch what's printed to the console. You should see something like this:

```
Request <NSMutableURLRequest: 0x7a2a17f0> { URL:
http://www.raywenderlich.com/, headers: {
    Accept =
"text/html,application/xhtml+xml,application/xml;q=0.9,*/*;q=0.8
";
    "User-Agent" = "Mozilla/5.0 (iPhone; CPU iPhone OS 8_0 like
Mac OS X) AppleWebKit/538.43 (KHTML, like Gecko)
Mobile/12A4318c";
} }
Request <NSMutableURLRequest: 0x787ba2a0> { URL:
http://www.facebook.com/plugins/like.php?&href=https://www.faceb
ook.com/raywenderlich&send=false&layout=button_count&width=60&he
ight=20&show_faces=false&action=like&colosheme=light, headers: {
    Accept =
"text/html,application/xhtml+xml,application/xml;q=0.9,*/*;q=0.8
";
    Referer = "http://www.raywenderlich.com/";
    "User-Agent" = "Mozilla/5.0 (iPhone; CPU iPhone OS 8_0 like
Mac OS X) AppleWebKit/538.43 (KHTML, like Gecko)
Mobile/12A4318c";
} }
```

At the time of writing this chapter, loading raywenderlich.com in a web view on an iPhone issues eleven requests; not all of them are related to the same host. For example, the second request loads some content from Facebook, whereas the last loads an advertisement from a CDN (Content Delivery Network). In fact, this is not atypical, as most web pages load content from different sources.

The key point is that with the new WebKit framework, you can hook into the loading process and tweak it according to the needs of your app.

The other interesting parameter of this delegate method is `decisionHandler`, a closure that takes a policy as a parameter and returns `void`. This allows the native code to specify a policy that can be:

- `.Cancel` to prevent halt the request in it's tracks
- `.Allow` to let the request go on it's merry way, and ultimately complete

In other words, `.Cancel` blocks any further action related to the loading of a URL, whereas `.Allow` – which is also the default behavior – goes on with the process.

Replace the existing implementation of `webView(webView:, decidePolicyForNavigationAction:, decisionHandler:)` with the following:

```
func webView(webView: WKWebView!,
decidePolicyForNavigationAction navigationAction:
WKNavigationAction!, decisionHandler:
((WKNavigationActionPolicy) -> Void)!) {
  println("Request \(navigationAction.request)")
  if (navigationAction.navigationType == .LinkActivated &&
!navigationAction.request.URL.host!.lowercaseString.hasPrefix("w
ww.raywenderlich.com")) {

UIApplication.sharedApplication().openURL(navigationAction.reque
st.URL);
    decisionHandler(.Cancel)
  } else {
    decisionHandler(.Allow)
  }
}
```

This code checks two conditions:

1. The action is initiated by a tap

2. The host is not raywenderlich.com.

When both are met, the URL opens in Safari, and the `.Cancel` policy stops any further activity. If both are not met, the page renders in the web view as usual.

Build and run. Tap the **Art** link at the top of the page. Safari will now take over and open the website http://www.gameartguppy.com

Conclusion

In this chapter, you've learned the basics of the new WebKit framework. You built a simple web browser from scratch that features many of the core functionalities of Safari, such as loading a URL, displaying progress, detecting errors while loading, and navigating through browsing history.

Last but not least, you learned about the internal URL loading process of the `WKWebView` component, and how to intervene at the appropriate time.

In the **Intermediate WebKit** chapter, you'll learn how to inject JavaScript into a web page to extract data that you'll then render in a native control.

Chapter 25: Intermediate WebKit

By Cesare Rocchi

With the new WebKit framework, your application can communicate directly with a web page hosted in an instance of `WKWebView`, and receive callbacks. This is a huge improvement over `UIWebView` which allowed only limited interaction between the web page and your code.

The WebKit framework allows you the freedom to customize how web pages look and behave when hosted your app. Just let that sink in for a moment – the realm of possibilities is, well, spectacular.

In this chapter, you'll learn two game-changing techniques:

1. How to modify the appearance of a web page directly from your code.

2. How to receive callbacks from JavaScript you've injected into a hosted web page.

In particular, you'll learn how to inject some JavaScript to parse the content of a web page and callback to your apps code when the operation is done. The content extracted will then be used to populate a table view. Moreover, you'll learn how to modify the look and feel of any hosted web page by injecting some custom CSS.

Say what? *Any* hosted web page?

Yes, you'll soon be an all-powerful master of the interwebs; changing and tweaking pages as you see fit when viewed within your app!

This chapter includes a starter project named **RWPedia**. It's a custom browser specifically for the Ray Wenderlich website.

Open the project in Xcode and build and run. At this point, it's basically a relatively simple, custom web browser. You'll see a navigation controller that shows the title of the page at the top, a web view similar to the one described in Chapter 24, **Beginning WebKit**, and standard back, forward and reload buttons in a toolbar at the bottom. Of course, it's tinted with Ray Wenderlich green :]

If you're not well acquainted with WebKit, I recommend working through the **Beginning WebKit** chapter first to find your feet.

This is how the app looks when it's running:

In this chapter, you'll add two new bespoke features to the app:

1. Hide the biography section of each profile page
2. Load the list of authors from the about page of the website and display it in a table view, which is displayed when you tap the **Authors** button in the navigation bar

To implement both features you'll learn:

1. How to initialize a web view with a configuration object
2. How to load and inject JavaScript into the hosted web page
3. How to set up callbacks so you can be notified when the script has finished

Setting up communication

Until recently – just before writing this chapter in fact – hosted web pages and native app code had an icy relationship. Communications were strained, and it resulted in a lot of frustration for developers. Fortunately, these two are now on much better terms, as long as you set them up to play nicely together.

To facilitate seamless communication between the native and the web parts of the application, you'll need to initialize the `WKWebView` component with a `WKWebViewConfiguration`.

You set up an instance of `WKWebViewConfiguration` with a collection of properties that allow for the creation of a *bridge* between your native code and your hosted web content. Creating a web view with a configuration is easy. Here is a simple example:

```
let webViewConfiguration = WKWebViewConfiguration()
let authorsWebView = WKWebView(frame: CGRectZero, configuration:
webViewConfiguration)
```

A `WKWebViewConfiguration` has some interesting properties, such as:

- `mediaPlaybackRequiresUserAction` to specify whether a video player starts playing automatically or requires a tap from the user
- `mediaPlaybackAllowsAirPlay` to specify whether the video player can stream content to AirPlay supported devices
- `preferences`, an instance of `WKPreferences`, which encapsulates further properties to configure the web view rendering like `minimumFontSize` and `javascriptEnabled`
- `userContentController` which is the facilitator that enables injecting user scripts into web pages and listening for a callbacks

The latter is the property you'll use to implement both new features in the app.

The most interesting, by far, is the ability to inject code into a page, and in the next section, you'll learn just how to do that.

Hide that biography, please

Open **Safari** on your iPhone or iPad and load up http://www.raywenderlich.com/u/funkyboy.

You have to scroll down quite a bit to see the tutorials written by this author, and it's less than elegant on a smaller screen than it is desktop. Wouldn't it be nice to hide the biography section and simply show the tutorials?

You'll implement this by injecting a user script that contains some custom CSS code. There are two steps than need to happen in order to achieve this:

1. Build a new CSS rule to hide the biography section
2. Inject the new CSS rule into the web page

But to build a new CSS rule, you need to know a bit about CSS and the structure of HTML pages.

Dissecting the tree

A HTML page is made up of tags that describe the document in a tree-like structure. `<html>` is the root tag that encloses everything. The direct children of the root are `<head>`, which contains metadata about the page, like the title and any styling, and `<body>`, which contains the actual content.

For example, this is an excerpt of the HTML for a profile page www.raywenderlich.com/u/funkyboy

```
<html>
  <head>
    <title>Ray Wenderlich | funkyboy Profile</title>
    <style type="text/css">
      ...
    </style>
  </head>
  <body ... >
    <section id="user-details">
    ...
    <article id="post-63283" ...>
    <article id="post-34050" ...>
  </body>
</html>
```

The `<style>` tag contains the CSS rules that describe the look and feel of elements in a web page. A CSS rule follows a relatively simple syntax:

```
selector {
  // description of font size, background color, etc.
}
```

CSS also allows styling of a specific tag in a web page, provided you give that tag a unique id. In this case, the selector is simply prefixed by a hash symbol:

```
#unique-id {
  // description of font size, background color, etc.
}
```

Open www.raywenderlich.com/u/funkyboy in **Safari** on your Mac. Right click on the white area right below the users profile picture and select **Inspect Element**. You'll see something like this.

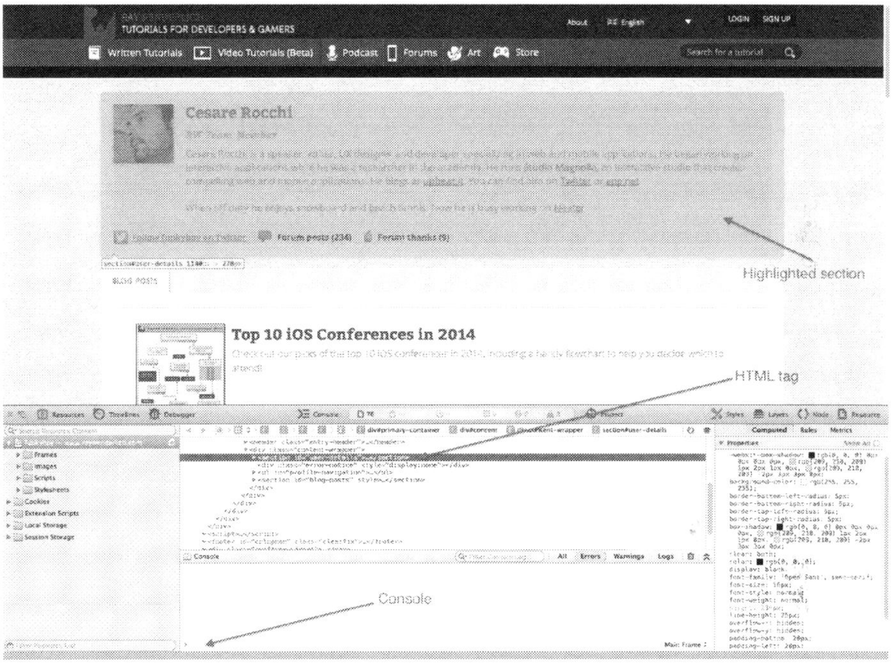

If this option is not available, open Safari's **Preferences**, select **Advanced** and check **Show Develop menu in menu bar**.

> **Note:** The screenshot reflects the web site at the time of this writing (August 2014). If you're reading this chapter beyond this point in time, there's a chance the site may look different. If so, please check the forums to see if they have any updated instructions for how to handle the new layout for use with this chapter.

Highlight the biography section on the top portion of the page and you'll see the **Element Inspector** highlight the corresponding HTML block in the middle window. At the bottom, the console is ready to execute JavaScript.

On the right side of the **Element Inspector**, you'll see the CSS for the line of HTML you've selected. Notice how the highlighted `<section>` tag has an id property named `user-details` that has no styling to speak of.

```
#user-details {
}
```

If the styles aren't visible, click the **Styles** button in the **Web Inspectors** toolbar to display them.

The CSS property that changes the visibility of an element in a web page is named `display`, and you'll use it now to hide the biography.

Create a new CSS rule by clicking the **New Rule** button.

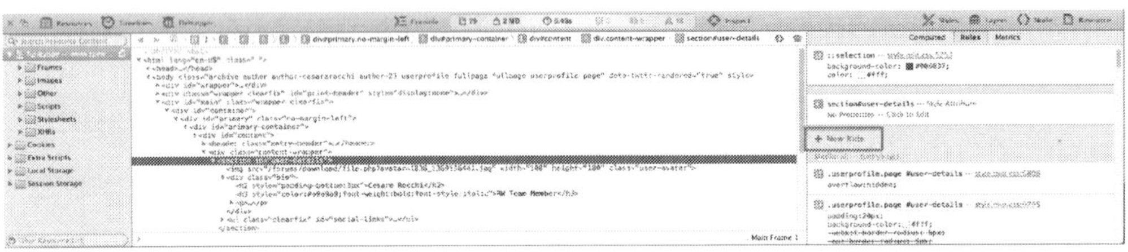

For the new rule, add the following:

```
display: none;
```

It will look like this in the Inspector:

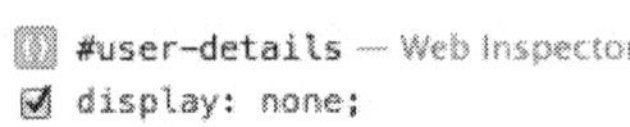

Next to the rule is a checkbox. When you uncheck it, the rule is no longer applid and the biography section reappears. Using checkboxes and playing around with the rules is an easy way to test various rules without committing to them or having to reload the page.

This CSS code is what you'll use to hide the biography section.

Careful with that needle

Before getting stuck into the app, you'll need to test the new CSS rule in Safari. It's considered best practice to make sure everything works in a standard browser before you work with it in your native app code. You'll then manipulate the DOM with JavaScript to inject the code.

Paste following code into the Safari console and press **Enter**:

```
var styleNode = document.createElement("style");
```

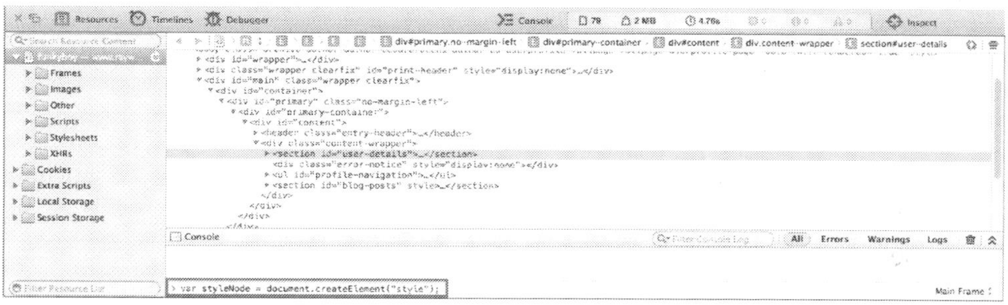

This creates an empty `style` element, but it's not yet part of the DOM. You can inspect it simply by typing its name in the console:

Now enter following line in the console:

```
styleNode.textContent = '#user-details {display: none;}';
```

This injects the CSS rule described above into the `style` element. Inspect it again by typing its name into the console to make sure the CSS is a direct child of the `style` element.

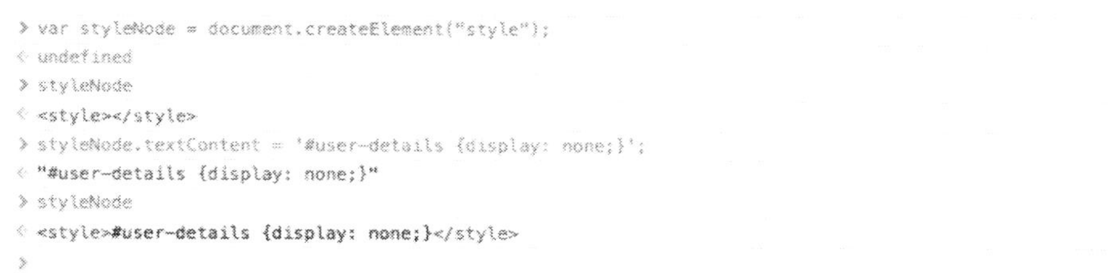

Finally enter this line into the console, and then press **Enter**:

```
document.documentElement.appendChild(styleNode);
```

This adds the newly created `style` element to the DOM, which is immediately reflected in the web page. As soon as the code is evaluated, the biography section of the web page disappears. *Step aside David Blaine!*

> **Note:** The Safari console is much like the Terminal app or the Swift REPL. It's simply a prompt where you can enter commands and have them execute.

Here's how the web page looks after executing the steps above:

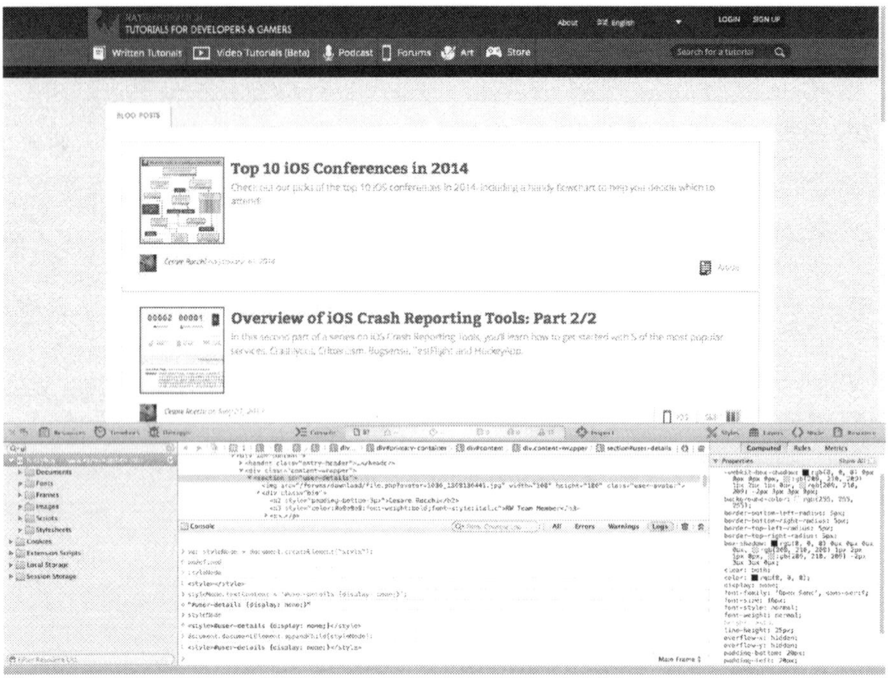

In short, there are three steps to inject CSS into a web page:

1. Create a new `style` element
2. Add the necessary CSS rules to it
3. Append the new `style` element to the DOM of the current web page

Go back to Xcode. Select **File\New\File...** then choose **iOS\Other\Empty** and click **Next**. Name the new file **hideBio.js**. Open it and add the following code:

```
var styleNode = document.createElement("style");
styleNode.textContent = '#user-details {display: none}';
document.documentElement.appendChild(styleNode);
```

Now, open **ViewController.swift** and replace the existing `init(coder:)` method with this one:

```
required init(coder aDecoder: NSCoder) {
  // 1
  let configuration = WKWebViewConfiguration()
  // 2
  let hideBioScriptURL =
NSBundle.mainBundle().pathForResource("hideBio", ofType: "js")
  let hideBioJS = String(contentsOfFile:hideBioScriptURL!,
encoding:NSUTF8StringEncoding, error: nil)
  // 3
  let hideBioScript = WKUserScript(source: hideBioJS!,
injectionTime: .AtDocumentStart, forMainFrameOnly: true)
  // 4
configuration.userContentController.addUserScript(hideBioScript)
  // 5
  self.webView = WKWebView(frame: CGRectZero, configuration:
configuration)
  super.init(coder: aDecoder)
  self.webView.navigationDelegate = self
}
```

These are the five steps needed to inject a custom script in a web page:

1. Create an instance of `WKWebViewConfiguration`
2. Load the JavaScript from a file into an instance of `NSString`
3. Wrap the JavaScript in an instance of `WKUserScript`
4. Add the user script to the configurations `userContentController`
5. Use the configuration to initialize the web view

When injecting a script there are quite a few variables to specify:

- the content of the script itself
- when it should be injected
- whether it acts on the whole page or a specific frame.

You specify all these values by wrapping the in an instance of `WKUserScript` (step 3). There are two options you can choose from for the `injectionTime` parameter:

- `.AtDocumentStart` which is when the page begins loading
- `.AtDocumentEnd` which is when the page has finished loading

Your code uses `.AtDocumentStart` so the biography section is hidden as soon as possible. You also specify whether the script affects all the frames of the page, or just the main one via the parameter `forMainFrameOnly`. In this case, the property is set to `true`.

> **Note:** A HTML page can host other HTML pages, even ones from different hosts. They are displayed via the `iframe` tag. For example, on raywenderlich.com, the Facebook plugin and Google Ads service use this technique to inject content in the page dynamically. When you create a user script, you can specify whether you want the script to act on just the main frame (the root `html` tag) or on all the child frames too.

Build and run. Tap a tutorial in the carousel at the top and then tap the avatar of the author. The biography section is now hidden, and the profile page simply lists all of that authors tutorials.

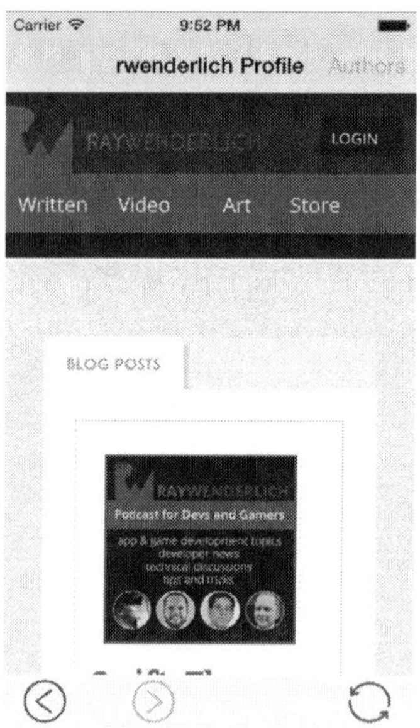

Pretty powerful, I think you'll agree. With user scripts, you can interact directly with the source of a web page, and even customize it before it's rendered.

You can do much more with this technique than I've shown here. For instance, injecting a script to process the content of a webpage and trigger a callback in the host app, passing the processed content.

Sounds interesting?

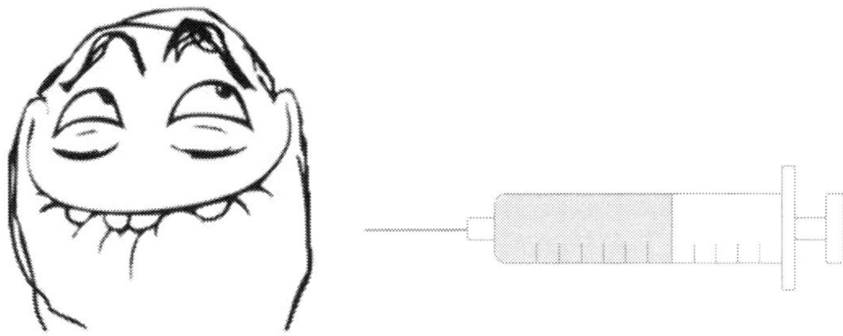

Of course, this technique does raise a few security concerns. Since it's possible to inject scripts into any web page the user loads, a malicious app developer has the potential to capture sensitive information, and even send it to a remote server.

> **Note:** The security of user data is absolutely paramount. You should always be conscious of this when utilizing any of the techniques I'm demonstrating in this chapter.

App calling web: Do you copy?

The web page www.raywenderlich.com/about contains a list of all the members of the Ray Wenderlich team. The app will inject a script into this page that fetches the members of the tutorial team, *the authors*, and trigger a callback to the apps native code. The callback will pass an array of the authors that you'll use to populate a table view. When a cell is tapped, the corresponding URL will open in the web view. The script will extract two properties for each author: their name and profile URL.

Open www.raywenderlich.com/about in Safari on your Mac. The page layout is structured like this:

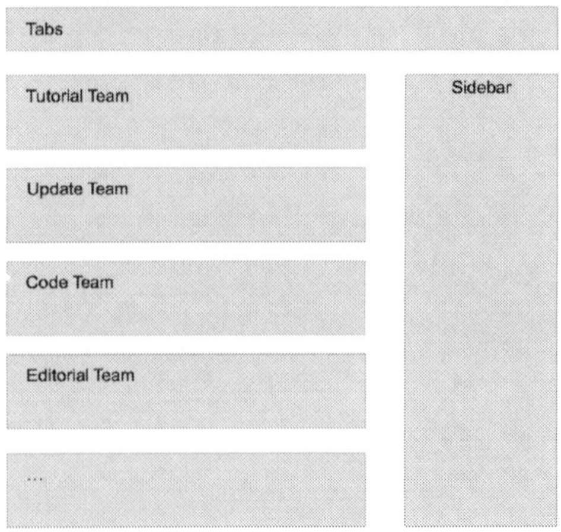

There is a list of team sections on left, and each is nestled inside a `<ul>` tag, all of which are marked with the class `team-members`. Whilst on the **About** page, open the **Web Inspector** using the menu **Develop\Show Web Inspector** and enter the following code into the console.

```
var teamAuthors = document.querySelector('ul.team-members')
```

Here the `teamAuthors` variable is set to point at the first `<ul>` tag with a class of `team-members`. The keyword `document` refers to the root element of the web page; `querySelector` is a function available on each DOM element and takes a CSS selector as a parameter, returning the first match from the DOM.

To inspect the variable, type the following:

```
teamAuthors
```

You'll see the `<ul>` element printed to the console, with a disclosure triangle. Expand the disclosure triangle to see the entire list of team members.

```
> var teamAuthors = document.querySelector('ul.team-members')
< undefined
> teamAuthors
< ▼<ul class="team-members">
    ▶<li id="darnaout">…</li>
    ▶<li id="sazarpour">…</li>
    ▶<li id="sbehera">…</li>
    ▶<li id="bbroom">…</li>
    ▶<li id="tcoron">…</li>
    ▶<li id="tdahbura">…</li>
    ▶<li id="sdaniel">…</li>
    ▶<li id="sdavies">…</li>
    ▶<li id="edekhayser">…</li>
    ▶<li id="jdistler">…</li>
>
```

The next step is to extract all the children from this list.

Type this code into the console, and then hit **Enter**:

```
var authors = teamAuthors.querySelectorAll('li')
```

This extracts all the children `<li>` tags from the parent `<ul>` tag. As you did before with the `teamAuthors` variable, inspect `authors` by typing the variable name into the console and hit **Enter**:

```
> var authors = teamAuthors.querySelectorAll('li')
< undefined
> authors
< [▶<li id="darnaout">…</li> , ▶<li id="sazarpour">…</li> , ▶<li id="sbehera">…</li> ,
  ▶<li id="bbroom">…</li> , ▶<li id="tcoron">…</li> , ▶<li id="tdahbura">…</li> , ▶<li id="sdaniel">…</li> ,
  ▶<li id="sdavies">…</li> , ▶<li id="edekhayser">…</li> , ▶<li id="jdistler">…</li> ,
  ▶<li id="ceberhardt">…</li> , ▶<li id="mfabri">…</li> , ▶<li id="cfulton">…</li> ,
  ▶<li id="mgalloway">…</li> , ▶<li id="sgardner">…</li> , ▶<li id="jgreene">…</li> ,
  ▶<li id="jgundersen">…</li> , ▶<li id="ahafizji">…</li> , ▶<li id="mhollemans">…</li> ,
  ▶<li id="jjordan">…</li> , ▶<li id="mkatz">…</li> , ▶<li id="clapollo">…</li> , ▶<li id="fmarsetti">…</li>
  , ▶<li id="clowe">…</li> , ▶<li id="mluedke">…</li> , ▶<li id="smcalister">…</li> ,
  ▶<li id="jmeyer">…</li> , ▶<li id="mmorey">…</li> , ▶<li id="kmuzykov">…</li> , ▶<li id="vngo">…</li> ,
  ▶<li id="nnorth">…</li> , ▶<li id="kpedersen">…</li> , ▶<li id="gpugh">…</li> , ▶<li id="prea">…</li> ,
  ▶<li id="breichart">…</li> , ▶<li id="rcepeda">…</li> , ▶<li id="krichter">…</li> ,
  ▶<li id="crocchi">…</li> , ▶<li id="dselander">…</li> , ▶<li id="ddesignatednerd">…</li> ,
  ▶<li id="jshapiro">…</li> , ▶<li id="psholtz">…</li> , ▶<li id="tstephens">…</li> , ▶<li id="atam">…</li> ,
  ▶<li id="atan">…</li> , ▶<li id="mtodorov">…</li> , ▶<li id="cwagner">…</li> , ▶<li id="nwaynik">…</li> ,
>                                                                                     Main Frame
```

Now inspect the structure of a single `<li>` tag by expanding the disclosure triangle. Here is a simplified version to highlight the relevant parts.

```
<li id="crocchi">
  <h3 name="teamname">Cesare Rocchi</h3>
  <a href="/u/funkyboy"> ... </a>
  ...
</li>
```

The name of the author is contained in the first element, a `h3` element, whereas the URL is a property of the `a` element. To extract the data required for the app you're going to need two separate CSS selectors:

1. A selector to fetch the `h3` element and extract its textual content
2. A selector to fetch the `a` element and extract the value of its `href` property

Eventually you'll write a JavaScript function that takes an array of `li` elements as input and returns an array of custom JavaScript objects, but for now you'll continue to write all the code in the console.

Back in Safari, enter the following into the console:

```
var dani = authors[0];
```

This points the variable `dani` to the first element in the `authors` array.

```
> var dani = authors[0]
< undefined
> dani
< ▶<li id="darnaout">…</li>
>
```

Now type this code to extract the name:

```
dani.querySelector('h3')
```

```
> dani.querySelector('h3')
< <h3 name="teamname">Dani Arnaout</h3>
> |
```

This extracts the `h3` element that contains the name of the author. Next, enter this into the console:

```
dani.querySelector('h3').textContent
```

As its name implies, the `textContent` property returns the textual content of an element, which in this case is the name of the author.

```
> dani.querySelector('h3').textContent
< "Dani Arnaout"
>
```

Okay, good work! You've completed the first few steps. Now onto extracting the URL.

Enter the following code into the console:

```
dani.querySelector('a').getAttribute('href')
```

A handy feature in JavaScript is that you can chain function calls. This above first fetches the `a` element and then extracts the value of its `href` property.

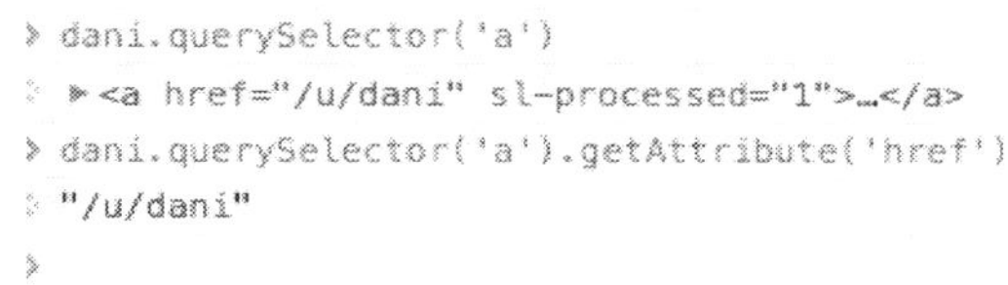

To make sure that the parsing is accurate you'll write a loop that includes a log statement.

Enter the following code into the console. To make it easier, write it in a text editor first, and then paste it into the console. Otherwise, while working in the console, you can press **shift+return** to create a new line without having JavaScript evaluated.

```
for (var i = 0; i < authors.length; i++) {
  var author = authors[i];
  var authorName = author.querySelector('h3').textContent;
  var authorURL = "http://www.raywenderlich.com" +
        author.querySelector('a').getAttribute('href');
  console.log("name is ", authorName, " URL is ", authorURL);
}
```

Select the **Logs** tab in the console, and then take a look at the result.

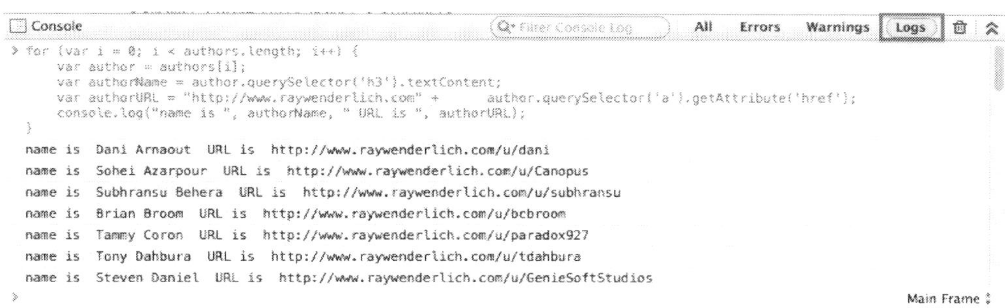

Notice that the URL of each author in the page is a relative path, e.g. `/u/dani`, so the host address is prepended to build the complete URL.

Return to Xcode. Select **File\New\File...** then choose **iOS\Other\Empty** and click **Next**. Name the new file **fetchAuthors.js** and click **Create**. Open it and add the following code:

```
var teamAuthors = document.querySelector('ul.team-members')
var authors = teamAuthors.querySelectorAll('li')

function parseAuthors() {
  result = []
  for (var i = 0; i < authors.length; i++) {
    var author = authors[i];
    var authorName = author.querySelector('h3').textContent;
    var authorURL = "http://www.raywenderlich.com" +
author.querySelector('a').getAttribute('href');
    result.push({'authorName' : authorName, 'authorURL' :
authorURL});
  }
  return result;
}

var authors = parseAuthors();
webkit.messageHandlers.didFetchAuthors.postMessage(authors);
```

This script fetches the first `ul` element it finds with the `team-members` class, extracts the name and profile URL of each author, and finally packs the result into an array.

The last line of code is critical to the JavaScript -> native code communication working. The first part – `webkit.messageHandlers` – is a global object that's setup by the framework to facilitate the triggering of callbacks in the native code. It's available in every `WKWebView`.

The communication between the two environments relies on the concept of named messages. Here, the object `didFetchAuthors` acts as proxy and is the representation of a message with the same name in the native code. The `postMessage` function actually triggers the callback, passing whatever data you supply through to the callback.

Time to integrate this with Swift.

Loud and clear web, go on

Back in Xcode, open **ViewController.swift** and add the following just below the import statements:

```
let MessageHandler = "didFetchAuthors"
```

This creates a constant with the same value of the message name specified in the JavaScript above.

Next, update the class declaration so that it conforms to the `WKScriptMessageHandler` protocol:

```
class ViewController: UIViewController, WKNavigationDelegate,
WKScriptMessageHandler {
    ...
}
```

Now add the following new property to the class, just beneath the `webView` property.

```
var authorsWebView: WKWebView?
```

Add the next block of code to the bottom of `viewDidLoad()`:

```
//1
let authorsWebViewConfiguration = WKWebViewConfiguration()
//2
let scriptURL =
NSBundle.mainBundle().pathForResource("fetchAuthors", ofType:
"js")
let jsScript = String(contentsOfFile:scriptURL!,
encoding:NSUTF8StringEncoding, error: nil)
//3
let fetchAuthorsScript = WKUserScript(source: jsScript!,
injectionTime: .AtDocumentEnd, forMainFrameOnly: true)
//4
authorsWebViewConfiguration.userContentController.addUserScript(
fetchAuthorsScript)
//5
authorsWebViewConfiguration.userContentController.addScriptMessa
geHandler(self, name: MessageHandler)
//6
authorsWebView = WKWebView(frame: CGRectZero, configuration:
authorsWebViewConfiguration)
//7
let authorsURL =
NSURL(string:"http://www.raywenderlich.com/about")
let authorsRequest = NSURLRequest(URL:authorsURL!)
authorsWebView!.loadRequest(authorsRequest)
```

This code performs seven steps:

1. Creates an instance of `WKWebViewConfiguration`
2. Loads the JavaScript into an instance of `NSString`
3. Wraps the JavaScript in an instance of `WKUserScript`, which this time is injected once the document has finished loading
4. Add the user script to the configuration
5. Subscribe to a messages named `didFetchAuthors`
6. Initializes the an instance of `WKWebView` with the configuration
7. Load a URL request and ask the web view to load it

The key step is 5, which sets the view controller as the handler for any messages dispatched from `authorsWebView`.

Now add the required `WKScriptMessageHandler` protocol method:

```
func userContentController(userContentController:
WKUserContentController, didReceiveScriptMessage message:
WKScriptMessage) {
  println("message is \(message)")
}
```

Build and run. You'll see the message printed in the console. It means the script is functioning as expected and messages are being sent from the JavaScript through to the native code.

Next, you'll build a model class that will house data for each author.

Select **File\New\File...** then choose **iOS\Source\Cocoa Touch Class** and click **Next**. Name the class **Author**, make it a subclass of **NSObject** and select **Swift** as the language. Click **Next** and then **Create**. Open the class and replace its contents with the following:

```
import UIKit

class Author: NSObject, Printable {
  var authorName: String = ""
  var authorURL: String = ""
  override var description: String {
    return "name: \(authorName) URL: \(authorURL)"
  }
```

```
  init(dictionary: Dictionary<String, String>) {
    self.authorName = dictionary["authorName"]!
    self.authorURL = dictionary["authorURL"]!
    super.init()
  }
}
```

The class has two properties for authors name and profile URL. There's also custom initializer, which accepts a dictionary and use that to populate the properties.

Notice that the names of the keys used in the dictionary, `authorName` and `authorURL`, match the ones used in the JavaScript. It also overrides the `description` property to make the object more readable in the console.

Now open **ViewController.swift**. Add the following property declaration below the other properties:

```
var authors: [Author] = []
```

This will hold all the author objects extracted from the web page.

Next, replace the `userContentController(userContentController:, didReceiveScriptMessage:)` method with the following:

```
func userContentController(userContentController:
WKUserContentController, didReceiveScriptMessage message:
WKScriptMessage) {
  if (message.name == MessageHandler) {
    if let resultArray = message.body as? [Dictionary<String,
String>] {
      for d in resultArray {
        let author = Author(dictionary: d)
        authors.append(author)
      }
      println("authors = \(authors.debugDescription)")
      authorsButton.enabled = true
    }
  }
}
```

This method compares the name of received message with the one you're expecting, and if it matches extracts the array of dictionaries attached to the message, which is stored in the `body` property. Each dictionary is used to create an instance of `author`, which is then added to the `authors` array. Eventually, it enables the **Authors** button.

Build and run. Wait until the **Authors** button is enabled, and then check the console. You should see something similar to the following:

```
authors = [name: Dani Arnaout URL:
http://www.raywenderlich.com/u/dani, name: Sohei Azarpour URL:
http://www.raywenderlich.com/u/Canopus, name: Subhransu Behera
URL: http://www.raywenderlich.com/u/subhransu, name: Brian Broom
URL: http://www.raywenderlich.com/u/bcbroom, name: Tammy Coron
URL: http://www.raywenderlich.com/u/paradox927, ...]
```

This is a big leap forward for the app. You've injected a script that parses some content and passes it back to the native code.

Pretty powerful, right?

Next you'll incorporate that data into the apps interface.

Show me the list

Open **Main.storyboard** and drag a new **Table View Controller** from the **Object Library** on to the canvas. Select it, and then embed it in a navigation controller using **Editor\Embed In\Navigation Controller**.

Now select the **Authors** button in the **View Controller Scene** and **ctrl-drag** to the new navigation controller, selecting **popover presentation** from the popup menu. Finally, select the segue between the controllers and set its **Identifier** to **showAuthors**.

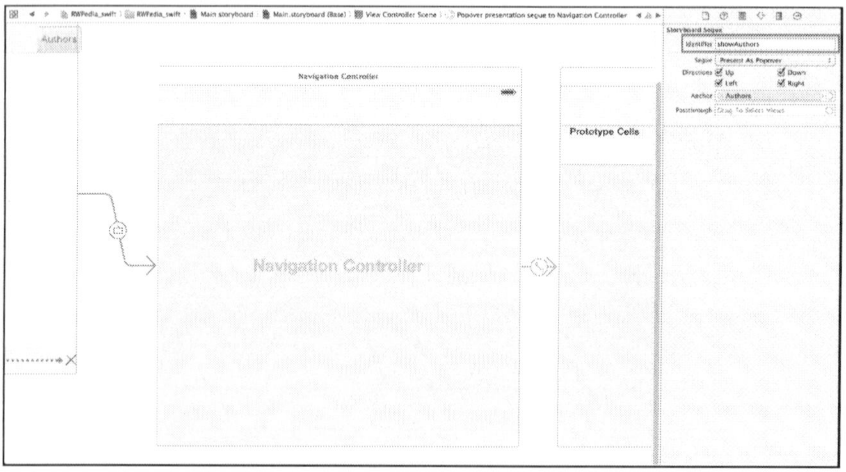

Build and run. Wait for the **Authors** button to become enabled, tap it and make sure an empty table view shows up.

Now you'll populate it.

Select **File\New\File...** then choose **iOS\Source\Cocoa Touch class** and click **Next**. Name it **AuthorsTableViewController**, make it a subclass of **UITableViewController** and make sure the **Langauge** is set to **Swift**. Click **Next** and then **Create**.

Now open **Main.storyboard**, select the **Table View Controller** and set its class to **AuthorsTableViewController** in the **Identity Inspector**.

While you're still in the storyboard, select the prototype cell in the table view, and in the **Attributes Inspector** set its **Identifier** to **authorCellID**.

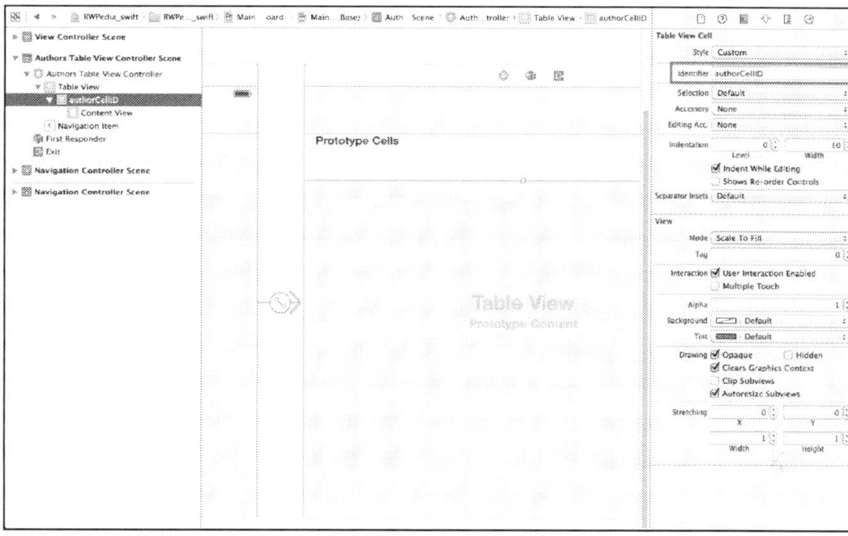

Next, open **AuthorsTableViewController.swift**. Replace the contents with the following:

```
import UIKit

class AuthorsTableViewController: UITableViewController {
  var authors: [Author] = []

  override init(style: UITableViewStyle) {
    super.init(style: style)
  }
```

```
  required init(coder aDecoder: NSCoder) {
    super.init(coder: aDecoder)
  }

  override func viewDidLoad() {
    super.viewDidLoad()
    self.title = "Authors"
    tableView.reloadData()
  }

  override func didReceiveMemoryWarning() {
    super.didReceiveMemoryWarning()
  }

  override func numberOfSectionsInTableView(tableView:
UITableView?) -> Int {
    return 1
  }

  override func tableView(tableView: UITableView?,
numberOfRowsInSection section: Int) -> Int {
    return authors.count
  }

  override func tableView(tableView: UITableView,
   cellForRowAtIndexPath indexPath: NSIndexPath) ->
    UITableViewCell {
    let cell =
tableView.dequeueReusableCellWithIdentifier("authorCellID",
forIndexPath: indexPath) as UITableViewCell
    let author = authors[indexPath.row]
    cell.textLabel.text = author.authorName
    return cell
  }
}
```

This is nothing more than a boilerplate table view controller with implementations for the mandatory data source methods. The `authors` variable contains the objects that are used to populate the table view, with each cell displaying the name of the author.

Now open **ViewController.swift** and add this method.

```
override func prepareForSegue(segue: UIStoryboardSegue, sender:
AnyObject!) {
  if (segue.identifier == "showAuthors") {
    let navController = segue.destinationViewController as
UINavigationController
```

```
    let authorsViewController = navController.topViewController
as AuthorsTableViewController
    authorsViewController.authors = authors
  }
}
```

This is called right before the table view controller is shown and it passes the list of authors that will be displayed in the table view to the table view controller.

Build and run. Once it's enabled, tap the **Authors** button and voila, the list of authors!

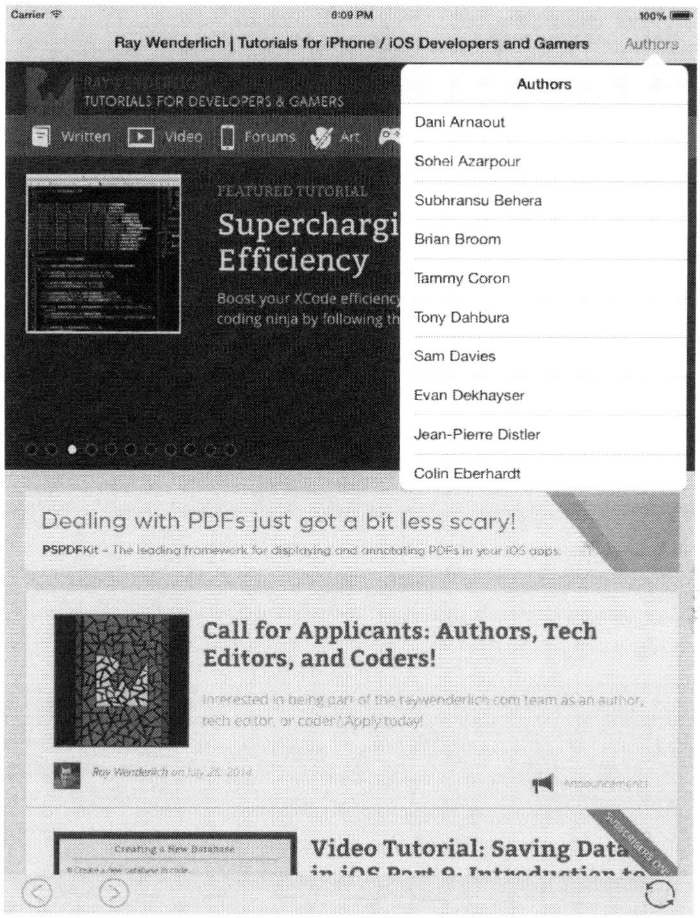

And that, my friends, is how you manipulate the look and feel of a web page without the need for pesky user names, passwords or wrangling with a troublesome CMS.

Next you'll load the corresponding authors profile page when you select a cell in the table view. And of course, you'll add a close button so your iPhone users won't be stuck in limbo.

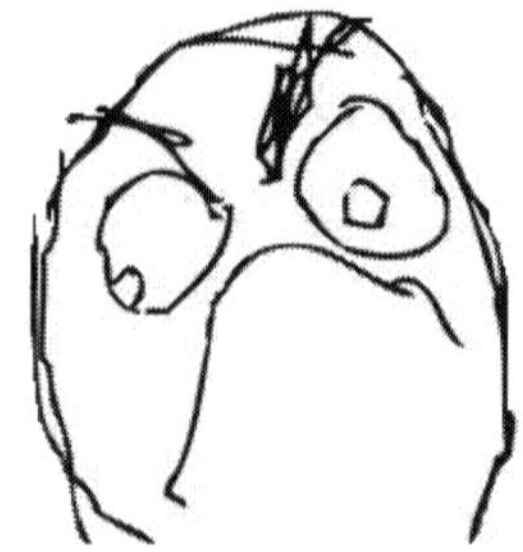

Y No Close Button?

Show me that profile

Open **Main.storyboard** and drag a **Bar Button Item** from the **Object Library** on to the right hand side of the navigation bar in the table view controller, and set its title to **Close**.

Open the **Assistant Editor**, making sure you're editing **AuthorsTableViewController.swift**, and **ctrl+drag** from the **Close** button to the class to create a new `IBAction`.

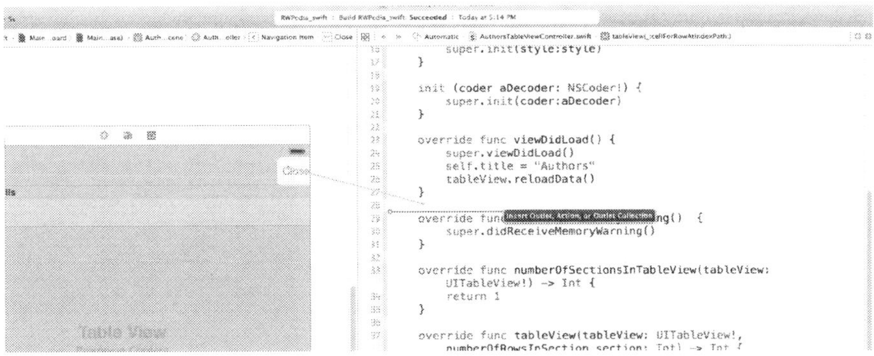

Make sure to set the **Connection** to **Action**, and **Name** to **close**. Then, add the following line to the method:

```
dismissViewControllerAnimated(true, completion: nil)
```

Switch to **ViewController.swift** and add this right below the import statements:

```
let AuthorSelected = "authorSelected"
```

This is a new constant for the name of a notification that'll be posted by the table view when the user selects a row. Head back to **AuthorsTableViewController.swift** and add the following method:

```
override func tableView(tableView: UITableView,
didSelectRowAtIndexPath indexPath: NSIndexPath) {
  let author = authors[indexPath.row]
NSNotificationCenter.defaultCenter().postNotificationName(Author
Selected, object: author)
  dismissViewControllerAnimated(true, completion: nil)
}
```

Any time a user selects a cell, this method is called. In turn, it posts a notification containing the corresponding author object.

Next, open **ViewController.swift** and add this at the bottom of `viewDidLoad`:

```
NSNotificationCenter.defaultCenter().addObserver(self, selector:
"authorSelected:", name: AuthorSelected, object: nil)
```

This sets the view controller as an observer of the notifications posted when you select an author in the table view. Finally add the following method to the bottom of the class:

```
func authorSelected(notification:NSNotification) {
  webView.loadRequest(NSURLRequest())
  let author = notification.object as Author
  title = author.authorName
  let URL = NSURL(string:author.authorURL)
  let request = NSURLRequest(URL:URL!)
  webView.loadRequest(request)
}
```

This pulls out the author object attached to the notification, sets the name as the title in the navigation bar and uses the `authorURL` property to build a new URL request which is then loaded in the web view.

Build and run. Select an author in the table view and watch as the profile is loaded.

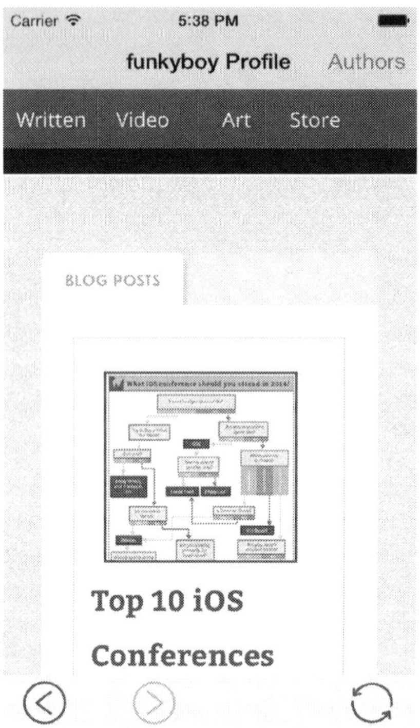

Where to go from here

In this chapter you've learnt how to use a very powerful feature of the new WebKit framework.

You now know how to be a master of the interwebs; well, maybe not. But at least you can customize the appearance of a web page and extract information from it so it can be blended seamlessly with your apps own interface.

There are many ways you can extend your learning by improving the app you just built. For example, you could also extract the avatar URL of each author and display it beside his or her name in the table view. Another improvement would be extracting all the members of the Ray Wenderlich team, not just the authors, and displaying them in different sections in the table view.

With the new WebKit framework, the potential to build cool apps that interact directly with hosted web pages has increased ten-fold. What are you waiting for? Go forth and build your next awesome app!

Section IV: Bonus Chapters

To thank you for purchasing this book, we've included some bonus chapters for you!

These bonus chapters come as an optional PDF download, which you can download for free here:

- http://www.raywenderlich.com/store/ios-8-by-tutorials/bonus-chapters

In these bonus chapters, you'll learn about further additions to your iOS developer tool belt. You'll implement some real-time blurring, take in-depth look at all things Xcode 6, before rounding out the section with an overview of the new and shiny bits Apple added to the testing framework introduced in iOS 7. You *do* test your apps, right? :]

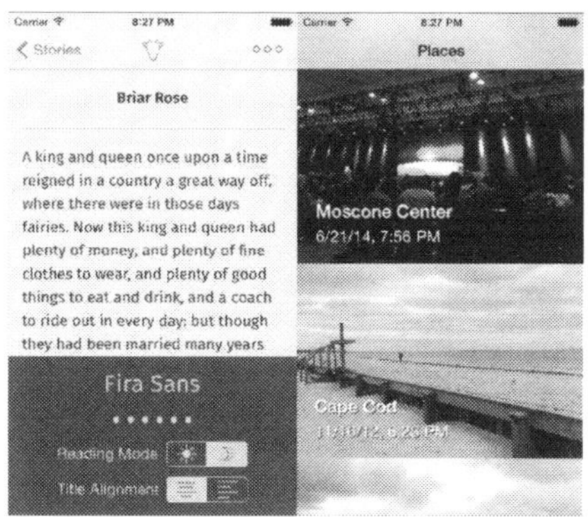

Chapter 26: iOS 8 Visual Effects

Chapter 27: An In-depth Look at Xcode 6

Chapter 28: Xcode 6 & Swift

Chapter 29: What's New with Testing

Chapter 30: What's New with iTunes Connect

Conclusion

We all sincerely hope you had a ton of fun reading this book. If you cherry-picked chapters according to your own interests and projects, that's great — hopefully you learned a lot and got your projects started off on the right foot. And if you read this entire book from cover to cover, then take a bow — you are a coding ninja!

You now have experience with the new APIs in iOS 8 and know what it takes to make your app's layout adapt to its environment and how to extend its functionality beyond the sandbox, along a whole host of other new and exciting concepts and techniques. If you're like us, learning about all these new technologies and concepts has you overflowing with ideas. We can't wait to see what you come up with!

If you have any questions or comments, please stop by our forums at http://www.raywenderlich.com/forums.

Thank you again for purchasing this book. Your continued support is what makes the tutorials, books, and other things we do at raywenderlich.com possible — we all truly appreciate it!

Best of luck with your iOS adventures,

- Soheil, Tammy, Jack, Ricardo, Mike, Chris W., Vincent, Nicholas, Sam, Cesare, Chris L., Jake, Ryan, Audrey, Scott, Brian, Wendy, Chris B., Mic, Ray, and Vicki

(The raywenderlich.com Tutorial Team and friends!)

37056200R00403

Made in the USA
Charleston, SC
27 December 2014